Strategic Information Technology and Portfolio Management

Albert Wee Kwan Tan
National University of Singapore, Singapore

Petros Theodorou
Athens University of Economics and Business, Greece

INFORMATION SCIENCE REFERENCE

Hershey · New York

Director of Editorial Content: Kristin Klinger
Director of Production: Jennifer Neidig
Managing Editor: Jamie Snavely
Assistant Managing Editor: Carole Coulson
Typesetter: Kim Barger
Cover Design: Lisa Tosheff
Printed at: Yurchak Printing Inc.

Published in the United States of America by
    Information Science Reference (an imprint of IGI Global)
    701 E. Chocolate Avenue, Suite 200
    Hershey PA 17033
    Tel: 717-533-8845
    Fax: 717-533-8661
    E-mail: cust@igi-global.com
    Web site: http://www.igi-global.com

and in the United Kingdom by
    Information Science Reference (an imprint of IGI Global)
    3 Henrietta Street
    Covent Garden
    London WC2E 8LU
    Tel: 44 20 7240 0856
    Fax: 44 20 7379 0609
    Web site: http://www.eurospanbookstore.com

Library of Congress Cataloging-in-Publication Data

Strategic information technology and portfolio management / Albert Wee Kwan Tan and Petros Theodorou, editor.

    p. cm.

  Includes bibliographical references and index.

  Summary: "The objectives of the proposed book are to provide techniques and tools appropriate for building application portfolios and develop strategies that increase financial performance"--Provided by publisher.

  Includes bibliographical references.

  ISBN 978-1-59904-687-7 (hardcover) -- ISBN 978-1-59904-689-1 (ebook)

  1. Information technology--Management. 2. Information technology--Cost effectiveness. 3. Strategic planning. I. Tan, Albert Wee Kwan, 1962- II. Theodorou, Petros.

  HD30.2.S7878 2009

  658.4'038--dc22

                          2008033947

British Cataloguing in Publication Data
A Cataloguing in Publication record for this book is available from the British Library.

All work contributed to this book is original material. The views expressed in this book are those of the authors, but not necessarily of the publisher.

Table of Contents

Section IV
Enterprise Architecture

Section V
Further Readings

Detailed Table of Contents

Section I
Emerging Concepts in SISP

Chapter I

    David Van Over, University of Wollongong, Dubai

This chapter focuses on the methods and means of creating a linkage between business requirements and the IT investments that can address those requirements. An ITIM framework is proposed, which addresses three key elements of ITIM: what decisions are to be made, who should make the decisions, and how decisions are to be made and monitored. ITIM is a management process that provides for the identification (pre-selection), selection, control, and evaluation of business driven IT investments across the investment lifecycle.

Chapter II

    Albert Wee Kwan Tan, National University of Singapore, Singapore

This chapter describes an industry approach to IS Planning that has been used effectively in Singapore to develop the IT capabilities of each industry. More specifically, the different stages in planning and executing an industry scale IT project for supply chain management are discussed here based on an example from Singapore. This generic framework proposed can be used in any industry where IT plays a strategic role for industry transformation.

Chapter III

    Teay Shawyun, Assumption University of Thailand, Thailand

This chapter proposes an externalized approach to IS Planning by identifying the market driven needs through the firm's value proposition to the customer derived from the product/service consumption.

The market based push-pull framework is to ensure that the push strategy of the firm in what it wants to offer and at a price that it intends to offer is matched with the pull strategy of the market in what it wants to buy and at a price it is willingly to pay. A case study of how a university revamp its Information Management System by aligning the external and the internal elements is used to illustrate this reconciliation in its market driven IS/IT planning.

This chapter describes a new approach to utilize a Fuzzy Cognitive Map to align strategic objectives with IS opportunities that exist at the level of business processes. It exemplifies fuzzy cognitive mapping in SISP, and illustrates how the strategic alignment between the business and IT domains can be realized.

Section II
Information Technology Portfolio Management

This chapter provides an introduction to advent of Information Technology Outsourcing (ITO) and its impact on portfolio management in modern day decision-making. Specifically, it outlines the use of the Application Portfolio Matrix (APM) by companies in formulating their strategic IT direction and why such techniques may be unsuitable for outsourcing decisions. It presents an analysis of ten outsourcing decision-making frameworks, identified from the literature, highlighting their commonalities, strengths, deficiencies, and the potential misalignment between the theory and practice of outsourcing as determined by focus group discussions.

The goal of this chapter is to present an adaptation of the scenario-based methodology for IT and Information Systems Planning. It describes in details each step of the proposed methodology and discusses a study case. Steps include the identification of different scenarios and their corresponding antecedent events, the determination of probabilities, and consequences of the events, how to calculate risks and how to plan Information Systems and IT resources to manage each scenario.

Chapter VII

This chapter describes the exploration of Information Technology Portfolio Management (ITPM) in conjecture with Modern Portfolio Theory (MPT). Yet, the standard MPT has proved unable to represent the complexities of real-world situations. This is the inception of the present work which focuses on the project portfolio optimization solution through a meta-heuristic approach, that is, application of algorithmic methods able to find near-optimal solutions in a reasonable amount of computation time.

Chapter VIII

This chapter presents the concept of strategic information technology portfolio management for development of innovation competences in a project-oriented company. It is a specific type of portfolio management, called project portfolio management. It takes into consideration the key aspects of IT − innovation relationship, and introduces the organizational support to the Portfolio Management Office. An established PMO that is actively supported at the executive level can help solve problems with project auditing and initiative approval.

Chapter IX

Developing countries, opting to pursue services-oriented economies, have invested in information and communication technologies (ICT) to enhance their competitiveness in the global environment. This has called for improved management in both public and private sectors and as a consequence governments, some of which have undertaken public sector reform, now seem ready to embrace E-government. However experience even in developed countries has shown that incorporating E-Government practices is not a sure means of attaining desired goals. This paper examines the position of Vietnam, as it becomes a member of WTO in implementing E-Government. Some E-Government initiatives taken are identified and an IT roadmap is recommended as a means of achieving a successful transformation. This roadmap emphasizes a holistic approach to analyze existing performance gaps and identify E-Government opportunities for Vietnam.

The chapter describes an IT Reengineering & Portfolio Management Model (RPM) offering a pragmatic, proven and plausible means for IT to deliver and demonstrate value to their organizations. The framework will address the question of "what is the value of IT?" and approach it in a more objective and dispassionate manner.

Section III
Capability Development

This chapter summarized a research conducted via postal survey of 202 pairs of CEOs and CIOs to investigate the effect of such frequency and channel richness on CEO/CIO mutual understanding of the impact of existing information systems and of the impact of the portfolio of planned information systems. It provided direction for CEOs and CIOs who may be interested in increasing their mutual understanding of the impact of IT, improving their relationship with each other, and thus improving their planning of new information systems.

This chapter proposes a "capacity and capability" model based on the management of technology approach and its technology capabilities approach to manage its human, information and organization capitals critical to the successful IS/IT implementation and utilization. To illustrate what capability and capacity dimensions need to be addressed, a university case study of how it refocused its Information Management System through its IS/IT capability and capacity management is used as an illustration.

The chapter will present the challenges in implementing information technology plan pertaining to two dimensions: literature and practical. It will also suggest ways to rectify and deflect the negative impact of the challenges. In addition, the chapter will show some of the challenges' manifestations shown in some case studies.

Section IV
Enterprise Architecture

This chapter discusses the importance of developing a system that not only works in support of, but hand-in-hand with the specific needs of a given business. Through the discussion of its main characteristics and its implementation, it will be shown that the Enterprise Architecture Approach (EA) meets this specific need, as it provides the "blue-prints" to strategically organize information.

This chapter presents a methodical strategic technology engineering planning (STEP) approach, to effectively cope with the design complexity in service-oriented architecture and manage the strategic planning of solution development of information systems. This overarching framework provides a comprehensive multi-disciplinary approach to conduct strategic and tactical technology planning for both near-term needs and long-term goals.

This chapter discusses the design pattern methodology and provides an example of how the methodology could be implemented to solve a business problem using the multivariate vector map (mvm). It applies the mvm pattern to the problem of choosing an it outsourcing strategy as a means to demonstrate its effectiveness to it managers and to it outsourcing vendors.

Section V
Further Readings

Chapter XVII

Zaiyong Tang, Louisiana Tech University, USA
Bruce Walters, Louisiana Tech University, USA

The authors trace historical developments in the fields of information technology (IT) and strategic management. IT's evolution from the mainframe era to the Internet era has been accompanied by a shift in the strategic emphasis of IT. In the early days, IT's contribution to the organization was largely information provision, monitoring and control. Current research at the intersection of IT and strategic management increasingly highlights the impact of IT in terms of informing strategic decisions and enabling information flow vis-à-vis all manner of organizational processes. We believe these fields are ripe for research focusing on their complementary impact on organizational performance.

Chapter XVIII

Ram Kumar, University of North Carolina – Charlotte, USA
Haya Ajjan, University of North Carolina – Charlotte, USA
Yuan Niu, University of North Carolina – Charlotte, USA

There is significant interest in managing IT resources as a portfolio of assets. The concept of IT portfolio management (ITPM) is relatively new compared to portfolio management in the context of finance, new product development (NPD) and research and development (R&D). This paper compares ITPM with other types of portfolio management and develops an improved understanding of IT assets and their characteristics. It presents a process-oriented framework for identifying critical ITPM decision stages. The proposed framework can be used by managers as well as researchers.

Chapter XIX

Brian H. Cameron, The Pennsylvania State University, USA

Information Technology Portfolio Management (ITPM) is a topic of intense interest in the strategic management of IT. In ITPM, IT synchronization with corporate business strategy is operationalized by the application of the principles of financial portfolio management to IT investments. This perspective is crucial to the continual alignment of business strategy and IT investments. Portfolio management is the discipline of managing projects together as a portfolio that meets stated corporate goals and objectives (Combe & Githens, 1999). It facilitates the optimization of resource allocation and development investment across multiple projects. This chapter investigates current techniques and issues for managing IT project portfolios and aligning those portfolios with the strategy of the business. The models and concepts presented are regarded as a starting point for dialogue and further research among IT project researchers and practitioners.

Chapter XX

This chapter is intended primarily for managers who are preparing to implement portfolio management concepts in an organisation and students of IT Project Management courses at the Masters level, who wish to understand the difference between Project and Portfolio Management. As IT Governance is gaining importance, the IT department should not be surprised if they are given a mandate from the senior management to implement a Governance framework. Portfolio Management principles are the foundations of building an effective governance. While there is literature available discussing portfolio management at the conceptual level, there is not enough available which translates these concepts into tactical implementation. This could be because implementation differs between organisations and there is no one size fits all solution. However, practitioners can benefit from discussing implementation approaches that can be tailored to suit individual needs. This chapter shows one of the many ways to implement a portfolio management framework.

Chapter XXI

Demand for mental healthcare increases. Simultaneously the need for more patient oriented processes increases and the market develops towards more competition among providers and organizations. As a result of these developments mental health care organizations are becoming more aware of efficiency and effectiveness. Often, they choose to transform to more process oriented organizations, which require changes in planning and control systems and Information Technology (IT). However, little is known about the required planning and control systems and IT for mental health care.

Despite the technological progress made by organisations in Namibia, the impact of IT has not been studied. The existing definition of IT is not comprehensive enough to include all relevant IT expenditures. No return calculations are made, though managers are showing growing concern at the increasing IT costs. The purpose of this article is to determine what organisations in Namibia use as basis for investing in IT. In interviews with six organisations in Namibia, it was determined how they define and manage their investment in IT. Some conclusions can be drawn, the first being that organisations need to look at their definition of IT to include all aspects of IT like communication systems, maintenance, etc. the second implication is that somebody must be appointed to take responsibility for managing the IT investment.

Preface

Strategic information systems planning (SISP) has been the subject of much attention over the past decade. While it has evolved in method and style, the thesis that SISP is important because it emphasizes the need to bring IT to bear on and sometimes influence strategic direction of the corporation is widely accepted by researchers. This is particularly true in today's dynamic environments where harnessing the power of technology resources could be critical for competitiveness. However, while there have been studies that examine the "what" questions of SISP, particularly concerning the issue of Information System and Business alignment, there has been little on the "how" questions, which include the process of planning and whether this yields effective outcomes. Furthermore, is it reasonable to presume that organizations will change their planning processes over time in an attempt to improve their effectiveness as well as leverage their investment based on SISP?

It is useful to examine evolution and maturing of planning processes as companies strive toward achieving more effective planning systems. This can serve the purpose of delineating changes in process characteristics that can lead to greater planning effectiveness over time. The authors in this book therefore attempt to address the fundamental questions: How does SISP evolve? Is it becoming more effective? If yes, can organizations optimize the planning of IT systems —particularly when there is a portfolio of IT systems that require investment and continual support? What adaptations do firms need to make in order to improve planning to leverage on enterprise architecture and global supply of IT resources?

The SISP concept has undergone significant evolution since the initial discussions of the 1980s. The changing technology and the recognition of its importance as a corporate resource drove this evolution. Specifically, the proliferation of E-Commerce, outsourcing, and enterprise resource systems tended to push developmental activities outside the exclusive domain of professional IS groups, creating challenges that did not exist when SISP was first conceived. Also, firms are aggressively searching for new ways to leverage information, knowledge, and IT in supporting strategic goals and competitiveness. Hence, SISP in many firms refers to both a proactive search for competitive and value-adding opportunities, as well as the development of broad policies and procedures for integrating, coordinating, controlling and implementing the IT resources.

This book which entitled "Strategic Information Technology and Portfolio Management" is organized in four sections to provide comprehensive coverage of topics in SISP such as: (1) Emerging Concepts in SISP; (2) IT Portfolio Management; (3) Capability development; and (4) Enterprise Architecture. The following provides a summary of what is covered in each section of this book:

SECTION I: EMERGING CONCEPTS IN SISP

This section focuses on new methods and concepts of creating a tighter linkage between business requirements and the IT investments that can deliver better IT plans. For example, David Van Over proposes a new framework in Chapter I to address three key elements of SISP: what decisions are to be made, who should make the decisions, and how decisions are to be made and monitored. Albert Wee Kwan Tan in Chapter II expands the SISP to develop the IT capabilities for an industry as part of industry development and transformation while Teay Shawyun in Chapter III argue the need for SISP to matches the market needs with the firm's value proposition to deliver the product/service. Finally, Dimitris and Bill in Chapter IV propose a new approach to utilize a Fuzzy Cognitive Map to align strategic objectives with IS opportunities as business needs are changing dynamically.

SECTION II: IT PORTFOLIO MANAGEMENT

This section examines some of the issues in IT portfolio management and have some of the authors propose new methods to maximize the value from managing the IT portfolio. Luke Ho and Anthony Atkins in Chapter V provides an introduction to advent of Information Technology Outsourcing (ITO) and its impact on portfolio management in modern day decision-making, highlighting the strengths and weaknesses in some of the common decision making frameworks for outsourcing. Stanley Loh, Ramiro Saldana, and Leo Failer Backer in Chapter VI presents a method that include the identification of different scenarios, and how to plan IS and IT resources to manage each scenario. Vassilis Syrris in Chapter VII describes the exploration of Information Technology Portfolio Management (ITPM) in conjecture with Modern Portfolio Theory and how its limitations can be overcome by a meta-heuristic approach to find near-optimal solutions in a reasonable amount of computation time. Dejan Petrović, Marko Mihić, and Biljana Stošić in Chapter VIII presents the concept of strategic information technology portfolio management for development of innovation competences in a project-oriented company that takes into consideration the key aspects of IT − innovation relationship, and introduces the organizational support to the Portfolio Management Office. Cuthbert, Tan and Tran in Chapter IX propose an IT planning framework for E-Government targeting the developing countries where infrastructures are poor and funds are limited. Finally, Anand Sanwal and Subhradeep Mohanty in Chapter X describe an IT Reengineering and Portfolio Management Model (RPM) that will address the question of "what is the value of IT?" and approach it in a more objective and dispassionate manner.

SECTION III: CAPABILITY DEVELOPMENT

This section examines the different approaches to develop capacity and capability to support IT organization as well as the challenges faced in SISP. Al Lederer and Alice Johnson in Chapter XI summarized a research work to investigate the effect of frequency and channel richness on CEO/CIO mutual understanding of the impact of existing information systems and of the impact of the portfolio of planned information systems. Teay Shawyun in Chapter XII proposes a "capacity and capability" model to manage its human, information and organization capitals critical to the successful IS/IT implementation and utilization. Finally, Evon M. Abu-Taieh, Asim A. El Sheikh, and Jeihan M. Abu-Tayeh in Chapter XIII discuss some of the challenges in implementing information technology plan and suggest ways to rectify and deflect the negative impact of the challenges.

SECTION IV: ENTERPRISE ARCHITECTURE

This section examines how enterprise architecture and design can assist in SISP. Anthony Ioannidis and Nikolaos Skarpetis in Chapter XIV expand the design further using the Enterprise Architecture Approach (EA) to meets specific need, as it provides the "blue-prints" to strategically organize information. Tony Shan and Winnie Hua in Chapter XV further propose a framework that provides a comprehensive multi-disciplinary approach to conduct strategic and tactical technology planning for both near-term needs and long-term goals. Finally, Eric Kenji Tachibana and David Ross Florey in Chapter XVI discuss how design pattern methodology can solve a business problem using the multivariate vector map.

SECTION V: FURTHER READINGS

Last but not least, some additional readings are included in this book to provide readers with a wider coverage of SISP and also serve as a supplement to the existing chapters in search of better methods for SISP. In fact, with the pervasiveness of IT and increasing pressure on firms to leverage their IT assets, the importance of SISP has never been stronger. SISP is more than a narrow methodology or sequence of steps. It is complex set of organizational activities that can be characterized by a number of process characteristics, which form an evolutionary pattern as they change as a firm's experience grows in adapting to a changing environment and technological base. Therefore, firms should take advantage of the latest techniques and methods in SISP proposed in this book to align their IT resources with business objectives.

Section I
Emerging Concepts in SISP

Chapter I
Use of Information Technology Investment Management to Manage State Government Information Technology Investments

David Van Over
University of Wollongong, Dubai

ABSTRACT

The expenditures of funds on IT has continued to expand and a significant proportion of the expenditures are hidden, unaccounted for, or never evaluated in terms of the business value derived from the expenditure. This chapter focuses on the methods and means of creating a linkage between business requirements and the IT investments that can address those requirements. An ITIM framework is proposed, which addresses three key elements of ITIM: what decisions are to be made, who should make the decisions, and how decisions are to be made and monitored. ITIM is a management process that provides for the identification (pre-selection), selection, control, and evaluation of business driven IT investments across the investment lifecycle. ITIM uses structured processes to minimize risks and maximize return on investments. Additionally, a high-level ITIM implementation plan is discussed.

INTRODUCTION

As the demands and expectations of citizens for services and information from the public sector have grown, the expenditure of funds on information technology (IT) has continued to expand and a significant portion of the expenditures are hidden, unaccounted for, or never evaluated in terms of the business value derived from the expenditure. For public sector organizations committed to improving strategic planning processes and outcomes, a critical component of strategic planning is deciding how IT can best support the execution of strategic business plans. IT investments are costly and it is important to fund IT initiatives that best support the strategic goals and objectives defined by the business strategic planning process. An information technology investment management (ITIM) process provides an integrated approach to the identification (pre-selection), selection, control, and evaluation of IT investments across the investment lifecycle. The ITIM framework is based on:

- The recognition that the business strategic planning process drives technology investment strategies;
- The concept that technology investments support and add value to the business of state government; and,
- The premise that technology investments should be prioritized, executed, and measured based on the benefits related to achieving business strategic goals and objectives.

This chapter focuses on the methods and means of creating a linkage between business requirements and the information technology investments that can address those requirements. An ITIM framework is proposed, which addresses three key elements of ITIM: what decisions are to be made, who should make the decisions, and how decisions are to be made and monitored. Additionally, a high-level ITIM implementation plan is discussed.

BACKGROUND

Information technology investment management (ITIM) traces its roots to the 1952 work of Harry Markowitz on Portfolio Selection (Markowitz, 1952). In this work, Markowitz proposed a new theory of financial investing based on a portfolio of investments balanced by a number of factors, with expected return, diversification, and risk being primary. Markowitz suggested that a portfolio with the proper balance of investments provided a higher return over time to the investor than simply evaluating each investment on its own merits. This theory is now referred to as Modern Portfolio Theory (MPT) and Markowitz received a Nobel Prize in 1990 for his work. MPT makes four key assumptions:

- A rational investor chooses greater value over less value.
- A rational investor chooses less risk over more risk.
- An investment goal may be supported by more than one optimal portfolio.
- The probability of success increases over time with diversification.

In financial markets, it is now standard and accepted practice to apply MPT to the development of investment instruments. Most retirement plans for example offer one or more versions of an investment strategy based on MPT.

In 1981, Warren McFarlan applied the concepts of MPT to evaluating and selecting information systems projects and development initiatives (1981). McFarlan focused on the area of risk assessment at both the project and portfolio level and noted that risk is inherent in any project or portfolio and, in and of itself, risk is neither good nor bad. It is the determination of the degree of risk and the risk compared to the potential reward that are the critical factors in project selection. At the portfolio level, a balance of risks should exist across all projects with some projects having low risk factors and other having higher risk. It is the balancing of risk that generates the highest return over time with an IT investment portfolio.

McFarlan's portfolio view of information technology projects as investments to be managed has been developed and enhanced over the last 25 years and is now the generally accepted model for technology investments in the private sector. However, it is interesting to note that in a 1986 survey article on IT and corporate strategy (Bakos & Treacy, 1986), no mention of portfolio development was described and MPT was not identified as an emerging model or general theory that could provide direction and insight into IT management and corporate strategy. The existence of information technology in government applications was not mentioned at all.

Portfolio management focuses on the strategic business goals of the organization and aggregate performance of the portfolio components rather than simply one or two projects. Fitzpatrick (2005) points out that it is rare for a business initiative to show a positive financial return from the start but that the implementation of portfolio management is a notable exception and, in his study of the field, he had difficultly finding an implementation that was considered a failure. Portfolio management has consistently shown positive impacts on IT investments by focusing first on selecting high business value projects while concurrently focusing on the elimination or avoidance of high risk, low return and duplicative projects.

The Project Management Institute (PMI) developed its portfolio management standard to provide a framework for the development of project portfolio management processes in organizations. The standard is an extension of the existing Project Management Standard developed by PMI. The Project Management Institute defines an IT portfolio as:

A collection of projects and/or programs and other work that are grouped together to facilitate effective management of that work to meet strategic business objectives. (The standard for portfolio management, 2004).

Rather than taking a more holistic approach to ITIM and addressing the full investment life-cycle, the PMI portfolio management standard focuses on the conceptualization, development, and delivery of investments, which closely mirrors the Project Management Standard. While the standard provides an excellent structure for portfolio management of projects, it lacks the comprehensive characteristics (projects, procurements, services, and assets) and range of lifecycle activities characteristic of a true IT portfolio.

At the beginning of the 1990's, Clemons (1991) discussed the concept of IT as an enabler of corporate business strategic investments and Weill (1990) studied the impact of IT strategic investments on corporate performance. This work was key to the development of the use of MPT in IT; however, the results from these and other later studies showed a limited connection between IT investments and corporate profitability and the issue of whether or not computers and technology actually improved productivity in businesses emerged as the productivity paradox (Brynjolfsson & Hitt, 1998). The solution to the paradox required among other things a consensus definition of "IT investment".

Later studies (Hitt & Brynjolfsson, 1996) expanded the definition of corporate impact and found a significant relationship between IT investments and productivity, value to consumers, and competitive advantage. Gartner predicted in 2002 (Harris & Casonato, 2002), that by 2005, more than two thirds of the IT investment decisions by leading-edge corporations would be based on non-financial or synergistic measures as the primary decision factors in investment selections. This represents a nearly complete reversal from the 1990s where the primary decision factor was financial return on investment. A comprehensive review of the empirical evidence of IT and economic performance (Dedrick, Gurbaxani & Kraemer, 2003) showed that the overwhelming preponderance of the evidence refuted initial findings of no association. These studies laid the foundation for a model of IT investments tied to corporate business goals and objectives.

In 1994, the U.S. Government Accountability Office released a report entitled "Improving Mission Performance Through Strategic Information Management: Learning from Leading Organizations (1994). This report described the select, control, and evaluate processes that are now the common factors in ITIM. In part due to the proven effectiveness of ITIM and portfolio management in the private sector, Congress passed the Clinger-Cohen Act of 1996 which mandated the adoption of an investment approach to IT projects in all Federal agencies. Most agencies began this process with some version of portfolio management focused on selecting and controlling IT projects.

As portfolio management matured and garnered widespread acceptance, shortcomings of the approach began to emerge. While corporations were realizing significant savings in IT projects, the expenditures in these areas were small relative to the overall IT expenditures. A broader based definition of IT investment was needed which extended beyond new initiatives and projects and incorporated ongoing operations, services, existing assets, and human capital. In this expanded model of IT investment management, the object is to maximize the return on IT assets while minimizing risks and meeting performance standards. The initial challenge to this approach was

that no consistent definition or conceptualization of 'IT investment' existed (Rai, Patnayakuni & Patnayakuni, 1997). This fact created difficulties in scoping the parameters of ITIM programs as well as defining appropriate measures and criteria for investment selection and monitoring.

The ITIM framework uses the following definition for IT investment:

Information technology (IT) investments are the hardware, software, and related systems operated by an organization to support the flow or processing of information in support of business activities. IT investments include hardware and software assets, projects, procurements and statewide contracts through which assets can be procured, and services. Figure 1 shows the types of IT investments that are managed through the ITIM processes.

An <u>asset</u> is the product of a completed and fully operational IT project or procurement. IT related contracts are also assets. Operations and maintenance (O&M) are activities associated with assuring that an existing asset continues to support an identified business need. O&M activities preserve existing functionality and assets in contrast to projects and procurements that create new assets or functionality. O&M expenditures

Figure 1. IT investment types

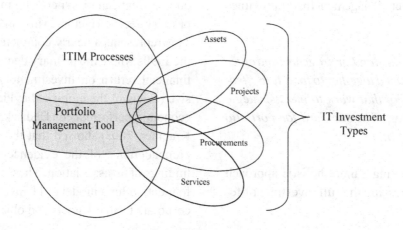

in and of themselves are not considered investments; however, O&M expenditures do support an underlying asset.

A project is a temporary endeavor undertaken to create a unique asset, service, or result.

A procurement is the process of acquiring an IT asset through the use of a purchasing mechanism. The procurement process is distinguished by the fact that the process culminates in the acquisition of a physical good.

A service facilitates a business activity. A service is intangible, perishable, and does not result in the creation of a tangible asset which distinguishes a service from a project or procurement.

While ITIM and portfolio management continued to be studied and evolved in the private sector throughout the 1990s, little work was done in the public sector. Much of the research, model development, and theory in the corporate sector was focused on economic performance; however, economic factors such as profitability and competitive advantage are not relevant factors in the public sector. Research in developing IT investment models in the public sector that reflects the unique public sector factors has been lacking. There are several reasons for this lack of research:

- A lack of funding and sponsorship of research in the public sector as it relates to public sector model and theory development.
- A lack of incentives in the public sector for participation in data collection.
- The perception that investment decisions are driven solely by political considerations and the intractability of that process.
- Broad and significant differences between diverse public entities in IT investment approach.

Based on data from all 50 states, 35 large cities, and 40 large counties, the Government Performance Project (*Government Performance Project State Survey*, 2001) was released in 2001 and was the first comprehensive study of its kind. Focused on government management capabilities, the study used data collected from 1996–2000 and included a sub-component focused on management information technology. Based on the data in the project, Dufner, Holley, and Reed (2005) proposed a four level model to explain state government strategic information system planning:

- Utility/Agency – IT planning is function wide.
- Middle-Up/Agency – IT planning is agency wide.
- Statewide Project Team – IT planning is project wide.
- Information Technology Commission – IT planning is state government wide.

As the strategic approach moves from Utility/Agency towards Information Technology Commission, the approach takes on more of an IT investment portfolio approach although portfolio management is possible to some degree in each model.

In 2004, the GAO issued its final framework for ITIM ("Information Technology Investment Management A Framework for Assessing and Improving Process Maturity," 2004). This framework incorporated changes and recommendations from the 2000 exposure draft of the document. The 2004 document reflects current best practices in ITIM and provides both an operational guideline for implementing ITIM and a progressive maturity model which provides direction on assessing and improving ITIM performance. This framework is the current directive under which U.S. Federal agencies implement ITIM.

The GAO ITIM model involves three phases: select, control, and evaluate. Although each phase accomplishes specific objectives, the ITIM process is a continual, interdependent management effort. Information from one phase supports the activities in the other two phases. ITIM model therefore is a fluid, dynamic process for continually monitoring proposed and ongoing projects, services, and assets throughout their life cycles, evaluating successful investments as well as terminated or delayed projects, and assessing the impact on future proposals and the benefits from any lessons learned ("Information Technology Investment Management A Framework for Assessing and Improving Process Maturity," 2004). A pre-select phase has been added to this process to link the organization's strategic planning process, align business needs with potential investments, and screen or triage investments to determine if they should be incorporated into the more rigorous select, control, and evaluate processes.

Within state government, there is a pervasive belief that the services that are provided by the public sector and supported by information technology cannot be measured or evaluated because of the nature of the services provided and that an effort to develop and implement a rational ITIM standard will most likely fail. Various reasons are given for this view of ITIM:

- A large percentage of the funding for State agencies does not come from State funds.
- Some State agencies are a part of a larger Federal or multi-state network.
- State agencies provide opportunities and services for citizens and it is more important to serve the needs of the citizens than to account for expenditures.
- It is to the potential benefit of all citizens that government exists to accomplish missions that serve smaller "specialized populations" where it might not be cost effective to do so.
- Cost effective measures utilized successfully by private industry are not congruent with accomplishing non-cost effective missions of government.

An alternate explanation for the resistance to ITIM rests in the history and traditions of some states. From a historical perspective, agencies in some states have enjoyed a significant degree of autonomy with little centralized oversight. Many agencies receive funding directly from sources other than the state legislatures and some agencies have independent governing boards reflecting this history of independence. In order for ITIM to be successful, agencies will be required to give up some autonomy and control over their IT expenditures and investments and many agencies are reluctant to do so.

THE ITIM FRAMEWORK

The ITIM framework uses structured processes to minimize risks and maximize return on IT investments and identifies the processes and required steps to assure IT investments are well thought-out, cost effective, and support the business plans of the organization.

The ITIM framework can be used with any public sector organization unit; however, generally, the lowest level organizational unit should have responsibility for strategic planning and management, development, purchase, operation, and use of information technology investments. A multi-tiered solution can be developed reflecting the hierarchical nature of public sector organizations, which fosters the synergies afforded by enterprise architectures and solutions. Complete implementation of the framework requires development of a tailored ITIM standard as well as development and rollout of a supporting guideline and tools for managing information technology at state agencies.

The Key Components of the ITIM Framework

The ITIM framework consists of the following key components.

- **Strategic Planning** – Strategic plans, including both agency plans and state strategic plans for technology; state long-term objectives; and the governor and legislative priority initiatives are used to align IT investments to ensure that IT directly and measurably supports business goals. Agency and state strategic planning processes establish a planning cycle, which generally aligns with the budgeting and ITIM processes.
- **Organization Management Collaboration** - Integration of the ITIM process into the broader strategic planning process requires a collaborative effort between the functional business managers and the IT organization within an organization and state. Staff responsible for strategic business plans must work closely with the staff responsible for managing IT investments.
- **Repeatable Process** – ITIM must be the primary process for making decisions about technology investments that best support business plans and needs; developing and analyzing the rationale for those investments; and monitoring and evaluating investments to assure continued business value. The ITIM process is repeated within the organizational unit on an annual basis and as part of the budget cycle.
- **Available Staff and Supporting Tools** – In order to fully implement ITIM, an IT Portfolio Management (PfM) tool to manage, track, and report IT investments is required. Additionally, sufficient staff resources must be applied to support ITIM processes. Each organizational unit must establish an ITIM management process to oversee the implementation and ongoing operation of IT investment management within the organization.
- **Investment Portfolio** – The investment portfolio is a management tool comprised of essential information about technology investments. The portfolio is structured to facilitate the evaluation of investment alternatives in support of strategic business plans, providing a single, consolidated source for information about IT investments.

ITIM Process Framework Overview

At the highest level, the ITIM process is a circular or repeatable flow of technology investments through four sequential phases. Identification of business needs and potential investments occurs in the Pre-Select Phase. Potential investments as well as existing investments are evaluated, scored, ranked, and chosen for investment (or continued investment) in the Select Phase. Selected investments are monitored in the Control Phase. In the Evaluate Phase, operational investments are assessed against performance measures and lessons learned are identified and documented to assist with future development and operational optimization. The flow of IT investment information moving through each phase is shown in Figure 2.

The ITIM process is implemented at each organizational level with strategic planning responsibility (generally agencies and the state levels) and each level has an associated investment portfolio. The agency portfolio encompasses all IT investments currently funded through the agency. Generally, portfolios at higher organization levels (e.g. the state level portfolio), are limited to higher cost or risk investments to maintain a focus on high cost, high risk investments.

Pre-Select Phase

Purpose

In the ITIM Pre-Select Phase the IT components of business needs are identified, analyzed, and documented. Potential technology solutions (investments) are also identified and evaluated in light of strategic plans, enterprise technology architecture, and other standards. The Pre-Select Phase begins the process of defining business objectives, associated costs, and performance measures that result in making an investment case for meeting a business need. The Pre-Select Phase activities are performed sequentially in order to complete the phase successfully. Completion of the Pre-Select Phase answers the question "What proposed IT investments potentially solve business needs?"

The Pre-Select Phase activities are displayed in Figure 3.

Pre-Select Phase Activities

Analyze Business Need

The Analyze Business Need Activity is a required part of the strategic planning process. Each organization with strategic planning responsibility must analyze its mission, long term goals, and current operations to identify business needs that are not adequately satisfied. After completing the initial analysis, the organization must determine if information technology can solve or contribute to the solution of the performance gap by fulfilling the business need. The specific mission, objective(s), and mandate(s) a potential IT investment addresses are identified as well as the potential investment's strategic alignment, benefits to the organization, and the potential for enterprise or collaboration opportunities.

Required Step: Each proposed IT investment includes an analysis of business need.

Figure 2. ITIM process overview

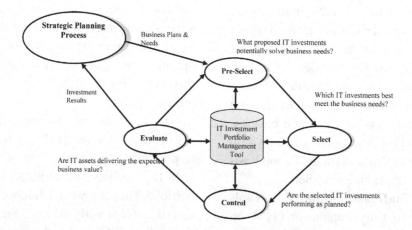

Figure 3. Pre-select activities

Analyze Investment

The purpose of the Analyze Investment Activity is to describe how a proposed investment will fill the performance gap identified in the Analyze Business Need Activity. The focus of the Analyze Investment Activity is on the analysis of the elements of risks of a proposed solution or investment relative to its estimated costs.

Each proposed IT investment includes an Analyze Investment Activity that addresses the contribution or potential contribution to the solution of a business need, including an analysis of the associated benefits and risks.

Required Step: Each proposed IT investment includes an investment analysis.

Develop Investment Case

The Develop Investment Case Activity provides sufficient information to evaluate, score, and rank a potential investment in the ITIM Select Phase. The Develop Investment Case Activity combines the outputs from the Analyze Business Need Activity and the Analyze Investment Activity.

Required Step: Each proposed IT investment includes an Investment Case.

Pre-Select Phase Deliverable

The output from the Pre-Select Phase is the Investment Case which answers the question "What proposed IT investments potentially solve business needs?" The Investment Case provides, at a high level and in a standardized format, the information necessary to evaluate a potential IT investment in the ITIM Select Phase.

Pre-Select Phase Deliverable: The output from the Pre-Select Phase is the Investment Case.

Select Phase

Purpose

The purpose of the Select Phase is to decide which investments best support an organization's mission, strategic goals, and mandates as well as strategic plans from among the investments identified in the Pre-Select Phase and other investments previously selected into the investment portfolio. In the Select Phase, all IT investments are scored and ranked. IT investments in the Select Phase include:

- proposed investments from the Pre-Select Phase

  - proposed projects
  - proposed contracts and procurements

- previously approved investments and assets

  - investments previously approved in the Select Phase but not yet in the Control Phase
  - investments currently in the Control Phase
  - assets

The Investment Case for a proposed investment is initially evaluated and scored after which the scores from the proposed investments are analyzed along with the scores from the organization's ongoing investments. Based on the organization's internal analysis, the organization ranks all its investments and subsequently selects the organization Investment Portfolio. Completion of the Select Phase answers the question "What IT investments best meet the business needs?" Select Phase activities are shown in Figure 4.

Activities

Investment Case Evaluation, Scoring, and Approval

The Investment Case for every proposed investment is evaluated, scored, and approved by the organization. The results of the evaluation and scoring activities are documented in the organization investment portfolio.

The final output from the Agency Investment Case Evaluation, Scoring, and Approval Activity is a decision by the designated organization approving authority on whether a proposed investment is:

- approved for planning
- approved for planning with contingencies
- deferred
- disapproved

Required Step: Each investment is evaluated, scored, and approved using standard criteria identified in the Agency ITIM Plan.

Maintain Investment Portfolio

The Maintain Investment Portfolio Activity includes investments currently in the investment portfolio which may include:

- investments previously approved in the Select Phase but not yet in the Control Phase
- investments currently in the Control Phase
- assets

These investments have been previously evaluated, ranked, and scored on the same basis as other investments. Current Control Phase monitoring and performance data or current performance data from the Evaluate Phase is used to maintain investments in the investment portfolio.

Required Step: Information about each is maintained in the investment portfolio.

Investment Portfolio Analysis and Investment Ranking

The Investment Portfolio Analysis and Investment Ranking Activity incorporates newly approved investments into the investment portfolio. The placement of an investment within the portfolio is determined by the process of ranking and ordering the entire portfolio. The organization consolidates proposed and on-going investments and completes an investment portfolio analysis. The final output from the Investment Portfolio Analysis and Investment Ranking Activity is a ranked investment portfolio for review and approval by the organization approving authority.

The portfolio analysis review includes:

- Investment type by business line and service area;
- Overall spending by business line, service area, and objective;
- Portfolio strategic alignment;
- Portfolio risk;
- Infrastructure spending; and,
- Budget growth/decline.

Required Step:

1. *The organization consolidates proposed and on-going investments and completes an IT Investment Portfolio Analysis.*
2. *The organization ranks the consolidated investment portfolio for review and approval.*

Portfolio Selection

The Investment Portfolio Analysis and the Investment Portfolio are approved by the organization's approving authority. The approved Investment Portfolio is the output from this activity.

Required Step: The organization's Investment Portfolio is approved by the agency approving authority.

Select Phase Deliverables

The output from the Select Phase is an approved Investment portfolio, which answers the question "What IT investments best meet the business needs?"

Select Phase Deliverable: The output from the Select Phase is an approved Investment Portfolio.

Control Phase

Purpose

The objective of the Control Phase is to ensure, through timely oversight, quality control, and executive review, that IT investments are developed and placed in operation using a disciplined, well-managed, and consistent process. During this process, the progress and performance of IT investment initiatives against projected cost, schedule, and performance metrics, are regularly monitored in accordance with the investment's planned review schedule. When issues or problems are identified, corrective action is taken. The Control Phase is characterized by decisions to continue, modify, or terminate investment initiatives. Decisions are based on reviews at

Figure 4. Select phase activities

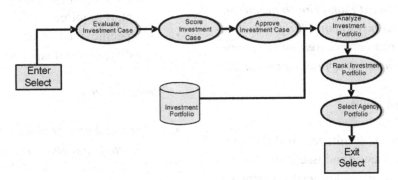

Figure 5. Control phase activities

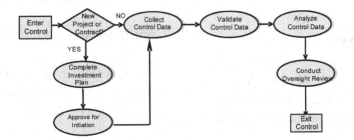

key milestones during the investment lifecycle and reviews conducted on pre-defined periodic schedule. The focus of these reviews changes and expands as the investment moves through the investment lifecycle and as projected investment costs and benefits change. Completion of the Control Phase answers the question "Are the selected IT investments performing as planned?" The Control Phase activities are displayed in Figure 5.

Activities

Complete Detailed Investment Plan

Every proposed IT investment as well as current investments with proposed changes will include a Detailed Investment Plan. The Detailed Investment Plan must be reviewed and approved by the appropriate approving authority prior to initiation of the investment.

Required Step:

1. *Each proposed IT investment includes a Detailed Investment Plan prior to initiation.*
2. *The Detailed Investment Plan for each investment must be reviewed and approved by the organization approving authority.*

Collect Control Data

After an investment is initiated in the Control Phase, it will be reviewed and assessed according to the schedule and control criteria contained in the Detailed Investment Plan.

Required Step: Control data for each investment in the Control Phase is collected on a defined schedule.

Validate Control Data

A validation review will be completed on control data for investments in the Control Phase. If investment control data fails to meet required control standards and guidelines, the organization will remediate the documentation and resubmit for review. If the control standards cannot be met by the organization, the investment will be placed on the investment watch list and a remediation plan will be developed.

Required Step: Control data for each investment in the Control Phase is validated.

Investment Oversight Review

On a quarterly basis, the control data for all organization investments in the Control Phase are consolidated into an Investment Control Analysis Report. For each investment in the Control Phase, the report will include:

- an IT investment control analysis
- any significant changes since the last report
- the identification of under-performing investments
- any recommended remediation plans
- a remediation plan status for each investment, if required
- a specific recommendation to continue, modify, or terminate each investment

Required Step:

1. *Control data is summarized, analyzed, and reported on a quarterly basis.*
2. *The Investment Oversight Review results in a decision to:*
   - *continue an investment*
   - *modify an investment*
   - *terminate an investment*

Control Phase Deliverables

The output from the Control Phase is the Investment Control Analysis Report. The report answers the question "Are the selected IT investments in the Control Phase performing as planned?" The report includes:

- an investment watch list of at-risk investments
- a decision for each investment to:
  - continue the investment without modification
  - modify the investment to better meet current needs, including accelerating deployment
  - terminate the investment based on a finding that the investment is consistently underperforming or no longer a business priority

Control Phase Deliverable: The output from the Control Phase is the Investment Control Analysis Report.

Evaluate Phase

Purpose

The purpose of the Evaluate Phase is to compare actual performance results and benefits of an investment to the results that were initially projected. The Evaluate Phase includes all investments that have been placed in operation.

In the Evaluate Phase, new assets receive a Post-Implementation Review (PIR). In addition, the key performance metrics of assets are monitored and "out of bounds" performance statistics trigger in-depth review and analysis.

Evaluate Phase results are collected and evaluated by the organization and reported to the organization approving authority. These results provide a better understanding of asset performance and identify necessary investment adjustments or the need for a replacement investment. The Evaluate Phase answers the question "Are IT assets delivering the expected business value?" The Evaluate Phase Activities are displayed in Figure 6.

Activities

Conduct Post Implementation Review

A post implementation review (PIR) is completed on each new asset within 6 – 12 months of the investment becoming an asset.

Required Step: All new assets have a PIR completed 6 – 12 months after being placed in operation.

Conduct Asset Evaluation

Asset Evaluations are performed on all assets. Asset Evaluations provide a method for timely

Figure 6. Evaluate phase activities

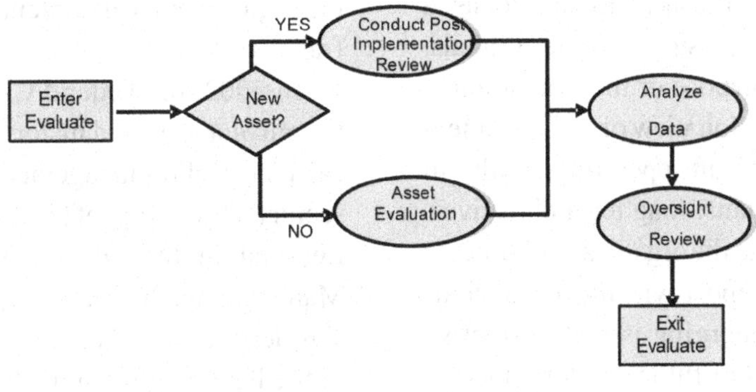

identification of sub-optimal asset performance. Each asset is assigned associated performance criteria, a monitoring schedule for the collection of performance data, and an identified range of acceptable performance. Using the criteria assigned to an asset, the asset is monitored for performance, outages, maintenance activities, costs, resource allocation, defects, problems, and system changes.

Out-of-range performance of an asset triggers a full evaluation of an IT asset including a root cause analysis and development of a remediation plan, if required.

Each Asset Evaluation includes a decision to:

• Continue the IT asset without modification;

• Modify the IT asset to better meet current business needs or performance criteria; and,

• Terminate the IT asset based on a finding that the asset is consistently underperforming or no longer a funding priority.

Required Step: Asset Evaluations are performed periodically on all assets.

Investment Oversight Review

Results from PIRs and Asset Evaluations are summarized and analyzed on an annual basis by the organization. The organization completes an Operating Results Analysis Report that summarizes and analyzes the investments focused on the organization's mission, long term goals, and mandates. The purpose of the evaluation is to provide an organization view of IT investment operating results; evaluate operating results in relation to strategic plans, long term objectives, and to provide input into the organization strategic planning cycle. The report will include accomplishments, trends, emerging issues, corrective actions, and a forecast of future performance.

Required Step: Operating results are compiled, analyzed, and subsequently reviewed by the organization approving authority.

Evaluate Phase Deliverables

The output from the Evaluate Phase is the Operating Results Analysis Report. The operating results for the investment portfolio are reviewed and approved by the organization approving authority. The Operating Results Analysis Reports answer the question "Are the selected IT assets delivering the expected value?"

Evaluate Phase Deliverable: The output from the Evaluate Phase is the Operating Results Analysis Report.

DEVELOPING AN ITIM PROCESS IN A PUBLIC SECTOR ORGANIZATION

Developing and implementing an organization ITIM process enables consistent IT investment performance within the organization and provides improved, long-term business value to the organization that, in turn, provides increased benefits to the its citizens. The ITIM framework is a structured approach that identifies the key practices for establishing and maintaining successful IT investment management processes. The ITIM framework describes *what* to do, not *how* to do it. Thus, specific implementation methods can and will vary by organization while meeting the requirements and intent set forth in the ITIM framework.

In 2002, the Federal CIO Council described the current state and history of ITIM and specifically portfolio management in the U.S. Federal sector (A Summary of First Practices and Lessons Learned in Information Technology Portfolio Management, 2002). The council listed nine lessons learned based on the experience of agencies in the Federal government:

- Understanding the differences and the relationship between portfolio management and project management and manage each accordingly.
- Gain and sustain the commitment of organization officials and senior business managers to make informed IT investment decisions at an enterprise level.
- Establish and maintain enterprise architecture to support and substantiate IT investment decisions.
- Integrate IT portfolio management with the organization's planning and budgeting policies, processes, and practices.
- Clearly define and communicate the goals and objectives to be served by the investment portfolio and the criteria and conditions for portfolio selection.
- Acquire and utilize portfolio, project management, decision support, and collaborative methodologies and tools.
- Routinely collect and analyze data and information to assess portfolio performance and make adjustments as necessary.
- Carefully consider the internal and external customers and stakeholders of the organization's investment portfolio.
- Pay very close attention to the inter-organizational aspects of the organization's investment portfolio.

ITIM Improvement

The ITIM framework includes an ITIM maturity model and maturity assessment process which:

- Identifies implemented ITIM processes within the organization;
- Provides an assessment of ITIM capability within an organization; and,
- Identifies gaps and areas for improvement.

The maturity model, developed by the U.S. GAO, includes five levels of maturity described in Figure 7. Each maturity level builds upon the previous level and enhances an organization's ability to manage IT investments.

The cornerstone to the success of ITIM at the organization level is the designation of an ITIM Manager and supporting staff to implement and maintain a well-documented organization ITIM process. The head of each organization with strategic planning responsibility resources and manages the organization ITIM process including development and implementation of an ITIM Improvement Plan. Senior management commitment is essential to ensure that an organization's ITIM process is adequate, well managed, and effectively implemented. Improvements to the ITIM process should occur continuously within the context of evolving business needs, strategic goals and objectives, and operating plans.

The ITIM maturity model (Figure 7) provides direction for improving IT investment processes in a systematic and organized manner. Continuous ITIM process improvements are intended to:

- Increase the business value and mission performance of IT investments;
- Ensure that IT investments are selected by a well-informed decision-making body based on the merit of the investment;
- Promote a better understanding and management of IT investment related risks; and,
- Improve the likelihood that planned investments will be completed on time and on budget.

The developmental nature of a maturity model requires a cumulative process for maturation. Lower level processes provide the foundation for upper level processes. As expertise with basic ITIM processes is developed, ITIM process improvements can be incorporated. Progressing through the maturity levels requires that the maintenance of previously implemented lower level critical processes.

Figure 8 describes the ITIM development, implementation, and improvement process. On a biennial basis, the organization completes an ITIM assessment, develops an ITIM Plan based on the assessment and the maturity model, and subsequently implements the plan.

ITIM Development Activities

Initial Implementation Activity

An organization initiates the ITIM development process by chartering and establishing an ITIM oversight organization appointed by the agency head. The organization designates one or more individuals to perform ITIM management functions (herein referred to as an ITIM Manager) and commits to the required training for the individual(s) appointed with the objective of implementing ITIM within their organization. The ITIM Manager will provide ITIM support to the ITIM oversight organization. ITIM oversight organization membership must include one or more senior business managers and may include members from other organizations, information technology managers, and citizens served by the organization who are familiar with ITIM processes and the mission of the agency.

The ITIM oversight organization systematically reviews, evaluates, and makes recommendations to the organization head on information technology investments which best support the mission, strategic goals, and objectives of the organization. For all phases of the ITIM pro-

Figure 7. The ITIM maturity model

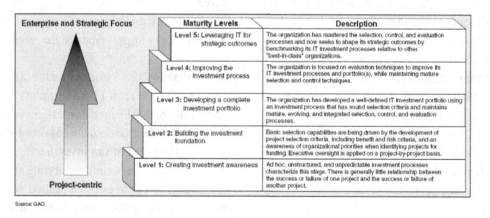

Source: GAO.

Figure 8. ITIM improvement process

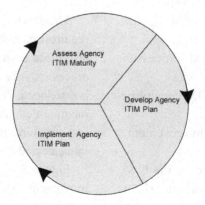

cess, the ITIM oversight organization conducts investment reviews and makes recommendations to the organization head. Members of the ITIM oversight organization complete initial ITIM training.

The responsibilities of the ITIM oversight organization are defined in the ITIM oversight organization charter and include:

- overseeing development and implementation of the ITIM process
- developing and maintaining multi-year IT investment plans
- guiding investment business case preparation and review
- identifying project integration and collaboration opportunities
- recommending investments to the organization head
- reviewing current investments to ensure that performance is satisfactory and the investment continues to deliver business value commensurate with the magnitude of the investment
- identifying deficiencies in program and project management including the oversight of corrective actions
- conducting periodic reviews of IT investment status for approved and funded investments

Required Steps:

1. *Designate an ITIM Manager.*
2. *Establish and charter an ITIM oversight organization.*
3. *Establish and manage an investment portfolio.*

Assess ITIM Maturity

The organization completes a comprehensive biennial ITIM process self assessment. The self assessment is used to both assess the maturity of the organization ITIM process and to evaluate adherence to the ITIM Plan. Individuals conducting the self assessment will first successfully complete ITIM assessment training.

As part of the initial ITIM implementation, an initial self assessment is performed prior to developing the initial ITIM Plan.

The following activities in the ITIM plan will be assessed:

- **Pre-Select**
  - Identifying business needs;
  - Screening proposed investments; and,
  - Investment analysis process.
- **Select Activities**
  - Analyzing and ranking all investments based on benefit, cost, and risk criteria;
  - Selecting a portfolio of investment;
  - Establishing investment review schedules and criteria;
  - Collecting data in the existing investment portfolio;
  - Scoring and prioritization outcomes;
  - Developing investment review schedules and criteria; and,
  - Deciding upon the mixture of investment in the overall IT investment portfolio.
- **Control Activities**
  - Consistently monitoring investments;
  - Involving the right people in control activities;
  - Documenting all actions and decisions;
  - Feeding lessons learned back into the selection phase;
  - Measuring interim results;
  - Updating analyses of each investment's costs, benefits, schedule, and risks;
  - Deciding whether to cancel, modify, continue, or accelerate an investment; and,

- Aggregating data and reviewing collective actions taken to date.
- **Evaluate Activities**
  - Assessing investment impact on mission performance and determining future prospects for the investment;
  - Measrements of actual vs. projected performance of investments;
  - Documented "track record" (investments and process);
  - Conducting post-implementation reviews using a standard methodology;
  - Feeding lessons learned back in to the Selection and Control phases; and,
  - Revising the selection and control phases based on lessons learned.

Required Step: Complete a comprehensive biennial ITIM process self assessment.

Develop ITIM Plan

The ITIM oversight organization develops and maintains an ITIM Plan which includes:

- The relationship of the ITIM process to the strategic planning activities;
- The ITIM improvement goals;
- The roles and responsibilities of the agency ITIM oversight organization and the agency ITIM Manager;
- A description of the agency ITIM process (Pre-Select, Select, Control, and Evaluate) which implements the ITIM framework; and,
- An implementation schedule including milestones for the ITIM Plan and the ITIM Improvement Plan.

Required Step: Establish a comprehensive Agency ITIM Plan.

The organization develops and implements an ITIM process improvement plan based on the findings of the ITIM maturity self assessment and reflecting goals, objectives, and strategies to advance through the ITIM Maturity Model.

The plan is reviewed, approved, and monitored by the agency ITIM oversight organization and includes the details necessary to track progress on a quarterly basis.

Progress reports are submitted to the ITIM oversight organization on a quarterly basis.

Required Steps:

1. *Develop and implement an ITIM process improvement plan reflecting goals, objectives, and strategies to advance through the ITIM Maturity Model.*
2. *Submit progress reports to the ITIM oversight organization on a quarterly basis.*

FUTURE TRENDS

The purpose of establishing an ITIM process is to improve the outcomes from IT investments in relation to their contribution to the strategic goals of the organization. In order to successfully implement an ITIM process, it must be both technically adequate and acceptable to users. From a technical perspective, the ITIM process is an exceptional example of state of the art best practices in the public sector. The ITIM framework builds on the project portfolio management best practice by incorporating assets into the portfolio management process. While this appears to be a minor addition, closer inspection reveals that IT assets constitute nearly 80% of the investments in the public sector and, historically, assets have been largely ignored until a catastrophic event occurs. The ITIM framework places assets into the investment selection process where assets must compete with other investments for scare resources and thereby creates transparency into the entire investment portfolio as opposed to simply selecting and controlling projects.

Sabherwal, Jeyaraj, and Chowa (2006) found that the key factors related to information system success are system quality and perceived usefulness. Clearly, a valid and reliable information system must be a minimum requirement for information system success and, without that basic foundation; an information system cannot be successful. Likewise, the system must include functions and features that are easy to use and result in more efficient work flows. An organization accomplishes both these requirements by implementing a portfolio management tool.

The ITIM framework requires fundamental organizational changes in the organization's approach to selecting and managing IT investments. Any plan for establishing and implementing the ITIM framework must adequately prepare for the organization changes that are required and address the potential for significant resistance from the organization. In order for an organization to realize the full benefit of the ITIM process, it must be adopted by the organization and its sub-components. It is not sufficient to simply "comply with the process" but instead requires a cultural change that adopts transparency of action and support for the enterprise strategic vision. Further, the general principle that information systems are composed of three elements: people, processes, and technology suggests that the people component of the equation as measured by user acceptance and satisfaction plays an important role in information system success.

Fernandez and Rainey (2006) examined the factors that are relevant to successful organizational change in the public sector. The authors identify eight factors as significant and, while others have viewed similar steps as stages or sequential processes, their view is that each of the factors is additive and can be performed in any order or in parallel. The model focuses on the human component of organizational change. The eight factors are:

- Verify and communicate the need for change;
- Disseminate a plan or roadmap to accomplish the change;

- Build internal support for the change through widespread participation in the process;
- Identify a champion for the change;
- Foster and develop external support for the change;
- Fully fund and resource the change process;
- Embed the change in the organizational processes and culture; and,
- Ensure that any change is sufficiently comprehensive enough to maintain congruence in the organization.

The authors also found that there are other unique challenges in the public sector in implementing these factors including frequent change in political appointments resulting in reduced continuity and shifting priorities, less delegated authority in the public sector, and public employees characterized as motivated by caution and security.

Gil-Garcia (2005) in a study of success factors in state website functionality stressed the importance of investigating both the technological factors and the surrounding social structures in explaining success as measured by state website functionality. His findings support the position that success factors include behavioral, social, and cultural aspects and these findings also support the general findings of Fernandez and Rainey (2006).

IMPLICATIONS AND FUTURE RESEARCH

User acceptance and fundamental cultural change are considered key to the success of any ITIM initiative. Additionally, while the portfolio management concept inherent in ITIM has been shown to be successful in the private sector, little empirical work has been done in the public sector despite the acknowledgement that the two sectors are driven by substantially different success factors.

Implementation of the ITIM process puts in place a system to allow a comprehensive evaluation process for both investments and the investment process. The ITIM process is implemented with a goal of improving prioritization of projects, more appropriately allocating scarce funds, and enhancing services through the identification, selection, control, and evaluation of high priority investments. Future research focused on the development and execution of an evaluation methodology to (1) assess the level of user acceptance of the ITIM process and (2) develop a portfolio evaluation model to assess ITIM effectiveness in improving IT investments would provide valuable information for refining the ITIM framework. The goal of this research is to explore the impact of user acceptance of ITIM on the success of portfolio management in the public sector.

Gartner's 2002 prediction (Harris & Casonato, 2002) that by 2005, more than two thirds of the IT investment decisions by leading edge corporations would be based on non-financial or synergistic measures as the primary decision factors in investment selections appears to have been accurate. This bodes well for evaluating public sector investments where measuring financial ROI is frequently not relevant.

The Gartner paper identifies several categories of return that may be appropriate in the public sector:

- Improved customer service;
- Increased employee effectiveness;
- Increased process effectiveness;
- Creation of intellectual assets;
- Connectedness;
- Asset utilization; and,
- Improved reputation.

The Center for Technology in Government published a public value framework for determining ROI for government IT (Cresswell, Burke, & Pardo, 2006). Return on Investment (ROI) has been a standard measure for assessing the value of potential information technology (IT) investments or expenditures for decades. The concept of using ROI to select investments was developed and matured in the private sector corporate environment where generally ROI is measured in financial terms. Using a standardized measure of ROI (dollars invested vs. dollars returned) made it somewhat easier to make comparisons between investments to arrive at an investment selection decision. Further, although corporations offer many different products and services, they share a common overarching mission of exiting to increase shareholder wealth which is generally measured in financial terms.

When the concept of ROI was moved to the government sector, problems arose with the traditional view of ROI as a financial measure. Many of the products and services government organizations provide show little or no financial ROI or financial ROI is so far removed from the investment that the connection is tenuous at best. The Center for Technology in Government proposes a public value framework for measuring ROI that encompasses a more complete set of criteria for assessing ROI from the public perspective. This approach to ROI determination in the public sector mirrors the predictions made by Gartner in 2002. A public value ROI approach is similar to the approach in the corporate environment where ROI is measured from the shareholder's perspective.

In the public value framework, the authors identify two broad categories of public value: directly delivered benefits and the value of government itself. Within these categories, value can be created in a number of different dimensions: financial, political, social, strategic, ideological, and stewardship.

In comparison, the corporate environment also divides ROI into two broad categories: tangible (generally financial) and intangible (generally results that are difficult to quantify). The public value framework categorizes and defines the intangible returns and then provides guidance on how those returns can be measured and quantified. Value measurements can include:

- Change in efficiency;
- Change in effectiveness;
- Enabling value creating activities; and,
- Intrinsic process enhancements.

CONCLUSION

ITIM is a management process that provides for the identification (pre-selection), selection, control, and evaluation of business driven IT investments across the investment lifecycle. ITIM uses structured processes to minimize risks and maximize return on investments. This chapter describes an ITIM framework focused on linking strategic business plans to the selection, control, and evaluation of IT Investments. The ITIM process delivers value to an organization through:

- More efficient utilization of resources by aligning technology investments with strategic business needs;
- Increased investment transparency which facilitates IT collaboration and partnerships;
- Increased workforce productivity through the use of technology to address business needs; and,
- Increased value for citizens through improved business processes.

Successful implementation of the ITIM framework requires fundamental organizational change and recognition that the ITIM process is iterative and requires a multi-year commitment to advance to a fully mature process. However, implementation of the ITIM framework will begin to pay dividends in the very early stages through the elimination of duplicative efforts; high risk, low return initiatives; and

non-business focused systems. The use of ITIM enables enterprise performance management and creates a business-results focused system for managing IT investments across the investment lifecycle.

REFERENCES

A summary of first practices and lessons learned in information technology portfolio management, Technical Report, Federal CIO Council, Best Practices Committee, 2002. Available via: http://cio.gov/Documents/BPC_Portfolio_final.pdf.

Bakos, Y., & Treacy, M. (1986). Information technology and corporate strategy: A research perspective. *MIS Quarterly, 10*(2), 107-119.

Brynjolfsson, E., & Hitt, L. (1998). Beyond the productivity paradox. *Communications of the ACM, 41*(8), 49-55.

Clemons, E. (1991). Evaluation of strategic investments in information technology. *Communications of the ACM, 34*(1), 22-36.

Cresswell, A. M., Burke, G. B., & Pardo, T. A. (2006) *Advancing return on investment analysis for government IT: A public value framework*. Albany, NY: University at Albany, SUNY, Center for Technology in Government. Retrieved September 17, 2006 from http://www.ctg.albany.edu/

Dedrick, J., Gurbaxani, V., & Kraemer, K. (2003). Information technology and economic performance: A critical review of the empirical evidence. *ACM Computing Surveys, 35*(1), 1- 28.

Dufner, D., Holley, L., & Reed, B. (2005). Models for U.S. state government strategic information systems planning. *Proceeding of the 38th Hawaii International Conference on Systems Sciences*, 1-9.

Fernandez, S., & Rainey, H. (2006). Managing successful organizational change in the public sector. *Public Administration Review, 66*(2), 168-176.

Fitzpatrick, E. (2005). *Planning and implementing IT portfolio management.* Gaithersburg, MD: IT Economics Corporation.

Harris, K., & Casonato, R. (2002). *Where is the Value on Investments in IT?* (No. SPA-17-2345): Gartner, Inc.

Improving Mission Performance Through Strategic Information Management and Technology: Learning from Leading Organizations. (1994). (pp. 1 - 50): United States Government Accountability Office, Washington, D.C.

Information Technology Investment Management: A Framework for Assessing and Improving Process Maturity. (2004). (pp. 1 - 138): United States Government Accountability Office, Washington, D.C. *The standard for portfolio management* (2006). Newtown Square, PA: PMI Publications.

Gil-Garcia, J. R. (2005). Exploring the success factors of state website functionality: An empirical investigation. *Proceedings of the 2005 national conference on digital government research* Atlanta, Georgia: Digital Government Research Center.

Hitt, L., & Brynjolfsson, E. (1996). Productivity, business profitability, and consumer surplus: Three different measures of information technology value. *MIS Quarterly, 20*(2), 121-140.

Markowitz, H. (1952). Portfolio selection. *The Journal of Finance, 7,* 77-91.

McFarlan, F. W. (1981). Portfolio approach to information systems. *Harvard Business Review* (September-October), 142-150.

Rai, A., Patnayakuni, R., & Patnayakuni, N. (1997). Technology investment and business

performance. *Communications of the ACM, 40*(7), 89-97.

Sabherwal, R., Jeyaraj, A., & Chowa, C. (2006). Information system success: Individual and organizational determinants. *Management Science, 52*(12), 1849-1860.

Weill, P. (1990). Strategic investment in information technology: An empirical study. *Information Age, 12*(3), 141-147.

KEY TERMS

Asset: An investment that has completed a final post implementation review or that was placed in service prior to the adoption of this standard and incorporated into the portfolio.

Information Technology Investment Management (ITIM): A business driven management process that provides for the identification (preselection), selection, control, and evaluation of IT investments across the investment lifecycle. ITIM uses structured processes to minimize risks and maximize return on investments.

Investment Portfolio: (1) A management tool comprised of essential information about technology investments, structured to facilitate the evaluation of investment alternatives in support of strategic business plans. (2) The hardware, software, and related systems operated by an organization to support the flow or processing of information in support of business activities.

New Asset: An investment that has been in operation less than 12 months.

Chapter II
An Information Technology Planning Framework for an Industry Cluster

Albert Wee Kwan Tan
National University of Singapore, Singapore

ABSTRACT

Strategic IS planning (SISP) has been found to be a key issue of concern for management across organizations in various industries. However, most SISP studies have been conducted in the context of large, for-profit organizations but not at the industry level. An industry approach to SISP has been found to be most effective in Singapore to develop the IT capabilities of each industry. This chapter introduces a framework for planning of information technologies (IT) for the industry cluster. More specifically, the different stages in planning and executing an industry scale IT project for supply chain management are discussed here based on an example from Singapore. This generic framework proposed can be used in any industry where IT plays a strategic role for industry transformation.

INTRODUCTION

According to Michael Porter, similar companies are not the only companies that tend to cluster together. It happens in virtually every business and it has to do with natural competitive advantages created by the clustering process (Porter, 1998). When companies cluster together, they tend to have a mutual reinforcement and the flow of information is enhanced when these companies work in the same field. It is much more efficient to do business within a cluster because companies can turn to suppliers or other companies who are near them, rather than creating everything from zero. It is also easy to find people, new business partners and it is a self-reinforcing process that tends to feed on itself.

In fact, the government plays a strategic role to improve the performance of each key industry through the development and deployment of such project. Carlsson and Mudambi (2003) find that one of the primary challenges for policymakers is to create a favorable climate for private entrepreneurship, often related to the formation of clusters. This however cannot be directed, only facilitated. Furthermore, once clusters have been formed, a comprehensive set of facilitating policies, from information provision and networking to tax codes and labor laws, are necessary (Braunerhjelm and Carlsson, 2003).

As such, the deployment of innovation is important from the national development point of view, and in order to benefit the stakeholders in the national economy, the deployment should take place in industry level instead of supporting individual companies only. From the companies' point of view, industry level is a natural environment to enhance their opportunities to do business with the supply chain partners. Therefore it makes sense to examine the IT planning and deployment at an industry level than enterprise level for economic growth.

The purpose of the chapter is to examine existing IT planning frameworks that are applicable to industry and if none are found, extend or adapt the frameworks to meet the industry needs. The framework will need to address the following questions:

- Is there existing IT planning frameworks for industry cluster available from the literature?
- What are the key activities involved and their duration in each phase of the framework?
- How does each actor add-value during implementation and the key measurements of success in each phase?

- Are there potential risks that can be avoided when implementing such industry cluster projects?

After reviewing the literatures for SISP, we were not able to find any framework that is meant for industry. We therefore are proposing a new framework to provide a systematic approach to deploy information technologies within an industry cluster. This framework is adapted from Lederer and Salmela (1996) framework and applied to a few industries in Singapore. A case study is used to illustrate its application.

LITERATURE REVIEW

Strategic information system planning (SISP) has consistently been identified as one of the most critical issues facing IS executives and academic researchers (King, 1995; Lederer and Salmela, 1996; Segars and Grover, 1999; Teo and Ang, 2000; Li and Chen, 2001; Basu et al., 2002; Lee and Pai, 2003; Newkirk et al., 2003; Brown, 2004). From the surveys of information systems management issues conducted during the recent decade, SISP remains one of the major issues facing IT/IS executives and corporate general managers (Brancheau et al., 1996; Watson et al., 1997; Chou and Jou, 1999; Gottschalk, 2001; Pimchangthong, 2003). SISP has been described as a managerial and interactive learning process for integrating information systems considerations into the corporate planning process, aligning the application of IS to business goals, developing detailed IS plans and determining information requirements to achieve business objectives (Earl, 1989; Galliers, 1991; Auer and Reponen, 1997; Teo and King, 1997; Cunningham, 2001; Lee and Pai, 2003).

Prior studies found that industry as a whole operates differently from individual enterprises in many aspects. Moreover, organizational theories that are applicable to each enterprise may not fit in an industry setting (Wesh and White, 1981; Lertwongsatien and Wongpinunwatana, 2003). Numerous results of studies target to these enterprises are not suited to the industry as whole since there are many different characteristics that exist between enterprises and industry (Blili and Raymond, 1993). Raymond (2003) indicated that as the result of globalization and e-business, industry faces new challenges and to enhance their competitiveness, industry must re-evaluate the business conditions and environment. Clustering has been a theme in international business research for several decades, but has only become a central concern in the last five to ten years. The line of thinking traditionally is to research on the impact of foreign direct investment on host-country productivity (Blomstrom, 1986; Cantwell, 1986; Caves, 1974; Kokko, 1992).

Porter (1990) argued that sustainability is a function of the dynamism of the cluster which, in turn, is a function of the interaction between the four elements of the cluster's "diamond" (demanding customers, related and supporting industries, factor endowments, and firm structure and rivalry). The supply chain deployment is hardly ever considered as purely technological innovations only but it involves several elements related to industry clustering process at the same time. The deployment may be considered for development of infrastructure, advanced carrier or cargo handling technologies, development of IT - or business processes. Therefore in the deployment of such projects, multiple skills and approaches are pre-requites for industry cluster. This will result in industry cluster development in addition to the companies dealing directly within the industry. It is common that consortiums are established for projects or development initiatives which later turn into industry cluster, where organizations from related industries and the surrounding society are represented.

AN INFORMATION TECHNOLOGY PLANNING FRAMEWORK FOR INDUSTRY

A planning process can defined as a set of partially ordered steps intended to reach a goal. A typical SISP process follows a series of well-defined steps. This process may differ substantially from one organization to another. Some organizations might choose to select or omit some particular steps or the tasks within them (Lederer and Salmela, 1996). Premkumar and King (1994) indicates that the SISP process is the set of activities in analyzing the external environment for opportunities and threats, assessing the internal environment to identify strengths and weaknesses, analyzing the business plan and its implications for the IS functions, forecasting IS technology trends and their effect on the industry and the organization, identifying the users information requirement, and developing an information architecture, and developing a set of strategic programs and plans for managing the IS functions.

Researchers have proposed numerous different SISP processes. For example, Mentzas (1997) proposed a five phases of SISP process including strategic awareness, strategic analysis, strategic conception, strategic formulation and strategy implementation planning (Table 1).

Lederer and Salmela (1996) proposed an information systems strategic planning theory that encompasses seven important constructs (external environment, internal environment, planning resources, information plan, plan implementation and alignment), as shown in Figure 1. This theoretical SISP framework hypothesizes external and internal environments as well as planning resources as constructs that affects the planning process. Furthermore, Lederer and Salmela (1996) indicated that numerous factors with respect to internal environment influence information systems strategic planning, including organization's corporate culture, organizational

Table 1. Phases and stages of the SISP process (Source: adapted from Mentzas, 1997)

Phases	Stages
Strategic awareness	☐Identification of strategic goals ☐Identification of business and IT systems ☐Definition of planning process objectives
Situation analysis	☐Analysis of business systems ☐Analysis of organizational systems ☐Analysis of external business environment ☐Analysis of external IT environment
Strategy conception	☐Scanning of the future ☐Identification of alternative scenarios ☐Scenario elaboration
Strategy formulation	☐Formulation of business architecture ☐Formulation of IT architecture ☐Formulation of organizational solutions ☐Synthesis and prioritization
Strategy implementation planning	☐Definition of action plan elements ☐Evaluation of plan ☐Definition of follow-up and control procedures

size, organizational structure (mechanistic vs. organic), management style, and maturity of organization's information systems management experience, information planning goals and objectives. Additionally, this framework showed that a more comprehensive planning process produces a more useful information systems plan. Moreover, it further suggested that a more useful information systems plan produces greater plan implementation, and greater plan implementation produces better alignment.

Figure 2 is a proposed framework that is adapted from Lederer and Salmela (1996) framework which can be apply to any industry clusters. The framework assumed a coordinator (a neutral party, for example World Bank, United Nation Council) to collaborate with industry and government departments to perform each planning process efficiently. The process phases are similar, irrespective of industry (except during pilot

implementation where there might be variants) and within each industry, business environment will need to be re-examine as part of industry analysis.

The phases/sub processes of the framework are discussed as follows:

Phase 1: Industry Scan

Market demand or requirements (potentially the more specific customer needs) and the ability to respond to these requirements determine the performance gaps in each industry. In this phase, the coordinator will conduct survey and gap analysis with industry to identify performance gaps within the industry. The gaps could be operational or strategic in nature. The instruments used can range from field surveys to focus group interviews. Survey can be conducted on a yearly basis to identify trends and best practices

Figure 1. A theoretical model of SISP (Source: Lederer and Salmela, 1996)

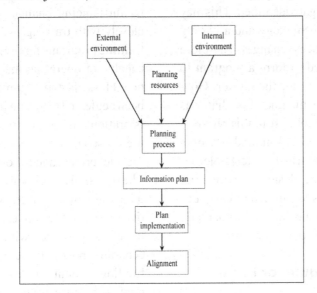

Figure 2. Framework to deploy information technologies for an indusry cluster

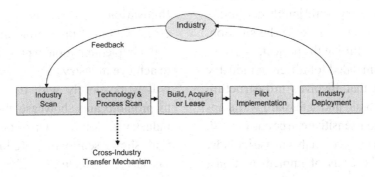

in each industry. The potential risk involved in this phase is that the interested party might take too long a time to complete the study. Economic or structural changes would have taken place that might make the initial study invalid.

Phase 2: Technology & Process Scan

The performance gaps detected during the previous phase may be addressed by technology, new organization and process, or a combination of these. The coordinator will seek advice from research institutes and technology providers for solutions to narrow those gaps identified. This may involve more than one technology and a variety of organizational and process changes. Therefore the coordinator will need to form a program to conceptualize the solution for the cluster. Government could also takes the role of mediator as it is in the government's interest in this phase to facilitate and establish mechanisms and networks required to transfer the information, technologies and knowledge within the cluster. The potential risk at this phase includes recommendation of unproven technologies or if the industry is not ready to embrace the new concept or technology.

Phase 3: Build, Acquire or Lease

In order to ensure that the solution is both economically and operationally feasible, it is crucial to consider its financing opportunities, scalabilities, risks and projected life cycle of the solution. The coordinator and industry could jointly determine whether to build, acquire or lease the solution. Depending on the nature of the project, different approach is recommended for different industry setting. Solution that involves infrastructure might be better to build and safeguard while applications that are non-sensitive can be outsourced. The potential risks involved at this phase include: underestimating the costs of implementations; difficulty in soliciting participation from the industry as they do not want to be guinea pig; or the participating companies may have hidden agenda to make use of this project to secure government funding.

Phase 4: Pilot Implementation

The pilot implementation is a test-bed for novel application (in a new environment) that may be based on new innovations and technologies. The coordinator and industry will identify suitable pilot companies to test the solution and manage the project till completion. The coordinator

helps to smoothen the implementation process by introducing change management and work closely with training institutes to establish new training programs for the industry so that they are capable of operating the IT systems using their new IT skills and capabilities. This has always been neglected resulting in strong resistance from operation staff in adopting the new system. Funding is used to motivate companies to take part in the pilot project and to co-share some of the risks. The potential risks involved in this phase include: pilot companies exiting the project for competitive reason as they are expected to share some of their best practices with other participants; for economic reason if the government changes the funding amount due to overwhelming response; pilot companies are not convinced that the solution is meeting their original objectives.

Phase 5: Industry Deployment

Innovation diffusion is the next phase after establishing the innovation or novel application (pilot implementation in practical terms) in order to achieve industry acceptance. The coordinator will work closely with the solution providers to promote and showcase the solution for the industry to follow. This can be done through trade shows, seminars, and education workshops. The last phase includes analysis of the results and experiences to be shared within the cluster. There is a feedback loop from this deployment experience as part of the input to a new deployment process. Thus a loop of continuous improvement is created at the industry level and innovation is spread widely with the potential to revolutionize the industry. The potential risks involved in this phase include getting buy-in from the industry to adopt the solution due to its high cost or the industry is not ready to make radical process change to adopt such solution.

The main activities of each phase, duration, key actors involved, outcome and potential risks for each phase are summarized in Table 2.

Table 2. Key activities, actors and outcomes for each phase in the framework

	Industry Scan	Technology and Process Scan	Build, Acquisition or Lease	Pilot Implementation	Industry Deployment
Main activities in each phase	• Field survey • Focus group interviews	• Gap analysis • Gather best practices • Technology tracking	• Develop Business case • Select companies to pilot • Evaluate IT solution	• Manage pilot project • Provide training for users	• Awareness and marketing programs • Document lessons learnt
Average duration	1 – 3 months	1 – 3 months	6 – 12 months	12-24 months	Ongoing
Key actors in each phase	• Coordinator • Government • Industry	• Research institutions • Coordinator • Technology providers	• Coordinator • Technology providers • Pilot companies	• Coordinator • Technology providers • Government • Pilot companies	• Coordinator • Technology providers • Government • Industry
Outcome from each phase	• Market demand • Performance gaps	• Potential solutions • Trends and best practices	• Project organization • Solution selected • Establishment of project objectives • Industry partners selected for pilot implementation • Financing plan for solution providers • Prototype	• Establishment of project team • Pilot implementation and skills development • Funding schemes and criteria for pilot companies • Analysis of results and potential pitfalls to avoid	• Scope of implementation • Marketing and promotion plans • Deployment strategies • Measurement of success • Analysis of results and follow up actions.
Potential Risks	• Study taken too long	• Unproven technology • Industry not ready for new technology	• Under-estimate the cost • Industry not keen to participate • Companies with hidden agenda • Solution too expensive	• Users not convince • Pilot companies quit project • Government changes funding criteria	• Industry not keen to adopt • Too costly solution even after government funding

CASE STUDY: IT PLANNING AND IMPLEMENTATION FOR THE LOGISTICS INDUSTRY IN SINGAPORE

The following example will illustrate how the proposed framework can be applied to the logistics industry in Singapore. The landscape of the logistics industry in Singapore is changing and is no longer just managing warehouses or offering isolated transport services. Instead, logistics companies in Singapore are offering integrated logistics services such as reverse logistics, product configuration and international procurement with regional coverage. With the increased demand for more information about the cargo shipments, more third party logistics companies are investing more IT into their businesses to meet this growing demand. As a result, an IT planning and implementation framework is needed to assist the industry in the transformation.

Phase 1: Industry Scan

In 1998, a study sponsored by the government was conducted by Accenture (formerly known as Andersen Consulting) to map out the essential IT functionality to support the logistics industry. The main objectives of this study were to:

- Establish an industry-wide logistics best practice using IT that could be adopted by the industry upon completion;
- Conduct an industry-wide analysis of the logistics sector to determine IT gaps and the functional requirements to narrow those gaps;
- Identify new EDI and Internet message standards that could be deployed to existing EDI networks; and
- Propose an IT implementation methodology as a guide for the logistics industry.

Eight third parties logistics companies (3PL) from the industry were selected for this study with the majority of them providing more than two types of logistics services (e.g. warehousing, transportation, etc). A focus group interview was conducted for each of these companies at their premises. Each interview lasted about one day and involved a site visit and software demonstration. The interviewees were mainly senior executives and operational managers. Accenture examined the internal processes of the eight companies, and the interactions between them and the other entities (such as the shippers, consignees, carriers and government agencies). The internal processes of the other entities (e.g., the procurement process of consignees and shipping process of shippers) were outside the scope of this study.

Within each of the eight 3PLs, key operational processes were relatively straightforward. The management of the eight companies had correctly focused their attention on the need to reduce the cycle time of each process. However, the lack of integrated IT systems to support these processes had resulted in:

- Duplication of work; and
- An absence of performance measurements to monitor overall process effectiveness.

Within this industry, there is a large number of interactions between the logistics companies and external entities, similar to a cluster. While most interactions with the government agencies are electronically linked, interactions between the companies and with commercial entities are still mainly paper-based. This had resulted in duplication of effort, increased chances of data errors and longer cycle times. Linking the entities electronically within the supply chain would help to reduce the overall cycle time and achieve higher standards, such as:

- A cycle time reduction from 5 hours to less than 2 hours to deliver goods from the manufacturers' premises to the airport; and
- A cycle time reduction from 8 hours to less than 4 hours to deliver goods from port to consignee.

It is found that most 3PL companies attempt to provide as wide a range of 3PL services to their clients as possible, with warehouse management and operation as the most commonly offered 3PL service. These companies also have extensive regional and international network, and serve a number of industries including the main ones like electronics, chemical, high-tech and computers, and consumer goods.

The 3PL industry in Singapore is viewed as growing and is ahead of many of its counterparts in Asia. The key strengths of the industry include numerous factors such as good connectivity and language skill, while its main weaknesses are a shortage of qualified staff and high operating cost. There are a number of concerns and issues raised, such as lack of qualified staff, oversupply of warehousing space in Singapore, competition from the influx of foreign 3PL firms to Singapore, and regulations on free trade zone, seaport and airport, all of which may have policy implications.

With regards to global trends, the move towards greater outsourcing is the most frequently singled out broad trend. Others cited include growing pressure from customers, the rise of mega 3PL companies, and the relentless drive towards greater use of IT and e-commerce in the industry. Most of these trends identified are noted to hold in Asia countries including Singapore. The exception is M&A activity that is unlikely to occur in Singapore, due to a lack of interest among the local firms on merger.

Responding to the trend towards greater globalization, all 3PL companies are noted to expand their overseas network. They however differ in their network expansion plan, with the foreign 3PL firms more likely to focus on global expansion and the local 3PL companies more likely to consider strengthening their Asia network.

Many companies are also taking the challenge arising from e-commerce seriously, and most have at least a few e-commerce services such as pre-alert service and track and trace on offer. While acknowledging that there is potential in B-to-C service, many companies do not appear keen to pursue opportunity in B-to-C actively.

The 3PL companies are able to identify various opportunities and challenges arising from the trends discussed. Greater awareness of the need to outsource and of the many capabilities the 3PL firms in rendering such services is the most frequently cited opportunity under the discussion on broad trends.

With the trend towards greater globalization, many companies see opportunity to follow their clients overseas to provide logistics support. They also expect globalization to result in greater complexity in network and higher logistics cost in Asia. This presents opportunity as well as challenge to the 3PL firms.

As the use of e-commerce proliferates, there is increasing opportunity to provide e-logistics services. The key challenge however is the difficulty in developing, operating and maintaining the e-commerce system due to both the difficulty in recruiting and retaining IT staff.

The challenges in providing supply chain management are many. The most frequently factors seem to relate to the various dimensions of customer relationship such as issues like customers not knowing their logistics functions well, customers withholding information, and customers providing unrealistic SCM implementation time frame.

To capitalize on the opportunities available and to meet the challenges, most companies are keen to position themselves as supply chain solutions providers and would like to leverage on e-commerce, information technology and information system. For the foreign companies, they would also like to position themselves as leading global players. The local companies on the other hand see themselves more as dominant Asia players or player with strong regional network and local knowledge.

The critical success factors invariably relate to resources, with having the right people being singled out as the most critical success factor of all. Others include information technology and process.

Arising from this study are several implications. With respect to globalization, the trend clearly favours 3PL companies that have extensive overseas network. This holds implication for those that lack the resources to establish such network, as is the case of many local 3PL companies in Singapore. For the larger 3PL local firms in Singapore, their preferred strategy is to expand organically and/or to forge alliances abroad, but not to merge with other local 3PL firms. For the many smaller 3PL local firms that this study has no time to investigate, it is not sure what will be their choices and responses.

On e-commerce, it is always said that the ability to fulfill order is key to the success of many dot. com companies. Yet this study reveals a general reluctance of many 3PL firms to service B-to-C

e-commerce, particularly those that are run by companies without good track record. Such being the case, one implication is that some dot. com companies, such as those that are new and lack the track record may experience difficulty in getting 3PL firms to support them.

Finally it is also observed that there is a certain level of concern and perhaps frustration voiced out by the 3PL companies against their clients. Invariably, this is detected from the various comments made by the 3PL firms during the personal interview, such as comments like customers do not understand the complexity of and difficulty in providing logistics support in Asia, customers lack the understanding of their logistics process, and customers withhold critical information. Taken together, these comments could imply expectation between the parties is not managed properly, or that there is a gap of understanding and communication between them.

Phase 2: Technology Scan

An IT functional framework describing the functional modules needed to support the industry was developed after the study by Accenture, with the aim of facilitating information sharing and exchange. This framework is shown in figure 3.

Figure 3. IT functional framework for logistics industry

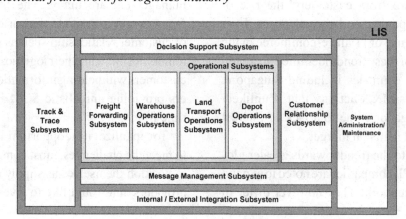

The core of this functional requirement framework consists of the Customer Relationship Subsystem and the Operational Subsystems. The Customer Relationship Subsystem will help logistics providers to provide integrated logistics services by maintaining contracts spanning all services, delivering a single bill to the customer, tracking performance and managing customer contacts. The Operational Subsystems – Freight Forwarding, Warehouse operations, Land Transportation Operations and Container Depot Operations – will enable end-to-end processing of the key business processes. The implementation of the Customer Relationship Subsystem and the Operational Subsystems will enable the logistics providers to improve customer service and process performance, and provide them with the means to monitor the efficiency of their operations.

To support the demand for value-added logistics services and increasing volume of business, a Decision Support Subsystem to model and simulate facilities, networks and customers' requirements is recommended to help logistics providers to utilize their assets more effectively and be more responsive to their customers. The Track and Trace Subsystem will help to monitor shipments at the level of detail needed by the customer and by selected milestones.

The logistics industry is characterized by numerous interactions between the entities and within each entity. The Internal/External Integration Subsystem and the Message Management Subsystem are thus required to manage the flow of information into and out of the core modules using specific integration methods (e.g., API, Servlet) and direct the requests to the appropriate subsystems. With these subsystems in place, there will be a reduction in the overall cycle time across logistics providers and the external entities and Singapore will be better positioned to conduct business electronically as eCommerce gathers momentum.

Accenture recommended that government agencies in Singapore to consider the following four recommendations to improve the flow of information within the logistics industry:

- The EDITRANS (EDI for Transportation System) Working Group should consider including additional EDI messages to facilitate information interchange between the logistics companies and other commercial entities. Currently, such information flows are paper-based with a standard format and thus can be automated;
- Encourage shippers, consignees and carriers to increase their electronic linkages so that the overall processing cycle times can be improved and data errors reduced;
- Assist logistics companies to develop an internet presence so that they will be well-positioned to provide logistics service within the region using Singapore as an eCommerce hub; and
- Provide financial assistance for logistics companies to acquire some of the subsystems identified in the IT functional framework, in particular, those that are common across service providers such as the External/Internal Integration Subsystem and the Message Management Subsystem.

Phase 3: Build, Acquire or Lease

Accenture's recommendation to exploit eCommerce for information and document exchange were implemented by the respective parties to cut down the overall cycle time. For example, Singapore Trade Development Board (TDB) and Infocomm Development Authority of Singapore (IDA) had initiated an IT Action Plan to identify key programs and deliverables to prepare the logistics industry in the face of new opportunities and challenges. The overall goal of this Action Plan was to provide an IT framework for the deployment and integration of information and technologies across the logistics industry.

The action plan is needed to meet the needs of the various logistics players with varying capabilities and this resulted in a three-pronged thrust in advancing the IT-readiness of the logistics industry. The three key thrusts were:

i) Facilitate intra-company integration to enhance logistics competencies
ii) Enhance inter-company connectivity to foster business collaboration
iii) Establish international linkages to position Singapore as the Asia Logistics Hub

The implementation would evolve in stages, namely internal integration, external integration and international linkages. Each stage would involve different sets of IT requirements and it was important for companies to migrate progressively from stage to stage to ensure that information from earlier stage will form the foundation for the next stage. Funding schemes were made available to attract logistics companies to participate in the pilot program. Potential IT solution identified in the previous phase would be selected by pilot companies for implementation.

Phase 4: Pilot Implementation

As a follow-up from Accenture study, EDI for Transportation System (EDITRANS) standard was launched (figure 4).

Seven EDI messages standards were developed in compliance with UN/EDIFACT in the initial phase.

The intention of EDITRANS was to enable freight forwarders to respond faster to shippers' needs and thus tighten the supply chain and resulting in better customer service. However, after more than a year of promotion and marketing to the shippers and logistics providers, the number of companies using EDITRANS was still relatively small. A closer look into the low penetration rate of EDITRANS revealed several causes:

a. Shippers did not engage logistics companies in the same proportion of buyers to suppliers. For example, shippers could use only one logistics company to manage their full logistics requirements.
b. Some shippers have the luxury of having order processing clerks from the logistics providers stationed at their premises to

Figure 4. Information flows between shippers and the logistics companies

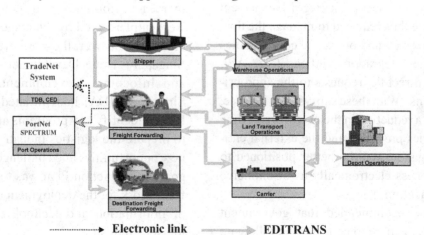

manage their export and import documentation. Therefore, EDI was not crucial in this context.

With a limited number of shippers interested in using EDITRANS, few logistics providers were keen to implement EDI as cost savings were low without a critical mass. This confirmed the fact that B2B eCommerce would prevail only when there is sufficient critical mass to warrant sustainability. In fact, the logistics industry has refocused their efforts to target shipping lines instead to use EDITRANS for exchanging Bill of Lading information between these shipping lines and freight forwarders. This shift in direction was logical since a single shipping line could be serving many freight forwarders.

Phase 5: Industry Deployment

An integrated IT project that manages the flow of trade-related information was launched in June 2004 to leverage on EDITRANS for shippers, freight forwarders, carriers and financial institu-

tions to facilitate the flow of goods within, through and out of Singapore. This single web interface for all trade-related IT systems as shown in Figure 5 will help logistics players cut down on multiple data entry steps with less duplication of manual efforts and reduction in human errors which will ultimately improve efficiency and time to market. The net effect is increased competitiveness for the logistics industry.

The integrated IT project will automate the creation and exchange of commercial and regulatory documentation necessary for trade. The Singapore government will invest up to S$50 million over five years to develop the system, which will cover project development expenditure, assistance for industry adoption and other project costs. Singapore has a number of electronic systems that manage the flow of regulatory and commercial information for trade. These include PortNet for sea logistics, Cargo Community Network for air logistics and Marinet for dangerous goods declarations. Most pervasively used is TradeNet, the world's first nationwide electronic trade documentation system which allows the trading community

Figure 5. TradeXchange for shippers, forwarders, banks, ports and governments

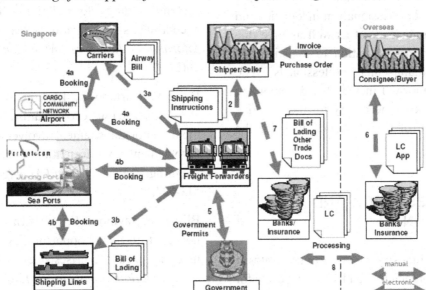

to submit permit applications electronically to the relevant government bodies for processing. TradeNet was launched in January 1989. These existing IT applications have served the trade and logistics communities well for the past 20 years, will be integrated with the platform.

When completed in end 2008, the integrated IT system will become the gateway to the new TradeNet system for trade permit applications. Such integration will enhance process and information flow in the entire trade and logistics community which will contribute to improving overall competitiveness of the sector. An Inter-Agency Steering Committee has been formed to oversee the development, implementation and adoption of the services offered under the integrated IT projected. A tender exercise was conducted to shortlist qualified vendors for the development of the IT systems. This will spin off many opportunities for IT solutions providers to build new and innovative technology capabilities

To support the continuous upgrading the capabilities of the logistics industry, the TDB and IDA have also initiated with the Chartered Institute of Logistics and Transport of Singapore and other relevant institutions to formulate a Certified Professional Logisticians or CPL programme. It will be used as the definitive standard for measuring competence and professionalism in logistics and supply chain management as well as give due recognition and accreditation to logistics and supply chain management professionals. The CPL programme will include the development of critical IT skills, necessary for the effective implementation of the IT Action Plan for the logistics industry.

FUTURE RESEARCH AND CONCLUSION

The logistics industry mentioned illustrates a systematic approach in the IT planning cycle for an industry cluster. It is apparent that in some clusters, the prerequisites to adopt innovations are more favorable than others due to a number of factors: product life cycle, competition, government policies and directions, etc. This is a limitation in the proposed framework that needs to be addressed. Further research work can be expanded to address these factors either individually or holistically.

Although the investigation in this case involves the logistics cluster only, the authors are confident that the framework proposed is generic enough for other industry cluster. By understanding the main activities and outcomes of each phase within the framework, better planning and allocation of resources can be achieved for both the company and the government. Furthermore, the potential risks identified in each phase can be used by project managers to validate the viability of the project before more investments are committed. What could be more appropriate and attractive would be to develop specific strategy at each phase to engage the companies within each cluster.

REFERENCES

Auer, T., & Reponen, T. (1997). Information systems strategy formulation embedded into a continuous organizational learning process. *Information Resources Management Journal,* *10*(2), 32-43.

Basu, V., Hartono, E., Lederer, A. L., & Sethi, V. (2002). The impact of organizational commitment, senior management involvement, and team involvement on information systems strategic planning. *Information and Management, 39*(6), 513-524.

Blili, S., & Raymond, L. (1993). Information technology: threats and opportunities for small and medium-sized enterprises. *International Journal of Information Management, 13*(6), 439-448.

Blomstrom, M. (1986). Foreign Investment and Productive Efficiency: The Case of Mexico. *Journal of Industrial Economics, 35*(1), 97-110.

Brancheau, J. C., Janz, B. D., & Wetherbe, J. C. (1996). Key issues in information systems management: 1994-95 SIM Delphi results. *MIS Quarterly, 20*(2), 225-242.

Braunerhjelm, P., & Carlsson, B. (2003). Introduction: Regional Growth, Clusters and Institutions. *Industry and Innovation, 10*(1), 1-3.

Brown, I. T. (2004). Testing and extending theory in strategic information systems planning through literature analysis. *Information Resource Management Journal, 17*(4), 20-48.

Cantwell, J. (1989). *Technological Innovation and Multinational Corporations*. Oxford: Basil Blackwell.

Carlsson, B., & Mudambi, R. (2003). Globalization, Entrepreneurship, and Public Policy: A System View. *Industry and Innovation, 10*(1), 103-116.

Caves, R. E. (1974). Multinational Firms, Competition and Productivity in HostCountry Markets. *Economics, 41*, 176-93.

Chou, H., & Jou, S. (1999). MIS key issues in Taiwan's enterprises. *International Journal of Information Management, 19*, 369-387.

Cunningham, N. (2001). a model for the role of information systems in strategic change within healthcare organizations. *Organizational Development Journal, 19*, spring, 93-105.

Earl, M. J. (1989). *Management Strategies for Information Technology*. Prentice Hall, Englewood Cliffs, New York.

Galliers, R. D. (1991). Information systems strategic planning myths reality and guidelines for successful implementation systems planning. *European Journal of Information Systems, 1*(1), 55-64.

Gottschalk, P. (2001). Key issues in IS management in Norway: an empirical study based on Q-methodology. *Information Resources Management Journal, 14*(2), 37-45.

Infocomm Development Authority of Singapore website: http://www.ida.gov.sg.

King, W. R. (1995). The payoff from IS strategic planning. *Information Systems Management, 2*(3), 66-68.

Kokko, A. (1992). *Foreign Direct Investment, Host Country Characteristics, and Spillovers*. Ph.D. dissertation, Stockholm School of Economics.

Lederer, A. L., & Salmela, H. (1996). Toward a theory of strategic information systems planning. *Journal of Strategic Information Systems, 5*, 237-253.

Lee, G. G., & Pai, R. J. (2003). Effects of organizational context and inter-group behaviour on the success of strategic information systems planning: an empirical study. *Behaviour and Information Technology, 22*(4), July-August, 263-280.

Lertwongsatien, C., & Wongpinunwatana, N. (2003). E-commerce adoption in Thailand: an empirical study of Small and Medium Enterprises (SMEs). *Journal of Global Information Technology Management, 6*(30), 67-83.

Li, E.Y., & Chen, H. G. (2001). output-driven information systems planning: a case study. *Information and Management, 38*(3), 195-199.

Mentzas, G. (1997). Implementing an IS strategy - a team approach. *Long Range Planning, 30*(1), 84-95.

Newkirk, H., Lederer, A. L., & Srinivasan, C. (2003). *Strategic information systems planning: too little or too much?, 12*, 201-228.

Pimchangthong, D., Plaisent, M., & Bernard, P. (2003). Key issues in information systems management: A comparative study of academics and practitioners in Thailand. *Journal of Global Information Technology Management, 6*(4), 27-44.

Porter, M. (1990). *The Competitive Advantage of Nations.* Free Press.

Porter, M. (1998). Location, Clusters, and the 'New' Micro-Economics of Competition. *Business Economics, 33*(1), 7-13.

Prekumar, G., & King, W.R. (1994). The evaluation of strategic information system planning. *Information and Management, 26,* 327-340.

Raymond, L. (2003). Globalization, the knowledge economy, and competitiveness: A business intelligence framework for the development SMEs. *Journal of American Academy of Business, 3*(1/2), 260-269.

Segars, A. H., & Grover, V. (1999). Profiles of strategic information systems planning. *Information Systems Research, 10*(3), 199-232.

Teo, T. S. H., & Ang, J. S. K. (2000). How useful are strategic plans for information systems. *Behavior and Information Technology, 19*(4), 275-282.

Teo, T. S. H., & King, W. R. (1997). Integration between business planning and information systems planning: an evolutionary-contingency perspective. *Journal of Management Information Systems, 14*(1), 185-224

Watson, R. T., Kelly, G. G., Galliers, R. D., & Brancheau, J. C. (1997). Key issues in information systems management: an international perspective. *Journal of Management Information Systems, 13*(4), 91-115.

Wesh, J., & White, J. (1981). A small business is not a little big business. *Harvard Business Review, 59*(4), 213-223.

Chapter III
Strategic Market Driven IS/IT Planning Model

Teay Shawyun
Assumption University of Thailand, Thailand

ABSTRACT

IS literature continues to highlight the issues of strategic business and IT planning alignment to achieve business performance. As an alternative to the mainstream models in the planning and implementation of the IS/IT by an organization, this chapter proposes an externalized approach by identifying the market driven needs through the firm's value proposition to the customer derived from the product/service consumption. The market based push-pull framework is to ensure that the push strategy of the firm in what it wants to offer and at a price that it intends to offer is matched with the pull strategy of the market in what it wants to buy and at a price it is willingly to pay. This externalized customer value is reconciled by the internalized firm's creation and delivery of the value as proposed by the firm based on the reconciliation of the market-pull and firm-push value proposition affecting customer satisfaction. Once the market pull and firm push strategy is identified, the alignment of the IT would be based on the push-pull effect of the business requirement to serve and satisfy not only the internal customer needs but also the more important external customer needs and requirements in term of the firm's value proposition. The IT as a key enabler would be the main enabling mechanism to create and deliver on the value as proposed to the customer. A case study of how a university revamp its Information Management System by aligning the external and the internal elements is used to illustrate this reconciliation in its market driven IS/IT planning. The "market driven IS/IT" planning model is the base of the strategic integration of the internal and external elements that is contended to address the key planning issues in a more integrated and comprehensive way.

INTRODUCTION

A McKinsey Survey of CIO agenda for 2007 suggested a trend of migration to service oriented architectures and lean manufacturing (Akella et.al, 2006) that embraces a global standard for interactions of internal and external partners. The interactions was defined clearly by Viswanathan's (2006) white paper that recommended the need of a move towards a single plan that is truly cross-functional and a multi-dimensional process that includes all elements of demand, supply and financial analysis in relation to the business planned goals and strategies with technology as the enabler of matching the market and the firm interactions. The emphasis on inter-disciplinary internal players of marketing, sales, finance and operations to manage the processes and support it with the right metrics and increased collaborations with customers is a must. LaValle and Scheld's (2004), 2005 CRM Done Right Executive Decision Maker Research and IBM's advocacy in the customer focused enterprise (Hefferman and LaValle, 2006) in support of the above highlighted the following:

- Decision makers emphasis on delivering on promises and improving the customer experience with 30% agreeing that ensuring promises and improving total customer experience as top concerns.
- Most companies have shortcomings in understanding their customer experience with 26% being superficial and 53% having generalized understanding.
- Marketplace leaders see real returns with 79% of consumers committing to a deeper product or service relationship with a brand after a satisfying experience due to the focus on the customers. 74% of the customer experiences are in the tactile/operational aspects that emphasized on the physical qualities of the interactions like consistency, availability or convenience. Only 17% focused on the emotive aspects that are more intangible and subjective like trustworthiness, genuine or emphatic.

With the trend of the firm leaning heavily towards customer focus (Hefferman and LaValle, 2006 and LaValle and Scheld, 2004), customer orientation (Kohli and Jaworski, 1990; Deshpandé and Webster 1998; Narver and Slater 1990; Deshpandé et al. 1993), the key issue is whether the traditional approach to IS/IT development and deployment (Lederer and Gardiner, 1992; Lederer and Salmena, 1996; and Rogerson and Fidler, 1994; Gliedman and Brown, 2004; Burn, 1991; Martin, 1989; and Premkumar and King, 1994; Lau and Pun, 2000) is still a valid approach.

As also noted by Akella et.al, (2006) and Viswanathan, (2006), interactions of internal and external partners and cross-functional and a multi-dimensional process is the new standard of the name of the new game. The issue would be whether the firm is properly aligned with the customer's focus and whether the IS/IT resources are actually well positioned to create and deliver on the value proposed. Based on this, the objective of this chapter is to explore a market driven IS/IT planning model that reconciliate the market's focus with the firm's push of its product and service offer that creates and delivers on the customer value proposition through the deployment of the IS/IT as enablers that are aligned with the cross-functional and multi-dimensional aims. This is important as the firm is an organic interaction and inter-play of all functional aspects and its operations systems and sub-systems to achieve the same goals of the firm.

INFORMATION SYSTEMS AND INFORMATION TECHNOLOGY PLANNING LITERATURE

In the main literature of Lederer and Gardiner (1992), Lederer and Salmena (1996) and Rogerson and Fidler (1994), the success of an organization depends heavily on the total strategic planning of the information system, technically called the SISP (Strategic Information System Planning) of which the 7 main constructs are: the external environment; the internal environment; planning resources; the planning processes; the information plan; the implementation of the information plan; and the alignment of the information plan with the organization's business plan. Based on these constructs and corporate development methodologies of Burn (1991), Martin (1989) and Premkumar and King (1994), Lau and Pun (2000) identified 3 key questions be answered when developing the SISP as follows: how to make a stable SIS in the face of changing needs; defining a strategic plan for design and development; and evaluating the impact of the SIS on sustaining competitiveness with a model that emphasized on determining the strategic prerequisites and strategic directions.

Gliedman and Brown, 2004, identified 4 steps of aligning the business and Information Technology plan as: Gather relevant business factors; Gather relevant factors; Determine the key value proposition for the overall IT portfolio; and Prioritize. At the same time, Williams (1997), identified the 4 aspects of planning as: identify the strategic objectives; identify the information systems to support them; analyze, in detail, the information systems requirements; and allocate resources and budgets to schedule projects.

A more recent framework calls for the use of the IT strategy maps for aligning IT and business strategies as adapted from the Balanced Scorecard of Kaplan and Norton (Symons, 2005). This means that a management information system presupposes modeling the entire management processes and activities to create and deliver on the value proposition and tailoring all the components of information technology to meet the needs of the organization (Kettunen and Kantola, 2005) and as noted above, that highlighted the General Accounting Office 1997 study that stated that failures

in information technology systems have more to do with poor management than with inadequate technology.

INFORMATION SYSTEMS AND INFORMATION DEFINITION

Duff and Assad (1980) provided a traditionally adequate definition of IS as "a collection of people, procedures, a base of data and (sometimes) hardware and software that collects, processes, stores and communicates data for transaction processing at operational level and information to support management decision making". Even though Salton (1975) highlighted that a computer system can be an information retrieval system, a question-answering system, a database system, a management information system and a decision support system, but this paper takes only the MIS stance that highlighted the 3 roles of IS as automate, informate and transformate (Schein, 1992 and Zuboff, 1988).

Argris (1991) defined MIS as "a system using formalized procedures to provide management at all levels in all functions with appropriate information based on data from both internal and external sources, to enable them to make timely and effective decisions for planning, directing and controlling the activities for which they are responsible". It will be noted that the emphasis was on "all functions" as a system as noted by Kempner (1976) as the organization as a pattern of ways engaging in a complexity of tasks, inter-relating to each other in the conscious and systematic establishment and accomplishment of mutually agreed upon purposes. It must also be noted that data from "internal and external sources" which means that these internal environmental requirements must be aligned with the external requirements to reach a mutually acceptable arrangement. Adeoti-Adekeye (1997) re-surmised the problem still facing a successful MIS as an organizational, behavioral and technical composite and key barrier of non-integrated applications and internal politics.

The MIS as a system is to generate information and Zorkoczy (1981) defined information, "as the meaning that a human expresses, or extract from representations of facts and ideas by means of known conventions of the representation used", that is used in this chapter.

PERFORMANCE MANAGEMENT OF THE IS/IT

It is inevitable that all firms have to assess whether the investments are beneficial to the firm and helps the firm achieve its stated goals and objectives that result in an enviable and coveted competitive position that it aims to stake out in the industry. As the IS/IT is a key enabler that generates both tangible and intangible benefits allowing the firm to access information to make decisions, affecting its efficiency in its resources allocation and uses through cost reductions, seize opportunities in the market to achieve its staked out position competitively (Dirks, 1994), the determinations of the measures is important.

But the literature as noted in the IS frameworks still focuses on the combination of hardware, software, communication networks, transformational or transactional applications (Weill and Broadbent, 2000) or "Traditional benchmarking in IT has been around technology silos such as desktop, mainframe, operating systems, and networking" as noted by the American Productivity & Quality Center (APQC, 2007). They still lean towards the hard measures as indicated in the quantitative IT measures of Open Standards Benchmarking Collaborative Database of APQC (2007) with emphasis on the IT functions and processes in terms of costs, productivity, efficiency, and cycle time. The main benchmarks being: Manage the business of IT; Develop and manage the IT customer relationships; Develop and manage business resiliency and risk; Manage enterprise informa-

tion; Develop and maintain IT solutions; Deploy IT resources; Deliver and support IT services; and Manage IT knowledge. These benchmarks at least covers the productivity aspects of the IT but not on the real "soft" measures of capacity and capability which are critical to the success of IS/IT as it is recognized that success is in the utilization that falls on the competency aspects of the human capital, information capital and organization capital as opposed to "having" the resources in the functions and processes.

The main questions of "measuring the value of IT" and "evaluating IS performance" have been dealt with extensively in Kueng et.al, (2000) who compare current value with historical values, Heo and Han (2003) who used a contingent evaluation approach to evaluate the impact of IS on Business Performance, Ives et.al (1988) who looked at IS effectiveness and satisfaction and Ranganathan and Kannabiran (2004) also touched on IS effectiveness and satisfaction but also IS role and overall business performance. But based on the literature above, it appeared that the "systems" approach of inter-linking the functional aspects of the organization to meet the market needs need to be addressed by identifying what and how the functional areas relate to each other to create and deliver on the market value.

RATIONALE OF MARKET AND FIRM RECONCILIATION

Market Pull

The marketing concept could be traced back to the early works of Drucker, 1954; Felton, 1959; Keith, 1960; Hise, 1965; Levitt, 1969; Barksdale and Darden, 1971; McNamara, 1972; Kotler, 1977 that belied a corporate state of mind and a fundamental business philosophy guiding and coordinating the operations of the entire organization. The inherent concepts was the beginnings of market orientation focused on the customer with products or services offered based on an understanding of customer preferences and business activities are organized to create customer satisfaction and loyalty by satisfying their needs. Kohli and Jaworski (1990) conceptualized market orientation as 'the organization-wide generation of market intelligence pertaining to current and future needs, dissemination of the market intelligence across departments, and organization-wide responsiveness to it' that has a distinct customer-focused culture (Deshpandé and Webster 1998; Narver and Slater 1990; Deshpandé et al. 1993) with three fundamental components: customer orientation, competitor orientation, and inter-functional coordination that are not exclusive of all other stakeholders such as owners, managers, and employees.

The customers' needs are driven by their inherent needs and the consumption of the products and services are the benefits or value derived from the consumption. It must be noted that the consumption is subject to the customers' willingness to pay for the perceived value or customer delivered value (Kotler, 1999), or customer benefits (Kotler, 2001) or customer value (Gale, 1994), the customers deemed appropriate to satisfy the needs. If the perceived value does not match with the needs, the search for a substitute will be initiated. Colton (2006) said that for Bell to deliver great customer experience, it is not just about meeting customer's needs and expectations, as it is about meeting their hopes and aspirations based on engagement (listen to understand), enlistment (make the customer feel like partners), enlightenment (integrate service and learning), empowerment (help customers feel confident and secure), enchantment (create a magical experience), entrustment (affirm that there is trust in the relationship), and endearment (connect with passion).

Market Value Proposition

The key to being market driven is to understand the components of the value sought. Kotler's 1999

definition of *Customer Delivered Value is Total Customer Value – Total Customer Cost*, whereby TCV is a function of *{Product Value, Service Value, Personnel Value, Image Value} and* TCC is a function of *{Monetary Cost, Time Cost, Energy Cost, Psychic Cost, and Opportunity Cost}*. Kotler (2003) included the relationship dimension in the original equation and called it as *Customer benefit = f (v, b, r, -c, -t) whereby v is Value of Market value, b is Value of Brand, r is Value of Relationship -c is Cost of Market Offering and -t is cost of time*. Gale, (1994) defined *Customer Value = f (Product Quality, Service Quality, Relationship, Image)/Cost*.

It is important to understand these components, as ultimately the decision to consume is based on all these components culminating in the value derived. This means that all the organizational systems must be aligned towards the maximization of the value at the minimal cost. The firm must define what its value proposition to the customer is. Kaplan and Norton (1996, 2001, and 2004) and Treacy and Wiersema (1995), identified 4 sets of value that an organization can propose to the customers as different value proposition has different customer objectives as shown in Figure 1.

Since there are 4 sets of value propositions, for each of the value proposition and its corresponding objectives, the composition of emphasis on the different components of the value equation is different. If an organization chooses Product leadership, it must excel in product quality and maintain its minimal industry standard in the other components of service quality, image and relationship. This would mean that the firm must excel (has distinctive competency over its nearest competitor) in the operation management of: Flexible robust processes; Supply capacity for rapid growth; Rapid introduction of new products; and In-line experimentation and Improvement as defined in Figure 2. At the same time, the firm must also maintain the minimal industry standards of flexibility, service, partnership and brand that underlie its customer selection, acquisition, retention and growth as shown in Figure 3.

A case study of Motorola in the late 90's whereby they were the best in product leadership through near perfect defect free product as the leading proponent of its Six Sigma imperatives, but they lost sight of its market needs, and they lost out to Nokia with Nokia gaining more that 35% global market shares dominance of the mobile phones. In late 2004, Nokia lost 3 % of its global market shares to the Korean's Samsung brand that is trendier. In its achievement, Nokia became complacent and also lost track of meeting the customers' need as was the case of Motorola. But in the late 2005, both Motorola and Nokia unleashed completely new series more attuned to the customer needs. This showed that in excelling in a staked out value proposition of which the firm must excel, it cannot afford to ignore or underperform in the other components of the value equation, whereby they must maintain the industry benchmark to sustain its competitiveness.

What and how the firm identifies the value proposition are dependent on the firm's market research system and market intelligence system to survey the competitors' value offers leading to the economies of knowledge through data-mining technologies that culminates in the market wisdom This is the ultimate competent curiosity *that is an inquisitiveness about happening in its markets that are of current and future importance, coupled with the ability to satisfy that curiosity with timely, relevant, reliable, accurate and cost-effective information* and competent wisdom *that concerns the ability to translate information into effective action by doing the right thing (EFFECTIVE) and doing it right (EFFICIENCY)* as propounded by Barabba and Zaltman (1991).

Firm Push

The firm's strategic position in the market industry is defined in the organization's vision (what it wants to be), its mission (what it can be based on its capabilities and capacity), its organization's goals and objectives that are translated into operational

Figure 1. Customer objectives for different value propositions

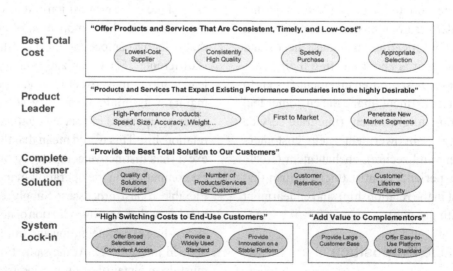

Source: Adapted from Kaplan, Robert S. and Norton, David P. (2004), Strategy Maps: Converting Intangible Assets into Tangible Outcomes, HBS Press, 2004

marketing goals and objectives, and its strategies to achieve what it wants to offer and is willing to offer. This means that the market's needs must be reconciled with the firm's needs as the firm must define clearly its position that it want to make a stake in. Based on the organization's reconciliation of the market's pull and the firm's push, the bottom line of the market orientation of the organization is the firm's aims for profit rather than sales volume as the motivation behind its marketing activities (Barksdale and Darden 1971).

The firm's competitive strategy is defined by the value it intends to propose to the customer. If it chooses to use Product Leadership as the strategic theme, its operational template would be similar to that shown in Figure 2.

According to Kaplan and Norton (1996, 2001 and 2004), the Product Leadership value proposition's objective is "Products and Services that expand existing performance boundaries into the highly desirable" by excelling in being the first to the market with a high performance product that outperforms its nearest competitors or reaching new market segment. In terms of its service quality, image and relationships, it must not under-perform but maintain a close parity with the industry standards as defined by the buying criteria of the market.

What is important is the imperative of the internal processes being able to create and deliver on the product leadership value as proposed. The internal processes of operation management, customer management, innovation management and regulatory and social management actually constitute the value chain activities that add value to the final product or service offer. The strategic cost component of each activity is used as an indicator of the over cost that contributes to the overall value equation as discussed earlier. Pepper and Rogers's white paper (2006) emphasized the imperative of striking a balance between cost-efficiency (lower-cost to serve) and customer effectiveness (a satisfying customer experience) through: considering all the economics; treating

Figure 2. Strategy map template for product leadership

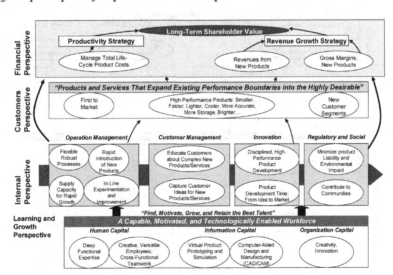

Source: Adapted from Kaplan, Robert S. and Norton, David P. (2004), Strategy Maps: Converting Intangible Assets into Tangible Outcomes, HBS Press, 2004

customer differently; letting the technology do the work and turning self-service into a customer insight machine. As shown in Figure 2, different value propositions will require different composition of key activities. With the processes and its activities and sub-activities defined based on the value proposition, the firm's capital assets can be aligned with the internal processes as shown in Figure 3. Figure 3 shows how the firm should manage its customers of which there are 4 main sub-activities of selection, acquisition, retention and growth.

What is important is that different activities will need different type of human capital competency, information needs and organizational systems. Once these are identified, the 3 sets of intangible capital assets of human capital, information capital and organization capital are inter-dependent as they are inter-twined together to use the processes and its activities to create and deliver on the value proposed to

the market. It must be noted that these 3 sets of intangible capitals forms the foundation of achievement of the market position as envisioned as propounded in Teay (2007) as they forms the capacity and capability of the organization that must be managed to implement the market strategies successful to achieve its market position.

The crux is that this shows the alignment of the capital assets of the firms used in the processes to create and deliver value as proposed to the market. The cause-effects linkages are strategically mapped out, and everyone in the organization knows what and how to contribute to the final product or service value as demanded by the market. This highlight the key link of the reconciliation of the firm's push with the market's pulls that brings about a mutually amicable and satisfactory exchange between the firm and the market as shown in Figure 4 of what a market based firm should be.

Figure 3. Learning and growth strategies for customer management

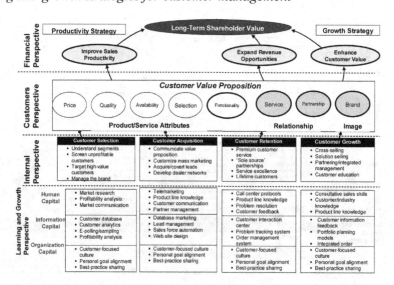

Source: Adapted from Kaplan, Robert S. and Norton, David P. (2004), Strategy Maps: Converting Intangible Assets into Tangible Outcomes, HBS Press, 2004

Figure 4. Reconciliation of the market pull and firm push

MARKET DRIVEN IT PLANNING MODEL: AN ALTERNATIVE

In planning for an IT system, Leek (1997) recommended a top-down holistic view of the IT functions as "supplying" to the "demands" of management with a cycle of activities of the business strategy influencing the information systems function. To better understand the planning and management of the IS, Williams, (1997), contended that there are 3 information systems culture: Innovator – actively pursue IS development and not regard cost as an obstacle; Follower – concentrate on efficiency of the system with tight cost control; and Dinosaur – try to save costs with minimal investment and develop IS based on a specific competitive strategy. This culture, the business life cycle and management level (strategic, tactical and operational) will interact to form complex decision parameters in the design of the information systems.

For the new age information and market driven economy, being a follower and a dinosaur could lead to the consequences of market share deterioration and losing out on the future customer support, satisfaction and loyalty. Based on the issues identified and the rationale of the reconciliation of the market pull and the firm push, this paper will propose an IT planning model that also takes into consideration of the power and effect of the customer on the design and deployment of the IS/IT to ensure that the IS/IT as enabler are used effectively to create and deliver on the value as needed by the market.

This means that the market pull equation and the firm push equation must be balanced and equated as shown in Figure 7. The common ground is found in the value proposition of the firm to the market that results in the customer value to meet and satisfy on the needs. First and foremost, customer needs must be defined through researching and understanding of the benefits or value the customers seek in the consumption of the product/service offered. This result in the Step 1 of the market pull equation which means defining and understanding what the customers want and is willing to pay for. In Step 2, the market pull is operationalized by the Gale, (1994) equation that defined *Customer Value = f (Product Quality, Service Quality, Relationship, Image)/Cost*. This means that the sub-components of the value are broken down into various aspects that can be traced back to the firm's operational processes that create and deliver on that sub-components of the value equation.

On the firm push equation, the firm would have defined its reason for existence through its strategic perspectives of its firm's vision, firm and market mission, its goals and objectives and its strategies that represents the "what and how to do" of achieving its staked out market position in the industry.

An example case is an academic institution's design of the market driven IT planning model of the university management to achieve its strategic theme of "education excellence" under the product leadership value proposition. In order to achieve its strategic theme, as highlighted in the Figure 2, two of the most basic strategies are productivity strategy and the revenue growth strategy.

To achieve the strategic theme of academic excellence, the institution will define its value proposition emphasizing on academic leadership through the productivity and revenue growth in Step 3. After 30 years in existence, the theory and practice of the management systems were disparate. Figure 5 showed that in practice, the key basic systems of planning, quality assurance and its information systems were not aligned as

should be in Figure 6.

In Step 4, an integrated management system must be developed to ensure that all the key processes are aligned together to achieve the value proposition of the institution. The integrated QMIPS (Quality Management, Information and Planning Systems) was developed to ensure that the output of one system becomes the input to the other systems. The 3 core systems of the QMIPS (Teay, 2007) are:

• **QMS (Quality Management System)**: The QMS forms the core of the quality management system of the institution based on the 9 sets of KPI and 27 sets of sub-KPI of CHE (Commission on Higher Education) and the external ONESQA (Office of National Edu-

Figure 5. University management in practice

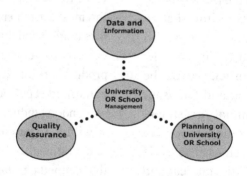

Figure 6. University management in theory

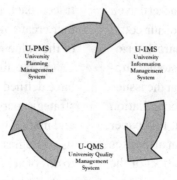

Figure 7. Market-driven IT planning model

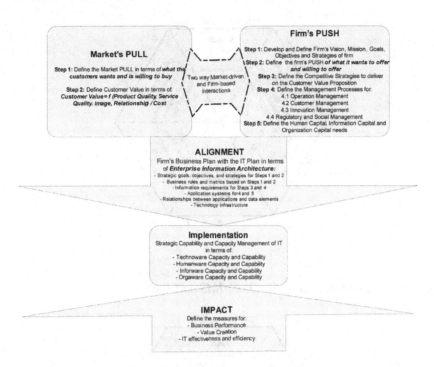

cation Standards and Quality Assessment) 7 Standards assessment criteria within the Malcolm Baldrige National Quality Award model.

- **IMS (Information Management System)**: The IMS forms the core of the information and statistics management system of the university to ensure that the planning and decision making of the units are supported by an evidence-based mechanism whereby the units can retrieve the rich database of the university ICT system.

- **PMS (Planning Management System)**: The PMS forms the core of the planning system of the university. The main objective is to ensure that all the 5 main management reports are streamlined, are coherent, are consistent and are aligned with each other.

The key linkages as shown in Figure 8 (Integrated Curriculum QMIPS) and 9 (school or institution integrated QMIPS) are via the key management reports for the curriculum is: *The*

Curriculum Annual Report (C-AR); The Curriculum Self-Assessment Report (C-SAR); The Curriculum Standards and Key Performance Indicators Report (C-SKPIR); The Curriculum Internal Audit and Assessment Report (C-IAAR); and *The Curriculum One-Year Plan and Budget (C-OYPB)*. The curriculum integrated reports will be the key input to the school and institution's main management reports of: *The Annual Report (AR); The Self-Assessment Report (SAR); The Standards and Key Performance Indicators Report (SKPIR); The Internal Audit and Assessment Report (IAAR);* and *The One-Year Plan and Budget (OYPB)*

In Step 5, the Strategic Skills and Competency and Performance Metrics must be defined. In the main stream strategic management literatures (Thomson and Strickland, 2004, Johnson and Scholes, 2003 and Prahalad and Hamel, 1999) to name a few, the edge to competitive advantage is the competency profile of the organization in terms of readiness (Kaplan and Norton, 2004). These competency are normally human based

Figure 8. Integrated curriculum QMIPS linkages of the QMS, IMS and PMS

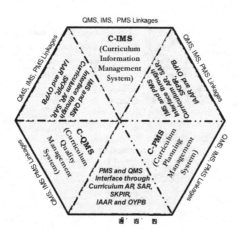

Figure 9. Integrated QMIPS linkages of the QMS, IMS and PMS

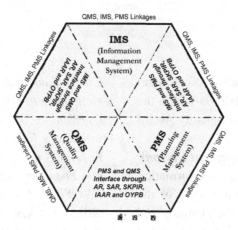

and is not on having the resources. The main competencies are:

- **Human Capital:** This comprises the knowledge, skills and values of the academic and administrative staffs in creation of educational value to the stakeholders.

- **Information Capital:** This comprises the QA-MIS systems, networks and databases that are horizontally and vertically integrated to support empowerment of the academic

and administrative personnel. A key competitive edge is the technology capabilities (Pramongkit and Teay, 2002) of the human sophistication in identifying, interpretation and integration of information into knowledge and market wisdom leading to competent curiosity and competent wisdom (Barabba and Zaltman, (1991).

- **Organization Capital:** This comprises the leadership, teamwork, alignment and culture as has been discussed above. This form the operating core for all the other aspects to function in an integrated total open system

The alignment of the Strategic Management Support Systems and Performance Metrics are the imperatives of successful IS/IT implementation and alignment to the business systems. The concepts of alignment are addressed in the "enterprise architecture" (Shupe and Behling, 2006) which comprises: the business architecture (business strategies, processes and functional requirements), the information architecture (defines the information entity independent of the IT view for management and performing operations), the application architecture (describes applications to support the business and allow efficient management of information entities) and the technical architecture (the actual technology used). In preparation for the development of the technology strategy, Shupe and Behling (2006) also emphasized that there must be committed executive-level involvement, structured decision making process and an effective model for organization-wide communication. This enterprise architecture will lead to the ERP (Enterprise Resource Planning) of the firm.

Traditionally for the firm, in the hierarchical and functional or departmental structure, the following computer-based information systems

exist independent of each other and underlies a political domain in itself.

- Strategic Information System
- Strategic Evaluation and Control System
- Strategic Innovation and Change system
- Strategic Human Resource System
- Strategic Financial and Accounting System

In the information age, to ensure the cause-effect linkages and inter-dependencies, they must be interlinked in a cause effect linkage as shown in Figure 10.

Kaplan and Norton's (2004), strategic mapping highlighted the main components of competency readiness as the Human Capital (skills, knowledge and values), Information Capital (QA-MIS system, Network, Database and Technology Capabilities) and Organization Capital (Culture, Leadership, Teamwork and Alignment – that has been discussed above) that forms the base competency foundation of the institution. This is encapsulated in the Strategic Human Resource and Strategic Information System, The Strategic Evaluation and Control System is the base for the quality assurance as defined in the QMIPS (Teay, 2005). The Strategic Innovation and Change system is the innovation manage-

Figure 10. Strategic support systems linkages

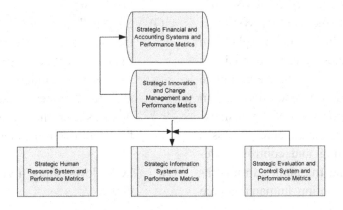

ment and the Strategic Financial and Accounting System is the financial perspective of the Kaplan and Norton Framework.

What is important in the linkages is the rationale that:

- Management must be measured through the performance metrics that are inherent in all the systems,
- There is a cause effect linkages of all the systems and their implicit performance metrics,
- It is the summation of the total and synergistic outcome that is more important than the individual system outcome.

In the normal firm environment, it will take the form of the ERP system which is a business management system that comprises integrated sets of comprehensive software, which can be used, when successfully implemented, to manage and integrate all the business functions within an organization. These sets usually include a set of mature business applications and tools for financial and cost accounting, sales and distribution, materials management, human resource, production planning and computer integrated manufacturing, supply chain, and customer information (Boykin, 2001; Chen, 2001; Yen et al., 2002). These packages have the ability to facilitate the flow of information between all supply chain processes (internal and external) in an organization (Al-Mashari and Zairi, 2000a).

Rosemann (1999), Gable (1998) and Watson and Schneider (1999) defined an ERP system as an integrated customizable, standard application software which includes integrated business solutions that seeks to integrate the complete range of business processes and functions in order to present a holistic view of the business from single information for the core processes (e.g. production planning and control, warehouse management) and the main administrative functions (e.g. accounting, human resource

management) of an enterprise that handles the majority of an enterprise's system requirements in all functional areas such as finance, human resources, manufacturing, sales, and marketing. It has a software architecture that facilitates the flow of information among all functions within an enterprise. The software component of the ERP model is the component that is most visible to the users and is therefore seen as the ERP product. It consists of several generic modules, some of which are listed below.

(1) *Finance.* The finance module is usually the backbone of the ERP system. It includes concepts such as the general ledger, accounts receivable, accounts payable, fixed assets and inventory control.

(2) *Human resources (HR).* HR forms an integral part of an ERP system. HR administration automates personnel management processes, including payroll, recruitment, and business travel and vacation allotments. It focuses on the automation of HR tasks from the employer's viewpoint. The focus of the administration function is to empower employees to manage their own employment terms and conditions. Mundane tasks like the allocation of leave days to an employee can be predetermined and assigned to an employee. The payroll is usually integrated with the finance module and handles all the accounting issues and preparation of cheques related to employee salaries, wages and bonuses.

(3) *Supply chain management (SCM).* SCM is the oversight of materials, information and finances as they move in a process from supplier to manufacturer to wholesaler to retailer to consumer (Alexandrou, 2002). SCM involves coordinating and integrating these flows both within and among companies.

a. SCM flows can be divided into three main flows:

i. the product flow;
ii. the information flow; and
iii. the finances flow.

b. The product flow includes the movement of goods from a supplier to a customer, as well as any customer returns or service needs. The information flow involves transmitting orders and updating the status of delivery. The financial flow consists of credit terms, payment schedules, and consignment and title ownership arrangements.

(4) *Supplier relationship management (SRM).* With an increasing reliance on contractors and suppliers for material, logistics and manufacturing capacity, the ability to manage these relationships has become critical. To maximize profitability, companies must be able to select the right suppliers quickly, establish strategic relationships and effectively collaborate with them as they help meet business goals. SRM describes the practices needed to establish the business rules for extended interaction with the suppliers of products and services. SRM enables companies and their suppliers to collaborate on strategic sourcing and procurement, while managing the overall process from an enterprise-wide perspective (Ganeshan and Harrison, 1995).

(5) *Customer relationship management (CRM).* CRM is a term for methodologies, software and usually internet capabilities that help an enterprise manage customer relationships in an organized and efficient manner (Lalakota and Robinson, 1999). An enterprise builds a database about its customers. This database describes relationships in sufficient detail so that management, salespeople and customer service representatives can access information, match customer needs with product plans and offerings, remind customers of

service requirements and know what other products a customer had purchased.

(6) *Business intelligence (BI).* BI applications are decision support tools that enable real-time, interactive access, analysis and manipulation of mission-critical corporate information (Cherry Tree & Co., 2002). Users are able to access and leverage vast amounts of information to analyze relationships and understand trends that ultimately support business decisions. These tools prevent the potential loss of knowledge within the enterprise that results from massive information accumulation that is not readily accessible or in usable form.

In the implementation of the aligned IS/IT systems with the market needs, two types of capacity needs (Teay, 2007) to be defined: Personal capacity which is the nuts and bolts of capacity building means the skills, knowledge, experience, personality and the ability not only to do something but also over a period of time to build up a reservoir of knowledge, experience and expertise that determines present and on-going performance; and Non-personal capacity or the administrative capacity provides the context (in essence the values, beliefs and ideals) in which personal capacity is developed as they work in the organizational setting which influence their mind-set.

Weill, Subramani and Broadbent (2002) also found that different strategic agility required distinct patterns of IT infrastructure capability that must be understood to derive performance and advantage. This research identified seventy services divided into ten capability clusters: channel-management services, security and risk-management services, communication services, data-management services, application-infrastructure services, IT-facilities-management services, IT-management services, IT-architecture-and-standards services, IT-education services, and IT R and D services that must be managed.

Within the IT context, a key Information Capacity is managing relationships as no individual or organization is able to achieve all the aims alone due to the volume of knowledge created leading to "cooperativity" (skills, attitudes and organizational culture and willingness to learn and share) across individuals and organization to make things happen. Individual and organizational ICT skills, awareness, readiness and capacity are the basic requirements and mechanisms to seamlessly tie together the relationships and the process to create and deliver on the value.

In the human capacity and capabilities context, the capabilities competency clusters (Thorton and Byham, 1982) can be categorized as: Intellectual – strategic perspective, analysis and judgment; Interpersonal – persuasiveness, decisiveness; Adaptability – resilience; Results orientation – initiative, business senses with 5 sets of skills and competencies profile Houtzagers, (1999), of: Professional knowledge, Customer Orientation, Business Awareness, Leadership and Planning and Organizing.

From the Inforware context, creating an information system without understanding what the knowledge professionals need or how they relate to others in the communities or the form of level of details they need did little to leveraging the knowledge leading to an information junkyard. To leverage knowledge, thinking of the information is needed, and the challenge lies not only in the technical side but also the social, management and personal. Kane et. al., (2006) identified knowledge into 2 groups of:

- Personal/Tacit – which are expertise, know-how that are manifested through action, acquired through practice and difficult to transfer based on personal beliefs, values, subjective insights or emotions that are contained in the container (technically the human's head) and is difficult to share.
- Public/Explicit – which are the rationalization of information that can be stored, codified and transmitted and can be articulated as facts represented in the form of documents, designs, patents, trademarks, business plans, formal language that are objective and rational and are about the container or embodiment of knowledge

In the Orgaware capacity and capability development aspects they would include: Skill enhancement – general education, on-the-job-training and professional deepening in crosscutting skills such as business, analysis and interpretation and IT; Organization strengthening – covering the process of institutional development or institution building implying an infrastructure mentality; Procedural improvements and Management – covering general functions changes or systems reforms that are on-going; Compatibility of the fit between the IS/IT architecture with the organization structure, with an emphasis on the interfaces between the organization and its stakeholders that might call for different structure depending on its "strategic fit with the business strategies".

IMPLICATIONS AND CONCLUSION

There are many existing models that looked at the design and development and implementation of the IS/IT systems to be aligned with the business needs, but the key issues would lie in 2 key areas:

- Whether the planned systems meet the real needs of the market in terms of its value proposition,
- Whether in the implementation, the alignment of the synergies of all the interactions and inter-dependencies are integrative to create and meet the market needs.

Based on this contention, the market-driven IS/IT planning model takes into account of:

- The identification of the real market needs by identifying the value needed to satisfy its needs,
- The identification of the customer value equation or the components of the value to be proposed in terms of the product quality, service quality, image, relationships and cost that culminates in the market pull equation,
- The firm push equation to create and deliver on all components of the value that it decides to propose to the customer with the value proposed as the key integrative agent to ensure all parts of the value are catered to by all the processes,
- The internal processes are aligned to create and deliver on the value as a "cause-effect" linkage in an integrative rather than independent process and system with the IS/IT as the key enabler,
- The capacity and capabilities are identified as they are the key competency needed for the success of the internal processes and that clearly defines the human, information and organization capital needed for the success of the implementation of the aligned business and IS/IT strategies of the firm.

In conclusion, the proposed model looks at the intricate aspects of the alignments of the capital assets to achieve and sustain the competitiveness firm as compared to the existing models that look at the design and development of the IS/IT from the technology perspectives. The existing models are good in the planning aspects that down-played the importance or over-looked the implementation side of the systems which is the crux and critical areas that need to be identified and managed. This proposed model deals not only with the planning aspects but also looks at the implementation aspect from an integrative approach.

REFERENCES

Adeoti-Adekeye, W. B. (1997). The importance of management information systems. *Library Review, 46*(5).

Akella, J., Kanakamedala, K., & Roberts, R. P. (2006). 2006 Survey on CIO agenda in 2007. McKinsey & Company, Silicon Valley.

Alexandrou, M. (2002). *Supply chain management (SCM) definition*. Retrieved on 18 February 2007, www.marioalexandrou.com/glossary/scm.asp

Al-Mashari, M., & Zairi, M. (2000a). Supply-chain re-engineering using enterprise-resource planning (ERP) systems: An analysis of a SAP R/3 implementation case. *International Journal of Physical Distribution & Logistics Management*, 30(¾), 296-313.

American Productivity & Quality Center (APQC, 2007). *Open Standards Benchmarking Collaborative Database for Information Technology*, APQC, Houston, TX, retrieved 18 March 2007 www.apqc.org..

Argris, C. (1991). Management information systems: The challenge to rationality and emotionality. *Management Science, 291.*

Barabba, V. P., & Zaltman, G. (1991). *Hearing the Voice of the Market: Competitive Advantage through creative use of Market Information*. Harvard Business School Press.

Barsdale, H., & Darden, B. (1971). Marketers' attitudes toward the marketing concept, *Journal of Marketing, 35*, 29-36.

Boykin, R. F. (2001). Enterprise resource-planning software: a solution to the return material authorization problem. *Computers in Industry, 45*, 99-109.

Burn, J. M. (1991). Stages of growth in strategic information systems planning (SISP). *Proceedings of the 24ᵗʰ Annual Hawaii International Conference on System Sciences*, Kanai, HI, Januatu.

Chen, I. J. (2001). Planning for ERP systems: analysis and future trend. *Business Process Management Journal, 7*(5), 374-86.

Cherry Tree & Co. (2002). Business Intelligence – the missing link. Retrieved 18 March 2007, www. cherrytreeco.com

Conlon, G. (2006). How do you create customer devotion? *1 to 1 weekly,* Issue December 11, 2006, retrieved 20 March 2007www. 1to1media. com/doc ID=29937,

Deshpandé, R., Farley, J. U., & Webster, F. E. (1993). Corporate culture, customer

orientation, and innovativeness in Japanese firms: a quadrad analysis. *Journal of Marketing, 57*(1), 23-37.

Deshpandé, R., & Farley, J. U. (1998). Measuring market orientation: generalization and synthesis. *Journal of Market-Focused Management, 2*(3), 213-232.

Dirks, P. (1994). MIS investments for operations management: relevant costs and revenues. *International Journal of Production Economics,* 35

Drucker, P. (1954). *The Practice of Management.* New York: Harper Collins Publishers, Inc.

Duff, W. M., & Assad, M. C. (1980). *Information Management: An Executive Approach.* London: Oxford University Press (p. 243).

Felton, A. (1959). Making the marketing concept work. *Harvard Business Review,* (pp. 55-65).

Gable, G. (1998). Large package software: a neglected technology? *Journal of Global Information Management, 6*(3), 3-4.

Gale, B. T. (1994). *Managing Customer Value: Creating Quality and Service that Customer Can See.* New York: The Free Press, Simon & Schuster.

Ganeshan, R., & Harrison, T. P. (1995). *An introduction to supply chain management.* Retrieved 22 May 2006, http://lcm.csa.iisc.ernet.in/scm/supply_chain_intro.html

General Accounting Office (1997). *High Risk Series. Information Management and Technology,* GAO/HR-97-9, February 1997

Gliedman, C., & Brown, A. (2004). *Defining IT Portfolio Management: Holistic IT investment Planning.* Cambridge, MA: Forrester Research Inc.,

Hefferman, R., & LaValle, S. (2006). Advocacy in the customer focused enterprise: The next generation of CRM done right. *Executive Handbook,* NY: IBM Global service, IBM Corporation.

Houtzagers, G. (1999). Empowerment, using skills and competence management. *Participation and Empowerment: An International Journal, 7*(2).

Hise, R. T. (1965). Have manufacturing firms adopted the marketing concept? *Journal of Marketing, 29,* 9-12.

Heo, J., & Han, I. (2003). Performance measures of information systems in evolving computing environment: An empirical investigation. *Information & Management, 40.*

Ives, B., Olson, M. H., & Baroudi, J. J. (1988). The measurement of user information satisfaction. *Communications of the ACM, 26*(10)

Kane, H., Ragsdell, G., & Oppenheim, C. (2006). Knowledge Management Methodologies. The Electronic Journal of Knowledge Management, 4(2).

Kaplan, R. S., & Norton, D. P. (1996). *Translating Strategy into Action: The Balanced Scorecard.* HBS Press..

Kaplan, R. S., & Norton, D. P. (2001). *The Strategy Focused Organization.* HBS Press.

Kaplan, R. S., & Norton, D. P. (2004). *Strategy Maps: Converting Intangible Assets into Tangible Outcomes.* HBS Press.

Keith, R. J. (1960). The marketing revolution. *Journal of Marketing,* January, 35-38.

Kempner, T. (1976). *Handbook of Management.* Penguin, Harmondsworth (p. 216)

Kettunen, J., & Kantola, I. (2005). Management information system based on the balanced scorecard. *Campus-wide Information System,* 22(5).

Kueng, P., Meier, A., & Wettstein, T. (2000). *Computer-based performance measurement in SMEs: Is there an option. Institute of Informatics,* Paper 00-11 (Internal Working Paper), University of Fribourg, Fribourg.

Kohli, A. K., & Jaworski, B. J. (1990). Market orientation: The construct, research propositions and managerial implications. *Journal of Marketing, 54*(April), 1-18.

Kotler, P. (1977). From sales obsession to marketing effectiveness. *Harvard Business Review,* November-December.

Kotler, P. (1999). *Kotler on marketing.* Simon & Schuster.

Kotler, P. (2003). Marketing management: an Asian perspective, Prentice Hall, 1999.

Lalakota, R., & Robinson, M. (1999). *E-business: Road-map for Success.* Reading, MA: Addison-Wesley.

Lau, C. W., & Pun. K. F. (2000). Assimilation of a strategic information system to gain competitiveness, *Logistics Information Management,* 13(5).

LaValle, S., & Scheld, B. (2004). *CRM Done Right: Executive Handbook for realizing the value of CRM.* NY: IBM Global service, IBM Corporation.

Lederer, L. A., & Gardiner, V. (1992). The process of strategic information planning. *Journal of Strategic Information Systems,* 1(2).

Lederer, L. A., & Salmena, H. (1996). Toward a theory of strategic information system planning. *Journal of Strategic Information Systems,* 5.

Leek, C. (1997). Information systems frameworks and strategy, *Industrial Management and Data Systems,* 97/3.

Levitt, T. (1969). Marketing Myopia. *Harvard Business Review,* July-August, 45-56.

Martin, J. (1989). *Strategic Information Planning Methodologies.* 2nd edition, Englewood Cliffs, NJ

McNamara, C. (1972). The present status of the marketing concept. *Journal of Marketing, 36,* 50-57.

Narver, J. C., & Slater, S. F. (1990). The effect of a market orientation on business profitability. *Journal of Marketing, 54*(October), 20-35.

Peppers & Rogers (2006). *Customer-Focused Self-Service: Building the Balanced Business Case.* white paper 2006, Peppers and Rogers, www.1to1.com.

Prahalad, C. K., & Hamel, G. (1990). The Core Competence of the Corporation. *Harvard Business Review,* May – June.

Pramongkit, P., & Teay, S. (2002). Strategic IT Framework for Modern enterprise by using Information Technology Capabilities. *Proceedings of 2002 IEEE International Engineering Management Conference (IEMC – 2002),* Cambridge UK

Premkumar, G., & King, W. R. (1994). The evolution of strategic information system planning, *Information & Management, 26.*

Ranganathan, C., & Kannabiran, G. (2004). Effective Management of Information Systems function: an exploratory study of Indian organizations. *International Journal of Information Management, 24*(3).

Rogerson, S., & Fidler, C. (1994). Strategic Information Planning System: its adoption and use. *Information Management and Computer Security, 2*(1).

Rosemann, M. (1999). ERP software characteristics and consequences. *Proceedings of the 7th European Conference on Information Systems,* Copenhagen.

Salton, G. (1975). *Dynamic Information and Library Processing.* London: Prentice-Hall International, (p. 523).

Schein, E. H. (1992). The Role of the CEO in the management of change: The case of information technology. In T. A. Kochan & M. Useem, (Eds), *Transforming Organizations.* Oxford: Oxford University Press.

Shupe, C., & Behling, R. (2006). Developing and Implementing a Strategy for Technology Deployment. *The Information Management Journal,* July and August 2006.

Symons, C. (2005). *IT Strategy Maps: A Tool for Strategic Alignment.* Cambridge, MA: Forrester Research Inc.

Teay, S. (2005). Quality Assurance and Strategic Implementation in educational institutions: A Holistic Alliance? *JIRSEA (Journal of Institutional Research South East Asia, 3*(1) 24-40.

Teay, S. (2007). Integrated Curriculum QMIPS – Curriculum Quality Management, Information and Planning Systems. *ASAIHL Journal, 10*(1).

Thompson Jr., A. A., & Strickland III, A. J. (2005). *Crafting and Executing Strategies – The Quest for Competitive Advantage: Concepts and Cases.* 14th Edition, 2005, McGraw-Hill Irwin.

Treacy, M., & Wiersema, F. (1995). *The Discipline of Market leaders: Choose your Customers, Narrow your Focus, Dominate your Market.* Reading, MA: Addison-Wesley.

Thorton, G. C., & Byham, W. C. (1982). Assessment centers and managerial performance. New York; Academic Press.

Viswanathan, N. (2006). *The Technology Strategies for Integrated Business Planning Benchmark Report.* Boston, MA: Aberdeen Group, www. Aberdeen.com.

Watson, E. E., & Schneider, H. (1999). Using ERP systems in education. *Communications of the Association for Information Systems,* 1, 2-44.

Wheelen, T. L., & Hunger, J. D. (2004). *Strategic Management and Business Policy.* 9th Edition, 2004, Pearson Prentice Hall

Williams, L. T. (1997). Planning and Managing the information system – A manager's guide. *Industrial Management and Data Systems,* 97/5.

Weill, P., & Broadbent, M. (2000). *Leveraging the New Infrastructure: How Market Leaders capitalize on the New Information Technology.* Boston: Harvard Business School Press.

Weill, P., Subramani, M., & Broadbent, M. (2002). Building IT Infrastructure for Strategic Agility. *MIT Sloan Management Review.*

Yen, D. C., Chou, D. C., & Chang, J. (2002). A synergic analysis for Web-based enterprise resources-planning systems. *Computer Standards & Interfaces, 24*(4), 337-46.

Zorkoczy, P. (1981). *Information Technology: An Introduction.* London: Pitman (p.157).

Zuboff, S. (1988). *In the Age of Smart Machines: The future of Work and Power.* New York, NY: Basic books.

Chapter IV
Fuzzy Modelling for Integrated Strategic Planning for Information Systems and Business Process Design

Dimitris K. Kardaras
Athens University of Economics and Business, Greece

Bill Karakostas
City University, UK

ABSTRACT

Strategic Information Systems Planning (SISP) has been a continuing top concern for IS/IT management, since the mid 1980's. Responding to the increasing interest in SISP, researchers have developed a large number of SISP methodologies and models. However, when organisations embark on planning for their information systems, they face difficulties and usually fail to gain the expected benefits. Strategic alignment and the identification of the business areas where the IT contribution is strategically important for the organisation are the most difficult problems in SISP. None of the existing SISP methodologies and models offers a complete solution. The approach presented in this chapter, utilises a Fuzzy Cognitive Map in order to align strategic objectives with IS opportunities that exist at the level of business processes. This chapter exemplifies fuzzy cognitive mapping in SISP, and illustrates how the strategic alignment between the business and IT domains can be realised.

INTRODUCTION TO STRATEGIC INFORMATION SYSTEMS PLANNING

Organisations experienced radical changes in their business and technological environment especially, during the 80's and 90's. The globalisation of the market and increased competition, in conjunction with a deep economic recession, and changes to the social and economic characteristics of the consumers, exert their pressure on companies. The struggle for further development, or even for survival in such an environment, has become increasingly difficult. However, during the same period an increasing number of research studies (Earl, 1989; O'Connor, 1993; Remenyi, 1991; Ward et. al., 1990) described successful IT initiatives that led companies to new ways of competing, and analysed the factors which led organisations to strategic planning for their IS. Briefly, the driving forces behind SISP are:

- Information technology is critical and strategically important to many organisations.
- The relative high growth in information systems budgets compared to that of other functions in organisations.
- Information technology is needed by our economic environment.
- Information technology is rapidly changing.
- Information technology infrastructure and architecture is critical for information systems integrity.
- Information technology involves many stakeholders.
- Top management support and user participation in IT-related decisions are needed.

It is high time that organisations begin to realise the potential of IT as the driving force to lead businesses out of the crisis and to improve organisational competitive performance. As a result, strategic planning for IS/IT has become a key activity which systematically addresses the IT issues in organisations, and can identify IT applications which exploit opportunities or counterthreats with substantial importance to business. Relevant literature argues that companies can not be competitive if their information systems strategies are not aligned with the business strategies (Avison et al. 2004).

In (Lederer and Sethi, 1988, 1991) a dichotomous definition of Strategic Information Systems Planning (SISP) is provided. On one side of the dichotomy, SISP is a process of identifying computer-based applications that support certain business activities, strategic plans and objectives. On the other side of the dichotomy, SISP is a process of identifying computer-based applications which are characterised by their high potential to lead the organisation to competitive advantage. It is a process which results in innovative IT applications that may alter the competitive scene in an industrial sector, spawn new products, raise entry barriers to new competitors, etc. In both the above adopted views, SISP also covers the definition of the technological infrastructure, i.e. databases, communications, and other systems which are required for the implementation of the identified IT applications.

It is argued however (Earl, 1989), that there exists a common confusion between the terminology which refers to information systems, information technology and their planning. Earl (1989) gives three definitions that delineate the concepts, and are adopted in this research work. These definitions are presented below:

Information Systems (IS) Strategy is concerned primarily with aligning IS development with business needs and with identifying and exploiting competitive advantage opportunities from IT. IS strategy deals with *what* to do with the technology.

Information Technology (IT) Strategy is concerned primarily with technology policies, such as the specification of analysis and development methods, security levels, technical standards, vendor policies, etc. The IT strategy is the architecture that drives, shapes and controls the IT infrastructure. IT strategy designates *how* technology can be applied in order to implement the IS strategy. The IT infrastructure consists of four elements: computer systems, communication systems, data and databases, and applications.

Information Management (IM) Strategy is concerned with the role and structure of IT activities in the organisation. It focuses on the relationships between users and specialists, decentralisation and centralisation, financing and appraising IT applications. IM strategy answers questions as to *who* does *what*, *where* regarding IT.

According to a survey conducted by (Earl, 1993), the five dominant objectives of an SISP study are the following:

- Align IS with business needs.
- Seek competitive advantage from IT.
- Gain top management commitment.
- Forecast IS resource requirements.
- Establish technology plan and policies.

Five types of planning for information systems are presented below (Remenyi, 1991; Synnott, 1987). Each type of planning reflects how the role and contribution of IT is conceived by the business and IT management. The focus of this classification is on the degree of integration between the business and IT planning process.

- *No Plan.* No formal planning takes place for either business or information systems. Small companies often do not develop any plans and normally react to every day events as they occur.
- *Stand-alone Planning.* Companies following this type of planning usually develop a business plan without considering the capabilities of IT. If they do develop a plan for their information systems, this takes place

in vacuum since there is no interaction with, or input from the business plan.

- *Reactive Planning.* Corporate managers develop their business plans and then ask from IT management to deploy IT in order to support the business plans. However, there is no communication or collaboration among business and IT managers. Therefore, IT management decides on the priorities and kind of support that IT systems should offer.
- *Linked Planning.* In this kind of planning, after the business planning has been completed, business and IT managers prepare together the IT plans in order to reflect the business needs.
- *Integrated Planning.* When planning is integrated, there is no distinction between business and IT plans. Instead, there is close collaboration between business and IT managers, who prepare the integrated plan together. As an example, while the business part of the plan is being prepared, IT managers suggest opportunities on how to advance business objectives and plans, achieve competitive advantage with IT systems, or suggest alternatives on how to support businesses. As the information systems part of the corporate plan is being prepared, the business managers suggest priorities and evaluate support alternatives.

Relevant literature argues that companies can not be competitive if their information systems strategies are not aligned with the business strategies (Teo & Ang, 1999; Avison et al. 2004). In fact, strategic alignment has been expressed by many different terms in the literature. The term *fit* is used in (Porter, 1996), *bridge* is found in (Coborra, 1997), *harmony* is suggested in (Luftman et al., 1996), *fusion* is proposed in (Smaczny, 2001) and *linkage* is reported in (Henderson & Venkatraman, 1993). In all cases, alignment implies the *integration* of IS and business strategic planning. Many authors advocate the integrated planning as the most suitable for realising the impact of business to IT and vice versa (Earl, 1989; Ward, et al. 1990; Remenyi, 1991; Synnott, 1987; Chen and Nunmaker, 1989; Hayward, 1987; Weil & Broadbent, 1998). However, (Galliers, 1993; Luftman, 1996; Papp, 2001; Tallon & Kraemer, 2003; Trainor, 2003) argue that despite the general agreement about the need of such integration, it is still the case that in many organisations the links between business and IT strategic planning are loose and IS strategic alignment not a top management priority. This chapter uses the terms *integration* and *alignment* of IS strategic planning interchangeably.

The research objectives of the approach described in this chapter follow:

- Develop a new model based on the theory of Cognitive Maps to facilitate SISP integrated planning.
- Integrate Fuzzy Cognitive Maps with business process models so that strategic IS alignment will be realised and strategic priorities will be translated into business process design options.
- Develop a methodology and associated models that draw on the principles of SISP, and Fuzzy Cognitive Maps.

The chapter continues with the discussion of the necessity of SISP, the problems pertaining to SISP and an introduction to fuzzy cognitive mapping. Then the chapter introduces and illustrates the proposed approach for integrated SISP and discusses the benefits from combining object-oriented and fuzzy cognitive mapping in aligning strategic objectives with process design suggestions.

THE NEED FOR INTEGRATED SISP

Although (Jarvenpaa & Ives, 1994), argue that tight IS strategic alignment may reduce strategic flexibility, integrated SISP appears to be the answer to the organisational concerns on how to succeed in an uncertain and turbulent environment (Earl, 1989; Remenyi, 1991; Ward, et al. 1990). SISP provides tangible and intangible benefits (O'Connor, 1993; Hackathorn & Karimi, 1988; Kearns & Lederer, 2000; Choe, 2003; Avison, et. al., 2004; Bryd, et. al., 2006) and more specifically:

- Ensures that information systems are aligned with the corporate business and IT strategic objectives and considers possible opportunities for the company to employ IT to advance its strategic objectives and plans and when possible to gain competitive advantage,
- Provides for the assignment of the systems development priorities, built on a solid base that depends on the corporate business needs,
- Fosters the new vision of information systems as investments and ensures the efficient management of the scarce IT resources,
- Facilitates top management and users participation to IT decisions as it encourages organisational learning i.e. raises the awareness of business users and management of information systems potential through out the organisation, as well as the knowledge of the IT staff about the organisation,
- Provides a basis for IT performance assessment,
- Ensures the co-ordinated development of information systems,
- Provides for the establishment of standards and prevents the piecemeal development of information systems, thus eliminating problems such as data redundancy, inaccuracy and inconsistency and systems incompatibility.

In summary, integrated SISP allows an organisation to realise its opportunities, to influence the future, thus developing a favourable environment, to focus on the business areas where the actual problem or opportunity is, and additionally provides top management and users' commitment and participation while ensuring the efficient management of the IT resources.

MODELS FOR INTEGRATED SISP

Researchers in their effort to improve SISP have developed several planning models which capture and formalise important aspects of the SISP process. (Earl, 1989) classified the planning models into three major categories namely:

- The *Awareness frameworks*, e.g. the *Information Intensity Matrix* (Porter & Millar, 1985), which demonstrate how IT can be used to inform executives for the potential impact of IT on their business and are more of a pedagogic nature. However, such models are generally of too high a level and too descriptive to guide the identification of specific IT opportunities (Earl, 1989).
- The *Opportunity frameworks*, e.g. the *Value Chain Model* (Porter & Millar, 1985), are explicitly designed to be analytical tools which can lead to firm-specific strategic advantage or clarify business strategies in order to demonstrate options for using IT strategically. However, there is need for tools used for searching for opportunities in particular application areas and for assessing specific technologies (Earl, 1989).
- The *Positioning frameworks*, e.g. the Strategic Grid by McFarlan and McKenney (Earl, 1989), are designed to help executives and planners to assess the strategic importance of the IT for a specific organisation and to show in quite general terms, how to manage the IT function. They indicate the nature of

the management but they are not useful in searching for opportunities (Earl, 1989).

In the SISP literature the following models have been extensively presented: The *Stage Model* by Richard Nolan (Earl, 1989; Ward et al., 1990; (King & Kraemer, 1984), The *Strategic Grid* proposed by McFarlan and McKenney (Earl, 1989), The *Growth Share Matrix* introduced by Boston Consultancy Group (Synnott, 1987), The *Information Intensity Matrix* (Porter & Millar, 1985), The *Information Weapon Model* proposed by (Synnott, 1987), The *Five Competitive Forces Model* developed by (Porter, 1980), The *Value Chain Model* was introduced by (Porter & Millar 1985), the *Strategic Option Generator* presented by (Wiseman, 1985), The *Customer Resource Life-Cycle Model* of (Ives & Learmonth, 1984), (Beaumont & Walters, 1991) proposed a framework for developing information systems strategies in the services industry, The *Strategic Alignment Model (SAM)*, has been proposed by (Henderson & Venkatraman, 1993; Luftman et al., 1993). A number of methodologies has also been discussed such as the *Information Engineering*, the *BRG-Model*, the *B-SCP*, (Bleistein, et al. 2006), the *Business Systems Planning (BSP)*, etc. (Synnott, 1987; Earl, 1989).

PROBLEMS WITH ALIGNMENT AND SISP

In order to carry out an SISP study, an organisation needs generally to embark on a major intensive study. It must apply one, or more of the several available methodologies or even invent its own, form committees of users and IS consultants and carry out the planning process for several weeks or months. While recognising the potential of SISP many organisations either fail to undertake planning or when they do so, planning fails. The literature provides little assistance on how to realise IS strategic alignment, how to evaluate the impact from alignment or misalignment on the business performance and what management can do to create an environment that fosters the culture for alignment (Hackathorn & Karimi, 1988, Lederer & Sethi, 1988; 1991; Mahmood & Soon, 1991; O'Connor, 1993; Henderson & Venkatraman, 1993; Luftman, 1996; Yetton, 1997; Hsaio & Ormerod, 1998; Burn, 1997). The main problems for integrated SISP are presented as follows:

- Methodologies do not follow a specific theoretical model.
- Despite the large number of models available for SISP, none of them offers a complete answer.
- Methodologies fail to take into account the organisational goals and strategies.
- Methodologies fail to provide a statement of the IS organisational objectives and to identify specific new projects. Identification of IS projects with determination of the business area where IS are needed, clarification of information needs, and proposal for development IT system, are the most difficult problems to be tackled.
- There is difficulty in communicating organisational objectives and strategies to the SISP team, and hence difficulty in ensuring alignment between business and information systems.
- Methodologies fail to assess the current information systems situation.
- The output of the methodologies is not flexible enough to consider unanticipated changes in the organisation and its environment.
- Inadequate computer support for planning methodologies.
- The time and cost involved in performing the SISP study is often considered excessive.
- Planning is inaccurately viewed as an one-off process rather as a continuous exercise. As a result SISP becomes outdated and inappropriate to the changing environment.

- There is difficulty in securing top management commitment for the plan implementation.
- SISP methodologies fail to produce an overall organisational data, applications, communications and hardware architecture.
- SISP output fail to take into account issues related to plan implementation and accomplishing as plan requires further analysis.
- SISP groups fail to consider the political side of the planning, i.e. the power of the participants and the possible changes to the balance of the power.

INTRODUCTION TO FUZZY COGNITIVE MAPS

Cognitive maps were first introduced by (Axelrod, 1976) in social sciences as signed oriented graphs, designed to capture the causal assertions of a person in a given area, in order to use them in the analysis of the effects of alternatives e.g. policies, business decisions etc. In a number of studies, they have been used to represent knowledge by presenting the cause – effect relationships that are comprehended to exist between the elements in a given context. Although the term "CM" is being used in various ways, all cognitive maps can be categorised depending on their world – objective (Hong & Han, 2002). One category is the physical and visible one. Another category includes the mental and invisible one (Zhang et al., 1992). The perception and understanding of a person about a problem may be presented on a cognitive map, comprising sets of elements associated with each other, representing the personal opinion of each individual about one's interests and concerns (Lenz & Engledow, 1986). In other words, it captures the beliefs of an individual or of a group about their subjective world, regardless of objective reality. A cognitive map is also defined as "a representation of the relations that are perceived to exist between the attributes and the concepts of a given environment" (Zhang et al., 1989). In another study (Eden et al., 1992), it is defined as "an oriented graph characterised by a hierarchical structure that is, most of the time, in the form of a means/ends graph". Alternative names such as cognitive map, cause map, and influence map have also used to describe a CM (Kwahk & Kim, 1998a). The three structural elements of a CM are the nodes, representing concepts, the directed arrows, symbolising the causal relation between two concepts, and the causality coefficient, which is either positive or negative.

(Kosko, 1986) introduced fuzzy cognitive maps (FCM) and substantially enhanced cognitive maps with fuzzy logic. Kosko used fuzzy values for cognitive map variables, in order to map causal relations. As people use fuzzy data, rules and sets, in a mathematical way, to represent fuzziness in their way of thinking (Bezdek, 1993), fuzzy cognitive maps can map human reasoning and model complex dynamic systems that are characterised by intense non linearity.

FCMs are a combination of fuzzy logic and Neural Networks. They combine the heuristic and common sense rules of fuzzy logic with the heuristic learning capabilities of neural networks (Stylios & Groumpos, 1999). In essence, they constitute Artificial Neural Systems (ANS) (Hilton,

1992) that mimic how the human brain relates and deals with various input data and events. (Kosko, 1986) defines the fuzzy cognitive map as "a fuzzy signed oriented map with feedback that models the world as a collection of concepts (or factors) and causal relations between concepts". In a subsequent study (Kosko, 1990) described a FCM as follows: "A FCM presents a causal picture. It maps events, things and processes with values, policies and objectives... allowing you to predict how complex events will impact on each other".

Typically, a FCM is a non hierarchical graph (Irani et al., 2002), where a change in a concept may result in a change throughout the network. Changes originate from a series of causal increases and decreases. These fluctuations are generally in the form of a ruled weighted measure, from −1 to +1.

A FCM is obtained from a CM by fuzzifying the strength of relations between concepts. In this way, fuzzy cognitive maps reflect most cases in a more logical manner. Therefore, a fuzzy cognitive map consists of nodes representing the factors that relate to the context being studied and of arrows indicating different fuzzy causal relations, whether positive or negative, between such factors (Figure 1).

Figure 1. Part of a FCM

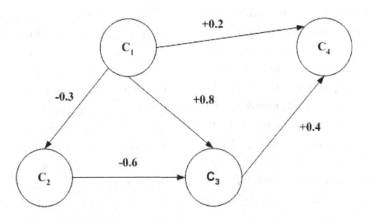

The FCM approach is, therefore, an inferential mechanism representing the existence of fuzzy causal relations between concepts and the monitoring of their effects (Lee & Han, 2000). In a similar way to CMs, if certain nodes are stimulated, the change will be conveyed through positive or negative weighted links throughout the map until equilibrium is reached.

A FCM can also be represented by using an *nxn* table of links E, where *n* is the number of nodes-concepts contained in the graph. Every value of this table represents the strength and direction of causality between various concepts. As already stated, the value of causality e_{ij} is from the interval [-1, +1]. Thus, according to (Schneider et al., 1998):

- $e_{ij} > 0$ indicates a causal increase or positive causality from node i to j.
- $e_{ij} = 0$ there is no causality from node i to j.
- $e_{ij} < 0$ indicates a causal decrease or negative causality from node i to j.

The representation of FCM with the use of a links' table allows the study of the impact of a given causal effect D_1 (Banini & Bearman, 1998), which can be represented with the aid of a vector. This impact is calculated through repeated multiplications: $ExD_1 = D_2$, $ExD_2 = D_3$ and so forth, that is, $ExD_i = D_{i+1}$, until a dynamic equilibrium is reached, which is the final result of the effect D_1.

Fuzzy cognitive maps have been used to model complex dynamic systems which are characterised by strong non linearity (Groumpos & Stylios, 2000). They have been used to capture the behaviour and reaction of virtual worlds by representing their needs such as "the search for food" or "the survival threat" (Dickerson & Kosko, 1994). Similar use is made in social systems, characterised by fuzzy causality grades (Taber, 1994). Another application of FCMs is in modeling dynamic systems with chaotic characteristics, such as social and psychological processes (Craiger

& Coovert, 1994), as well as in the behaviour of organisations (Craiger et al., 1996). Moreover, they have been used for planning and decision making in the fields of international relations and political developments (Taber, 1991). From a different perspective, FCMs have been used in factory control (Gotoh et al., 1989), in modelling distributive systems' supervisors (Stylios et al., 1997), in designing EDI (Lee & Han, 2000), in strategic planning (Kardaras & Karakostas, 1999a) and in the evaluation of information systems (Kardaras & Karakostas, 1999b). In addition, they have been used in managing relations in airline services (Kang et al., 2004), in supporting urban planning (Xirogiannis et al., 2004), in the differential diagnosis of specific speech disorders (Georgopoulos et al., 2002), as well as in many other fields.

THE PROPOSED APPROACH: FUZZY MODELLING FOR INTEGRATED SISP AND BUSINESS PROCESSES DESIGN

Overview of the Approach

This chapter proposes an approach for integrating strategic planning for IS with business strategic planning and for translating the resulting strategic objectives into business processes improvement suggestions. FCMs represent the strategic priorities, which are expressed in terms of increase or decrease of business performance issues such as cost, customer satisfaction, market share, etc. FCMs also offer the modelling mechanism for linking the strategic objectives with the Object Oriented (*OO*) model that represent the business processes. The proposed approach advocates the integration of business and SISP planning that allows complex interrelationships between business and IT to be systematically identified and managed. The realisation of the integration in the planning process can be seen as the foremost objective of the methodology.

The following diagram depicts how FCMs are linked with the OO business models.

Figure 2 shows that strategic objectives (Si) are linked with each other, thus are forming a FCM that represents how the objectives impact on each other. Furthermore, the dotted arrows in Figure 2 represent relationships among strategic objectives and tasks (ti) of the OO business process model. The proposed modelling supports the simulation of planning at strategic level, as well as the simulation of the strategic impact at the process level. The following sections of this chapter illustrate in detail the proposed approach.

Step 1: Modelling Strategic Objectives with the Strategic-FCM (S-FCM)

Fuzzy cognitive mapping of strategic objectives starts with the identification of the concepts to be modelled. Such concepts belong to broad business and technological areas of strategic interest, for example, 'Customers', 'Suppliers', 'Competition', 'IT Products and Services'. The *variables* of the *S-FCM* are therefore key concepts pertaining to the identified target areas and specifying the business and technological factors affected by IT affects and also how IT contributes to organisational performance improvement. A factor can be quite broad and therefore relevant to more than one target areas. The concepts of 'cost', 'efficiency', 'quality', 'customer satisfaction', 'speed of service delivery', etc. are some examples of variables. In fact, the S-FCM variable represent business performance factors as a series of increases or decreases to the values of the variable reflect the strategic choices of a company.

Fuzzy cognitive mapping of strategic objectives continues with the identification of the *Relationships* of the S-FCM variables that show how a variable affects one or more other variables. The relationships are represented as the arrows in the S-FCM. Each relationship is assigned a (+) or a (-) sign that indicates the causal direction of the impact that a variable exerts to another, and a fuzzy weight that indicates the perceived degree of the strength of the relationship (Kosko, 1986).

The S-FCM is a tool for planners to be used in order to formulate the strategy and develop a consensus regarding the strategic choices. After the S-FCM is finalised and agreed by the strategic planners, it shows what is needed to be achieved.

Figure 2. FCMs link strategies with business process tasks

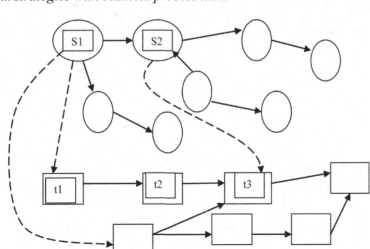

Figure 3 below, shows part of a S-FCM. The fuzzy weights shown in the figure in bold represent the strategic objective. Strategic objectives are defined in a subset of the S-FCM set of variables. The formulation of the strategy would not necessarily use all the variables in the model.

Therefore, the strategic objectives (Si) shown in figure 3 are:

- S1: To increase customer satisfaction by **(strong)**
- S2: To decrease product price by **(medium)**
- S3: To increase individualised attention by **(strong)** and
- S4: To increase availability of products by **(strong)**

The rest of the variables that constitute the S-FCM do not represent a strategic objective.

Each strategic objective is then defined by the following attributes:

- Its current achievement (ca)
- its target (tr)
- its impact on other variables (im)
- its links with the tasks that are responsible for the realisation of the objective (lk).

Each attribute of an S(i) is a fuzzy set, taking values from the set of linguistic variables {little, medium, strong}, which, after defuzzification, take values from the [0,1] range (Kosko, 1986; Tanaka, 1997).

Each strategy (SP) is also a fuzzy set, and is represented by a series of strategic objectives (Si), i.e. as:

$$SP(i) = [S_1(ca, tr, im, lk), S_2(ca, tr, im, lk), S_3(ca, tr, im, lk), \ldots, S_n(ca, tr, im, lk)].$$

Figure 3. Part of the S-FCM and its linking with the process model

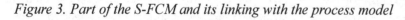
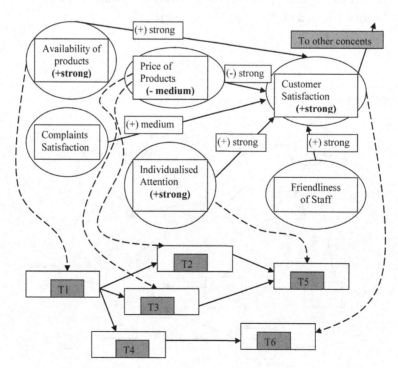

The above model of a strategy (SP), allows the planners to know the current level of achievement of each strategic performance variable, but also which business areas performance is critical and to what extent. The links between the S-FCM and the business model, provide the necessary modelling technique for IS alignment.

Step 2: Aligning Strategies with Business Processes

Drawing on figure 3, each variable in the S-FCM is linked with one or more tasks in the business process models. Such links represent allow the alignment of strategies with business process design and IS applications development. Business processes are modelled as OO models. The performance of each process and each task of a process is assessed in terms of the S-FCM variables.

For example, *availability of products* is a strategic target (S4) that needs a *strong increase*. The performance of this strategic objective depends, as shown in figure 3, on the performance of task (T1). Because of this relationship, it is important not only to focus the attention for improvement on task T1, but also to measure and assess its performance in terms of the availability of products. Similarly, *price of products* needs a *medium drop*. The achievement of this objective depends on the performance of tasks (T2) and (T3). The performance metrics for each task constitute part of the tasks' attributes.

The impact of the performance of each task to other tasks is propagated through the model by using the *FCM* relationships that link task attributes together. These relationships are shown in figure 3 as solid arrows connecting tasks in the process model. The attributes that reflect the object's performance are linked to attributes of the *S-FCM*. The *S-FCM* that supports the integrated business and SISP represents the organizational performance at a strategic level and is a *FCM* itself.

Step 3: Compare Current Business Performance and Strategic Objectives and Identify Areas of Improvement

Consider the two vectors *(Sca(i))* and *(Str(i))* that represent for each (i), the current achievement and the target performance of strategic objectives respectively, where (i) is a strategic objective. The Gap (GP) in performance of a firm is defined as the distance (di) between two elements (vi) of the vectors i.e. as:

$$(GP) = di = |\chi 1(Sca(i)) - \chi 2(Str(i))|,$$

where $\chi 1$ and $\chi 2$ is the degree of membership for the (i) element of the vectors *(Sca(i))* and *(Str(i))* respectively. For a company to be competitive, it needs to minimise the distance between current achievement and strategic target.

By looking at the value of *gap* in performance, the proposed approach locates the business areas where initiatives for improvement are needed.

However, as our approach does not aim to manage differences in performance automatically; there is no need to specify a threshold for "accepted" or not differences. It rather encourages strategic decision makers to develop alternative scenarios based on their assumptions for the company. The differences indicate to strategic planners, the performance areas and subsequently the tasks they should focus on their attention. So, if there are areas that do not perform as expected, the management can trace the business tasks that are responsible for delivering the required performance and decide the appropriate actions. Any changes or initiatives that they may propose, possibly altering the performance of tasks or changing the process design, can be fed back to the S-FCM and simulated.

STRATEGIC SIMULATION OF IS ALIGNMENT

All concepts in S-FCM and tasks in business processes are interrelated. These interrelationships are implemented as a matrix (***Strategy-Task Matrix***), which has as columns and rows all strategic concepts and tasks performance measures, respectively. The following table shows the structure of this matrix.

The numbers in the first row of Table 1 show how each concept affects or is affected by other concepts and task performance. The values are in the interval [-1, 1] and reflect the perception and beliefs of the IS planning team.

New strategic initiatives can be modelled as a vector, *Strategic Initiatives*= [S1(tr), S2(tr), ... , Sn(tr)], that is taking into consideration only the targets for each strategic objective.

By considering the vector *Strategic Initiatives*, and its multiplication with the *Strategy-Task Matrix*, (i.e. strategic initiatives vector constitutes a row of the matrix), the above matrix indicates which tasks in which process(es) should change and in what direction (+ or –), in order to satisfy the strategic requirements.

Several simulation runs will provide detailed examination of different strategic scenarios, as well as their evaluation in terms of required process design changes and performance improvements.

CASE STUDY

This section illustrates the applicability of the proposed approach for IS strategic alignment with a case study. For simplicity reasons, the complexity of the case is been kept to a minimum. Thus, only two strategic objectives and only two business tasks will be modelled.

Let us consider company (X) which aims at realising the following two strategic objectives:

- S1, from a medium current level of achievement increase market share to a high and
- S2 from a low current level of achievement increase customer satisfaction to a very high.

The defuzzification process (Ross 2004), depending on the technique, could assign for example values to the linguistic expression of the strategic objectives as follows:

- Low=0.2
- Medium=0.5
- High=0.7
- Very High=0.9

Table 1. Strategy-task matrix that integrates strategy and tasks performance

	S_1	$S_2...S_n$	Task_1 performance	Task_2 performance...	Task_n performance
S_1	0	0.5	0.7	-0.4	0.8
S2, ..., Sn					
Task_1 performance					
Task_2 performance...					
Task_n performance					

Then the gap of performance for S1= (0.7-0.5) = 0.2 and for S2= (0.9-0.2) = 0.7.

S2 target is assigned a higher priority to S1, since the gap of performance for S2 is bigger than the gap of S1. The top priority for S2 indicates that all changes required at the process level and the IS that could be proposed for development in order to support S2, should have a higher priority from the changes and IS that would support S1.

Company (X) then need to increase its customer satisfaction by 0.7 and to increase its market share by 0.2.

The S-FCM for the above case is shown in the figure below:

Figure 4 shows that the realisation of target S1 depends on the performance of task T1, as measured in terms of task T1's cost (T1-C) and time for completion (T1-t) as well as it depends on the cost (T2-C) of task T2. Similarly, the objective S2 depends on the cost (T2-C), time (T2-t) and friendliness (T2-F) of task T2 and the cost (T1-C) of task T1. The above figure also shows that target 2 affects target S1.

Next consider the Strategy-Task matrix in the following table that represents the above FCM.

The *Strategic Initiatives (StrI)* vector, which is shown below, is identical to a row of S-FCM and represents the strategic objectives that company (X) aims to achieve.

Therefore company (X) aims at increasing S1 by 0.2 and S2 by 0.7 respectively.

The multiplication of the StrI vector with the S-FCM indicates how strategic alignment can be achieved at the process and the IS level. The result of the multiplication is the *Strategic Alignment vector StrA*, which is identical to the StrI vector.

The results show that in order to achieve target S! and target S2, company (X) needs to reduce very strongly (-0.95) the time of completion of task T1, to strongly reduce the cost of task T2, to slightly reduce the time of task T2 and to increase the friendliness of task T2 by medium.

The proposed approach then identifies the areas where changes are needed (e.g. tasks T1 and T2) as well as specifies what kind of changes

Figure 4. S-FCM for company (X)

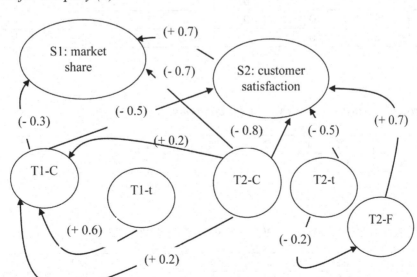

are required thus indicating the information systems that are needed in order to implement the strategic targets and achieve strategic alignment. Multiplication continue with each resulting StrA vector with the S-FCM until all cells values equal to (0), implying that there is no further impact to consider in the model.

Several scenarios can be studied for alternative strategic objectives by changing the values in the StrI vector (thus changing the priorities for the objectives) or adding more objectives to be considered.

FUTURE TRENDS

The proposed approach opens up new opportunities for research in IS strategic alignment. The intangible nature of strategic thinking as well as

the different and many times contradicting views of stakeholders can be represented using fuzzy logic models. Further research could focus in incorporating concepts from resource dependencies theory (Clemons & Row, 1991) into fuzzy models. Moreover, the resources dependencies theory is promising in investigating the resources necessary for the development of strategies and the realisation of competitive advantage.

Another direction for future research may be towards the investigation and modelling of strategic thinking principles and guidelines that would improve knowledge on strategy formulation, integration and pre-development IS assessment. Finally, the development and use of IS evaluation metrics is an important research task; one that may change the way that IS is modelled and managed. Such a set of metrics could include the definition and measurement of concepts such as

Table 2. The strategy-task matrix for company (X)

	S1	S2	T1-C	T1-t	T2-C	T2-t	T2-F
S1	0	0.7	-0.3	0	-0.7	0	0
S2	0	0	-0.5	0	-0.8	-0.5	0.7
T1-C	0	0	0	0.6	0.2	0	0
T1-t	0	0	0	0	0	0.2	0
T2-C	0	0	0	0	0	0.3	0
T2-t	0	0	0	0	0	0	0
T2-F	0	0	0	0	0	-0.2	0

Table 3. The strategic initiatives (StrI) vector for company (X)

S1	S2	T1-C	T1-t	T2-C	T2-t	T2-F
0.2	0.7	0	0	0	0	0

Table 4. The strategic alignment vector (StrA) vector for company (X)

S1	S2	T1-C	T1-t	T2-C	T2-t	T2-F
0	0.14	-0.95	0	-0.7	-0.35	0.49

'compatibility', 'reusability', 'suitability', 'competitiveness', etc.

CONCLUSION

The proposed fuzzy causal strategic design model provides the means to consider the business objectives and to associate them with specific business areas, which can be benefited by IT. In contrast to other strategic design and management approaches, the proposed model is dynamic, exhibits flexibility and responsiveness to business environment changes, customisability to specific organisational context, and allows for the development of planning scenarios.

The approach discussed in this chapter suggests that the introduction of fuzzy attributes and fuzzy associations to process models will facilitate the representation of inexact and soft concepts involved in SISP and process design. The proposed framework not only provides flexibility by accommodating non-financial measures, but it also allows the development of the systems and methods for representing, analysing, and communicating aspects of business performance information. Moreover, as it is argued in this chapter, integrated business and strategy *FCM* models allow the consideration of alternative business process re-design suggestions and their comprehensive evaluation in terms of organisational effectiveness related issues.

This chapter discusses the importance of developing frameworks for the integrated SISP that can conceptually support business process design under different IT architectures. It suggests the use of fuzzy logic and its reasoning techniques in strategic planning and processes modelling techniques. Among the benefits of the approach is its potential

- to facilitate the development of a consensus among the planners and decision makers when developing strategies,

- to integrate business and IS planning,
- to translate strategic objectives into business processes design options,
- to suggest IT architecture options that would implement the suggested by the proposed model IS strategies.

The proposed methodology provides planners with the means to cope with the complex and turbulent external environment. In order to accomplish the required external consistency, it exhibits *responsiveness* and *flexibility* so that

- environmental changes are adequately taken into consideration during the planning process,
- their impact on the organisation and its IS can be estimated and
- IS plans which reflect the latest development in the environment are produced.

With regard to the model's internal consistency, the *translation* of the organisational strategic plans into specific IS plans, takes place through various levels of abstractions of business and IT concepts. The translation is achieved by linking business and IT factors at the strategic level, with corresponding ones at specific business units and business functional areas. *Scenarios* can be developed during the planning session in order to:

- incorporate stakeholders' differing viewpoints. This also facilitates the development of an organisational learning culture as business and IT experts, co-operatively develop the scenarios, get an insight on the organisational and technological matters and experience a multi-dimensional approach to planning and
- cope with the full availability of information and alleviate the drawbacks of the rational model adopted in the planning process.

The proposed approach provides the conceptual framework in order to accommodate the rather intangible and qualitative nature of the SISP process. Fuzzy linguistic terms are suggested to describe concept attributes and associations and add flexibility to the SISP and process models as well as facilitate the communication among planners.

REFERENCES

Avison, D., Jones, J., Powell, P., & Wilson, D. (2004). Using and validating the strategic alignment model. *Journal of Strategic Information Systems, 13*, 223-246.

Axelrod R. (1976). *Structure of Decision: The Cognitive Maps of Political Elites*. Princeton, NJ: Princeton University Press.

Banini, G. A., & Bearman, R. A. (1998). *Application of fuzzy cognitive maps to factors affecting slurry rheology. International Journal of Mineral Processing, 52*, 233 – 244.

Beaumont, J. R., & Walters D. (1991). Information management in service industries: Towards a strategic framework. *Journal of Information Systems, 1.*

Bezdek, J. (1993). Editorial, Fuzzy models - what they are, and why. *IEEE Transactions on Fuzzy Systems, 1.*

Bleistein, S., J., Cox, K., Verner, J., & Phalp, K.T. (2006). B-SCP: A requirements analysis framework for validating strategic alignment of organisational IT based on strategy, context, and process. *Information and Software Technology, 48*, 846-868.

Burn, J. (1997). Information systems strategies and the management of organizational change. *Journal of Information Technology, 8,* 205-216.

Byrd, T. A., Lewis, B. R., & Bryan, R. W. (2006). The leveraging influence of strategic alignment on IT investment: An empirical examination. *Information & Management,* (43), 308-321.

Chen M., & Nunmaker J. (1989). *Integration of organisation and information systems modelling: An object-oriented approach*. In Proceedings of the 22nd Hawaii International Conference on Systems Science, Jan.

Choe, J. (2003). The effect of environmental uncertainty and strategic applications of IS on a firm's performance. *Information & Management, 40*, 257-268.

Ciborra, C., (1997). De Profundis? Deconstructing the concept of strategic alignment. *IRIS conference* (http://iris.informatik.gu.se/conference/iris20/60.htm).

Clemons E. K., & Row M. C. (1991). Sustaining IT advantage: The role of structural differences, *MIS Quarterly*, September.

Craiger, J. P., & Coovert, M. D. (1994). Modeling dynamic social and psychological processes with fuzzy cognitive maps. *Proceedings of the IEEE International Conference on Fuzzy Systems,* 1873 – 1877.

Craiger, J. P., Goodman, D. F., Weiss, R. J., & Butler, A. B. (1996). Modeling organizational behavior with fuzzy cognitive maps. *International Journal of Computational Intelligence and Organizations, 1*, 120 – 123.

Dickerson, & Kosko, B. (1994). Fuzzy virtual worlds. *AI Experts*, 25-31.

Earl, M. J. (1989). *Management Strategies for Information Technology*. Prentice Hall.

Earl, M. J. (1993). Experiences in strategic information systems planning. *MIS Quarterly/* March.

Eden, C., Ackerman, F., & Cropper, S. (1992). *The analysis of cause maps. Journal of Management Studies, 29*(3), 309 – 324.

Galliers R. D. (1993). Towards a flexible information architecture: integrating business strategies, information systems strategies and business process redesign. *Journal of Information Systems, 3*.

Georgopoulos, V. C., Malandraki, G. A., & Stylios, C. D. (2002). A fuzzy cognitive map approach to differential diagnosis of specific language impairment. *Artificial Intelligence in Medicine, 679*, 1-18.

Gotoh, K., Murakami J., Yamaguchi, T., & Yamanaka, Y. (1989). Application of fuzzy cognitive maps to supporting for plant control. *Proceedings of the SICE Joint Symposium of 15th Systems Symposium and 10th Knowledge Engineering Symposium*, (pp. 99-104).

Groumpos, P. P., & Stylios, C. D. (2000). Modeling supervisory control systems using fuzzy cognitive maps. *Chaos, Solitons & Fractals, 11*, 329-336.

Hackathorn R. C., & Karimi J. (1998). A framework for comparing information engineering methods. *MIS Quarterly*/June.

Hayward, R. G. (1987). Developing an information systems strategy. *Long Range Planning, 20*(2).

Henderson, J. C., & Venkatraman, N. (1993). Strategic alignment: Leveraging information technology for transforming organisations. *IBM Systems Journal, 32*(1).

Hilton, E. (1992). How neural networks learn from experience. *Scientific American 267*, 144 – 151.

Hong, T., & Han, I. (2002). Knowledge-based data mining of news information on the Internet using cognitive maps and neural networks. *Expert Systems with Applications, 23*, 1-8.

Hsaio, R., & Ormerod, R. (1998). A new perspective on the dynamic of IT-Enabled strategic change. *Information Systems Journal, 8*(1), 21-52.

Irani, Z., Sharif, A., Love, P. E. D., & Kahraman, C. (2002). Applying concepts of fuzzy cognitive mapping to model: The IT/IS investment evaluation process. *International Journal of Production Economics, 75*, 199-211.

Ives, B., & Learmonth, G. P. (1984). The information system as a competitive weapon. *Communications of the ACM, 27*(12), December.

Jarvenpaa, S. L., & Ives, B., (1994). The global network organization of the future: Information management opportunities and challenges. *Journal of Management Information Systems, 10*(4), 25-57.

Kardaras, D., & Karakostas, B. (1999a). The use of fuzzy cognitive maps to stimulate the information systems strategic planning process. *Information and Software Technology. 41*(4), 197-210.

Kardaras, D., & Karakostas, B. (1999b). A Modeling Approach for Information Systems Evaluation Based on Fuzzy Cognitive Map. *Proceedings of the 5th International Conference of the Decision Sciences Institute. Integrating Technology and Human Decisions: Global Bridges into the 21st Century*. Athens, Greece.

Kang, S., & Choi, L. J. (2003). Using fuzzy cognitive map for the relationship management in airline service. *Expert Systems with Applications, 26*, 545-555.

Kearns, G. S., & Lederer, A. L. (2000). The effect of strategic alignment on the use of IS-based resources for competitive advantage. *Journal of Strategic Information Systems, 9*, 265-293.

King J. L., & Kraemer K. L. (1984). Evolution and organisational information systems: An assessment of Nolan's stage model. *Communications of the ACM, 27*(5).

Kosko, B. (1986). *Fuzzy Cognitive Maps. International Journal of Man-Machine Studies, 24*, 65-75.

Kosko, B. (1990). *Fuzzy Thinking: the New Science of Fuzzy Logic*. Flamingo Press.

Kwahk, K.-Y., & Kim, Y.-G. (1998). A Cognitive Model Based Approach for Organizational Conflict Resolution. *International Journal of Information Management, 18*(6), 443-456.

Lederer A. L., & Sethi V. (1998). The implementation of strategic information systems planning methodologies. *MIS Quarterly*/September.

Lederer A. L., & Sethi V. (1991). Critical dimensions of strategic information systems planning, *Decision Sciences, 22.*

Lee, S., & Han, I. (2000). Fuzzy cognitive map for the design of EDI controls. *Information & Management, 37,* 37-50.

Luftman, J. N., Papp, R., & Brier, T. (1996). *Business and IT in harmony: Enablers and Inhibitors to alignment.* (http://hsb.baylor.edu/ramsowner/ais. ac.96/papers/papp.htm Oct 2000).

Mahmood, M. A, & Soon S. K. (1991). A comprehensive model for measuring the potential impact of information technology on organisational strategic variables. *Decision Sciences, 22.*

O'Connor, A. D. (1993). Successful strategic information systems planning. *Journal of Information Systems, 3.*

Remenyi, D. S. J. (1991). *Strategic Information Systems Planning.* NCC Blackwell.

Papp, R. (2001). *Strategic information technology: Opportunities for competitive advantage.* IDEA publishing Group.

Porter M. E. (1980). *Competitive Strategy.* Free Press.

Porter M. E., & Millar V. E. (1985). How information gives you competitive advantage. *Harvard Business Review*, July-August.

Porter, M. E. (1996). What is strategy? *Harvard Business Review*, Nov-Dec., 61-78.

Ross, T. (2004). *Fuzzy Logic with Engineering Applications.* John Wiley, 2nd edition.

Schneider, M., Shnaider, E., Kandel, A., & Chew, G. (1998). Automatic construction of FCMs. *Fuzzy Sets and Systems, 93,* 161-172.

Smaczny, T. (2001). IS an alignment between business and IT the appropriate paradigm to manage IT in today's organization? *Management Decision, 39*(10), 797-802.

Stylios, C. C., & Groumpos, P. P. (1999). Fuzzy Cognitive Maps: a model for intelligent supervisory control systems. *Computers in Industry,* (39), 229 – 238.

Synnott, W. R. (1987). The Information Weapon. Wiley.

Taber, R. (1991). Knowledge processing with fuzzy cognitive maps. *Expert Systems with Applications, 2*(1), 83 – 87.

Taber, R. (1994). *Fuzzy cognitive maps model social systems. AI Expert, 9,* 18-23.

Tallon, P., & Kraemer, K. (2003). *Investigating the relationship between strategic alignment and business value.* Hershy, PA: IDEA Publications (pp. 1-22).

Tanaka, K. (1997). *An Introduction to Fuzzy Logic for Practical Applications.* Springer Verlag.

Teo, T., & Ang, J. (1999). Critical Success Factors in the alignment of IS plans with business plans. *International Journal of Information Management, 19,* 173-185.

Trainor, E. (2003). From the president's desk. *SIM Top Ten List* (http://www.simnet.org).

Xirogiannis, G., Stefanou, J., & Glykas, M. (2004). A fuzzy cognitive map approach to support urban design. *Expert Systems with Applications, 26,* 257-268.

Yetton, P. (1997). False prophesies, successful practice, and future directions in IT management. In C. Sauer, P. Yetton, et al., (Eds), *Steps to the Future.* San Francisco: Jossey-Bass.

Zhang, W. R., Chen, S. S., & Bezdek, J. C. (1989). *Pool2: a generic system for cognitive map development and decision analysis, 19*(1), 31-39.

Zhang, W. R. Chen, S. S., Wang, W., & King, R. S. (1992). A cognitive-map-based approach to the coordination of distributed cooperative agent. *IEEE Transactions on Systems, Man, & Cybernetics, 22,* 103-114.

Ward, J., Griffiths, P., & Whitmore, P. (1990). *Strategic Planning for Information Systems.* Wiley.

Weill, P., & Broadbent, M. (1998). *Leveraging the new Infrastructure.* Harvard Business School Press.

Wiseman, C. (1985). *Strategy and Computers,* Dow Jones Irwin.

Section II
Information Technology
Portfolio Management

Chapter V
IT Portfolio Management:
A Holistic Approach to Outsourcing Decisions

Luke Ho
Staffordshire University, UK

Anthony S. Atkins
Staffordshire University, UK

ABSTRACT

This chapter provides an introduction to the advent of Information Technology Outsourcing (ITO) and its impact on portfolio management in modern day decision-making. Specifically, it outlines the use of the Application Portfolio Matrix (APM) by companies in formulating their strategic IT direction and why such techniques may be unsuitable for outsourcing decisions, which are inherently complex and multi-faceted in nature. Consequently, there is a need for alternative decision support tools to enable companies to determine how to "best-source" various aspects of their business. This chapter subsequently presents an analysis of ten outsourcing decision-making frameworks, identified from the literature, highlighting their commonalities, strengths, deficiencies and the potential misalignment between the theory and practice of outsourcing as determined by focus group discussions. This chapter gives a background introduction to the practitioner-driven Holistic Approach {Business, Information, Organizational} (HABIO) Framework, which adopts a holistic approach to outsourcing that examines underlying issues from the business, information (i.e. technical) and organizational perspectives. The framework adopts a "card/deck" analogy in its design, allowing for the flexibility and scalability required to accommodate the intricacies of heterogeneous outsourcing decisions in varying industry and context. The chapter outlines its application to two case studies, involving multi-million contracts from the finance and retail sectors, which is of particular interest to academics seeking accounts of current practices and practitioners seeking a systematic guide to ITO portfolio management.

INTRODUCTION

The outsourcing of Information Technology (IT) and business services has been receiving increased attention since the late 1990s, particularly in 1999 where there was a particular surge in offshore outsourcing as companies sought to resolve the Y2K problem (i.e. millennium bug). Since Eastman-Kodak's mega-deal (i.e. outsourcing contracts with total worth of over $1bn) in 1989, where outsourcing was perceived to be first formalized as a strategy, over 78 other mega-deals have been publicly announced. This meteoric rise is also reflected in the statistics and analyst predictions, which indicate that 88% of IT companies in UK currently utilize some form of outsourcing and that Business Process Outsourcing (BPO) will reach a market worth of $650bn by 2009 (Ravi, Bingham, Rowan, Danilenko, & McStravick, 2005).

The traditional concept of geographical boundaries has diminished in recent years, as advances in communication technology and the subsequently deregulation of telecommunications facilities have resulted in the ability for economically-viable international communication via data and voice networks (Namasivayam, 2004; Weinstein, 2004). With proliferated access to computing capabilities and emergence of collaborative groupware tools as a catalyst, the concept of virtual teamwork is now a reality, particularly for service-related functions (e.g. call centre operations and medical transcription). Hence, such functions are now being outsourced to knowledge workers around the world more on virtue of skills and capabilities and less on physical proximity.

At present, there are indications of Computerized Axial Tomography (CAT) scans from US hospitals being remotely analyzed in Israel and Magnetic Resonance Imaging (MRI) scans from UK hospitals being transmitted for analysis in Spain, which offers not only commercial revenue, but also altruistic opportunities for knowledge sharing. In such healthcare setups, the CAT scans are first taken within the US hospital, following which the digitized information is then transmitted via data networks to remote doctors based overseas in Israel, where the analysis and subsequent recommendation(s) on whether to operate can be made. Such information can be reviewed quickly because of the difference in time zones, thus allowing the CAT scans to be analyzed overnight (working day in Israel). This setup also provides coverage for the US hospital to deal with emergency cases arriving at night which require urgent attention. Due to the seamless integration of information interchange, boundaries between the US-based components and Israeli-based components are indistinct, and hence patients are often unaware that the hospital is essentially a virtual organization.

There is an increasing propensity for companies to consider offshore outsourcing, largely due to the promise of significant cost reductions (primarily from labor cost arbitrage), but also the potential to maintain round-the-clock availability (by exploiting time zone differences) and leverage foreign expertise. This has made countries such as India and China attractive offshoring locations for a myriad of industries, ranging from laptop production to remote tutoring. Niche markets have also developed, such as Taiwan for research and development of Personal Digital Assistant (PDA) components and South Africa for insurance claims processing.

Despite the various realizable benefits associated with outsourcing, it is not without its risks, just like any other business moves (Aubert, Patry, & Rivard, 1998; Earl, 1996). Hence, companies which fail to consider outsourcing as a strategic decision (often eliciting to rely solely on computational cost analysis instead) tend to encounter financial consequences, as illustrated by a supermarket group's cancellation of its $3.3bn outsourcing contract in 2006, which resulted in termination costs of $128m (Hadfield, 2006).

The recent growth in outsourcing uptake has accentuated the increasing challenge to achieve successful outsourcing, with as many of 50% of outsourcing deals running into complications and indications of $7.3bn being wasted by European companies on poorly managed contracts (Cohen & Young, 2005; Deloitte, 2006; Overby, 2006). This is further highlighted by the Computerweekly's 2006 survey of Chief Information Officers (CIOs), in which 75% of the 140 respondents disagreed that outsourcing has provided expected benefits (Computerweekly, 2006). These figures highlight a number of critical concerns for corporate IT portfolio management, one of which is the need for rigorous and methodical process by which outsourcing is incorporated into the planning process as a strategic investment, rather than a simple procurement decision.

IT PORTFOLIO PLANNING PROCESS

Companies should adopt a systematic approach to IT portfolio management (as shown in Figure 1) in order to ensure that decisions involving such projects (including that of outsourcing operations) are considered in an objective manner, which takes into account the longer term impact on the organization as a whole.

Stage 1: Prepare IT Strategy

Initially, companies need to clearly articulate defined long-term business objectives, and then develop an Information Technology (IT) strategy which will enable them to progress and align with such business goals. At this stage, decision support tools, such as the Application Portfolio Matrix (APM), are often utilised to analyse each function's (or application's) strategic importance, contribution to business value or/and other specific criteria. A rigorous review of legislative implications is also needed to determine the legal implications of the associated project (e.g. *"do the national labour laws inhabit implementation of a 24/7 operation?"*). In instances where outsourcing is being considered, a through evaluation is needed to identify the mission-critical elements for strategic retention and the level of internal expertise required in order to prevent loss of organizational competencies, and hence safeguard against the risk of vendor lock-in.

Stage 2: Resource Planning

The next stage in the process is resource planning, in which the resources (both personnel and equipment) currently required for maintaining the functions (or applications) are identified. The

Figure 1. IT portfolio planning process

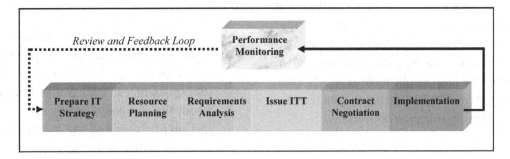

identification facilitates the creation of a resource utilization table (e.g. breakdown into volume of data transmission, processor capacity required, etc.) in which the resource commitment for the various functions can be detailed, thus allowing resource-intensive functions/applications to be flagged. Subsequently, these resource-intensive functions/applications can then be evaluated for suitability for streamlining (e.g. Business Process Re-engineering) or elimination (e.g. outsourcing to external service providers).

At this stage, an understanding of the internal cost metrics is required in order to establish a "base case" against which submitted tenders can be evaluated. This is increasingly formulated using the Activity-Based Costing (ABC) method, which seeks to objectively assign costs by identifying cause and effect relationships via the concept of "cost drivers" (Massy, 1999). In the event of outsourcing, it is important that human resource issues are not overlooked, due to the definite impact that outsourcing has on staff morale. Companies may hence have to commit more resources (typically financial) to make corresponding adjustments in order to maintain internal work efficiency. In some instances, it may be appropriate to utilize consultants to help identify or redefine the company's strategic intention, particularly if this has yet to be clarified in the previous stage. It is also important that issues concerning ownership of equipment and other resources are clarified beforehand in a defined exit strategy, in order to pre-empt complications resulting from a later change in service provider or reversal of decision (i.e. bringing the outsourced function/application back in-house). In the event of outsourced software development, further consideration concerning copyright of the final product will have to be taken into account in addition to the legal implications (e.g. UK Data Protection Act of 1998) relating to data transfer outside of the organization or overseas.

Stage 3: Requirements Analysis

Requirements definition is a vital part of the IT portfolio management process, as inaccurate definition can result in resource waste, misalignment to business objectives, implementation delays and client dissatisfaction. Requirement analysis should begin with business requirements which are then translated into performance requirements for the respective function/application. The exact method to be utilized will be specific to the context of individual companies; some may prefer the use of formal project methods while others may prefer the use of informal brainstorming sessions as the basis. Typically, companies have found it helpful to utilize Service Level Specifications to set measurable requirements and performance criteria (Sorteberg and Kure, 2005). Completed requirements analyses should be reviewed by a select management committee at this stage before further progression, as individuals may inevitably omit the required clarity and details, which results in ambiguous definitions that consequently lead to complications during implementation.

Stage 4: Issue Invitation To Tender (ITT)

The Invitation To Tender (ITT) stage, also known as Request For Proposal (RFP) stage, is a procurement procedure where clients invite potential service providers to tender for a particular function/application. The key component of this stage is the ITT/RFP document, which should comprise of the following sections:

- ***Introduction***, e.g. industrial context, goals and objectives, and the procurement timetable
- ***Background***, e.g. background information about the company, details of the technical environment and the current business systems in place

- *Scope and scale of functions*, e.g. detail and scope of the function/application under tender, such as number of users, number of transactions and data transmission volume
- *Key requirements*, e.g. the most important requirements, such as legal adherence to data protection legislations
- *General requirements*, e.g. description of service provision and type of client-provider relationship to be established, such as strategic partnership
- *Detailed functional requirements*, e.g. full description of what is specifically required from the service provider
- *Technical requirements*, e.g. details on technological direction, software and hardware
- *Cost information required*, e.g. details of costs for various activities, such as licensing, training, consultancy, development, customization and implementation
- *Service provider information required*, e.g. contact details, parent company name, financial backing details, company audits and evidence of ability to deliver
- *Implementation requirements*, e.g. timescales, preferred project methodology and resource utilization
- *Instructions to service provider*, e.g. format and content of tender responses, selection criteria and submission deadlines
- *Appendices*, e.g. organizational charts, glossary of terms and business process diagrams

It is particularly important for companies to ensure that service providers maintain the strict numbering in the ITT/RFP document, which makes it easier to verify if respective service providers have replied to each defined requirement. At this stage, companies often also opt to include a compliance grid for tendering service providers to complete, which facilitates an intuitive and hence quicker review of requirements fulfilled. In order to meet scheduled timeframes, it is important for

companies to state a clear cut-off date for tender submission and emphasize that tenders received after such date will be rejected outright.

Stage 5: Contract Negotiation

This stage involves negotiating with the selected service provider to reach a suitable contractual agreement, which often requires a mix of tact, diplomacy and knowledge of relevant market dynamics (e.g. typical implementation cost of technology X, availability of alternative options, etc.). After a potentially time-consuming selection process, there is often a natural tendency for companies to desire a speedy negotiation to reach a suitable contractual agreement. This is, however, a potential pitfall that companies should safeguard against, as it typically results in the haphazard drafting of contracts which may lead to complications, and subsequently a costly and time-intensive remediation process. In this stage, the service provision issues that should be discussed are performance standards, compliance monitoring, change management procedures, technological review periods and penalties for non-compliance, which are typically addressed by the establishment of Service Level Agreements. Acceptance testing should also be included in the contract, as a means of ascertaining whether pre-defined client requirements have been adequately met. Ideally, various safeguards should also be worked into the contract, such as the following:

- Non-disclosure clause for information identified as confidential or company secret
- Unambiguous definition of Intellectual Property (IP) rights
- Requirement for implementing a recognized code of practice on information security
- Ability to veto the use of sub-contractors (i.e. further outsourcing of functions)
- Exit clause in the event the contract termination is deemed necessary

- Procedures to account for business changes where both parties share any potential savings from new technology or process streamlining (i.e. mutual goal sharing)

There should be a clear escalation hierarchy and dispute resolution procedures in terms of problem resolution. In instances where traditional pricing arrangements are deemed inadequate, companies can opt to utilize escrow arrangements, where a third party intermediary acts as a security buffer between the client and the service provider. During this stage, the contract negotiation should be built on trust and not developed in an adversarial way. Overall, companies should have a good understanding of the market, and thus have a grasp of their bargaining power in the contract negotiation with service providers.

Stage 6: Implementation

The implementation stage involves the establishment of monitoring procedures and ascertaining the compliance of performance standards in the service provision. In order for the client-provider relationship to be truly effective, constant communication is a must, and hence it is particularly important that communication channels and feedback procedures are established to facilitate constant and open communication. It is also important that formal procedures are developed to resolve issues in a convivial rather than adversarial way. In the interest of long-term business benefits, companies should build up a strategic client-provider relationship, which is based on trust, and work towards designing contracts that account for the velocity business changes.

Stage 7: Performance Monitoring

Performance monitoring is an essential post-implementation stage in ensuring that pre-defined requirements and performance criteria for the function/application are being met, and that its implementation is contributing towards the business objectives of the organization. This stage is often extended by the establishment of a feedback loop via means of review sessions (typically 4-6 weeks after implementation), in which companies can seek to identify any best practices and isolate problem areas. This is important as it provides review information which can be utilized in future implementations to pre-empt potential problems and can facilitate knowledge transfer, through documented practices, from experienced staff to those in training. Such practices can be further extended by the use of web-based monitoring systems, which integrate with varying service management software (e.g. BMC Remedy) to provide a consolidated view of service compliance, thereby facilitating a pro-active approach to performance monitoring. An example of this application is outlined later in the chapter.

APPLICATION PORTFOLIO MATRIX (APM)

The concept of IT portfolio management was first proposed by McFarlan (1981), beginning initially on a project-centric basis, and then evolving towards the inclusion of "steady-state" portfolio entries such as application maintenance and support. Although analogous to financial portfolio management, there are significant differences between the two, particularly as IT investments typically involve a "harvest period" (i.e. returns are not immediate) and can be measured using by both quantitative and qualitative measurements. Consequently, a range of decision support tools specific to IT portfolio management have been developed by academics and practitioners, one of which is the well-known Application Portfolio Matrix (APM) by McFarlan and McKenneys (1983) that provides for systematic management of an organization's IT portfolio by assessing the scope of its current, planned and potential applications. The APM is a 2x2 framework which allows for

Figure 2. Application portfolio matrix

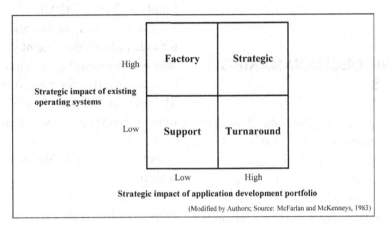

(Modified by Authors; Source: McFarlan and McKenneys, 1983)

analysis of each respective application's strategic impact on existing operating systems against its strategic impact on the application development portfolio

In addition to the APM, there were also other traditional techniques that are utilized for IT portfolio management, such as:

- Strength, Weakness, Opportunity, Threat (SWOT) Analysis, resultant from Stanford University's research led by Albert Humphrey (Learned, Christensen, Andrews, & Guth, 1965), is a strategic planning tool which is utilized to generate strategic alternatives from a situation analysis, by identifying the strengths and weaknesses of an organization along with the opportunities and threats in the environment.
- Value Chain Analysis by Porter (1985), which is a systematic approach to examining the development of competitive advantage by decomposing a company's sequence (i.e. chain) of business functions into specific activities (e.g. inbound logistics and procurement) and analyzing their links to the organization's competitive position, thereby identifying opportunities for value adding. This has been updated for the Internet Era as

the "value web chain" (Laudon and Laudon, 2004).

- Porter's 5 Forces by Porter (1979), which is a business management framework for diagnosing an industry's structure through the analysis of five competitive forces that erode its long-term average profitability (i.e. Suppliers, Potential Entrants, Buyers, Substitutes and Industry Competitors). The 5 Forces framework has been refined over the years by academics and strategists (Laudon and Laudon, 2004), including the addition of a 6th force known as 'complementors' which helps to explain the reasoning behind strategic alliances.

Although anecdotal evidence suggests that the above-mentioned techniques are still very much in use for IT portfolio management in general, the increasingly diverse nature of outsourcing and the myriad of domains of application (ranging from micro-scale logistics outsourcing to large-scale private military operations) indicates a need for refined frameworks, tools and techniques specific to outsourcing decision-making. Since the Eastman Kodak mega-deal in 1989 which brought outsourcing into the public eye, there has been an increasing (in line with the growth of outsourcing) number of such frameworks developed by both academics and practitioners for outsourcing decision support.

OUTSOURCING DECISION-MAKING FRAMEWORKS

In place of the Application Portfolio Matrix (APM), there are a number of other frameworks which can be utilized for outsourcing decision-making. Table 1 outlines the key features of ten such frameworks identified from the literature (excluding commercial sources such as paid access consultancy reports).

Analysis of the identified frameworks highlighted a lack of quantitative measurement in the frameworks, similar to the case of the APM. In terms of making definite comparisons, the use of quantitative measures can provide a more distinct yardstick over relative descriptive properties (*'10 compared to 8'* against *'very high compared to high'*). As such, quantitative measurement within a framework approach is considered to be important, as it increases the precision of decision-making by increasing objectivity in the decision-making process (Yang and Huang, 2000)

The analysis also highlighted a lack of financial costing tools within the frameworks, which is considered to be contradictory as reducing operational costs is commonly identified as one of the top reasons for outsourcing (Mills, 2004). Hence, the lack of a defined costing method will result in challenges for companies seeking to ascertain whether such projected cost savings have been achieved post-implementation. Research by McIvor (2000) attempts to include financial costing within a framework but does not provide examples or procedural guidelines in its application. This is considered to be a crucial component for framework approaches, as it facilitates the ability of the business to benchmark its internal cost position against external service providers, and hence provides a comprehensive financial

justification for outsourcing decisions (Farbey, Land and Targett, 1993).

The reviewed frameworks appeared to only provide partial coverage of the domains associated with outsourcing decision-making, i.e. business, technical (information) and organizational. Majority of the frameworks were focused on issues within the business domain (e.g. in-house economics of scale and contribution to business value), and do not adequately address issues within the technical and organizational domains (e.g. retention of internal expertise and political influences from labor legislations). These shortcomings were the motivation behind the development of a new outsourcing framework, which incorporates a holistic approach that considers the organization as a whole rather than carrying out an analysis of separate parts (i.e. emphasizes the importance of the whole and the interdependence of its parts). This framework, known as the Holistic Approach {Business, Information, Organizational} (HABIO for short), is named after its tri-perspective grouping of issues, which is detailed in the following section.

HABIO FRAMEWORK

Figure 3 illustrates the proposed HABIO framework, which is based on the Information Systems Strategy Triangle (ISST) by Pearlson (2001) - a framework for understanding the impact of Information Systems (IS) on organizations that relates *Business Strategy* with *Information Strategy* and *Organizational Strategy*. It advocates that the corner of the triangle are interlocking, hence a change in one strategy will require re-evaluation of the other two strategies so that corresponding adjustments can be made to ensure that balance is preserved. Changes in *Business Strategy* without consideration of the corresponding effects on *Information Strategy* and *Organizational Strategy* will result in the business struggling until balance can be restored (Pearlson and Saunders, 2004).

Table 1. List of alternative outsourcing decision-making frameworks

Willcocks Frameworks (Willcocks, Feeny & Islei, 1997)	☐ Matrix Analysis (Strategic Grid/Boston Matrix) ☐ Empirically derived frameworks which focus on critical factors ☐ Set of three frameworks ☐ Business Matrix / Economic Matrix / Technical Matrix
Yang-Huang Decision Model (Yang and Huang, 2000)	☐ Utilizes Analytic Hierarchy Process method ☐ Hierarchical format which works on the principle of decomposing complex problem into sub-problems
De Looff Framework (De Looff, 1995)	☐ Descriptive framework in the form of a checklist ☐ Provides for systematic description of outsourcing options
Perry Matrix Framework (Perry, Stott, & Smallwood, 1993)	☐ Matrix Analysis (Strategic Grid/Boston Matrix) ☐ Based on concept of Unit Competitive Advantage ☐ Analyses a function's abilities to value-add
Systems Audit Grid (Earl, 1989)	☐ Matrix Analysis (Strategic Grid/Boston Matrix) ☐ Involves an Information Systems audit which incorporates both the business user perspective and technical specialist perspective
Cox Methodology (Cox, 1996)	☐ Based on Relational Competence Analysis ☐ Involves assessment of asset specificity
McIvor Framework (McIvor, 2000)	☐ Integrates key theories such as core competency thinking, value chain perspectives and supply base influences ☐ Involves core activity definition, value chain analysis, total cost analysis and relationship analysis
Four Outsourcing Relationship Type (FORT) Framework (Kishore, Rao, Nam, Rajagopalan & Chaudhury, 2003)	☐ Matrix Analysis (Strategic Grid/Boston Matrix) ☐ Classifies client-provider relationships into Reliance, Alliance, Support and Alignment types
Market, Competence and Advantage Model (MCA) (Cullen and Willcocks, 2004)	☐ Matrix Analysis (Strategic Grid/Boston Matrix) ☐ Considers supplier and market maturity, organization's relative competence and sustainable competitive advantage
Outsourcing Decision Tree (Cullen and Willcocks, 2004)	☐ Based on traditional decision flowchart technique ☐ Involves high-level analysis of six issues such as the potential for a monopolist supplier market

Similarly, changes in *Information Strategy* or *Organizational Strategy* alone with prior consideration of corresponding impacts will cause an imbalance. This is analogous to the concept of strategic alignment (Luftman, Lewis and Oldach, 1993).

The choice of the Strategic Triangle concept (i.e. the ISST) for mapping the outsourcing decision-making process is based on merit that the Strategic Triangle concept (such as the ISST) is both a well-documented concept and a well-known convention (Frenzel and Frenzel, 2004;

Figure 3. ISST and the HABIO framework

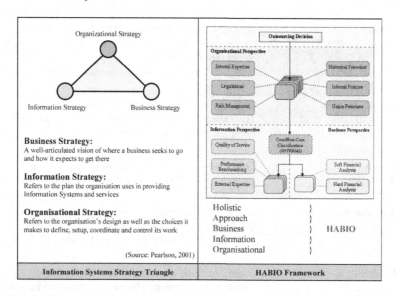

Robson, 1997). The resultant HABIO framework design, illustrated in Figure 3, provides a tri-perspective approach (akin to the ISST's tri-strategy) approach to outsourcing decision-making which addresses issues within a range of domains.

Developed with inputs from a leading financial institution and a large UK retail group (profiled in a later section), the framework's tri-perspective approach advocates the logical grouping of issues to be considered under the Business, Information (i.e. technical) and Organizational context. This logical grouping adopts the analogy of a deck of cards, in which each issue is depicted as a "card", which can be added or removed to the corresponding "deck" (i.e. perspective) as appropriate to the organization under consideration. The resultant flexibility is an intentional design as outsourcing decisions are not necessarily homogenous between companies (Dibbern, Goles, Hirschheim, & Jayatilaka, 2004), thus customization is essential to facilitate adaptability for specific context and industry.

The HABIO Framework (Ho, Atkins, & Eardley, 2005) is normally comprised of 11-12

"cards" (depending on the inclusion of core/non-core classification), as listed in Table 2. However, due to its holistic approach, the framework can be extended to include additional or modified "cards" that relate specifically to the organization under consideration. An example of this is a government agency that may choose to expand the Organizational Perspective to factor in the issue of 'political sensitivity' and the Information Perspective to factor in the issue of 'defense systems integration'.

The concept of core/non-core classification relates to the theory of "core competence", which has been frequently mentioned in connection with outsourcing decision-making since the work of Prahalad and Hamel (1990). Popularized by the notion of strategic outsourcing (Quinn and Hilmer, 1994), the concept argues that companies should focus on core competencies, while contracting with other companies for support services and ancillary functions (i.e. outsource). Core competencies are deemed to underpin the ability of the organization to outperform the competition (McIvor, 2000), thus convention suggests that

Table 2. "Cards" (i.e. issues considered) within HABIO framework

Organizational Perspective	Information Perspective	Business Perspective
☐ Internal Expertise	☐ Quality of Service	☐ Soft Financial Analysis
☐ Legislations	☐ Performance Benchmarking	☐ Hard Financial Analysis
☐ Risk Management	☐ External Expertise	
☐ Historical Precedent		
☐ Internal Policies		
☐ Union Pressures	☐ Additional / Modified "Card"	

they should be defended and nurtured (i.e. kept in-house). However, such convention appears to be designed for a stable and well-defined environment, which is far from a live environment where technologies, priorities, finances and demands are more volatile (Healy and Linder, 2004).

Non-core functions have traditionally been labeled as prime candidates for outsourcing (Willcocks *et al*, 1997), but the clear identification of functions by such core/non-core classification remains a challenge as it is subject to an organization's strategy, which can change quickly. In such classification, some organizations may perceive that nothing is sacristan and hence everything can be outsourced, while other organizations may perceive it as crucial to be retained in-house. Furthermore, distinguishing between core and non-core functions is a complex task (McIvor, 2000) and to some degree a subjective process. For example, the processing of tax records may be considered by some as a core function of the UK Inland Revenue, thus its outsourcing mega-deal with the Cap Gemini Ernst & Young consortium (Cullen, 2003) could be deemed as contradicting the convention that core functions should be retained in-house. In addition, studies have found no support for the argument that organizations retain strategic (i.e. core) functions and that such functions are indeed outsourced (Dibbern et al., 2004; McLellan, 1995; Nam, Rajagopalan, Rao,

& Chaudhury, 1996). This challenges the concept of core competency and introduces the need to reconsider its relevancy in modern outsourcing decision-making practices. Hence, the HABIO framework considers core/non-core classification to be an optional process, which can be included or excluded as deemed appropriate by the organization.

In instances where core/non-core classification is considered within the outsourcing decision, it is important to take into account both the (technical) specialist and (business) user perspectives in the analysis, due to the possibility of differences between individual perceptions (Earl, 1989). In order to reflect this, the core/non-core classification process is illustrated in the HABIO framework as spanning both the information (i.e. technical) and business (i.e. user) perspectives.

The framework adopts a Weight and Score (W&S) technique that provides a systematic approach by which the outsourcing decision can be evaluated. This involves a three stage process outlined as follows:

- Assign weights to each of the three perspectives (to indicate priorities)
- Assign scores to each of the issues (according to specific assessment method)
- Determine weighted score which indicates propensity for successful outsourcing

Each perspective is first assigned a weight to indicate its overall priority in the outsourcing decision, e.g. a higher weight assigned to the Business Perspective indicates that the hard and soft financial costing aspects are of greater emphasis. Each issue within the framework is then measured by its respective assessment method, involving either a grid or scale evaluation technique (as illustrated in Figure 4). This involves only the measurement of issues which are prevalent to the company under consideration, e.g. the issue of union pressure is not measured if considered to be inconsequential for a company's outsourcing operations. The three perspectives of the HABIO Framework and their underlying issues are described in the following sections.

Organizational Perspective

The Organizational Perspective involves the consideration of organizational issues and political influences, which includes:

Internal Expertise

One commonly cited risk associated with the use of outsourcing is the loss of internal expertise, which increases the level of dependence that an organization has on the external service provider(s). The organization thus risks being more locked into the service provider(s), and is therefore more vulnerable to business disruptions from service provision failures. As such, in outsourcing decisions, it is important for a company to take into account the degree of internal expertise which it intends to retain to ensure business continuity in the event of complications in the outsourcing arrangement. The need to retain internal expertise is particularly crucial in instances where outsourcing has been utilized in domains that relate to national security. At present, US Private Militaries Companies (PMCs), which take up 1/3 of the $87bn budget earmarked for US military operations in the Middle East, are responsible for maintaining over 28% of all US weapon systems (Eyal, 2004; Traynor, 2003). This is a particularly worrying statistic as PMCs can legally withdraw their employees when faced with danger in a combat zone. Thus, without retaining some degree of internal expertise, the US military may be stranded in a combat zone with complex weapon systems that they no longer have the skill or knowledge to operate (Yeoman, 2003).

Figure 4. HABIO framework - Grids and scales

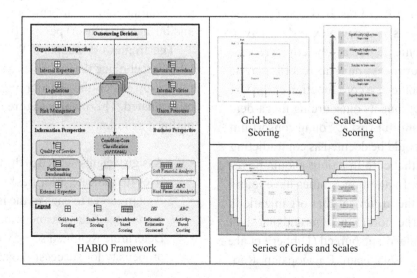

Legislations

In each country, there are different legislations (e.g. US Sarbanes-Oxley Act 2002 and UK Data Protection Act 1998) that shape the operating environment for businesses, which in turn enforces a unique set of constraints on the outsourcing decision-making process. An example of national legislation that affects the outsourcing decision is the UK Transfer of Undertakings (Protection of Employment) Regulations 1981 (TUPE), which applies where there is a transfer of undertaking from one person to another. The purpose behind the legislation is to provide special protection for employees when the business in which they work is transferred to a new employer. This was revised in mid-2006 to include first generation outsourcing (i.e. 1st customer to 1st service provider), second generation outsourcing (i.e. 1st service provider to 2nd service provider) and contracting in (i.e. bringing the service back in-house). Under the legislation, employees involved in the undertaking automatically continue in their jobs with their existing terms and conditions, thus preserving continuity of employment. In addition, TUPE requires that recognized trade unions and elected employee representatives are informed and consulted about the potential transfer and its corresponding implications. As such, due to TUPE, the outsourcing decision-making process within the UK has to take into account additional time required for the consultation period (with trade unions and employee representatives) and potential requirement for staff transfers across the organizations (e.g. from the company to the external service provider). Although seemingly an obvious consideration, confusion over TUPE regulations has resulted in a number of high-profile disputes, such as the cancelled contract between Atos and Lucent (Benett, 2002), and employer compensations of up to 13 weeks of pay as illustrated by the case of Sweetin v Coral Racing (2005).

Historical Precedent

This relates to evolutionary game theory (Fisher, 1930) where players are able to observe the actions and subsequent outcomes of previous games, and base their future actions upon these observations. Actions which cumulate to positive outcomes are perceived to be better and hence more likely to be adopted, thus "past perception dictates future performance". Similarly, the outsourcing decision can be influenced by an organization's history (Dibbern et al., 2004), as decision-makers evaluate the consequences of past decisions and base their future decisions upon such knowledge. For example, if the previous outsourcing of the payroll function has resulted in cost savings and increased service quality, it is perceived to be successful (i.e. positive outcome), thus outsourcing of the payroll function is likely to continue and similar functions (e.g. human resources administration) may be considered for outsourcing.

Internal Policies

A company is a political coalition (March, 1962) and like any other human organization, there are some individuals who have more influence in key decisions than others (Dahl, 1958). The nature of a business organization endows the management level with higher authority (i.e. political influence) than others in the organizational strata and hence internal policies by the management level tend to take precedent in decision processes. Initial case studies by Palvia (1995) and Goodstein Goodstein, Boeker, and Stephan (1996) have illustrated that different stakeholders have different motivations for and against outsourcing within an organization, and that power and politics play a role in the outsourcing decision. Interpretative results from multiple case studies of Lacity and Willcocks (1995) also concur that such political factors may influence the outsourcing decision. In some instances, managers were found to have manipulated or instrumentalised the benchmarking process in order to prove the efficiency of internal capabilities, expose exaggerated outsourcing claims or justify the need for new resources (Hirschheim and Lacity, 2000).

Union Pressures

Union pressure is a factor commonly overlooked in outsourcing decision-making frameworks, which varies from country to country, depending on factors such as the percentage of unionization, industrial context and political clout. In certain countries such as the UK, the strength of trade unions is highly visible as demonstrated by their willingness to utilize strike action (Oates, 2004, Richardson, 2004) and legal action to achieve their objectives. The literature indicates that such trade unions have disrupted outsourcing attempts by a number of companies (McIvor, 2000), and that union pressure is considered one of the most significant hurdles to overcome among obstacles to effective outsourcing (Healy and Linder, 2004; Verhoef, 2005). Hence, this is a critical factor that could potentially undermine the entire outsourcing operation or/and result in severe financial impact (primarily from compensation claims) if left unaddressed.

Risk Management

This refers to the process of identifying, assessing and controlling risks that may result in financial loss or organizational impact in the outsourcing process. Risk management strategies include risk avoidance, risk abatement (e.g. contingency planning), risk retention, risk transfer (e.g. corporate insurance or indemnification provisions) and risk allocation (e.g. joint venture). Risk is commonly defined as probability against impact. More specifically in the context of outsourcing, risk is defined as the probability of an undesirable outcome against the importance of potential loss (Aubert, Dussault, Patry, & Rivard, 1999).

Information Perspective

The Information Perspective involves the consideration of technical issues, which includes:

Quality of Service (QoS)

This refers to the degree to which the service provided is fit for purpose, i.e. fitness for intended use. The International Organization for Standardization defines three components of quality of service, which are outlined as follows:

- *Effectiveness* relates to whether the service provided fulfils the requirements of its intended users
- *Efficiency* relates to whether the service provided allows its intended users to perform their required tasks effectively with a minimum of effort (i.e. without unnecessary effort)
- *Satisfaction* relates to whether the service provided meets the expectations of its intended users (i.e. the intended users are content with the service provision)

It is important to note that although managers claim rational economic benefits when making outsourcing decisions, they may in fact be bounded in their rationality by their perception of the quality experienced as the users (Fowler and Jeffs, 1998). As such, if an accurate measure of quality of service for an internal function were to be derived, its actual users should be involved in the evaluation process, rather than management representation alone.

In some instances, organizations have pre-assessed potential service providers based on QoS practices and standards such as the IT Infrastructure Library (ITIL), Capability Maturity Model Integration (CMMI) model and Six Sigma. This is taken a step further in some organizations, which also evaluate QoS based on the number of service provider staff who are certified to relevant accreditations, such as those of the Information Systems Examinations Board (ISEB) which is administered by the British Computer Society (BCS). Some of these practices, standards and accreditations are outlined as follows:

- Information Technology Infrastructure Library (ITIL) is widely adopted around the world as the de facto standard for best practices in IT service management. It is essentially a series of consistent documentation, which are used to aid in the implementation of a framework for IT service management. ITIL was revised in 2000 by the Office of Government Commerce (OGC) to operate in synergy with related standards such as BSI Management Overview (PD0005), BS15000-1 (Specification for Service Management) and BS15000-2 (Code of Practice for Service Management). It is divided into a series of sets, which can be classified under two main categories of Service Support and Service Delivery.
- Capability Maturity Model® Integration (CMMI) is a model which provides a structured view of process improvement across an organization. It seeks to integrate traditionally separate organizations, set process improvement goals and priorities, provide guidance for quality processes, and provide a yardstick for appraising current practices. CMMI defines six capability levels by which an organization's capability, relative to a particular process area, can be measured. It is similar to ISO 9001, which specifies an effective quality system for software development and maintenance, but differs in the sense that ISO 9001 specifies minimal acceptable quality levels while CMMI establishes a framework for measuring continuous process improvement.
- Six Sigma (6σ), developed by Motorola, is a rigorous and systematic data-driven methodology that utilizes management information and statistical analysis to measure and improve a company's operational performance, practices and systems. The fundamental objective of the methodology is the implementation of measurement-based strategies, which focus on variation reduction and process improvement through Six Sigma improvement projects. This can be achieved through the use of two systems, known as the DMAIC (Define, Measure, Analyze, Improve, Control) and DMADV (Define, Measure, Analyze, Design, Verify) respectively.

Performance

This refers to the standard of measurements which is applied in the evaluation of the activities being considered for outsourcing. There exists a myriad of metrics which can be used to track areas such as system response and to measure compliance with set performance standards. Each activity being considered for outsourcing should be benchmarked against the capabilities of all potential service providers of the activity. This will enable the organization to identify its relative performance for each activity along a number of selected measures (McIvor, 2000; Willcocks, Fitzgerald, & Lacity, 1996). Although the benchmarking process may be time consuming and expensive, it can provide useful detailed information to validate the relative capabilities of the organization, and hence determine the need for outsourcing. With increasing emphasis by companies on establishing reliable, measurable and defined levels of performance from service providers, Service Level Agreements (SLAs) have gained wider acceptance as a primary governance tool for performance monitoring and service compliance management.

External Expertise

This refers to the market availability of the required skill sets, i.e. the ability of external service provider(s) to supply the required skill sets at a price considered affordable by the company. For example, the company may require outsourced services provided by highly specialized medical experts, such as in the field of epilepsy surgery (Malmgren, 2003), which is limited in availability and hence potentially expensive. This lack of market availability and affordability of the required skill sets can thus constrain the decision-making process for outsourcing (Mueller, 2001).

Business Perspective

The Business Perspective involves the consideration of financial issues related to the outsourcing decision. This can be a major determinant of profitability, making a significant contribution to the financial health of the company (Yoon and Naadimuthu, 1994). Thus, financial feasibility is a key consideration in the decision-making process, and there is consequently a need for financial costing to allow the company to benchmark its cost position relative to potential service providers (i.e. comparison of costs associated with keeping activities in-house against outsourcing). This facilitates the identification of economic disparity between the internal and external service providers of the activities (McIvor, 2000), which in turn provides the financial justification required for the outsourcing decision. Distinction is made between two types of financial costing (i.e. "soft" and "hard" financial analysis) which are outlined as follows:

Soft Financial Analysis refers to financial analysis via the use of costing methods that utilize qualitative (i.e. relative) metrics, which provide measurement for intangible aspects such as research and development work. A candidate costing method for this is the Information Economics Scorecard (IES). The IES (Parker, Benson, &

Trainor, 1998) is an investment justification tool which is based upon the concepts of value and two-domain analysis of business and technology factors (General Services Administration, 2003). It provides an evaluation of investment alternatives by identifying, evaluating, scoring and ranking potential positive and negative aspects for each investment.

Hard Financial Analysis refers to financial analysis via the use of costing methods that utilize quantitative (i.e. absolute) metrics, which provide measurement for tangible aspects such as the product delivery work. A candidate costing method for this is Activity-Based Costing (ABC). The ABC method, developed by Cooper and Kaplan (1988), is based on the principle that overheads do not just occur, but that they are caused by activities, such as data processing, that "drive" the costs (Atrill and McLaney, 2004). It utilizes an approach for assigning overheads to products and computing product costs, which claims to provide activity-oriented product cost information that is useful for decision-making purposes. ABC-based systems acknowledge that companies need to understand the factors that drive each major activity, their costs and how these activities relate to products. Such understanding is also crucial to the outsourcing decision-making process.

Analysis of "Cards" (HABIO Grids and Scales)

Figure 5 provides an example relating to the Risk Management issue (one of six issues within the Organizational Perspective listed in Table 2), within a financial services context, in which various potential risks have been plotted on the positioning grid. In this example, the company first begins by identifying a list of risks that it considers relevant to its organization, namely:

- Transition costs - cost of switching service providers (e.g. internal to external)

- Contractual amendments - flexibility in updating contract for business changes
- Cost escalation - risk of opportunistic price hikes by service provider
- Management costs - cost of monitoring and supervising the outsourcing operation
- Disputes and litigations - risk of legal complications
- Loss of organizational competencies - risk of tacit knowledge loss
- Lock-in - risk of captive contract by monopolist service provider
- Service debasement - risk of performance degradation in service provision

The company then categorizes identified risks into high and low impact on a scale of 1 to 5 (as illustrated in Table 3), based on assessment of how disruptive the respective risks are to its day-to-day operations (i.e. importance of potential loss).

This is typically conducted via use of a risk assessment questionnaire which guides practitioners through a systematic review of risk factors (e.g. *"how integrated is the outsourced IT function with business operations?"*), although it can alternatively be assessed by comparison with risks of previous projects of a similar nature. In this example, the company is particularly concerned about the impact from lock-in, which would severely increase its reliance on a specific service provider (and its propriety technologies, definition of standards, etc), and any potential complications from likely contractual amendments (i.e. flexibility of contract in accommodating business changes) given its dynamic and highly competitive operating environment.

Subsequently, the company categorizes identified risks into high and low probability on a scale of 1 to 5 (as illustrated in Table 4) based on assessment of the likelihood of occurrence of the respective undesirable outcomes. Similarly, this is typically conducted via use of a risk assessment questionnaire which guides practitioners through a systematic review of risk factors, although it may also be useful for decision-makers to review historical statistics to identify recurring trends. In this example, the company has identified contractual amendments (given its dynamic and highly competitive operating environment) and transition costs (given that this is a recurring issue

Figure 5. HABIO risk management Grid example

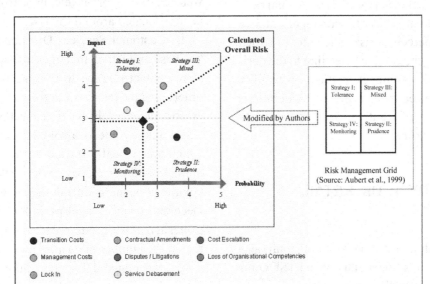

Table 3. High and low impact risks

High Impact	Low Impact
○ Lock In (4.0)	○ Management Costs (2.6)
○ Service Debasement (3.4)	● Disputes / Litigations (2.0)
● Cost Escalation (3.2)	● Loss of Organizational Competencies (2.8)
○ Contractual Amendments (4.0)	● Transition Costs (2.5)

Table 4. High and low probability risks

High Probability	Low Probability
○ Contractual Amendments (3.2)	○ Lock In (2.1)
● Transition Costs (3.5)	● Cost Escalation (2.5)
	○ Service Debasement (2.1)
	○ Management Costs (1.5)
	● Disputes / Litigations (2.1)
	○ Loss of Organizational Competencies (2.8)

of concern in previous outsourcing initiatives) to be high probability risks.

In such instances involving multiple plottings, the overall scoring for the Risk Management issue can be derived by two techniques: algorithmic determination of the average of all individual risks or plotting of a combined risk factor representative of the overall perceived risk. The latter of which was utilized by the company, leading to the derivation of a medium-impact, medium-probability overall risk (after factoring in considerations such as the use of incentive-based contracts) as illustrated in Figure 5.

CASE STUDY 1: UK RETAIL GROUP (UKRG)

UKRG is a leading retail company with total sales of over £3.5bn. It is a subsidiary of an FTSE company that focuses on three key activities, namely general merchandise retailing, information and customer relationship management, and luxury goods retailing. As part of the company strategy, customers are provided with a multi-channel approach to shopping: through its direct retail website, in store or via telephone to one of its call centers located around the UK.

Its Customer Services Division (CSD) is the business unit which manages all aspects of non-store contact relating to this, such as handling orders over the telephone and contacting customers to arrange a delivery time for their items. The CSD is responsible for all of UKRG's call centers, which are typically staffed entirely by internal human resources. However, due to the increasing volume of business during the months of July to December (typical "peak period"), additional call center agents were required to cope with the sharp rise in the number of customer calls.

As the demand for such human resources was only seasonal, UKRG decided to outsource this overflow to an external service provider, rather than hiring new personnel, who would be otherwise underutilized during the later "lull period". It was determined that the outsourcing arrangement would initially begin with a capacity of 25 "seats" (i.e. call center agent positions), which will then be incrementally ramped up to 100 "seats" by December.

This would involve a full outsourced service, in which the service provider handles all aspects of the call centre operation, including facilities, equipment, staff, overheads and the necessary infrastructure. This type of outsourcing was deemed to be in line with the company's overall strategic aim of achieving higher cost efficiency throughout the organization. The cost basis of UKRG's call center operations was approximately $59m, of which $37m was attributed to direct people cost. It is anticipated that outsourcing will deliver costs savings of $4-6m in the long run, primarily from ensuring efficient staffing and cost reductions from provision of amenities and staff benefits (Sharp, Atkins, Ho, Kothari, & Paul, 2005).

Figure 6 illustrates the executive summary view of UKRG's outsourcing decision evaluated using the HABIO Framework, in which the overall weighted scores for only 3 vendors (anonymously labeled "A", "B", and "C") that qualified for the final selection phase are shown for brevity. In this instance, the weights have been assigned as 3/10 (30%), 3/10 (30%), and 4/10 (40%) respectively, indicating a higher emphasis on the Business Perspective which relates to financial costing. This is reflected in the tiered baseline of the diagram, which indicates a step-up in the Business Perspective sector in accordance with its higher weighting. In this particular case, although service provider (i.e., vendor) C was marginally prevailing in terms of weighted scores (69% compared to B's 68%), UKRG opted instead to contract with service provider B due to concerns regarding the former's corporate stability, having recently undergone ownership changes. This indicates that a single factor may have an overriding effect in the overall outsourcing decision, particularly in instances where the final scores are similar, which underscores the importance of flexibility (to accommodate such intricacies) in outsourcing decision-making frameworks.

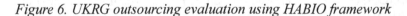

Figure 6. UKRG outsourcing evaluation using HABIO framework

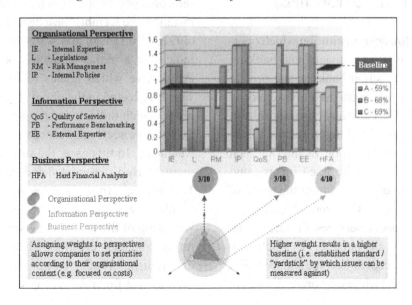

The UKRG case study presents an interesting paradox: although there was a higher emphasis on financial costs in the outsourcing decision, its evaluation suggests a contradiction, as the financial basis of the decision appears to be below baseline (i.e., internal operating costs) as illustrated in Figure 6. This is because the arrangement involves a fully outsourced service (including personnel, software and amenities), which results in a high start-up cost that UKRG anticipates to make cost savings on in the longer term. In general, the evaluation of UKRG's outsourcing decision via the HABIO Framework yielded similar results and the same ordering as UKRG's in-house system of rating various criteria on a scale of 1-3 (Vendor A, B, C : HABIO's weighted scores of 59% / 68% / 69% as compared to UKRG's ratings of 17 / 21 / 23), which illustrates its mappability to UKRG's decision system. In this instance, the application of the HABIO Framework is particularly advantageous to UKRG as it allows for adaptability at any stage of the selection process, e.g., the Risk Management issue can be decomposed into sub-issues to accommodate consideration for corporate stability.

CASE STUDY 2: INTERNATIONAL FINANCIAL INSTITUTION (IFC)

IFC is a leading financial institution which operates in the areas of asset management, banking and securities, transaction banking and private wealth management, with assets exceeding $1000bn in total. The company has a significant private and business banking franchise globally, and a prominent position in international foreign exchange along with fixed income and equities trading. In order to address the needs of its wide customer base, IFC offers a broad range of banking and financial services. Private clients are provided with an all-round service (including asset management, account-keeping and securities investment advisory) while corporate clients are provided with the full assortment of services of an international corporate and investment bank. This includes payments processing, advisory relating to Mergers and Acquisitions (M&As) and support with Initial Public Offerings (IPOs).

In order to provide opportunities for its staff to move up the value chain (i.e. to positions of more strategic value) and achieve higher cost-efficiency, IFC decided to evaluate the use of outsourcing. In particular, the company was keen to explore the potential of Remote Infrastructure Management (RIM), which is essentially an extension of Infrastructure Management Services (IMS). IMS refers to the day-to-day management of the IT needs of an organization, such as managing network operations, desk and server management (e.g. configuration, updates and maintenance), security requirements and a 24x7 technical help-desk. RIM differs from IMS in the sense that the management of infrastructure is conducted remotely, typically in a lower cost country such as India, thereby allowing for labor cost arbitrage (Ho, Atkins, Prince, & Sharp, 2006).

Figure 7 illustrates the executive summary view of IFC's outsourcing decision evaluated using the HABIO Framework, in which the overall weighted scores for only 2 vendors (anonymously labeled "X" and "Y") that qualified for the final selection phase are shown for brevity. In this instance, the weights have been assigned as 3/10 (30%), 3/10 (30%), and 4/10 (40%) respectively indicating a higher emphasis on the Business Perspective which relates to financial costing. This is reflected in the tiered baseline of the diagram, which indicates a step-up in the Business Perspective sector in accordance with its higher weighting. In this case, the weighted scores are more clearly differentiated, indicating that Vendor Y is the preferred choice at 87% compared to Vendor X at 74%. This is because of the higher weighting of the Business Perspective (incorporating financial costing) which unequivocally distinguishes Vendor Y due to its cost basis. This typifies that financial cost is still a major factor in outsourcing decision-making, although recent literature indicates that companies are progressively more aware and hence more inclined to consider strategic implications such as knowledge retention (Ho et al., 2006).

In general, the evaluation of IFC's outsourcing decision via the HABIO Framework yielded similar results and the same ordering as IFC's in-house system of rating various criteria on a scale of 0-4 (Vendor X, Y : HABIO's weighted scores of 74% / 87% as compared to IFC's ratings of 27 / 32), which illustrates its mappability to IFC's decision system. In this instance, the key benefit of the HABIO Framework is its concise executive summary format that facilitates quick visual review and intuitive analysis, which is advantageous to IFC's directorial level decision-makers who are often time-constrained by hectic schedules. In addition, electronic interpretation of the "cards" in the HABIO Framework makes it amenable for comparing initial framework assessments against post-implementation performance evaluations.

WEB-BASED DATA COLLATION AND ANALYSIS INTERFACE

Figure 8 illustrates conceptual views of a web-based interface that is currently being developed for integration with the HABIO Framework, which will automate data import (e.g. performance metrics and QoS measurements) from varying service management software (e.g. BMC Remedy), in turn minimizing manual collation efforts. The web-based nature of the system will facilitate accessibility across locations (i.e. geographically diverse decision-makers) and promote data consistency by serving as a central point of interaction.

The system will involve a "wizard" type of interface, which allows users to easily add and remove issues to be considered under each perspective as appropriate to their specific organizational context. This accentuates the flexibility provided by the framework, thereby facilitating adaptiveness in live environments where technologies, priorities, finances and demands are ever-changing. Besides providing for dynamic customizations of the framework "on the fly", the web-based system is intended to include visualization algorithms,

Figure 7. IFC outsourcing evaluation using HABIO framework

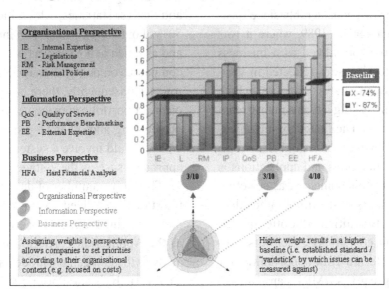

Figure 8. Web-based data collation and analysis system (Conceptual Views)

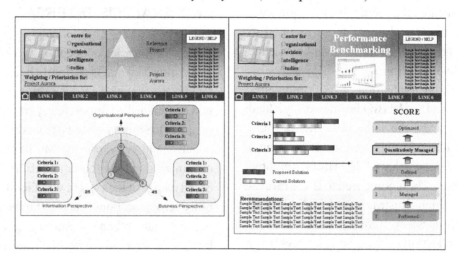

which will assist in the weighting process. This will be potentially extended by the incorporation of software agents to provide intelligent analysis and expert recommendations in outsourcing decision-making processes.

CONCLUSION

Outsourcing has grown considerably since Eastman-Kodak's mega-deal in 1989, where it was perceived to be first formalized as a business strategy. This meteoric rise is reflected in various media reports and analyst statistics, which also highlight its increasing use as a mainstream management practice. Facilitated by advances in technology and enablers of virtual teamwork, global sourcing of functions and applications is now a commonplace phenomenon, as selection priorities shift towards best-skilled rather than physical proximity. In addition to the often quoted benefit of significant cost savings, such outsourcing practices also offer altruistic opportunities for knowledge sharing (e.g. CAT/MRI scan analysis)

and provision of round-the-clock support (e.g. Enterprise Software Systems such as SAP/R3), which has further increased the appeal of outsourcing, and consequently its uptake. However, despite such realizable benefits, outsourcing is not without its risks, particularly in instances where it has not been considered as a strategic decision. This increasing challenge to achieve successful outsourcing is also reflected in media reports and analyst statistics, which indicate that up to 50% of outsourcing deals run into complications and as much as $7.3bn was wasted by European companies on poorly managed outsourcing contracts. Consequently, there is an increased focus on the IT portfolio management process by which outsourcing and other IT projects are assessed, which should involve a systematic and objective approach, such as the 7-stage planning model.

There are a number of decision support tools traditionally utilized for IT Portfolio Management, ranging from grid-based approaches such as the Application Portfolio Matrix and SWOT analysis to management models such as the Value Chain Analysis and Porter's 5 Forces. However, with its increasingly diverse nature and expanding domains of application, the assessment of outsourcing as an option for the IT Portfolio requires refined tools and techniques, which has been addressed in part by various frameworks developed by sourcing theorists and practitioners such as Willcocks (1997).

Analysis of such frameworks identified from the literature indicates a potential misalignment between theory and practice, as majority of the frameworks do not include quantitative measures, performance benchmarking and clear methods of financial costing, which is contradictory given that service improvements and cost savings are often quoted as the top drivers of outsourcing. Consequently, the HABIO Framework was developed following professional insights from industrial collaborators and theoretical accounts from the literature. The framework proposes a tri-perspective approach, which advocates the logical grouping of decision factors (i.e. issues)

under the Business Perspective, Information Perspective and Organizational Perspective by adopting a "card/deck" analogy. This encapsulates the holistic concept which provides for the customizability and adaptability required to address heterogeneous outsourcing decisions in various context and industries. Each issue within the framework is assessed using a grid or scale-based method, which is weight-adjusted according to the company's defined priorities, and subsequently summated to provide an overall indicator value that represents its propensity for successful outsourcing.

This chapter provided an overview of the framework's application to two industrial case studies, involving the application of Business Process Outsourcing (BPO) to call centre operations of a retail group and Information Technology Outsourcing (ITO) to infrastructure management of a financial institution. Evaluation of these outsourcing decisions via the HABIO Framework

Figure 9. Decision support tool use in the IT portfolio planning process

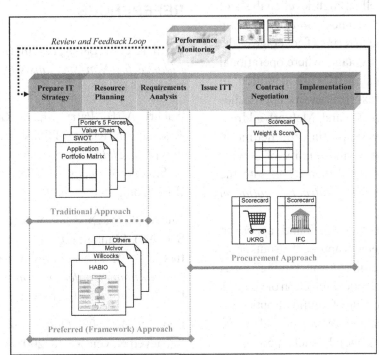

produced similar results to assessment using the companies' distinct sets of in-house decision criteria, indicating the framework's versatility and mappability to varying context and industry. In particular, decision-makers have noted the framework's intuitiveness in application, and its executive summary format which allows them to quickly identify areas of concern.

The current development of a web-based interface for automated data collation and issue analysis makes the HABIO Framework amendable for comparing initial assessments against post-implementation results, thereby widening its coverage of the IT Portfolio Planning Process (as illustrated in Figure 9) to include *Performance Monitoring*. This can be extended in future by the use of software agents to provide intelligent analysis and expert recommendations in the outsourcing decision process.

There appears to be a lack of decision support tools which span the entire advocated IT Portfolio Planning Process, indicating a potential disparity between theory and practice. Traditional tools such as the Application Portfolio Matrix and SWOT analysis (as indicated from the literature) provide excellent high level analysis of the *Prepare IT Strategy* and *Resource Planning* stages, but are limited in terms of coverage of the *Requirements Analysis* stage, where operational level requirements and metrics are identified. In the outsourcing context, framework approaches (e.g. HABIO, Willcocks and McIvor) address this shortcoming by supporting the definition of service performance and quality of service criteria, but do not extend themselves into the later stages of *Issue ITT*, *Contract Negotiation* and *Implementation*.

Organizations, on the other hand, appear to be adopting a procurement approach to outsourcing, involving a more short-term "buying" focus which prioritizes the tactical selection of vendors over the strategic selection of candidate outsourcing functions/applications (as advocated in the *Prepare IT Strategy* stage). In such approaches,

the function/application to be outsourced is tenuously selected prior to the decision process, which instead focuses on the evaluation and subsequent identification of an ideal service provider by means of a weight and score or scorecard method. This is reflected in both case studies (i.e. UKRG and IFC), where the companies have initiated the outsourcing decision from the *Issue Invitation To Tender (ITT)* stage, thereby bypassing the earlier stages of the advocated IT Portfolio Planning model, which seek to analyze the high level needs of the organization and align its IT portfolio (including the use of outsourcing) with its overall business objectives.

As such, there is a need for an extended framework to provide guidance throughout the IT Portfolio Planning Process to help align advocated portfolio management principles with actual business practices. This could be potentially established by expanding an existing framework or by an amalgamation of existing decision support tools and techniques, and will benefit greatly from the incorporation of ITIL best practices.

REFERENCES

Atrill, P., & McLaney, E. (2004). *Accounting and Finance for Non-Specialists* (4th ed.). England: Prentice Hall.

Aubert, A. B., Patry, M., & Rivard, S. (1998). Assessing the Risk of IT Outsourcing. In *Proceedings of the 31st Hawaii International Conference on Systems Sciences* (pp. 685-692). Washington: IEEE Computer Society.

Aubert, A. B., Dussault, S., Patry, M., & Rivard, S. (1999). Managing the risk of IT Outsourcing. In *CD-ROM Proceedings of the 32nd Hawaii International Conference on System Sciences*. Los Alamitos: IEEE Computer Society.

Bennett, M. (2002). *Outsourcing overlooks staff.* Retrieved November 18, 2005, from http://www.

computing.co.uk/itweek/news/2084685/outsourcing-overlooks-staff

Cohen, L., & Young, A. (2005). *Multisourcing: Moving Beyond Outsourcing to Achieve Growth And Agility*. Boston: Harvard Business School Press.

Cooper, R., & Kaplan, R. S. (1988). Measure costs right: make the right decisions. *Harvard Business Review, 66*(5), 96- 103.

Cox, A. W. (1996). Relational competence and strategic procurement management: towards an entrepreneurial and contractual theory of the firm. *European Journal of Purchasing and Supply Chain Management, 2*(1), 57-70.

ComputerWeekly (2006, May 9). Computer-Weekly CIO Index, *ComputerWeekly*, 14-15.

Cullen, D. (2003). *Inland Revenue sacks EDS*. Retrieved January 17, 2004, from http://www.theregister.co.uk/content/archive/34454.html

Cullen, S., & Willcocks, L. P. (2004). *Intelligent IT Outsourcing: Eight Building Blocks to Success*. Great Britain: Butterworth-Heinemann.

Dahl, R. A. (1958). A Critique of the Ruling Elite Model. *American Political Science Review, 52*(2), 463-469.

De Looff, L. A. (1995). Information Systems Outsourcing decision-making: A framework, organisational theories and case studies. *Journal of Information Technology, 10*, 281-297.

Deloitte (2005). *Calling a Change in the Outsourcing Market: The Realities for the World's Largest Organizations*. Retrieved January 08, 2006, from http://www.deloitte.com/dtt/cda/doc/content/us_outsourcing_callingachange.pdf

Dibbern, J., Goles, T., Hirschheim, R. A., & Jayatilaka, B. (2004). Information Systems Outsourcing: A Survey and Analysis of the Literature. *The DATA BASE for Advances in Information Systems, 35*(4), 6-102.

Earl, M. J. (1989). *Management Strategies for Information Technology*. New Jersey: Prentice-Hall.

Earl, M. J. (1996). The Risks of Outsourcing IT. *Sloan Management Review, 37*(3), 26-32.

Eyal, J. (2004). *Armies Inc.* Retrieved June 08, 2004, from http://straitstimes.asia1.com.sg/world/story/0,4386,255062,00.html

Farbey B., Land F., & Targett, D. (1993). *How to Assess your IT Investment: A Study of Methods and Practice*. Oxford: Butterworth-Heineman.

Fisher, R. (1930). *The Genetical Theory of Natural Selection*. Oxford: Clarendon Press.

Frenzel, C. W., & Frenzel, J. C. (2004). *Management of Information Technology* (4th ed.). Cambridge: Course Technology.

Fowler, A., & Jeffs, B. (1998). Examining Information Systems Outsourcing: A Case Study from the United Kingdom. *Journal of Information Technology, 13*, 111-126.

General Services Administration (2003). *Performance-Based Management: Eight Steps to Develop and Use Information Technology Performance Measures Effectively*. Retrieved May 06, 2005, from http://www.gsa.gov/gsa/cm_attachments/GSA_DOCUMENT/eight_steps_R2GX2-u_0Z5RDZ-i34K-pR.doc

Goodstein, J., Boeker, W., & Stephan, J. (1996). Professional Interests and Strategic Flexibility: A Political Perspective on Organizational Contracting. *Strategic Management Journal, 17*(7), 577-586.

Hadfield, W. (2006). *Sainsbury's transfers IT back in-house*. Retrieved May 09, 2006, from http://www.computerweekly.com/Articles/2006/05/09/215869/Sainsbury%e2%80%99s+transfers+IT+back+in-house.htm

Healy, T.J., & Linder, J.C. (2004). *Outsourcing in Government: The Path to Transformation*.

Retrieved June 23, 2004, from http://www. accenture.com/xdoc/en/ideas/institute/pdf/outsourcing_in_gov.pdf

Ho, L., Atkins, A., & Eardley A. (2005). Emergent Trends of Outsourcing and Strategic Framework Techniques. In G. Kotsis, D. Taniar, S. Bressan, I.K. Ibrahim, & S, Mokhtar. (Eds.), *Proceedings of the 7th International Conference on Information Integration and Web-based Application & Services* (pp. 433-444). Austrian Computer Society.

Ho, L., & Atkins, A. (2006). IT Outsourcing: Impacts and Challenges. In B. Walters and Z. Tang (Eds.). *IT-Enabled Strategic Management - Increasing Returns for the Organization* (pp. 244-274.). United States of America: Idea Group Inc.

Ho, L., Atkins, A., Prince, I., & Sharp, B. (2006). Alignment of a Strategic Outsourcing Framework to Practitioner Case Studies. In Z. Irani, O. D. Sarikas, J. Llopis, R. Gonzalez, & J. Gasco (Eds.), *CD-ROM Proceedings of the European and Mediterranean Conference on Information Systems*. EMCIS Press.

Kishore, E., Rao, H. R., Nam, R., Rajagopalan, S., & Chaudhury, A. (2003). A Relationship Perspective on IT Outsourcing. *Communications of the ACM, 46*(12) 87-92.

Lacity, M. C., & Willcocks, L. P. (1995). Interpreting Information Technology Sourcing Decisions from a Transaction Cost Perspective: Findings and Critique. *Accounting, Management and Information Technologies, 5*(3/4), 203-244.

Learned, E.P., Christensen, C.R., Andrews, K.R., & Guth, W.D. (1965). *Business Policy: Text and Cases*. Homewood: Irwin.

Luftman, J.N., Lewis, P. R., & Oldach, S. H. (1993). Transforming the enterprise: The alignment of business and information technology strategies. *IBM Systems Journal, 32*(1), 198-221.

Malmgren, K. (2003). *Epilepsy Care Across Europe and Key Concerns*. Retrieved June 22, 2004, from http://www.bbriefings.com/pdf/14/lth031_p_MALMGREN.PDF

March, J. G. (1962). The Business Firm as a Political Coalition. *Journal of Politics, 24*, 662-678.

Massy, W.F. (1999). *The ABCs of Course-Level Costing*. Retrieved May 08, 2005, from http://www.nwmissouri.edu/sloan/CostBook/CourseLevelCosting.html

McFarlan, F.W. (1981). Portfolio Approach to Information Systems. *Harvard Business Review, 59*(5), 142-150.

McFarlan F.W., & McKenney J.L (1983) *Corporate Information Systems Management: The issues facing senior executives*. Illinois: Richard D. Irwin Inc.

McIvor, R. (2000). A practical framework for understanding the Outsourcing process. *Supply Chain Management: An International Journal, 5*(1), 22-36.

McLellan, K. L., Marcolin, B. L., & Beamish, P. W. (1995). Financial and Strategic Motivations Behind IS Outsourcing. *Journal of Information Technology, 10*(4), 299-321.

Mills, C. (2004). *Outsourcing - The latest research from the public and private sectors*. Retrieved January 07, 2005, from http://www.conferencepage.com/outsourcing4/downloads/CliffMills.pdf

Muller, N. J. (1999). Managing Service Level Agreements. *International Journal of Network Management, 9*(3), 155-166.

Nam, K., Rajagopalan, S., Rao, H. R., & Chaudhury, A. (1996). A Two-Level Investigation of Information Systems Outsourcing. *Communications of the ACM, 39*(7), 36-44.

Namasivayam, S. (2004). Profiting from Business Process Outsourcing. *IT Professional, 6*(1), 12-18.

Oates, J. (2004). *Inverclyde IT staff fight outsource threat*. Retrieved June 03, 3004, from http://www.theregister.co.uk/2004/06/15/inverclyde_strike/

Overby, S. (2006). *Outsourcing: Big Deals, Big Savings, Big Problems*. Retrieved February 08, 2006, from http://www.cio.com/archive/020106/outsourcing.html

Palvia, P. C. (1995). A Dialectic View of Information Systems Outsourcing: Pros and Cons. *Information & Management, 29*, 265-275.

Parker, M. M., Benson, R. J., & Trainor, H. E. (1988). *Information Economics: Linking business performance to Information Technology*. New Jersey: Prentice Hall.

Pearlson, K. E. (2001). *Managing and using Information Systems: A Strategic Approach*. New York: John Wiley & Sons Inc.

Pearlson, K. E., & Saunders, C. S. (2004). *Managing and using Information Systems: A Strategic Approach* (2nd ed.). United States of America: John Wiley & Sons.

Perry, L. T., Stott, R. C., & Smallwood, W. W. (1993). *Real Time Strategy: Improvising Team Based Planning for a Fast-Changing World*. New York: John Wiley & Sons Inc.

Porter, M.F. (1979). How Competitive Forces Shape Strategy. *Harvard Business Review, 57*(2), 137-145.

Porter, M.F. (1980). *Competitive Strategy*. New York: The Free Press.

Porter, M.F. (1985). *Competitive Advantage*. New York: The Free Press.

Prahalad, C. K., & Hamel, G. (1990). The Core Competence of the Corporation. *Harvard Business Review, 68*(3), 79-91.

Quinn, J. B., & Hilmer, F. G. (1994). Strategic Outsourcing. *Sloan Management Review, 35*(4), 43-55.

Ravi, R., Bingham, B. J., Rowan, L., Danilenko, A., & McStravick, P. (2005). *Worldwide and U.S. Business Process Outsourcing (BPO). 2005-2009 Forecast: Market Opportunities by Horizontal Business Functions*. 33815, IDC.

Richardson, T. (2004). *Bradford IT staff vote to strike*. Retrieved June 02, 2004, from http://www.theregister.co.uk/2004/01/21/bradford_it_staff_vote/

Robson, W. (1997). *Strategic Management & Information Systems* (2nd ed.). London: Pitman Publishing.

Sharp B., Atkins A., Ho L., Kothari H., & Paul D. (2005). Intelligent Agent Concepts for Outsourcing Decision-Making in Customer Service Operations. In P. Iasias, & M. B. Nunes (Eds.), *Proceedings of the IADIS International Conference WWW/Internet* (Vol I., pp. 215-221). IADIS Press.

Sorteberg, I., & Kure, O. (2005). The use of service level agreements in tactical military coalition force networks. *IEEE Communications Magazine, 43*(11), 107-114.

Sweetin v Coral Racing (2005). *Industrial Relations Law Reports (UK) Vol. 252*.

Traynor, I. (2003). *The Privatisation of War*. Retrieved June 08, 2004, from http://www.guardian.co.uk/international/story/0,3604,1103566,00.html

Verhoef, C. (2005). Quantitative aspects of outsourcing deals. *Science of Computer Programming, 56*(3), 275 - 313.

Ward, J., & Peppard, J. (2002). *Strategic Planning for Information Systems* (3rd ed.), New York: John Wiley & Sons Inc.

Weinstein, L. (2004). Inside Risks: Outsourced and out of control. *Communications of the ACM, 47*(2), 120.

Willcocks, L. P., Fitzgerald, G., & Lacity, M. C. (1996). To Outsource IT Or Not? Recent Research on Economics and Evaluation Practice. *European Journal of Information Systems, 5*(3), 143-160.

Willcocks, L. P., Feeny, D., & Islei, G. (1997). *Managing IT as a Strategic Resource*. Berkshire: McGraw Hill Book Company.

Yang, C., & Huang, J. (2000). A decision model for IS Outsourcing, *International Journal of Information Management, 20*, 225-239.

Yeoman, B. (2003). *Soldiers of Good Fortune*. Retrieved June 08, 2004, from http://www.motherjones.com/news/feature/2003/05/ma_365_01.html

Yoon, K. P., & Naadimuthu, G. (1994). A make-or-buy decision analysis involving imprecise data. *International Journal of Operations and Production Management, 14*(2), 62-69.

Chapter VI
A Scenarios–Based Methodology for IT Portfolio Planning

Stanley Loh
Catholic University of Pelotas and Lutheran University of Brazil, Brazil

Ramiro Saldaña
Catholic University of Pelotas, Brazil

Leo Faller Becker
Catholic University of Pelotas, Brazil

ABSTRACT

One of the main topics in IT Portfolio Management, according to IT Governance models, is to plan and control information systems that are aligned with the company mission and objectives. The goal of the IT Portfolio Planning is to define which information systems are necessary and with which priority. In general, planning methodologies trace directions from a present point to a future and desired target. However, in many cases, companies can not control situations; events may occur that can not be avoided. A scenarios-based planning methodology can help managers to identify future events, their probability and consequences. A scenario represents a future situation that can not be controlled nor can be avoided. However, the study of future scenarios can help managers to plan reactions, so that company can create mechanisms for avoiding problems or for minimizing bad consequences. The goal of this chapter is to present an adaptation of the scenario-based methodology for IT and Information Systems Planning. The chapter will describe in details each step of the proposed methodology and discuss a study case. Steps include the identification of different scenarios and their corresponding antecedent events, the determination of probabilities and consequences of the events, how to calculate risks and how to plan Information Systems and IT resources to manage each scenario.

INTRODUCTION

One of the main topics in IT Portfolio Management, according to IT Governance models, is to plan and control information systems that are aligned with the company mission and objectives. The goal of the IT Portfolio Planning is to define which information systems are necessary and with which priority. In general, planning methodologies trace directions from a present point to a future and desired target. However, in many cases, we are not able to control situations; events may occur that company can not avoid. In this last situation, companies can preview these events and can prepare themselves to manage future and adverse situations.

A scenarios-based planning methodology can help managers to identify future events, their probability and consequences. A scenario represents a future situation that can not be controlled, that is, the company cannot avoid its occurrence. Although a scenario cannot be avoided, they allow managers to trace future directions, so that company can create mechanisms for avoiding problems or for minimizing bad consequences. A potential adverse situation can become an opportunity for a company if this company is prepared for that. For example, the lack of supplies in a specific market is a bad situation in general; but if the company can find alternative supplies, it can overcome its competitors and achieve a better position. The challenge for the company is to preview the situation before competitors and then to prepare itself for the future. Scenarios may be related to a future market (external view) or to an internal status in the company (internal view).

The goal of this chapter is to present an adaptation of the scenario-based methodology for IT and Information Systems Planning. Scenario-based methodologies are usually employed for organization planning. For IT planning, this methodology may be adapted to generate results in terms of Information Systems and IT resources necessaries in the future. The chapter will show how this can

be accomplished. It will also describe in details each step of the proposed methodology and discuss a study case. Steps include how to identify different scenarios and their corresponding events, how to determine probabilities and consequences of the events, how to calculate risks and how to plan Information Systems and IT resources to manage each scenario.

BACKGROUND

In general, planning methodologies such as Balanced Scorecard (Kaplan & Norton, 1992; Kaplan & Norton, 1997) trace directions from a present point to a future and desired target. In this case, companies intend to control variables that lead to the goals. If the company accomplishes the variables, goals will be achieved and the desired future will be made real. This kind of planning methodology works with known and controllable variables.

However, in many cases, we are not able to control situations; events may occur that company can not avoid. In this case, companies can preview these events and can prepare themselves to manage future and adverse situations. Although companies can not control or avoid the events, they can plan reactions (for example, contingency plans) so that bad consequences could be minimized. In the same way, companies can proactively prepare their ways and trace directions to react to undesired events. The challenge is to know which events may occur, when they may occur and which their consequences are. This is the goal of a scenarios-based planning methodology. It helps planners to determine which scenarios may affect the company, when and under which degree.

Scenarios do not conflict with other methodologies; they are complementary. Traditional methodologies are useful to determine directions for desired situations and scenarios-based methodologies can help to trace directions for undesired situations. When both kinds are used jointly the results tend to be more reliable and precise, leading to a broader image of the company future.

Scenarios are widely used in planning tasks, especially for analyzing market directions and economic situations (Fahey & Randall, 1998; Kahn & Wierner, 1968; Schwartz, 1991; Van Der Heijden, 2005; Wilkinson, 1995). However, this methodology is not usually used for IT Governance. Organizations prefer to use methodologies like Balanced Scorecard.

For IT Governance, scenarios are useful to help IT managers in determining priorities for Information Systems development. With the advance of IT research and wide use of IT resources, there are many possibilities for IT applications in companies. Deciding which systems will be developed first is a difficult task. Furthermore, IT investments are more controlled nowadays and are being decided according to their return (tangible of intangible). A scenarios-based methodology can help managers to evaluate which events are more probable and generate greater risks, so that managers can plan the development of information systems.

When using scenarios for planning, a special attention must be given to the risk of each scenario. The risk depends on the probability of the occurrence of the scenario and on the size of the impact if the scenario occurs.

Hubbard (2007, p.46) states some concepts for avoiding misunderstandings. Risk is "a state of uncertainty where some of the possibilities involve a loss, catastrophe, or other undesirable outcome". Risk may be measure by quantified probabilities and quantified losses. In the proposed methodology, the risk of a scenario is calculated by the probability of the scenario versus the impact of its occurrence.

MAIN THRUST OF THE CHAPTER

This section presents the steps of the scenarios-based methodology for IT portfolio planning.

1. Identification of Scenarios

Scenarios are future situations that affect companies and that can not be avoided. In general, they are external conditions. A scenario is a set of events. For example, the lack of energy for one day is an event, but a sequence of these events composes a scenario.

The first step in the methodology is to preview future scenarios that will influence the company performance (external or internal).

In this initial step, it is not necessary to determine if a scenario is good or bad for the company. For example, if a competitor opens a filial next to the company, this event may be good or bad depending on how the company and the market react to this event. In some cases, this event may benefit the company, bringing more customers to the region. The next steps in the methodology will help in determining how a scenario affect the company and with which degree.

There may be many scenarios. The ideal situation is to identify and analyze all of them. However, costs make that only those that significantly affect the company be considered.

2. Determination of Each Scenario Probability

For this step, it is necessary to identify antecedent events, that is, those that indicate that the scenario may occur in a brief future or that the scenario is already occurring. Knowing these events allows monitoring them to quickly react to the events.

The calculus of the scenario probability depends on each event probability and how much the event causes the scenario (conditional probabilities). Individual and jointly probabilities must be estimated.

Probability of each event occurring has to be determined. After, we have to determine the probability of the event influencing the scenario, that is, the probability of the scenario occurring if the event occurs (conditional probability). The multiplication of these two probabilities generates a combined probability for each event.

Also, it is necessary to determine the probability of two or more events jointly (probability of the scenario conditioned by more than one event). This is necessary because one event alone may not lead to the scenario, but two events jointly may increase the probability of a scenario occurring or even may make real the scenario.

The final probability of the scenario is the greatest probability for all combinations, because if there is a probability of 100% of occurring the scenario, it is not necessary to consider other probabilities.

This analysis of probabilities must be made for all scenarios and over all events of each scenario. It is important to correctly identify all events. If an important event is left out, the final probability may be wrong. The calculus must be made only for future events and not for events that ever occurred.

Following, we explain the step through an example.

Example

Considering that for a given scenario X, there are the following antecedent events: event A, event B and event C.

The result of determining probabilities is:

*   Probability of event A occurring = P(A) = 70% (or 0.7)
*   Probability of event B occurring = P(B) = 80% (or 0.8)
*   Probability of event C occurring = P(C) = 60% (or 0.6)

When two events are conflicting, that is, if one occurs, the other does not occur (i.e., increase of customers X decrease), their probabilities must be complementary (the sum must be 100%).

Now, we have to verify the conditional probability of the scenario in relation to the events. Considering that the event A is independent of

the others events, that is, there is no relation between A and other event. Let us consider that the probability of the scenario X occurring when the event A occurs is 100% (that is, if the event A occurs, we have certainty that the scenario will occur).

$$P(X \mid A) = 1.0$$

But, as the probability of the event A occurring is 70%, we have

$$P(A) \times P(X \mid A) = 0.7 \times 1.0 = 0.7$$

That is, the combined probability of the scenario considering only the event A is 70%.

Now, we have to determine probabilities related to events B and C.

Considering that these two events are influenced one by each other, we have to calculate the probability of scenario X occurring when one of the occurs and the other does not and also to calculate when both occur. Let us assume that the probability of the two events occurring jointly is 50%. So:

$$P(B \text{ and } C) = 50\%$$

For the conditional probability of the events, let us estipulate some values:

$$P(X \mid B \text{ and } C) = 100\%$$
$$P(X \mid B) = 80\% \text{ (only event B occurs)}$$
$$P(X \mid C) = 70\% \text{ (only event C occurs)}$$

$P(X \mid \text{not B and not C})$ = probability related to other events;
in this case $= P(X \mid A)$

So, we have to multiply these conditional probabilities versus the probabilities of the events (positive or negatives):

P(X | B and C) . P(B and C) = 1 x 0.5 = 0.5
P(X | B) . P(B) = 0.8 x 0.8 = 0.64
P(X | C) . P(C) = 0.7 x 0.6 = 0.42

Conditions	Combined Probabilities
Event A	70%
Event B and Event C	50%
Event B and not Event C	64%
Event C and Not Event B	42%

Resuming, the final probability of the scenario is 70%. We consider the greatest value among the combined probabilities because if one alternative is more probable than others than this alternative may cause the scenario.

3. Determination of the Impact of Each Scenario

The calculus of the impact of a scenario is made by analyzing consequent events, that is, those that occur as consequence of the scenario concretization. Depending on how many consequences the scenario has and on how much these consequent events affect the company, it is possible to determine the impact of the scenario.

The impact of a scenario is calculated by integrating the probability and the impact of the consequent events. If the scenario generates more probable events and with greater impacts, its impact is greater.

First, we have to identify all events that are consequence of the occurrence of the scenario. After that, we have to estimate the probability and the impact of each event. The impact of an event is not related to a good or bad consequence, but it is related to how much the company have to change itself to react to the event. For example, the increase in the number of customers may be good (if the company is prepared to attend the demand) or bad (if the company does not have enough resources to satisfy customers). The impact depends on how the company is prepared to react to the event; the greater the changes, the greater the impact. We suggest using a range from 1 to 10 to determine the size of the impact.

After that, we multiply the probability of the event by its impact to obtain the risk of each event.

Finally, the impact of a scenario is the total sum of the impacts of its consequent events. We utilize the sum because the more events may occur and the greater their impacts, the greater the impact of the scenario. The impact of a scenario is given by a numeric value representing how bad the scenario occurrence may be to the company (the greater the value, more bad consequences to the company may happen).

4. Determination of the Risk of Each Scenario

As stated early, the risk of a scenario is a combination of its probability with its impact. In the proposed methodology, we calculate the scenario risk by multiplying the probability of the scenario by its impact, as determined in steps 2 and 3.

The final risk of a scenario is a numeric value (number of points) representing the chance of something happening that will have an impact upon the organization.

5. Definition of the IT Portfolio

This step concerns the selection of Information Systems and IT infra-structure to support the future scenarios. The goal is to determine which Information Systems are more necessary to minimize problems relative to the occurrence of the scenarios.

Although many systems are possible, analysts have to focus on priorities. Priorities may be determined by the scenarios with greatest risk (most probable and with greater impact).

Another way to select priority systems is to concentrate efforts on supporting more than one scenario. In this case, we can concentrate on the information systems that support a great number of scenarios. Other alternative is to determine information systems that can minimize a great number of consequent events.

Special attention has to be given to information systems that monitor antecedent events, so that organization can be aware of a scenario that is becoming concrete or starting to happen.

The selection of which information systems are necessary is intuitive and experience-dependent. There is no methods for helping analysts to determine the correct systems. We propose the selection of systems by the analysis of information needs and of the kind of process necessary. We have a classification with 31 kinds of information systems, each one having special characteristics and dedicated to hold some kinds of information (structured, text, geographical, multimedia, etc.). Each kind of information system has a different goal. For example, there is a kind to deal with transactional data, other to deal with workflow, other for Data Warehouse, other for pervasive and ubiquitous data, other for mining data, other for recommendations and so on. Depending on the kind of information need and on the goal proposed by the scenarios, we can determine which kinds of information systems are more adequate to support the results of the methodology.

Finally, after defining the necessary information systems, we can determine which technologies (infra-structure) are necessary to support the information systems. Also this kind of task is still much dependent on analysts knowledge, experience and intuition and there is no systematic way to perform this task.

THE CASE STUDY

This section presents a case study conducted to analyze the application of the methodology in a real case. The section discusses each step of the methodology in details.

The methodology was applied in a real Meat Plant Company.

This company is located in Rio Grande do Sul, a southern state of Brazil. This state has borders with other states but also has border with two countries: Argentina and Uruguay.

1. Identification of Scenarios

Using Delphi method, experts from the company suggested the following scenarios:

- Scenario A: Lack of cattle due to incidents of Aftosa fever
- Scenario B: Entry of a competing company in the local market
- Scenario C: Devalue of dollar

Due to limits of space in this chapter, we decide to show only de development of one scenario. The scenario chosen to be described in this chapter was scenario A, related to the lack of cattle due to Aftosa Fever. However, a complete and real IT Portfolio Management must address all identified scenarios.

2. Determination of the Scenario Probability

Using Delphi method, the following antecedent events and their respective probabilities were identified by experts from the company:

- **Event A:** Incidents of Aftosa fever in neighbor countries
  - Registered cases of Aftosa fever in herds from neighbor countries
- **Event B:** Incidents of Aftosa fever in neighbor states
  - Registered cases of Aftosa fever in herds from neighbor states
- **Event C:** Badly made vaccination
  - Lack of vaccine, vaccines with defect or badly applied vaccines.

Now we have to determine the independence of the events in relation one to each other. Analyzing the possibilities, we found that events A, B and C are independent, that is, the occurrence of one does not influence the occurrence of others.

Probabilities of the events, considering independent conditions:

- Probability of event A occurring = P(A) = 0.60
  Probability of event B occurring = P(B) = 0.40
- Probability of event C occurring = P(C) = 0.10

Conditional Probabilities (Probability of the scenario in relation to the events):

As the three events are independent, we have that:

- P(Scenario | A and not B and not C) = P(Scenario | A)
- P(Scenario | B and not A and not C) = P(Scenario | B)
- P(Scenario | C and not A and not B) = P(Scenario | C)

Experts determined the conditional probabilities of the scenario as:

P(Scenario | A) = 0.30
This equation must be interpreted as "there are 30% of chances of lack of cattle if incidents of Aftosa fever occur in neighbor countries".

P(Scenario | B) = 0.9
This equation must be interpreted as "there are 90% of chances of lack of cattle if incidents of Aftosa fever occur in neighbor states".

P(Scenario | C) = 1.0
This equation must be interpreted as "there are 100% of chances (quite certainty) of lack of cattle if exist problems in vaccination".

Combined Probabilities:

- P(A) x P(Scenario | A) = 0.60 x 0.30 = 0.18
- P(B) x P(Scenario | B) = 0.40 x 0.90 = 0.36
- P(C) x P(Scenario | C) = 0.10 x 1.00 = 0.10

Conditions	Combined Probabilities
Event A	18%
Event B	36%
Event C	10%

The final probability of the scenario A is of 36% of occurring.

In this case study, we carried out the second step for all possible scenarios. However, due to space limits, we only show details for the scenario A, as an example. Table 1 shows the final probability for each scenario identified in this study case, after the execution of the second step of the proposed methodology. We can see in table 1 that Scenario A has the highest probability.

3. Determination of the Impact of the Scenario

The calculus of the impact is made by analyzing the probability and the impact of the consequent events, that is, events that can occur if the scenarios happen. In this case study, consequent events for the Scenario A – Lack of cattle due to Aftosa fever were identified by experts from the Company. The probability related to each event was determined by experts and means how probable is the event if the scenario happens. For each consequent event, the impact of the event is determined in a scale from 1 to 10 (10 meaning the greatest impact).

Event K: Suspension of Meat Exportation:

Other countries cancel acquisition of meat from areas suspected of Aftosa fever; so if the scenario happens, there 100% of chances of this event occurring. As 50% of the sells of this Meat

Table 1. Comparing the probability of the scenarios

Scenarios	Final Probability of the Scenario
Scenario A: Lack of cattle due to incidents of Aftosa fever	36%
Scenario B: Entry of a competing company in the local market	31%
Scenario C: Devalue of dollar	23%

Plant are to external market, the impact of this event is high. Probability of the event = 100%; Impact = 10.

Event L: Suspension of Sells to Other States

Other states also suspend meat acquisition to avoid contamination. As this kind of sell represents only 15% of the total, the impact is not so high. Probability of the event = 100%; Impact = 5.

Event M: Decrease in the Meat Price

Usually, the meat price is devalued due to low demand and bogged down commodities. The plant has to sell with minor prices. Probability of the event = 90%; Impact = 7.

Event N: Suspension of Work and Sackings in Some Plants

Due to low supplies of cattle, some plants may dismiss employees or even finish their activities. Probability of the event = 80%; Impact = 10.

The risk of each event is calculating by multiplying the probability of the event by its impact. Table 2 resumes information about the consequent scenarios for this case; note that the total risk of the scenario is calculated by summing the risk of each event. It is important to observe that as many events associated to the scenario, more risks to the company.

In this case study, we do not explained details for all possible scenarios. We used the scenario A as an example. However, in this step of the methodology, we have to compare the risk for all possible scenarios. Table 3 shows the total risk for each scenario identified in this study case, after the use of the proposed methodology. We can see in table 3 that Scenario A has the highest risk.

4. Determination of the Risk of the Scenario

As stated early, the risk of a scenario is a combination of its probability with its impact. In the proposed methodology, we calculate the scenario risk by multiplying the probability of the scenario by its impact, as determined in steps 2 and 3.

5. Definition of the IT Portfolio

The most worrying scenario is that with highest probability or highest risk. If both characteristics are present in a scenario, then this scenario deserves more priority. In our case study, Scenario A (Lack of cattle due to incidents of Aftosa fever) is the scenario that will be treated as priority.

If there is not a unique scenario with top probability and top risk, the methodology proposes that the top scenarios in both cases must be faced as priority.

The four step of the methodology concerns the identification of priority scenarios (made below) and the definition of an IT Portfolio Planning. This planning is made by determining which Informa-

Table 2. Analysis of consequent events and impact of the scenario

	Consequent Events	Probability of the Event	Impact of the Event	Risk of each event
K	Suspension of meat exportation	100%	10	1000
L	Suspension of sells to other states	100%	5	500
M	Decrease in the meat price	90%	7	630
N	Suspension of work and sackings in some plants	80%	10	800
	Total impact of the scenario =			2930

Table 3. Comparing the impact of the scenarios

Scenarios	Impact
Scenario A: Lack of cattle due to incidents of Aftosa fever	2930
Scenario B: Entry of a competing company in the local market	2700
Scenario C: Devalue of dollar	1300

Table 4.

Scenarios	Probability of each scenario	Impact of each scenario	Risk of each scenario
Scenario A: Lack of cattle due to incidents of Aftosa fever	36%	2930	1054.8
Scenario B: Entry of a competing company in the local market	31%	2700	837
Scenario C: Devalue of dollar	23%	1300	299

tion Systems have to be developed to minimize the problems caused by the chosen scenarios.

One of the activities is to trace an action plan to the company. In this case study, experts from the Meat Plant Company have selected the following actions to face the scenario A:

- More control over focus of Aftosa in neighbors;
- Diversify the line of products;
- Plan work schedule and collective vacations of employees;

- Decrease costs and more control over production costs;
- Diversify suppliers, registering and qualifying suppliers in other regions.

After defining the actions, the final task is to define actions for the IT Sector. Actions will be represented by Information Systems necessary to support the action plan defined previously.

Information Systems to support Action Plan for the Scenario A:

- Develop an Information System for Competitive Intelligence. The goal of this system is to monitor the formation of the scenario, looking in Internet for news related to the antecedent events. This system helps the company to identify events before the occurrence of the scenario, so that the company can make decisions quickly to minimize bad effects of the scenario occurrence.
- Create infra-structure of telecommunications to connect plants all over the country. The goal is to facilitate the exchange of information about market among the plants present in all regions of the country, in order to diversify the products of the company, to minimize decrease of sells if the scenario occurs.
- Implement a database of working hours. The goal is to develop this system integrated to the existing Human Resources System, controlling working hours, extra-hours, vacations and compensations. This system will be useful to better plan collective vacations due to low activities in the plant (due to low sells), when the scenario occurs.
- Implement Information System for Costs Control. The goal is to support decisions of cutting costs when the scenario get true.
- Implement Information System for Suppliers. The goal is to acquire and register new suppliers and to evaluate the quality of their products and services. This alternative sup-

pliers will be used if the scenario happen in the state, so that suppliers from other regions (not affected by the Aftosa) may supply cattle to the company.

CONCLUSION

This chapter showed a scenarios-based methodology for IT Portfolio planning. The main result is a way to plan and control information systems to be aligned with the company mission and objectives.

The methodology is based on the analysis of future scenarios. A scenario represents a future situation that can not be controlled nor can be avoided, but it may be investigated. In general, planning methodologies trace directions from a present point to a future and desired target. However, in many cases, there are situations that can not be controlled or avoided. Scenarios are useful to help companies to prevent problems, to minimize consequences and to react quickly to undesired situations.

The analysis of the scenarios probability and risk helps determining which scenarios are more worrying and deserve more attention. This may lead companies to concentrate efforts in priority areas instead of using all resources in too many directions.

As argued by IT Governance models (like COBIT), companies have to align IT to business goals and directions. The methodology presented here follows this orientation by driving IT systems and infrastructure towards actions and initiatives planned by the company to prepare itself for the future scenarios. Furthermore, as established by COBIT, the methodology helps companies to plan the IT investments by selecting priority information systems.

FUTURE TRENDS

One of the limitations of the methodology is the four step, where analysts have to decide which information systems and IT resources are necessary to support the planned actions of the company to react to the scenario. This is still a subjective task, too dependent on the analyst experience and feeling. We need systematic methods and tools to support analysts to conduct this task. One possible way is a database of benchmarking cases (best practices), with kinds of actions and respective kinds of IT technologies to support that actions.

Furthermore, the methodology may be extended to help experts in the identification of scenarios and the events related to them. Today, this is a task that depends on the expert vision of the future in a certain domain. The definition of probabilities is important because a scenario may be disregarded if determined that its probability is low; however the consequences, that is, the risk of the scenario may be disastrous.

REFERENCES

Fahey, L., & Randall. R. M. (1998). *Learning from the future*. London: John Wiley.

Hubbard, D. (2007). *How to measure anything: finding the value of intangibles in business*. John Wiley & Sons.

Kahn, H., & Wierner, J. (1968). *The year 2000: a framework for speculation on the next 33 years*. New York: Macmillan.

Kaplan, R. S., & Norton, D. P. (1992). The Balanced Scorecard - Measures that Drive Performance. *Harvard Business Review*, (Jan-Feb), 71-79.

Kaplan, R. S., & Norton, D. P. (1997). *Balanced scorecard*. 17. ed. Rio de Janeiro: Campus.

Schwartz, P. (1991). *The art of the long view*. New York: Doubleday.

Van Der Heijden, K. (2005). *Scenarios: the art of strategic conversation*. 2.ed. London: John Wiley.

Wilkinson, L. (1995). How to build scenarios. *Wired*, (September), 4-10.

Chapter VII
Information Technology Portfolio Management:
A Meta–Heuristic Optimization Approach

Vassilis Syrris
Aristotle University of Thessaloniki, Greece

ABSTRACT

This study involves the exploration of Information Technology Portfolio Management (ITPM) in conjecture with Modern Portfolio Theory (MPT). The ITPM constitutes an indispensable part of the Strategic Information System which is an integrated multi-functional structure having its origin in works of Anthony (1965) and Gibson & Nolan (1974). ITPM attempts to resolve the project selection problem concerning the majority of project-centric organizations. Roughly speaking, projects must compete for the scarce resources which are only available for the fittest ones. Although a large proportion of portfolio selection decisions are taken on a qualitative basis, quantitative approaches to selection such as MPT or its variants are beginning to gain wide application. Yet, the standard MPT has proved incapable of representing the complexities of real-world situations. This issue generates the present work which focuses on the project portfolio optimization problem through a meta-heuristic approach, that is, application of algorithmic methods able to find near-optimal solutions in a reasonable amount of computation time. The ultimate goal is the enhancement of IT portfolio management which has become a significant factor in the planning and operation of information-based organizations, thus, offering a competitive advantage.

INTRODUCTION

Recently the role of information systems in an organization has advanced to the level of its application in information management and in strategic decision-making assistance. The so-called Strategic Information Systems (SIS[1]) align with the organization strategy and culture, contributing significantly to the realization of its overall objectives and the increase of competitive advantages. Yet, a crucial point to consider is that as they are often linked with higher-risk projects[2], they should be handled through an effective portfolio management. This is currently underpinned across all industries that seek ways to improve the decision making processes as far as undertaking specific projects is concerned.

Rigorous mathematical methodologies have not yet successfully treated the project portfolio management and its prominent issue of projects selection[3]. The closest attempt is the Modern Portfolio Theory which has been extensively applied in financial portfolio management. According to this theory a portfolio is defined as mean-variance efficient if it has the highest expected return for a given variance (risk), or if it has the smallest variance (risk) for a given expected return. However, in practice, mean-variance model has proved unable to represent realistic conditions due to inherent computational complexity and uncertainty issues.

Current information system takes a much more sophisticated and strategic direction with the aid of meta-heuristic optimization techniques. Advances in the field of meta-heuristics (the domain of optimization that compounds traditional mathematics with artificial/computational intelligence and methods based on biological or evolutionary processes) have improved the traditional methods by introducing more pragmatic assumptions and providing a more sophisticated analysis with flexible and robust forecasting tools. The techniques employed in meta-heuristics are mostly general purpose search methods that do not derive the solution analytically but by iteratively searching and by testing improved or modified solutions until some convergence criterion is met; usually, they result in near-optimal[4] solutions. Since they usually outperform traditional numerical procedures, they are well suited for empirical and computational studies.

The objective of this work is to investigate the ability of some meta-heuristic methods to deliver high-quality solutions for the mean-variance model when confronted with additional practical constraints. The optimization problem herein is the project portfolio selection with cardinality constraints stated as: in business, there exist many more project proposals than funding can support; selection processes must intelligently choose a subset of projects that meet the company profit goals while abiding by budgetary restrictions. Finally, an alternative meta-heuristic approach is presented and compared with Genetic Algorithm and Monte Carlo methods through experimental analysis.

STRATEGIC INFORMATION SYSTEMS AND IT GOVERNANCE

A Strategic Information System (SIS) is a system which manages information in respect to company strategy and its operational planning. It assists decision making, adds value and ensures business viability through its alignment with the strategic goals[5]. Such a system responds faster to environmental changes and thus provides a competitive advantage.

The main components of a SIS is: a) The Information System (IS), that is, the means by which the information is collected, codified, stored, organized in computational structures and processed, with a final aim, to be exploited and disseminated, b) The Information Technology (IT) which provides the integrated platform (hardware, software, networking, protocols) upon which the IS can operate consistently, quickly and robustly.

The information is a major capital asset, and are the systems that support it. SISs improve the internal operational procedures, facilitate the executive management, support and control the creation of new innovative and enhanced products and services, refine the relationship between company and customers/suppliers, open new markets (through Internet), advance the human resources (by on/off line e-learning programs) and improve productivity and effectiveness. Moreover, there is evidence, that, in some organizations, IT strategic planning functions as drive to corporate planning, and that IT can actively assist in the creation of business opportunities, rather than just support them (Oesterle, 1991).

The dependency of today's organizations on SIS is immense. Such a valuable business module needs a rational and organized development framework. As the SIS evolves, a systematic supervision ought to relate and fit business needs with IT/IS competency. New projects and investments must be evaluated, prioritized and selected especially when balanced cost/benefit issues or business—short or long—strategic objectives are involved. A successful project that does not contribute to the goals accomplishment is simply a waste of resources.

According to Rosser & Potter (2001), the alignment of IT and business strategy is the number one concern of chief executive officers (CEOs) today; similarly, the misalignment of strategic planning and tactical operations is particularly acute in many IT organizations today (Bonham, 2005). CEOs of fast-growth companies frequently indicate that IT is crucial for their success. The implication is that companies are working at a competitive disadvantage when their IT management is not aligned with business strategy.

The adoption of SIS leads a company to IT Governance, that is, the principled and justified decision making philosophy, which provides consistent and transparent processes flow. IT Governance answers the questions: what should IT focus on? (alignment with business goals) and how should IT manage to do it? (IT management pertinence). It links business management with IT potentiality in a transparent way, i.e., clear targets, communication among business departments which leads to mutual comprehension of the way they work, objective projects evaluation and understanding of their impact into the company. Today, a great part of IT Governance is visible through IT project portfolio management; the latter continuously proves to be an effective tool for establishing the strategic asset allocation policy and, hence, enhances the business portfolio and wealth. Moreover, portfolio management provides a consistent means for regular progress monitoring to ensure that portfolio performance is on track in terms of strategic allocation of funds targets and a justified and objective way to stop projects that have run off the rails.

IT PROJECT PORTFOLIO MANAGEMENT

Most organizations operate in a complex environment with many programs and projects running simultaneously. It has been observed that many of these organizations have little oversight over their projects course and employ non-repeatable planning processes without a constant rule-based reasoning. Despite the limit on the number of resources, many businesses lack a systematic approach on projects conduction and suffer from poor project selection, prioritization and acceptance criteria that could enhance the successful delivery of the organization strategic objectives. This in turn leads to a lack of comparability and difficulty in cancelling projects and reallocating resources.

All these issues can be tackled successfully by Project Portfolio Management (PPT) which can be defined as a dynamic decision-making process involved with the selection and management of a mix of projects (portfolio) and aiming at creating wealth in business and accomplishment of mission goals. While Project Management concentrates primarily on the challenge "doing projects right", Project Portfolio Management focuses on the "doing the right projects" (Linenberg et al., 2003). By extension, the objective of IT Portfolio Management is to optimize the organization's IT investments portfolios in order to contribute to the whole successful performance of this organization and its sustained viability, value, and growth. ITPPM appears to be of immediate necessity as, according to some studies such as the research realized in the United States (TechRepublic & Smith, 2000), 40% of Information Technology investments fail to deliver their intended results.

The IT project selection problem (Bonham, 2005; Muralidhar et al., 1988; Santhanam & Kyparisis, 1995; Schniederjans & Santhanam, 1993; Walter et al., 2007) is classified into two streams: a) the management science stream which focuses on the implementation and managerial aspects of the subject and b) the financial optimization stream which is a quantitative framework for maintaining a profitable trade-off between portfolio expected return and its associated risk.

In this study, we have adopted the latter approach. This kind of management enables an efficient set (frontier) of projects to be sustained capable of maximizing the return in terms of financial performance, as well as progress towards strategic goals, while minimizing both the cost and risk to the organization.

BENEFITS

The skilled application of ITPPM can deliver numerous benefits. A concise list is presented below:

- Ensures alignment with business strategy and improves mission performance. Overall spending reflects the strategic priorities of the business.
- Reduces projects duplication, checks for obsolete investments and interoperability.

In general, a strong reluctance to stop or reject projects has been observed, due to no consistent criteria, unreliable information and politics among the business departments. PPM overcomes these obstacles and permits the re-allocation of funds in projects that provide increased capabilities and better support current priorities and mission goals, achieving, hence, their full potential.

- Blocks the scarce resources to be divided into too many projects and allows planners to schedule resources more efficiently. Also, it provides transparency of the entire cost structure and resolves conflicts and contentions for scarce and costly resources.
- Warrants ongoing successful delivery of programs and projects.
- Provides central oversight of budget and progress by maintaining a common project inventory.
- Balances the portfolio via a number of specific parameters, i.e., risk/return, short-term/long-term, markets-customers-technologies etc.
- Supports risk management.
- Maintains the business competitive position by being able to respond quickly to changes in the environment. Portfolios can be constantly reviewed and altered if necessary, to produce the highest returns based on changing conditions.

On the whole, we stress that the ITPPM is indispensable in today's organizations resulting in a balanced enviable portfolio of high value projects which support business short and long-term pursuits.

MODERN PORTFOLIO THEORY

Much of modern portfolio management has been motivated by the seminal work of Harry Markowitz (1952) and his efficient risk-return curve optimization model. The introduction of the portfolio optimization process was an important step in the development of what is now considered to be Modern Finance Theory. MPT and its variants have been widely used in practice for more than fifty years. Markowitz (1952, 1959) formulates the portfolio optimization model over two dimensions: investment benefits (expected return) versus risk (positive or negative deviation from the expected return). The goal is double-folded: mediate the portfolio risk and for a specific level of risk catch the maximum return. The key concept to reach the goal is through the diversification of portfolio investments. MPT proposes two ways to handle profitably the risk[6]:

- A group of investments encompass less risk than a single one. The variability of the portfolio as an entity is smaller than the average variability of the investments that form it, without negatively affecting expected returns. Adding more investments in the portfolio is equivalent to spreading the total risk into multiple smaller and diverse risks.

- The criterion used for the investments selection is to be co-evolved in a diverse way, that is, to have reciprocal progress. This criterion is represented mathematically by two statistical measures: the *covariance* and the *correlation coefficient* (see next section); two variables move in a diversified way in case where their covariance is negative or their respective correlation coefficient is negative and tends to -1.

Thus, the concept of an efficient portfolio emerges in accordance with the above two dimensions: trade-off between return and risk. The objective now can be described as: given a set of candidate investments and a set of constraints (such as capital budget limit or revenue horizon), find out the weightings of those investments that minimize the variance of a portfolio

and ensure a return equal to or bigger than the expected return.

Portfolio Optimization Problem Definition According to MPT

For each investment the rate of return is a random variable; in the simplest case, the returns can be described with the normal distribution. The risk and return of a portfolio P consisting of n risky investments can be treated as a convolution of the individual investment returns and variances. It is a necessary precondition that the included investments are described by the distributions of their respective returns. The two features outlining the portfolio P are calculated as shown in Exhibit A.

Maximizing portfolio return or minimizing portfolio risk without a specific objective in mind is seldom interesting to an investor. The previous formulation is known as *unconstrained optimization* portfolio problem. In practice, efficient diversification to establish an optimal set of portfolio investments is ultimately a *constrained optimization* problem; its mathematical definition appears with many variants but the principal objectives can be summarized as:

1. Minimize risk (portfolio variance) for a specified expected return, that is:

   $\min_{w_i}(\sigma_P^2)$ subject to (1.1) and conditions (1.3), where $r_P = r^*$ specific value.

2. Maximize the expected return for a specified risk, that is:

   $\max_{w_i}(r_P)$ subject to (1.2) and conditions (1.3), where $\sigma_P^2 = \sigma^*$ specific value.

3. Minimize the risk and maximize the expected return simultaneously (multi-objective optimization). Because there is no obvious way for an investor to determine the

Exhibit A.

$$\text{Expected return (P)} = \sum_{i=1}^{n} w_i \cdot E\left(r_i\right) = r_P \tag{1.1}$$

$$\text{Variance(P)} = \sum_{i=1}^{n}\sum_{i=1}^{n} w_i \cdot w_j \cdot \sigma_{ij} = \sigma_P^2 \text{ (risk measure)} \tag{1.2}$$

Where: $\tag{1.3}$

$E(r_i)$ is the expected value (per period) of the return corresponding to investment i, $\min_{i}(r_i) \leq r_P \leq \max_{i}(r_i)$

and $\exists i \neq j$ such that $r_i \neq r_j$

σ_i^2 is the variance of investment i, $\sigma_i > 0, \forall i$

$\sigma_{ij} = \sigma_{ji} =$ the real-valued covariance of expected returns of investments i and j

- $\sigma_{ij} = \dfrac{1}{m}\sum_{q=1}^{m}\left(r_{qi} - \overline{r}_i\right)\left(r_{qj} - \overline{r}_j\right)$, where m the number of samples for the variables r_i and r_j, $\overline{r}_i$ and $\overline{r}_j$ are the averages of r_{qi} and r_{qj}, $q = 1, 2, ..., m$, respectively.

- $\sigma_{ij} = \sigma_i \cdot \sigma_j \cdot \rho_{ij}$, where $\rho_{ij} \in \left[-1, 1\right]$ is the correlation coefficient.

- $\sigma_{ii} = \sigma_i^2$

$\sum_{i=1}^{n} w_i = 1$, w_i is the share of investment i in P

$w_i \in R_0^+, \forall i \tag{1.4}$

"correct" trade-off between risk and return, someone is frequently interested in looking at the trade-off between the two. We can deal with both objectives simultaneously in the following way:

$\max_{w_i} \left(\alpha \cdot r_P - (1-\alpha) \cdot \sigma_P^2\right)$ subject to (1.1), (1.2) and conditions (1.3), where $0 \leq \alpha \leq 1$ denotes an investor-specific parameter which can be interpreted as a risk-aversion coefficient. Solving the problem for different values of α, the efficient curve of diverse portfolios can be identified. As the trade-off parameter $\alpha \to 1$, portfolios with high return are detected. In case of $\alpha \to 0$, portfolios with low risk would be identified.

The problems above are essentially equivalent mathematically and their solutions are called Mean-Variance (MV) efficient. The efficient points in the Return-Risk figure are called the Efficient Frontier (Fig.1). Points under the Efficient Frontier curve represent inefficient portfolios. Any point above the Efficient Frontier is not possible. Portfolios along the curve are said to be efficient because the maximum value from the available constraints is achieved.

Some subsequent objectives:

- Minimize the risk regardless of the expected return.
- Maximize the expected return regardless of the risk.
- Minimize the expected return regardless of the risk.

The constraint (1.4) inhibits an analytic solution and additionally, it makes the standard Markowitz model NP-hard (Garey & Johnson, 1979). However, when n is sufficiently small, quadratic optimization software can solve numerically the problem within reasonable time (Jagannathan & Ma, 2003).

Figure 1. Efficient frontier

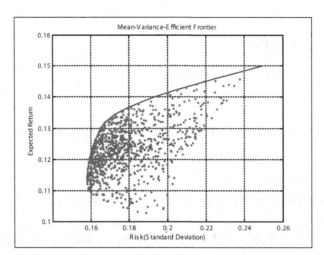

The Efficient Frontier

The Efficient Frontier is a simple analysis tool which supports the visualization -in a graphical representation- of the result of a portfolio risk-return approach. Concisely, this handy tool can give information about:

- Trade-offs between portfolio value and cost. Scenarios concerning different levels of expected returns, risks and diversification tactics.
- Comparisons with already running portfolios. Detection of mismatches between supply and demand.
- Influence of constraints and comprehension of the relationships among resources, policies, strategies and goals. Answers to which factors move the portfolio position away from the efficient curve.
- Possible improvements or compromises that could be considered about a potential portfolio.

Modern Portfolio Management Criticism

The critical issues of MPT application are summarized below:

- There is the need for inputs (expected returns, standard deviations and correlations) to be estimated. The normal distribution underlying assumption for the model variables is too simplistic and affects the quality of the resulting strategic allocations; the estimation of return and covariance from historical data is very sensitive to measurement errors whereas small perturbations of uncertain data can make the suggested optimal solution heavily infeasible and as such – practically meaningless (Rachev et al., 2004).
- The computational difficulty of the quadratic programming model is not tolerable (Elton et al., 1976; Konno &Yamazaki, 1991).
- The computational requirements of the covariance matrix usage for large portfolios can become quite cumbersome or inefficient.

- Risk minimization requires the investor to set a minimum level for expectation, a readily understandable quantity, while the interpretation of a maximum risk level in expected value maximization may not always be clear.
- MPT has no significant practical value due to its unsophisticated constraints.

Model Parameters Estimation

There is a critical implementation decision that the analyst/investor must consider: How the model required inputs (expected returns, variance, correlations, revenue projections, costs) can be estimated; even small changes in the parameter inputs lead to large changes in the implied portfolio holdings. Unfortunately, there is not any standard method to cope adequately with this matter. In practice, the following approaches are utilized with the respective strengths and drawbacks:

- Expert evaluation: Many firms rely on the intuitive feelings and past experience of experts on the particular domain to help identify potential project risks and returns. It is about a quantitative approach the success of which depends on the experts' experience, knowhow, wide and deep analytical ability and good market-information. The *Delphi* scheme is the most applicable judgment technique for deriving a consensus among a panel of experts to make predictions about future developments. The sufficient number of experts ensures the objectivity of the considerations and the reduction of the fault diagnoses.
- Historical data: A very common method used in financial portfolio management. The key assumption here is the existence of regularities during the movement of an asset related to time. In simple words, past events could be repeated in a similar way in future time. Unfortunately, historical records can

be found rarely in project management since a project is not a routine procedure which can be identically replicated; this is the rule especially in innovative projects where the originality is the foremost eligible trait.
- Simulation (see section: Monte-Carlo Simulation): A standard technique for exploring phenomena where the input variables do not take exact values, leading hence, to the generation of multiple outcomes. In other words, simulation reflects the way the uncertainty induced in model parameter estimates affects the future results. The key idea is to run numerous different input-output scenarios and wrap up with a statistically valid model. Despite its analytical power, simulation has a critical drawback: it is time consuming.

These approaches must be applied with caution because the practice has proved that estimation errors in the input parameters frequently outweigh the benefits of the mean-variance model.

MPT IN IT PROJECT PORTFOLIO MANAGEMENT

The mathematical framework of MPT and its management extensions were appealing for many researchers who attempted to induct it into coherent fields. McFarlan (1981) is considered to be the first to propose Portfolio Management approach to IT assets and investments. Further contributions have been made by (Aitken, 2003; Benson et al., 2004; Kaplan, 2005; Moskowitz & Kern, 2003; Weill & Broadbent, 1998). The idea behind these efforts is that a company while conducting a portfolio of projects reduces risks through risk diversification (hedging) in the same way that an individual can reduce financial investment risks by investing in a portfolio of diversified stocks.

The straightforward MPT application in ITPPM is not easy due to extra complexities and peculiarities associated with project management in general. In a relatively recent interview (Harder, 2002), Markowitz analyzed several dissimilarities:

"Perhaps portfolio theory–as is–is not applicable. An investment manager doesn't have to run companies he purchases. Also, he doesn't jeopardize the prospect of the companies whose shares he buys if he invests a small fraction of his portfolio in this one and a small fraction in that one. But if a company manager subdivides his resources too finely among many projects in order to diversify, he may give each project too little to succeed."

"There are different constraints regarding projects, like management expertise, human skill sets, physical production capabilities and other factors that come into play. Understanding how an organization's experience in one product area may be applicable to other markets is not very clear."

"As far as returns from these projects, part of the uncertainty is market uncertainty as with securities. But part of the uncertainty also has to do with skills available. In order to evaluate the potential of a project, the company must estimate whether it can design and produce a product of a quality and price sufficient to be sold in the face of present and future competition."

It is generally accepted that IT portfolio management has not reached the same level of standardization as investment portfolio management. Financial portfolio assets typically have consistent measurement information enabling accurate and objective comparisons. In project management, the basic problem is that each organization develops its own philosophy, adopts variant metrics and posts different priorities. Some evaluation measures are quantitative, like estimated return on investment, while others are qualitative, like alignment with company strategy. Unlike financial portfolio risks, there is typically no direct way to

measure the statistical dependence among the risks of conducting potential projects. Also, the vital activities of project selection and prioritization, resource allocation and project implementation can be carried out in various ways in pursuit of the strategic goals. Finally, other serious factor is the problem constraints definition. Goldman (1999) highlights that incorporating constraints is a key step in the portfolio alignment process and he mentions four types of constraints that should be managed: scarce human resources, staff capabilities, budgets and infrastructure; such constraints are extrinsic to financial portfolio management.

Value of IT Projects/Investments

An IT investment benefit is not a return rate that compensates time and risk; it is unique in terms of timing, the existing operating expertise and fitting into the overall operation of the organization. However, in the present enterprise computing environment, it becomes more and more important to be able to demonstrate financial gains of IT investments compared to their cost (Kersten & Verhoef, 2003). The valuation of IT investments is challenging because it is characterized by long payback periods, uncertainty, and changing business conditions. Organizations have used several evaluation metrics when making capital budgeting decisions such as Net Present Value (NPV), Return On Investment (ROI), Internal Rate of Return (IRR) and pay-back period (Archer & Ghasemzadeh, 1999; Barney & Danielson, 2004; Benaroch, 2002; Kwak & Ibbs, 2000; McGrath & Macmillan, 2000). While finance professionals have worked for decades with metrics to capture return and risk of assets, the use of these methods for IT projects still seems uncommon for many organizations (Jeffery & Leliveld, 2003). The major criticism concerns their weakness to capture every objective of an organization; there are intangible objectives in organizations such as customer satisfaction and brand image that cannot be quantified without problems.

In our study, we follow the NPV approach to measure the project expected return and its variance to represent the associated risk. NPV is the present value of future cash returns, discounted at the appropriate interest rate, minus the present value of the cost of the investment. NPV is an effective way of expressing how much value a long term project investment will result in. However, there are some limitations to NPV measurement that the reader has to consider: a) it does not account for uncertainty after the project decision has been made, b) it is unable to deal with intangible benefits; this inability decreases its usefulness for handling strategic issues and projects. Despite these drawbacks, NPV has become an industry standard method.

Practical Implementation Issues

In order for the mean-variance optimization problem to be solved, it is important to note the major traits distinguishing the project portfolio problem: a) The investment variables are 0/1, reject/approve decision variables, b) It is much less obvious how one develops the covariance matrix describing the project intercorrelation risks[7]. This matter is tackled by the *Delphi* technique and a similarity matrix approach (see section: Cluster Analysis), and c) There may be logical constraints among the projects, reflecting project interdependencies, overlapping, prerequisites etc. Herein, the problem is solved with an additional project cardinality constraint.

RISK

In management and financial sciences the term *risk* is employed to express ambiguity in decision making and to depict the intrinsic uncertainty of the future outcomes. Risk does not contain necessarily a negative hue; future results or conditions could be better than expected and usually are called opportunities.

There are many types of risks related to states, organizations and people; their complete study is out of the scope of this work. We would better concentrate on the risks confronted by the companies which execute Information Technology projects[8]. The risk is swotted in four broad categories:

- Technology risk: available infrastructure and supplied materials, design/architecture suitability and feasibility, time consistency, implementation knowhow, competent staff or outsourcing, maintenance capability, statutory and regulatory obligations, technology obsoleteness or inadequacy.
- Financial risk: financial endorsement (loan, financial/leveraged lease), cash flows, liquidity, credits, payment periods, replacement/maintenance costs, cost of capital, inflation, external sources of funds, expected revenues.
- Market risk: project outcome utility and acceptance, timing, results distribution, quality level, competitors.
- Corporation risk: changes in business strategy or operational processes, project interdependencies or overlapping, problematic communication among stakeholders[9], management support, realistic expectations and proper planning, clear visions, objectives and scope definitions.

These risks have an impact on the company's ability to obtain the payback from its IT assets and cause fluctuations in expected benefits. Systematic and profound risk analysis could anticipate several sudden situations. This could be summarized in four activities:

- Risk identification: the most common techniques used herein are: brainstorming, *swot* analysis, interviewing and experts committee (*Delphi* approach).
- Evaluation of factors that affect the projects implementation and results. Best and worst

scenarios are carried out in order for the range of potential outcomes to be determined.

- Establishment of a plan of actions to be considered in every step of project cycle. These actions would mitigate negative responses and they would enhance fine performance.
- Constant control, adjustments and reconsiderations during the project implementation cycle.

IT project portfolio management aims to maneuver the risk associated with single project implementation by providing an integrated platform for monitoring, controlling and improving the simultaneous execution of a large number of projects, mitigating the risks through diversification and achieving, hence, the best possible returns. However, a successful portfolio composition presupposes one fundamental feature: the investor attitude against risk. The technical terminology that is used to describe the amount of satisfaction or pleasure received from a potential payoff is the risk utility or risk tolerance. A risk-averse investor presents low risk tolerance and seeks for investments with the lowest possible risk[10]. Established organizations tend to be risk averse, for the most part, whereas start-up companies are frequently risk seeking. Thus, the portfolio manager would select those projects which result in a portfolio risk that meets the investor risk tolerance.

THE PROJECT PORTFOLIO SELECTION PROBLEM – MATHEMATICAL FORMULATION

The problem model is considered as an object with three attributes: decision variables and their domains, objectives and constraints (linear or nonlinear, equality and inequality). Portfolio selection or capital allocation models can be formulated either in terms of rates of return and portfolio weights, like in Markowitz-type formulations (see Exhibit B1) or by using a budget constraint, expressing the initial *wealth level*, and maximizing the investor's *terminal wealth level* (see Exhibit B2).

When properly applied, both approaches yield identical results. Despite the fact that the second approach is more suitable and easily implemented to a project portfolio selection setting, we choose the first formulation in order to keep the correspondence with the financial portfolio analysis.

Both mathematical descriptions can be extended straightforwardly to handle many complexities addressed in the real world. We can examine three real situations:

- Conflicting project goals: in this case when a project A is selected then the project B cannot be conducted. The following constraint ensures that when w_A is 1 then w_B must be 0: $w_A + w_B \leq 1$.
- Project prerequisites: in this case there is a precedent relationship between projects A and B, i.e. A can be conducted only if B is implemented. The next constraint secures that both projects must be 1: $w_A - w_B \leq 0$
- Mandatory projects: strategic benefits or wide-influence projects like operations re-engineering impose the kickoff or the continuation of specific projects. In such cases, the respective weights must stay equal to 1 in the whole optimization process.

In this work we attempt to solve the cardinality constraint problem (single-period problem) which states that an organization wishes or is able to administer at most k different projects in its portfolio. The cardinality constraint[11] is presented in the following form:

$$\sum_{i=1}^{n} w_i \leq k$$

(2.9)

Exhibit B1.

$$\max\left(\alpha \cdot r_{NPV} - (1-\alpha) \cdot \sigma_{NPV}\right) \qquad (2.1)$$

Subject to:

$$\sigma_{NPV}^2 = \sum_{i=1}^{n}\sum_{j=1}^{n} w_i \cdot w_j \cdot \sigma_{ij} \qquad (2.2)$$

$$r_{NPV} = \sum_{i=1}^{n} w_i \cdot r_i \qquad (2.3)$$

$$\alpha \in [0,1] \qquad (2.4)$$

$$w_i = \begin{cases} 0, & i \text{ project is rejected} \\ 1, & i \text{ project is accepted} \end{cases} \qquad (2.5)$$

$$i = 1,2,...,n \text{ projects}$$

Where:

r_{NPV} is the mean of the distribution of the *NPV* values of the portfolio for one period

σ_{NPV} is the expected risk (standard deviation) of the portfolio for one period

r_i is the mean return of project *i*

σ_i is the risk (standard deviation) of project *i*

σ_{ij} is the covariance of projects *i* and *j*

$w_{i=1,2,...,n}$ are the decision variables

α is the risk-aversion coefficient

Exhibit B2.

$$\max\left(\sum_{i=1}^{n} b_i \cdot w_i\right) \qquad (2.6)$$

Subject to:

$$\sum_{i=1}^{n} c_i \cdot w_i \leq C \qquad (2.7)$$

$$w_i = \begin{cases} 0, & i \text{ project is rejected} \\ 1, & i \text{ project is accepted} \end{cases} \qquad (2.8)$$

$$i = 1,2,...,n \text{ projects}$$

Where:

C is the total available budget for one period

b_i is the benefit of the *i*'th project

c_i is the cost of the *i*'th project

$w_{i=1,2,...,n}$ are the decision variables

The projects are assumed to not be correlated (they are independent)

Where:

$2 \leq k \leq n$ (*k* could not be 1 because in such case the project portfolio is out of meaning)

Thus, the optimization problem we attempt to solve is that consisting of relationships (2.1)-(2.5) and (2.9).

EXHAUSTIVE SEARCH

When the number of projects becomes large, the project portfolio optimization problem cannot be solved straightforwardly with an exact, analytic solution. The approach that needs the least optimization skills would be complete enumeration where all the possible values for the decision variables are tested. This method would lead to the global optimum when there is enough time for all the testings and the set of candidate solutions is finite. If not, the latter can be discretized defining a suitable discretization step so as not to exclude the actual optimum while allowing for the number of feasible solutions to be tractable.

The original optimization problem where $\forall i = 1, 2, ..., n, w_i \in R_0^+$, is practically insolvable through complete enumeration since there could be found $n \cdot c, c \to \infty$ possible solutions which confront the constraints (c is the number of trials). Additionally, the cardinality constraint imposes new complexities in the initial problem. There are

$$\binom{n}{k} = \frac{n!}{k!(n-k)!}$$

different combinations for selecting k out of n solutions; hence, the complexity of the cardinality constraint optimization problem explodes to

$$O\left(\binom{n}{k} \cdot (k \cdot c)\right).$$

In project portfolio optimization the state space[12] is smaller. The valid values for the decision variables are binary, that is, a solution $w \in \{0, 1\}^n$ would contain n bits of type 0 and 1. The size of the set with all the solutions -all the possible combinations of 0 and 1- would be 2^n (including the trivial solution where all the values are zero). The cardinality constraint reduces further the state space into:

$$C(k), 2 \leq k \leq n \qquad (3.1)$$

where $C(l)$ is defined by the recursive formula:

$$C(l) = \begin{cases} 2^n, \text{when } l = n \\ C(l+1) - \binom{n}{l+1}, \text{when } k \leq l < n \end{cases}$$

$$(3.2)$$

Nevertheless, the problem complexity is still high and makes the state space very easily outsized and uncontrollable. For example, a problem with *n=50* projects and cardinality constraint *k=32*, would enclose a complexity of rank 1.107×10^{15}. As a last note, exhaustive search can be applied to any state space. However, the overwhelming size of the state space met in realistic problems makes this approach practically impossible.

MONTE-CARLO SIMULATION

Monte-Carlo is considered the most popular simulation analysis technique capable of examining various scenarios of type *what if*. It tests several theories and actions repetitively and records systematically the model output in order to assign to it a probability of occurrence. Moreover, it facilitates the realization of a sensitivity analysis which is interpreted as the detection of the factors that cause changes within the model under consideration, the discovery of results most likely to occur, those that are least likely to occur and best-case and worst-case results. This reinforces the justification required in decision making by resolving many of the conflicts between sponsors and project managers and by building confidence among the company stakeholders.

Three crucial points regulate the successful application of Monte-Carlo simulation:

- Inputs are defined as probability distributions, so their choice has to approximate as accurately as possible the realistic conditions. The information that would permit the accurate definition of distribution parameters must be extracted very carefully by the project managers, the sponsors and the market consultants.
- In order to achieve diversification, it is important to account for any correlation between input variables. Correlation would

occur when the sampling of two or more input distributions are chosen to be related.

- Answers have to be accompanied by statistical validity, that is, a specific confidence percentage associated with the estimates.

To conclude, Monte Carlo simulation, when performed with skill, is a proven, effective decision-making technique requiring only enough time and a computerized random number generator (Kelton & Law, 1991; Winston, 2000).

Monte-Carlo Algorithm Description

Let $f(x_1, x_2, ..., x_n)$ a parametric model where $x_1, x_2, ..., x_n$ are n decision variables for which: $\forall i, x_i \sim D_j$, $D_{j=1,2,...}$ are known probability distributions like Normal, Uniform, Lognormal, Poisson, Binomial, Triangular etc., and k is the number of simulations (see Listing 1).

META-HEURISTICS

In many real-world problems, the complexity of computational resources (time, hardware capacity etc), information inadequacy (limited precision or failing in estimating instance parameters) and multiplicity of possible results renders the analytical methods unable to attain feasible solutions. Recently, many researchers and practitioners have focused on flexible, approximate algorithms, such as heuristic and meta-heuristic optimization techniques which can cope with more realistic assumptions.

Heuristics are algorithmic strategies applied to very complex problem spaces attempting to detect optimal or near optimal solutions. An elementary heuristic algorithm consists of two modules: the heuristic measure which evaluates the quality of a candidate solution and an algorithm that employs it to search the state space. Unfortunately, heuristics are fallible. They are only an informed guess of the next step to be taken in solving a problem and consequently, they can lead a search algorithm to a suboptimal solution or fail to find any solution at all (Garey and Johnson, 1979).

Meta-heuristics constitute a wide extension of traditional heuristics. They successfully combine notions and techniques from several fields like traditional mathematics, artificial intelligence, biology, cognitive science etc. These advances as well as the recent facilities in terms of implementation tools have led to the construction of efficient optimization methodologies which carry out iteratively an intelligent, non-monotonous and multi-criteria trial and error approach in order to explore the state space and localize the optimal solutions. The term *meta* indicates their capability to guide other search procedures to overcome the trap of local optimality for complex optimization problems. In general, these solving strategies can not prove the optimality of the returned solution, but they are usually very efficient in finding approximate optimal

Listing 1. Monte-Carlo simulation algorithm

```
t = 0;
repeat
        each x_i takes a random value based on its respective probability distribution;
        enter all x_i in the parametric model, calculate and record the outcome;
        t = t + 1;
until t = k;
analyze the results by computing the statistics of the distribution of the model outcomes;
```

solutions (Blum & Roli, 2003; Hoos & Stützle, 2004). The most known meta-heuristics that have been applied extensively with satisfactory success in the portfolio optimization problem is *simulated annealing, tabu search* (Glover & Laguna, 1997), *scatter search* (Glover et al., 2003) and evolutionary techniques such as *genetic algorithms* (Davis, 1987; Doerner et al., 2002; Medaglia et al., 2007).

Genetic Algorithms

GAs (Holland, 1975) are algorithms for optimization, based loosely on several features of biological evolution (Darwin's Theory of Evolution). These algorithms maintain a constant size population of candidate problem solutions represented as string structures (called chromosomes); in an iterative way, some genetic operators are applied to them (the parents) in order to form better solutions (the children). The solutions quality is measured by their influence on the optimization function (maximization or minimization) which is called now fitness function. Thus, GAs are search algorithms based on the survival of the fittest among string structures (Goldberg, 1989); high fitness increases the chances of reproduction while low fitness will eventually lead to extinction. The selection is probabilistic, that is, weaker candidates are given a smaller likelihood of reproducing but are not eliminated outright. A weak candidate may continue to contribute to the makeup of better candidate solutions when still including some essential component of a solution; in that case, reproduction may extract it. The process continues until an appropriate termination criterion is satisfied, such as the maximum number of iterations (generations) or the amount of time devoted to the search.

A genetic algorithm requires five components:

- A way of encoding the solutions/chromosomes.
- An evaluation function which returns a rating for each chromosome given to it.
- A way of initializing the population of chromosomes.
- Operators that may be applied to parents to alter their genetic composition. Standard operators are *mutation* (random replacement of one or more bits in a solution vector), *crossover* (exchange of values between solution vectors) and *elitism* (preservation of the fittest parents).
- One or more termination criteria.

Genetic Algorithm Description

Let $P(t) = \{x_1(t), x_2(t), ..., x_n(t)\}$ a population of candidate solutions at time t and $f(x_i(t))$ a fitness function that returns an evaluation of the $x_i(t), i = 1, ..., n$ candidate's fitness at time t (see Listing 2).

Strengths and Weaknesses

GAs are more demanding to implement than any single-agent heuristic method. Also, they are more time-consuming because of their computational costs for administrating the population of candidate solutions. However, they are less likely to get stuck in local optimum. The genetic operators guide the search to an (near) optimal solution; the population will converge to one containing only chromosomes with good fitness. In brief, GAs implement a powerful form of hill climbing that maintains multiple solutions, eliminates unpromising solutions and improves gradually good solutions.

Cluster Analysis

A typical clustering method attempts to find natural groups (clusters) of data samples based on a similarity or dissimilarity measure. The

Listing 2. Standard genetic algorithm

```
t = 0;
initialize P(t);
repeat
        evaluate fitness of P(t) on f ;
        select pairs of solutions and individuals according to the quality of their evaluation;
        generate the offsprings of these pairs and/or individuals using genetic operators;
        replace the weakest candidate solutions with the offsprings;
        t = t + 1;
until termination condition met;
```

elements of a cluster are more similar among them and less similar compared to the elements of the other clusters. The key idea for applying cluster analysis in PPM is to reduce the problem complexity by compressing the sample space. This is interpreted to the following actions: identify similar projects based on their attributes (the respective expected return and variance), form suitable project groups and, finally, select the most representative and distinctive project of each group. In that way the initial sample space gets reduced into a smaller but representative space[13]. Then, the selection procedure would be applied only among the representative projects.

While the problem complexity is resolved satisfactorily, it is noteworthy to mention that the clustering approach can hardly lead to the global optimum; at best, the returned solutions constitute local optima. However, experimental analysis demonstrates that a few steps of local search may improve substantially the first approximate solutions.

The Clustering Algorithm

The clustering algorithm presented here originates from the author's previous work (Syrris & Petridis, 2008; Petridis & Syrris, 2007). There are two factors which customize the model upon the samples dataset and affect its overall performance: a) the metric function (similarity) and b) the proximity

value (how close two projects can be in order for them to be considered similar).

Each project is represented by a vector: $\vec{x}_i = [x_{i1}, x_{i2}]^T \in R^2$, where x_{i1} is the expected return and x_{i2} is the standard deviation of project i (the symbol T signifies the transpose operation). The sample space is defined as a set $D = \{x_{ij} \mid i = 1,...,n \text{ and } j = 1,2\}$, where n the total number of projects. The similarity measure is chosen to be: $S(\vec{x}_1, \vec{x}_2) = e^{-\|\vec{x}_1 - \vec{x}_2\|^p}$, where the *norm* is the Euclidean distance:

$$\sqrt{\sum_{j=1}^{m}(x_{1j} - x_{2j})^2},$$

where $m=2$ the number of attributes. The proximity parameter p is computed in the following way:

$$p = \left| \frac{\min(s_1,...,s_m)}{\max(s_1,...,s_m)} - \frac{1}{m}\sum_{j=1}^{m} s_j \right|,$$

where $s_j = \sqrt{\dfrac{1}{n-1}\sum_{i=1}^{n}(x_{ij} - \bar{x}_j)^2}$

the sample standard deviation of D with

$$\bar{x}_j = \frac{1}{n}\sum_{i=1}^{n} x_{ij}$$

and $j = 1, ..., m$. For the proximity value holds: $0 < p \leq L$, where $L = |b - a|$, $0 \leq a \leq b \leq 1$ or $-1 \leq a \leq b \leq 1$ and $[a, b]$ is the range of entries of all samples belonging to D. This criterion measures somehow the projects variance and conducts the cluster formation by grouping projects presenting similar variance.

The algorithm partitions the samples space in one pass. The only precondition is to have all the data available from the beginning; this is necessary in order to calculate the threshold p. This parameter is essential for the algorithm performance since it guides the space partitioning and retains the time complexity in affordable levels: $O(n(n - 1)/2)$, where n the number of samples.

The similarity function measures the vicinity of projects in the two dimensional space (see fig.14). In cases where the correlation coefficient matrix is missing or it is difficult to be estimated, we can employ instead the similarity matrix (see Listing 3: Function Similarity_Matrix) as a broad approximation of the projects correlation.

The output of the clustering algorithm is an index vector denoting the project groupings. The representative project of each cluster is considered to embody the average characteristics of all the projects comprising the cluster, and therefore, it is suggested for further validation. The rest of the projects of the cluster are assumed not to have an important role for the portfolio, so their respective decision variables (their contribution) are set zero. As a result, the number of candidate projects for investigation has reduced significantly and other heuristics (depending on the complexity of the produced sub-problem) like exhaustive search or genetic algorithms can be used to optimize the selection procedure.

EXPERIMENTAL ANALYSIS

In order to have a complete picture of the techniques described previously, we apply and test

them upon a real project portfolio problem (Table:1). The NPVs are considered to follow normal distribution, while the correlations among projects are extracted from IT experts. We have selected a few projects problem (n=10 candidate projects) because we would like to run the exhaustive search algorithm and handle its results as a comparison template.

The optimization problem consists of relationships (2.1)-(2.5) and (2.9), where:

- The parameter $\alpha \in [0,1]$ is discretized with step 0.05, i.e., 21 different values.
- The decision variables $w_{i=1,2,...,10}$ can only take two values: 0, meaning project exclusion from the portfolio and 1 meaning project incorporation.
- The k cardinality constraint threshold is chosen to be 8 projects.
- The state space (according to (3.1) & (3.2)) of the problem is 1,013 possible solutions.

The experimental procedure, the considerations and the analysis of results are demonstrated in the following tables and figures:

The template results of exhaustive search are displayed in Table 2 and Fig.2.

Monte-Carlo simulation is applied in two ways: a) All the parameters (returns, risks, correlations, weights) of the problem are deemed as variables and they are estimated by various probability distributions. Next, a statistical analysis is done for the forecasts evaluation (Table:3, Fig.3-7), b) The values of Table:1 are adopted and only the decision variables (weights) are estimated by the standard uniform distribution. The number of trials is kept below the state space size (Tables:4-5, Fig.8-9).

The results of the Genetic Algorithm are shown in Tables:6-7 and Fig.10-11 The genetic operators are applied with the following proportion: *elitism*:30%, *crossover*:30%, *mutation*:20%. An alternative operator is used additionally, called *injection*:20%, which balances exploitation and

Listing 3. Clustering algorithm

Function Clustering;
-define set D and normalize the data in range $[-1,1]$;
-compute p;
-n = number of D rows;
-t = 1;

-initialize the index vector of clusters $Ind(1) = 1$;

-initialize the matrix of clusters C with $C(1) = \begin{bmatrix} x_{11} & x_{12} \end{bmatrix}$. The $C(l)$ notation means that $C(l)$ is the submatrix

of C consisting of all vectors i belonging to cluster l, i.e. $Ind(i) = l, i \in N^*$;

-consider the representative vector of the first cluster $\vec{R}_1 = \begin{bmatrix} x_{11} & x_{12} \end{bmatrix}^T$;
-repeat
   $t = t + 1$;
   k = the number of clusters already created;
   for $l = 1$ to k

      $\vec{R}_l$ = Representative($C(l)$);

      compute similarity $S(\vec{x}_t, \vec{R}_l)$ between $\vec{x}_t$ and the representative vector $\vec{R}_l$ of each

      cluster l and record it into a list $sim(l) = sim(1,...,l-1) \cup S(\vec{x}_t, \vec{R}_l)$;
   next l;

  $K = k$;

  Label_1: find the maximum similarity $\max\limits_l(sim(1),..,sim(l),..,sim(K))$ and retrieve the

      respective cluster $C(l) = \left(\vec{x}_{l_1},...,\vec{x}_{l_j},...,\vec{x}_{l_L} \right), \forall l_j : Ind(l_j) = l$, where L is the

      number of vectors containing in $C(l)$;

  if $\frac{1}{2}\left(\left|\min(x_{1l_1},...,x_{1l_L},x_{1t}) - \max(x_{1l_1},...,x_{1l_L},x_{1t})\right| + \left|\min(x_{2l_1},...,x_{2l_L},x_{2t}) - \max(x_{2l_1},...,x_{2l_L},x_{2t})\right| \right) < p$ then

$C(l) = \left(\vec{x}_{l_1},...,\vec{x}_{l_j},...,\vec{x}_{l_L},\vec{x}_t \right), \forall l_j : Ind(l_j) = l$, $Ind(t) = l$ and $L+1$=the new cardinality
    of $C(l)$;
  else
      $K = K - 1$;
    if $K = 0$ then
          $C(k+1) = \vec{x}_t$;
          $Ind(t) = k+1$;
    else
          $sim(K) = sim(K+1) - S(\vec{x}_t, \vec{R}_l)$;
          go to Label_1;
    end if
  end if
-until $t = n$;

-return Clustering = $Ind(j), j = 1,...,k$;
end function

---

continued on following page

Listing 3. continued

```
Function Representative(Set_of_Clusters)
-      Representative = the vector x⃗ = [x₁  x₂]ᵀ ∈ Set_of_Clusters with maximum x₁ / x₂ ,
       where x₁ represents the expected return and x₂ its respective standard deviation;
-return Representative;
end function


Function Similarity_Matrix(Data, Similarity_func)
-n = the number of Data rows;
-for i = 1 to n
     for j = 1 to n
          Similarity_Matrix(i,j)=Similarity_func(Data(i,all_columns),Data(j,all_columns));
     end if
-end if
-return Similarity_Matrix;
end function
```

exploration. It generates such solutions that are dissimilar, based on Hamming distance[14], to the elite solutions found so far; the aim is to explore as much as possible more diverse regions of the state space. The combination of generations and population size values do not surpass in total the limit of 900 solutions, i.e., generations × population size ≤ 900. Furthermore, the experiments show that improved efficient portfolios frontiers are produced in cases where the population size is high enough despite the smaller number of generations; this provides evidence for the algorithm impotence to conduct adequately the optimization steps. That is, a big number of random solutions could probably be converged more quickly than a small number of solutions created through the application of genetic operators.

The clustering algorithm is tested (Tables: 8-11, Fig.12-15) in conjunction with exhaustive search (alternatively to complete enumeration, someone could use other heuristic methods such as genetic algorithm, in the stage after the clustering process termination). The initial dataset of 10 projects is compressed by 30%. The state space of the reduced dataset is $2^7 = 128$. In larger datasets, someone could adjust (increase) the proximity threshold in

order to achieve more compression; the exchange would be the decline of the solutions quality. Tables:10-11 and Fig.14-15 display the results after the utilization of similarity matrix in place of correlation matrix. This case can be exploited when the correlation among the variables is missing or it is difficult to be estimated, two scenarios not far away from the reality surrounding the IT project portfolio management. However, we keep in mind that the complexity of similarity matrix calculation is $O(n^2)$.

The IT Project Selection problem is located in the heart of combinatorial optimization; several alternative algorithms can be implemented attempting to balance among execution time, problem dependency, quality of solutions and transparency of results. We could not propose a unique method, since, in real world conditions, the solution optimality is practically unattainable. However, the available computational processing power permits a satisfactory testing and comparison of different methodologies which could be customized upon the specific problem domain. Based on the experimental procedure, this work suggests a two steps approach: a clustering application first in order to

Table 1. Ten candidate IT projects with their return-risk-correlation estimates

	Pr.1	Pr.2	Pr.3	Pr.4	Pr.5	Pr.6	Pr.7	Pr.8	Pr.9	Pr.10
NPVs (x10^4€)	15	12	11	18	13	10	17	9	8	21
Standard Deviations (x10^4€)	3.6	2.1	4.5	3.9	2.5	1.8	5.1	1.8	2.3	3.9
Correlation Coefficients	1	0.4842	0.1313	0.3049	0.1739	0.3457	0.4556	0.3033	-0.4229	0.8822
	0.4842	1	0.1333	0.3859	0.0101	0.5334	0.1880	-0.4155	-0.7680	0.1332
	0.1313	0.1333	1	-0.4882	0.1251	0.3243	-0.6974	0.2010	-0.8762	0.6272
	0.3049	0.3859	-0.4882	1	0.4063	0.2750	0.4110	-0.7557	0.7088	0.2616
	0.1739	0.0101	0.1251	0.4063	1	0.6847	0.2757	-0.4670	-0.5528	0.3167
	0.3457	0.5334	0.3243	0.2750	0.6847	1	0.3031	0.1259	-0.9178	0.2501
	0.4556	0.1880	-0.6974	0.4110	0.2757	0.3031	1	0.4546	0.3445	0.3020
	0.3033	-0.4155	0.2010	-0.7557	-0.4670	0.1259	0.4546	1	0.3315	0.1968
	-0.4229	-0.7680	-0.8762	0.7088	-0.5528	-0.9178	0.3445	0.3315	1	0.1898
	0.8822	0.1332	0.6272	0.2616	0.3167	0.2501	0.3020	0.1968	0.1898	1

Table 2. Selected projects generated by exhaustive search

Pr.1	Pr.2	Pr.3	Pr.4	Pr.5	Pr.6	Pr.7	Pr.8	Pr.9	Pr.10	Obj. Func.	Parameter α
0	1	0	0	1	0	0	1	1	0	0.95957	0
0	1	0	0	1	0	0	1	1	0	1.1884	0.05
0	1	0	0	1	0	0	1	1	0	3.3364	0.1
0	1	1	1	1	1	1	1	1	0	6.8536	0.15
0	1	1	1	1	0	1	1	1	1	12.484	0.2
0	1	1	1	1	0	1	1	1	1	18.516	0.25
0	1	1	1	1	0	1	1	1	1	24.549	0.3
1	1	1	1	1	0	1	1	0	1	31.026	0.35
1	1	1	1	1	0	1	1	0	1	37.563	0.4
1	1	1	1	1	0	1	1	0	1	44.099	0.45
1	1	1	1	1	0	1	1	0	1	50.636	0.5
1	1	1	1	1	1	1	0	0	1	57.243	0.55
1	1	1	1	1	1	1	0	0	1	63.882	0.6
1	1	1	1	1	1	1	0	0	1	70.522	0.65
1	1	1	1	1	1	1	0	0	1	77.162	0.7
1	1	1	1	1	1	1	0	0	1	83.801	0.75
1	1	1	1	1	1	1	0	0	1	90.441	0.8
1	1	1	1	1	1	1	0	0	1	97.081	0.85
1	1	1	1	1	1	1	0	0	1	103.72	0.9
1	1	1	1	1	1	1	0	0	1	110.36	0.95
1	1	1	1	1	1	1	0	0	1	117	1

Figure 2. Efficient portfolios produced by exhaustive search

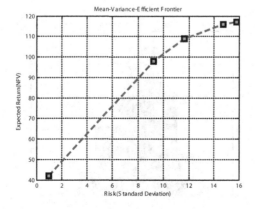

Figure 3. The normal distribution of project 3 likely returns (1000 samples)

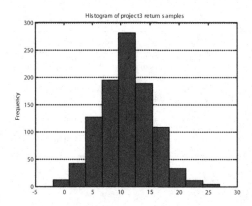

Figure 4. The gamma distribution of project 5 likely returns (1000 samples)

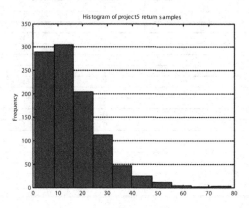

Figure 5. The poisson distribution of project 7 likely returns (1000 samples)

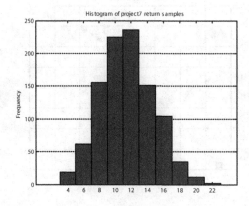

Figure 6. The exponential distribution of project 10 likely returns (1000 samples)

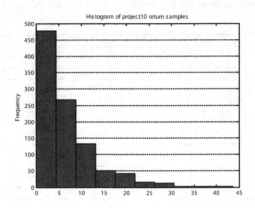

Table 3. Statistics of the simulation process displayed in Fig.7

Statistics	Forecasts
Trials	3,800
Mean	15.05
Median	15.29
Standard Deviation	3.79
Skewness	-0.4299
Kurtosis	2.6
Minimum	4.90
Maximum	21.84
95% Confidence Interval	[14.93,15.17]

Figure 7. Simulation forecast for a portfolio risk

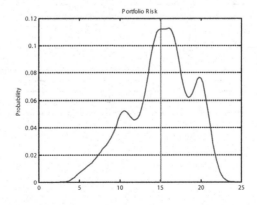

Table 4. Selected projects generated by Monte Carlo simulation. The decision variables are assumed to follow the standard uniform distribution on the interval [0,1]. Number of trials: 200.

Pr.1	Pr.2	Pr.3	Pr.4	Pr.5	Pr.6	Pr.7	Pr.8	Pr.9	Pr.10	Obj. Func.	Parameter α
0	0	0	0	0	1	0	0	1	0	0.96468	0
0	1	0	0	0	1	0	0	1	0	-0.17195	0.05
0	1	0	0	0	1	0	1	1	0	-1.7676	0.1
0	1	1	1	1	0	1	1	1	0	-6.4063	0.15
0	1	1	1	0	1	1	1	1	1	-11.921	0.2
1	1	1	1	1	0	1	0	1	1	-18.04	0.25
1	1	1	1	1	0	1	0	1	1	-24.504	0.3
1	1	1	1	1	0	1	1	0	1	-31.026	0.35
1	1	1	1	1	0	1	1	0	1	-37.563	0.4
1	1	1	1	1	0	1	1	0	1	-44.099	0.45
1	1	1	1	1	0	1	1	0	1	-50.636	0.5
1	1	1	1	1	0	1	1	0	1	-57.172	0.55
1	1	1	1	1	0	1	1	0	1	-63.708	0.6
1	1	1	1	1	0	1	1	0	1	-70.245	0.65
1	1	1	1	1	0	1	1	0	1	-76.781	0.7
1	1	1	1	1	0	1	1	0	1	-83.318	0.75
1	1	1	1	1	0	1	1	0	1	-89.854	0.8
1	1	1	1	1	0	1	1	0	1	-96.391	0.85
1	1	1	1	1	0	1	1	0	1	-102.93	0.9
1	1	1	1	1	0	1	1	0	1	-109.46	0.95
1	1	1	1	1	0	1	1	0	1	-116	1

Table 5. Selected projects generated by Monte Carlo simulation. The decision variables are assumed to follow the standard uniform distribution on the interval [0,1]. Number of trials: 800.

Pr.1	Pr.2	Pr.3	Pr.4	Pr.5	Pr.6	Pr.7	Pr.8	Pr.9	Pr.10	Obj. Func.	Parameter α
0	1	0	0	1	0	0	1	1	0	0.95957	0
0	1	0	0	1	0	0	1	1	0	-1.1884	0.05
0	1	0	0	1	0	0	1	1	0	-3.3364	0.1
0	1	1	1	1	1	1	1	1	0	-6.8536	0.15
0	1	1	1	1	0	1	1	1	1	-12.484	0.2
0	1	1	1	1	0	1	1	1	1	-18.516	0.25
0	1	1	1	1	0	1	1	1	1	-24.549	0.3
1	1	1	1	1	0	1	0	1	1	-30.968	0.35
1	1	1	1	1	0	1	0	1	1	-37.432	0.4
1	1	1	1	1	0	1	0	1	1	-43.896	0.45
1	1	1	1	1	0	1	0	1	1	-50.36	0.5
1	1	1	1	1	0	1	0	1	1	-56.824	0.55
1	1	1	1	1	0	1	0	1	1	-63.288	0.6
1	1	1	1	1	0	1	0	1	1	-69.752	0.65
1	1	1	1	1	0	1	0	1	1	-76.216	0.7
1	1	1	1	1	0	1	0	1	1	-82.68	0.75
1	1	1	1	1	0	1	0	1	1	-89.144	0.8
1	1	1	1	1	0	1	0	1	1	-95.608	0.85
1	1	1	1	1	0	1	0	1	1	-102.07	0.9
1	1	1	1	1	0	1	0	1	1	-108.54	0.95
1	1	1	1	1	0	1	0	1	1	-115	1

Figure 8. Efficient portfolios produced by Monte Carlo simulation. The decision variables are assumed to follow the standard uniform distribution on the interval [0,1]. Number of trials: 200.

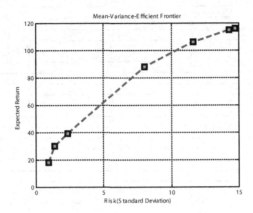

Figure 9. Efficient portfolios produced by Monte Carlo simulation. The decision variables are assumed to follow the standard uniform distribution on the interval [0,1]. Number of trials: 800.

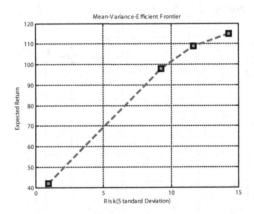

Table 6. Selected projects generated by GA (Generations=100, Population=5)

Pr.1	Pr.2	Pr.3	Pr.4	Pr.5	Pr.6	Pr.7	Pr.8	Pr.9	Pr.10	Fitness Func.	Parameter α
					Chromosomes						
0	0	0	0	1	0	0	1	1	0	-2.6391	0
0	0	0	0	0	1	0	0	1	0	-0.01645	0.05
0	1	1	1	1	1	0	1	1	0	2.2803	0.1
0	0	1	1	0	1	1	1	1	1	4.7264	0.15
1	0	1	1	1	1	1	1	1	0	11.385	0.2
0	1	1	1	1	1	1	1	1	0	17.577	0.25
1	1	0	1	0	1	0	1	1	1	20.131	0.3
1	1	0	1	1	0	1	1	1	1	29.856	0.35
1	1	0	1	1	1	1	1	0	1	36.654	0.4
0	1	1	1	1	0	1	1	1	1	42.645	0.45
1	1	1	0	1	1	0	1	0	1	39.025	0.5
1	1	1	1	0	0	1	1	1	1	54.89	0.55
1	1	1	1	0	0	1	1	1	1	61.124	0.6
0	1	1	0	1	1	1	1	1	1	61.85	0.65
0	1	1	1	1	0	1	1	1	1	72.807	0.7
1	0	1	1	1	1	1	0	1	1	81.136	0.75
1	0	1	1	1	0	1	1	1	1	86.815	0.8
1	1	1	1	0	0	1	1	1	1	92.297	0.85
1	1	0	1	1	1	1	0	1	1	101.04	0.9
1	1	1	1	1	1	0	1	0	1	102.86	0.95
1	0	1	1	0	1	1	0	1	1	100	1

Table 7. Selected projects generated by GA (Generations=60, Population=15).

Pr.1	Pr.2	Pr.3	Pr.4	Pr.5	Pr.6	Pr.7	Pr.8	Pr.9	Pr.10	Fitness Func.	Parameter α
				Chromosomes							
0	1	0	0	1	0	0	0	1	0	-1.51	0
0	1	1	0	0	0	1	0	1	0	-1.0281	0.05
0	1	0	0	1	0	0	1	1	0	3.3364	0.1
1	1	1	1	1	1	0	1	1	0	6.8236	0.15
0	1	1	1	1	1	0	1	1	1	12.201	0.2
0	1	1	1	1	1	1	0	1	1	18.096	0.25
0	1	1	1	1	1	1	1	0	1	24.234	0.3
1	1	1	1	1	1	1	0	0	1	30.684	0.35
1	1	1	1	1	0	1	1	0	1	37.563	0.4
1	1	1	1	1	0	1	0	1	1	43.896	0.45
1	1	1	1	1	0	1	1	0	1	50.636	0.5
1	1	1	1	0	1	1	1	0	1	57.172	0.55
1	1	1	1	1	1	1	0	0	1	63.882	0.6
1	1	1	1	1	1	1	0	0	1	70.522	0.65
1	0	1	1	1	0	1	1	1	1	74.222	0.7
1	1	1	1	1	0	1	1	0	1	83.318	0.75
1	0	1	1	1	1	1	1	0	1	88.193	0.8
1	1	1	1	1	1	1	0	0	1	97.081	0.85
1	1	1	1	1	1	1	0	0	1	103.72	0.9
1	1	0	1	1	1	1	1	0	1	108.47	0.95
1	1	0	1	1	1	1	1	0	1	115	1

Figure 10. Efficient portfolios produced by GA (Generations=100, Population=5).

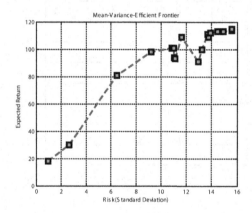

Figure 11. Efficient portfolios produced by GA (Generations=60, Population=15).

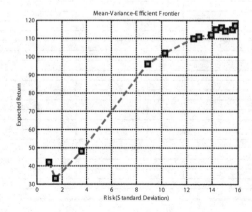

Table 8. Clustering result

Vector	NPV	Risk	Cluster	Representative project
1	15	3.6	1	1
2	12	2.1	2	2
3	11	4.5	2	
4	18	3.9	3	4
7	17	5.1	3	
5	13	2.5	4	5
6	10	1.8	5	6
8	9	1.8	5	
9	8	2.3	6	9
10	21	3.9	7	10

Figure 12. The candidate solutions indicated by clustering. The symbol # can take any of the two digits 0 and 1.

Pr.1	Pr.2	Pr.3	Pr.4	Pr.5	Pr.6	Pr.7	Pr.8	Pr.9	Pr.10
#	#	0	#	#	#	0	0	#	#

Table 9. Selected projects generated by cluster analysis and exhaustive search

Pr.1	Pr.2	Pr.3	Pr.4	Pr.5	Pr.6	Pr.7	Pr.8	Pr.9	Pr.10	Obj. Func.	Parameter α
0	0	0	0	0	1	0	0	1	0	0.96468	0
0	1	0	0	1	0	0	0	1	0	0.21551	0.05
0	1	0	0	1	0	0	0	1	0	1.941	0.1
0	1	0	0	1	1	0	0	1	1	4.3191	0.15
1	1	0	1	1	1	0	0	1	1	9.7068	0.2
1	1	0	1	1	1	0	0	1	1	15.163	0.25
1	1	0	1	1	1	0	0	1	1	20.618	0.3
1	1	0	1	1	1	0	0	1	1	26.074	0.35
1	1	0	1	1	1	0	0	1	1	31.53	0.4
1	1	0	1	1	1	0	0	1	1	36.986	0.45
1	1	0	1	1	1	0	0	1	1	42.442	0.5
1	1	0	1	1	1	0	0	1	1	47.898	0.55
1	1	0	1	1	1	0	0	1	1	53.353	0.6
1	1	0	1	1	1	0	0	1	1	58.809	0.65
1	1	0	1	1	1	0	0	1	1	64.265	0.7
1	1	0	1	1	1	0	0	1	1	69.721	0.75
1	1	0	1	1	1	0	0	1	1	75.177	0.8
1	1	0	1	1	1	0	0	1	1	80.633	0.85
1	1	0	1	1	1	0	0	1	1	86.088	0.9
1	1	0	1	1	1	0	0	1	1	91.544	0.95
1	1	0	1	1	1	0	0	1	1	97	1

Figure 13. Efficient portfolios produced by cluster analysis and exhaustive search

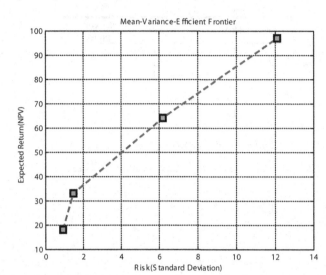

Figure 14. Projects 4 and 7 are more similar than project 1

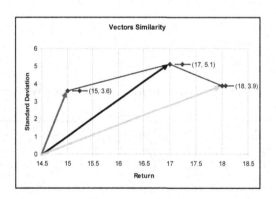

Table 10. The similarity matrix of the project vectors

Similarities										
1	0.3536	0.5085	0.7819	0.5833	0.1683	0.3981	0.1298	0.1686	0.4127
0.3536	1	0.1177	0.1298	0.9209	0.8801	0.0203	0.7819	0.6748	0.0447
0.5085	0.1177	1	0.2747	0.2093	0.0671	0.3737	0.0625	0.1366	0.0822
0.7819	0.1298	0.2747	1	0.2694	0.0435	0.5755	0.0291	0.0366	0.8081
0.5833	0.9209	0.2093	0.2694	1	0.6750	0.0572	0.5720	0.5453	0.1070
0.1683	0.8801	0.0671	0.0435	0.6750	1	0.0057	0.9766	0.8299	0.0113
0.3981	0.0203	0.3737	0.5755	0.0572	0.0057	1	0.0040	0.0083	0.4035
0.1298	0.7819	0.0625	0.0291	0.5720	0.9766	0.0040	1	0.8909	0.0066
0.1686	0.6748	0.1366	0.0366	0.5453	0.8299	0.0083	0.8909	1	0.0072
0.4127	0.0447	0.0822	0.8081	0.1070	0.0113	0.4035	0.0066	0.0072	1

Table 11. Selected projects generated by Cluster Analysis and Exhaustive Search. In place of correlation matrix, the similarity matrix of project vectors is used.

Pr.1	Pr.2	Pr.3	Pr.4	Pr.5	Pr.6	Pr.7	Pr.8	Pr.9	Pr.10	Obj. Func.	Parameter α
0	1	0	0	0	1	0	0	0	0	3.782	0
0	1	0	0	0	1	0	0	0	0	2.4929	0.05
0	1	0	0	0	1	0	0	0	1	0.66263	0.1
0	1	0	1	1	1	0	0	1	1	2.6832	0.15
1	1	0	1	1	1	0	0	1	1	8.2193	0.2
1	1	0	1	1	1	0	0	1	1	13.768	0.25
1	1	0	1	1	1	0	0	1	1	19.317	0.3
1	1	0	1	1	1	0	0	1	1	24.866	0.35
1	1	0	1	1	1	0	0	1	1	30.414	0.4
1	1	0	1	1	1	0	0	1	1	35.963	0.45
1	1	0	1	1	1	0	0	1	1	41.512	0.5
1	1	0	1	1	1	0	0	1	1	47.061	0.55
1	1	0	1	1	1	0	0	1	1	52.61	0.6
1	1	0	1	1	1	0	0	1	1	58.158	0.65
1	1	0	1	1	1	0	0	1	1	63.707	0.7
1	1	0	1	1	1	0	0	1	1	69.256	0.75
1	1	0	1	1	1	0	0	1	1	74.805	0.8
1	1	0	1	1	1	0	0	1	1	80.354	0.85
1	1	0	1	1	1	0	0	1	1	85.902	0.9
1	1	0	1	1	1	0	0	1	1	91.451	0.95
1	1	0	1	1	1	0	0	1	1	97	1

Figure 15. Efficient portfolios produced by Cluster Analysis and Exhaustive Search. In place of correlation matrix, the similarity matrix of project vectors is used.

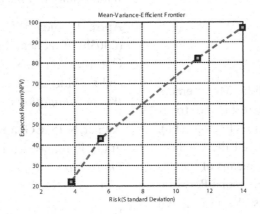

reduce the problem complexity in reasonable size (the algorithm identifies the projects that could significantly contribute to the efficient frontier generation) and a heuristic application secondly to discover the range of possible solutions among the most representative projects extracted in the previous phase.

FUTURE TRENDS

The testing of simulation and meta-heuristics establish their ability to cope effectively with the inherent difficulties of the Mean-Variance application and more particularly, when this is applied in Project Portfolio Selection problems. The complexities and uncertainties in real world conditions are the primary reason that simulation is often chosen as a basis for handling the decision problems. Yet, when the number of projects becomes high, the simulation alone is insufficient to identify the optimal solution; the use of simulation, cluster analysis and heuristic optimization exhibits a noteworthy evidence for a successful combination.

CONCLUSION

Information Technology Portfolio Management (ITPM) is a topic of intense interest in the strategic management of Information Technology (IT). In this work, we have considered the business strategy to be incorporated by means of the application of the principles of Financial Portfolio Management to IT investments. We have shown that the Modern Portfolio Theory can be applied acceptably in ITPM while informing the reader about the necessary modifications, considerations and limitations of this theory.

In order to tackle the inherent complexities of IT Portfolio Optimization Problem, we have experimented with some meta-heuristic techniques and have demonstrated their suitability

by solving a numerical project selection problem as an example.

Finally, the scope of this study was to convince the reader about the principles of IT portfolio management which has proved to be a significant tool for the decision making improvement, providing a controllable framework for handling uncertainty and for justifying enterprise reasoning.

REFERENCES

Aitken, I. (2003). *Value-driven IT management.* Computer Weekly: Professional Series. Oxford, Butterworth-Heinemann.

Anthony, R. N. (1965). *Planning and Control Systems: A Framework for Analysis.* Graduate School of Business, Harvard University.

April, J., Glover, F., & Kelly, J. (2003a). Optfolio-A Simulation Optimization System for Project Portfolio Planning. In S. Chick, T. Sanchez, D. Ferrin & D. Morrice (Ed.), *Proceedings of the 2003 Winter Simulation Conference* (pp. 301-309).

April, J., Glover, F., Kelly, J., & Laguna, M., (2003b). Practical Introduction to Simulation Optimization. In S. Chick, T. Sanchez, D. Ferrin and D. Morrice, (Ed.), *Proceedings of the 2003 Winter Simulation Conference* (pp. 71-78).

Archer, N. P., & Ghasemzadeh, F. (1999). An Integrated Framework for Project Portfolio Selection. *International Journal of Project Management,* 17(4), 207-216.

Barney, L. D., & Danielson, M. (2004). Ranking Mutually Exclusive Projects: The Role of Duration. *The Engineering Economist, 49,* 43-61.

Benaroch, M., (2002). Managing Information technology Investment Risk: A Real Options Perspective. *Journal of Management Information Systems, 19*(2), 43-84.

Benson, R. J., Bugnitz, T., & Walton, B., (2004). *From business strategy to IT action: right decisions for a better bottom line.* Hoboken, N.J., Wiley.

Blum, C., & Roli, A., (2003). Metaheuristics in combinatorial optimization: Overview and conceptual comparison. *ACM Computing Surveys, 35*(3), 268–308.

Bonham, S. S. (2005). *IT Project Portfolio Management.* Norwood, MA: Artech House.

Clemons, E. K. (1991). Evaluating strategic investments in information systems. *Communications of the ACM, 34,* 22–36.

Dai, Q., Kauffman, R. J., & March, S. T. (2004). Valuing IT middleware infrastructure with real options. Working paper, *Carlson School of Management, University of Minnesota,* Minneapolis.

Davis, L. (1987). *Genetic Algorithms and Simulated Annealing.* London: Pitman.

Doerner, K., Gutjahr, W. J., Hartl, R. F., Strauss, C., & Stummer, C., (2002). *Pareto Ant Colony Optimization: A metaheuristic approach to multiobjective portfolio selection.* Kluwer Academic Publishers, Printed in the Netherlands.

Elton, E. J., Gruber, M. J., & Padberg, W., (1976). Simple Criteria for Optimal Portfolio Selection. *The Journal of Finance, 31*(5), 1341-1357.

Garey, M., & Johnson, D., (1979). *Computers and Intractability: A Guide to the Theory of NP-Completeness.* San Francisco: H.W. Freeman & Company.

Gibson, C. F., & Nolan, R. L., (1974). Managing the Four Stages of EDP Growth. *Harvard Business Review, 52*(1), 76-88.

Glover, F., & Laguna, M., (1997). *Tabu Search,* Kluwer Academic Publishers, Boston.

Glover, F., Laguna, M., & Marti, R. (2003). Scatter Search. *Advances in Evolutionary Computing: Theory and Applications.* New York Springer-Verlag, (pp. 519-537).

Goldberg, D. E. (1989). *Genetic algorithms in search, optimization and machine learning.* New York: Addison-Wesley.

Goldman, C. (1999). Align Drive–Expert Advice. *CIO Magazine,* January, 5.

Harder, P. (2002). *A Conversation with Dr. Harry Markowitz,* Retrieved by Gantthead.com.

Holland, J. H. (1975). *Adaptation in natural and artificial systems: an introductory analysis with applications to biology, control and artificial intelligence.* University of Michigan Press.

Hoos, H. H., & Stützle, T. (2004). *Stochastic Local Search: Foundations and Applications.* Elsevier/Morgan Kaufmann, San Francisco, CA.

Jagannathan, R., & Ma, T. (2003). Risk Reduction in Large Portfolios: Why Imposing the Wrong Constraints Helps. *The Journal of Finance, 58*(4), 1651–1638.

Jeffery, M., & Leliveld, I., (2003). Best Practices in IT Portfolio Management. *Sloan Management Review,* 45.

Kaplan, J. D. (2005). *Strategic IT portfolio management: Governing enterprise transformation.* Pittiglio Rabin Todd & McGrath (PRTM), Inc.

Kelton, W. D., & Law, A., (1991). *Simulation Modeling & Analysis.* New York: McGraw Hill, Inc.

Kersten, B., & Verhoef, C., (2003). IT Portfolio Management: A Banker's Perspective on IT. *Cutter IT Journal, 16*(4), 34-40.

Konno, H., & Yamazaki, H., (1991). Mean-Absolute Deviation Portfolio Optimization Model and its Applications to Tokyo Stock Market. *Management Science, 37*(5), 519-531.

Kwak, Y. H., & Ibbs, C.W., (2000). Assessing Organization's Project Management Maturity. *Project Management Journal, 5*, 32-43.

Linenberg, Y., Stadlker, Z., & Arbuthnot, S., (2003). Optimising Organisational Performance by Managing Project Benefits. *PMI Global Congress 2003*, Europe.

Markowitz, H. (1952). Portfolio selection. *Journal of Finance, 7*, 77-91.

Markowitz, H. (1959). *Portfolio Selection, Efficient Diversification of Investment.* (2nd edition in 1991), Basil Blackwell, New York.

McFarlan, F. W. (1981, Sept-Oct). Portfolio approach to information systems. *Harvard Business Review*, 142-150.

McGrath, G. R., & Macmillan, I. C. (2000). Assessing Technology Projects Using Real Options Reasoning. *Research Technology Management, 43*(4), 35–49.

Medaglia, A. L., Graves, S. B., & Ringuest, J. L. (2007). A multiobjective evolutionary approach for linearly constrained project selection under uncertainty. *European Journal of Operational Research, 179*(3), 869-894.

Moskowitz, K., & Kern, H. (2003). *Managing IT as an Investment.* Prentice Hall.

Muralidhar, K., Santhanam, R., & Schniederjans, M., (1988). An optimization model for information system project selection. *Journal of Management Science and Policy Analysis, 6*(1), 53–62.

Oesterle, H. (1991). Generating Business Ideas Based on Information Technology. In Clarke R. & Cameron J. (Ed.), *Managing Information Technology's Organisational Impact II.* Elsevier/North-Holland, Amsterdam.

Petridis, V., & Syrris, V., (2007). Machine Learning Techniques for Environmental Data Estimation. In V. G. Kaburlasos, &G. X. Ritter (Ed.), *Computational Intelligence Based on Lattice Theory* (pp. 195-214).

Rachev, S. T., Ortobelli, S., & Schwartz, E. (2004). The Problem of Optimal Asset Allocation with Stable Distributed Returns. In Krinik, A., & Swift, R. J. (Ed.), *Stochastic Processes and Functional Analysis. Dekker Series of Lecture Notes in Pure and Applied Mathematics* (pp. 295–361).

Rosser, B. & Potter, K., (2001). *IT Portfolio Management and Survey Results.* Stamford, CT: Gartner Research.

Santhanam, R., & Kyparisis, G. J., (1995). A multiple criteria decision model for information system project selection. *Computers and Operations Research, 22*(8), 807–818.

Schniederjans, M., & Santhanam, R., (1993). A multi-objective constrained resource information system project selection method. *European Journal of Operational Research, 70*(2), 244–253.

Strassmann, P. A. (1990). The Business Value of Computers-An Executive's Guide. *The Information Economics Press.* Connecticut, USA: New Canaan,

Syrris, V., & Petridis, V. (2008). Classification through Hierarchical Clustering and Dimensionality Reduction. *IEEE World Congress on Computational Intelligence*, Hong Kong.

Tate, P. (1999, Dec 98-Jan 99). The Big Spenders. *Information Strategy*, 30-37.

TechRepublic & Smith, T. (2000). *IT Project Management Research Findings.* Louiville, KY: TechRepublic.

Walter, J., Gutjahr, S. K., & Reiter, P. (2007). A VNS Algorithm for Noisy Problems and Its Application to Project Portfolio Analysis. In J. Hromkovic et al. (Ed.), *Lecture Notes in Computer Science, Stochastic Algorithms: Foundations and*

Applications 4665 (pp. 93-104), Springer-Verlag Berlin/Heidelberg.

Weill, P., & Broadbent, M. (1998). *Leveraging the New Infrastructure: How Market Leaders Capitalize on Information Technology.* Cambridge, MA, Harvard Business School Press.

Winston, W. (2000). *Financial Models Using Simulation and Optimization: A Step-By-Step Guide With Excel and Palisade's Decision tools Software.* Palisade.

Zhu, K., & Weyant, J. P. (2003). Strategic decisions of new technology adoption under asymmetric information: A game-theoretic model. *Decision Sciences, 34*(4), 643–675.

ENDNOTES

[1] Structure of IT activities defined by Anthony (1965): strategic planning, management control and operational control.

[2] Projects are crucial to organization growth as they are investments for the future.

[3] In bibliography, the projects selection problem can be found also as project prioritisation or project portfolio optimization.

[4] The optimality could not be proven.

[5] What an organization is trying to achieve and how it plans to achieve it.

[6] In this context, the term risk is associated with the uncertainty being enclosed in the future course of investments. In Markowitz model this type of risk is considered controllable in contrary with the market risk which is affected by exogenous factors.

[7] It has been shown that Mean-Variance is not an appropriate risk measure for a portfolio, and in practice, Mean-Variance efficient portfolios have been found to be quite unstable (April et al., 2003a, 2003b). Also, there is evidence showing the absence of correlations between any kind of return and the intensity of IT investments. There are companies -in the same enterprise branch- each spending about the same on IT, of which the one makes high profits, and the other makes huge losses (Strassmann, 1990; Tate, 1999).

[8] Some indicative references: (Benaroch, 2002; Clemons, 1991; Dai et al. 2004; McGrath & MacMillan, 2000; Zhu & Weyant, 2003).

[9] Stakeholders are the people involved in or affected by project activities and include the project sponsors, executives, project team, support staff, customers, users, suppliers. These stakeholders often have very different needs and expectations.

[10] Risk and return preserve a linear relationship for the investor, that is, he/she expects a high benefit from a high risk investment and vice-versa.

[11] The more general definition of cardinality constraint could be:

$$k_l \le \sum_{i=1}^{n} w_i \le k_u,$$

where $2 \le k_l \le k_u \le n$, k_l is the lower cardinality bound and k_u is the upper cardinality bound.

[12] The set of all the legal solutions.

[13] It keeps on containing sufficient information that characterizes the initial sample space.

[14] The number of bits that differ between two binary sequences:

$$\sum_{i=1}^{n} |x_i - y_i|, x_i, y_i \in \{0,1\}$$

Chapter VIII
Strategic IT Portfolio Management for Development of Innovative Competences

Dejan Petrović
University of Belgrade, Serbia

Marko Mihić
University of Belgrade, Serbia

Biljana Stošić
University of Belgrade, Serbia

ABSTRACT

This chapter presents the concept of strategic information technology portfolio management for development of innovation competences in a project-oriented company. It is a specific type of portfolio management, called project portfolio management. The chapter begins with a strategic basis of project-oriented company, links it to the modern portfolio theory and then expands it into the IT project portfolio management (IT PPM). The role of the IT PPM is to ensure that the group of IT projects supports the achievement of the goals of the corporate strategy. The chapter takes into consideration the key aspects of IT – innovation relationship, and introduces the organizational support to the IT PPM – the Portfolio Management Office. An established PMO that is actively supported at the executive level can help solve problems with project auditing and initiative approval.

INTRODUCTION

The market is constantly forcing the product or service line to change. Extremely dynamic technology changes bringing radical innovations with domination of information technology (IT), are said to have produced new and almost entirely different means of communication and doing business, especially having in mind e-business and Internet. Together with globalization processes, the *high-tech* reality and *information society* coming from the end of the 20th century gained the powerful possibility to create new industries and to transform the existing ones. Such pressures to decrease the life cycle and increase the quality of products and services directly affected how the executives want from IT to improve the efficiencies of their units. Also, today executives want to have tools that would help them to prioritize the projects so they would know which ones were healthy contributors to the corporate strategy and which ones could be cancelled. Today market is slowing down, and they want to centralize corporate governance and cut unnecessary IT projects. They also knew that some IT projects are critical to the growth and ongoing operations of the company, and they couldn't simply eliminate any project.

This paper presents the concept of strategic information technology portfolio management for development of innovation competences, which are said to be the key driver of a long-term competitiveness, profitability and business success of the company, national and global economy. In European Commission's Green Paper on Innovation (1995), innovation is defined as the renewal and enlargement of the range of products and services and the associated markets; the establishment of new methods of production, supply and distribution; the introduction of changes in management, work organization, and the working conditions and skills of the workforce. In that sense, the relation between strategic information technology portfolio management and innovative

competencies should be aimed at development and improvement of the capability of the firm to innovate - create new products, services, processes, organization, marketing, i.e. to manage innovation process from idea to implementation and achieving market superiority. Information technology portfolio management is examined in a project-oriented company and because of that paper presents project portfolio management as a specific type of portfolio management.

BACKGROUND: STRATEGIC BASIS OF PROJECT-ORIENTED COMPANY

Generally, strategy is defined as a means to achieve individual or organizational goals (Grant, 2007). In this definition, *means* is defined as a plan or policy determining concrete actions. Ansoff (2007) finds that, regardless of the complexity of the managerial problem, it is possible to identify a number of strategic variables that will determine the solution to this problem. According to him, strategy means a set of decision rules as well as guide to achieve organizational goals in the future (Ansoff, 1987). On the other hand, Porter (1996) maintains that the essence of the strategy is a clever selection of varied sets of activities that will ensure a unique combination of values for the organization. In other words, the basis of the strategy is a difference in comparison to the competitors. Chandler (1962) defines strategy as a process of determining the long-term goals of the company, defining the direction of activities and allocating resources necessary in achieving these goals. The definition is supported by Grant's (1991) attitude that strategy is the choice the organization makes between the resources and competence on one hand and opportunities and differences in the environment, on the other.

Globalization, the technological development and the geopolitical changes in this century call for the change in the organization's strategic orientation as well. Growth in profits, as one of the basic goals, is being exchanged for the growth in value for the shareholders, for the respect for the business ethics and for the establishment of the socially responsible business (Smith, 2003). The turbulent and unpredictable development of technology has also had an impact upon a fierce competition in certain markets, such as e-trade, where the winner captures the entire or a major share of the market (e.g. eBay in the Internet auctions).

In answer to these challenges it is necessary that such a management system in the organization be defined that will pool the needs for change in the form of a different number and size of projects and programmes to be realized as well as the strategy these projects are comprised in. By applying the concept of the project-oriented organization as a frame for such a management system, if it is supported by an appropriate organization, team work and project culture, it is possible to achieve a substantial improvement in the business results.

The project-oriented company can be defined as a business entity that conducts its activities on the principle of the project organization of work, implementing contemporary achievements of project management, i.e., using programme management or project management (Mihić & Petrović, 2004). The organization and processes executed by the project-oriented company (POC) are characterised by a complex structure, by the dynamics reflected in constant changes in the number and size of the programmes and projects, by flexibility, as well as by a large number of permanently or temporarily employed participants.

The basic features of the project-oriented organization may be listed as follows (Gareis, 2003):

The project-oriented organization

- takes project management as its strategy;
- uses temporary organization to perform complex processes and activities;
- has a separate permanent organization that functions as integrator;
- manages a project portfolio consisting of different types of projects;
- implements a new management paradigm;
- is characterised a specific project culture;
- considers itself as project-oriented.

Basically, the project-oriented company uses the concept of project management. According to Loo (1996), project management is a new management approach since the projects:

- are focused upon results,
- require efficient leadership,
- are a meeting point of different stakeholders in the company,
- serve as a synergy factor uniting multidisciplinary teams towards a defined goal, with definite time and resource limitations,
- are the basis for individual development within the team,
- serve as a team membership enhancing factor.

On the other hand, in their detailed research on PM processes, technologies and skills that in which they explored over 3,500 articles, journals and reports, Kloppenborg and Opfer (2002) defined the following trends related to the project management evolution:

- standardization of processes and tools,
- broader use of Web-based technologies for corporate communication and collaboration,
- implementation of generally accepted PM practices and methodologies,
- clear „outsourcing" in the execution of the projects of the largest companies,
- larger share in the non-profit sector projects,
- evolution of project manager's role into a leader's role,

- adjusting the project scope to the demands of business and measurable benefits,
- increasing importance of project selection and prioritization,
- stress on formal PM trainings and accreditation,
- increasing focus upon risk management, communications management and stakeholder management, especially in the planning phase.

Webster (1999) states that in the conditions of temporary organizational structures and an ever present scarcity of resources, today's organizations recognize project management as a method to achieve an adequate system flexibility and the desired business results. This attitude is supported by Hebert (2002), who views project management as a flexible, efficient and strategic *management system* to achieve planned results in the traditional management structures. Similarly, he maintains that the present role of project managers is primarily strategic (50%), then managerial (40%) and in the least technical (10%). These views are shared by Cicmil (1997), who thinks that project managers should reposition the role of project management from the medium and operative management discipline into a business philosophy whose task is to support strategic organizational change in the company.

Project management is therefore no longer viewed as an approach to planning and monitoring a project, but rather as a way to achieve the company's strategic goals in a new business environment. This means implementation of modern PM disciplines that stress the strategic aspect of project management. The company in which project management is pronounced to be strategically important is defined as project-oriented company.

The boundaries and contents of a project-oriented company are changing in character (Gareis, 2003). This is reflected, on one hand, in constant changes in the number and size of projects, in the engagement of temporary or permanent resources and in the use of virtual teams for the tasks of coordination and management. On the other hand, relations are established with various strategic partners, so that the projects and programmes are realized in the conditions of different social environments to which the company has to adapt. In order to adequately respond to challenge that takes on the character of project-oriented enterprise, it is necessary that a unique identity of the company be defined, however, it should be flexible enough not to endanger the company's dynamic character.

When analysing the project-oriented organization strategy, we must by all means take into consideration the Hamel and Prahalad's (1989) research, in which they challenge the conventional approach to adjusting the company's capacity to the demands of the environment. According to the research, less successful companies try to realize their strategic intentions within the resources available. They support the attitude that the strategic balance and sustainable competitive advantage are achieved by implementing one of the available generic strategies. Such an approach results in repetition and imitation. On the other hand, the most successful companies focus upon using key competences in a new and innovative way, in order to achieve the goals that at first sight seem unattainable. The resources are used in a creative way, different demands are put to the environment, while the company continually improves key competences and undertakes organizational change. It is these features that make the strategic basis of the project-oriented company. Its key project management competences are functional in the realisation of strategic intentions.

Creating the project portfolio, which is the first step towards taking action is considered to be a most important element of the project-oriented organization strategy. The aim of linking the strategy to the project portfolio is to bring into accord the project and the priorities with the defined strategy and strategic priorities (Killen,

Hunt, & Kleinschmidt, 2008). This is primarily important in adjusting the portfolio size to the company's capacity and presenting the projects in the portfolio as key events in the process of achieving a desired future state.

In the context of the project-oriented company, the project portfolio is viewed as a set of projects a company executes in a given period of time (Jovanović, Mihić, & Petrović, 2007). To this group belong research projects, development projects, work processes improvement projects, IT projects, cost reduction projects, product and services improvement projects, projects for ordering parties, etc.

The portfolio management is critical for the success of the project-oriented company. It covers areas such as project selection, project prioritization, resources allocation and the company's business strategy implementation. Thus it has to answer the following questions (Cooper, Edgett, & Kleinschmidt, 1998):

- Which projects should be realized?
- How should projects be most efficiently organized as regards achieving desired goals?
- Which is the right relationship between projects?
- Which project mix can give best results?
- Which projects are of highest priority?
- How should resources be distributed among different projects?

The project portfolio forming process is necessary in order that the right projects should have a chance to be realized (Mikkola, 2001). The company must first identify the possibilities, estimate its organizational adjustment, analyse costs, benefits and risk, and finally, develop and select the portfolio. Every company must undergo this process if it seeks to create an appropriate project mix. The methods and techniques used may differ according to the maturity of the company, project types and the experience in forming the project mix. The project portfolio management is an important factor of a long-term strategic success of project-oriented companies.

IT PORTFOLIO IN PROJECT-ORIENTED COMPANY

The task of the IT project portfolio management is to ensure a consistent approach to the classification, selection, prioritization and planning of the right IT projects and programmes in the company (Reyck, Grushka-Cockayne, Lockett, Calderini, Moura, & Sloper, 2005). The aims of IT project portfolio management are as follows:

- Optimization of IT project portfolio results (not an individual project or portfolio);
- Harmonization of IT projects and programmes with the company's strategy;
- Selection of IT projects and programmes to be realized;
- Defining IT projects and programmes priorities;
- Discontinuing or stopping IT projects or programmes;
- Coordination of internal and external resources for IT projects and programmes; and
- Organizational learning between IT projects and programmes.

An efficient realisation of an IT project is said to be a key factor of the company's business success. This is, however, only partly true. The achived competitive advantage is not the result of efficient work on a project only. The fact that companies conduct real IT projects is important. IT project portfolio management is meant to ensure a successful execution of the company's strategy through the most effective and most efficient execution of respective IT projects possible (Verhoef, 2002). It is closely related to the role of the top management in the company and with the key decision makers in creating the environment in which set goals can be achieved.

According to Cooper, Edgett and Kleinschmidt (1997), works dealing with the issues of project portfolio have appeared since 1970. In these works, elements such as "selection of research-developmental projects", "resource allocation in research-developmental projects", "project prioritization"and "portfolio management" are analysed.

The majority of works on this topic deal with the problem of portfolio management by defining the optimization methods and techniques (Cooper, Edgett, & Kleinschmidt, 1998). According to these works, the portfolio management problem appears to be a limited optimization in the conditions of uncertainty: multiproject and multilevel model of decision making should be achieved by means of mathematical programming. The starting models for the selection of projects were mathematically oriented and they used techniques such as linear, dynamic and full number programming. The aim was to develop a portfolio of new and existing projects to maximize some function goals (e.g., the expected profit) as the issue of setting resource limitation.

The application of these methods immediately revealed some difficulties in solving the problems of IT portfolio management (Verhoef, 2002). Contrary to the many methods developed in an early stage of the approach to this problem, none of these could be adequately implemented in the IT project portfolio management.

The IT projects are recognized as a vital fact for any company. The influence of the IT projects upon the future of any company is certainly strong since they are related to all the important events and processes in the company, be it the development of a new product, the implementation of a new service process, the change in organizational structure or the launching of a new business (Russell, 2003). The IT project portfolio is a collection of projects which together with other projects make the strategy of the company's investments.

The project portfolio management means the implementation of knowledge, skills, methods and techniques upon a set of projects in order that the needs and expectations of the company's investment should be attained and even exceeded (Dye & Pennypacker, 1999). This calls for a balance to be made between strategic and tactical requirements. The IT project portfolio management usually requires that a definition should be made of what is possible and what is necessary. Balancing between the possibilities and the needs generally results in finding the best possible solution within limited resources.

There is a gap today between a majority of management models and the environment in which the IT projects are executed. These models emerged in the circumstances in which it was possible to predict the consequences of certain decisions and the project's impact upon the company and the community in general. A successful IT project portfolio in the project environment nowadays is characterised by a number of non-economic features, uses an iterative budgeting process and what appears to be the best decision for an organization may not be viewed as such for all its stakeholders. Today's the IT project environment is much more complex compared to a majority of management models, and such a complexity must be taken into account in defining „the best" IT project portfolio to be executed.

The IT project portfolio management focuses upon a clear definition of the values the projects bring to the company (Kaplan, 2001). The IT project portfolio management is applied to all projects, to making decisions as regards the selection and prioritization, which is in accord with the strategic goals and the development of the company.

Alongside decision making on the IT projects execution within a portfolio, there is another process of the final approval of the very beginning and of some specific phases in the IT project execution underway. There certainly must exist a lower level of decision making that takes place in the real time of the IT project execution. Decisions within the IT portfolio are made during the given time intervals, all the projects being discussed together, whereas at a lower level decisions are made on individual IT projects at any moment the project passes from one execution phase into another. All this may cause conflicts between the two levels of decision making, since in decision making processes we most frequently deal with different people, even different criteria.

Decision making at the portfolio level, although taking all the IT projects together and making a comparison among them, does not pay enough attention to individual projects (Levine, 1999). On the other hand, the lower level of decision making focuses upon only one IT project, leaving out all the other IT projects. It is of great importance for the company that these two different decision making processes be integrated and harmonized. The dominance of either of the two is unwelcome in any company.

The weakness of the IT portfolio model appears to be insufficient accuracy or relevance of the facts on the basis of which the processing, the analysis, and the conclusion procedures are conveyed and then a final decision is made. The models used in IT portfolio decision making are by far more advanced compared to the input data. Financial indicators, criteria and the processing and presentation methods themselves may be well created and functional for making the final decision. However, all these calculations and use of the seemingly appropriate criteria may lead to a wrong decision, if the data used are incorrect, inaccurate or unreliable (Morris, 1997). If we wish to enhance the success of an IT portfolio decision making process, we must ensure that we have as high a quality of input data.

In their research Cooper, Edgett and Kleinschmidt (1997) have found that the main problems the companies encounter in the project selection and portfolio management are the following:

1. The project portfolio does not reflect the strategy of the company;
2. The portfolio quality is poor;
3. The checking procedures and the decision making procedures at check points are inefficient;
4. Scarce resources and lack of focus;
5. Simplification of the product development projects.

The issue raised in the companies that apply the project-oriented organization concept is whether the undergoing IT projects should be discontinued or deprioritized in favour of certain better quality projects that we become acquainted with. On one hand, we should try to keep the resources engaged in IT projects flexible and capable of shifting from one project to another, as the need may be. The reason for such an attitude is found in the need that the company's management be granted an opportunity to allocate resources in a best possible way, regardless of their current use. On the other hand, there are attitudes that the resources involved should remain in the project all along, regardless of whether there is a more attractive project in sight. Here the issues of continuity and the morale of the project team and the project manager appear to be considerably more important than an optimal allocation of resources. Such a view resulted from the attitude that discontinuing and restarting the project would mean a substantial loss of resources and time, that a shift from one project to another would by all means affect the projects and that a launch and discontinuation or a final suspension of a project would all need additional time and costs (Wysocki, 2004).

The new IT projects always appear better than those under way, therefore the resources in the projects that are in the final phases are usually transferred as a support to new projects. Such support sometimes results in the projects deprived of resources in this way being never completed (Thomas, 1993). The far-reaching consequences and damages for the company fail to be perceived in that moment.

There is no universal rule on how we should act or set the company policy in such cases (Norton & Kaplan, 2003). It is certain that the long-term IT projects call for a continuity in order that satisfactory results should be obtained. On the other hand, there is a need that the company responds to changes in the market by introducing a flexible model of resources distribution. Many companies find that using only financial methods and criteria in giving priorities to IT projects prove inappropriate. The reasons most frequently lie in the financial simplification, which results into an unreliable image of the project, especially prior to the launching of the project, when the prioritizing is most necessary, but also, during the execution of the project. Analyses carried out upon executions of projects have shown that the evaluations of key parameters on the bases of which decisions are made were significantly incorrect.

Statistical implications of the portfolio choice are complex and varied. They include the analysis of both internal and external factors of the company, the company's market position, the strengths and weaknesses of the company. These analyses may be used to create a wide perspective of strategic directions as well as specific initiatives for achieving competitive advantage (Cleland, 1999). Such a procedure may be used in developing focused goals of the IT project portfolio and determining the necessary resources for its support. In estimating the strategic position of the company a portfolio matrix is used, where the different criteria for the company positioning are presented in one or more graphs within two description dimensions. A decision maker may use such a presentation to estimate the current position as well as the position the company wishes to occupy in the future. It is clear that the company's strategic direction must be defined prior to the analysis of the individual projects for the IT project portfolio. Successful organizations conduct a broad strategy preparation and planning before individual projects are analysed.

Upon determining the strategic direction, it is necessary that IT projects be selected and resources allocated. The IT projects selection includes the identification of opportunities, the estimate of organizational fitting, the cost analysis, the cost and risk analysis, the forming and the selection of the portfolio. The success of the IT project portfolio depends on the readiness and the support of the company's management (Verhoef, 2002). This is more important, sometimes even crucial, than just the selection of the method to be used in project selection.

A periodical review of IT project portfolio is absolutely necessary (Bridges, 1999). This means that each active project should be checked, those on the waiting list as well, and should be compared to another. The aim of this check is to find out whether there is the right set of active projects and whether these projects are still in accord with the strategic goals of the company.

To aid the decision making process it is necessary that general criteria are established, as well as the evaluation of each IT project related to those criteria. Since a majority of decisions are based on multiple factors, it is necessary to evaluate each criterion in order to establish a relative importance of each of them. Thus we could identify what is most important for the company, and every project could be measured as regards the criteria that are defined as important (George et al., 2005).

The company must establish an unbiased mechanism of monitoring and control of IT projects (Reyck, Grushka-Cockayne, Lockett, Calderini, Moura, & Sloper, 2005). Measuring may be based on the revenue from the project in relation to the resources invested; then there is measuring of a number of projects within the project portfolio and a continual adjustment to the overall goals of the company. It is very important that there exists an agreement from the start on the process of authority determination. Only when the company defines its overall goals and the investment strategy into the IT projects, will it be able to create an optimal group of projects or an IT project mix to implement its strategy and achieve goals.

In order to achieve a respective relation between the risk and the extent of revenue from the investment into IT projects, it is necessary that each project be evaluated on the basis of its two characteristics: technical difficulties and added value. The secret of a successful IT project management is in understanding critical relations between the probability of success and the values the project will earn if successful. This provides a good basis for quality decision making on the input portfolio of IT projects.

A majority of portfolio decisions is aggravated by a long time horizon, high level of uncertainty and a large number of variables affecting each project (Ghasemzadeh & Archer, 1999). The tools most commonly used in developing a business model that would predict a potential project value are a learning diagram, a sensitivity analysis and a decision tree.

The purpose of the decisions related to the IT project portfolio is not only the selection of right projects; it is also the inclusion and strengthening of appropriate personalities and their groups who are to realize these decisions efficiently and effectively. Creating an adequate level of participation between cross-functional teams allows for a constructive dialogue between decision makers and those who are in charge of enacting them, which leads to coordination of ultimate actions to be conducted (Englund, Graham, & Dinsmore, 2003).

The portfolio analyses and deals with the future events and possibilities where the majority of information necessary in the selection of projects is at best uncertain, and at worst is largely unreliable. The decision making environment is dynamic, and the status and the perspective of the IT projects in a portfolio constantly change in accordance with the inflow of new information and technologies. The IT projects in a portfolio are in different phases of execution and compete for available resources. However, the comparison among the IT projects is made with varied quantities and reliability of information. The resources distributed among the projects are limited, which is to say that the decision on resource allocation to one project means depriving another project of resources, and the transfer of resources from one project to another usually leaves deep scars.

SELECTION OF IT PROJECT PORTFOLIO

The selection of IT project portfolio is one of the crucial steps in the portfolio management process. It is a periodical activity of choosing one portfolio among the available project propositions and projects which are underway, and which achieve the defined organizational goals in a desired way, without exceeding the resources available or breaking other limitations (Archer & Ghasemzadeh, 1996). IT projects selecting directly guides and adjusts business activities to the strategic guidelines of the company. It is within this process that decisions are made on the future execution of IT projects as well as on any vital aspects of their realization.

By undertaking a proactive approach to the IT project selection and real performance management the companies significantly enhance the achievement of IT project goals as regards time, quality and costs, as well as making sure that these projects will facilitate the overall business success. Using quality principles in decision making on evaluation and management of IT project portfolio profitability and productivity may be significantly improved. The IT projects, however, include factors that account for the complexity in the process of project portfolio harmonization. One of the most important among them is the interaction of the projects within the portfolio

(Mantel & Meredith, 1999). IT projects are not independent, they overlap and are related to each other by depending critically on each other, in different ways.

Although there are numerous methodologies to be used in selecting an IT portfolio, so far the consensus on which one is most effective has not been reached (Reyck, Grushka-Cockayne, Lockett, Calderini, Moura, & Sloper, 2005). As a consequence, every company tends to choose a methodology that corresponds to the existing organizational culture and allows for the analysis of project attributes it considers the most essential.

The conventional methods of measuring IT values, the estimation of what is easily measurable – costs – and the expectation that an automatic cost saving or cost avoiding practice will pay the investment off do not, in fact, represent the real value IT earns to the company. The problem is reflected in the IT professionals' inability to establish a link to the business value of the proposed IT solution which consequently fail to get the manager's support until it is too late. The problem of inadequate communication is often largely based on the fact that IT managers do not have an effective access to the data they need in order to approach the benefits of a certain IT initiative.

Numerous IT managers estimate IT investments solely on the basis of IT costs saving. While this approach is valid in case the critical factors of success are directed towards reducing exploitation costs in time, it may prove problematic when it is necessary to take into consideration the overall value created by an innovative application of information technologies in business (Sommer, 1999; Stošić, 2004).

As a consequence, the strategic role of investments in new IT initiatives that may lead towards new business opportunities for an organization is neither recognized nor measured. One of the key problems in the total cost scenario implementation is the lack of communication between business activities and technology management, when decision making on implementing new information technologies and the resulting specific business benefits are concerned.

Without the knowledge of where and how IT earns value for the organization, it is impossible to measure this value in concrete quantitative terms. Also, without financial guidelines in defining the value of increased business flexibility, it is difficult to develop a meaningful proposition of values to invest in any IT initiative.

In preparing the input data for the portfolio selection it is necessary to analyse whether the project is worth the risk undertaken (Cooper, Edgett, & Kleinschmidt, 1998). This means conducting an overall identification of potential risks, risk estimation, the analysis on the impact the risk may have on the project, a discussion on the moves to reduce risk and estimation as to whether the project is still justified after the risk reduction costs are added.

The input information for portfolio selection is to allow for (Levine, 1999):

- finding out which of the projects proposed bears the greatest value for the company, so that the priorities in resource allocation may be defined.
- an estimation of the projects proposed in view of their importance for the overall portfolio, especially as regards the availability of resources and the realization of other projects.
- identifying projects which lag behind the planned terms by 25 percent or more and analysing influences upon the entire portfolio in case these projects are discontinued (depending on the availability of resources and the realization of other projects).

The choice of the method to be used in the project estimate depends on the purpose of the project. The most frequently used methods of project estimate of individual IT projects are the following:

- economic revenue – net current value, internal profit-making rate, return on capital, pay off terms, expected value
- benefit-cost techniques – include the calculation of the benefit-cost ratio, where the inputs represent the total value of all benefits and costs
- risk analysis – a combination of the probability of events (usually undesired events) and consequences related to the event. Every project carries a certain risk of failure to reach the desired goals
- potential project success – specific measuring of the probability of project success
- degree of acquaintance with the organizational strategy
- degree of acquaintance with the activities of competition
- degree of acquaintance with the organizational financial goals.

Individual projects may be estimated as good, however, they may be negative from the point of view of the company (Kerzner, 2003). Therefore it is essential that the project be analysed not only from the aspect of its success, but from the aspect of its contribution to the overall goal of the company as well. The project must not endanger the existing benefits and advantages the company has. No decision on the project requires all the analyses possible, nor is every element equally important.

Strategic decisions affecting the IT portfolio focus should be executed in a broad context that takes into account both external and internal business factors, and before the project portfolio is selected. The frame of the project selection should be flexible enough to allow for prior selecting of individual techniques and methodologies that are adequate for the relevant data analysis and deci-

sion making on the selection in a certain type of projects (Markowitz, 1991).

The project portfolio selection and adjustment is an iterative process (Meta Group, 2002). The existing projects require resources from the set available therefore the time of execution and resources are interdependent and affect new projects. It is a general practice that the review of the estimate of the project key elements is conducted at the end of each phase, in order to determine whether the project is eligible to be continued.

As regards the plan and the input information we have when we enter the decision making and the project execution processes, further execution may change many things. The best project may prove to be only average, and sometimes it is necessary to discontinue the project since it does not promise satisfactory results (Ghasemzadeh & Archer, 1999). During the execution stage it is therefore necessary that requireded adjustments be made, in accordance with the changes that appeared in the process.

The current IT projects that reached a certain key event should be reviewed again at the same time when new projects are analysed to be selected into the IT project portfolio. Thus it is possible to, in accordance with the resources available, generate a combined portfolio in regular intervals, and this is defined by:

- project completion or project abandoning
- new project proposition
- changes in strategic focus
- review of available resources
- changes in the environment

Problems related to the project failure and project discontinuation may be reduced if those working on the project approval are better organized and more careful in the decision making process. Within the IT project portfolio the scopes of performances for each project must be identified. It is necessary that certain acceptable values that would serve as an alarm tool within the IT project portfolio management system should be defined in advance.

KEY ASPECTS OF IT: INNOVATION RELATIONSHIP

In today's *knowledge-based* economy (European Commission, 2004) with increasingly dependence on knowledge and information (OECD, Eurostat, 2005), innovations and innovative competences are said to be the key driver of a long-term competitiveness, profitability and business success of an enterprise, national and global economy - and this should be considered as a widely accepted hypothesis, supported by a numerous research and literature (Tidd, 2001, Narayanan, 2001, Kleinknecht & Mohnen, 2002, European Commision and Enterprise DG, 2004). Innovation as a specific form of change and novelty presents a very extensive concept, which can be defined from different aspects - as the basic element of technological progress, economic growth and entrepreneurship, enabling the company to gain *competitive advantage* based on capability to realize successful innovation projects.

One of the key innovation management goals in the company is producing and development of company's *innovative competences* - capabilities mainly related to *the knowledge* accumulated by the company to create and introduce new products, services, processes, business that will lead to competitive advantage and market superiority. Among numbered and various innovation definitions, one that describes how important this field is considered to be nowadays, has been given in the guidelines for collecting and interpreting innovation data, well-known in the innovation field as the "Oslo manual" (OECD, Eurostat, 2005), saying that innovation represents the implementation of a new or significantly improved product (good or service), or process, or a new market-

ing or organizational method. Unlike the prior versions of this basic document, here it has been provided an expanded measurement framework (above all, recognizing the role of linkages between firms in the innovation process and giving more relevance to the service sector - less R&D intensive industries). This happened especially due to the changes in the basic identification of the types of innovation - now four main types, mentioned above:

- product/service innovation;
- process innovation;
- marketing innovation;
- organizational innovation.

In that sense, innovation presents both *the process* of transformation the idea into new product/service etc., and *the output* of that process, which is highly connected with three functions: research and development (R&D), production and marketing - Figure 1.

For a long time, in the area of building innovation models dominated linear approach, which treated innovation as a series of sequentially established phases without any feedback. Today's integrative models of innovation processes and innovation management are based on one of the basic innovation management relations, as in the Kline and Rosenberg "chain-linked model" (Kline, Rosenberg, 1986), which represents an interaction between capabilities of the company and market opportunities with the *strategy as a mediating force*, in order to achieve goals of competitiveness and effectiveness. This essential relation was the basis for a later upgrade of conventional, linear-sequential models of innovation - the company is responding to the market requests by means of its strategic concept - Figure 2.

This means that successful innovation management should start from defining *innovation strategy*, which is to be coordinated with other strategies - business, technology, marketing, intellectual property. Strategy is often said to be the

Figure 1. Key functions that influence innovation in the company (Trott, 2005)

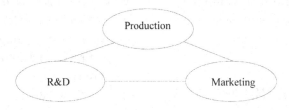

Figure 2. Achieving innovative competences through company's strategy

architecture for building competences. Successful innovation requires a clearly defined innovation strategy that corresponds to the current realities in the company, taking into account vital internal factors - technical capabilities, organizational capabilities, success of the current business model, top management vision, and most important external factors - capabilities of external network, industry structure, competition (Davila, 2006). One of the basic indicators of the innovative competences of the company can be followed through relations connecting invention, innovation, performances and business success (neither all of inventions lead to successful innovations, nor all innovations mean business success). Company can be said to achieve innovative competences if its innovations result in its potential to contribute continuously (time aspect) to growth, through stability and adaptation (Tidd, 2001). The key is

in using the results of innovations evaluation, in a way that the next time company will be ready for responding to challenges of changes.

Innovative competences are highly connected to a *degree of novelty* that a company is capable to implement and successfully introduce to market, meaning different competences when implementing incremental and/or radical innovation; this assumes different innovation strategy and innovation management model (starting from the differences in the first stage of ideation, i.e. how is company to evaluate incremental vs. radical ideas, how to recognize the value of idea fragments etc.), depending on the company's strategic goal to launch so-called "new-to-the-world" products or services or to enter the market with the evolutionary innovations such as line extension or small improvements. Typically, innovation portfolio is dominated by incremental

Figure 3. An average product innovation portfolio (Adapted from P. Trott (2005), "Innovation Management and New Product Development", Third edition, pg. 396)

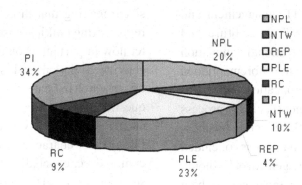

innovations: New product lines - NPL, Product line extension - PLE, Reducing costs - RC, Repositioning - REP, Product improvements - PI, while radical i.e. New to the world - NTW innovations participate with smaller amount - Figure 3.

Incorporation and use of IT can be identified as one of the key preconditions for successful implementation of radical innovations, since the degree of novelty thus introduced is so high as to demand the existence of high IT competences in the company involved. IT is inevitable in the domain of coordination of innovative activities, communication and exchange of information and knowledge, which presents the intellectual capital of the company and the core innovative competence. It can be showed that the knowledge is one of the key resources in today's global economy, so that knowledge is to be treated as the basic innovative competences factor and strategic dimension driving competitiveness and long-term profitability. The most innovative economies of today, are, actually, knowledge-based. The conclusion is that so-called knowledge-intensive organizations are potential innovation management drivers, where knowledge is built as their primary value-adding process.

In line with the "Oslo" guidelines, different kinds of innovation surveys have been implement-ed in extremely large number of countries - EU, OECD, non-OECD countries in different regions and continents. Generally, in Europe, methodology and research known as Community Innovation Survey (CIS), so far has been conducted in four intervals and in various countries, and is aimed to collect data to recognize the range of *innovation activities* as wide as possible - such as R&D expenditures, product design, trial production, market analysis, innovation *input/output factors* and indicators like patents, introduction of new products, processes and organizational changes and variety of different factors that influence *innovation process* - hampering and stimulating innovation, like sources of knowledge, reasons for innovating, strength of various appropriability mechanisms (Kleinknecht & Mohnen, 2002).

However, while there exist different results in the domain of innovation in IT (Huizenga, 2005), there cannot be found much of the research conducted in the direction of the IT being the factor of influence on innovative competences development; this is why it is so important that the latest "Oslo" document emphasizes this aspect of relationship between IT, innovation and innovative competences, suggesting that innovation surveys should focus on the use of IT (in the sense of so-called "front-office"- like

Web page, call centre etc, and "back-office" applications - company's internal operations that support or automate core and critical activities or processes) and the ultimate purpose of IT usage, existence of internal IT management and development capabilities, IT expenditure and its relationship with organizational innovation (Oslo, 2005). Considering the aforementioned innovation typology, IT application and diffusion is recognized to be either service or process innovation, depending on the concrete business function and organization; finally, it is concluded that successful strategic management of IT should produce higher innovative competences, which is the key hypothesis of this paper.

Some elements of this relation have been proven by findings of one of the recent exploratory research based on case study method, which is, according to its authors, one of the first to examine the influence of IT on innovation processes, starting from the fact that IT is more frequently understood as a support for innovation rather then its antecedent. In this study, several competences associated to IT have been identified: information and knowledge management, project management, collaboration and communication, and business involvement, which are likely to improve company's ability to innovate and, consequently, innovative competences thus developed (Gordon & Tarafdar, 2007).

Having in mind numbered sophisticated and complex innovation models developed to support innovation management and improve innovative competences, starting from conventional technology-push and market-pull towards modern integrative network models (Cooper, 2001, Trott, 2005), the innovation process here presented has been simplified at three broad stages - "Initiation", "Development" and "Implementation", in order to noticeably identify the relationship between these extensive stages and selected IT attributes. It should be interesting to point out that this study found no relevant impact of IT competence concerning information and knowledge management on the first "Initiation" phase, while all other analyzed IT attributes have recognized to be of strong influence at all innovation process components.

This can be the case because of the sample size, meaning that three innovative companies representing multiple case methodology, no matter how important, shouldn't be enough to reach convinced relation in all aspects. On the other side, this research indicates that one of the considerable questions in this area can arise when making a clear distinction between intrinsic attributes of IT and those characterizing wider organizational competence, concluding that most of them often span departmental limits (for instance, knowledge management as the organizational competence can be reasonably observed as the consequence of IT competence in the area of knowledge management, since it significantly depends on company's IT learning curve).

Whatever the complexity of IT attributes might be, it should be said that relation between IT and innovation is more then obvious, knowing that the recent changes and development of IT, bringing the *high-tech* reality and *information society* has highlighted the variety of ways in which companies in different sectors and countries can develop innovative competences (Whitley, 2002). Speaking of complexity, it should be important to identify the relationship among "hardware/software part" of IT and ability to innovate; hardware can be analyzed through company's introducing a technologically new or improved piece of IT equipment that support innovation capabilities, while the development, production, adaptation and use of software is a more complex matter, as these activities should be analyzed throughout the economy as a whole. It should be recommended that more serious survey should relate to the use of IT, aiming at differentiating situations between various countries (high developed or developing countries etc.), since so far only a partial studies and surveys can be found on this subject.

ORGANIZATIONAL SUPPORT TO IT PORTFOLIO MANAGEMENT: PORTFOLIO MANAGEMENT OFFICE

Companies usually have a large number of different projects within their portfolio and the more these differ, the more complex their management process becomes (Englund, Graham, & Dinsmore, 2003). In order that a successful execution of an individual IT project be supported and its compliance with the goals of other projects and with the overall organizational strategy be ensured, there must exist a specific integrative structure, e.g., strategic centre, expert group, centre for competence in project management or a portfolio office (Block & Frame, 2001; Bolles, 2002; Dinsmore, 1993; Miranda, 2003). Some of these may be virtual organizational units (Gareis & Huemann, 2000; Seltzer, 1999).

The hierarchically highest level is the Portfolio Management Office. The Portfolio Management Office defines projects and programmes in accordance to the general organizational strategy and goals. Its basic role is managerial and is related to the project portfolio management process phases, from defining the portfolio and categories of projects (such as IT projects) to the control and periodical review of the existing priorities and plans. The Office can also be viewed as the director or managing board headquaters, with an impact upon the strategy and a general direction of the company's development. Though primarily engaged in the activities on the strategic management level, it works together with the members of the Project Management Office on the operational jobs related to coordination of project activities, developing and spreading the project management principles throughout the company in certain situations (changes in plans, radically changed business conditions, delay caused by lack of resources, etc.).

The strategic role of the PMO is primarily concerned with the project portfolio development and management and its coordination with the organizational strategic goals. Hence the PMO provides the basis for a quantitative estimate of the portfolio management success in the organization and promotes the awareness of the portfolio management value.

The PMO provides numerous benefits for the organization that implements it, in view of the portfolio management process standardization, project execution improvement, professionalism building, improvement of organizational performances, etc. However, the other part of the PMO implementation has negative aspects that diminish the importance of the benefits listed above. Its significant weaknesses are: implementation costs, stress and conflicts, dualism in decision making, lack of clearly defined responsibilities, delays in execution, etc.

In a large number of organizations the implementation of the PMO remains, unfortunately, at the operational level, therefore the support of modern PM concepts in strategic planning and management is minimized. The management of such an organization will have to make additional efforts towards restructuring, changing the business methods and improving the PM competence level in their employees in order to position the PMO on a strategic level, that is, on project management as a basic competence of the company. Only in this way will the advantages of corporate project management be fully visible.

CONCLUSION AND FUTURE TRENDS

Modern companies rely on their IT to a large extent and this cannot be denied. It is almost impossible nowadays or in future to imagine a successful business without an equally successful IT. On the other hand, the link among these structures is often not strong enough so as to make this relation useful for new investments and joint projects.

In order to understand why some organizations earn greater financial value from implementing the same information technologies compared to some others, numerous research have been conducted. Among the best practices certainly is the joint vision of valuable opportunities that exist both in the IT and in business units, quality business planning for any initiative and an effective linking of projects and programmes. The basis of all these is the portfolio management with its process of work.

In the project-oriented organization, strategic management is implemented by way of project portfolio management. Classification, selection, prioritization, planning, monitoring and control of programmes and projects are defined and analysed as basic elements of project management. The IT project portfolio management is to allow for a consistent approach to classification, selection, prioritization, planning and execution of the right IT projects and programmes in the company. The IT project portfolio management is characterised by uncertainty as well as by changing information, dynamic possibilities, manifold goals, strategic analyses, interdependence of projects, manifold decision making and group decision making. Defining and managing the IT portfolio is today one of the most demanding processes in modern business.

The development of an efficient portfolio approach is not an easy task. There is no unique appropriate approach to the portfolio that can be implemented in any company. Some research (Archer & Ghasemzadeh, 1999) show that the most successful companies, as regards the portfolio performances, do differ in their approach to numerous elements in comparison to the companies whose performance is poorer. A general conclusion is that there is no approach to project portfolio management that holds a monopoly either in its implementation or in its features.

The development and selection of the IT project portfolio is a process which helps optimize a set of IT projects, not just one project. The approaches in IT portfolio development vary from simple ranking, based on a cost reduction rate, to very complex methodologies that take into consideration the interrelations among the projects. Organizations tend to select a methodology appropriate to their organizational identity and allowing for the analysis of project attributes they consider the most essential. Regardless of the model chosen, the goals should be related to the portfolio optimization, not only the optimization of individual projects. The choice of IT project portfolio mostly depends on the company's strategic direction, its capabilities, limitations and the complexity of the project.

We can predict that modern organizations will need a better coherent strategic frame for planning, monitoring and implementation of IT requirements in the future business activities such as IT portfolio management. Information technologies change their reach and impact upon modern business. Managers can either sit and wait for the consequences or organize preventively in order to answer the challenge and achieve a real *ROI* and increase the value of shares. Our firm recommendation is the latter approach.

REFERENCES

Ansoff I. (1987). *Corporate Strategy.* London, UK: Penguin Books.

Ansoff I. (2007). *Strategic Management.* Classic edition. London, UK: Palgrave Macmillan.

Archer, N. P., & Ghasemzadeh, F. (1996). *Project Portfolio Selection Techniques: A Review and a Suggested Integrated Approach* (Innovation Research Working Group Working Paper No. 46). Hamilton, Ontario: McMaster University.

Archer, N. P., & Ghasemzadeh, F. (1999). An Integrated Framework for Project Portfolio Selection. *International Journal of Project Management, 17*(4), 207-216.

Block T. R., & Frame J. D. (2001). Today`s Project Office: Gauging Attitudes. *PM Network*, *15*(8), 50-53.

Bolles D. (2002). *Building Project Management Centers of Excellence*. New York, NY: AMACOM.

Bridges, N. D. (1999). Project Portfolio Management: Ideas and Practices. In Dye, D. L., & Pennypacker S. J. (Eds.), *Project Portfolio Management* (pp. 45-54). West Chester, PA: Center for business Practices.

Chandler, A. D. (1962). *Strategy and Structure*. Cambridge, MA: MIT Press.

Cicmil, S. J. K. (1997). Critical factors of effective project management. *The TQM Magazine*, *9*(6), 390-6.

Cleland, I. D. (1999). The Strategic Context of Projects. In Dye, D. L., & Pennypacker S. J. (Eds.), *Project Portfolio Management* (pp. 3-22). West Chester, PA: Center for Business Practices.

Cooper, R. (2001). *Winning at New Products: Accelerating the Process from Idea to Launch*. New York, NY: Harper Collins Publishers.

Cooper, R. G., Edgett, S. J., & Kleinschmidt, E. J. (1997). Portfolio Management in New Product Development: Lessons from the Leaders, Phase I. *Research Technology Management, 40*(5), 16-28.

Cooper, R. G., Edgett, S. J., & Kleinschmidt, E. J. (1998). Best Practices for Managing R&D Portfolios, *Research Technology Management, 41*(4), 20-33.

Davila, T., Epstein, M.J., Shelton, R. (2006). *Making Innovation Work - How to Manage IT, Measure IT and Profit from IT*. Upper Saddle River, NJ: Wharton School Publishing.

Dinsmore, P. C. (1993). *The AMA Handbook of Project Management*. New York, NY: AMACOM.

Dye, L. D., Pennypacker, J. S. (1999). An Introduction to Project Portfolio Management. In Dye, L. D., & Pennypacker J. S. (Eds.), *Project Portfolio Management* (pp. xi-xvi). West Chester, PA: Center for Business Practices.

Englund, R. L., Graham R. J., & Dinsmore, P. C. (2003). *Creating the Project Office: A Manager's Guide to Leading Organizational Change*. The Jossey-Bass Business & Management Series. New York, NY: Wiley.

European Commission, (1995). *Green Paper on Innovation*. COM (95) 688 final. European Commission.

European Commission, (2004). Innovation Management Studies: Published Studies: Innovation Management. *Innovation Management and the Knowledge-Driven Economy*. Retrieved February 3, 2006, from http:/cordis.europa.eu/int/innovation-policy/studies/im_study6. htm.

European Commission, Enterprise DG (2004). *The Enterprise Directorate General - Activities and goals, results and future directions*. European Commission.

Gareis, R. (2003). *Competencies in the Project-oriented organization*, IPMA World Congress, Moscow, Russia.

Gareis, R., Huemann, M. (2000). Project Management Competences in the Project-oriented Organisation. In Turner J. R., & Simister S. J. (Eds.), *The Gower Handbook of Project Management*. Aldershot, UK: Gower.

George, M. et al. (2005). *Fast Innovation - Achieving Superior Differentiation, Speed to Market and Increased Profitability*. New York, NY: McGraw-Hill.

Ghasemzadeh, F., Archer, N. (1999). Project Portfolio Selection Techniques: A Review and a Suggested Integrated Approach, In Dye, D. L., & Pennypacker S. J. (Eds.), *Project Portfolio*

Management (pp. 207-238). West Chester, PA: Center for business Practices.

Gordon, S., & Tarafdar, M. (2007). How do a company's information technology competences influence its ability to innovate?, *Journal of Enterprise Information Management, 20*(3), 271-290.

Grant, R. (1991). The Resource-Based Theory of Competitive Advantage: Implications for Strategy Formulation. *California Management Review, 33*(3), 114-135.

Grant, R. (2007). *Contemporary Strategy Analysis.* VI edition. Oxford, UK: Blackwell Publishing.

Hamel, G., & Prahalad, C. K. (1989). Strategic Intent. *Harvard Business Review, 67*(3), 63-78.

Hebert, B. (2002). Tracking Progress. *New Zealand Management, 49*(1), 24-27.

Huizenga, E. (2005). *Innovation Management in the ICT Sector.* New York, NY: John Wiley & Sons.

Jovanović, P., Mihić, M., & Petrović, D. (2007). Social Implications of Managing Project Stakeholders. In Feng Li (Ed.), *Social Implications and Challenges of e-Business* (pp. 130-144). Hershey, PA: Information Science Reference.

Kaplan, J. D. (2001). White Paper: Strategically Managing Your IT Portfolio. *PRTM's Insight,* April 1.

Kerzner, H. (2003). *Project Management.* Eight edition. New York, NY: John Wiley & Sons.

Killen, C., Hunt, R., & Kleinschmidt. E. (2008). Project portfolio management for product innovation. *International Journal of Quality & Reliability Management, 25*(1), 24-38.

Kleinknecht, A., & Mohnen, P., ed. (2002). *Innovation and Firm Performance - Econometric Explorations of Survey Data.* Hampshire, UK: Palgrave.

Kline, S. J., & Rosenberg, N. (1986). An Overview of Innovation. In Landau, R., & Rosenberg, N., (Eds.), *The Positive Sum Strategy* (pp. 275-305). Washington, DC: National Academy Press.

Kloppenborg, T., & Opfer, W. (2002). The current state of project management research: Trends, interpretations and predictions. *Project Management Journal, 33*(2), 5-18.

Levine, H.A. (1999). Project Portfolio Management: A Song without Words? *PM Network, 13*(7), 25-27.

Loo, R. (1996). Training in Project Management a powerful tool for improving individual and team performance. *Team Performance Management: An International Journal, 2*(3), 6-14.

Meredith, R. J., & Mantel, J. S., Jr. (1999). Project Selection. In Dye, D. L., & Pennypacker S. J. (Eds.), *Project Portfolio Management* (pp. 135-168). West Chester, PA: Center for Business Practices

Markowitz, H. M. (1991), *Portfolio Selection.* London, UK: Basil Blackwell.

Meta Group (2002). *Centralizing Management of Project Portfolios.* Meta Group, January 29.

Mihić, M., & Petrović, D. (2004). Project-oriented managers – results of the new approach to managers' education. In proceedings of International Scientific Days, *European Integration: Challenge for Slovakia* (pp. 720-725). Nitra, Slovakia: Slovak Agricultural University.

Mikkola, H. (2001). Portfolio management of R&D projects: implications for innovation management. *Technovation, 21*(4), 23-35.

Miranda, E. (2003). *Running the Successful Hi-Tech Project Office.* Boston, MA: Artech House.

Morris, P. (1997). *The Management of Projects.* London, UK: Thomas Telford.

Narayanan, V. K. (2001). *Managing Technology and Innovation for Competitive Advantage.* Upper Saddle River, New Jersey: Prentice-Hall.

Norton, D., & Kaplan, R. (2003). *The Strategy-Focused Organization.* Boston, MA: Harvard Business School Press.

OECD, Directorate for Science, Technology and Industry, Industry Committee (1991). *OECD Proposed Guidelines for Collecting and Interpreting Technological Innovation Data.* Paris, France: OECD.

OECD, Eurostat (2005). *Oslo Manual - Guidelines for Collecting and Interpreting Innovation Data,* Joint Publication, 3rd Edition. OECD/European Communities.

Porter M. (1996). What Is Strategy? *Harvard Business Review, 74*(60), 61-78.

Reyck, B. D., Grushka-Cockayne, Y., Lockett, M., Calderini, S., Moura, M., & Sloper, A. (2005). The impact of project portfolio management on information technology projects. *International Journal of Project Management, 23*(7), 524-537.

Russell, A. (2003). *Managing High-Technology Programs and Project.* New York, NY: John Wiley & Sons.

Seltzer, L. (1999). The Virtual Office. *PC Magazine.* October 19.

Smith C. (2003). Corporate Social Responsibility: Whether or How? *California Management Review, 45*(4), 52-76.

Sommer, R. (1999). Portfolio Management for Projects: A New Paradigm. In Dye, D. L., & Pennypacker S. J. (Eds.), *Project Portfolio Management* (pp. 55-60). West Chester, PA: Center for business Practices.

Stošić, B. (2004). Application of PATTERN Method in Innovation Projects Management. In I. Travnik (Ed.), *3rd Central and South East Europe Project Management Network Conference, Project Management Paving the Way to European Union,* (E:\papers\p22.pdf). Bratislava, Slovakia: SENET.

Thomas, R. J. (1993). *New Product Development: Managing and Forecasting for Strategic Success.* New York, NY: Wiley.

Tidd, J., Bessant, J., & Pavitt, K. (2001). *Managing Innovation.* Chichester, UK: John Wiley & Sons.

Trott, P. (2005). *Innovation Management and New Product Development.* London, UK: Prentice Hall.

Verhoef, C. (2002). Quantitative IT portfolio management, *Science of Computer Programming, 45*(1), 1–96.

Webster, G. (1999). Project definition – The missing link. *Industrial and Commercial Training, 31*(6), 240-244.

Whitley, R. (2002). Developing innovative competences: The role of institutional frameworks, *Industrial and Corporate Change, 11*(3), 497-528.

Wysocki, R. (2004). *Project Management Process Improvement.* Boston, MA: Artech House.

Chapter IX
Developing an E–Government Roadmap for Developing Countries

Cuthbert Shepherdson
KDI Asia Pte Ltd, Singapore

Albert Wee Kwan Tan
National University of Singapore, Singapore

Van Nam Tran
National Economics University, Vietnam

ABSTRACT

Developing countries, opting to pursue services-oriented economies, have invested in information and communication technologies (ICT) to enhance their competitiveness in the global environment. This has called for improved management in both public and private sectors and as a consequence governments, some of which have undertaken public sector reform, now seem ready to embrace e-Government. However, experience even in developed countries has shown that incorporating e-Government practices is not a sure means of attaining desired goals. This paper examines the position of Vietnam, as it becomes a member of WTO in implementing E-Government. Some E-Government initiatives taken are identified and an IT roadmap is recommended as a means of achieving a successful transformation. This roadmap emphasizes a holistic approach to analyze existing performance gaps and identify E-Government opportunities for Vietnam.

INTRODUCTION

Over three decades ago the potential of information and communication technology to enhance the socioeconomic development of developing countries (DCs) was recognized by some international institutions. Since then DCs all over the world have been increasing their investment in ICT and extending its application into all sectors of their economies. In the private sector there is the issue of the 'productivity paradox' in the utilization of ICT in enterprises with apparently little measurable productivity gains being attained after considerable ICT investment. Many governments have also not been noticing the expected improvements after their considerable investments (Ciborra, 2005). This has been a difficult pill to swallow for some DCs which are least able to afford such unprofitable investment when their populations sometimes lack basic necessities in their social systems. The reality gap between the hype about ICT and the actual performance must therefore be confronted by governments in DCs (Heeks, 2003).

To narrow the gap on how government should plan and implement e-Government, we drew upon the literature on strategic information systems (SIS) and strategic information systems planning (SISP). SIS refers to the use of information systems to change the way a firm competes in the industry or change the structure of the industry (Neumann, 1994). Extensive research was conducted on the nature, driving forces, critical success factors, problems and barriers of SIS. However, most of these studies were conducted in the context of the private sector, where firms compete with each other in an open free market. Alternatively, public organizations like governments do not operate on the same principles as the private counterparts. In the absence of competitive forces of the market, one may question the relevance and applicability of the concept of SIS to the public sector. We believe that today governments are under increasing pressure to operate more like private firms. Internally, they are challenged to improve efficiency by legislative mandates or budget constraints (Fountain, 2001). Externally, the public – citizens and business – exerts increased pressure on government to improve the way it delivers services. Having witnessed and gotten used to the convenience and power of electronic commerce in the private sector, the public has become less tolerant with the level of services provided by governments. All these forces – by making government more efficient, responsive, and accountable – have the potential to change the way government operates and alter the political structure. We believe that information technologies have much to offer in the process, just like the way SIS has the power to modify the market structure. We therefore conjecture that e-Government is a strategic IS issue because it has the potential to change the way government operates and its political structure.

This paper addresses one aspect of a larger project undertaken by two of the authors on ICT, governance and modernization, reviews some initiatives towards e-Government taken by the Government of Vietnam and proposes an IT roadmap that can be used to enhance our understanding of how many of the failures experienced elsewhere might be avoided. Note is taken of the literature concerning models on ICT application and, more recently on e-Government adoption. Unfortunately these have tended to be about developed countries such as Canada, emerging economies like Singapore and large DCs like South Africa and India. The situation in Vietnam has special characteristics and requires specific consideration.

Hunter and Long (2002) in examining the challenges faced in the application of IT to small businesses utilized the Entrepreneurial Process and that work has been closely studied in preparing this paper. Likewise the contributions of Heeks (2001(a), 2001(b)) have been useful in the study of efforts to re-engineer administrative processes within government and to seek to implement such processes. In his work he has generally been cognizant of the failure of e-Government and other ICT initiatives in DCs and has proposed steps to attain e-readiness. Finally one of the authors has recently advised the Vietnam government on national IT planning as a precursor to e-Government introduction. That involvement has given great insight into many of the hindrances in the efforts towards successful ICT utilization in DCs. It is hoped that the roadmap can be useful or at least insightful for other developing countries in their thrust towards e-Government.

E-GOVERNMENT IN DEVELOPING COUNTRIES: THE CURRENT SITUATION

Globally there has been dissatisfaction with the provision of services by governments and moves towards public sector reform have been undertaken by DCs. As the private sector has become more involved in matters once reserved for the public sector the issue of governance has become paramount. The current preoccupation with and hype about electronic government or e-Government have therefore reached the DCs. Bhatnagar (2004) questions the justification for the expense of IT in an environment where many basic needs are not met and many basic rights often violated. Ultimately it is accepted that the real question is not how to use IT or whether to use IT but rather under what circumstances, if any, can IT be utilized to meet such needs and rights. Heeks (2001b) has stipulated that e-Governance projects must show sensitivity to the reality of developing country values, structures, and infrastructure. Simply pulling private sector solutions off-the-shelf and trying to impose them on public sectors in DCs will be like driving square pegs into round holes. E-Governance solutions must be adapted, not simply adopted, to ensure that the design of those solutions matches realities. There has been uneven progress in DCs towards

the provision of online access to information especially in Asia (Yong, 2005). Some general barriers have been identified in the successful implementation of e-Government. These include organizational, political and technical factors. In particular the need to redesign existing services and improve their coordination and integration has been highlighted.

Lee-Kelley and James (2003) examined the extent to which e-Government implementation might lead to the exclusion of certain groups in the community. Results suggest that:

- A citizen's socio-economic status, language and ethnic background, computer skills and e-Government vision are significantly related to the willingness to utilize e-Government services.
- Internet availability and confidence in its use tend to determine one's willingness to use e-Government services.

While these results relate to a UK study, they would appear to be even more applicable to a typical DC. In particular, one must acknowledge that whereas e-Government services must be made available to all citizens, a citizen makes a conscious decision to become involved with commercial services involving the private sector. Hence the matter of universal access to information technology becomes a crucial factor in the adoption of e-Government. It may be that, until such access is assured, the citizen should be allowed some choice in the type of technology that is employed in their dealings with the public sector.

E-GOVERNMENT CHALLENGES

Heeks (2001a) has identified two other challenges facing developing countries as they undertake e-Government application: lack of e-readiness and large design-reality gaps.

Contrary to the impression given by the hype surrounding e-Government, realizing its benefits takes more than the mere creation of a Web presence. Getting citizens online and transacting their business with assurance in a secure environment should be the goal of those contemplating e-Government. Successful implementation of e-Government or indeed of any ICT strategy is dependent on the support of the public sector officials and other stakeholders. Hewitt (2003) sees the protection of "turf" by public sector functionaries as a key hindrance within departments and ministries. He asserts that the enthusiastic and sustained leadership of the Head of government is perhaps the best way to achieve national consensus and commitment in an undertaking like IT planning. He advocates that the articulation of such a strategy should be done ideally by the chief executive of government.

RESEARCH METHODOLOGY

This research focuses on Vietnam e-Government development. Based on inputs from some of the key stakeholders in Vietnam, the following research questions were formulated and grouped into four key issues:

e-Governance

- What should be the key e-Government strategies for Vietnam?
- What are the roles of key ministries and agencies in central government, cities and provinces?
- How can ICT organizations in government agencies manage e-Government initiatives?
- How can ICT management in government agencies be improved?

e-Government ICT Opportunities

- How can government agencies share common applications system to improve productivity and efficiency compared to the weaknesses of the current state computerization program?
- What are the opportunities for e-Government services especially in the cities of Hanoi, Danang and Ho Chi Minh City?
- How can government agencies improve data sharing and collaboration?
- What are opportunities for improving productivity and working environment for government employees?
- How can e-Government reach out to rural areas?

Building e-Government Awareness in Government and Publics and How to Build e-Government Competencies?

- How to create e-Government awareness for leaders, officials and staff?
- How can the government communicate effectively to the public about the value of e-Government in providing online information and e-services?
- What relevant training programs are available and what are the key competencies for e-Government?
- How can the mindset of government employees be changed for e-Government especially in adopting a new way of working?

e-Government Delivery

- What are components of an e-Government roadmap?
- How can the government develop an effective implementation plan for e-Government?

- What are the various strategies for implementing e-Government initiatives and programmes?
- How can Vietnam learn from the lessons of countries implementing e-Government?

In order to answer these research questions, a 3 phase approach is undertaken for this study as shown in Figure 1:

a. **Analysis Phase**

Activities include research and analysis of best practices and lessons learnt from leading exponents of e-Government and developing countries that have embarked on e-Government. Case studies on e-Government implementation from Singapore, India and South Korea would be examined. In all, two separate study tracks with stakeholders would be conducted. The first track is for selected government agencies / cities / provinces while the other is for citizens, businesses and non-government organizations. Gap analysis was performed to examine Vietnam's current e-Government state and challenges faced through focus group interviews and surveys.

b. **Design Phase**

An e-Government Roadmap Framework would be developed to provide a complete view and key considerations for the development of e-Government in Vietnam. With performance gaps identified during the analysis phase, potential e-Government opportunities and solutions (G-to-G, G-to-E, G-to-B and G-to-C as well as other related areas) would be sought and evaluated. Metrics are recommended to measure the success of these e-Government projects.

Figure 1. e-Government study approach

	Analysis Phase	**Design Phase**	**Implementation Planning Phase**
Task	• Identify performance gaps • Gather best practices • Assess e-readiness • Challenges and barriers in e-Government	• Develop an e-Government roadmap • Identify potential projects for e-Government • Develop metrics for success	• Identify donors for funding • Prepare funding paper for budget • Setup committees to oversee the projects • Assess the viability of each project for sustainability • Prepare user training plan • Identify processes for reengineering to meet project objectives • Recommend new laws to support e-Government
Duration	3 months	5 months	9 months to 2 years depending on scale of each project
Outcome	• List of best practices suitable for Vietnam • Performance gap report	• An e-Government roadmap • List of potential projects for e-Government • List of metrics	• A budget paper for the overall e-Government plan • Steering and working committees for e-government

c.   Implementation Planning Phase

This phase would include activities such as considering issues of E-Governance (e-Government management) and implementation planning for the e-Government Roadmap. Relevant strategies and recommendations including the lead role of coordinating body for integrated government services, other key agencies and key focus areas would also be covered.

This study was funded by the Asia Development Bank (ADB) and part of the information in this paper was extracted from the study report submitted to ADB (Shepherdson and Nam, 2005).

ANALYSIS PHASE: CURRENT STATE OF VIETNAM e-GOVERNMENT DEVELOPMENT

Progresses of ICT Development in Vietnam government agencies in terms of the ICT infrastructure, LANs and Data Integration centres have been implemented in the Offices of Peoples Committees (Provincial / City Government) as well as in the government ministries. Most of the Offices of the Peoples Committees are connected to Vietnam Government Wide Area Network (CPNet). The CPNet was built in 1997 for government agencies (state administrative organisations). The existing CPNet nodes are connected to the Office of the Government (OOG) offices in Hanoi and Ho Chi Minh City (HCMC), 30 ministries (or equivalent level organizations), 61 Peoples Committees' Offices of cities and provinces.

Currently CPNet supports electronic mail, online public journals search and exchange of official texts (government documents). All application software running on CPNet was developed in the Lotus Notes 4.2 environment. However, the workflow functions of Lotus Notes and different databases have not been fully exploited.

The biggest challenge for CPNet is network performance when many users are simultaneously trying to connect or when the quantity of sending data is large. There are no public online services to citizens and businesses as CPNet is not connected directly to the Internet and has only limited data security protection. Cities like HCMC separately have started enhancing their own network infrastructure and explored a few online services.

Due to the lack of common ICT standards and information architecture, many applications running on LANs and developed by ministries, cities and provinces cannot communicate with each other. Most ministries have their private LANs not directly connected to CPNet. The existing 2-tier client-server architecture of the existing IT applications is not scalable coupled by the inflexible 8-bit Vietnamese character code for older IT system applications. Many government ministries, cities and provinces have also developed internal IT system applications (some web-based) from their own budgets.

There appears to be a number of Government Portals (from government ministries, provinces and cities) in Vietnam, including the popular Hanoi City Web portal and the Ho Chi Minh City Web portal. Most of these local government websites are not true portals. They tend to be centrally-mandated and organized around government bureaucracy. Many are static Web pages authored by the various government departments within the local government. As such, they are "supply driven" rather than "demand driven". In 10 Jan 2006, the Vietnam government launched the Official Vietnam Government Information Portal (www. vietnam.gov.vn) using portal technology from Oracle. Managed by OOG, this portal provides the key channel in the course of communication with members of the Vietnamese public in and out of the country and the world community. The portal informs them of the Vietnamese Government's policy and instructions, performance of the Government, ministries and local authorities as well as what happens in Vietnam in the fastest and formal manner.

The opportunities for e-Government are mainly in the towns (provincial capitals) of provinces and more connected districts (in the rural areas) which are primarily farming / agriculture communities. The Ministry of Agriculture and Rural Development (MARD) and donors such as United Nations Development Programme (UNDP) assist these communities in programs such as poverty alleviation schemes. The heart of the government in rural areas is providing information and services in the districts and communes. Access to relevant information has the potential to transform economic opportunities and improve the livelihoods for rural households. Information access can do this by facilitating improved farming techniques, improving crop selection in response to market needs, reducing exploitation in pricing, improving efficiency of transportation, improving access to financial services, and improving delivery of health and educational services. But as a start, access to Internet and literacy are the key building blocks for e-Government in rural areas.

The Ministry of Post and Telematics (MPT) was formed in November 2002 to oversee ICT and its development in Vietnam. This consisted of the former Department General of Post and Telecommunications which was upgraded to the level of a ministry. MPT was tasked to lead the ICT master plan for ICT Usage and Development approved by the Prime Minister in August 2002 which identified major ICT areas and projects. Currently, MPT is working with World Bank to implement a master plan for ICT Development in Vietnam. The objective is to bring greater availability of and access to information about government policies, services and procedures. The project also aims to increase the effectiveness, transparency and accountability of govern-

ment agencies and contribute to better provision of public services. The project comprises five subprojects in three areas: (a) leadership in ICT and modernization of the Ministry of Post and Telematics; (b) modernization of the General Statistics Office, (c) and E-applications for the cities of Hanoi, Ho Chi Minh and Danang. In August 2007, the Ministry of Information and Communication was established from MPT and the Ministry of Culture of Information State Media Branch.

The State Administration Computerisation (SAMCOM) 112 Programme (2001-2005) was managed by OOG. Information systems have been developed (shared applications of SAMCOM deployed at provinces / cities down to department /districts) to serve as a tool for management activity in government agencies including the building of IT infrastructure and data centres. There are 3 common software applications that have been piloted / used in the provinces: a) Documents and File Management System, b) Internal Website for Executive Management and lastly, Socio-Economic Information Management System

The state of e-Government is still in its early stages. There is a need for government policies and practices to adopt modern administrative changes to fully embrace use of ICT. Fundamentally, there is a need for a change in mindset to adopt ICT as part of work practices in government agencies. There is a need for government agencies in the central government including key cities to provide more services and information to businesses and citizens to improve Vietnam's competitiveness with the entry into the World Trade Organisation (WTO) in Dec 2006.

DESIGN PHASE: e-GOVERNMENT ROADMAP FOR VIETNAM

By examining best practices from Singapore, South Korea and India and overcoming challenges faced, an e-Government Roadmap is developed by the authors with the objectives as shown in Figure 2 are as follows:

- To define the areas of focus for the e-Government Study
- To focus on identified key issues and challenges during analysis
- To provide a holistic and consistent approach for study activities
- To examine and explore opportunities for the various e-Government components

In addition, the study team would also conduct an assessment of the Law on E-Transactions and the Law of IT as well as related sub-laws, if required. This would highlight any potential gaps and issues that are needed to be considered for e-Government.

e-GOVERNANCE

E-Governance (or e-Government Management) is usually one of the biggest challenges in e-Gov-

ernment initiatives found in many countries. In Vietnam's context, this covers the following:

e-Government Leadership and Strategies

Strong leadership is required from top government leaders for e-Government, i.e. Prime Minister, deputy prime ministers and the cabinet. In examining leading countries such as Singapore and Korea, early studies have shown that individual strong leadership and direction for e-Government is required. One example includes the prime minister leading initiatives supported by a strong executive steering committee. In large countries such as Korea, India and the United States, strong support and commitment is essentially and visibly obtained from central government agencies and local governments. For Vietnam, support and commitment is required from central government ministries / agencies and within cities and provinces, Peoples Committees and their departments. Clear goals and focused strategies must be defined in the e-Government Roadmap. Key strategies should highlight different opportunities

Figure 2. e-Government roadmap for Vietnam[1]

e-Government Roadmap			
E-Governance	**e-Government Operating Model**	**E-Govt Capability & Awareness**	**E-Govt Delivery**
e-Government Leadership & Strategies	Integrated E-Services & Info (Citizens/ Business)	e-Government Competencies, Training, Education & E-Learning	Implementation Strategies
Roles of lead / support agencies in Central Govt & Cities / Provinces	Govt to Govt Collaboration (Data Hub, E-Govt Intranet and common applications)		e-Government Operating Model Pilots and recommendations
Role of Coordinating Body	Governance Employee Performance Support (E-Apps & E-Govt Competencies)	e-Government Best Practice Capture and Sharing	Phase Implementation Plan for pilot, projects and programmes
e-Government Programme Management		Government Change Communication	
e-Government ICT Organisation and Management	e-Government Infrastructure and Network	E-Govt Awareness and Public Communication	Projected Budgets and Estimates
			Critical Success Factors
E-Government Legal Assessment			
Assessment of Laws on a) E-Transactions & b) Information Technology (IT) and related Sub-Laws			

[1] *E-Government Roadmap adapted from E-Government Framework, Vietnam E-Government Roadmap Study (2005).*

in the central government, cities and provinces. E-Government programmes, projects and pilots should cover relevant areas in order to have adequate coverage throughout the country including urban and rural areas. It must be noted that with Vietnam's size and the large number of provinces, e-Government cannot be fully implemented easily throughout the country. Focus must be given on cities and provinces which have the resources (including foreign direct investment) and critical success factors to successfully implement e-Government. This should be done through start-small, scale-fast strategies.

Role of Lead / Support Agencies (Central Government and Cities / Provinces)

There is a need to provide direction and coordinate e-Government initiatives for central and local government agencies. These are roles at two levels in Vietnam, i.e. central government as well as cities / provinces. At the central government level, key ministries must take up lead roles and collaborate to cover different aspects of e-Government, not just ICT development. Other agencies and ministries have support roles in charge of their specific domains. At the cities / provinces level, the Peoples Committees and their departments have the roles of lead and support agencies that need to be clearly defined in order to avoid confusion and conflict in implementing e-Government initiatives.

Role of Coordinating Body in e-Government initiatives (especially for E-Services to the Public)

There are coordinating bodies at the central and state government level in countries such as Australia, India and the United States. In Vietnam's context, the coordinating body at the central government level refers to the programme management role comprising of planning, budgeting and coordination to launch e-Government programmes for the general public. At the city / provincial level, the role of the coordinating body is to facilitate the development of E-Services to coordinate and elicit requirements between government departments and citizens / businesses to build an e-Government model for integrated E-Services. It is also useful to have a coordinating body for initiatives within central government ministries.

e-Government Programme Management

In countries such as Singapore and Victoria State (Australia), the roles of managing e-Government programmes are clearly defined and separate from the government agency in charge of ICT and implementation. The reason for this structure to broadly manage overall programmes (public administrative reforms, e-Government programmes and impact to government policies and processes) separately from the e-Government technical implementations. In Vietnam's context, the e-Government programme management role needs to be clearly defined and separated from the technical implementations. The programme management role should comprise of planning, budgeting, coordination, management and monitoring of various e-Government initiatives at central government and at provinces / cities. This role also facilitates collaboration and working arrangements with other ministries to strategies and programmes for e-Government implementation. A reporting structure and monitoring capability is essential to track e-Government initiatives at all levels.

e-Government ICT Organisation and ICT Management within Government Ministries and Agencies

In many developed countries, government operations and administration together with ICT are seen as a coordinated strategy for e-Government. ICT plays a key enabling role in public administration further enhanced by Chief Information Office (CIO) function to increase government efficiency and effectiveness. This is apparent in United States, Europe as well as in Singapore. In Vietnam's case, there is an insufficient understanding of the CIO role and increasingly importance of ICT. Top management needs to understand and recognize the role of the ICT departments within government agencies and their key contributions in e-Government. This is from both the technical and CIO perspective. Once Government leaders and department heads understand the strategic opportunities and challenges for ICT, there can be a more effective approach to ICT management with the adoption of ICT standards. The SAMCOM Training Standards have been developed to provide standards and training in key areas of ICT management. By leveraging on these standards in the area of ICT management, this would help to support and facilitate e-Government initiatives.

e-GOVERNMENT OPERATING MODEL

In order to apply e-Government in public administration with ICT as a key enabler, various operating models for e-Government applicable for Vietnam can be determined. These should start as pilots before scaling them up to full projects and programmes.

Integrated E-Services Model for Citizens and Businesses (G-to-B / G-to-C)

Lessons learnt in countries such as Malaysia and Thailand embarking on e-Government, show that there is a need to demonstrate development and progress of E-Services to the media and public. The traditional approach emphasizes that governments need to reengineer existing operations and have internal ICT systems first in place before implementing E-Services is no longer a valid explanation. This is because it takes too long as the media and general public want to see visible results. The latest e-Government trends show that the traditional approach does not facilitate cross-agency collaboration and E-Services provided are not fully integrated from a citizen perspective but more from individual agency perspectives. This can be seen in Singapore and Australia where integrated portals are been developed. These two countries started with development of E-Services from specific agencies. For Vietnam case, the approach recommended is to facilitate the development of an e-Government Operating Model for integrated E-Services that is open and flexible. This allows government agencies to plan their own schedule for reengineering together with the ICT system implementation (Tan, 2007). The premise is that a new channel is provided for government agencies to have E-Services on the Internet through a centralized infrastructure at the provincial / city government level.

In the interim before reengineering and ICT system implementation, an electronic workflow can support agencies by allowing data submitted from electronic forms by citizens / data on the Internet or Kiosks to be shared and exchanged with various agencies. This would reduce duplicated data entry by citizens and business owners who submit their request(s) and do not need to re-enter their personal particulars. This centralized infrastructure can be seamlessly integrated when the new ICT systems belonging to other agencies are implemented. Such an implementation can be done by a coordinating body.

Government to Government Collaboration Model for Data Hub and e-Government Intranet for Common Applications (G-to-G)

In many countries that have made good progress in e-Government, the common challenge is data sharing between government agencies. There is a need for a common data hub and exchange system that allow government agencies to share and exchange data (especially common data such as citizens and businesses). The first critical ingredient is the setting up of the data / information architecture and exchange standards.

In Vietnam's case, many government agencies are still in the preliminary stage of ICT development. The concept of data hub and relevant standards would facilitate data sharing with the e-Government Operating Models for integrated E-services, operational ICT systems being developed and lastly common applications being planned in provinces and cities. A pilot data hub project should start with a key central government ministry and a city planning integrated E-services to plan and deploy data sharing and exchange standards. The data sharing pilot implementation should be a centralized infrastructure that is scalable and shares data through a publishing and subscription model. Cecchini and Raina (2004) state that it is imperative for e-Government projects to establish the service and information needs of the community that it serving, and that the technology itself should be developed in collaboration with local staff.

For common applications in Vietnam, the current implementation approach has to be improved through a start-small and scale-fast strategy with identified pilot provinces and cities. The implementation strategy for these common applications must consider deployment through a centralized infrastructure and their readiness for e-Government. The common applications for the respective provinces and cities can be launched within the e-Government Intranet. Emphasis would be on placing controls for implementation which should be aligned with the Training of Trainers (TOT) for the SAMCOM Standards in ICT management. As a number of ministries in central government have plans to build new ICT systems or enhance existing systems through funding from central government or donors, specific G-to-G (domain) applications for ministries in the central government would not be covered in this study.

Government Employee Performance Support (G-to-E)

In advanced countries, the onus is usually given to individual ministries in the central or state governments in improving employee performance with Intranets and employees support systems (ESS). In Singapore, such initiatives have been on a government wide deployment such as the government personnel information system and the government employee claims system (petty cash, transport claims, etc). Not many developing countries have yet to see the strategic importance of G-to-E applications in improving employee productivity and motivation. Government leaders and civil servants in Vietnam may not fully appreciate the value of Intranets or ESS. Furthermore, few ministries / agencies in the central government have advanced ICT infrastructure. The two agencies that have advanced ICT systems are the State Bank and Ministry of Finance. Emphasis should be placed on identifying opportunities in advanced agencies in the central government and in cities of Ho Chi Minh, Hanoi and Danang, to explore ESS and Intranets. Such initiatives can be aligned with the public administration reforms as pilot implementations.

e-Government Infrastructure and Network

E-Government provides development opportunities for stakeholders in rural and poorly developed communities. More than 75% of the population in Vietnam lives mainly in rural areas in the provinces. Opportunities for e-Government include providing government information and application forms in provincial Internet websites. Such information can be made available with specially designed sites which provide Internet access whether through PCs, thin clients or even kiosks. Such sites should be assisted by trained operators who can assist citizens who need information on government services or have needs for IT literacy and Internet training. This is extremely useful in remote areas and poorly developed communities.

ICT infrastructure is recognized to be one of the main challenges for e-Government. Many developing countries suffer from the digital divide, and they are not able to deploy the appropriate ICT infrastructure for e-Government deployment (World Bank, 2003). Due to a lack of infrastructure in most developing countries, the telecommunications costs can be high, thereby nullifying this benefit (Schware and Deane, 2003). In situations such as this, it may be more appropriate to look at low-tech solutions that fit in with the existing infrastructure (Cecchini & Raina, 2004). Therefore for Vietnam, instead of rebuilding the government network, the approach should be on a needs basis as infrastructure and network investments are high capital expenditures. Emphasis should be placed on enhancing government network connectivity in cities or provinces with new ICT system requirements as well as strategic pilot projects or programmes. Opportunities with the private sector companies through private-public partnership should be explored especially for

upgrading the government network infrastructure. The Government should consider strategies with the private sector to leveraging on existing public telecommunication networks to link government agencies and explore the use of Virtual Private Networks (VPN). The Government can also explore opportunities for WIMAX wireless technology in rural areas than is more cost effective than laying fibre-optic cables.

e-GOVERNMENT CAPABILITY AND AWARENESS

Besides addressing the governance issues and operating models for E-Governance, a key area is building up e-Government capabilities for government agencies and creating awareness for e-Government not only within the government but also among the general public and businesses. This covers the following areas:

e-Government Competencies, Training, Education and E-Learning

Jaeger and Thompson (2003) assert that an e-government system would fail if the government did not take an active role in educating citizens about the value of e-government. Linked to this is the lack of skills and training which are required to effectively use an e-government system that are available to government officials and citizens (Heeks, 1999; Moon, 2002; Ho, 2002). It is a particularly significant problem in developing countries due to the chronic lack of qualified staff and training schemes, which are necessary conditions for the existence of successful e-government schemes (Ndou, 2004). In order to support e-Government, countries such Singapore, Korea and Canada have created programmes to build e-Government competencies. This includes areas such as training, education and even e-learning. In Vietnam, there are key needs to increase e-Government capability as the government moves towards public administrative reforms and e-Government initiatives. An important consideration is to structure and launch these programmes in an effective manner to ensure sustainability and work with the industry and local universities. One example is to create e-Government / ICT Competencies for the following:

- Project Management
- Quality Management
- Procurement
- Process Reengineering
- System Development
- Operations, Maintenance and Support
- Technical Audit

e-Government Best Practice Capture and Sharing

Since e-Government initiatives are relatively new in some countries like Sri Lanka and Philippines, there have been initiatives to setup specialized centres to capture and share best practices. Such centres capture best practices from other countries as well as lessons learnt and practices from various e-Government initiatives in the country. In Vietnam case, this is also an essential element in developing internal capability. Such lessons learnt and best practices learnt should be coordinated and shared not only with government agencies but also supported by academic research at selected local universities at key centres in the country. Such learning can be shared and deployed on an e-Government Intranet or Internet.

Government Change Communication

Countries like Canada, United States and Singapore, have learnt that as they embark on e-Government, there is a need to embark on change management / change communication programmes. In many countries, the government usually lags behind the private sector in business processes and customer centricity. With e-Government attempting to leverage on ICT to improve government operations and efficiency as well as improving public services, many government civil servants feel threatened by these changes such as business process reengineering (Tan, 2007) and ICT projects. A lot of effort is required to put in place change communication programmes to explain the need for change to improve transparency, reduce bureaucracy and red-tape and increase productivity (Yong, 2005). What is also fundamental is the need for government operations managers and ICT Project Managers to challenge existing assumptions and mental models (on current laws and regulations leveraging on international best practices) and explore innovative solutions. The public sector must change its mental models and reengineer its processes to adapt to the new technology and culture of an e-Government (Ebrahim and Irani, 2005).

e-Government Awareness and Public Communications

One of the biggest challenges that countries face when implementing e-Government is to create awareness of e-Government as well as to gain public confidence in e-Government initiatives. A properly coordinated public communication programme can be effective in communicating key messages to the public and correct any incorrect perceptions presented by the media (Yong, 2005). New capabilities in public communication are required, not only for e-Government but also for general government communication. This includes handling issues from the public and other major events and incidents. Consistent e-Government collaterals should be developed for communication, not only in hardcopy but also online. This has to involve leading agencies in e-Government working together to develop a set of generic public communication materials. Another area is communicating awareness about new e-Government services. The key is in getting public buy-in and support and has to be part of 2-way government communication channels. Such government consultative channels (Internet, etc) with citizens obtain feedback and provide inputs for government policies and services.

e-GOVERNMENT DELIVERY (PART OF IMPLEMENTATION PLANNING PHASE IN FIGURE 1)

The key deliverables include the following: a) implementation strategies; b) key study recommendations; c) various pilots for the e-Government Operating models; d) phase implementation plan for pilot, projects and programmes. The implementation should also include the projected budgets and estimates for the successful rollout of the implementation plan.

Implementation Strategies

In identifying the focus areas for the e-Government Delivery, there is a need to have defined strategies for the implementation and define the rationale and/or key principles. In identifying the focus areas for the e-Government delivery, there is a need to define strategies for implementation and their rationale and/or key principles.

e-Government Operating Model Pilots and Recommendations

Various pilots recommended would cover the following: integrated E-services model; common application pilots and centralized infrastructure implementation; data hub studies and infrastructure pilot; and lastly, Internet access pilot projects for government information and IT literacy training in rural areas. In terms of programmes and specific recommendations, areas covered are from the following areas: E-Governance, e-Government Operating Model and e-Government Capability and Awareness.

Phase Implementation Plans for pilots, projects and programmes

The phase implementation plan would cover the 5-year timeframe from 2006-2010. The key approach would be to start recommendations as pilots first before making an assessment to scale them to full projects and programmes. Pilots shall be recommended only in cities or provinces that meet certain pre-defined criteria (i.e. readiness assessment). Key essential elements also include change communication for government agencies affected, public communications, training and education programmes for civil servants and even for the general public. One of key challenges in implementing the E-Roadmap is ensuring the suitable project/programme structure for implementation and getting relevant expertise including adequate project management and staff resources.

Projected Budgets and Estimates

E-Government projects in developing countries are usually driven by individual government departments that frequently depend upon on aid from donors. Once this financing ceases, there is often insufficient funding to continue the project (Schware & Deane, 2003). Thus, projected budgets and estimates should be projected for both technology and non-technology recommendations. For the technology recommendations, they include sizing for the infrastructure which includes hardware and software as well as the cost for infrastructure setup, development and implementation services. If there are several components for a pilot, the costs and estimates are broken correspondingly into separate activities. As an e-Government Roadmap or blueprint is a high level study, figures provided are budgetary for planning purposes and based on assumptions made for sizing and determination of scope. Before implementing the recommendations into specific pilots / projects / programmes, a preliminary study (e.g. pre-technical assistance programme) should be done to determine the terms of reference including the scope and budget as part of a procurement process before awarding to the suitable candidate solution providers for the implementation.

Critical Success Factors

These are critical success factors for the successful implementation of the e-Government roadmap. They would cover specific areas of concern and highlight implications to the stakeholders responsible for e-Government initiatives, and who make use of the e-Government roadmap study.

The following are the critical success factors that need to be considered:

- Strong Leadership and determination to embrace and adopt changes
- Developing of Competencies for e-Government for Government Agencies
- Reengineered Government Processes and Streamlined Administrative Procedures
- Cross Agency Collaboration
- Core ICT systems and ICT infrastructure for key agencies to be implemented
- Provision of vital information and essential E-services for stakeholders to appreciate and understand e-Government
- Awareness and communications programmes for public to understand e-Government
- Set of related laws to implement and support e-Government

e-GOVERNMENT LEGAL ASSESSMENT

In most countries, there are no specific laws for e-Government unless there is a need to facilitate collaboration between government agencies and to clearly spell out roles and responsibilities. There has been a common view in Vietnam that

the government should embark on e-Government pilots especially in the area of E-Services in various cities and make government information easily accessible. Only after the implementation of such pilots, should an assessment be made to determine whether an e-Government law or decree needs to be formulated. Another consideration is alignment of the One Stop Shop decree and a new decree / regulations after studying the relationship in provision of E-services impacting backroom and front office of government agencies in key cities.

However, it has been observed that regulations supporting various e-Government programmes are necessary to bring up the management capacity of ICT in government especially in planning, budgeting and administration including the role and responsibility of the Chief Information Office (CIO). One of the biggest challenges is in ensuring proper ICT Planning for ministries, cities and provinces. Fundamentally, the Government has to establish IT manpower cost norms for ICT services from consultants, developers and project managers, these are not only local but international expertise. This is extremely important as Vietnam embarks on e-Government making use of made of government funds as well as loans and technical assistance from international donors and aid agencies.

CONCLUSION

An e-Government initiative brings with it much hope and even hype that citizens and institutions will benefit from the services provided by the government. However, before this can be realised, much planning and coordination must take place. The government of a developing country must devise a national strategy in consultation with all stakeholders.

At the national level, at the regional level and internationally, particularly with DCs which have contemplated or undertaken such initiatives, there must be partnerships and alliances so as to optimise the limited human and financial resources available in the search for such a complex technological solution.

The roadmap presented here could assist governments in Vietnam and similar developing countries in their e-Government initiatives as they seek to achieve the best for their citizens and institutions. Vietnam should pursue a more active role in the formulation of national policies and strategies to promote the information economy, to reap huge benefits in terms of economic and social growth/development. E-Government does not only facilitate market- led initiatives but it also plays a major role in initiating the process of capability building and in coordinating the actions of a large number of interested stakeholders (Mansell and Wehn, 1998). The roadmap offers the potential of reshaping the public sector activities and processes, building relationships between citizens and the government, enhancing transparency, increasing government capacity and providing a "voice" for those outside the government.

REFERENCES

Allen, A. B., Juillet, L., Paquet, G., & Roy, J. (2001). E-Governance and Government Online in Canada: Partnerships, People and Prospects. *Government Information Quarterly, 18*, 93-104.

Bhatnagar, S. (2004). E-Government: Lessons from Implementation in Developing Countries. *Regional Development Dialogue, 24*, UNCRD, Autumn Issue 164-174.

Cecchini, S., & Raina, M. (2004). Electronic Government and the Rural Poor: The Case of Gyandoot. *Information Technologies and International Development, 2*(2), 65–75.

Ciborra, C. (2005). Interpreting e-government and Development Efficiency, transparency or governance at a distance? *Information Technology and People, 18*(3). 65-75.

Cuthbert S., & Tran V. N. (2005). *Vietnam E-Government Roadmap Study.* ADB Technical Assistance 4080 Program for Vietnam Office of the Government (OOG), Decision 112 State Administration Computerisation Committee (SAMCom).

DeLisi, P. S (1990). Lessons from the Steel Axe: Culture. Technology and Organisation Change. *Sloan Management Review, 32*, (1), 83-93.

Ebrahim, Z., & Irani, Z. (2005). E-Government adoption: architecture and barriers. *Business Process Management Journal, 11*(5), 589-611.

Fountain, J. F. (2001). *Building the Virtual State: Information Technology and Institutional Change.* Washington, DC: Brookings Institution Press.

Hassard, J., & Sharifi, S. (1989). Corporate Culture and Strategic Change. *Journal of General Management, 15*(2), 4-19.

Heeks, R. (Ed.) (1999). Reinventing Government in the Information Age: International Practice in IT-Enabled Public Sector Reform. Routledge: London.

Heeks, R. (2001a). *Understanding e-Governance for Development.* Working Paper Series Paper No. 11 IDPM U. of Manchester.

Heeks, R. (2001b). *Building e-Governance for Development: A Framework for Nation and Donor Action.* Working Paper Series Paper No. 12 IDPM U of Manchester.

Heeks, R. (2003). *Most e-Government-for-developing Projects Fail: How Can Risks Be Reduced?* iGovernment Working Paper Series, Paper no. 14.

Hewitt, E. (2003). A National Strategy for Developing Countries. *COMNET-IT Forum Newsletter of Comm Network of IT for Development.*

Ho, A.T-K. (2002). Reinventing local governments and the e-government initiative", Public Administration Review, 62(4), 434-44.

Hunter, M. G., Long, W. (2002). Information Systems and Small Business: Lessons from the Entrepreneurial Process. In M. Khosrow-Pour (Ed.), Issues and Trends of IT Management in Contemporary Organisations. Idea Group Press

Jaeger, P. T., & Thompson, K. M. (2003). E-Government around the world: Lessons, challenges, and future directions. *Government Information Quarterly, 20*, 389–394.

Lee-Kelley, L., & James, T. (2003). E-Government and Social Exclusion: An Empirical Study. *Journal of Electronic Commerce in Organisations, 1*(4), 1-16.

Lin, M., Zhu, R., & Hachigian, N. (2001). *Beijing's Business E-Park*. World Bank.

Mansell, R., & Wehn, U. (1998). Knowledge Societies: Information Technology for

Sustainable Development. Oxford University Press.

McClure, D. L. (2001). *Electronic Government: Challenges Must Be Addressed with Effective Leadership and Management*. GAO-01-959T, Testimony before the Senate Committee on Governmental Affairs, on behalf of the U.S. General Accounting Office.

Moon, M. J. (2002). The evolution of e-government among municipalities: rhetoric or reality. *Public Administration Review, 62*(4), 424-33.

Ndou, V. D. (2004). E-Government for Developing Countries: Opportunities and Challenges. *Electronic Journal of Information Systems in Developing Countries, 18*(1), 1-24.

Neumann, S. (1994). *Strategic Information Systems: Competition Through Information Technologies*. New York, NY: Macmillian College Publishing.

OECD (2001). Engaging Citizens in Policy-Making: Information, Consultation and Policy Participation. *Puma Policy Brief No. 10.*

Schware, R., & Deane, A. (2003). *Deploying E-Government programs: The strategic importance of 'I' before 'E'"*, info, *5*(4), 10-19.

Tan, A. (2007). Business Process Reengineering in Asia: A Practical Approach. Second Edition, Prentice Hall.

Tapscott, D. (1996). The Digital Economy. New York: McGraw Hill.

World Bank (2003) World Development Indicators, http://www.worldbank.org/data/wdi2003/

Yong, J. (2005). *E-Government in Asia*. Second Edition, Times edition.

Chapter X
Adopting the IT (RPM) Model to Enhance the Value of IT

Anand Sanwal
Brilliont, USA

Subhradeep Mohanty
American Express, USA

ABSTRACT

In a day and age that has been deemed the "Information Age", it is ironic that one of the most common questions that organizations continue to grapple with is "what is the value of Information Technology?" Despite mercurial debate on the question, it remains unanswered with most IT organizations unaware of how they can demonstrate this value. Interestingly, the question posited this way drives you to one immediate, and potentially false, conclusion – that IT, in fact, is driving value, and therefore, it is just a matter of determining or solving for this value. Most of us probably know (but may be unwilling to admit) that the reality is not so. Just like not all people are above average, not all IT organizations demonstrate value. We would argue that the "what is the value of IT?" question is the wrong question. The more important question that IT organizations should ask themselves is "how can IT deliver more value?" A satisfactory resolution to this question will also handle the "what is the value of IT?" question. But by posing the question this way, you approach it in a more objective and dispassionate manner. The IT Reengineering & Portfolio Management Model (herein, IT (RPM)) offers a pragmatic, proven and plausible means for IT organizations to deliver and demonstrate value. In introducing you to the IT (RPM), we aim to:

- *Discern between those investments which are valued by the business and those which are not, e.g. expenses versus investments*

- *Develop a plan to reengineer low value IT expenses in an effort to create additional investment capacity within IT and/or for the larger organization for strategic, business-enhancing projects and investments*
- *Utilize a portfolio management discipline to select the best investments, e.g. those that maximize strategic and financial value per unit of risk*
- *Provide an understanding of the process and behavioral elements required to enable IT (RPM)*

BACKGROUND

Reengineering

Reengineering as a discipline has emerged into the corporate psyche because of proponents like Michael Hammer and James A. Champy who authored *Reengineering the Corporation* and *Reengineering Management*. Their basic assertion is that far too much time and effort is wasted on tasks and there is very little focus on the value that these tasks deliver for the customer

Despite their lofty and mostly accurate aspirations, reengineering has earned a less than savoury reputation because it has come to be associated with reducing the efforts - mass layoffs and corporate restructuring – rather than redirecting those efforts to something more constructive. This is due to the fact that many organizations don't actively reengineer their business on a continuous basis, but instead they make large cuts under the banner of reengineering when business or economic conditions worsen. For public companies, reengineering pressures also can mount due to the self-inflicted pressure companies can place on themselves to meet arbitrary earnings expectations. These knee-jerk efforts are not true reengineering but despite this, the public relations harm to the term reengineering remains.

Our view of reengineering, informed but not limted by the likes of Hammer and Champy, is that reengineering is simply a practice and discipline of evaluating processes to determine if they can be done better in some other fashion. By better, this may imply the process is done cheaper, faster, in a less risky way, or sometimes the process is eliminated altogether. These benefits may be realized through the utilization of technology, labor arbitrage and/or a variety of methods which maybe employed to make the organization more productive. In essence, reengineering examines processes that result in unproductive organizational complexity and seeks to improve or remove them altogether.

Portfolio Management

Portfolio management has emerged or come into vogue mainly due to an army of consultants, academics and software vendors who espouse this discipline's benefits. While their means to achieve this are dubious at best, their high-level definitions of portfolio management are largely on the mark.

Portfolio management applied to the corporation is based on the realization that organizations spend vast sums of money on discretionary projects - or rather investments - whether in IT, marketing, R&D, sales, operations or any other business function. And in order to properly allocate resources to these investments, it is worthwhile to evaluate these investments as part of a portfolio, with a clear understanding of the trade-offs between risk, return and timing.

One notable departure from the "experts'" definition is that we aim to employ portfolio management to discretionary operating expenses (OpEx) and capital expenditures (CapEx) – not just capex which is customary. Most often, portfolio management is utilized for larger, multi-year projects which are categorized as CapEx, but in our view, this misses a huge category of discretionary investments. The Corporate Portfolio Management Association's research (www.corporateportfoliomanagement.org) indicates that between 25-40% of OpEx is in fact discretionary which points to a huge opportunity to optimize both OpEx and CapEx as part of the portfolio management effort.

The portfolio management discipline ultimately is about optimizing an organization's allocation of resources to discretionary investments. And there is a financial benefit of doing this. A McKinsey study of 2000 corporations determined that companies with the highest growth over a 10 year period achieved it as a result of organic growth and resource allocation efficiency. The top consistent growth companies - of which there were only 9 - did so without relying significantly on mergers & acquisitions and instead focused on taking a deliberate and thoughtful approach to their resource allocation decisions and organic growth.

Historically, reengineering and portfolio management have not been considered together and have been managed as two distinct specialized areas. However, in practice, they are closely intertwined and corporations can generate more value if they take an integrated approach towards these disciplines. It seems intuitive that the effort to rationalize the resources expended in one part of the business (reengineering) should be tied to the effort to reinvest those same resources in another area (portfolio management) .

MAIN THRUST OF THE CHAPTER

The need for a pragmatic and proven model like IT (RPM) is necessitated by a few key drivers and issues, some specific to IT, some to the overall organization and some due to other larger macroeconomic and environmental factors.

- IT value remains a perplexing issue – This question persists and IT and the larger organizations of which they are a part do not appear to be closer to measuring or more importantly ensuring they are driving this value. Despite numerous efforts that claim to do this, no generally useful or scalable model or framework has been created to answer the value question. Part of the issue as already discussed is the implicit assumption that IT drives value which it may not. Dangerous assumptions lead to dangerous outcomes.

- Accountability and measurability are top priorities – This move towards measurability is not relegated or specific to IT. All areas of the corporation are being asked by senior management, the Board of Directors, customers and in many cases, external parties focused on governance, environmental impact and other issues about how their organizations are measuring these dimensions. "What am I getting for my investment?" is an increasingly asked question of marketers, R&D researchers and IT organizations. An inability to provide a satisfactory answer to this question can result in decreased investment in the area, career limitations, lessened organizational influence, etc. It is also not just about the promise of results but also about the ability to deliver the performance. And as a result, accountability and tracking of results is becoming more important to demonstrate that performance is really being delivered against the promise.

- Inconsistent language – In line with the move towards accountability and measurability is the need to move away from the highly specialized language of IT when talking to business partners and other organizational constituents, e.g., finance, risk, operations, etc. It is not the job of others in the organization to understand the language of IT but for IT to articulate their actions in the language of business – dollars, euros, pounds, etc and the resulting revenue, profit and cash flow that are used to measure corporate performance.

- IT as an expense – By thinking and presenting themselves as an expense, IT organizations have been perpetually considered something to be minimized. Investments get managed and optimized – expenses do not.

- The heightened pace of change – Although every generation probably claims this, it maybe argued with some merit that we've reached a new inflection point in the way technology is changing entire industries, business models, etc. IT organizations must continue to grapple with and in some instance embrace and accommodate these changes while keeping the proverbial "machine" running.

- IT as a victim – Too many IT organizations have adopted a victim psychology often resulting in an adversarial relationship with other parts of the organization. Relying on common retorts such "We just do what the business tells us" or "Technology is a key competitive advantage in today's world", a philosophy of IT victimization has permeated many IT organizations taking them away from conversations about and contributions to value and unfortunately has made them more focused on safeguarding turf, e.g., people, money, etc.

- Too many experts – Contributing significantly to many or most of the above issues and confusion is an army or ecosystem of consultants, vendors, and other self-proclaimed experts who have created a cottage industry around this issue of IT value. Despite or rather, in spite of their efforts, these assorted luminaries have not delivered

upon their oft-ambitious goals. More often that not, they've resulted in organizational inefficiency (time and money lost) as organizations move towards the supposed "best practices" they highlight. A recent example of the dubious nature and quality of these expert sources was illustrated by a January 30, 2008 Wall Street Journal column which found that Aberdeen, a prominent IT consulting & research firm had major conflicts of interest between the research findings they promote and the sponsors who support them. The Wall Street Journal columnist wrote, "…If much of your top line is dependent on getting tech companies to sponsor your research reports, you've got quite an incentive to design questionnaires that will yield the kind of reports tech vendors will want to sponsor. In that regard, Aberdeen delivers. The reports seem to invariably discover that "best in class" companies use, or are thinking about using, or somehow embody, whatever technology the report happens to be discussing." These conflicts are not exclusive to Aberdeen and have actually infested much of the IT ecosystem.

Solutions and Recommendations

In order for IT to deliver value, one of the central realizations that must first occur is that today's IT organization may not be driving value and second, that not all dollars spent on IT are valued by the business. And if not valued by the organization, they are not really valuable. Value is a perception and is therefore in the eye of the beholder.

While there might not exist immediate solutions to the 'value' problem, a good way to start working towards a resolution is by asking the business team the following questions :

1. How much are you willing to pay for this service?

   or

2. Are you ready to pay the amount required to perform this service?

Through a combination of open & direct discussions, and an efficient practice of usage-based chargeouts to the business, answers to the above questions can be sourced in either a direct or indirect way.

However, that might not necessarily throw up the most accurate answers as the perceived value might not reflect the real value to the business. Many aspects of IT have come to be expectations (stability, reliability, speed, etc) and so much like the ante in a game of poker, these are the minimum expectations of an IT organization to "play the game". These IT expenses are like electricity – obviously essential but not inherently considered valuable. Whether this is the appropriate 'value' system is an esoteric and unsolvable debate, but like it or not, this is the reality. In order to guide the organization to a common & more realistic understanding of value, all IT services should be invoiced to the business and the business should be encouraged to 'switch off' a service if they feel that it is over-priced. This would ensure that services that continue to be 'switched on' are perceived to be priced right. This would, to a certain extent, ensure a better alignment between the cost and efforts of the IT organization and the value to the business.

After ensuring that only value-added activities are being handled by the IT organization, it becomes important to separate lower value expenses

Exhibit A.

Magnitude (funding, time, risk)		
Large	**NA**	**Portfolio Management**
Small	**Reengineering**	**Portfolio Management**

Criticality to Organization:

Low	High
Expenses – Keeping the lights on, e.g., day to day business operations	Investments – Used for growth, innovation and business flexibility

from higher value investments. A central tenet of IT (RPM) is that it advocates a departure from managing IT solely as an expense to be mitigated and minimized, and instead, it pushes for different but inter-related disciplines to manage IT expenses as well as IT investments. Investments are those projects that genuinely and actively contribute to the future health of the business through contributions to growth, innovation and/or flexibility. As a result, the IT (RPM) model looks at investments as shown in Exhibit A.

While the reengineering and portfolio management disciplines will be discussed in further detail further on, it is worth noting the NA (not applicable) in this framework. In essence, no project or initiative which is of a large magnitude should be categorized as an expense. Projects in this area tend to be large multi-year capital expenditure projects to upgrade capabilities, build redundancy, increase flexibility, etc and so they should be considered and actively managed as investments and therefore as part of the portfolio management effort. Doing this also prevents gamesmanship which may occur by those hoping to avoid investment scrutiny by including large initiatives in the expense category.

At its most basic level, the model pushes for active reengineering of IT expenses. The resources (money to fund projects or employees engaged in low-value efforts) that are freed up from reengineering initiatives can then be used for IT investments which focus on growth, innovation and business flexibility/agility. Now we will explore the reengineering and portfolio management disciplines to be used with IT expenses and investments, respectively, in greater detail.

REENGINEERING IT EXPENSES

IT reengineering, as a source for generating additional investment resources, has found wide acceptance across a broad range of industries. However, in practice, very few firms have been able to exploit its full potential. The biggest implementation hurdle that managers have faced is self-created – defining a very narrow scope of what reengineering can deliver.

Reengineering initiatives can broadly be divided into two categories - strategy driven and profitability driven. We define strategy driven reengineering as focused on improving capabilities or product offerings to gain a competitive advantage, and profitability driven reengineering as an attempt to improve the bottom line.

The reengineering mandate invariably originates as a reactive, profitability driven measure. In its bi-annual Management Tools and Trends 2007 Survey, Bain & Company has identified reduction of costs & cycle time as a primary use of reengineering tools. As has been stated earlier in this chapter, IT is largely considered an expense and companies, in the early stages of a reengineering program, focus on minimizing the 'unit cost' of IT efforts

The results are typically encouraging in the beginning with redundant efforts and costs being eliminated. However, after removing the 'low-hanging fruit', this approach proves difficult to sustain and could prove disastrous at times. Bain & Company's 2007 survey highlights that the overall satisfaction score for reengineering tools had been declining since 2004. In an effort to keep reducing 'unit costs', companies might start compromising on more critical elements that drive customer engagement, financial control, etc. and the business impact of these measures can be severe.

Strategy driven reengineering, on the other hand, is focused more on improving processes and practices that are critical to the company's success. Instead of 'unit cost', the key parameters defining the desired outcome are customer experience and satisfaction, level of control and compliance, etc. While they might have a positive & significant business impact, such projects are difficult to value as the benefits are largely intangible. Additionally, they might have longer-term returns and might negatively impact the bottom line in the first year. (See Exhibit B.)

.Both of these approaches, in isolation, have huge drawbacks. But a balanced reengineering portfolio would prove to be ideal. The profitability driven reengineering initiatives get easier organizational buy-in and can serve as the platform to understand the strategic opportunities. The strategy driven reengineering initiatives, in turn, will help position the IT organization as a strategic partner. Therefore,

a pre-planned, proactive reengineering program moving on both fronts will deliver the best results.

IT reengineering initiatives have broadly been focused on the categories in Exhibit C.

The various types of reengineering initiatives differ in the amount of management effort required, implementation difficulty, size of sustainable benefits that they deliver and the implementation time frame. Managers have to be aware of the trade-offs and have clarity on the end objectives. (See Exhibit D.)

Exhibit B.

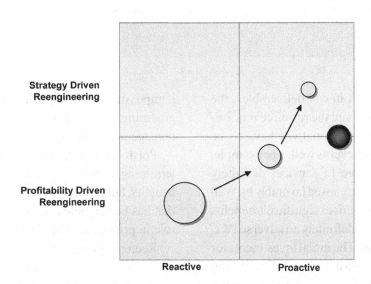

Exhibit C.

Category	Examples of Strategic Objectives	Examples of Financial Objectives
Automation	- Value-added services for customers - Reduce operational & financial risk	- Lower manpower costs
Offshoring	- Access to new talent pool - Develop operating knowledge of untapped markets	- Access to low-wage labor pool
Outsourcing	- Improve time-to-market & operational flexibility - Develop a Champion-challenger situation for in-house operations	- Lower overhead costs
Process Improvement	- Develop new capabilities	- Reduce cost of rework

Exhibit D.

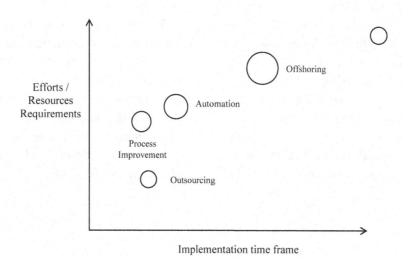

Given the trade-offs in end deliverables, the investment time frame and the resource requirements, IT reengineering initiatives have to be managed at a portfolio level as well. For example, while a plan to offshore IT services definitely makes headlines, is often viewed favorably by Wall Street analysts and promises significant benefits in the long run, there is definitely an adverse P&L impact in the short run. The initial investments for setting up a new infrastructure and dismantling an existing one are high. A smart reengineering team would then aim to supplement that with a few small-scale IT process improvement projects that would deliver immediate benefits and help absorb the negative short-term impact of the large-scale initiative.

Therefore, having a broad set of well-defined reengineering projects is just half the battle. The bigger challenge is to understand the timing and size of the benefits, and establish a framework to utilize those most efficiently. They could either help close short-term gaps in the company's profitability or be reinvested for long-term objectives (growth, innovation and flexibility). This makes it impossible to uncover the full potential of reengineering initiatives without a focused portfolio management program.

Portfolio management will not only help in determining the most optimal use of the reengineering benefits, but the incremental investment capacity that has been created but will also play a critical role in prioritizing areas of reengineering.

Reengineering can prove to be a double-edged sword and has to be handled very skillfully. As outlined earlier, reengineering has to be focused on non-critical processes and efforts, and a lack of awareness of criticality of functions can result in ill-advised reengineering plans. Criticality assessment can be based on the degree of separation from the customer (customer-facing functions are more critical than those that are non customer-facing) and the portfolio management team can help define the prioritization of the non customer-facing costs.

Reengineering can also have important implications from an organizational standpoint. Certain plans might result in teams being impacted and may result in employee dissatisfaction and organizational whiplash. Doing what is right for the company might suddenly feel not right for you. In such instances, the handling of change becomes easier if the reengineering plans are linked to the portfolio management plans. Providing the context of the portfolio needs facilitates better organizational buy-in and also helps present a more rational, dispassionate view to the impacted teams.

In short, Reengineering and Portfolio Management are two wheels of the organization's growth vehicle and they need to coordinate well to sustain a high growth trajectory. With the investment capacity generated by your IT reengineering program, you can take a look at how portfolio management can be applied to the investment side of IT.

APPLYING CORPORATE PORTFOLIO MANAGEMENT FOR IT INVESTMENTS

Our discussion of portfolio management for IT investments takes a decidedly financial view as it is dollars, euros, Yuan, pounds, etc and the resulting cash flow, revenue, profit, NPV, etc which define the language of business. IT portfolio management as it has come to be known has been tightly tied to software tools and project management capabilities which while potentially useful are not tied appropriately to overall business goals and requirements.

Corporate portfolio management in the context of the IT (RPM) model provides the organization with the ability to frequently and actively manage the company's IT investments as a portfolio of discretionary projects. It leverages data on projections as well as tracked actual results and actively involves investment owners in a discipline that lets companies select the best investments to meet their strategic, financial and risk goals. Data and information are fundamental to removing the personality-driven elements of resource allocation as it relates to IT investment. Ultimately, corpo-

rate portfolio management's underlying belief is, as the adage goes, that what gets measured gets managed. To enable this measurement, portfolio management relies on modern portfolio theory, but it is not so myopic in its use of data that it ignores critical behavioral and cultural elements. As a result, corporate portfolio management is predicated on and requires balancing two critical dimensions: modern portfolio theory and organizational behavior. (See Exhibit E.)

Note: Corporate portfolio management is often referred to by different terms so as a point of reference, terms such as IT portfolio management, enterprise portfolio management, product portfolio management, project portfolio management, resource allocation and investment optimization are similar. In fact, these all are slices or subsets of corporate portfolio management which will be used synonymously with the term portfolio management throughout the remainder of this chapter.

Modern Portfolio Theory (aka the Process)

This is what people generally think of when they think of corporate portfolio management. It is comprised of:

1. Investment valuation - This includes defining what an investment is. As mentioned earlier, it is worthwhile to take an expansive definition of what comprises an investment because this is not just capital expenditures (CapEx), but also should include more recurring operating expenses (OpEx) within IT of which 25-40% are discretionary in nature. Investment valuation also requires consistency of valuation methodology which necessitates using driver-based models to create projections and also looking past NPVs and ROIs to consider strategy, risk and other qualitative aspects that drive investment 'value'. By consideration of the

Exhibit E.

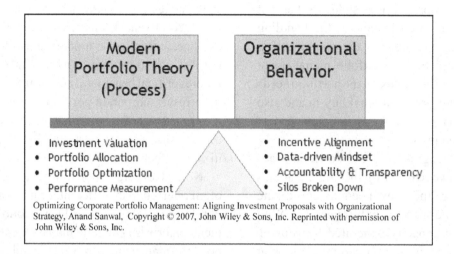

Optimizing Corporate Portfolio Management: Aligning Investment Proposals with Organizational Strategy, Anand Sanwal, Copyright © 2007, John Wiley & Sons, Inc. Reprinted with permission of John Wiley & Sons, Inc.

financial, strategic and risk parameters, you will have a more complete view into investment value.

2. Portfolio allocation - This requires determining investment areas/themes and the associated allocations. Basically, what are my strategic priorities for investment and how much will go to each area? For example, 25% in customer acquisition, 20% in innovation, 55% in customer retention. The allocation should also consider the risk profile of investments, e.g., 60% in low risk, 30% in medium risk and 10% in high risk.

3. Portfolio optimization - This requires selecting the best investments to support the portfolio allocation and periodically rebalancing the portfolio to ensure consistency with desired portfolio allocations. The aim is to maximize strategic and financial return per unit of risk.

4. Performance measurement - A key element of successful corporate portfolio management is capturing actual investment results to enable promise vs. performance. Doing this ultimately allows an organization to hold investment/initiative owners accountable and lets an organization improve ongo-

ing investment valuation based on actual results. Based on this, the organization can rebalance the portfolio based on performance achieved.

The problem with most of the discussion of portfolio management is that it assumes that people behave according to a theoretical/rational construct. While various experts like to offer platitudes saying things like, "Just manage your company's IT investments like you manage your own investments," they fail to realize that many individuals may not even manage their own personal portfolios as they should or that even 50% of "smart" mutual fund managers underperform on average. Managing like a portfolio of stocks is simplistic advice with potentially poor results. We may know what we should do but emotions, intuition, and other external influences take us off this rational path. What often leads us astray in our personal portfolio is what leads us astray in an organizational setting - behavior. The challenge in an organization is magnified by the fact that it is hundreds or even thousands of people whose behavior that needs to be considered. And so this is the second fundamental lever of corporate portfolio management - organizational behavior.

Organizational Behavior

In order to optimize one's corporate portfolio, the behavioral elements must be understood with:

- A data-driven mindset - Organizations often make decibel- or intuition-led decisions and corporate portfolio management, like 6-Sigma, requires data and analytical decision making.
- Silos removed - Corporate portfolio management success requires people thinking about what is best for the organization and not just what is best for "my world" - silos and organizational dynasties need to be broken down.
- Incentive alignment - People should be motivated by similar short- and long-term incentives.
- Accountability & transparency - There should be a willingness to share information and effectively create a marketplace for investments.

Moving organizational behavior is the larger challenge and this takes time to change. At American Express, for example, they have actively focused on changing organizational behavior and have made significant inroads, but it has not happened overnight. They have conducted cross unit investment reviews, sponsored an internal corporate portfolio management conference and even utilized a portfolio management simulation/game to visibly demonstrate the benefit of corporate portfolio management. Portfolio management ultimately is a large change management effort, and it requires education and influence to impact behavior and culture.

A Four-Step Roadmap to Corporate Portfolio Management Success

Armed with a high-level understanding of the tenets of portfolio management, the question then becomes one of how to bring and build such a discipline. The following four-step model offers a roadmap to doing this followed by discussion of each of the four phases. (See Exhibit F.)

Phase 1: Analyze

Simply stated, you cannot know where you are going if you don't know where you are or where you have been. The purpose of the analyze phase is to understand what your organization is good at across three dimensions related to resource allocation:

1. Process, discipline & systems
2. Organizational behavior
3. Attitude & readiness

Process, discipline and systems. Within this category, you must answer several key questions in determining whether your company is ready for portfolio management. First is: What does the IT organization consider to be a discretionary investment? This question is sure to engender significant debate. Individuals inherently want to believe that what they do is not discretionary; everyone wants their domain to be core to corporate operations. At this point, you are just taking stock of what people across the organization view as discretionary. Try to take an expansive view with the expectation that other IT stakeholders will try to narrow your definition down the road. The more you consider discretionary, the more room you'll have to negotiate down the road when you move to the standardize phase of the portfolio management initiative.

Second, you must select a credible "nerve center" to manage the portfolio management effort. No function is necessarily the best place to house portfolio management, but certain attributes and skills are required of the central body that can manage portfolio management's development and, ultimately, the processes that result from it. This central body needs to be viewed as credible and

Exhibit F.

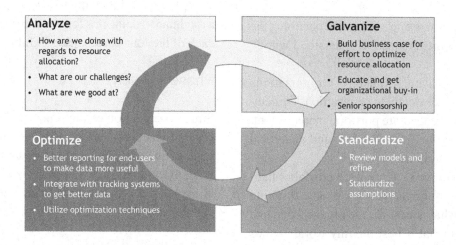

impartial. In terms of skills, the team needs to be able to assess the financial, strategic, and risk attributes of an investment, so members of the team need corporate finance and strategic planning skills. Putting your portfolio management ambitions in the hands of a project management team is generally not advisable.

One more question that can help determine whether a company's processes are ready for portfolio management is: Are core metrics widely accepted throughout the organization? Portfolio management is about a data-driven mind-set, so agreement on what information is most important in investment decisions will be critical as the project moves forward. If there is widespread consensus in your company about which metrics are key in evaluating investments, your company will have a head start.

Organizational behavior. Take a pragmatic view of the inevitable organizational politics. Know who your supporters and detractors are, and develop game plans to deal with each. Then ask yourself: What is the organization's patience level? It is vital that you understand how quickly others will want to see results? Portfolio management is not an overnight or fast-acting elixir so you should understand your organization's patience

level before deciding which area to focus on first. Also, consider what incentives your company has in place to foster organizational and individual success. Portfolio management will mean that some individuals may lose investment dollars from their CapEx and OpEx areas, while those who have more attractive opportunities may gain. If incentives promote success of the organization as a whole, these actions will be less disruptive.

Attitude and readiness. One question you must answer is: Who will champion portfolio management? When embarking on a project that is this transformational, you need a highly regarded senior champion who can help shepherd and sell the idea around the organization. You also need to think about your personal ambitions as they relate to portfolio management. This is a major effort within any IT organization, so anyone who takes a lead role in the project needs to understand up front why he or she is getting involved and whether the perceived personal rewards will be worth the effort that is required.

Phase 2: Galvanize

After you spend some time understanding where your organization stands, your efforts should shift to galvanizing support. Your aim is to create momentum and excitement for corporate portfolio management. Some key tactics during this phase include the following:

1) Leverage your champion. Harness this executive's power for credibility. Make sure he or she is talking about portfolio management far and wide. Ask the project champion to build support for incorporating portfolio management objectives into people's personal goals, and to develop an incentive system in which achievement of portfolio management-related objectives drive compensation.

2) Build a coalition. Seek like-minded people from other parts of the organization. Brainstorm with them, and solicit their input. Give them access to your champion.

3) Avoid confronting or embarrassing detractors. Head-on conflicts will come back to bite you. More important, a portfolio management initiative is about inclusion, and buy-in must be widespread for the project to be successful. Focus instead on the promoters of portfolio management, so that you don't have to spend a lot of time defending your efforts.

4) Win small, win early, and win often. People like associating with winning initiatives. Conduct a successful pilot in one portion of the IT organization and then advertise your victories.

5) Understand the challenges you face. Listen to your supporters and to those in the trenches. Acknowledge the obstacles and opposition confronting the initiative. Develop answers to detractors' concerns and solutions to the real problems that might hamper success.

6) Compare yourself to other organizations your company admires. Social comparison theory is a psychological theory which says that individuals evaluate their own opinions and desires by comparing themselves to others. In essence, point to how portfolio management can make you more like organizations that you admire. This type of upward social comparison will create a favorable impression of your portfolio management effort.

7) Change organizational behavior on an ongoing basis. Focus on ongoing education and reinforcement. Continuously re-evaluate incentives and the effectiveness of efforts to inform people about portfolio management.

8) Determine the ROI of portfolio management. Corporate portfolio management is about data, so demonstrate your understanding of it. If you were able to improve the effectiveness of investments by just 1 percent, what dollar value would the portfolio management effort be contributing to your company? Use this information to show the bottom-line impact of portfolio management within the IT organization.

Phase 3: Standardize

When the Analyze and Galvanize phases of your portfolio management initiative are under control (even if they're not complete), you can shift part of your energy to the extremely critical standardize phase. The intent in this phase is to create a means for people to speak the same language when they propose and evaluate IT investments. You likely uncovered numerous questions during the analyze phase that you will need to resolve during your work to standardize investments. The most important questions include the following:

1. What is a discretionary OpEx investment? Determining which operating expenses will be considered discretionary will involve negotiation with the managers who control each area of spending, and the definition of "discretionary" must be finalized during the standardize phase. It is important to avoid singling out a particular area of expenses as a target. It is also important to work with different stakeholders to come to your

definition. Once you have a clear definition of discretionary investments, ensure that you have the approval of all the appropriate people before you move on.

2. Which metrics are important, and which are not? There is a metrics zeitgeist these days which would have you believe that the measurement of anything and everything is good. You will need to work with your business partners to understand which metrics either truly indicate success or else offer reliable predictive value.

3. How should we standardize the modeling of projects? Reframing discretionary expenses as investments requires modeling, when possible, the returns associated with these investments. So creating standardized cost-benefit analyses is critical, especially once the company begins comparing prospective investments against one another. Standard driver-based models in which the drivers and certain business assumptions are controlled at some central level are required to drive consistency of valuation and ensure parties believe comparisons. For example, a business unit might define its expected response rates for marketing campaigns while the corporate group managing the portfolio management effort might control the discount rates, foreign exchange rates and calculation logic used in financial projections. By doing this, conversations can occur about the value and selection of the right investment and not be derailed by questions and protests about the integrity of the data.

4. What will we do with OpEx investments that do not generate returns? Many discretionary OpEx investments in IT will have not clearly identifiable financial returns. This is why standardizing qualitative or execution-related investment parameters — such as risk and strategic scoring of investments or stage-gated milestones — will be useful. Consider an IT investment that is intended to improve the reliability of internal systems. This may not have a directly quantifiable benefit associated with it, but it does have a risk or strategic rationale that can be articulated. Also, although no financial benefit can be ascribed to this investment as part of a cost-benefit analysis, the investment does have costs and project milestones. Capturing costs and deliverables, then holding people accountable for them, is a good idea for all investments, but it is critical for projects without an obvious return metric.

5. How will we collect the information? This is an organizational decision, but our recommendation is to not buy a software tool at the beginning of the portfolio management initiative. While numerous vendors are hawking "portfolio management" and "portfolio optimization" software panaceas, these are a distraction and waste of money when you initially implement portfolio management. . A spreadsheet and a simple database should suffice in the beginning. When American Express built its leading portfolio management discipline, this worked for a number of years; not jumping right into a software purchase helped ensure that the company understood the process and outcomes they wanted from their portfolio efforts.

6. How often should we collect portfolio information? As mentioned in *The 7-1/2 Deadly Sins of Managing Your Corporate Investment Portfolio* from <u>Optimizing Corporate Portfolio Management,</u> one of the key sins to avoid is viewing IT resource allocation as a New Year's resolution. Your portfolio of OpEx investments must be viewed on a more frequent basis so that the portfolio can be rebalanced by killing underperforming projects and funding promising projects throughout the year. The frequency of reviews and rebalancing will be driven by the nature of the organization's investments. At American Express, for example, these

reviews are done quarterly.

7.   How do we compare actuals with projections? One of the other deadly sins is making your portfolio view all about the projections. Ultimately, projections are just an individual's or a team's best guess. You must set up a standardized means for capturing actual investment results. This may mean manual tracking of investments or tapping into automated systems, but it is critical that you demonstrate to initiative owners that they will be held accountable for investment results. More important than the accountability is the fact that tracking results enables the performance of past investments to inform future projections. If a marketing investment is projected to have a 10 percent response rate but ends up with only a 3 percent response rate, portfolio management managers can use the tracking of actual results to inform and improve future-year projections. This closed loop on investment performance improves projections and, ultimately, decisions on investments.

Phase 4: Optimize

With your business case for corporate portfolio management established and sold, and with a standardized view of what an investment is, how to project investments' costs and benefits, and how to collect the information, you can enter the optimize phase of a portfolio management initiative with a true view into the portfolio of your organization's investments. In this phase, you can propose resource allocation tradeoffs within the IT portfolio. The nerve center managing the portfolio management effort can help propose tradeoffs, but ultimately it is not realistic to believe this nerve center can force these reallocations. Ideally, business units whose resources are being considered should be part of and driving this decision. At American Express, an investment review team was convened bringing participants from the business units together with the group negotiating with one another for resources. This ensured a level of sponsorship and engagement to the resource tradeoff decision process. Ultimately, it led to tens of millions of dollars being reallocated across business divisions.

More generally, the tradeoffs may involve shifting investment dollars to more risky projects or to projects that will grow a historically underfunded business unit or strategy. As you look to optimize the portfolio, be sure not to take a one-size-fits-all approach by boiling all decisions down to ROI or NPV. As investment amounts get larger and time periods and results become more predictable, the decisioning criteria and frameworks you employ will also have to change.

One of the key aspects of the optimize phase is that you must kill underperforming projects, and you must not fund unattractive projects. Making these tough decisions gives the portfolio management discipline credibility. If every proposal that starts as part of the portfolio gets funded, you're just creating bureaucracy. The idea behind portfolio management is to create a strategic discipline for picking meritorious IT investments. Certain investments that are started don't turn out as expected, and some proposals seem less promising once they are put through a rigorous process for projecting their benefits. These projects deserve to be stopped or not started. The first time the corporate portfolio management process kills an initiative, people will sit up, take notice, and begin to take portfolio management very seriously—which will force better decisions around discretionary investments and, ultimately, enhance the company's value.

THE BENEFITS OF IT (RPM)

IT (RPM) is not an esoteric, complicated model or theory which points to potential value creation, and herein lays one of its key strengths – it is easy to articulate and engage people on. When implemented successfully, its benefits are numerous including:

- Flexibility – In the course of business, performance challenges may dictate that costs need to be controlled. Instead of indiscriminate cost cutting, looking at IT expenses as customer and non-customer facing allows you to focus on cutting back on those projects which are least customer-relevant. This ensures that IT expenses always maintain a consistent growth orientation.

  Conversely, if incremental investment funding becomes available within the organization, IT now, through its corporate portfolio management effort, has unfunded investments that they can trigger. IT now has become a credible source for receipt of incremental funding because of the flexibility and agility with which it can respond to such opportunities and requests.

- Strategic IT organization – With decreased IT expenses and more IT investments oriented towards growth, innovation and flexibility, the IT organization is now one that is working in tandem with the business to realize and evolve its strategy. The proverbial goal of "IT as a strategic partner to the business" is achieved.

- Control & Accuracy: With increased flexibility, and the ability to monitor & influence costs more regularly, there exists increased control over the budget and also helps improve forecasting accuracy.

FUTURE TRENDS

Increasingly, IT organizations will be forced to clearly articulate and support the value they provide. The trend, as mentioned, is not relegated to IT but all areas of the organization will have to demonstrate this. The intuitiveness of the IT (RPM) model can get both the IT organization and its essential business partners aligned on how to demonstrate this value. The ability of even the layperson to understand this model aids in its viability and adoption. The main pitfall that organizations adopting the IT (RPM) model must avoid is focusing on the process elements to the exclusion of the cultural and behavioral components. As the CIO of Medtronic has said, "Culture eats strategy for lunch." The best laid out strategies are prone to being derailed without an appropriate plan in place to influence individual behavior and inspire engagement.

To this end, we feel that some care should be taken in determining or modifying the organizational construct in a way that is conducive to adoption of the IT (RPM) model and discipline. The following outlines a high-level view of what roles & responsibilities may look like. (See Exhibit G.)

Communication and accountability are critical to a successful IT (RPM) deployment. All stakeholders should be engaged and there should exist a common understanding of the desired benefits of the program and the resources available for execution. And individual teams should have clear, distinct responsibilities and goals related to make the IT (RPM) program a success.

IT (RPM) adoption will require a balancing of the ambitious optimism and practical pessimism which often accompany any new initiative. And this will require involving all the stakeholders in the beginning to put the organization in a place to realize the benefits of IT (RPM). The strategy and operations team would lay out the business needs to IT and the Finance & HR teams can work with IT to help identify resource constraints – people and money. In addition, the Finance & HR teams will also evaluate the impact of tactical plans from a control, compliance and employee standpoint.

Once the plans are finalized, all the stakeholders need to sign up for their individual roles in execution, monitoring and reporting. The three activities are closely linked and vitally important.

Exhibit G.

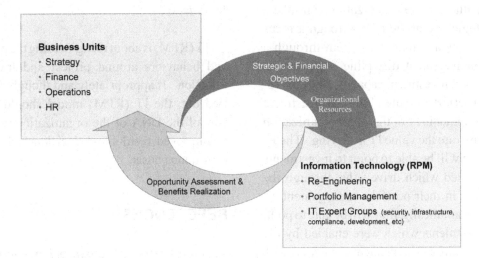

A lack of focus on any one of them might adversely affect the success of the program. Though the importance of execution is universally understood, many companies underestimate the power of effective monitoring and reporting in sustaining the execution momentum. It is important to use monitoring and reporting to keep management and stakeholders informed of the IT (RPM) efforts being undertaken by the IT organization. For those with a senior champion advocating for the IT (RPM) model, the reporting and monitoring provides a means to update their champion, keep them motivated and also allow the champion to look good.

The IT (RPM) team should take the primary responsibility for execution and consolidated monitoring and reporting. However, other teams like Finance, HR and Operations need to own and manage the metrics for their individual areas. Performance management practices like the use of scorecards can prove to be very effective in ensuring an appropriate level of engagement from all parties.

Establishing a well-defined communication and governance structure is just half the battle.

More often than not, the best-laid plans begin to break under the pressure of differing priorities and perspectives. At this juncture, the level of executive participation proves to be the defining element by satisfying the need for an arbitrator and providing the necessary push for the program to go ahead.

Managing the workplace dynamics to implement a successful IT (RPM) program might appear like a mammoth task. But a well-defined implementation plan and governance structure, backed by a strong executive mandate, can transform organizational noise into organizational momentum.

CONCLUSION

Moving to a psychology which seeks to demonstrate value versus prove value is more conducive to long term IT organizational success. And demonstrating value is possible through the adoption of the IT (RPM) model. By taking a pragmatic look into the IT organization's areas of focus to discern those efforts which are expenses and those which are investments, the organization can create an active reengineering plan for expenses. Coupled with this, the organization can take a more strategic seat at the table through a focus on investments and managing them through a portfolio management discipline. Ultimately, utilizing freed investment capacity from the reengineering effort to create additional investment capacity, whether in IT or the larger organization will demonstrate the value IT is driving. The IT organization will be able to point to investments they've enabled which drive value through the data resident in their portfolio management effort. More dramatically, they will be able to point to new investments which were enabled by the creation of additional investment capacity that IT reengineering enabled. There is not a better or more effective way of demonstrating value.

Although quite intuitive, the IT (RPM) model does require significant rigor in investment valuation, prioritization as well as in shaping organizational culture and behavior. Utilizing partners in the organization, whether in the business, finance, etc to develop your thinking and to help overcome some of these hurdles is suggested and probably required to become successful. IT (RPM) is not a gimmick which points to a scorecard, dashboard, software or quick framework to 'drive corporate performance'. Ultimately, heeding the advice of McKinsey who ironically are often creators of these frameworks maybe advisable:

"Executives should eschew simplistic organizational solutions. Popular techniques such as management incentives and key performance indicators (KPIs) are strikingly ineffective. Advice from experts on organizational performance often falls into either of two traps. Some of these authorities fail to give the full picture because they assume that companies already have a number of complementary building blocks in place and therefore systematically overestimate the impact of a single practice. Others have a preference for one big, visible intervention they regard as more

effective than a combination of less dramatic initiatives."

IT (RPM) is about reengineering the processes and behaviors around project and investment selection. If appropriately and thoughtfully carried out, the IT (RPM) model should become part of the DNA of the organization and result in improved results and decision-making on a continuous basis.

REFERENCES

Champy, J. (1996). *Reengineering Management: The Mandate for New Leadership.* New York/NY: HarperCollins.

Champy, J., & Hammer, M. (2001). *Reengineering the Corporation: A Manifesto for Business Revolution.* New York/NY: Harper Collins.

Corporate Portfolio Management Association. (2007). *CPMA Member Survey Results & Research.* Retrieved November 1, 2007, from http://www.corporateportfoliomanagement.org.

Devan, J., Klusas, M., & Ruefli, T. (2007). *The Elusive Goal of Corporate Outperformance. The McKinsey Quarterly,* Retrieved October 25, 2007 from http://www.mckinseyquarterly.com/The_elusive_goal_of_corporate_outperformance_1994.

Leslie, K., Loch, M., & Schaninger, W. (2006). Managing Your Organization by the Evidence. The McKinsey Quarterly, Retrieved August 14, 2007 from http://www.mckinseyquarterly.com/Managing_your_organization_by_the_evidence_1829.

Sanwal, A. (2007). *Optimizing Corporate Portfolio Management: Aligning Investment Proposals with Organizational Strategy.* New York/NY: John Wiley & Sons, Inc.

Chapter XI
CEO/CIO Communication and
the Strategic Organizations

Section III
Capability Development

Chapter XI
CEO/CIO Communication and the Strategic Grid Dimensions

Alice M. Johnson
North Carolina A&T State University, USA

Albert L. Lederer
University of Kentucky, USA

ABSTRACT

McFarlan's strategic grid postulated that the impact of existing information systems and impact of the portfolio of planned information systems constitute two dimensions on which the chief executive officer and chief information officer could assess their information technology. But what predicts their agreement on those impacts? Mutual understanding between an organization's CEO and CIO is an important factor in the organization's efforts to gain the greatest value from information technology, a factor that communications theory predicts, moreover, can be the product of greater communication frequency and channel richness. This research used a postal survey of 202 pairs of CEOs and CIOs to investigate the effect of such frequency and channel richness on CEO/CIO mutual understanding of the impact of existing information systems and of the impact of the portfolio of planned information systems. More frequent communication between the executives predicted mutual understanding about the current and future impacts of IT. However, the use of richer channels did not predict mutual understanding about the current impact, but did predict it about the future impact when the extent to which the organization relied on IT to support future projects was used as a covariate. Moreover, the finding that CEOs and CIOs perceived e-mail to be a richer communication channel than telephone was an unexpected outcome of the research. From a research perspective, the study extended theory about communication frequency, media richness, mutual understanding, and the impact of IT in organizations. It also provided additional validation of existing instruments that can be used to help future researchers of communications and IT. It provided direction for CEOs and CIOs who may be interested in increasing their mutual understanding of the impact of IT, improving their relationship with each other, and thus improving their planning of new information systems.

INTRODUCTION

Mutual understanding between the chief executive officer and chief information officer is critical to an organization's effective application of information technology. Such understanding can facilitate the organization's alignment of IT with business strategy (Keen 1991; Preston et al. Rowe 2006; Tan and Gallupe 2006), which predicts both improved IT performance and business performance (Chan et al. 1997).

On the other hand, the lack of mutual understanding between the two executives can cause problems. For example, if the CIO fails to understand business objectives or the CEO fails to understand the value of IT and how to employ it to achieve those objectives (Nath 1989; Neo 1988), then strategic information systems planning will be adversely impacted (Feeny et al. 1992; Keen 1991). Furthermore, failure to achieve such understanding can impede the organization's ability to acquire support for IT investments and the information systems function (Earl 1996). The Information Systems department's budget, after all, does depend on top management's understanding and perception of the impact of IT (Raghunathan et al. 1989).

McFarlan et al. (1983) established current strategic impact of IT and the future strategic impact of IT as meaningful and useful constructs in information systems practice and research. They defined the two impacts within their now well-known strategic grid framework. According to the authors, organizations should have developed and thus be employing a portfolio of current information systems with strategic impact, and organizations should be planning a portfolio of future systems with such impact. The grid was intended to provoke self-evaluation and the creation for information systems with strategic impact.

Mutual understanding of that impact, at both the current time and in the future, is critical (Applegate et al. 1996). An understanding of the current impact increases the likelihood of the proper support for critical, existing functions that rely on IT for daily operations. However, IT support for current functions does not guarantee support for future operations. In fact, plans and strategies for an organization's current IT may be counterproductive for future corporate strategies (Applegate et al. 1996). Therefore, mutual understanding — often referred to as convergence — about the future impact of IT is also important.

Convergence between the CEO and CIO is important, but few studies have investigated the process through which it is achieved. The objective of this chapter is to examine the role of communication in achieving convergence in the CEO/CIO relationship. The research question is: Do the frequency of communication and the richness of the communication channel between the CEO and CIO influence convergence about the current and future impact of IT in an organization? Figure 1 illustrates the research model.

COMMUNICATION FREQUENCY, CHANNEL RICHNESS, AND CONVERGENCE

Communication frequency, channel richness, and convergence are the constructs in this research. Each is now defined along with its importance to IT management.

Frequency

Communication is defined as a process in which individuals share and create information in order to reach a mutual understanding (Rogers and Kincaid 1981). Through frequent communication, they develop common definitions of situations and build consensus (Van de Ven and Walker 1984). Such communication is referred to as an "adjustment process" (Warriner 1970, p. 126), through which relationships are transformed over time (Singlemann 1972). Similarly, it is described as a

Figure 1. Research model

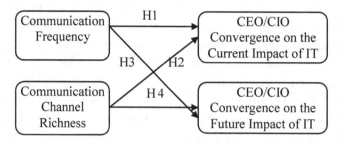

facilitator of gradual convergence of meanings and opinions about situations (Berger and Luckmann 1966; Van de Ven and Walker 1984).

Frequent communication is important in IT management in several respects. First, it helps IT personnel and their users have a common understanding of the organization's business functions and how IT can be used to support these functions (Lind and Zmud 1991).

Second, it positively affects an organization's competitive use of IT. For example, when CEOs communicate frequently with IT managers, the organization is more progressive than its competitors in its use of IT (Jarvenpaa and Ives 1991).

Third, frequent communication between IT and business executives positively influences the alignment of IT with business strategy. A case study of organizations in the insurance industry identified such communication as a factor that influenced alignment (Reich and Benbasat 1996).

Channel Richness

Communication channel richness refers to the extent to which media have the ability to overcome different frames of reference, clarify ambiguous issues, and thus facilitate understanding between communicating individuals (Daft and Lengel 1986). Certain communication media have a greater capacity than others to facilitate understanding. Thus, they are termed richer media or channels (Daft and Lengel 1986; Daft et al.,

1987). (The terms media and channels are used synonymously.)

According to media richness theory, a rich medium is one that enables immediate feedback, supports multiple cues such as facial and nonverbal expressions, accommodates language variety (e.g., numbers, natural language, etc.), and allows communication participants to tailor a message to fit personal requirements. Based on these four characteristics, an initial hierarchy was developed to indicate the following channel classifications in order of decreasing richness: (1) face-to-face, (2) telephone, (3) personally addressed media such as letters and memos, (4) non-personally addressed media such as telegrams, and (5) unaddressed media such as flyers and bulletins (Daft et al., 1987). Subsequent hierarchies confirmed that face-to-face and telephone communication, respectively, were the richest modes of communication. However, they further indicated that e-mail communication was slightly higher in richness than other traditional written communication (King and Xia 1997; Zmud et al., 1990). This may be because e-mail richness is in part a function of social factors (e.g., peer acceptance of e-mail) and the user's experience (e.g., with the topic) (Carlson and Zmud 1999; Higa et al. 2000; Lee 1994; Markus 1994).

Media richness theory argues that performance improves when richer media are used for equivocal tasks. More specifically, when the communication channel matches the message content or task, performance is greater (Daft et al. 1987; Kahai and Cooper 2003). This implies that in order to achieve optimal performance, the media selected should depend on the nature of the communication. The theory has generally been confirmed when tested with traditional media such as face-to-face, telephone, and letters (e.g., Daft et al. 1987), and partially supported for such new media as e-mail and voice mail (Karahanna and Limayem 2000; Kock 2001; Straub and Karahanna 1998).

Media selection is important in IT management. The use of richer channels to communicate strategic information systems planning requirements helps IT managers minimize the complexity of the planning task (Watson 1990). Similarly, when IT personnel and their users employ rich communication channels, they jointly understand the organization's business functions and how IT can be used to support these functions (Lind and Zmud 1991).

Convergence

Convergence is defined as the tendency for two or more individuals to move toward one point, and to unite in a common interest or focus. According to Rogers and Kincaid (1981), it is the objective of communication. Their convergence model describes communication as a dynamic process of idea and knowledge generation, which occurs over time through interaction with others. Such interaction leads to mutual understanding and collective action.

The IT function and the organization in general can benefit from convergence. When an organization's technology providers and users converge on both the importance of the firm's activities and the potential for technology to support the activities, more innovative proposals for using IT result (Lind and Zmud 1991).

Convergence between IT and business executives is also beneficial. It exists when business executives understand IT objectives and IT executives understand business objectives. Convergence between these executives supports the development of a shared vision of the role and contribution of IT to the organization (Reich and Benbasat 1996) and it facilitates IT success (Sabherwal and Kirs 1994).

IS and business executives have agreed that the most critical issues in IS management are improving IS strategic planning, using information systems for competitive advantage, and facilitating organizational learning so that new IS technologies are integrated into the entire operation of the firm (Brancheau and Wetherbe 1987). Considering that such issues are strategy-oriented and thus presumed to be equivocal (Webster and Trevino 1995), convergence between IT and business executives about those issues would result from frequent iterations of interpretations and reasonings based on rich media.

In terms of McFarlan et al.'s (1983) strategic grid framework of a current and a future impact of IT, recent research has shown that the current impact has one dimension whereas the future impact has three (Reghunathan et al. 1999). The current impact dimension, of course, represents the organization's reliance on IT at the present time. The managerial support future impact embodies how organizations direct their planned systems development projects to support decision making and organizational efficiency. The differentiation future impact focuses on the use of such projects to help the organization make its products and services unlike those of its competitors. The enhancement future impact represents how firms plan to use IT to facilitate the maintenance of existing systems. These strategic grid dimensions thus offer a target for convergence by the chief executive officer and the chief information officer of the organization.

HYPOTHESES

Rogers and Kincaid's (1981) convergence model described communication as a cyclical process, which involved the repetitive exchange and sharing of information between two or more individuals in order to reach a mutual understanding. They stated (p. 64):

By means of several iterations or cycles of information-exchange, two or more participants in a communication process may converge toward a more mutual understanding of each other's meaning, obtain greater accuracy, and come within the limits of tolerance required for the purpose at hand.

Each cycle of information exchange results in incremental changes in an individual's accuracy regarding a point of interest. Thus, frequent communication would allow communicating individuals eventually to "zero in on" (McLeod and Chaffee 1973, p. 482) the attribute that is salient for each of them.

Lind and Zmud (1991) suggested further that frequent contact between communicating individuals implied a certain level of intimacy, which had the potential for reducing barriers to achieving convergence. They investigated the influence of convergence between IT providers and users of technology on innovation. Their study of a large multinational firm found that frequent communication between those parties resulted in a higher degree of convergence regarding the importance of business activities and the potential for IT to support these activities.

The convergence model of communication (Rogers and Kincaid 1981) and Lind and Zmud's (1991) findings can be extended to CEO/CIO communication. Frequent communication between the CEO and CIO would provide greater opportunity for exchanges of information. Such exchanges would promote mutual trust, reduce barriers between the functional roles, and thus facilitate convergence.

More specifically, frequent communication between the CEO and CIO would promote mutual understanding about functions that the organization is critically dependent upon for daily operations. Furthermore, such communication would help ensure that IT resources are used to support these critical daily activities. Therefore:

- H1: When an organization's CEO and CIO communicate more frequently with each other, the degree of convergence about the current impact of IT is higher.

Likewise, it is reasonable to expect that frequent communication between the CEO and CIO would result in exchanges of information about the organization's future domain. Frequent exchanges would promote mutual trust and understanding about the organization's strategy and how IT could be deployed to support or enable that strategy. Therefore:

- H2: When an organization's CEO and CIO communicate more frequently with each other, the degree of convergence about the future impact of IT is higher.

An individual's choice of communication channels could also affect convergence. Because communication channels vary in their ability to convey information (Daft and Lengel 1984, 1986), they probably differ in their ability to facilitate convergence (Lind and Zmud 1991). More specifically, richer channels (e.g., face-to-face communication) would more likely facilitate convergence than less rich channels (e.g., printed reports, charts, and graphs). Rich channels have the capacity to transmit body language, tone of voice, and other physical cues that affect the understanding and interpretation of communication. Physical cues can be as important to understanding a message as the actual words (Short et al. 1976).

Empirical evidence has supported the proposition that communication channels vary in their capacity to convey a variety of cues (Daft et al. 1987). That evidence supported a relationship between task and media selection. Specifically, managers preferred richer media for equivocal communication tasks and less rich media for unequivocal ones. Additionally, high performing managers were more sensitive to the need to use rich channels for equivocal messages than were low performing managers.

Equivocality (i.e., ambiguity) exists when managers have multiple and conflicting interpretations about organizational situations (Daft et al. 1987; Weick 1979). It has been associated with lack of convergence between managers. It is high between managers from different functional areas of an organization because their frames of reference differ (Daft et al. 1987). Thus, it is often high between an organization's CEO and CIO (Earl and Vivian 1993; Jones et al.1995; Keen 1991; Miller and Gibson 1995; Reich and Benbasat 1996; Watson 1990). It is reasonable to expect that by providing multiple ways to convey a message, rich media would diminish equivocality, facilitate mutual understanding, and thus increase convergence.

Moreover, use of richer communication channels would improve decision quality by providing faster feedback (Dennis and Wixom 2001-2002; Kahai and Cooper 2003). Such feedback would help CEOs and CIOs to more quickly resolve misunderstandings about the impact of IT in the organization. The ability to provide faster feedback would be particularly valuable when applying IT to support the organization's current operations. Inability to quickly resolve misunderstandings about the current impact of IT could result in disruptions in company operations.

The opportunity for faster feedback about the current impact of IT would increase convergence and thus ensure that existing IT resources are used, as needed, to maintain smooth company operations. The CIO would better understand the business and how IT should be used to support daily activities. Likewise, the CEO would better understand IT and its ability to support current company operations. Therefore:

- H3: When an organization's CEO and CIO use richer channels to communicate with each other, the degree of convergence about the current impact of IT is higher.

As a result of using richer channels to communicate with the CEO, IT managers are less concerned with strategic planning issues (Watson 1990). This suggests that IT managers who use rich communication channels have a better understanding of organizational goals and strategy and consequently find strategic planning a less difficult task. A further implication is that the use of richer channels to communicate with the CEO reduces equivocality and thus increases convergence about the organization's strategy and the significance of IT in the future.

Likewise, it is reasonable to expect that the use of richer channels to communicate strategic planning information would also enable the CEO to better understand IT and its future impact in the organization. Therefore:

- H4: When an organization's CEO and CIO use richer channels to communicate with each other, the degree of convergence about the future impact of IT is higher.

METHODOLOGY

This study used a postal survey consisting of two questionnaires. The CEO of the organization completed one and the CIO or top IT executive completed the other. Each subject provided responses about their frequency of communication with each other, the richness of the channels they used to communicate, and their perceptions of the impact of IT in the organization.

The content validity of each questionnaire was examined prior to the mailing of the survey

(Boudreau et al. 2000, Straub 1989). Five IT professors initially reviewed each instrument. Their comments and suggestions were used to revise the surveys. Next, five sets of executives (one CEO and one CIO per set) pilot tested the surveys. The senior author met with each subject individually while he or she filled out the survey. After completion of each one, the executive provided feedback and comments about it. The discussion and comments were used to iteratively revise the survey.

Operationalization of Variables

The communication frequency construct was measured with Jang's (1989) single item scale. Subjects responded on a 1 (very infrequent) to 5 (very frequent) scale about their communication during a typical month via five channels. The measure contained one item for each of the channels and one for overall communication. The CEO and CIO responses to the items about their frequency of communication for the channels were summed. This sum was used for hypothesis testing. (The appendix contains all of the items used in this research.)

An adapted version of Bacharach and Aiken's (1977) communication frequency measure was used to validate Jang's construct. The Bacharach and Aiken measure required subjects to respond to an item with the number of times they used each communication channel during a typical month.

The Bacharach and Aiken measure may have been a more objective measure of communication frequency, but fewer subjects responded to it than to the Jang (1989) measure. Thus, the Jang measure of communication frequency was used for hypothesis testing.

The media richness construct was measured with an adapted version of Webster and Trevino's (1995) instrument over five channels. Subjects responded on a 1 (no extent) to 5 (great extent) scale about the extent to which a channel had the ability to give and receive timely feedback, convey multiple types of information, transmit varied symbols, and tailor messages to fit the sender or receiver's requirements when communicating with each other.

This study used Rice et al.'s (1998) five channels, namely face-to-face, telephone, e-mail, business memo, and voice mail. Zmud et al.'s (1990) list of fourteen channels appeared more comprehensive, but they mapped into Rice et al.'s five and thus permitted a more parsimonious instrument.

Twenty items (i.e., four characteristics for each of the five channels) measured richness. Responses for these 20 items were used for two purposes.

First, they were used to determine the richness rating for each medium across all CEOs and all CIOs. Subjects' responses to the four richness items for a specific medium were averaged to determine the richness rating for that specific medium for his or her group (CEO or CIO). For example, the richness rating for face-to-face communication for CEOs was computed by averaging all CEO responses to the four items about the richness of the medium.

Second, the 20 channel richness items were used in the following calculation to determine a standardized communication channel richness measure for each respondent:

- The appropriate richness rating for each CEO for each medium was multiplied by that respondent's answers to Jang's (1989) item about how frequently he or she used the medium to communicate with the CIO; this produced the respondent's weighted measure of communication channel richness for each medium. An analogous computation was done for each CIO for each medium.

- The weighted measures of communication channel richness were summed across each participant's responses for all media and then divided by the sum of the communication frequency responses for the participant.

This produced a single standardized communication channel richness measure for each participant.

These calculations were consistent with Lind and Zmud's (1991) measure for communication channel richness. However, because multiple informants were used in the current study, an average of the CEO's and CIO's standardized communication channel richness score provided the overall communication channel richness measure used for hypothesis testing.

The current and future impact of IT constructs were measured with Raghunathan et al.'s (1999) strategic grid instrument. The current impact of IT construct was comprised of one factor. Subjects indicated on a scale of 1 (strongly disagree) to 5 (strongly agree) the extent to which they agreed to six items about the current portfolio of information systems for their organization. CEO/CIO convergence about the current impact of IT for each item was determined by calculating the absolute value of the difference between the CEO and CIO response for that item.

The future impact of IT construct contained three factors, which represented how organizations were directing their system development projects. The managerial support factor, the differentiation factor, and the enhancement factor respectively contained four, three, and two items. Subjects indicated on a scale of 1 (low significance) to 5 (high significance) the significance of nine specific types of projects as they related to the firm's future portfolio. CEO/CIO convergence about the future impact of IT for each item was determined by calculating the absolute value of the difference between the CEO and CIO response for that item. Smaller differences indicated more convergence for both the current and future impact of IT.

Data Collection

The participating organizations were headquartered in two southeastern states. The Chamber of Commerce in the largest city within the sampling area had agreed to endorse the research. That endorsement included the active solicitation and encouragement of organizational executives and Chamber members to participate in the research. It also included the use of their membership list.

In addition to the Chamber of Commerce list, two other resources were used to identify potential participants. One was a database of major employers in the sampling area. The other was the American Business Index.

Organizations headquartered in the sampling area were selected as potential subjects if they had at least 50 employees or if the Chamber data indicated the presence of an IT function within the firm. These criteria resulted in the identification of 1,011 organizations.

CEOs of the 1,011 organizations were then contacted to solicit their participation in the research via an initial letter on Chamber of Commerce stationary signed by a Chamber official. It included a postage-paid return postcard to be completed by the CEO. CEOs willing to participate were required to write the name of the organization's top IT manager on the postcard. The survey packets were then mailed directly to the CEO and CIO of the organization.

Five hundred twenty-one CEOs (52%) returned the postcard and 228 (23%) agreed to participate. Subjects then returned 204 matched surveys for a response rate of 20%. Two of the matched surveys were unusable due to incomplete responses so 202 were used as the sample for the study.

Table 1 summarizes the industries represented. Those that accounted for at least 5% of the sample are categorized.

The average gross revenues for the 202 organizations were $3 billion and average total assets were $13 billion. The mean number of employees was 3,569.

Table 1. Industries represented

Industry Type	Percent
Manufacturing	20.3
Medicine/Law/Education	13.4
Finance/Insurance	10.4
Wholesale/Retail	8.4
Construction	7.9
Government/Utilities	5.4
Real Estate	5.4
Other – specified	16.3
Other – unspecified	12.4

The CEOs had an average of 26 years of industry experience, 19 with their organization, and 13 in the CEO position. The CIOs had an average of 14 years of industry experience, nine with the organization, 15 in the IT field, and six in the CIO position.

Approximately 37% of the CEOs had postgraduate degrees. An additional 35% had undergraduate degrees. Of the CIOs, 22% had postgraduate and 43% had undergraduate degrees.

Table 2 provides the mean and standard deviation for each construct in the model. It shows that CEOs and CIOs ranked face-to-face and e-mail, respectively, as the most frequently used and richest media. Business memo was the least frequently used and telephone had the lowest richness.

A time-trend extrapolation (Armstong and Overton 1977) was used to assess the presence of non-response bias. Its premise is that non-respondents are more similar to late respondents than early ones. Therefore, using the first 25 percent of the returned surveys as early respondents and the last 25 percent as surrogates for non-respondents, a multivariate analysis of variance of the fifteen current and future impact of IT variables was performed to determine if differences in response time were associated with different responses. The results indicated no significant differences for the CEO responses (Wilks' Λ = .87, p=.25) or CIO responses (Wilks' Λ = .85, p=.23) (Compeau and Higgins 1995).

ANALYSIS

Reliability and Validity

The research model contained four constructs. Reliability and validity tests were done for each.

Communication Frequency

Correlation analysis was used to validate the communication frequency construct. Jang's (1989) scaled item for each channel correlated highly with Bacharach and Aiken's (1977) item for the corresponding channel, but not so highly with items for other channels. This provided some support for convergent and discriminant validity (Campbell and Fiske 1959).

Further, a paired t-test indicated there was no difference in CEO and CIO responses about their overall frequency of communication with each other. These results provided additional support for convergent validity (Campbell and Fiske 1959).

Table 2. Means and standard deviations for constructs

Construct	CEO		CIO	
	Mean	Std	Mean	Std
Communication Frequency				
Face-to-face	4.08	1.06	3.85	1.21
Telephone	2.83	1.04	2.72	1.04
E-mail	3.08	1.35	3.09	1.36
Business memo	2.04	1.05	1.87	0.90
Voice mail	2.62	1.12	2.56	1.18
Channel Richness				
Face-to-face	4.31	0.80	4.29	0.75
Telephone	2.64	0.76	2.45	0.70
E-mail	3.81	1.04	3.95	1.33
Business memo	2.70	0.82	2.81	0.70
Voice mail	2.78	0.79	2.77	0.78
Current Impact of IT	3.77	0.62	3.82	0.65
Future Impact of IT				
Managerial Support	84.	0.62	3.73	0.54
Differentiation	67.	0.68	3.48	0.76
Enhancement	3.44	0.69	3.42	0.57

Communication Channel Richness

Confirmatory factor analysis (CFA) with the software package EQS, version 5.2, was used to validate the channel richness construct. The maximum likelihood method of parameter estimation and robust statistics were employed. A model was deemed a good fit for the data if the Satorra-Bentler scaled chi-square to degrees of freedom ratio (SBSχ^2/df) was less than 3 (Carmines and McIver 1981), the non-normed fit index (NNFI) and robust comparative fit index (RCFI) were at least .90 (Bentler 1995), the LISREL adjusted goodness of fit index (AGFI) was greater than .80 (Gefen et al. 2000), the standardized root mean square residual (RMR) was less than .10 (Gefen et al. 2000), and the root mean square error of approximation was less than .08 (Browne and Cudeck 1993).

CEO and CIO data were independently fitted. Modification indices were observed for each execution. To prevent overmodification of the model, only one change was made during a single execution (Joreskog and Sorbom 1989).

Initial statistical results indicated that respecifications were required to achieve a good fit for the CEO channel richness model. Examination of the residual matrix provided some evidence that the voice mail and business memo factors were misspecified. Furthermore, during the study, two CIOs had inquired (via a telephone conversation) about the channel richness items and one CEO had written comments on the survey to further clarify the completed responses. In each case, the subjects had expressed some difficulty in differentiating between e-mail and business memo communication and between telephone and voice mail communication. They further suggested that e-mail was frequently used to send attached business memos and the telephone was used to support voice mail communication. Thus, responses for e-mail items could include e-mail with and without business memo attachments. Similarly, responses for telephone items could include traditional telephone use and use that resulted in a voice mail message. Based on this evidence, the voice mail and business memo factors were dropped from the model. Tables 3 and 4 show the details of the modification process for the revised three-factor CEO and CIO channel richness models, respectively. (The appendix shows the variable names with their respective items in the questionnaire.)

Current Impact of IT

The current impact of IT construct was a single-factor model. Tables 5 and 6 show the details of the modification process for the CEO and CIO data, respectively.

Table 3. CEO channel richness confirmatory factor analysis

Face-to-face	Telephone	E-mail	Fit Indices
Initial Model This shows the indicators associated with the constructs.			
FACE1, FACE2, FACE3, FACE4	TELE1, TELE2, TELE3, TELE4	EM1, EM2, EM3, EM4	SBSχ^2/df = 5.55 NNFI = .75 RCFI = .81 AGFI = .71 RMR = .10 RMSEA = .14
Iteration 1 Item TELE4 was a complex variable, which appeared to be influenced by both the telephone and face-to-face factors, and was therefore dropped.			
FACE1, FACE2, FACE3, FACE4	TELE1, TELE2, TELE3	EM1, EM2, EM3, EM4	SBSχ^2/df = 3.90 NNFI = .85 RCFI = .89 AGFI = .78 RMR = .07 RMSEA = .10
Iteration 2 Item TELE1 was a complex variable, which appeared to be influenced by both the telephone and the e-mail factors, and was therefore dropped.			
FACE1, FACE2, FACE3, FACE4	TELE2, TELE3	EM1, EM2, EM3, EM4	SBSχ^2/df = 3.03 NNFI = .89 RCFI = .92 AGFI = .83 RMR = .05 RMSEA = .08
Final Model and Iteration 3 Item EM2 was a complex variable, which appeared to be influenced by the telephone and face-to-face factors was therefore dropped.			
FACE1, FACE2, FACE3, FACE4	TELE2, TELE3	EM1, EM3, EM4	SBSχ^2/df = 2.38 NNFI = .94 RCFI = .96 AGFI = .89 RMR = .03 RMSEA = .06

Table 4. CIO channel richness confirmatory factor analysis

Face-to-face	Telephone	E-mail	Fit Indices
Initial Model This shows the indicators associated with the constructs.			
FACE1, FACE2, FACE3, FACE4	TELE1, TELE2, TELE3, TELE4	EM1, EM2, EM3, EM4	$SBS\chi^2/df = 7.76$ $NNFI = .51$ $RCFI = .62$ $AGFI = .51$ $RMR = .10$ $RMSEA = .12$
Iteration 1 The factor loading for TELE1 was low (.21). Therefore, it was dropped in the next iteration.			
FACE1, FACE2, FACE3, FACE4	TELE2, TELE3, TELE4	EM1, EM2, EM3, EM4	$SBS\chi^2/df = 7.12$ $NNFI = .59$ $RCFI = .69$ $AGFI = .53$ $RMR = .09$ $RMSEA = .10$
Iteration 2 The Lagrange multiplier test indicated a high error correlation between items EM1 and FACE1. This was reasonable because recent studies have found e-mail to be a relatively rich channel (e.g., Lee 1994; Schmitz and Fulk 1991). Therefore, some of the characteristics normally associated with face-to-face communication may also be attributed to e-mail communication. After including the correlation, the model parameters were re-estimated.			
FACE1, FACE2, FACE3, FACE4	TELE2, TELE3, TELE4	EM1, EM2, EM3, EM4	$SBS\chi^2/df = 4.44$ $NNFI = .75$ $RCFI = .79$ $AGFI = .76$ $RMR = .08$ $RMSEA = .09$
Iteration 3 Item TELE4 was a complex variable, which appeared to be influenced by both the telephone and the face-to-face factors, and was thus dropped.			
FACE1, FACE2, FACE3, FACE4	TELE2, TELE3	EM1, EM2, EM3, EM4	$SBS\chi^2/df = 3.09$ $NNFI = .82$ $RCFI = .85$ $AGFI = .82$ $RMR = .05$ $RMSEA = .08$
Iteration 4 Item EM2 was involved in five of the six largest residuals (including the second largest), and was therefore dropped.			
FACE1, FACE2, FACE3, FACE4	TELE2, TELE3	EM1, EM3, EM4	$SBS\chi^2/df = 3.02$ $NNFI = .86$ $RCFI = .89$ $AGFI = .84$ $RMR = .04$ $RMSEA = .06$
Final Model and Iteration 5 The Lagrange multiplier test indicated a high error correlation between items EM1 and FACE2. This was reasonable because recent studies have found e-mail to be a relatively rich channel (e.g., Lee 1994; Schmitz and Fulk 1991). After including the correlation, the model parameters were re-estimated.			
FACE1, FACE2, FACE3, FACE4	TELE2, TELE3	EM1, EM3, EM4	$SBS\chi^2/df = 2.63$ $NNFI = .90$ $RCFI = .95$ $AGFI = .88$ $RMR = .03$ $RMSEA = .05$

Future Impact of IT

The initial EQS execution for the CEO future impact of IT construct (comprised of the managerial support, differentiation, and enhancement factors) indicated that respecifications were necessary to achieve a good fit. The residual matrix showed that the two indicators comprising the enhancement factor was involved in seven of the ten largest residuals. Furthermore, it appeared that one of the two items (*projects focusing on routine maintenance to meet evolving business needs, new regulatory or legal requirements*) could be contained within the other item (*projects focusing on existing systems enhancements*). The removal of any one of the items would have resulted in a single item factor, which is not recommended (Hatcher 1994). Therefore, the enhancement factor was dropped from the model. The resulting model, which was now comprised of the managerial support and differentiation factors, was used to perform the CFA for the CEO and CIO data.

The revised model indicated an excellent fit for the CEO and CIO data. The SBSχ^2/df, NNFI, RCFI, AGFI, RMR, and RMSEA for the CEO data were 2.31, .92, .95, .92, .04, and .07 respectively. Likewise, they were 1.91, .92, .95, .93, .04, and .07 for the CIO data.

Reliability and Validity Statistics

Table 7 shows Cronbach alpha (α) and composite reliability (ρ_c) indexes for each construct. Most are well above .70, which is the preferred level of reliability. All were at least .60 which is the minimum acceptable level (Hatcher 1994).

Convergent validity was shown by the significance of the factor loading (p < .001) for all indicators for each factor (Hatcher 1994). All variance extracted tests performed supported discriminant validity.

Hypothesis Testing

Structural equation modeling was performed to test the hypotheses in Figure 1. Communication frequency (based on Jang's (1989) item) and communication channel richness (based on Lind and Zmud's (1991) calculations) were each represented by a manifest variable. Convergence about the current and future impact of IT contained latent variables, which were determined by calculating the absolute value of the difference between the CEO and CIO response for that variable.

A two-step approach recommended by Anderson and Gerbing (1988) was followed. The first step used CFA to develop an acceptable measurement model. The second was to specify a structural model, which represented the hypothesized relationships. Table 8 shows details of the model development process.

The research model demonstrated acceptable reliability. Cronbach alpha and composite reliability indexes for the current impact of IT convergence factor were both .82. They were .65 and .66, respectively, for the future impact of IT. All factor loadings were significant at p < .001. Thus, convergent validity was supported. A variance extracted test supported discriminant validity between the current and future impact of IT convergence factors.

H1 (the effect of communication frequency on CEO/CIO convergence about the current impact of IT) and H2 (the effect of communication frequency on CEO/CIO convergence about the future impact of IT) were supported. H3 (the effect of the use of rich communication channels on CEO/CIO convergence about the current impact of IT) was not supported. H4 (the effect of the use of rich communication channels on CEO/CIO convergence about the future of IT) was marginally supported. Table 9 shows the path coefficients for each hypothesis.

Table 5. CEO current impact of IT confirmatory factor analysis

Single-Factor Construct	Fit Indices
Initial Model This shows the indicators associated with the constructs.	
CUR1, CUR2, CUR3, CUR4, CUR5, CUR6	SBSχ^2/df = 2.10 NNFI = .95 RCFI = .98 AGFI = .89 RMR = .03 RMSEA = .05
Final Model and Iteration 1 The factor loading for CUR1 was low (.41), and was therefore dropped.	
CUR2, CUR3, CUR4, CUR5, CUR6	SBSχ^2/df = 2.30 NNFI = .93 RCFI = .98 AGFI = .88 RMR = .04 RMSEA = .07

Table 6. CIO current impact of IT confirmatory factor analysis

Single-Factor Construct	Fit Indices
Initial Model This shows the indicators associated with the constructs.	
CUR1, CUR2, CUR3, CUR4, CUR5, CUR6	SBSχ^2/df = 1.43 NNFI = .98 RCFI = .99 AGFI = .93 RMR = .03 RMSEA = .06
Final Model and Iteration 1 The factor loading for CUR1 was low (.30), and was therefore dropped.	
CUR2, CUR3, CUR4, CUR5, CUR6	SBSχ^2/df = 1.90 NNFI = .97 RCFI = .98 AGFI = .92 RMR = .02 RMSEA = .07

Table 7. Reliability statistics

Construct	Latent Variable	CEO α / ρ_c	CIO α / ρ_c
Channel Richness	Face-to-face Telephone E-mail	.90 / .90 .79 / .81 .91 / .91	.79 / .84 .76 / .72 .83 / .84
Current Impact of IT	N/A (Single Factor)	.90 / .91	.92 / .92
Future Impact of IT	Managerial Support Differentiation	.75 / .71 .62 / .65	.69 / .71 .60 / .61

Table 8. Development of the measurement and structural models

Channel Richness	Communication Frequency	Current Impact Of IT Convergence	Future Impact Of IT Convergence	Fit Indices
Initial Model This shows the indicators associated with the constructs.				
RICH	FREQ	CUR2, CUR3, CUR4, CUR5, CUR6	FUT1, FUT4, FUT5, FUT6, FUT7, FUT8, FUT9	SBSχ^2/df = 3.00 NNFI = .68 RCFI = .75 AGFI = .76 RMR = .10 RMSEA = .11
Iteration 1 Item FUT8 was a complex variable, which appeared to be influenced by both the current and the future impact of IT, and was thus dropped.				
RICH	FREQ	CUR2, CUR3, CUR4, CUR5, CUR6	FUT1, FUT4, FUT5, FUT6, FUT7, FUT9	SBSχ^2/df = 2.96 NNFI = .71 RCFI = .78 AGFI = .78 RMR = .10 RMSEA = .11
Iteration 2 The Lagrange multiplier test indicated a high error correlation between items CUR4 and CUR2. This was reasonable because both items addressed the effect of IS breakdown on the organization. After including the correlation, the model parameters were re-estimated, as shown below.				
RICH	FREQ	CUR2, CUR3, CUR4, CUR5, CUR6	FUT1, FUT4, FUT5, FUT6, FUT7, FUT9	SBSχ^2/df = 2.41 NNFI = .79 RCFI = .85 AGFI = .82 RMR = .08 RMSEA = .09
Iteration 3 The Lagrange multiplier test indicated a high error correlation between items CUR5 and CUR3. This correlation was reasonable; therefore it was included in the model. The parameters were re-estimated, as shown below.				
RICH	FREQ	CUR2, CUR3, CUR4, CUR5, CUR6	FUT1, FUT4, FUT5, FUT6, FUT7, FUT9	SBSχ^2/df = 2.21 NNFI = .87 RCFI = .93 AGFI = .88 RMR = .07 RMSEA = .07
Final Measurement Model and Iteration 4 Item FUT6 was a complex variable, which appeared to be influenced by both the current and the future impact of IT, and was therefore dropped.				
RICH	FREQ	CUR2, CUR3, CUR4, CUR5, CUR6	FUT1, FUT4, FUT5, FUT7, FUT9	SBSχ^2/df = 1.62 NNFI = .90 RCFI = .95 AGFI = .90 RMR = .06 RMSEA = .06
Structural Equation Model The structural model was a good fit. Thus, no further modifications were required. The model parameters are shown below.				
RICH	FREQ	CUR2, CUR3, CUR4, CUR5, CUR6	FUT1, FUT4, FUT5, FUT7, FUT9	SBSχ^2/df = 1.61 NNFI = .90 RCFI = .94 AGFI = .90 RMR = .07 RMSEA = .07

Table 9. Results of hypotheses tests

Hypothesis	Independent Variable	Dependent Variable	Path Coefficient	t	p
H1	Communication frequency	Current impact of IT	.19	2.95	.01
H2	Communication frequency	Future impact of IT	.36	4.30	.001
H3	Channel richness	Current impact of IT	.00	0.06	NS
H4	Channel richness	Future impact of IT	.11	1.32	.10

DISCUSSION OF FINDINGS

The study supported the notion that frequent communication between an organization's CEO and CIO predicted greater convergence about the dimensions of the strategic grid, and in particular about current and about two of the future impacts of IT, namely differentiation (H3) and enhancement (H4). Support for both H1 and H2 was consistent with previous research. For example, the convergence model of communication (Rogers and Kincaid 1981) posited that frequent communication between two or more individuals enabled them to converge towards a more mutual understanding. Similarly, Lind and Zmud's (1991) study of communication in a large multinational firm confirmed that more frequent communication predicted convergence between providers and users of technology regarding the importance of business activities and the potential for IT to support those activities.

In general, support for H1 and H2 in this study showed that the relationship between frequency and convergence was generalizable to IT management settings. It also confirmed the value of frequent communication between a dyad of highly ranked executives. Further, the study extended the concept across a sample of multiple organizations and industries.

Lack of support for H3 (the use of richer communication channels predicts more convergence about the current impact of IT) might have oc-

curred because the current impact of IT may be low in equivocality (i.e., ambiguity), and low equivocality does not require richness to facilitate convergence. That is, information would most likely be available about the organization's current operations and the impact of IT to support them. This information would reduce uncertainty (Daft et al. 1987) and thus decrease equivocality about the current impact of IT. With low equivocality, the use of rich channels would not be as necessary to produce convergence (Daft et al. 1987), and the H3 path coefficient would be low.

The weak support for H4 (p < .10), which predicted that the use of richer channels to communicate would promote greater convergence about the future impact of IT, may have occurred because some organizations planned to use IT as a strategic resource to support future operations, whereas others did not. The future impact of IT would reasonably be more equivocal for organizations that plan to use IT to support future operations than for those that do not. The weak support for H4 may reflect this difference.

Therefore, ANCOVA was used to explore whether the relationship between communication channel richness and convergence about the future impact of IT was influenced by the organization's plans to use IT to support future operations. Communication channel richness was the independent variable. Convergence about the future impact of IT was the dependent variable. The covariate was the future impact of IT because it represented data about the organization's planned use of IT to support future operations. The CEO and CIO provided a different set of responses about the future impact of IT, so an ANCOVA using each set was performed.[1] Both showed that convergence about the future impact of IT was significantly related to the organization's future plans to use IT ($F(1,29) = 5.60$ for CEO responses; $F(1,29) = 4.31$ for CIO responses) at the .05 level. The main effect for communication channel richness was also significant for both ($F(169,29) = 2.07$, $p < .01$ for CEO responses; $F(169,29) = 1.83$, $p < .05$ for CIO responses). Thus, as the ANCOVA results in Table 10 show, the relationship between channel richness and convergence about the future impact of IT was influenced by the organization's plans to use IT to support future operations.

Finally, although not directly related to the hypotheses, Table 2 did reveal that CEOs and CIOs ranked face-to-face and e-mail, respectively, as the richest media. Telephone had the lowest richness. A closer analysis of the individual richness items showed that both CEOs and CIOs ranked e-mail richer than telephone for all four items ($p<.001$). This was interesting because previous research had ranked telephone as richer than e-mail (Zmud et al. 1990) and had found that the telephone, not e-mail, was a substitute for face-to-face communication (Straub and Karahanna 1998).

The analysis also showed that CIOs perceived no difference in the extent to which e-mail and face-to-face channels had the ability to provide timely feedback (based on one of the richness items), but did perceive e-mail as richer than face-to-face in terms of the ability to transmit varied symbols (another richness item; $p < .05$). These findings are contrary to media richness theory; it predicted face-to-face as the richest medium. Perhaps, CIOs' technical experience and knowledge about e-mail advancements (e.g., its ability to transmit a variety of attachments such as images and sound bytes) influenced their perceptions of e-mail richness. After all, an individual's experience with a medium does affect his or her

evaluation of its attributes (Carlson and Zmud 1999; King and Xia 1997).

IMPLICATIONS

Implications for Researchers

Lack of support for H3 and minimal support for H4 indicated that research is needed to further examine the relationship between communication channel richness and CEO/CIO convergence. Although theories and post hoc analysis provided some preliminary answers, further research is needed to empirically examine the effect of equivocality on the current impact of IT. Such research is also needed to identify other potential reasons why communication channel richness did not predict convergence at anything beyond the .10 level of significance.

This study found evidence that frequent communication predicted more CEO/CIO convergence. These results might stimulate further research about other factors that could affect this relationship. Perhaps, the combined effects of communication frequency and content of the communication is more important than the single effect of communication frequency. Perhaps, the duration of the communication episodes would affect the results of the study.

Other implications relate directly to the constructs. In general, the study indicated that the constructs were more complex than initially thought. For example, the CFA for the channel richness construct was unable to fit data for two of the channels (voice mail and business memos) to the initial model. Thus, they were dropped. Although theory provided an explanation for the lack of fit, research is needed to improve and validate the channel richness construct. Perhaps, some of the media are not distinct.

Although the components of the convergence construct were validated well in previous research,

Table 10. ANCOVA with convergence about the future impact of IT as dependent variable

Variable	CEO Responses		CIO Responses	
	F	p	F	p
Independent Variable: Richness	2.07	.01	1.83	.03
Covariate: Future Impact of IT	5.60	.02	4.31	.04
Adjusted R-squared	*.48*		*.45*	

the enhancement factor for the future impact of IT had to be dropped from the analysis. Future research should examine the validity and reliability of this factor. Additional items are probably needed to improve its reliability.

The measures in this research were based on each subject's perception. Some, particularly communication frequency, might have benefited from an objective assessment. However, that would have required considerable record keeping of communication activity. Given the decision to employ a large sample and the executive status of the participants, a less intrusive method was chosen so as to increase the response rate. Future research might, however, attempt objective record keeping across a large sample.

This study examined convergence between the CEO and CIO. Although past research has acknowledged the importance of their relationship, future work should consider convergence between other key executives. Similarities or differences in findings might facilitate an understanding not only of convergence, but also of communication between CEOs and CIOs.

Finally, e-mail was richer than telephone for both CEOs and CIOs, and was unexpectedly rich (in contrast to face-to-face communication) for CIOs. Although the current study offered potential explanations, further research is needed to investigate them.

Implications for Managers

Support for H1 and H2 suggested that frequent dialogue between an organization's CEO and CIO was valuable because it predicted convergence. This has two implications for practicing managers.

First, it implies that organizations might benefit by becoming more involved in encouraging activities that produce frequent communication between the CEO and CIO. Perhaps, firms might sponsor more activities to discuss and inform managers of the impact of IT.

Second, it implies that CEOs and CIOs might be more successful if they possessed certain communication attributes. More specifically, it reinforces the popular notion that individuals both comfortable with and willing to communicate frequently might be more suitable for the positions of CEO and CIO.

Preliminary findings (i.e., the covariate analysis) indicated that the use of richer channels to facilitate convergence about the future impact of IT might be more beneficial for managers in some organizations than others. It seems reasonable that the use of rich channels would be more important for managers in those that plan to use IT to support future operations. Thus, managers in these organizations might more diligently consider using richer channels to communicate about the future impact of IT because such use may facilitate more convergence.

An important yet unexpected outcome of the research was the richness of e-mail. Thus, managers might consider using e-mail rather than the telephone when they require rich communication.

CONCLUSION

Mutual understanding between a CEO and CIO about the impact of IT is invaluable to an organization. This study confirms the usefulness of the strategic grid dimensions as well as the impact of more frequent communication on convergence concerning the current, enhancement future, and differentiation future impacts of IT. It also draws attention to the context in which communication richness might have more or less impact. In particular, when planning future strategy not only is frequent communication critical, but richness in communication also plays a impact. Such findings are not only consistent with communications theory, but can also be used to stimulate better mutual understanding among top executives.

REFERENCES

Anderson, J. C., & Gerbing, G. W. (1988). Structural Equation Modeling in Practice: A Review and Recommended Two-step Approach. *Psychological Bulletin, 103,* 411-423.

Armstrong, J. S., & Overton, T. S. (1977). Estimating Nonresponse Bias in Mail Surveys. *J. Marketing Res., 14,* 396-402.

Applegate, L. M., McFarlan, F. W., & McKenney, J. L. (1996). *Corporate Information Systems and Management: Text and Cases.* Boston, MA: Richard D. Irwin..

Bacharach, S. B., & Aiken, M. (1977). Communication in Administrative Bureaucracies. *Acad.*

Management J., 20(3), 365-377.

Bentler, P. M. (1995). *EQS Structural Equations Program Manual.* Multivariate Software, Inc. Encino, CA.

Berger, P. L., & Luckmann, T. (1966). *The Social Construction of Reality.* Garden City, NY: Anchor Books.

Boudreau, M., Gefen, D., & Straubm D. W. (2001). Validation in Information Systems Research: A State-of-the-Art Assessment. *MIS Quart., 25*(1), 1-24.

Browne, M., & Cudeck, R. (1993). Alternative Ways of Assessing Model Fit. K. A. Bollen & J. S. Long (Eds.), *Testing Structural Equation Models.* London, UK: Sage Publications.

Campbell, D. T., & Fiske, D. W. (1959). Convergent and Discriminant Validation by the Multitraitmultimethod Matrix. *Psychological Bulletin, 56*(1), 81-105.

Carmines, E. G., & McIver, J. P. (1981). Analyzing Model with Unobserved Variables. In G. W. Bohrnstedt and E. F. Borgatta (Eds.), *Social Measurement: Current Issues.* Beverly Hills, CA: Sage Publications.

Carlson, J. R., & Zmud, R. W. (1999). Channel Expansion Theory and the Experiential Nature of Media Richness Perceptions. *Acad. Management J., 42*(2), 153-170.

Chan, Y. E., Huff, S. L., & Barclay, D. W. (1997). Business Strategic Orientation, Information Systems Strategic Orientation, and Strategic Alignment. *Inform. Systems Res., 8,* 125-150.

Compeau, D. R., & Higgins, C. A. (1995). Computer Self-Efficacy: Development of a Measure and Initial Test. *MIS Quart.,* 189-211.

Daft, R. L., & Lengel, R. H. (1984). Information Richness: A New Approach to Managerial Information Processing and Organization Design. In B. Staw and L. Cummings (Eds.), *Research in Organization Behavior.* Greenwich, CT: JAI Press.

(1986). Organizational Information Requirements, Media Richness, and Structural Design. *Management Science, 32*(5), 554-572.

Trevino, L. K. (1987). Message Equivocality, Media Selection, and Manager Performance: Implications for Information Systems. *MIS Quart., 1*(1), 355-366.

Dennis, A. R., & Wixom, B. H. (2001-2002). Investigating the Moderators of the Group SupportSystems Use with Meta-Analysis. *J. Management Information Systems, 18*(3), 235-257.

Earl, M. J. (1996). The Chief Information Officer: Past, Present, and Future. In M. J. Earl (Ed.), *Information Management: The Organizational Dimension.* New York: NY: Oxford University Press, Inc.

Earl, M., & Vivian, P. D. (1993). *The Role of the Chief Information Officer: A Study of Survival.* London: London Business School.

El-Shinnawy, M., & Markus, M. L. (1998). Acceptance of Communication Media in Organizations: Richness or Features? *IEEE Transactions On Professional Communication 41*(4), 242-253.

Feeny, D. F., Edwards, B. R., & Simpson, K. M. (1992). Understanding the CEO/CIO Relationship. *MIS Quart.,* 435-448.

Gefen, D., Straub, D. W., & Boudreau. M. (2000). Structural Equation Modeling and Regression: Guidelines for Research Practice. *Comm. AIS, 4*(7), 1-78.

Hatcher, L. (1994). *A Step-by-Step Approach to Using the SAS System for Factor Analysis and Structural Equation Modeling.* Cary, NC: SAS Institute.

Higa, K., Sheng, O. R. L., Shin, B., & Figueredo ,A. J. (2000). Understanding Relationships Among Teleworkers' E-Mail Usage, E-Mail Richness Perceptions, and E-Mail Productivity Perceptions Under a Software Engineering Environment. *IEEE Transactions On Engineering Management, 47*(2) 163-173.

Jang, S. Y. (1989). Influence of Organizational Factors on Information Systems Strategic Planning. *Unpublished Dissertation.* University of Pittsburgh.

Jarvenpaa, S. L., & Ives, B. (1991). Executive Involvement and Participation in the Management of Information Technology. *MIS Quart.,* 205-227.

Jones, M. C., Taylor, G. S., & Spencer, B A. (1995). The CEO/CIO Relationship Revisited: An Empirical Assessment of Satisfaction with IS. *Inform. & Management, 29,* 123-130.

Joreskog, K. G. D., & Sorbom, D. (1989). *LISREL 7: A Guide to the Program and Applications.* 2nd Ed., SPSS, Inc, Chicago, IL.

Kahai, S. S., & Cooper R. B. (2003). Exploring the Core Concepts of Media Richness Theory: The Impact of Cue Multiplicity and Feedback Immediacy on Decision Quality. *J. Management Information Systems, 20*(1), 263-299.

Karahanna, E., & Limayem, M. (2000). E-Mail and V-Mail Usage: Generalizing Across Technologies. *J. Organizational Computing and Electronic Commerce, 10*(1), 49-66.

Keen, P. G. W. (1991). *Shaping the Future: Business Design Through Information Technology,* Boston, MA: Harvard Business School Press.

Kenny, D. A. (1987). *Statistics for the Social and Behavioral Sciences.* Boston, MA: Little, Brown, and Company.

King, R. C., & Xia, W. (1997). Media Appropriateness: Effects of Experience on Communication Media Choice. *Dec. Sci., 28*(4), 877-910.

Kock, N. (2001). Compensatory Adaptation to a Lean Medium: An Action Research Investigation of Electronic Communication in Process Improvement Groups. *IEEE Transactions On Professional Communication, 44*(4) 267-285.

Lee, A. S. (1994). Electronic Mail as a Medium for Rich Communication: An Empirical Investigation Using Hermeneutic Interpretation. *MIS Quart.,* 143-150.

Lengel, R. H. (1983). Managerial Information Processing and Communication-Media Source Selection Behavior. *Unpublished Dissertation.* Texas A&M University.

Lind, M. R., & Zmud R. W. (1991). The Influence of a Convergence in Understanding Between Technology Providers and Users on Technology Innovativeness. *Organization Sci., 2*(2), 195-217.

Markus, M. L. (1994). Electronic Mail as the Medium of Managerial Choice. *Organization Sci. 5*(4), 502-527.

McLeod, J. M., & Chaffee, S. H. (1973). Interpersonal Approaches to Communication Research. *American Behavioral Scientist,* 469-499.

Miller, M. D., & Gibson, M. L. (1995). The CIO as an Integrative Strategist. *Information Strategy: The Executive's Journal,* 35-40.

Nath, R. (1989). Aligning MIS with the Business Goals. *Inform. & Management, 16,* 71-79.

Neo, B. S. (1988). Factors Facilitating the Use of Information Technology for Competitive Advantage: An Exploratory Study. *Inform. & Management, 15,* 191-201.

Preston, D., Karahanna, E., & Rowe, F. (2006). Development of Shared Understanding between the Chief Information Officer and Top Management Team in U.S. and French Organizations: A Cross-Cultural Comparison. *IEEE Transactions on Engineering Management. 53*(2), 191-206.

Raghunathan, T. S., Gupta, Y. P., & Sundararaghavan P. S. (1989). Assessing the Impact of IS Executives' Critical Success Factors on the Performance of IS Organizations. *Information & Management, 17,* 157-168.

Raghunathan, B., Raghunathan, T. S., & Qiang, T. (1999). Dimensionality of the Strategic Grid Framework: The Construct and its Measurement. *Information Systems Research 10*(4) 343-355.

Reich, B. H., & Benbasat, I. (1996). Measuring the Linkage Between Business and Information Technology Objectives. *MIS Quart., 20*(1), 55-81.

Rice, R. E., D'Ambra, J., & More, E. (1998). Cross-Cultural Comparison of Organizational Media Evaluation and Choice. *J. Communication, 48*(3) 3-26.

Rogers, E. M., & Kincaid D. L. (1981). *Communication Networks.* New York: The Free Press.

Sabherwal, R., & Kirs, P. (1994). The Alignment Between Organizational Critical Success Factors and Information Technology Capability in Academic Institutions. *Decision Sci., 25*(2) 01-330.

Schmitz, J., & Fulk, J. (1991). Organizational Colleagues, Media Richness, and Electronic Mail. *Communication Res., 18*(4), 487-523.

Short, J., Williams, E., & Christie, B. (1976). *The Social Psychology of Telecommunications.* London: Wiley.

Singlemann, P. (1972). Exchange as Symbolic Interaction: Convergences Between Two Theoretical Perspectives. *American Sociological Rev., 37,* 414-424.

Straub, D., & Karahanna, E. (1998). Knowledge Worker Communications and Recipient Availability: Toward a Task Closure Explanation of Media Choice. *Organization Sci., 9*(2) 160-175.

Straub, D. W. (1989). Validating Instruments in MIS Research. *MIS Quart., 13*(2), 147-169.

Tan, F., & Gallupe, R.B. (2006). Aligning Business and Information Systems Thinking: A Cognitive Approach. *IEEE Transactions on Engineering Management, 23*(2), 223-237.

Van de Ven, A. H., & Walker, G. (1984). The Dynamics of Interorganizational Coordination. *Admin. Sci. Quart., 29*, 598-621.

Warriner, C. K. (1970). *The Emergence of Society.* Dorsey, Homewood: IL.

Watson, R. T. (1990). Influences on the IS Manager's Perceptions of Key Issues: Information Scanning and the Relationship with the CEO. *MIS Quart.,* 217-231.

Webster, J., & Trevino, T. K. (1995). Rational and Social Theories as Complementary Explanations of Communication Media Choices: Two Policy Capturing Studies. *Acad. Management J.,* 1544-1572.

Weick, K. (1979). *The Social Psychology of Organizing.* Reading, MA: Addison Wesley.

Zmud, R. W., Lind, M. R., & Forrest, W. Y. (1990). An Attribute Space for Organizational Communication Channels. *Inform. Systems Res., 1*(4) 440-457.

ENDNOTE

[1] Convergence is comprised of CEO and CIO responses about the future impact of IT. Because the correlation between the two responses was not considered high (.32, $p <$ .05), according to Kenny (1987), ANCOVA was reasonable. However, the correlation between CEO and CIO responses about the current impact of IT was high (.67, $p <$ .01).

Appendix - Instructions to Respondents and Relevant Survey Items

The CIO survey contained the following items. The CEO items were identical, but they required the subject to respond based on communication with the CIO. (Upper case letters beside each item have been added to indicate the variable name.)

Communication Frequency

Please answer the following about your communication frequency with the CEO about important issues as accurately as possible.

In general, about how frequent has your communication with the CEO been in a typical month?

		Very Infrequent			Very Frequent
FRFACE1:	face-to-face	1 2 3 4 5			
FRTELE1:	telephone	1 2 3 4 5			
FREM1:	e-mail	1 2 3 4 5			
FRBM1:	business memo	1 2 3 4 5			
FRVM1:	voice mail	1 2 3 4 5			

During a typical month, about how many times have you used the following channels to communicate with the CEO?

	Channel	**Number of times**
FRFACE2:	face-to-face	_____
FRTELE2:	telephone	_____
FREM2:	e-mail	_____
FRBM2:	business memo	_____
FRVM2:	voice mail	_____

Communication Channel Richness

Most business communications travel on face-to-face, telephone, e-mail, business memo, and voice mail channels. Please answer the following about the richness of these channels based on your experience communicating with your organization's CEO about important issues in a typical month. If you have never used a particular channel, please leave the scales blank.

To what extent has **face-to-face** communication with the CEO had the ability to:

	No Extent		Great Extent		
FACE1: Give and receive timely feedback.	1	2	3	4	5
FACE2: Convey multiple types of information (verbal and nonverbal).	1	2	3	4	5
FACE3: Transmit varied symbols (e.g., words, numbers, pictures).	1	2	3	4	5
FACE4: Design messages to your own or others' requirements.	1	2	3	4	5

To what extent has **telephone** communication with the CEO had the ability to:

	No Extent		Great Extent		
TELE1: Give and receive timely feedback.	1	2	3	4	5
TELE2: Convey multiple types of information (verbal and nonverbal).	1	2	3	4	5
TELE3: Transmit varied symbols (e.g., words, numbers, pictures).	1	2	3	4	5
TELE4: Design messages to your own or others' requirements.	1	2	3	4	5

To what extent has **e-mail** communication with the CEO had the ability to:

		No Extent			Great Extent	
EM1:	Give and receive timely feedback.	1	2	3	4	5
EM2:	Convey multiple types of information (verbal and nonverbal).	1	2	3	4	5
EM3:	Transmit varied symbols (e.g., words, numbers, pictures).	1	2	3	4	5
EM4:	Design messages to your own or others' requirements.	1	2	3	4	5

To what extent has **business memo** communication with the CEO had the ability to:

		No Extent			Great Extent	
BM1:	Give and receive timely feedback.	1	2	3	4	5
BM2:	Convey multiple types of information (verbal and nonverbal).	1	2	3	4	5
BM3:	Transmit varied symbols (e.g., words, numbers, pictures).	1	2	3	4	5
BM4:	Design messages to your own or others' requirements.	1	2	3	4	5

To what extent has **voice mail** communication with the CEO had the ability to:

		No Extent			Great Extent	
VM1:	Give and receive timely feedback.	1	2	3	4	5
VM2:	Convey multiple types of information (verbal and nonverbal).	1	2	3	4	5
VM3:	Transmit varied symbols (e.g., words, numbers, pictures).	1	2	3	4	5
VM4:	Design messages to your own or others' requirements.	1	2	3	4	5

Current Impact of IT

Please indicate the extent to which you agree or disagree with the following statements as they relate to your portfolio of existing information systems.

		Strongly Disagree			Strongly Agree	
CUR1:	IS is not vital to our organization.	1	2	3	4	5
CUR2:	IS breakdown for extended periods will affect organizational activities severely.	1	2	3	4	5
CUR3:	Our company relies heavily on IS for efficient operation.	1	2	3	4	5
CUR4:	IS breakdown will critically affect one or more of our functional departments.	1	2	3	4	5
CUR5:	IS breakdown will affect our database access.	1	2	3	4	5
CUR6:	IS breakdown will affect overall coordination within our organization.	1	2	3	4	5

Future Impact of IT

Please indicate the significance of the following items as components of your portfolio of planned systems development projects.

		Low Significance			High Significance	
FUT1:	Projects involving applications of new technologies.	1	2	3	4	5
FUT2:	Projects focusing on routine maintenance to meet evolving business needs, new regulatory or legal requirements.	1	2	3	4	5
FUT3:	Projects focusing on existing system enhancements.	1	2	3	4	5
FUT4:	Projects whose primary benefit is providing new decision support information to top management.	1	2	3	4	5
FUT5:	Projects whose primary benefit is providing new decision support information to middle and lower levels of management.	1	2	3	4	5
FUT6:	Projects which will allow the company to develop and offer new products and services for sale.	1	2	3	4	5
FUT7:	Projects which enable development of new administrative control and planning process.	1	2	3	4	5
FUT8:	Projects which offer significant tangible benefits through improved operational efficiencies.	1	2	3	4	5
FUT9:	Projects which appear to offer new ways for the company to compete.	1	2	3	4	5

Chapter XII
Strategic Capital Capacity and Capability Management of IS/IT

Teay Shawyun
Assumption University of Thailand, Thailand

ABSTRACT

As IS/IT are technology enablers in the creation and delivery of the value, it is contended that all the core processes enabled by its technology should be aligned through the "ways and means" and the "what and how" value is added through the IT enabled processes. The management and implementation of the IT is dependant on the capacity and capability of the firm, and these are human and organizational based, that ultimately defines the firm's competency affecting successful implementation and utilization of the IS/IT. This chapter proposes a "capacity and capability" model based on the management of technology approach (the management of its Technoware, Humanware, Inforware and Orgaware) and its technology capabilities approach to manage its human, information and organization capitals critical to the successful IS/IT implementation and utilization. The "capacity and capability" model is the base of the integrated strategic capability driven implementation model that is contended to address the key implementation issues in a more integrated and comprehensive way. The capability and capacity management of the IS/IT is contended to better address the utilization success based on the inter-twined THIO that addresses the human and organizational issues as compared to the traditional approach of having the MIS resources.

INTRODUCTION

A successful information technology system must contribute to an organization's business functions (Ghoshal and Kim, 1986; Simon, 1990; Miller, 1991), and satisfy its operational, tactical and strategic needs. Rockart and Morton, (1984 and 1989) summarizes it as: "Information technology has become inextricably intertwined with the business. It has therefore become the province of not only IS professionals but of every manager and member in the organization no matter what his or her level is". The dynamics of information technology must run parallel with the business, product life cycles, and the globalization process which are defined by corporate restructuring, corporate freedom to make strategic moves and ability to organize operative functions that optimizes synergy of different SBUs which calls for fast moving and fast reacting management (Koski, 1988). The location of information technology decision making is best determined by and should align with business strategies (Boynton et al., 1992).

Bjornsson and Lundegard (1992) said that the most important criterion for a successful implementation of information technology in a business is that the effects and implications of information technology are in line with corporate strategy. The main task is to evaluate the role of information technology and its effect on corporate performance. Whereas in 1991, Sankar, said that the successful implementation of information technology requires a conceptual model of the change process and the organization to enable managers to plan the change. It calls for managing the domains of behavioral, technical and process, management systems and structure which constrains the implementation of information technology. It expands the relationship of each of the domains and management of change to bring about successful implementation of information technology.

Based on the imperative to manage the successful implementation of the firm's IS/IT within the context of alignment with the firm's strategic intent, it is the objective of this chapter to identify the strategic capital assets of the human, information and organization from the management of technology approach. The aim is to come up with an integrated approach for the strategic management of the capacity and capability of the IS/IT that address the issues of the human and organization that had impinged on implementation issues but had been addressed independently of each other. This model will identify the key competency components that need to be addressed "as a whole and in totality" to strategically manage the IS/IT implementation.

INFORMATION TECHNOLOGY: COMPETITIVE NECESSITY OR ADVANTAGE

The continuing raging battle as to whether IT is a competitive necessity or competitive enabler still rage on today. In Carr's "IT does not matter" (Carr, 2003), he argued that IT had become a commodity through its ubiquity (as IT are easily available and affordable), replicability (as processes are embedded in the software) and necessity (as IT is the minimal enabler to support the business) that had lost its strategic value in being a scarce resource to enable an organization to compete and survive in the market thus becoming an infrastructure technology. In counter-arguments by various authorities in IT to Carr's viewpoints through the Letters to the Editor (HBR, 2003), Brown and Hagel III stated that extracting value from IT requires innovation from business practices through rigorous investment requirements that actually brings about differentiation in the new practices or as called by Alter – the work system and not the IT or IS itself. This is also echoed by McFarlan and Nolan through understanding IT and its economics of how IT can change the rules and assumptions about competition. Strassmann challenged Carr point by point and said that the competitive advantage is gained through effective management and managerial capabilities as echoed by Gurbaxani through skilled and highly motivated people and the value is in the message, not IT as the conduit of conveyance to extend the value of the firm's knowledge capital.

In other letters (HBR, 2003), the "how" to use IT of Lewis, intelligent and innovative application of information or what is inside the box of Broadbent, McDonald and Hunter, with Skaistis and Zwass of using IT to streamline and optimize the critical processes that are embedded in the organizational and inter-organizational processes and combined with other capabilities. It appeared that the common theme in these perspectives were that, "value created and delivered" to the customers through the critical processes are dependent on the organizational mechanisms and capabilities.

In using information technology for maximal benefits, regardless of its use to attain a competitive edge or as a competitive necessity, it is an imperative to overcome the constraints to the success in the utilization of the IS/IT as discussed below:

- The lack luster success or failures of information technology can be attributed to *behavioral* (Cecil and Goldstein, 1990), *political* (Davenport et al., 1992) or *organizational* (Rockart and Short, 1989) issues rather than to technical characteristics of information technology which are explained by the behavior of people either building or using systems or by factors in the organizational setting instead of the specific mix of hardware and operating systems.
- Managing the change enabled by information technology is at least as important as bringing information technology to the organization. People must be trained in a change process that takes into account the

unique challenges presented by information technology (Parson, 1983; Jackson, 1989).
- Information problems and issues from executives are primarily management related. Effectively managing information politics requires a shift in organizational culture; new technology and even new executives alone are not enough to make this happen. Information "state" and politics must be identified and managed and it is something all managers must care and participate in (Davenport et al., 1992). To manage well, key assessment and indicators must be identified (Parsons, 1983; Bjornsson and Lundegard, 1992; Agarwal and Tanniru, 1992).

To surmise, Allert and Kleiner, (1997), identified management and organization as key inhibitors in successful implementation of computer integration with Lee and Bai (2003), reiterating that the IS/IT issues were not merely technological but also the interrelationship of IS/IT within the organizational context.

INFORMATION TECHNOLOGY PLANNING AND MANAGEMENT MODELS

To ratify the above, models for managing IS/IT was developed. Parsons (1983) presented a three level framework to assess the current and potential impact of information technology on business at the industry, firm and strategic level. It underlines the problem in understanding how information technology affected business and not in developing information technology. By understanding *when, where and how* information technology impact a firm, management can develop an explicit information technology strategy that makes the necessary tradeoffs and direct resources to take advantage of opportunities and mitigate threats. At the same time, McFarlan (1984) introduced a 5 questions framework to assess the impact of information technology based on barriers to entry, build in switching cost, basis of competition, change balance of power in supplier relationships and generating new products. The challenge lies in integrating management and user dialogue plus imagination which was complicated by the fact that information technology products were strategically used and the potential benefits are very subjective and not easily verified. Agarwal and Tanniru (1992) also proposed a holistic assessment of the organizational consequences of information technology. The impact is assessed along on breadth (local and global effects) and depth (direct and induced effects) of the effect of the information technology had on the organization. Kovacevic and Majluf (1993) introduced a six stages fifteen steps information technology strategic management framework as they argued that an organization's primary concern should be to integrate the information technology strategic planning process with the general management process.

Framel (1990) introduced the Information Asset Management (IAM) concept to manage an organization's total information resources as an asset rather than as an expense. This is a total management approach that will fully assimilate and integrate all information function and technologies into the total organization. Benjamin and Levinson (1993) drew upon general change management literature to develop an eight principles framework for managing information technology-enabled change which is different from change driven by other concerns. This framework focuses on value change in processes and outcomes rather than inputs. In, Tapscott and Caston (1993), *Paradigm Shift: The New Promise of Information Technology*, promises were made but still unachieved.

In the examination of the promises and constraints of these models affecting the successful utilization of information technology to realize the benefits of information technology and of the factors leading to the failures of information tech-

nology, a few key constraints stood out. In fact, the majority of the key concepts or frameworks are aimed at these few key constraints. Regardless of the contemporary or controversial perspectives, the literatures do perceive the importance and need to manage a few critical areas:

- *Behavioral and learning cycle aspect of people*
- *Organizational aspect of the implementation of information technology*
- *Strategic aspect of information technology*
- *Assessment and measurement aspects of information technology*

RATIONALE OF CAPITAL AND COMPETENCY AS THE STRATEGIC MANAGEMENT DIMENSION

The issue of whether information technology still creates a competitive advantage or is just a competitive necessity is still open to debate. It must be recognized that information technology in itself is only a tool or is an enabling agent that supports the organization to be able to operate and survive in a highly competitive arena. As such, it can be said that information technology in itself does not necessarily bring about any competitive advantage, and this advantage can be created through its being used creatively and intelligently. It must also be noted that such an edge is easily lost through imitation by the competitors as the same set of information technology as a resource is easily available to all who have the means to acquire it. A competitive edge created by leveraging the strategic utilization can last longer and withstand imitation as they are not that easily imitated or are available in the market.

With this rationale, it seems that complete competitive advantage lies not in the information technology or in its configuration but in its utilization that determines the competency of the organization to utilize the IS/IT and information as the differentiating distinctive competence. It is contended that the competitive edge lies in the utilization of the IS/IT and information that represents the strategic capital competency of the organization to achieve competitive advantage. This highlighted the twinned fundamentals of "capacity and capability" that are human based and organization based.

In 1980, Drucker wrote that "information is the manager's main tool, indeed the manager's capital, and it is he who must decide what information he needs and how to use it". This calls for the need of quality information and indicates that there is a logical relationship between information quality and an organization's or an individual's ability to achieve its objectives. The relationship premise is that: Individual success is a function of management quality; Management quality is a function of decision quality; and Decision quality is a function of information quality and quantity and exclusiveness. Churchman (1971) also noted that "Knowledge resides in the user and not in the collection. It is how the user reacts to the collection of information that matters." which reminds us that as we move from intelligence to knowledge, we move from the domain of the providers to the domain of the users.

In the past, the strategies to achieve the goals lie in increasing the amount and analysis of information which finally result in information overload. The new strategy is to achieve more with less through synthesizing higher quality information into wisdom guiding not only the manager's decision but also the customer's decision to bond with a specific product/service offers. The basis for such argument lies in the modified version of Haeckel's conception of an information hierarchy (Haeckel, 1987); the basic objective is to achieve more with less. Codified observations (DATA) are put in CONTEXT - through a processor to derive INFORMATION; which by applying INFERENCE (judgment) to contextual information to generate

INTELLIGENCE; as we gain CERTITUDE (greater certainty and acceptability) it leads to KNOWLEDGE; and by applying SYNTHESIS - holistically bringing together knowledge parts - we create WISDOM. This will result in better utilization of information to serve the market itself and to bond the market to the firm in a two way communication flow from firm to customer and vice-versa.

As Davenport (1994) has put it succinctly, "effective information management must begin by thinking about how people use information - not with how people use machines". Information technology glorification is the past. The future lies in the human psychology of effective and efficient use of information as we can no longer disregard how people actually go about acquiring, sharing, and making use of information. Benjamin et al., 1984, 1990 and 1993 iterated that to maintain competitive advantage, it is not from the use of technology but by instilling a mindset that focuses on customer values that supports a process that continuously innovates and adds value to the customer. They must learn how to integrate the technology effectively into their organizations in such a way that can continuously add capabilities to the system while deriving cost savings from increased productivity and decreased overhead. IS/IT can create value by:

- Facilitating business processes in operations, management, and strategic planning
- Enhancing product characteristics and product delivery
- Increasing process quality and product quality through improvement and innovation

The effective use of information requires two special competencies (Barabba and Zaltman, 1991). The first is called "competent curiosity." It is inquisitiveness about the happenings in its markets that are of current and future importance, coupled with the ability to satisfy that curiosity with timely, relevant, accurate, and cost-effective information. The second competence is called "competent wisdom." It concerns the ability to translate information into effective action by doing the right thing and doing it right. The two competencies are closely linked: Competence in one requires competence in the other. Poor information cannot be used wisely, nor can good information compensate for poor judgment or deficient wisdom.

STRATEGIC CAPITAL AND COMPETENCY MANAGEMENT

Using Kaplan and Norton's learning and growth perspectives (Kaplan and Norton, 1996. 2001 and 2004), the above discussions highlighted the fact that the foundation of the organization lies in the competency of the human capital, information capital and organization capital as the foundation of organization success from which competitive advantage can be acquired. The learning and growth perspective describes the organizations intangible assets which can be classified into the following three categories and their roles in the strategy map as shown below.

i.   *Human Capital (HC):* This comprises the knowledge, skills and values of people in creation of value to the stakeholders.

ii. *Information Capital (IC):* This comprises the IS/IT systems, networks and databases that are horizontally and vertically integrated to support empowerment of the academic and administrative personnel. A key competitive edge is the technology capabilities (Pramongkit and Teay, 2002) of the human sophistication in identification, interpretation and integration of information into knowledge and market wisdom leading to competent curiosity and competent wisdom (Barabba and Zaltman, 1991).

iii. *Organization Capital (OC):* This comprises the leadership, teamwork, alignment and

culture that form the operating core for all the other aspects to function in an integrated total open system.

As these strategic capital assets are intangible, Kaplan and Norton (2004) used "strategic readiness" as the proxy for the measure of these capital assets to successfully implement the strategy. In the Human Capital, there is a need to determine the competency profile of the individual in terms of knowledge, skills and values in terms of its strategic readiness to successfully implement strategy. In the Information Capital, the strategic readiness is determined in terms of the gap difference of the existing and needed information requirements and information infrastructure of the database, applications and communication network. For the Organization Capital, the strategic readiness is determined in terms of the gap differences of the existing and needed leadership, culture, teamwork and alignment of the synergies of all the strategic business units. The use of the "strategic readiness" as the proxy of measure for the intangible capital assets highlighted the "capacity and capability" issue that must be managed strategically.

As discussed above, managing the strategic capital above is an imperative for the success of the organization. As the existing information capital of Kaplan and Norton used the traditional approach for the IT dimension as discussed above, the integrated framework as proposed would incorporate the management of technology approach of the TCOMPS (Technology Components) and TCAPS (Technology Capabilities) (Sharif, 1995) aspects to better manage (as shown in Figure 1 below that highlights the dynamic interaction of the technology components) the 3 sets of capital and its competency and to integrate these 2 fundamental management framework into a strategic capital management model for IS/IT in the framework.

MANAGEMENT OF TECHNOLOGY APPROACH TO IT MANAGEMENT

As defined by the U.S. National Research Council (1987), "The management of technology links engineering, science and management disciplines to plan, develop and implement technological capability to shape and accomplish the strategic and operational objectives of the organization", whereby the unit of analysis is the technological capabilities of the portfolio of technologies on the firm. Badawy, (1998) suggested that the management of technology is the practice of integrating technology with business strategy. Technology is only a human-made tool (enabling agent) or means to:

1. enhance either the physical or mental capacities of human beings
2. amplify group capacities
3. enable human to evolve from purely basic needs satisfaction to engage in superior functions and competition.

Figure 1 shows the dynamics of the technology utilization that calls for the interaction of the humanware (H) in using the technoware (T) to generate the human-based inforware (I) are carried out within the orgaware (O) context and mechanisms for their work. This shows that the imperative of the THIO must be managed. It should be noted that the Kaplan and Norton's 1996, 2001 and 2004 strategic capital management of the human capital, information capital and organization capital are intertwined dependently rather than independently. The strategic capital assets HC/IC/OC intangible interdependency is clearly illustrated in Figure 1. With this in mind, the underlying theme for the organization management of IT are that the strategic capital assets of the HC/IC/OC must be integrated and

Figure 1. Dynamically integrating technology components

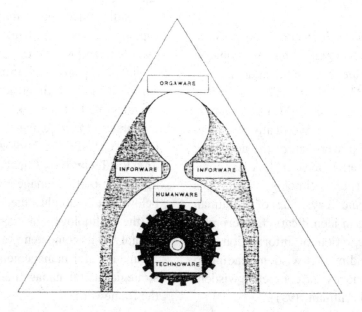

Source: Sharif, N. (1995), The Evolution of Technology Management Studies: Techno-economics to Techno-metrics, Professorial lecture at Asian Institute of Technology, 23 March 1995

viewed within the dynamics of the technology components that are inter-locked together into an integrated model of managing the two competent "capacity and capability" aspects of the strategic capital. This integrated framework is contended to better manage the key capabilities of what and how the human capital's degree of competency, uses the information capital capacity within the organization capital to leverage the use of IS/IT for better success through a set of metrics (adapting the APQC metrics for IT) for each of the capital set. The major fundamentals of Technology Components (TCOMPS) and Technology Capabilities (TCAPS) are highlighted below. The major dimensions of Technology Components (TCOMPS) are:

1. TECHNOWARE: Object-embodied physical facilities (tools, equipment, machinery, structure) → amplifies human powers and controls transformation processes

2. HUMANWARE: Person-embodied human abilities (skills, craftsmanship, expertise, dexterity and creativity) → degree of human sophistication increases the level of competence defined in terms of knowledge, skill, values, productivity orientation, achievement orientation, creativity orientation, and motivation.

3. INFORWARE: Record-embodied documented knowledge (facts, formulae, design parameters, specification, manuals, theories) → enables quicker learning and acquisition of knowledge in terms of time and resources through the tacit (individual that is human-based) and explicit (public that is organization based) knowledge

4. ORGAWARE: Institution-embodied organizational frameworks (methods, techniques, organizational frameworks and management practices) → to achieve coordination of activities and resources utilization towards achieving desired results.

STRATEGIC CAPACITY AND CAPABILITY ALIGNMENT WITH IS/IT

Agenda 21 defined (Chapter 37, UNCED, 1992) capacity building "the human, scientific, technological, organizational, institutional and resource capabilities" and UNDP Briefing paper (1991) emphasized the creation of an enabling environment with appropriate policy and legal framework and human resources development and strengthening of managerial systems and organizational development of management structure, processes and procedures, and also relationships. Basically capacity building focuses on "a series of actions directed at helping participants in the development process to increase their knowledge, skills and understandings and to develop the attitudes needed to bring about the desired changes" as noted by FAO (www.capacity.org, 2007).

Succinctly, Mentz, (1997) highlighted the capacity to achieve whereby the issue lies in the institutional capacity (capacity utilization) rather than technical capacity (availability of skills, methods, systems and technology). In operational terms, Cohen (1993b) highlighted "to strengthen targeted human resources (managerial, professional and technical) that can be marshaled and sustained effectively" or "the ability to perform appropriate tasks effectively, efficiently and sustainably" (Hiderbrand and Grindle, 1994). These complemented Berg's (1992) three main capacity building of skill upgrading – both general and job-specific; procedural improvements and organizational strengthening.

As applied to the IS/IT, information-infrastructure capacity must be aligned to the strategic needs of the organization (Prahalad and Krishnan, 2002) as IT must be an integral part of the strategy of the firm. To balance the tension between innovation and stability Prahalad and Krishnan (2002) developed the applications-portfolio scorecard to audit the current applications, identify priorities, to assess the linkages and interdependence with a focus on collaboration. This balanced approach will lead to both efficiency and flexibility with the IS/IT supporting the strategy.

As shown in figure 2, the IS/IT capacity and capability must be aligned with the firm's vision, mission, goals, objectives and strategies (at the corporate level and at the competitive level) as the IS/IT are the enablers to support the achievement of the firms strategies. The key alignment areas are: Orgaware Capacity and Capability (that creates the organization environment and foundation for the other aspects); Humanware Capability (the human capacity and capability to use the IS/IT and information); Inforware Capacity (that goes into the tacit and explicit knowledge domains and knowledge management and learning of the individual and organization); and the Technoware Capacity (that covers the mechanistic aspects of the hard infrastructure of the networks, applications, database and the "container of knowledge".

These components must interact dependently rather than independently to achieve a long-term sustainable competitive advantage. As noted in Figure 1, they exist as a "total" inter-locked mechanism as the T, H, I and O interacts within the organization context which is the orgaware

foundation. A strong orgaware foundation will lead to a longer term and more sustainable organization competence that cannot be duplicated by others as they are internalized and unique to the organization.

Orgaware Capacity and Capability foundation

Strategically, competencies is the combination of resources and capabilities (Hitt, Ireland and Hoskisson (2005), and they become core competencies when they are valuable, rare, difficult to imitate and substitute. Haanes (2000) stated that the competencies are the means by which a firm deploys its tangible and intangible resources that integrate the individual professional skills and knowledge with the organizational competencies which can be the firm's knowledge, culture, functions, processes or routines that Prahalad and Hamel (1990) called core competencies. The intangible organization resources are the knowledge, reputation and culture, whereas the intangible human resources are embedded as the capabilities of people in the form of knowledge,

Figure 2. Strategic capacity and capability management of IS/IT

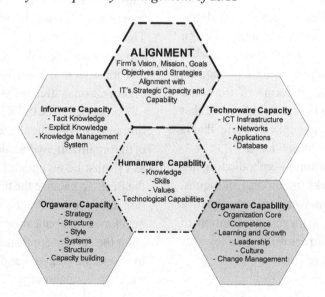

skills, and motivation and communication abilities affecting job performance. Andriessen (2001) classified these unique bundles of intangible assets or the core competencies into: collective values and norms (client focus, reliability, and quality), processes (leadership and control, communication, management of information technology) and explicit knowledge (patents, manuals, and procedures) and skills and tacit knowledge (know-how, talent and competencies).

In the learning and growth aspect, organizational level competencies are embedded in the employee-level competencies; the crux is in the capacities of the organization and its individuals to access and utilize the information and knowledge effectively to create value. This utilization calls for the individual and organization capacity and capability to understand and interpret the information. Mentz, (1997) and Turner and Crawford (1994) proposed 2 layers of capacity and competencies of the sustainability of the on-going processes to create and deliver on the value:

*   Personal capacity which is the nuts and bolts of capacity building means the skills, knowledge, experience, personality (de Jager and Clarke, 2001) and the ability not only to do something but also over a period of time to build up a reservoir of knowledge, experience and expertise that determines present and on-going performance. This underlies the "motive, trait, and skill, aspect of one's self-image or social role, or a body of knowledge which he or she uses" (Boyatzis, 1982).
*   Non-personal capacity or the administrative capacity provides the context (in essence the values, beliefs and ideals) in which personal capacity is developed as they work in the organizational setting which influence their mind-set. This would mean in management terminology organizational learning of the collective wisdom, expertise and experience of all the individuals

working in the corporate environment. This corporate capacity refers to the size, scope and scale of the performance of the total corporate system, the efficiency and rationality (exercise of reason and judgment) of the implementation and sustainability of maintaining the level of output over time. This refers to the internal structures, procedures and policy frameworks and collective capabilities of the staff and external environmental factors (de Jager and Clarke, 2001) or sets of behavior pattern needed to perform (Woodruffe, 1992).

In the Orgaware capacity and capability development aspects they would include:

*   Skill enhancement – general education, on-the-job-training and professional deepening in crosscutting skills such as business, analysis and interpretation and IT (Berg, 1992). These capabilities enhancement include intelligence, skills, knowledge and mental sets (Loubser, 1993).
*   Organization strengthening – covering the process of institutional development or institution building implying an infrastructure mentality (Berg, 1992) that could mean the values and cultural aspects of institution building (Morgan, 1993). Williams (1997) re-iterated that different business culture can support or hinder information development and utilization. He identified three IS/IT cultural hypothesis as: innovator – actively pursue IS/IT development regardless of investment; follower – concentrate on operation efficiency to ensure competitiveness; dinosaur – do not see investment in IS/IT as beneficial or has competitive use.
*   Procedural improvements and Management – covering general functions changes or systems reforms that are on-going (Berg, 1992 and Morgan, 1993). It must be noted that the value of information and IS/IT is

derived from the actions of the management and their utilization to get the work done. Organizations achieve these work through planning, designing, sequencing and mobilizing resources (Loubser, 1993). The organization mechanisms used include group interactions, knowledge management, organizational learning and change management, culture, experience and skills of the organization (Lee and Bai, 2003).

- Mukherji (2002), highlighted the compatibility of the fit between the IS/IT architecture with the organization structure, with an emphasis on the interfaces between the organization and its stakeholders that might call for different structure depending on its "strategic fit with the business strategies". Tavakolian (1989), in their study of 58 firms verified the strategy-structure relationship with a particular type of IS/IT. Leifer (1988) identified 5 types of organization structure that corresponded with 5 types of IS/IT architecture: simple structure – for stand alone PC; machine bureaucracy – for centralized systems; professional bureaucracy – for centralized and distributed systems; divisionalized form – for centralized, distributed and decentralized systems; advocacy – for decentralized systems. The newer networked structure would demand interfaces of the firm's IS/IT with the stakeholders to allow flexible work-group, centrality of customers, close collaboration with suppliers, and the ability and flexibility to respond to change that would lead to the integration of systems that makes boundary less relevant.

Within the IT context, a key Information Capacity is managing relationships (Ballantyne, 2000) as no individual or organization is able to achieve all the aims alone due to the volume of knowledge created leading to "cooperativity" (skills, attitudes and organizational culture and willingness to learn and share) across individuals and organization to make things happen. Individual and organizational ICT skills, awareness, readiness and capacity are the basic requirements and mechanisms to seamlessly tie together the relationships and the process to create and deliver on the value (Mancey, 2000).

In defining the ICT capacity development indicators, the International Institute for Communication and Development (IICD) uses the 3 "P" (de Jager and Clarke, 2001) of:

- Product – the actual capacities that needs to be improved or achieved.
- Performance – substantive/defined program outcomes.
- Permanence – the sustainability of the product.

Powell, (1999), considers information management "as a task to enable and support the creation of value out of knowledge and skills of people working on the front line and allowing them access to information and mainstreaming their knowledge within their organization and that the "customers" are the fundamental target. The knowledge base of the organization needs to be nourished and sustained. The ICT transform the way tasks are done, alliances and relationships are formed and the way the organization operates. The human attitudes and skills through the knowledge base is the organization mechanism to continue to foster and sustain the knowledge that forms the foundation of orgaware capacity and capability.

Humanware Capability

The International Labor Organization in their 2004 study, categorized 3 dominant job activity as: tacit – complex interactions; transactional – routine interactions and transformational – conversion of raw materials, and their study showed that jobs requiring tacit interactions were becoming more important especially in developed countries (41%) and developing countries (26%). Beardsley, Johnson and Manyika, (2006), suggested that these tacit interactions unique to an organization involved the exchange of information, the making of judgment, and the need to draw from multi-faceted forms of knowledge with co-workers, customers and suppliers are central to the economic activity. Managing for effective tacit interactions means managing the changes, learning, collaboration, shared values and innovation aspects of the organization.

The capabilities competency clusters (Thorton and Byham, 1982) can be categorized as: Intellectual – strategic perspective, analysis and judgment; Interpersonal – persuasiveness, decisiveness; Adaptability – resilience; Results orientation – initiative, business sense. Houtzagers, (1999), identified 5 sets of skills and competencies profile of: Professional knowledge, Customer Orientation, Business Awareness, Leadership and Planning and Organizing. These 5 profiles had 10 entities of: Professional knowledge, Orientation, Relationships, Coaching, Leadership, Communications, Business Awareness, Analysis and decision making, and Planning and organizing that are difficult to be copied in an organization. To identify and develop individual competencies, Cardy and Selvarajan (2006) proposed 4 frameworks as:

1. job-based that is static and focused on what gets done;
2. future-based that is directional and focused on what needs to be done;
3. person-based that is broad and emergent;
4. value-based that is process focused on how things are done.

Using the value-based approach, the technology capabilities can be improved through learning by DOING and learning by CHANGING of the individual and the organization. Under such a circumstance, the major Dimensions of Technology Capabilities (TCAPS) (Sharif, 1995)

of the individual and the organization could be classified as:

1. TRANSFORMING CAPS: *(Operating and Supporting Capabilities)* the utilization of available technology for the transformation process → corresponds to the improved operation, monitoring and maintenance of all technology components to respond to different market niches
2. VENDING CAPS: *(Marketing and Servicing Capabilities)* the distributing, selling and servicing of outputs using technology → concerned with the market-driven aspects of technological capability of providing customers with utility and convenience
3. ACQUIRING CAPS: *(Sourcing and Procuring Capabilities)* the acquisition of technology components and the capability to prepare specifications for upgrade → results in capability to undertake technological change management
4. MODIFYING CAPS: *(improvising and Improving capabilities)* the continuous improvement of all activities and technology components → capability to adapt technoware and orgaware for better efficiency, carry out minor and incremental improvement for superior outputs
5. DESIGNING CAPS: *(Conceiving and Devising Capabilities)* the actual utilization of product development technologies → product design, redesign and modifications, capability to introduce creativity and creation of new product for future market
6. GENERATING CAPS: *(Innovating and Commercializing Capabilities)* the utilization of process development technologies → the capability to carry out research and development work for product-process innovations → advancement indicates the realization of crucial self-reliance and control for effective market competition in the face of rapid technological changes

Inforware Capacity

McDermott (1999), distinguished knowledge from information which is an object in that knowledge is a human act, is the residue of thinking created and recreated in the present moment as information is fully made and is in a storage, and knowledge belongs to and circulate through communities, and knowledge is created at the boundaries of the old. Muller-Merbach, (2006), used Immanuel Kant's 3 kinds of actions: technical action, pragmatic action and ethical action, to distinguish a trisection of knowledge as follows:

- Knowledge for technical action requires an appropriate technical literacy, its familiarity with the subject which is technical competence.
- Knowledge for pragmatic action requires interest, intimacy and affection in people and emotional relations with individuals and groups.
- Knowledge for ethical action is a matter of judgment and evaluation, reflections rather than "facts or figures".

Creating an information system without understanding what the knowledge professionals need or how they relate to others in the communities or the form of level of details they need do little to leveraging the knowledge leading to an information junkyard. To leverage knowledge, thinking of the information is needed, and the challenge lies not only in the technical side but also the social, management and personal sides.

The human element of knowledge (Chatzkel, 2002; Davenport and Prusak, 1998; Fowler and Pryke, 2003; Hildreth et.al. 1999) were reflected in Blackler's (1995) description of knowledge as "multifaceted and complex, being both situated and abstract, implicit and explicit, distributed and individual, physical and mental, developing and static, verbal and encoded". This led to imperatives of tacit knowledge residing in people (Hendriks

and Vriens, 1999; Myers, 1996). Kane et. al., (2006) categorized knowledge into 2 groups of:

- Personal/Tacit – which are expertise, know-how that are manifested through action, acquired through practice and difficult to transfer based on personal beliefs, values, subjective insights or emotions that are contained in the container (technically the human's head) and is difficult to share.
- Public/Explicit – which are the rationalization of information that can be stored, codified and transmitted and can be articulated as facts represented in the form of documents, designs, patents, trademarks, business plans, formal language that are objective and rational and are about the container or embodiment of knowledge (Manesh and Surash, 2004) which is the organizational memory (Anand et.al, 1998) or systematic memory. They are captured in the organization's manuals, procedures, databases, operational models and systematic rules that are easily shared.

Organizational knowledge is a mixture of both tacit and explicit knowledge and knowledge management role is to unlock them and leverage them as organization asset. Knowledge Management is essentially the transfer of knowledge to others who need it for carrying out their responsibilities in the organization. This transfer is a synchronous communication between "speaker" and "listener" whereby the information must be interpreted and integrated into knowledge (Haeckel, 1987) with the rest of the knowledge that he or she possesses (Mahesh and Suresh, 2004). leading to market wisdom. Knowledge transfer is about connection (Davenport and Prusak, 1998) and not collection (Dougherty, 1999) and von Krogh et. al (1996) referred it to "knowledge connection" that is made up of formal and informal relationships. Amidon (1997) went one step further to describe "knowledge innovation – as the creation, evolution, exchange and applications of new ideas into marketable goods and services"

Technoware Capacity

In their research studies on 89 enterprises, Weill, Subramani and Broadbent (2002) also found that different strategic agility required distinct patterns of IT infrastructure capability that must be understood to derive performance and advantage. This research identified seventy services categorized into ten capability clusters: channel-management services, security and risk-management services, communication services, data-management services, application-infrastructure services, IT-facilities-management services, IT-management services, IT-architecture-and-standards services, IT-education services, and IT R and D services. Over investment or under investment at different period and situation need to be balanced to create the capability needed to achieve the strategic agility and business performance. Melarkode, From-Poulsen and Warnakulasuriya, 2004 defined agility as "the capacity to anticipate changing market dynamics and adapt to those dynamics and accelerate enterprise change faster than the rate of change in the market to create economic value". They believed that there are 5 levers of agility which need to be used together. The five levers are quality and efficiency that are the prices to play, while visibility, velocity and flexibility are the factors that differentiate enterprises and that IT must be managed to the agility theme.

Human takes central role in knowledge management, not the computer systems as they augment the human thinking (Nonaka, 1991; Nonaka and Takeuchi, 1995) and cannot replace individuals by even the most powerful "thinking machines". Huber (1991) and Malhotra (1996) considered IT as a tool to enable organizational memory and can serve the organizational learning processes. This calls for leveraging the information processing capacity of advanced technology to produce information that must be translated into action by the human's creativity and innovation. IT can be utilized in all the 4 phases on knowledge management of knowledge capture (database systems, data warehouse, digital library), knowledge development (data mining, OLAP, competitive intelligence), knowledge sharing (group support system, Intranet) and knowledge utilization (GUI with animation, multimedia technology) (Lee and Hong, 2002). On another perspective, Goh (2004), noted that three kinds of physical IT systems are needed for knowledge management practices in order to be effective: capture tools (e.g. intelligence database), communication tools (e.g. distributed networks), and collaboration tools (e.g. interactive web pages).

MANAGERIAL IMPLICATIONS

The volumes of literature on IS/IT management, its interdependence and alignment with business strategies coupled with the strategic management concepts and frameworks has brought about a diverse set of approaches and frameworks or models implement IS/IT successful. In essence, IS/IT regardless of being a competitive necessity or advantage must be managed strategically in alignment with its strategic management discipline. As noted above, the crux of success lies in the intangibility of the strategic capital of the human capital, information capital and the organization capital that must be integrated and managed in totality rather than as piecemeal jigsaw. The three strategic capital must complement each other to successfully implement the IS/IT. The major implications here are that:

i.   The planning and management approach for the IS/IT must be "market oriented" towards the internal customer (internal use and interpretation of the information to create and deliver values to the market) and the external customer (the derivation of value from the product service offer through the information and IS/IT infrastructure) which are human-based and organization-based.

ii. Since value creation is individual and organization based and that they fall into the human "faculty" domain, it is important to understand the tacit and explicit knowledge of both the individual and organization through individual and organization mechanisms.

iii. These individual and organization mechanisms do not work in a vacuum. On the contrary, they exists within a rich and diverse organization system that are the style of management, values and culture, leadership, relationships and interactions, organization structure and organization strategy that must be strategically dealt with and managed as a "whole and total" in terms of context and content.

iv. It must be noted that the "ends and means of the firm" must be matched or aligned. This means that the IS/IT as the means or the key enabler must be matched with or aligned with the firm's desired outcome which is represented by its performance through it strategies enabled by technology.

v. What had been neglected was the "capacity and the capability" of the human capital in their use the information capital within the organization capital context. These cannot exist independent of each other nor be managed independently and they had been treated superficially that neglects the real issue of the individual and organization competence.

vi. What had also been lacking was that these issues were not tackled in an integrated manner. This will mean that the future direction of the research into aligning the IS/IT with the business perspectives must be dealt at the individual and organization

"capacity and capability" level. Taking this approach could mean that the IS/IT once aligned and integrated would be more fruitful and beneficial within the human and the organization context to really create and deliver on the value as required by the customers.

FUTURE TRENDS AND RESEARCH

Based on the proposed paradigm and the strategic management of the capacity and capability, especially the organization capacity context which had a rich literature in the public management context but had not been applied nor researched within the private firms' or the business context, it is recommended that further researches should be conducted in these areas of:

• Business organization capacity and capability as the basis of its strategic management in the operational areas of marketing, finance, human resource, information systems and operations as all of them are key strategic resources that contribute to the success of the firm.

• The intangible aspects of the human capital, information capital and the organization capital (that forms the strategic foundation of the firm to leverage the internal organization processes and resources to create and deliver value to the customers to achieve the firm's financial value) that will affect the implementation of IS/IT or for that matter all the other operational areas.

• Using the management of technology approach to research into the THIO and TCAPS of the organization as they form a stronger foundation as compared to the existing use of Hardware, Software and Peopleware that do not really address the intangible aspects of capacity and capability that are human and organization based.

CONCLUSION

As discussed in the implications above, managing the organization strategically or the use of the IS/IT as the enabler to achieve the organization's business objectives, the "ends and the means" must be strategically managed. In this case, the ends represented by the achievement of the business performance and outcomes are realized by the strategic management of the means as the key enabler which is the IS/IT.

This would mean that the issues or the "capacity and capability" of the strategic capital assets competence of the human, information and organization, must be identified, recognized, planned and managed through an integrated and aligned mechanism. Failing which the prevalent issues will still prevail under existing approaches that do not really manage these strategic capitals in an integrated approach.

The "strategic management of the capacity and capability" model as described here is aimed at looking at the IS/IT management and implementation in an integrated and total approach that complement and supplement each other in terms of its technoware, humanware, inforware and orgaware or THIO capacity and capability that forms the foundation of success as they go into the human and organization domain that are and will always be "intangible" in nature and must be realistically and strategically approached and managed. The firm cannot afford to shy away from these lingering and pending issues. Tackled head on in a holistic approach will bring about more success to the organization in terms of not only market but also organization benefits.

REFERENCE

Agarwal, R., & Tanniru, M. (1992). Assessing the organizational impacts of Information technology. *ITJM, Special Issue on the Strategic Management of Information and Telecommunication Technology* (pp. 626-643).

Allert J., & Kleiner, B. H. (1997). Developments in Computer-based information systems, *Logistics Information Management, 10*(5).

Amidon, D. M. (1997). *Innovation Strategy for the Knowledge Economy: The Ken Awakening.* Boston, MA: Butterworth-Heinemann.

Anand, V., Manz, C., & Glick, H. (1998). An organizational memory approach to information management. *Academy of Management Review, 23*(4).

Andriessen, D. (2001). *Weightless wealth.* Paper for the 4th world congress on the management of intellectual capital. Mc Master University, January 17 – 19, Hamilton, Ontario.

Ballantyne, P. (2000). Managing Relationships: A Key Information Management Capacity. *Information and Capacity Building, 7,* October 2000, ECDPM

Barabba, V. P., & Zaltman, G. (1991). *Hearing the Voice of the Market: Competitive Advantage through creative use of Market Information.* Harvard Business School Press.

Badawy, M. K. (1998). Technology management education: alternative models. *California Management Review, 40*(4).

Beardsley S. C., Johnson, B. C., & Manyika, J. M. (2006). Competitive advantage from better interactions. *The McKinsey Quarterly, 2.*

Benjamin, R. I., Rockart, J. F., Morton, M. S. S., & Wyman, J. (1984). Information Technology: A Strategic Opportunity. *Sloan Management Review,* (pp. 3-10).

Benjamin, R. I., & Levinson, E. (1993). A Framework for managing IT enabled Change. *Sloan Management Review,* (pp. 23-33).

Benjamin, R. I., de Long, D. W., & Morton, M. S. S. (1990). Electronic Data Interchange: How much Competitive Advantage? *Long Range Planning*, 23(1), 34-40.

Berg, E. (1993). *Rethinking technical cooperation: reforms for capacity building in Africa*. Washington, DC: UNDP/DAL

Bjornsson, H. & Lundegard, R. (1990). Corporate Competitiveness and Information Technology. *European Management Journal*, 10(3), 460-475.

Blackler, F. (1995). Knowledge, knowledge work and organizations: An overview and interpretation. *Organization studies*, *16*(6).

Boynton, A. C., Jacobs, G. C., & Zmud, R. W. (1992). Whose Responsibility is IT management? *Sloan Management Review*, (pp. 32-38).

Boyatzis, R. (1982). *The Competent Manager*. New York: Wiley.

Bureau of Labor Statistics (2004). *Global Insights, International Labor Organization*. United Nations, World Bank.

Carr, N. C. (2003). IT doesn't matter. *Harvard Business Review*, May 2003.

Cardy, R. L., & Selvarajan, T. T. (2006). Competencies: Alternative frameworks for competitive advantage. *Business horizons, 49*. Elsevier.

Cecil, J., & Goldstein, M. (1990). Sustaining competitive advantage from IT. *McKinsey Quarterly, 4*, 74-89.

Chatzkel, J. (2002). Conversation with Alex Bennet, former deputy CIO for enterprise integration at the U.S. Dept. of Navy. *Journal of Knowledge Management, 6*(5)

Churchman, C. W. (1971). *The Design of Inquiring Systems: Basic Concepts of Systems and Organizations*. New York: Basic Books.

Cohen, J. M. (1993b). *Building sustainable public sector managerial, professional and technical capacity: A framework for analysis and intervention*. Development Discussion Paper 473. Cambridge. MA: Harvard Institute for International Development.

Davenport, T. H., & Prusak, L. (1998). *Working Knowledge, How Organizations Manage What They Know*. Boston, MA: Harvard Business School Press.

Davenport, T. H., & Short, J. E. (1990). The new Industrial Engineering: Information Technology and Business Process Redesign. *Sloan Management Review*, Summer 1990, pp 11-26.

Davenport, T. H., Eccles, R. G., & Prusak, L. (1992). Information Politics. *Sloan Management Review*, Fall 1992, pp. 53-65.

Davenport, T. H. (1994). Saving IT's Soul: Human-Centered Information Management. *Harvard Business Review*, March-April 1994, pp. 119-131.

De Jager, A., & Clarke, D. (2001). Building Local and Sustainable Capacities for ICT Development. *Approaches to ICT Development, 10*, July 2001, ECDPM.

Dougherty, V. (1999). Knowledge is about people, not databases. *Industrial and Commercial Training, 31*(7).

Drucker, P. F. (1980). Managing the Information Explosion. *The Wall Street Journal, 10*, 25-30.

Drucker, P. F. (1995). The information that executives truly need. *Harvard Business Review*, January-February 1995, pp. 54-63

Fowler, A., & Pryke, J. (2003). Knowledge management in public service provision: The child support agency. *International Journal of Service Industry Management, 14*(3).

Framel, J. E. (1990). Managing Information costs and Technologies as Assets. *Journal of Systems Management*, 41(2), 12-19.

Ghoshal, S., & Kim, S. K. (1986). Building effective Intelligence Systems for Competitive Advantage, *Sloan Management Review*, Fall 1986, pp. 49-58.

Goh, A. (2004). Enhancing Organizational Performance through Knowledge Innovation: A Proposed Strategic Management Framework. *Journal of Knowledge Management Practice*, October 2004.

Hannes, K. (2000). Linking intangible resources and competition. *European Management Journal*, *18*(1).

Haeckel, S. H. (1987). *Presentation to the Information Planning Steering Group*. Cambridge, MA: Marketing Science Institute.

HBR (2003). Does IT Matter?: An HBR Debate. *Harvard Business Review*, June 2003.

Hendriks, P. H. J., & Vriens, D. J. (1999). Knowledge-based systems and knowledge management: friends or foes? *Information and Management*, *35*(2).

Hiderbrand, M. E., & Grinde, M. S. (1994). *Building sustainable capacity: challenges for the Public Sector*: Cambridge, MA: Harvard Institute for International Development/UNDP.

Hildreth, P., Wright, P., & Kimble, C. (1999). Knowledge Management: are we missing something? In *Information Systems – The Next Generation*, L. Brooks & C. Kimble (Eds.), pp. 347-356.

Hitt, M. A., Ireland, R. D., & Hoskisson, R. E. (2005). *Strategic Management: Competitiveness and Globalization* (6th Edition), Versailles, KY: South-Western.

Houtzagers, G. (1999). Empowerment, using skills and competence management, *Participation and Empowerment: An International journal,* 7(2).

Huber, G. H. (1991). Organizational learning, the contributing process and the literature, *Organization Science*, *2*(1).

Kane, H., Ragsdell, G., & Oppenheim, C. (2006). Knowledge Management Methodologies. *The Electronic Journal of Knowledge Management*, *4*(2).

Kaplan, R. S., & Norton, D. P. (1996). *Translating Strategy into Action: The Balanced Scorecard*, HBS Press 1996.

Kaplan, R. S., & Norton, D. P. (2001). *The Strategy Focused Organization*, HBS Press 2001.

Kaplan, R. S., & Norton, D. P. (2004). *Strategy Maps: Converting Intangible Assets into Tangible Outcomes*, 2004 HBS Press.

Koski, T. H. A. (1988). Competitive Advantage and the IT Industry. *European Management Journal*, *6*(2), 340-357.

Kovacevic, A., & Majluf, N. (1993). Six stages of IT Strategic Management. *Sloan Management Review*, Summer 1993, 77-87.

Lee, G., & Bai, R. (2003). Organizational mechanisms for successful IS/IT strategic planning in the digital era. *Management Decision* 41/1, (2003).

Lee, S. M., & Hong, S. (2002). An enterprise-wide knowledge management system Infrastructure. *Industrial Management and Data Systems*, 102/1.

Leifer, R. (1988). Matching computer-based information systems with organizational structures, *MIS Quarterly*, *12*(1).

Lounser, D. K. (1991). *Capacity development – A conceptual overview*. Paper presented at a workshop on Capacity Development at the Institute of Governance, Ottawa, Canada.

Mancey, A. (2000). Building a National Information and Communication Network. *Information and Capacity Building*, 7, October 2000, ECDPM.

Mahesh, K., & Suresh, J. K. (2004). What is the K in KM Technology? *The Electronic Journal of Knowledge Management*, *2*(2).

Malhotra, Y. (1996). Organizational learning and learning organizations: An overview. available at: http:/brint.com/papers/orglrng.htm

McDermott, R. (1999). Knowing is a Human Act: How Information Technology Inspired but cannot deliver Knowledge Management. *California Management Review*, Summer 1999.

McFarlan, F. W. (1984). Information Technology changes the way you compete, *Harvard Business Review*, May-June 1984 pp. 210-226.

Melarkode, A., From-Poulsen, M., & Warnakula-suriya, S. (2004). Delivering Agility through IT, *Business Strategy Review*, Autumn 2004.

Mentz, J. C. N. (1997). *Personal and Institutional Factors in Capacity Building and Institutional Development*, ECDPM Working Paper No. 14, Maastricht: ECDPM.

Morgan, P. (1993). *Capacity development: An Overview* Paper presented at a workshop on Capacity Development at the Institute of Governance, Ottawa, Canada.

Mukherji, A. (2002). The evolution of information systems: their impact on organizations and structures. *Management Decision*, 40/5.

Muller-Merbach, H. (2006). Three kinds of knowledge, reflecting Kant's three kinds of action, *Knowledge Management Research and Practice, 4.*

National Research Council (1987). *Management of Technology: The hidden competitive advantage*, Report of the Task Force on Management of Technology. Washington: National Academy Press..

Nonaka, I. (1991). The Knowledge-Creating Company, *Harvard Business Review*, November – December 1991.

Nonaka, I., & Takeuchi, H. (1995). *The Knowledge-Creating Company: How Japanese Companies Create the Dynamics of Innovation*. New York: Oxford University Press.

Parsons, G. L. (1983). Information Technology : A new competitive weapon, *Sloan Management Review*, Fall 1983, pp. 3-14.

Prahalad, C. K., & Hamel, G. (1990). The core competencies of the corporation. *Harvard Business Review*, May – June 1990.

Prahalad, C. K., & Krishnan, M. S. (2002). The Dynamic Synchronization of Strategy and Information Technology. *MIT Sloan Management Review*, Summer 2002.

Pramongkit, P., & Teay, S. (2002). Strategic IT Framework for Modern enterprise by using Information Technology Capabilities. *Proceedings of 2002 IEEE International Engineering Management Conference (IEMC – 2002).* Cambridge UK

Pramongkit, P., Teay, S., & Boonmark, S. (2000). Analysis of Technological Learning for Thai Manufacturing Industry *Technovation: The International Journal of Technological Innovation and Entrepreneurship*, 20(4), 189 – 196.

Rockart, J. F., & Short, J. E. (1989). IT in the 1990s: Managing Organizational Interdependence. *Sloan Management Review*, Winter 1989, pp. 128-136.

Rockart, J. F., & Morton, M. S. S. (1984). Implications of Changes in Information Technology for Corporate Strategy. *Interfaces,* Jan 1988 pp. 84-95.

Sankar, Y. (1991). Implementing Information technology: A Managerial Audit for Planning change, *Journal of Systems Management, 42*(11), 32-37.

Sharif, N. (1995). *The Evolution of Technology Management Studies: Techno-economics to Techno-metrics*. Professorial lecture at Asian Institute of Technology, 23. March 1995

Tapscott, D., & Caston, A. (1993). *Paradigm Shift : The New Promise of Information Technology*. McGraw-Hill Inc.

Tavakolian, H. (1989). Linking the information technology structure with organizational strategy: a survey. *MIS Quarterly, 13*(3).

Thorton, G. C., & Byham, W. C. (1982). *Assessment centers and managerial performance.* New York: Academic Press.

Turner, D., & Crawford, M. (1994). Managing current and future competitive performers: The role of competency. In G. Hamel and A. Heene (Eds.), *Competency-based competition: Strategic Management series* (pp. 241 – 254). Chichester, England: Wiley.

UNCED (1992). *Capacity Building – Agenda 21's definition* (Chapter 37, UNCED, 1992)

UNDP (1991). Symposium on "A Strategy for Water Sector Capacity Building" Deft, The Netherlands in 1991.

Von Krogh, G., Roos, J., & Slocum, K. (1996). An Essay on corporate epistemology. In G. von Krogh and J. Roos (Eds), *Managing Knowledge: Perspectives on Cooperation and Competition.* London: Sage Publication.

Weill, P., Subramani, M., & Broadbent, M. (2002). Building IT Infrastructure for Strategic Agility. *MIT Sloan Management Review,* Fall 2002.

Williams, L. T. (1997). Planning and Managing the information system – a manager's guide. *Industrial Management and Data Systems,* 97/5.

Woodfuffe, C. (1992). What is meant by competency? In R. Boam & P. Sparrow (Eds.), *Designing and achieving competency.* New York: McGraw-Hill.

Chapter XIII
Challenges in Implementing Information Technology Plan

Evon M. O. Abu-Taieh
The Arab Academy for Banking and Financial Sciences, Jordan

Asim A. El Sheikh
The Arab Academy for Banking and Financial Sciences, Jordan

Jeihan M. Abu-Tayeh
Ministry of Planning and International Cooperation, Jordan

ABSTRACT

The chapter will present the challenges in implementing information technology plan pertaining to two dimensions: literature and practical. The chapter will also suggest ways to rectify and deflect the negative impact of the challenges. In addition, the chapter will show some of the challenges' manifestations shown in some case studies.

INTRODUCTION

The implementation of an information technology plan defined by (Hoffer, George, & Valacich, 2005) as a phase of the systems development plan that includes six major activities: Coding, Testing, Installation, Documentation, Training, and Support, in order to convert final physical system specifications into working and reliable software. In this regard, the phase of implementation follows many phases comprising of planning and analysis, followed by the design of the solution, as such, it is imperative that the work being done during the implementation phase is to be documented, in view that documenting the implementation phase will provide help not only for current but also for future efforts in the same field.

In this context, there should be a list of what must be done over the course of implementation of an IT plan (Hoffer, George, & Valacich, 2005), as follows: First; coding, testing and system conversion, second; preparing the test plan for the information system, third; installing the system, then preparing the documentation and training the user. The implementation of the IT project is usually followed by a maintenance phase, which may take up to 70% of the system development life cycle as claimed by (Hoffer, George, & Valacich, 2005).

CHALLENGES IN IMPLEMENTING INFORMATION TECHNOLOGY PLAN

Although text books in the field of *"Software Engineering"* discuss the implementation phase as any other phase in the development life cycle, nonetheless, lucidly such an idea is only a summer's night dream. In fact there are many challenges that face the implementation of information technology plan, where challenges stem from certain sources, *inter alia*: money, technology, time, culture, environment, project location/site, and human, as illustrated in Figure 1. In the next paragraphs, the sources of challenges will be discussed.

Money

Money is the most important source of challenges that face implementing information technology plan. As a matter of fact, many system development life cycles came to life because IT projects usually run over budget. Within this context, money has two aspects to a project: expenditure and revenue. Retrospectively, in order for projects to generate revenue, there should be cost incurred, whether that may be in terms of time or manpower

(i.e. effort/ operating cost) that are, ultimately, translated into money. Accordingly, there are three main challenges that stem from this first source of challenges, namely: budget, spending regulations, and currency exchange rate.

Furthermore, the issue pertaining to *project run over budget* can be attributed to either miscalculations in time of the project, and/or efforts needed for the efficient completion of the project, and/or the over promising made by the sales department (Millett, 1996).

However, vis-à-vis the time of the project, if estimated to be 10 months, for instance, would not necessarily entail that the efficient completion of the project will be 10 months. In this context, many rationales could cause the delay; as such an adept contingency plan (Cadle & Yeates, 2004) should be in place.

Moreover, with respect to estimating the effort needed for the project, many justifications can be identified; although mainly attributed to human error and technical miscalculations, for example, what programmer X can do in 19 working hours while programmer Y may take 25 working hours.

Likewise, a propos the spending regulations, which may be attributed to red tape, particularly when dealing with government agencies, can be source for the challenges of implementing IT projects. This can be time consuming, especially if dealing with red tape; it is noteworthy, nonetheless, that such feature is customarily never included in the original estimation of the timeline of the project. More importantly, it is noteworthy that such rationale may be reflected as delay, cost, yet unaccounted for in terms of effort. Thus the sufficient funding and financial independence is essential in the implementation of information systems projects (Plattner, 2004).

Similarly, in connection with currency exchange rates being relatively unstable, thereby many projects may account for unforeseen expenses, if it entails purchasing technology (hardware and software) from other countries with different

Figure 1. Sources of challanges in implementing information technology project

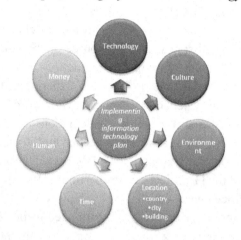

currency, for example if the US Dollar went up by two percent while the deal of purchasing Sun Server for a certain project is undergoing then such change would be a major hurdle if the project manager did not expect such change.

Technology

Implementing information systems transpires collectively with change and new technology. Both are a source of challenge, with new technology comes the fear of failure in speed (Gbaje, 2007), compatibility, software, hardware, and bugs. Moreover, Chaffey (2004) states "New system fails after changes over" due to speed or too many crashes, thereby citing that the failure of new technology stems from speed compatibility issues, hardware and software issue and the bugs that never discovered until implementation. Although customarily the only advice given to such challenges is testing, yet testing, validation and verification do not come at the cost of money, time and effort. On another note, implementation of new systems is indeed concomitant with the challenge of "change".

Time

Vis-à-vis time as being one of the challenges that face the implementation of information technology plan, indeed it is considered the most challenging resources to control, predict and monitor, when planning for or implementing a project, in terms that many things taken for granted would be a hurdle and radical source of challenge.

In this context, estimating the time can be an impediment when computing cross border vacation versus working time is lapsed. While other countries have different national holidays, for instance, in the USA where the 4th of July is a national day off, however, that does not hold when talking about other countries for example in Saudi Arabia or Korea. Whereas, many countries have varied working hours, where many nations work 8:00 a.m.-5:00 p.m., other countries work 8:00 a.m.-3:00 p.m., and others work on two shifts (6:00 a.m.-12:00 p.m. and from 4:00 p.m.-8:00 p.m.) as the case in the Arab Gulf countries.

Although the aforementioned is only to indicate the variation among countries, the same may go for multinational organizations, where people work in shifts. As such, when estimating time, the working hours and local habits governed by the country, nation, and organization, thereby the project manager must take these things into account when planning, monitoring, and implementing a project.

Another issue that pertains to time is predicting the time needed to carry out the IS project. The following methods, as suggested in (Cadle & Yeates, 2004), should help in this issue:

1. Analogy methods
2. Analysis effort methods
3. Programming method
4. Direct estimation based on project break down
5. The Delphi technique
6. Constructive cost model (COCOMO)
7. Function point analysis(FPA)

Cultural Aspects and Communication

Indeed, when considering implementation of information technology plan, culture and norms would be major challenge, from three facets; communication (language), traditions and habits, within this context, (Hariharan & Cellular, 2005) listed 15 challenges when implementing knowledge management projects, among which, culture was predominant, whereas (Millett, 1996) cited culture as one of Expert systems development problems.

Moreover, communication that is considered radical challenge in implementing Information systems, which transpires, by itself, into three dimensions; the regional dialect, the working language, and the colloquial speech. As for the regional dialect, the challenge stems from having two different languages used for communication, for example, when using English and Arabic to communicate, in view that ideas would have to be translated from one language to another, which is not an easy job. Accordingly, when planning for a project implementation in a country with

different language, such an issue should be taken into account.

While another aspect is the working language, which translates into having variation between the project owners's language and that of the implementer, for example, an IS project being implemented in a bank, the word "system" would carry a different meaning than that intended depending on the addressee, whereby, the bank may think of the system as the business process, while the IT personnel may consider it in terms of the hardware and software. This would eventually lead to misunderstanding and accordingly, making inappropriate decisions.

The final aspect that should be considered is the colloquial speech, i.e. common language, and thereby both parties would refer to a certain idiom by using the same expressions, vocabulary, etc. while holding the same meaning.

Nevertheless, it is worthwhile to note that both parties, planners of the IS project and the implementers, may not have that common language even if they both have similar language and business language, for instance, the communication challenge is obvious in the case by (MacKenzie, 2003) when implementing a GIS project in Texas.

When IS project requires business process re-engineering, it is of utmost importance to consider that the habits and traditions would be another challenge during implementation phase, particularly since people have the tendency to rely on what is familiar and the status quo at the work environment. In this context, the major hurdle would be the resistance to new technology (Millett, 1996), however, the challenge can be tamed by change management and change resistance tools.

On another note, it is worthwhile to note that in some cultures the word is the boss, as it is much stronger than a document. Therefore employees rely on the instructions of the boss rather than the documents and the laws; the idea is very clear in a study carried by (EL-MAHIED & ABU-TAIEH, 2005).

Environment

Another source of challenge is the environment, where the implementation of information technology plan would take place, in this regard; the environment can be categorized into three intersecting facets: working (inner and/or immediate) environment, living (intermediate) environment and outer environment as illustrated in Figure 2.

In regards to the working (inner and/or immediate) environment is where the team (user, developer, and customer) of the ITP will be conducting their tasks. The working environment include many surroundings, *inter alia*: the office space and equipments that act as the means needed to carry out the task, including the room, desk, chair, PC, etc. The location of the office compartment, i.e. the room, where such an office will be located, as well as the room environment including: air, space, ventilation etc., indeed the environment would encompass the people, as well as their relation, who occupy the room.

While, with respect to the living (intermediate) environment is closely related to the inner environment. This environment includes the organizational environment, as well as the people surrounding such an environment, taking into account their varied level of income and spending patterns, in this regard, when implementing an IT project for mobile telecommunication business organization, for example, it would be worthwhile to study the people income level and their spending patterns, particularly in view that in many countries the income is low and the people are conservative in spending, thereby the environmental implications would transpire in different set of challenges than that faced in a country with higher income rates.

Finally, vis-à-vis the outer environment, which includes, yet not exclusive to: laws, regulations of the country, in addition to the taxation system of the country, and the contractors and sub-contractors and the type of contracts allowed in the country itself (Hoffer, George, & Valacich, 2005), an employer in some countries such as Syria, for example, may force an employee (by contract) not to divulge any trade secrets that pertains to the

Figure 2. ITP different environments

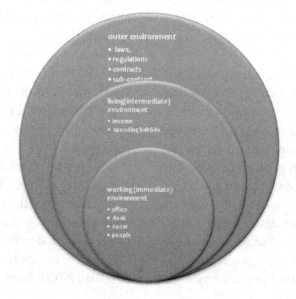

business secrets or knowledge, as such contracts prevent the employee from working for another firm of the same nature for a period of 5 years following the termination of the contract, noting that such contract is upheld in the Syrian courts.

Location/ Project Site

Naturally, the location or the project site is an instrumental source of challenge that may be faced during the implementation of information technology plan, within this context; the project site can be recapitulated into three elements: country, city, and vicinity.

A propos the country, the challenge arises in terms of the advancement achieved, since some countries are more advanced than others regarding the availability of communications infrastructure, i.e. lines, roads, for instance the implementation of Voice Over IP project in country X, where all infrastructures is based on fiber optics, would not necessarily entail the same level of challenges

arisen when attempting to do the same in country Y, where all communication lines are copper based as stipulated in (Gbaje, 2007).

Similarly, in connection with city, while considering some cities in the same country are richer than others, as such, urban cities are customarily more advanced in terms of the availability of infrastructure than in rural cities; for example New York City cannot be compared with a smaller less advanced and equipped city, accordingly, the infrastructure of one city is more advanced than other as stipulated by (Plattner, 2004).

Finally, vis-à-vis the building of an organization, where the implementation site is centralized and/or distributed, taking into account the age of the building (i.e. old or new), and the construction material of the building (i.e. concrete, steel structure, brick, wood), noting that older sites tend to be more challenging when installing a computer network in concrete building, for example, where much drilling must take place as the building is not designed for such incorporating such technol-

Figure 3. The different types of locations/projects sites

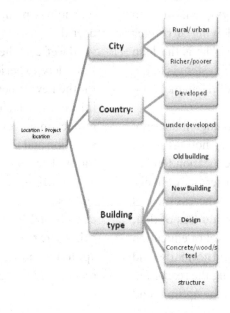

ogy, yet, older buildings that are made of steal structure, for example, where the ducting is much easier, highlighting that if the project (e.g. building a computer network) is implemented at one site only, then it becomes easier to implement from a distributed site.

Human

Needless to highlight the fact that the human factor is a radical source of challenge that may be faced during the implementation of information technology plan, bearing in mind that there are many facets for such factor; *inter alia:* End user of IT, Developer, and Customer. Indeed with each type, there are attributes that either hinders or encourages the process of the implementation of information technology plan; the attributes include but not exclusive to: education level, employment level (top management, middle management, and worker), level of experience, the type of activity carried by the employee under this plan whether technical, or non-technical, in addition to the level of understanding the goal of the implementation of information technology plan, as well as the time availability.

In this context, the end user is usually the one that uses the end product of the implementation of information technology plan, and can be classified based on the following attributes based on whether, for example, s/he is the loan officer in the bank, where the IT system is being implemented, or the customer of the bank using the system.

First, the education level, although it does not necessarily mean computer literacy, noting that the end users with high caliber of education tend to demand more advanced level of service delivery and hopefully are apt to change, whereas the end users with lower education demand less of that, while, the end users with low level of education with high computer literacy would normally tend to demand more without knowing the reasoning behind such a demand, as such, the optimal end user would be the highly educated with high computers literacy.

Second, the employment level, which is further categorized into three levels: top management, middle management, and worker. The top management usually has a better understanding of the macro-level strategic view of the implementation of information technology plan (Hoffer, George, & Valacich, 2005) thereby, there will be instantaneous help extended to the project manager in hindering the obstacles. However, the middle management end user would be coherent towards the goal (Hoffer, George, & Valacich, 2005) of the implementation of information technology plan, as such; there will be instant interest in conducting the job albeit with some reservations. In conclusion, the worker end user would be interested in conducting the task at hand in a more efficient manner promptly; whose satisfaction is the most important, as stipulated by (Hoffer, George, & Valacich, 2005).

Third, the level of experience of the end user; which spans from high to low; given that the highly experienced end user would habitually be most challenging since the way of conducting business has been set long ago albeit such end user is the best source of information for lessons learnt over the course of the implementation of information technology plan. Although the less experienced user does not have much of knowledge to offer yet the effect "the empty bowel" can be observed, since low experienced end user would be open for the new experience of the implementation of information technology plan. Accordingly, the project manager must take advantage of such situation and teach such user and make a convertor out her/him.

Fourth, the type of activity conducted by the end user under this plan, which can be further categorized into either technical or non-technical, where the technical workers are usually more apt to technology, thereby entailing less elusive mode of challenge.

Fifth, the understanding of the goal of implementation of information technology plan, whereby the more understanding on part of the end user to the goal the less challenge the project manager will face, thereby, better understanding of the goal would insistently open reliable channels of communications.

Sixth, the time availability, whereby the end user would have the time and the dedication to adapt to the change brought by the implementation of information technology plan, since drastic change over short period time entails expected level of challenge, as tackled by (Cadle & Yeates, 2004).

THE MANIFESTATION OF ITP CHALLENGES

The aforementioned sources of challenges faced upon implementation of information technology plan manifest in numerous ways, along those lines, (O'Shaughnessy, 2002) listed the following challenges when implementing a Geographic Information System (GIS) used in an oil and gas project:

1. Lack executive management support
2. Lack of user involvement
3. Lack of business-oriented strategy
4. No clear statement of requirements
5. Insufficient awareness of technology

Table 1. Human types in ITP and their attributes

Attributes\human type		End user	developer	customer
education level	High	Demand more Apt to change	Less challenge	Less challenge
	Medium			
	Low	Demand less Less apt to change		
employment level	top management			
	middle management			
	worker			
level of experience	High	More challenging , set in his way, status quoi	Less challenge	Less challenge
	Medium			
	low	Empty bowl effect		
types of work carried by the employee	technical			
	non-technical			
Understanding of the IS goal	High	Less challenge	Less challenge	Less challenge
	Medium			
	low	More challenge	More challenge	More cost
Availability and time (Chaffey, 2004)	More time	Less challenge	Less challenge	More cost
	Less time	More challenge	More challenge	Less cost

257

6. Lack of competent skills
7. Unrealistic expectations
8. Insufficient staff to implement data capture
9. Inadequate financial resources
10. Poor data quality
11. No clear GIS applications implementation plans
12. GIS/IT responsibilities unclear
13. Lack of ownership

Furthermore, (Chaffey, 2004) listed the following challenges when implementing Knowledge management (KM) project:

1. Lack of understanding of KM and its benefits
2. Lack of employee time for KM
3. Lack of skill in KM techniques
4. Lack of encouragement in the current culture for sharing
5. Lack of incentives/rewards to share
6. Lack of funding for KM initiatives
7. Lack of appropriate technology
8. Lack of commitment from senior management

However, (Chaffey, 2004) listed the following challenges when implanting an E-business project:

1. Insufficient senior management commitment
2. High staff turnover/key staff leave
3. Project milestones not met, overrun budget
4. Problems with new technology delaying implementation (bugs, speed, compatibility)
5. Staff resistance to change
6. Problem with integrating with partner's systems (e.g. customers or suppliers)
7. New system fails after changeover (too slow or too many crashes)

In addition, (Conroy, 2007) listed the following manifestation of challenges in context of management implementation project:

1. Control and Management
2. Migration
3. Gaining Approval
4. The People Factor
5. Fear of Obsolescence
6. Document Ownership

CONCLUSION

This chapter has presented the challenges in implementing information technology plan pertaining to two dimensions: literature and practical, in terms of categorizing the sources of challenges facing the implementation of IT projects into money, technology, time, culture, environment, project location/site, and human. The chapter explained each of these sources and their subcategories, thereby suggesting ways to rectify and deflect the negative impact of such challenges. In addition the chapter showed the manifestations of these challenges.

First source of challenges is money, this challenge manifest itself in the following pictures: budget, spending regulations, and currency exchange rate. The second challenge was technology and with new technology comes the fear of failure in speed, compatibility issues in software, hardware, and bugs. Such challenge is never discovered until the implementation. The third source of challenges is time, it is considered the most challenging resources to control, predict and monitor.

Culture and norms would be major challenge, from three facets; communication (language), traditions and habits. Communication that is considered radical challenge in implementing Information systems, which transpires, by itself, into three dimensions; the regional dialect, the working language, and the colloquial speech.

The environment, the fifth source of challenge, can be categorized into three intersecting facets: working (inner and/or immediate) environment, living (intermediate) environment and outer environment. Furthermore, the location or the project site is an instrumental source of challenge that may be faced during the implementation of information technology plan, within this context; the project site can be recapitulated into three elements: country, city, and vicinity.

The seventh source of challenge was human factor. Human factor is a fundamental source of challenge that may be faced during the implementation of information technology plan, bearing in mind that there are many facets for such factor; including: End user of IT, Developer, and Customer.

In the end of the chapter, the authors explained how the challenges manifest themselves during the Information technology project whether the project is Geographic information system (GIS), Knowledge Management (KM), E-business.

REFERENCES

Cadle, J., & Yeates, D. (2004). *Project Management for Information Systems* (4E ed.). Prentice Hall.

Chaffey, D. (2004). *E-Business and E-Commerce* (2 E ed.). Prentice Hall.

Conroy, J. (2007). *7 Challenges of Implementing a Content Management System.* Retrieved 12 30, 2007, from http://www.cmswire.com/cms/enterprise-cms/7-challenges-of-implementing-a-content-management-system-001848.php

El-Mhied, M. T., & Abu-Tieh, E. M. (2005). *Knowledge Management: Nurturing Culture, Innovation And Technology.* North Carolina, USA: World Scientific Publishing Co. Pte. Ltd.

Gbaje, E. S. (2007). Implementing a National Virtual Library for Higher Institutions in Nigeria. *LIBRES Library and Information Science Research Electronic Journal, 17*(12), 1-15.

Hariharan, A., & Cellular, B. (2005). Crtical Success Factors for Knowledge Mnangemnt: Fifteen Common Challanges and how to overcome them. *KM review, 8*(2), 16-20.

Hoffer, J., George J., & Valacich J. (2005). *Modern System Analysis and Design 5th Ed.* NewYork, USA: prentice hall.

MacKenzie, L. (2003). The Challenges of Implementing Enterprise GIS at the City of Fort Worth. *ESRI International Users Conference .* ESRI.

Millett, D. (1996). Critical Success Factors in Expert System Development: Case Study. *Sigcpiu sigmis '96,* (pp. 214-222). Denver Colorado USA: ACM.

O'Shaughnessy, B. (2002). *Challenges of Implementing GIS in a gas utility.* Retrieved 12 30, 2007, from GIS for Oil & Gas Conference : http://www.gisdevelopment.net/proceedings/gita/oil_gas2002/papers/boshauhnessy.asp

Plattner, B. (2004). Crtical Success Factors in Engineering Education: Some Observation and Examples. *Information Knowledge Systems Management,* (4), 179-190.

Section IV
Enterprise Architecture

Chapter XIV
Optimizing IT Implementation by Using the Enterprise Architecture Approach (EA):
The Case of a Telecommunications Operator

Anthony Ioannidis
Athens University of Economics and Business, Greece

Nikolaos Skarpetis
University of the Aegean, Greece

ABSTRACT

Businesses world-wide are faced with similar challenges including changing business conditions, shrinking profit margins, and competitive pressures. An organization is affected daily by the vast amounts of information received and stored from both external and internal environments. This information when not organized or standardized in a strategic manner, leads to the fragmentation of this same information. In turn, this fragmentation negatively affects an organization's productivity, competitive advantage and thus its profitability. This chapter discusses the importance of developing a system that not only works in support of, but hand-in-hand with the specific needs of a given business. Through the discussion of its main characteristics and its implementation, it will be shown that the Enterprise Architecture Approach (EA) meets this specific need, as it provides the "blue-prints" to strategically organize information.

INTRODUCTION

Increasing business efficiency and agility in the face of competitive pressure, shrinking profit margins and changing business conditions are top priorities for large organizations. Corporate Strategy, Organizational Structure, Business Processes and Information Systems are expected to completely support an organization in order to seize opportunities and overcome barriers that could threaten the same organization's development or even survival. In this chapter we focus on how process orientation, and more specifically the Enterprise Architecture Approach (EA), can support organizations to design, develop and maintain Information Systems. Furthermore, how Information Systems can fully align with business processes in order to match the overall strategy of the company and in this way achieve Strategic Fit.

This chapter is organized into three sections: Initially outlined are the external and internal environments that affect large organizations, forcing them to incorporate new approaches and best practises for IS development. In the second part, the characteristics, implementation, and benefits of Enterprise Architecture Approach (EA) are discussed, and finally presented is a case study that shows how the implementation of a process-oriented work-flow system can be achieved through the integration of the e-TOM reference model and the EA Approach.

BACKGROUND

Challenges for Business and IT: Agility

Changing business conditions such as globalization, expansion into other markets, mergers and acquisitions, and compliance with new regulations are some of the greatest challenges for large organizations. Increasing business efficiency and agility as a solution to competitive pressure and

shrinking profit margins, combined all translate into a single challenge of internal organization (structure, processes, IS and IT infrastructure, etc.). Since nowadays organizations "live and breath" because of their Information Systems, as well as their Technologies and Applications, the dynamics of the external environment raises expectations for Enterprise IT - it must be more responsive to business needs. Enterprise IT is very complex, making it difficult for an organization to respond to changing business needs (Filenet P8, 2006). Meeting changing business needs requires unprecedented responsiveness from business and in turn from IT in order to build and deploy business-critical applications and services while leveraging existing IT investments. The overall exercise becomes even more complicated due to the so-called "gap between business and IT" (Filenet P8, 2006; Scheer, 1998; Kirchmer & Scheer, 2004). The business may not understand the technology and technical constrains or challenges that IT faces, and similarity IT usually does not have the insight to appreciate the business' issues and challenges (Filenet P8, 2006; Kirchmer & Scheer, 2004). As a result, what IT builds quite often is neither what the business wants nor does it entirely meet the requirements of the business. In order to meet these challenges, new innovative approaches are needed together with the employment of best practices, new disciplines and technologies such as business process management, service-oriented architecture and enterprise architecture (Filenet P8, 2006; Kirchmer & Scheer, 2004; and Scheer, July 2004).

Information Fragmentation: IS Consolidation

Many large enterprises are faced with the problem of fragmentation of information. Although many companies have achieved double digit growth rates, many have done so at the expense of relaxing rules of IT architecture, since flexibility in IT systems is the easiest enabler in meeting customer and business needs in the shortest possible time frame. Companies collect, generate and store vast quantities of data which are usually not kept in a single repository. Information flow is spread across dozens or even hundreds of separate application systems, each housed in an individual business unit, office or desktop (Figure 1).

Most of these are the result of an end-user development effort. Each of the so-called legacy systems may provide invaluable support for a particular business function or a specific activity, but in combination they represent one of the heaviest weights on business productivity and performance, as well as in management control over an organization's operations. Maintaining many different computer systems leads to enormous costs for storing and rationalizing redundant data, for re-keying and reformatting data from one system for use in another, for updating and debugging obsolete software code, for programming communication links between systems to automate and transfer data.

It can be stated that more important than the direct cost of information fragmentation are the indirect hidden costs. Lack of process-oriented information systems result in fragmented business processes that lead to organization fragmentation. This type of fragmentation not only creates non-value adding and un-coordinated activities, it typically produces business processes that are out-of-date, ineffective, and unresponsive to customer needs. Fragmentation eventually and inevitably increases the complexity of operations to a point that makes operations' management opaque. This subsequently leads to the loss of management and cost control over operations, the loss of flexibility in serving the customer and an inability to acquire a cost advantage over the competition. As business gradually leads to maturity, companies facing the fragmentation problem should determine breakthroughs. A solution to this reality is IT consolidation or de-fragmentation of information. This in turn streamlines IT operations and IT spending which leads to cost leadership and competitive advantage - growing out of an entire system of value-chain functions/activities. The fit among functions/activities substantially reduces costs and increases differentiation. Therefore, the consolidation of numerous applications into major strategic information platforms becomes the vehicle for value-chain integration, and the achievement of a competitive advantage.

Figure 1. Information / application silos with hidden and inflexible processes

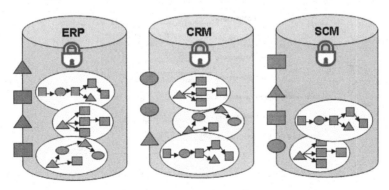

(Source: IBM – Filenet, 2006)

Integrated Information System Development: Process Orientation

Every organization performs distinct activities in designing, producing, marketing, delivering and supporting its products and services. Each of these activities contributes to the organization's overall strategy and creates a basis for differentiation. In order to analyze the sources of competitive advantage, a systematic way of examining these activities and how they interact is necessary. Process view or process orientation has attracted the interest and support of top management in large organizations as it fully guarantees the alignment of strategy, business, and IT (Kirchmer & Scheer, 2004; Scheer, July 2004; and Scheer, 2004). Integration of the value chain and consolidation of information systems, which in turn leads to optimization of IT spending, is best achieved through "process view," (Scheer, 1998; Maurer & Büch, 2007; and Kanungo, 2005).

Process-oriented information system development re-structures and organizes all the information shared within an organization which then in turn significantly impacts the organizations' competitive advantage. A successful design or redesign of business processes leads to improvements in time, quality and cost of products and services offered (Figure 2). (Scheer, 1998).

Strategic Fit among the business process activities is fundamental not only for competitive advantage but also for the sustainability of this advantage. It is harder for a competitor to match the integrated information system, which supports an array of interlocked activities, than to imitate a particular sales-force approach, match a process technology or replicate a set of product features. Positions built on systems of activities are far more sustainable than those built on individual activities, especially information systems that are built to support individual activities and integrate complete activities, namely business processes. Thus, it can be said that integrating process-oriented information systems into business processes aids in the reduction of complexity and cost, and provides an organization with the ability to respond quickly, efficiently and

Figure 2. Process orientation and IT investments

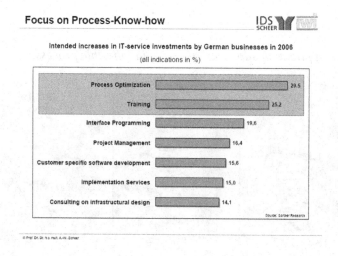

(Source: IDS Scheer EMEA, 2006)

effectively not only to its competitors, but also to market conditions.

A Holistic Approach: Enterprise Architecture

Major trends and challenges imply that a new business model, where Information Systems' support, design, consolidation or replacement, becomes strategic. Becoming strategic means that IT strategy should reflect corporate strategy. IT strategy should shape the architecture of the existing IT systems (core or satellite) aiming to group stand-alone applications under the umbrella of well-integrated platforms and enforce IT consolidation practices. This can be achieved successfully only when IT strategy is supported by the appropriate IT Architecture, which consequently inter-links with business processes. Since complex systems always require good building plans, an organizations' business processes should be used as the foundation of the IT environment.

Enterprise Architecture (EA) provides for a strategic integrated approach. The description and implementation of EA was initially defined as the process of developing an enterprise's Information Technology Architecture. EA focuses on a holistic and integrated view of the "why, where and who" uses of IT systems and "how and what" they are used for within an organization (Zachman, 1987, 1997). An Enterprise Architect designs the strategy for the development and implementation of IT systems in order to support business operations as well as assess, select and integrate technology into the organization's infrastructure.

FROM BUSINESS LEVEL TO EXECUTION (IT) LEVEL BY UTILIZING THE ENTERPRISE ARCHITECTURE APPROACH

Issues, Controversies, Problems

Despite the extensive standardization and homogenization of a company's IT world, IT landscape remains complex consisting of many different applications and systems built using heterogeneous technologies, on various middleware, using multiple databases and running on many platforms. This large number of different systems means that much data is redundant, that there are many interfaces, and that different networks have different protocols, etc. The variety is more likely to increase rather than decrease, due in large part to many mergers and acquisitions. This heterogeneity inevitably leads to weak spots: If a component fails, many companies do not know what effect it will have on a business process, individual jobs and employees. This means that reaction times are extremely long, which is risky. As a result, companies look for solutions to make the complexity transparent, to manage it, and to optimize it. Moreover, the maintenance of and change to any of these systems may be very resource intensive and expensive. It requires that the IT staff be well-versed in a wide range of technologies, programming languages and commercial products.

In the past, there was much discussion about EA, but nothing much was accomplished beyond the production of a few paper tigers. Company management was making demands for greater standardization and at the same time more efficient support from IT for business processes. As long as the systems and applications were not described by their pertinence for business processes, EA was hardly more than an inventory list. The relevance of IT first becomes clear to many companies when it fails and critical workflows grind to a halt. This can be avoided only when the chaos is controlled and the IT department defines rules and standards for process-related IT management. Nowadays, as shown in the examples above, EA has become very popular and it is quickly becoming an umbrella term, creating a relationship between the IT landscape and the world of processes. The growing importance of business processes makes it possible to define an IT system environment that corresponds to business needs. Recent EA discussions deal with the central question of how to organize IT so that it supports business processes and drives business. EA makes the dependencies between IT and business processes transparent and ensures secure business process management (Maurer & Büch, 2007). Moreover, EA creates the necessary transparency to support IT managers who are faced with the dilemma of less money at their disposal to manage systems and applications.

Evidence, Solutions, Recommendations

Enterprise Architecture is essential to achieve business integration in today's complex and dynamic business environment. The adoption of Enterprise Architecture (EA) as an IT practice began 10 to 20 years ago, predominately in banking, manufacturing, and government organizations (particularly US agencies). Recently, additional drivers have reinforced the use of EA and increased its importance (Peyret, 2007; Maurer & Büch, 2007):

- While becoming more global, companies seek more local efficiency and agility. Organizations not only share products and services between countries and regions, but also processes and applications — in addition to the IT infrastructure that many firms have already consolidated. Standardization and consolidation are not applied blindly; EA repositories and modeling tools allow analysis and modification of shared processes and applications.

- Executives increasingly face pressure for more rapid decision-making. The challenge of minimizing risks from change becomes greater as IT complexity increases. EA tools, which have multiple models that track links and dependencies, offer impact and risk analysis and summary dashboards, as well as help, prioritize different initiatives.

- Competing strategic initiatives require a common source of information. Simultaneous, enterprise-wide, strategic initiatives such as business process management, business service management, project portfolio management, IT governance implementation, strategic planning processes, Service Oriented Architecture (SOA) adoption and application or process rationalization are more likely to be successful if they reuse common strategic information — an ideal task for the EA repository.

- Business processes are based on highly sophisticated enterprise-wide IT systems. Enterprise Architecture (EA) has emerged as the key tool for documenting, analyzing and managing these complex structures, in turn forming part of an architectural framework that describes the information required for a complete architecture.

Recent evidence indicates the growing importance of EA for organizations, as well as the reasons for planning EA activities within these organizations [(as depicted in Figures 3 and 4) (Institute For Enterprise Architecture, 2005)].

With EA, IT managers can get an overall picture of their IT landscapes and how their IT affects business processes. On this basis, they can focus their IT directly on strategic corporate goals which is a reliable alternative to muddled systems, lack of transparency, "patch-work quilts," and resource squandering. EA provides answers to strategic and operational IT challenges. EA's strategic goal is to efficiently and specifically adopt IT that has a positive effect on costs

Figure 3. EA importance

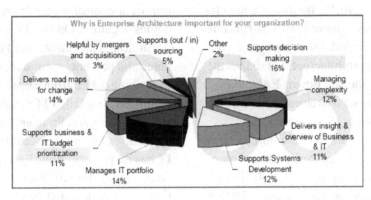

(Source: Institute For Enterprise Architecture, Trends in Enterprise Architecture 2005)

Figure 4. Reasons for planning EA activities

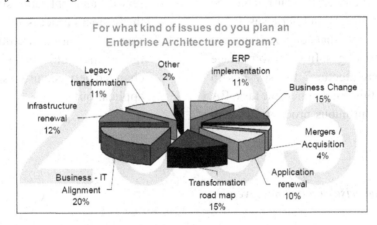

(Source: Institute For Enterprise Architecture, Trends in Enterprise Architecture 2005)

and flexibility and create a standardization that results in major cost reductions in the operation of an entire IT landscape. Creating a standardized IT environment is impossible without first standardizing business processes. For this reason, the methods and integration tools used for IT architecture management must create a structure that is fully synchronized with process management. The objective is to be aware that system architectures are a means to an end, and not actually an end themselves. The highest priority is to derive real IT needs from processes. EA also answers other questions, such as how costly a migration is, how system interruptions affect the business, and how many systems are redundant and superfluous. System management is the task of centrally managing all IT resources — data, systems, networks, hardware and software. EA encompasses more than just runtime IT resources; it also includes the connection with the business-process architecture that shapes the IT landscape from the top down. EA makes it clear that IT and process architecture, are two sides of the same coin.

Furthermore, EA works as an umbrella term covering the documentation, analysis, and management of organizations, processes, and information systems. It is a comprehensive blueprint that illustrates a company's business processes, data, systems and applications, and their connections with each other. EA should not be a static entity. This distinguishes EA from an architect's plan for a building, which is sketched once and then built as drawn. A company's EA must form a framework in which the structures can be changed dynamically. For all intents and purposes, EA is a "working architecture" that adapts to business and organizational changes. In order to manage such a "working architecture" the key lies in understanding that this is not a one-time task. EA management is a continuous process. Efficient

planning, management, and control of the EA require a control center from which everything comes together. On the IT side, EA allows for portfolio management, sets IT standards, eliminates and prevents redundancy, protects system-describing data and develops emergency plans for dealing with a failed IT system. On the process side, EA analyzes, for example, how expensively or quickly a business process runs and what effect IT has on the workflow. Enterprise Architecture compromises four different architecture descriptions as it is depicted in Figure 5 (Scheer, July 2004; Maurer & Büch, 2007):

1. The business architecture defines business strategies and describes organizational structures and business processes.
2. The application architecture describes the services and application systems that support the business processes.
3. The information architecture describes the business objects and data that are exchanged between process participants and applications.

Figure 5. Basic enterprise architecture levels

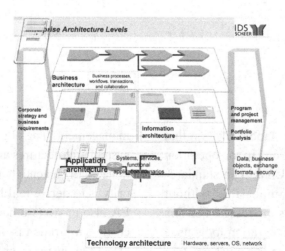

(Source: IDS Scheer EMEA, 2007)

4. The lowest level is the infrastructure architecture, which is used to describe the physical landscape — the hardware and networks that support the application systems.

This type of description highlights the impact of business process changes in the associated IT systems. System redundancy can be detected and new IT requirements identified. Similarly, the business processes affected by system shutdowns and infrastructure changes can be easily identified. Such architecture can be successfully implemented only if supported by an object-oriented approach that allows reusing architectural artifacts across different views and levels and if there is a common repository where all objects are solitarily defined. This makes it possible to recognize how corporate strategy, business processes, and IT architectures interact and build the necessary bridges. By creating such a seamless interconnection between IT and process architecture in a single repository, from strategy through to infrastructure level, for the first time it is possible to fully align IT systems with business needs. Benefits include the following:

- Ability to identify which critical business processes, at which locations, are affected and will therefore need to be part of the migration project when replacing an IT system.
- Planners and IT managers can navigate the entire enterprise architecture, following object relationships, and make informed decisions based on a holistic view of the company and a shared methodology.
- Users can compare the IT standards and target architectures defined in the repository with the actual situation and create a roadmap for future development.
- Facilitation of organization-wide enterprise architecture management by supporting distributed teams.

- EA related content can be re-used to set up processes and IT portals.
- Bringing together business process design and IT architectures allows coordinated management of these two areas, enabling the kind of integrative approach that is particularly important for successful enterprise architecture management, given the interdependency of processes and IT structures.

CASE STUDY: PROCESS-ORIENTED WORK FLOW IMPLEMENTATION BY INTEGRATING E-TOM REFERENCE MODEL AND THE EA APPROACH AT AURORA[1]

Project Scope and Desired Results

Aurora, a European cellular telecommunications operator, operating in a very competitive market (with 25 percent of the market), launched a project aiming at the development of an Enterprise Architecture focused on the Technical Division of the organization in mid-2007, which would serve as:

1. The central repository for all process-related information.
2. The framework and methodology for process design and process re-engineering.
3. The framework for process-oriented IS implementation (re-engineering, development or consolidation).
4. The approach and methodology for the re-engineering of a core process running in a work-flow application ("Co.Pr.").
5. A pilot for testing and evaluating the group-wide adoption of the Enterprise Architecture Approach.

The project implementation team consisted of members that came from the Telecom Operator as well as from consulting companies specializing in business process management and business process automation.

The Enterprise Architecture to be developed should be able to meet the above-mentioned expectations, while it should also incorporate the eTOM Framework[2] and eTOM's recommendations for the specific business area.

The project's scope included not only EA development, but business and study software platform and ARIS Methodology of IDS Scheer AG (Scheer, 1998).[3] ARIS Methodology is the market leader of Business Process Analysis (Blechar & Sinur, 2006) and Enterprise Architecture (Scheer, 2004) and fulfils the requirements of an object-oriented design approach.

During implementation, ARIS proved essential in defining, analyzing, validating and designing the current business of the Technical Division, while ARIS methodology efficiently served the documentation of both the business and technical aspects of the processes in question. It also facilitated the documentation of the changes recommended for the underlying workflow applications.

Implementation Details

The project had three main deliverables:

1. The Enterprise Architecture of the Technical Division
2. The design and detailed documentation of the "Co.Pr."
3. The re-design and detailed documentation of the "Co.Pr." ("blueprint")

The development of the Enterprise Architecture followed the phases illustrated in Figure 6, i.e., plan, design, build, populate.

The "Plan Phase" included:

1. The identification of the various stakeholders of the architecture-related information.
2. The understanding of the existing problems, constraints and rules.
3. The collection, documentation and review of objectives and requirements.
4. The determination of a time-line for the following phases.

Figure 6. Basic phases in developing and maintaining enterprise architecture

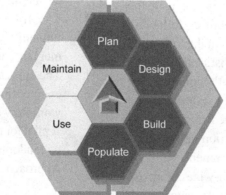

(Source: IDS Scheer EMEA, 2006)

5. The assignment of resources and responsibilities.
6. The communication of plans to the affected organizational units.

The "Design Phase" included:

1. The translation of requirements into technical needs.
2. The review and evaluation of the existing documentation.
3. The development and review of the Architecture meta-models and the related documentation samples.
4. The determination of the ARIS methodology conventions (model types, object types, relationship types and attribute types).
5. The design of the logical grouping structure within the "ARIS repository" (central repository for all process-related information).
6. The definition of the Architecture standards and generation of brief modeling guidelines.

The "Build Phase" included the development of the structure of the following:

1. The so-called static views, i.e., the organizational structure, the information systems' structure, the products/services map and the documents' list. Concerning the information systems' deliverable, the TAM categorization[4] was also followed.
2. The so-called dynamic view, where (a) the eTOM reference model was documented up to the 4th level of detail, (b) a gap analysis was performed comparing the existing situation within the Technology Division with the eTOM recommended functions, and (c) a cross-departmental and cross-eTOM building blocks Process Model that incorporated all processes of the Technology Division and realized a process-oriented approach.

The "Populate Phase" included the following:

1. The further analysis and content enrichment of the Process Model up to the 3rd level of detail.
2. The detailed business and technical analysis of the "Co.Pr" (including the reverse engineering of the application system where part of the process was running).
3. The detailed business and technical analysis ("blueprint") of the "to-be" process.

All the necessary information was gathered mainly via interviews. All the models and related documentation that was produced during the project implementation was also evaluated via interviews. These interviews were conducted with process owners, data owners, team leaders, applications' owners, organizational units' directors, etc. For the design of the models, a top-down approach was followed (Figure 7) that allowed the easy navigation from the business level down to the technical level as well as navigation from the eTOM framework to the Process Model.

Project Deliverables

There were three deliverables:

1. The Enterprise Architecture of the Technical Division. The EA included all views (Figure 8):

   - Organizational View
   - Data/Document View
   - IT Systems/Applications View
   - Products/Services View
   - Risk and Controls View
   - Process View.

While all information was gathered in a central repository, EA was established in the organization's intranet, serving as the basis for the development of a Knowledge Management System. The results of the gap analysis between eTOM requirements and the organization's "as-is" situation were used as input on "how compliant the organization was to the eTOM reference model."

2. The design and detailed documentation of the "Co.Pr." The document included all findings of the reverse engineering analysis:

• Business emphasizing business findings that resulted from the analysis

Figure 7. Top-down approach in modeling

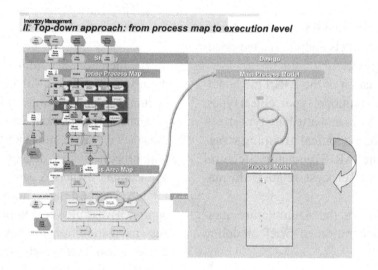

(Source: IDS Scheer EMEA, 2006)

Figure 8. Enterprise architecture views

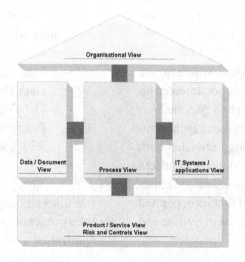

- Technical data
- Related data - mostly related to the applications design and implementation

3. The re-design and detailed documentation of the "Co.Pr." ("blue-print"). The "blue-print" document included all findings and recommendations of the "Co.Pr." further development. Moreover, it included all the business and technical details (i.e., new processes, new data structures, new functions, etc.) required for the implementation of new IT Systems.

Future Steps

Three specific steps were identified and proposed to take full advantage of EA's contribution to the Technical Division of Aurora:

1. The population of Aurora's EA with content, which could take the form of EA expansion to other Division(s) as well as the detailed documentation of all existing processes.
2. The automation of the new re-engineered "Co.Pr." process.
3. The implementation of a pilot project that will employ the EA as the driving framework for an organization-wide IT System implementation.

Findings and Conclusion

In line with best practices, this project resulted in an Enterprise Architecture, which (a) proved that it can support the development and maintenance of an integrated environment linking the business world with the IT world and continuous process improvement, (b) supported the Organization to clarify the existing content related to organizational positions, documents used, systems and applications involved, and risks and controls related to process implementation, and (c) supported the Technical Division of the

Organization in understanding complex business logic and identifying points of integration across all information silos.

EA-based top-down analysis and reengineering of the "Co.Pr." resulted in identifying areas of improvement including (a) the abolition of unnecessary functions, (b) the identification of unutilized work-flows and / or application interfaces of the existing IT application, (c) the identification of control points and related KPI's, and (d) changes in the Organization's "Co.Pr."–related business model.

Once the new "Co.Pr." is automated, it is expected to result in an overall performance increase of 20% as well as in a payback period of one and a half years (for the whole investment – analysis, re-engineering and implementation).

After all, the project leads to a solution that will suffice, although it might not necessarily be the best possible solution. It does, however, provide a viable solution that is widely supported by all stakeholders, and leads to business changes and implementations of target systems in every case where it was applied.

REFERENCES

Anderson, M. C., Banker, R. D., & Ravindran, S. (2003). The new productivity paradox. *Communications of the ACM, 46*(3).

Blechar, J. M., & Sinur, J. (2006). Magic Quadrant for Business Process Analysis Tools.

Brynjolfsson, E., & Hitt, L. M. (1998). Beyond the productivity paradox. *Communications of the ACM, 41*(8).

Filenet P8. (2006, November). *The Synergy between BPM and SOA*. White Paper.

Groot, R., Smits, M., & Kuipers, H. (2005). A Method to Redesign the IS Portfolios in Large Organizations. *The 38th Hawaii International Conference on System Sciences.*

Institute For Enterprise Architecture, Trends in Enterprise Architecture 2005 (2005, December). *How are organizations progressing? Report of the Third Measurement Developments, Edition 1.0.*

Kanungo, S. (2005). Using Process Theory to analyze direct and indirect value-drivers of information system. *Proceedings of the 38th Hawaii International Conference on System Sciences.*

King, W. R. (2002). IT capabilities, business processes and impact on the bottom line. *Information Systems Management, 19*(2).

Kirchmer, M., & Scheer, A.W. (2004). Business Process Automation — Combining Best and Next Practices. In A. W. Scheer, F. Abolhassan, W. Jost, & M. Kirchmer, (Ed.), *Business Process Automation — ARIS in Practice*, Berlin, New York and others.

Maurer, D., & Büch, P. (2007, March). From Business Process Design to Enterprise Architecture, ARIS Expert Paper.

Peyret, H. (2007, April 25). *The Forrester Wave™: Enterprise Architecture Tools, Q2 2007.*

Scheer, A. W. (1998). *ARIS — Business Process Frameworks*, 2nd edition, Berlin, New York and others.

Scheer, A. W. (2004). 20 years of business process management: From ideas to innovation. Process World.

Scheer, A. W. (2004, July). ARIS Value Engineering Concept, White Paper.

Sowa, J. F., & Zachman, J. A. (1992). Extending and formalizing the framework for information systems architecture. *IBM Systems Journal,* 31(3).

Zachman, J. A. (1987). A framework for information systems architecture. *IBM Systems Journal,* 26(3).

Zachman, J. A. (1997 March). Enterprise architecture: The issue of the century. *Database Programming and Design*, pp. 2-5.

ENDNOTES

[1] "Aurora" is a pseudonym that has been adapted by the authors to protect the anonymity of the mobile telecommunications operator presented in this case

[2] Business Process Framework for Telecommunications companies formulated by the TM Forum. eTOM describes the full scope of business processes required by a service provider and defines the key elements and how they interact.

[3] www.ids-scheer.com.

[4] TAM is the Telecom Applications Map produced by the TM Forum. It describes and categorizes BSS and OSS applications typically used by service providers to manage communications networks and infrastructure. The Telecom Applications Map is not a part of either the SID or the eTOM definitions but links to both in an easily understandable way and also provides a mapping between the telecom application map eTOM and SID.

Chapter XV
Strategic Technology Engineering Planning

Tony C. Shan
IBM, USA

Winnie W. Hua
CTS Inc., USA

ABSTRACT

This chapter presents a methodical strategic technology engineering planning (STEP) approach, to effectively cope with the design complexity in service-oriented architecture and manage the strategic planning of solution development of information systems. This holistic model comprises four modules: Want-Is-Target (WIT) model, Transition and Alignment Grid (TAG), Comprehensive Architecting Process (CAP), and Joint Analysis & Roadmapping (JAR). The characteristics and features of the constituent elements in the STEP model are articulated in great detail. The WIT model defines three stages of architecture states – current, target, and end state. TAG specifies two dimensions for architecture planning, namely current-to-future state transformation and IT-to-Business alignment. CAP presents an overarching method for step-by-step engineering and design in system architecture and portfolio optimization. JAR comprises the best-of-breed strategic analysis techniques, accompanied by a hybrid method with strategy-driven and initiative-driven planning streams. Applying the framework in planning and future trends are also discussed in the context. This overarching framework provides a comprehensive multi-disciplinary approach to conducting strategic and tactical technology planning for both near-term needs and long-term goals.

INTRODUCTION

The e-business models in today's dynamic business world demand increasing flexibility and responsiveness of information systems applications. It becomes mandatory for the information technology (IT) group in an organization to provide a higher level of services and better quality products at a lower cost for the business to compete and succeed in a globalized economy. The reality is that IT must build more complex, interoperable, scalable, reusable, innovative, forward-thinking, and sustainable technical solutions, to satisfy the ever-growing business needs.

Most large companies like worldwide financial institutions have built, acquired, or purchased virtually hundreds, if not thousands, of IT systems through the years to provide electronic services for external customers and internal staff, resulting in heterogeneous technologies and architectural platforms to satisfy diverse functional requirements from different lines of business. In the banking industry, the business process generally contains different business sectors that address retail, small business, commercial, corporate investment, wealth management, and capital management markets. In particular, services are delivered through a variety of channels. In order to effectively manage the architectural assets and design high-quality IT solutions in such a diverse environment, a highly structured methodology is crucial to achieve an array of goals – separate concerns, divide responsibilities, encapsulate complexity, utilize patterns, leverage best practices, control quality, ensure compliance, and establish operationalization processes.

A majority of today's information system development planning is still ad hoc, manual, subjective, incomprehensive, and error-prone, which inevitably leads to chaotic outcomes and failures in the execution. According to recent surveys, a vast majority of information systems projects are behind schedule, over budget, or canceled. A lack of a systematic framework describing the key design practices and disciplines in the planning of service-oriented information systems is a major cause of this situation.

A new model is proposed in the next section, with more detailed descriptions of the key characteristics and features of the components presented in the section that follows. The subsequent section discusses how to apply the framework in planning, followed by sections on future trends and related work. The chapter is concluded in the last section.

BACKGROUND

Most of the previous architecture planning methods reveal the architectural aspects of a software application to some extent at a fairly high level or from a restricted perspective. A comprehensive approach to architecting the end-to-end information system solutions has become a necessity, calling for a systematic disciplined mechanism. To meet this growing need, a highly structured method is designed in this article to present a comprehensive and holistic view of the core architectural elements, components, knowledge, platforms, planning, and their interrelationships. Design procedures are established accordingly in this methodical approach to facilitate the creation, organization, and management of the architectural assets and solutions at different levels in a large organization.

Design Philosophy

Developing the disciplined mechanism followed a set of key design principles, partly derived from TOGAF (The Open Group, 2008), but significantly modified/expanded to be tailored to the services-oriented development process of information systems.

Business Principles

- **Primacy of principles**: All stakeholders and relevant groups in an organization must follow these principles of technology planning.
- **Maximize benefits**: Maximum benefits will be achieved for the entire organization, rather than individual divisions.

- *Business continuity*: Business operations are not interrupted despite system and process changes.
- *Active engagement*: All stakeholders are actively involved in the process to accomplish business objectives.
- *Compliance with regulations*: The architecting processes comply with all relevant regulations, policies, and applicable laws.
- *IT accountability*: The IT group owns and implements the IT processes and infrastructure that build solutions to satisfy business requirements for functionality, service levels, cost, quality, delivery timelines, and operations supports.
- *Innovations*: The stimulation and protection of the corporate innovations is enforced in the IT architecture, design, management, and governance processes.

Technical Principles

- *Flexibility*: The technical model is agile and adaptive to be nimble in quick response to future business needs.
- *Incremental change management*: Changes to the corporate architecture/infrastructure environment are planned and implemented in a phased approach.
- *Requirement scope control*: The scope creep and waterfall approach are avoided.
- *Technology standardization*: Technological diversity is controlled to minimize immature and proprietary products, platforms, and solutions.
- *Interoperability*: Software, hardware, network and infrastructure should conform to established standards and policies that promote compatibility for data, applications, services, communications, integration, security and technology.

Solution Principles

- *Ease of use*: Solutions are straightforward to implement and use. The complexity of the underlying technology is abstracted from users, so they are able to focus on business functionalities and processes.
- *Technology independence*: Technical solutions are immune from specific technology choices and hence can run on different technology platforms.
- *Common services and processes*: Minimize the redundant development of similar functionalities to promote common services and processes across the organization.

Data Principles

- *Data asset*: Data is an asset that has a business value to the enterprise and is managed in a federated fashion.
- *Data ownership*: Each data element is owned by an entity accountable for the data quality.
- *Common vocabulary and metadata*: The data definition is consistent throughout the organization, and the metadata are standardized and available to all authorized users.
- *Shared data*: Data is shared across business lines for individual applications and systems to perform their duties.
- *Data access*: Data is accessible for users to perform the business transactions.
- *Data security*: Data is protected from unauthorized access and disclosure. This includes the protection of pre-decisional, sensitive, and proprietary information, besides the traditional aspects of national security classification.

General Model

The Strategic Technology Engineering Planning (STEP) approach is developed in this article as a multi-disciplinary framework. It defines a comprehensive analysis and planning method to control the application design and development practices for the quality delivery of information systems. The *STEP* model is a holistic structure to facilitate analyzing and optimizing the strategies, thought processes, methods, tradeoffs, and patterns in the IT design.

STEP forms a foundational knowledgebase to plan service-oriented architecture, integration, process and management in information systems. Its primary focuses are on architecture, execution environment, application frameworks, domain modeling, business process, information, integration, methodology, system management, security, quality of services, and governance. *STEP* is a cohesive set made of four modules, as illustrated in Figure 1:

- *Want-Is-Target (WIT) Model*: a triangle model intended to denote the staged approach of technology evolution and inter-relationships of the constructs and artifacts in the strategic technology engineering planning, and further build consensus with regard to the roles and responsibilities in the planning process.

- *Transition and Alignment Grid (TAG)*: a quadrant model with two dimensions for technology migrations from current state to future state, and seamless IT-to-business alliance.
- *Comprehensive Architecting Process (CAP)*: an overarching method for the step-by-step engineering and design in system architecture and portfolio optimization.
- *Joint Analysis and Roadmapping (JAR)*: a pragmatic analysis technique for all stakeholders and parties, and subsequent future planning to construct a roadmap and action plans.

STEP FRAMEWORK CONSTITUENTS

Want-Is-Target Model

The Want-Is-Target (WIT) model for IT planning is shown in Figure 2. In spite of its apparent simplicity, the value of the model is actually its strength of abstraction at a high level. The "Is" component represents the current-state architecture we have built or acquired via mergers. The "Want" component describes the end-state

Figure 1. Strategic technology engineering planning

architecture we wish to have in the long run. The "Target" component prescribes the target-state architecture that is feasible and reachable in the near future. The target state phase is typically a tactical approach to migrate the exiting portfolio to a strategic position through a multi-generation plan in an incremental fashion.

To fully understand the existing situation, investigate the near-term possibilities, and explore the long-term potentials, it is not only important but also necessary to leverage tools to help analyze and investigate the details in depth. As an analogy, various tools are illustrated in the diagram. For example, when evaluating the "Want" component, a telescope is needed to see things from a distance, whereas a pair of eyeglasses may be sufficient to observe the near-term state. On the other hand, in order to inspect greater details of the "Is" component, a microscope is necessary as a magnifying glass would not reveal the fine points at the level of granularity desired. Nevertheless, these tools still can not disclose the internal structure. To overcome this limitation, more advanced tools must be used, such as X-ray or Magnetic Resonance Imaging (MRI) instruments. Likewise, more sophisticated tools

(radar and satellite) augment what a telescope is capable of providing.

In reality, it is not uncommon that, due to time constraints and lack of acquaintance with tools, different parties misuse tools inadvertently from time to time when investigating various aspects in different domains. It is, however, critically important to utilize appropriate tools to look into the details of the components for analysis and synthesis. The metaphor indicates that we need not only "do things right", but also "rely on right tools to help do things right". Some tools, methods, and techniques for strategic planning will be articulated further in the sections that follow.

The Balanced Approach, represented as a triangle in the middle of the diagram, is the architecture planning process that balances the pros and cons, and resolves the conflicts with tradeoffs and compromises to lay out a reasonable path to the needed changes. Usually the balanced approach takes a hybrid approach to meet the immediate needs in the near term, but still aligning the architecture efforts with the strategic goals and vision.

Arguably, the most important factor in the strategic planning efforts are the "Stakehold-

Figure 2. Want-is-Target model

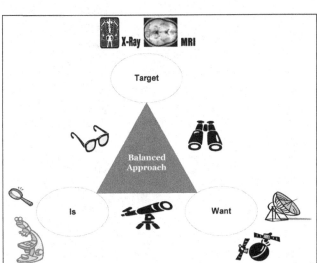

ers", which are all of the relevant people who have impacts on or are significantly affected by the architecture decisions and changes. The key stakeholders comprise the client users, business partners, business analysts, architects, developers, testers, system administrators, DBAs, network engineers, system managers, security specialists, risk officers, vendors, standards organizations, legal entities, consultants, and other subject matter experts. They may be for a change, be against it, be neutral, or not even know about it yet. Due to the different interests, relevant expertise, and roles played from various parties, the decision-making process must inevitably deal with conflicting forces and factors.

The process to establish the inventory of the "Is" component and define the models of the "Want" and "Target" components in a large organization is typically iterative. The current, end and target states can be represented in various formats from different viewpoints, such as business, technology, infrastructure, risk, finance, compliance, and standards.

Transition and Alignment Grid

Based on this triangle model, a Transition and Alignment Grid (TAG) is constructed to identify the key artifacts and design concerns in technology planning, as depicted in Figure 3. There are two dimensions defined – current-to-future state transition, and business-to-IT alignment.

In the transition dimension, the "Is" component is mapped to the current state assessment, which collects the input data and analyzes the existing environment. Similarly, the "Target" and "Want" components are mapped to the future state definition, which combines the vision of the near-term state and the end state. The future state specification serves as a blueprint of the desired form. The gap analysis is subsequently conducted to bridge the three states. A roadmap is thus defined to transit the current state to the future state in a controlled manner. Usually the transitions are staged in multiple phases in an incremental fashion. Depending on the timeframe desired, the end state vision is typically strategic and targeted to the long term. However, tactical

Figure 3. Transition and Alignment Grid

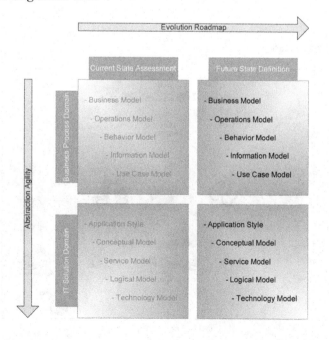

solutions are often needed to deliver required business functionalities in a short period of time. This creates a dilemma between the strategic and tactical needs. It is of vital importance to have the end-state vision well defined, so that the strategic goals are not deserted when pragmatic approaches are crafted for the short-term demands in the target state.

This approach serves as a use-case driven pattern-based procedure for iterative architecture planning. Round-trip architecture engineering is enforced to articulate the multi-perspective views, using the industry standards on visual modeling and semantic ontology, such as UML, SysML/DSL, BPMN, XPDL, BPEL, and OWL. Loosely-coupled interface and integration are imposed in the principle of design by contract. The 80-20 rule is leveraged in the use case drill-down for objective sizing and empirical estimation in the service-centered paradigm.

To provide better abstraction and individual agility, the spectrum in the alignment dimension is divided into two areas: Business Process Domain and IT Solution Domain. The goal is to make IT responsive and adaptive, so it will be nimble and flexible to support the business operations for quicker changes. The Business Process Domain captures the information pertinent to the static and dynamic structure on which the business runs – the business process, the operations method, the behavioral process, the information requirements, and the usage scenarios. The IT Solution Domain describes the IT systems supporting and realizing the business operations. The key artifacts in the IT Solution Domain are application domain styles, conceptual model, service model, logical model, and technology model. The gap between the business model and IT model is daunting in almost every large organization. There have been constant conflicts in the alignment of IT models with business models due to delivery schedules, resources, skillset, risks, and budgets. The strategy to alleviate this pain is to seamlessly integrate the models in these two areas. The engaging of end-to-end round-trip engineering principles with traceability and auditability is a necessity to make IT models adaptive, and eventually proactive in the long run.

The key drivers in the alignment dimension are value proposition, expectations, goals, end-to-end process, degree of complexity, lean models, situational context, purpose-driven adaptation, quality, and consistency.

Comprehensive Architecting Process

A pragmatic Comprehensive Architecting Process (CAP) is further defined in Figure 4 to facilitate the current state evaluation and future state specification. The key activities are grouped in 8 steps in the procedure:

- Step 1 – Operations Model.
- Step 2 – Use Case Model.
- Step 3 – Business Process Flow.
- Step 4 – Business Data Requirements.
- Step 5 – Application/Architecture Patterns.
- Step 6 – Domain-specific Modeling.
- Step 7 – Conceptual Model.
- Step 8 – Technology Model.

Operations Model

The operations model copes with the alignment and facilitation between the business operations

Figure 4. Comprehensive architecting process

and information systems. It is the business driver to all other technical models in the stack, forming the foundation of the strategic alignment of technical models with the business process mission. The in-depth analysis of the business processes often leads to the reengineering effort to improve the business operations in such a way that different divisions in a large organization can share common solutions for the business needs. The commonalities of the technology components and business logic modules are identified and reusable assets are constructed, resulting in reduced portfolio total cost of ownership (TCO) and increased operational efficiency. Business patterns are generally identified to group processes into different categories in the business domain. Common business languages are usually used.

Use Case Model

A use case model is a specification describing the functional requirements of an information system. Use cases convey the usage scenarios that characterize how the system interacts with the actors, what the system boundaries are, and how the use cases are related to each other, thereby describing the total functional behavior and specific business goals of the system.

No standard template exists for documenting use cases in detail. Different schemes and formats have been proposed, and individual teams tend to adapt from what is available or create a customized template that works for their specific situations. Standardization may be enforced at appropriate level, depending on the maturity and applicability, e.g., project, portfolio, domain, division, enterprise, industry sector, etc.

Although terminologies, section structure, and orderings may differ significantly, most use cases share an underlying similarity, so that the core sections in a use case specification look alike. Typical sections in a use case specification include: use case name, ID, version, description, actors, iteration, dependency, preconditions, postconditions, triggers, happy-path flow, alternative paths, business rules, errors, notes, author and date. Different templates may have supplementary sections, such as assumptions, exception handling, recommendations, technical constraints, and non-functional requirements. Other industry or project specific sections may be included as well. Figure 5 depicts a use case diagram for a supply chain management application.

Figure 5. Use case diagram example

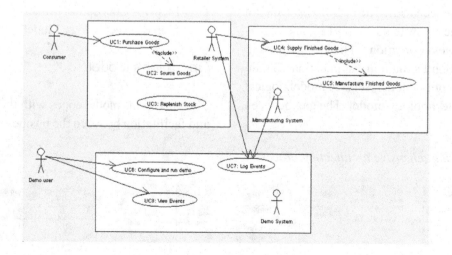

Business Process Flow

The use cases are further decomposed to capture the details in the business process flows. Flow charts are traditionally used to illustrate the logic flow in an informal but intuitive manner. The UML activity diagram provides a standard way to specify the workflows in the Use Case Model. As an example, Figure 6 shows an activity diagram for Use Case 2 defined in Figure 5.

Other notations and standards are maturing and available for business process design and execution, such as BPMN, XPDL, and BPEL. The Business Process Modeling Notation (BPMN) is a standard graphical notation for visualizing business processes in a workflow. The standardization of BPMN for the description of business processes bridges the gap in communications, which often arises between the business process design and implementation, thereby facilitating the interactions between all business stakeholders, including the business analysts who identify and specify the operations, the technical designers who defines the process orchestration or choreography using a process engine, the solution developers who are responsible for implementing the process scripts, and the business managers who monitor and manage the processes in execution. Therefore BPMN is designed to serve as a common language that is understandable by all stakeholders involved. Figure 7 displays a BPMN diagram for an email voting process.

The XML Process Definition Language (XPDL) is a standard format designed by the Workflow Management Coalition to exchange the definitions of business processes between different workflow products such as the workflow engines and modeling tools. A XML schema is defined in XPDL to specify the declarative part of workflow. XPDL is created to interchange the process design, both the graphical representations and the semantics of a business process workflow. The elements contained in XPDL hold the X and Y position of the activity nodes, together with the coordinates of points along the lines that link these activity nodes. By contrast, although BPEL is a process definition format as well, it is solely for the executable parts of the process. The elements to represent the graphical aspects of a process diagram do not exist in BPEL.

In the open source space, tools are available for BMPN, XPDL and BPEL, such as Intalio BPMN Modeler, JaWE, and ActiveBPEL, respectively.

Figure 6. Source Goods Activity Diagram Example

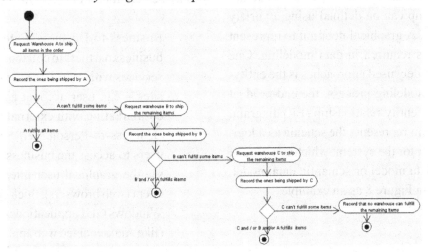

Figure 7. BPMN diagram example

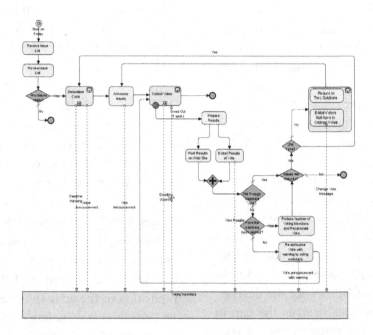

Business Data Requirements

The business data requirements are captured to specify the information requirements for the system. A logical data model is constructed with all the necessary definitions of data elements. A detailed data flow diagram specifies the data exchange and processing in the business operations. A schema is designed to map the business data to a persistence repository, predominantly a relational database system. The data structure and relationship can be defined using a variety of techniques. A graphical notation to represent data models is required in data modeling. One of the most widely used approaches is the entity-relationship modeling process, the end-product of which is an entity-relationship (ER) diagram. An ER diagram represents the schema as a logical data model for the system, which is a type of conceptual data model or semantic data model, as displayed in Figure 8 as an example.

Application/Architecture Patterns

Application/Architecture patterns are high-level artifacts that are used to describe the principal business purpose and architectural style of a solution. They identify the high-level participants who interact in the solution based on the primary objectives of the solutions, and define the nature of the interactions between the participants. In the banking sector for example, the primary patterns may be classified in the following list.

- Business-to-Business Enterprise: enable business partners to collaboratively provide services with seamless navigation between sites – e.g. user account aggregation, and co-marketing with external vendors.
- Business-to-Person Self-Service: enable users to access the business functionalities via the graphical user interfaces of a thin client (web browsers), thick client (typically Windows GUI applications), and rich client (like Ajax-enabled web applications) as well

Figure 8. Entity-relationship diagram example

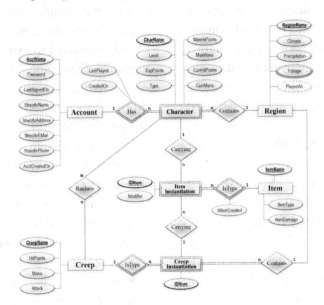

as other pervasive platforms like personal digital assistants (PDA) and mobile devices such as cell phones – e.g. money transfer between accounts, and bill payments.

- Person-to-Person Collaborations: enable users to communicate with other people like loan officers or brokerage account managers electronically – e.g. emails, and web-based instant messaging.
- Person-to-Data Data Aggregation: enable users to access product information, service details, directory, branch locations, and data summary – e.g. check images, and interim account statements.
- Person-to-Application Access Integration: enable the integration of front ends of servicing applications, typically at the web server tier – e.g. Single Sign-On (SSO), and portal services.
- Application-to-Application back-end Integration: enable inter-system integration – e.g. asynchronous messaging middleware, and web services.

The pattern categories serve as a baseline to classify various information systems into appropriate groups. The cataloging effort builds a common taxonomy for the technology portfolio, and facilitates the further technology planning and technical design. Commonalities among similar systems help rationalize the portfolio and optimize the asset use in the IT environment.

Domain-Specific Modeling

Domain-Specific Modeling (DSM) is a way of designing and developing systems, via the systematic use of a graphical Domain Specific Language (DSL) to represent the various facets of a system. The support of higher-level abstractions distinguishes the DSM languages from the general-purpose modeling languages, meaning that they require less effort and fewer low-level details to specify a given system.

A DSM environment automates creating program components that are otherwise expensive to construct from scratch, such as domain-specific editors, browsers and components. All a domain expert needs to do is to define the domain specific rules and constructs, and the DSM environment provides a modeling tool tailored for the target portfolio. Consequently, the overall cost of obtaining tool support for a DSM language can be considerably reduced by means of a well-designed DSM environment.

Almost all existing DSM activities leverage DSM environments, via commercial tools like MetaEdit+, open source tools like GEMS, and academic tools like GME. Thanks to the increasing popularity of DSM, DSM frameworks have been bundled into existing IDEs, as seen in the Eclipse Modeling Framework Project with Graphical Modeling Framework and Graphical Editing Framework, and in Microsoft's DSL Tools for Software Factories.

Conceptual Model

A conceptual architecture model is designed in Figure 9. The layering architectural pattern is applied to organize the internal structure of an application. The structure extends the concept of the well-known Model-View-Controller (MVC)

design pattern to form a generic skeleton of service-oriented component-based application architecture. For example, the scope of the application *View* is expanded to include the portal for easy customized navigation and content aggregation, as well as the interaction services to deal with multiple pervasive computing devices. Likewise, the application *Controller* is extended to deal with process choreography and collaborations.

The application structure is made of a stack of 5 layers and 1 vertical block. The *Access & Interaction Layer* supports various devices, handles user interface processing, and integrate single sign-on and authorization. The *Business Process & Coordination Layer* deals with process choreography, orchestration, human workflow, collaborations as well as complex events. The *Composite Services Layer* hosts the aggregated services, service transformation, itinerary routing, semantic web services, and advanced services such as transaction, reliable messaging, and secure conversation. The *Services & Component Layer* contains atomic services, foundational services, business rule engine, service registry/repository, and other servicing components. The *Enterprise Resources Layer* has enterprise ODS, federated

Figure 9. Conceptual model

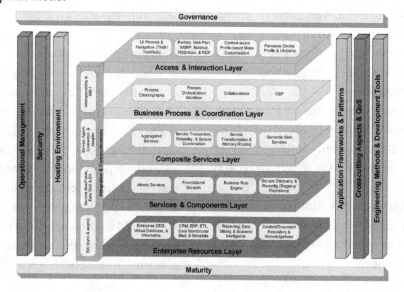

database, CRM, ERP, data warehouse/marts, content/document repository, reporting, and analytics suites. The *Integration & Communications Block* copes with inter-application integrations, interoperability, service bus/fabric, data grid, EII, and service agent/connector/broker that encapsulates the integration logic to access internal data sources and external services.

In addition, the *Security, Hosting Environment* and *Operational Management* pillars are across the layers in the runtime environment, whereas the *Application Frameworks & Patterns, Crosscutting Aspects & QoS* and *Engineering Methods & Development Tools* pillars are pertinent to various aspects in the development construction. The *Governance* and *Maturity* modules are for the overall program management, policies & standards, conformance enforcement, and evolution measurements.

Technology Model

The technology model defines a detailed structure chart with complete module specifications, and system architecture of servers, nodes, and communications lines. Infrastructure network and topology of data centers is a key part of the technology model. Figure 10 illustrates an end-to-end enterprise infrastructure in a hosting environment for both Internet and Intranet as well as Extranet communications, which includes remote access, routers, switches, firewalls, Domain Name Service (DNS), print services, certificate authority, storage, database, web services, middleware, proxy, Virtual Private Network (VPN) services, high-availability failover, and backup services.

Joint Analysis and Roadmapping

All stakeholders and parties are engaged to conduct a joint analysis on the current, target, and end states. Based on this comprehensive study, the strategic planning is kicked off to construct a roadmap and action plans. A combination of best-of-breed roadmapping methods are used in this effort.

SWOT

The Strengths, Weaknesses, Opportunities, and Threats (SWOT) technique is employed to con-

Figure 10. Technology model example

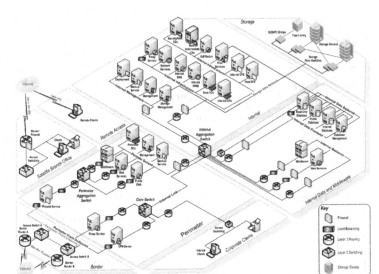

duct a thorough inspection on each major factor and option. The analysis reveals the requirement conflicts and design constraints as well as presumptions from a particular stakeholder's point of view. Focus on a single factor is meant to minimize risks only from that attribute perspective at a fine level. This is often insufficient when a variety of conflicting attributes play an equivalently important role in the system and a balance between these interacting attributes must be established. The outcome of the SWOT exercise is the key to the unbiased justification of tradeoffs in a balanced approach. The harmonious approach resolves the conflicts in local/individual attributes to reach a global optimization.

As shown in Figure 11, SWOT is used as inputs to generate possible strategies. Based on the results, a hierarchy of objectives, strategies, and tactics (HOST) diagram can be drawn to facilitate the drill-down on each major objective. By assessing the what, when, why, who, where, which, and how (6W+1H) on these objectives and strategies, the top rank objectives can be identified and prioritized. Dependencies and interrelationships among the objectives and strategies are also elaborated in this exercise.

Porter's Models

The Porter's Five Forces Analysis is a more robust framework than a SWOT analysis for business management. The concepts designed in Industrial Organization (IO) economics are utilized to derive 5 forces that determine the attractiveness of a market, as demonstrated in Figure 12. A change in any of these 5 forces generally triggers a reassessment of the marketplace for an organization. The four primary forces are the bargaining power of suppliers, the bargaining power of customers, the threat of new entrants, and the threat of substitute products. The fifth force – the level of competition in an industry – is influence by the four primary forces in combination with other variables. An extension to Porter's 5 forces model is called Six Forces Model, in which the sixth force is introduced, namely the government or public.

Porter also introduced a value chain model and a generic strategies framework in his seminal work. The value chain model consists of a sequence of value-generating activities that are common to a variety of companies. The principal activities are marketing, sales, inbound logistics, operations, outbound logistics, and service. The support activities comprise infrastructure, human resources management, technology development,

Figure 11. SWOT diagram

SWOT Analysis		Internal Analysis	
		Strengths	Weaknesses
External Analysis	Opportunities	S-O strategy: Build new methods that fits the organization's strength	W-O strategy: Remove weaknesses to embrace new opportunities
	Threats	S-T strategy: Take advantage of strength to defend threats	W-T strategy: Construct approaches to shun weaknesses that could be targeted by threats

Figure 12. Porter's 5 forces analysis

and procurement. The value chain model helps define a company's core competencies and the activities that a company can undertake to pursue cost advantage or differentiation. On the other hand, the generic strategies framework is composed of cost leadership, differentiation, and market segmentation. The three strategies can be further mapped to three basic value disciplines – product innovation, customer intimacy, and operational excellence. The cost leadership may be implemented as either a low cost strategy or a best cost strategy.

These two models are useful to align the technology strategies to the overall business strategies in an organization. The generic strategies help define the key drivers for the technology domain, while the value chain model helps identify the key activities in the technology area.

Portfolio Planning (BCG Growth-Share Matrix)

Bruce Henderson of the Boston Consulting Group designed a portfolio planning model called the BCG Growth-Share Matrix, founded on the observation that the business units in an organization can be categorized into four types – dogs, question marks, stars, and cash cows, depending on combinations of market growth and market share (growth-share) relative to the prevalent competitor in the market. The market growth is an indicator for industry attractiveness, whereas relative market share signifies the competitive advantage. Thus the Growth-Share Matrix demonstrates the positioning of a business unit along with the two most important determinants of profitability.

The original design of the Growth-Share Matrix was targeted towards allocating resources among different business lines in an organization. It can also be leveraged in the resource allocation for the products in a portfolio. The single diagram in a simple format helps visualize the relative positions of the entire business portfolio in an organization, as illustrated in Figure 13. However, the model has some limitations. Firstly, there are other important factors in the industry attractiveness and competitive advantage share

Figure 13. BCG growth-share matrix

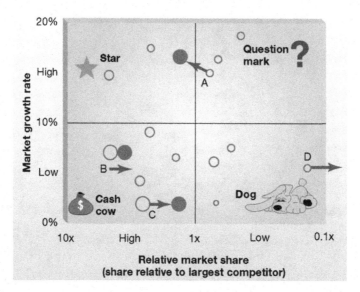

that are not included in the matrix. Secondly, the business divisions on the chart are presumably independent from each other. The inter-relationship between the units is not addressed in the model. Lastly, the breadth of the market definition has a big impact on the positioning of a business group, which may dominate its small niche, but have a very low market share in the overall industry.

Scenario and Situation Planning

The Scenario Planning was originated in the military strategy studies, when Herman Kahn founded the scenario-based planning in his work related to the possible scenarios associated with thermonuclear war (Kahn, 1985). Pierre Wack transformed the scenario planning into a business tool in the development of a scenario planning system at Royal Dutch/Shell. The efforts made Shell well-prepared to cope with the oil shock in late 1973 and significantly enhanced the company's competitiveness in the industry during the oil crisis and the subsequent oil glut.

Scenarios are efforts to detail a hypothetical succession of events that could conceivably lead

to the circumstance envisioned. The Scenario Planning is essentially about making choices now with an understanding of how the selections might turn out. A common misconception about the Scenario Planning is that it is perceived as a tool of accurate future prediction or forecast. Instead, it is an approach to laying out the possible situations and combinations, leading to a set of distinct but plausible future states, which help formulate plans and tactics to cope with each of the possible circumstances.

The key benefits of scenario planning are to force the stakeholders to break their routine thinking mode, in order to identify the blind spots that might otherwise be neglected in other normal approaches. Scenarios are recognized in an early stage, enabling informed decision-making and well-preparedness for the difficult situations. The source of disagreements can be better communicated, understood, and resolved when different scenarios are analyzed and walked through.

The Scenario Planning sessions are usually conducted with the key stakeholders such as executive sponsors, technical leaders, industry specialists, program/project managers, and subject matter experts. This enables a sufficient range of perspectives to be considered without leaving out important details or situations. Inputs, participation, and contributions from those who will formulate and implement strategies derived from the scenario analysis are critical to aptly address the issues and pain points that are vital to the teams who will later execute the strategy.

Figure 14 outlines the typical steps that constitute a process of scenario planning.

A matrix of scenarios is created for the analysis of the interaction between the variables, using the two most important variables and their possible values. As displayed in Figure 15, each cell in the matrix represents a single scenario. For straightforward reference in discussions and communications, it is a good practice that each scenario has a descriptive name. In case there

are more than two critical factors, a multidimensional matrix is developed. However it is hard to visualize beyond 2 or 3 dimensions. Instead, factors can be taken in pairs to generate several two-dimensional matrices.

PEST Analysis

The Political, Economic, Social, and Technological (PEST) analysis is a framework of macroenvironmental factors used in environmental scanning.

As a part of the external analysis in market research, it provides an overview, to a large degree, of the different macroenvironmental factors worth consideration by an organization. The political factors focus the areas of employment laws, environmental regulations, trade restrictions, tariffs, tax policy, and political stability. The economic factors include the economic growth rates, interest

Figure 14. Scenario planning process

Figure 15. Scenario planning matrix

		Variable 1		
		Outcome 1A ↓	Outcome 1B ↓	Outcome 1C ↓
Variable 2	Outcome 2A →	**Scenario I**	**Scenario II**	**Scenario III**
	Outcome 2B →	**Scenario IV**	**Scenario V**	**Scenario VI**
	Outcome 2C →	**Scenario VII**	**Scenario VIII**	**Scenario IX**

rates, exchange rates and inflation rates. The social factors are usually related to the cultural aspects, consisting of health consciousness, population growth rate, age distribution, career attitudes and emphasis on safety. The technological factors comprise ecological and environmental aspects that determine the barriers to entry, minimum efficient production level and outsourcing decisions. The core elements include the R&D activities, automation, technology incentives and the rate of technological changes.

From a technology engineering planning perspective, the prominent factors in technological analysis are recent technology advancements, technological impact on solution offerings, influence on cost, effect on the value chain model, and rate of technology diffusion. These PEST factors and other external micro-environmental factors can be categorized into the opportunities and threats cells in a SWOT analysis.

Hybrid Roadmapping Method

To effectively conduct strategic planning to meet the needs in both short and long terms, a hybrid method is necessary to take account of all factors and interests from different parties. Two streams are defined in this hybrid method – initiative-driven and strategy-driven.

The strategy-driven roadmapping is conducted at four levels:

- Macro-level: trend analysis
- Meso-level: competitor analysis
- Micro-level: enterprise analysis
- Nano-level: portfolio analysis

The technological trend analysis identifies the technological factors/trends that have impact on the organization. The competitor analysis determines the competition levels, analyzes competitive forces, examines competitor behavior, and identifies competitor strategies. The enterprise analysis analyzes the internal environment and

identifies its competencies. The portfolio analysis investigates the conditions and maturity in a technology domain. The results of these analyses can be captured in a set of SWOT matrixes.

The initiative-driven roadmapping deals with the requests from the current initiatives, which are typically for immediate needs and near-term goals. The activities include supporting the existing business operations, replacing obsolete vendor technologies, making minor modifications to meet regulatory requirements, retiring outdated applications, and adding short-term feature enhancement in the existing information systems. A target state is defined to build out these capabilities, which serves as a transformation step towards the end state as described in the foregoing section. A value chain model can be used to assess the impact and margins in the initiative-driven efforts.

Based on the results of the strategy-driven and initiative-driven streams, a roadmap is devised, which is usually in the format of a multi-generation plan. It outlines the long-term goals, and details the specific strategies and pragmatic goals that are to be pursued. The strategic and tactical concerns and challenges are articulated and addressed in depth. Areas of risks are analyzed and specific means for mitigating those risks are adopted.

APPLYING STEP IN PLANNING

The *STEP* framework forms a coherent set of components that can be used to compose a pragmatic approach for technology planning in the real-world context. The *WIT* module serves as a basic structural model to assess the current state and define the end state as well as the intermittent target states. The *TAG* module deals with the business-to-IT alignment and roadmap transforming the current state to future state, which is the outcome of the *WIT* module. An array of models are used in the *TAG* module to describe the prominent aspects and attributes of a domain, such as business, operations, behavior, information, use case, application, conceptual, service, logical, and technology. Further, the *CAP* module provides a practical process with 8 steps grouping the activities and artifacts in this effort. Some models introduced in the *TAG* module are articulated in greater detail in this process. Templates, checklists, UML diagrams, ER diagrams, reference architecture, and patterns may be used to facilitate the standardization of the notations and practices in this procedure. Finally, a range of roadmapping methods presented in the *JAR* module can be leveraged to conduct tradeoff analysis of the roadmaps developed in the *TAG* module, and balance the constraints and conflicts to reach a compromised agreement among the stakeholders with different interests and priorities.

FUTURE TRENDS

As the advance in the technology field continues at an unprecedented pace, a practical approach is to be adaptive and build out the strategy plan in an incremental manner. An iterative process should be established to refresh the plan and re-examine the internal and external influencing factors. The strategic planning tends to become semi-automated, with a pragmatic mechanism in place to monitor the changes and trigger necessary reassessment. Various techniques and methods will converge to formulate a complete strategic framework for the digital age, from concept to execution to termination. The focal point will be on the future and people, who are involved in planning and developing the strategy and measures, so that the execution can be accelerated. It can be foreseen that a more balanced approach will be taken between the tactical actions and strategic activities, resulting in lower cost, well-managed risk, efficient alignment, higher flexibility, enhanced quality, and faster time-to-market. The matured methodology and disciplines are expected to make a real difference, create values, and build sustainable competitive advantages in an organization.

RELATED WORK

Previous studies in the last few decades have strived to tackle the issue of architecture design complexity, which has grown exponentially as the computing paradigm has evolved from a monolithic to a service-oriented architecture. The Zachman Framework (Zachman, 1987) is a logical structure for categorizing and organizing the descriptive representations of an enterprise IT environment. In the form of a two-dimensional matrix, it has achieved a level of penetration in the domain of business and information systems architecture and modeling. It is largely used as a planning or problem-solving tool. Nevertheless, it tends to implicitly align with the data-driven approach and process-decomposition methods, and it operates above and across the individual project level. Extended Enterprise Architecture Framework (E2AF) (IEAD, 2004) takes a very similar approach seen in the Zachman Framework. Its scope contains business, information, system, and infrastructure in a 2-D matrix. E2AF is more technology-oriented. Both of these approaches are heavyweight methodologies, which set a fairly steep learning curve for a team to learn and successfully adopt either method.

Rational Unified Process (RUP) (Kruchten, 2003) made an effort to prevail over these shortcomings by leveraging the Unified Modeling Language (UML) in a use-case driven, object-oriented and component-based approach. The concept of 4+1 views interprets the overall system structure from multiple perspectives. RUP is more process-oriented, and is generally a waterfall approach. RUP barely addresses software maintenance and operations, and lacks a broad coverage on physical topology and development/testing tools. It essentially operates at the individual project level. RUP has recently been expanded to Enterprise Unified Process (EUP) and part of it has become open source – OpenUP in Eclipse.

Another heavyweight approach, The Open Group Architecture Framework (TOGAF), is a detailed framework with a set of supporting tools for developing an enterprise architecture to meet the business and information technology needs in an organization. The three core parts of TOGAF are Architecture Development Method (ADM), Enterprise Architecture Continuum, and TOGAF Resource Base. The scope of TOGAF covers Business Process Architecture, Applications Architecture, Data Architecture, and Technology Architecture. The focal point of TOGAF is at the enterprise architecture level, rather than the individual application architecture level. On the other hand, Model-Driven Architecture (MDA) (Object Management Group, 2008) takes an agile approach, aiming to separate business logic or application logic from the underlying platform technology. The core of MDA is the Platform-Independent Model (PIM) and Platform-Specific Model (PSM), which provide greater portability and interoperability as well as enhanced productivity and maintenance. MDA is primarily for the software modeling part in the development lifecycle process.

Other related works on IT architecture frameworks are for the most part tailored to specific domains. They are useful references when a team intends to create their own models for their organization. The comprehensive architectural guidance for the various Commands, Services, and Agencies within the U.S. Department of Defense are documented in the C4ISR Architecture Framework (DoD, 1997), for the sake of interoperability endurance and cost-effectiveness in military systems. The Federal Enterprise Architecture (FEA) framework (Federal Office, 2007) gives direction and guidance to U.S. federal agencies for designing enterprise architecture. The Treasury Enterprise Architecture Framework (TEAF) is to guide the planning and development of enterprise architectures in all bureaus and offices of the Treasury Department. The Purdue Enterprise Reference Architecture

(PERA) (Purdue University, 2008) is aligned to computer integrated manufacturing. ISO/IEC 14252 (a.k.a. IEEE Standard 1003.0) (IEEE, 1995) is an architectural framework built on POSIX open systems standards. The ISO Reference Model for Open Distributed Processing (RM-ODP) (Putnam, 2001) is a coordinating framework to standardize the Open Distributed Processing in heterogeneous environments. It creates an architecture that integrates the support of distribution, networking and portability, using five "viewpoints" and eight "transparencies". The Solution Architecture of N-Tier Applications (Shan & Hua, 2006) presents a multi-layer and multi-pillar model for web-based applications.

CONCLUSION

To effectively manage the complexity in service-oriented architecture and perform strategic technology planning in information systems, a comprehensive model is a necessity to abstract concerns, define methods, and present a holistic view of the planning aspects in a highly structured way. The Strategic Technology Engineering Planning (STEP) model introduced in this article is a holistic framework to facilitate planning information systems applications strategically and tactically. It provides comprehensive coverage of the planning artifacts from both analysis and execution perspectives. It defines a comprehensive multi-disciplinary approach to conduct strategic and tactical technology planning for both near-term needs and long-term goals.

The design principles of the framework are presented in the context. The model comprises an array of multiple modules: Want-Is-Target (WIT) model, Transition and Alignment Grid (TAG), Comprehensive Architecting Process (CAP), and Joint Analysis & Roadmapping (JAR). The characteristics and features of the constituent elements in the SETP model are articulated in great detail. The WIT model defines three stages of architecture states – current, target, and end state. TAG specifies two dimensions for architecture planning, namely current-to-future state transformation and IT-to-Business alignment. CAP presents an overarching method for step-by-step engineering and design in system architecture and portfolio optimization. JAR comprises the best-of-breed strategic analysis techniques, accompanied by a hybrid method with strategy-driven and initiative-driven planning streams. Furthermore, the elements and features of each module are detailed and the future trends are discussed.

The comprehensiveness and agility of this coherent framework has made it possible for the model to be extensively used in the service-oriented application planning in one format or another, and its usage has proved to be an enormous success. Furthermore, this structure is so scalable and flexible for dynamic extensions and expansions that the model can serve as a meta-framework to incorporate other general or specialized frameworks.

REFERENCES

DoD C4ISR Architecture Working Group (1997). *C4ISR Architecture Framework*, Version 2.

Federal Office of Management and Budget (2008). *Federal Architecture Framework*. Retrieved May 18, 2008 from http://www.whitehouse.gov/omb/egov/a-2-EAModelsNEW2.html

IEEE Standard 1003.0-1995. (1995). *IEEE Guide to the POSIX Open System Environment*. http://standards.ieee.org/reading/ieee/std_public/description/posix/1003.0-1995_desc.html

Institute for Enterprise Architecture Developments. (2004). *Extended Enterprise Architecture Framework*. Retrieved May 18, 2008, from http://www.enterprise-architecture.info

Kahn, H. (1985). *Thinking about the Unthinkable in the 1980s*. New York: Simon & Schuster.

Kruchten, K. (2003). *The Rational Unified Process: An Introduction*. 3rd Edition, Massachusetts: Addison Wesley.

Object Management Group (2008). *Model Driven Architecture*. Retrieved May 18, 2008 from http://www.omg.org/mda

Purdue University (2008). *The Purdue Enterprise Reference Architecture*. Retrieved May 18, 2008 from http://pera.net

Putman, J. R. (2001). *Architecting with RM-ODP*. New Jersey: Prentice Hall PTR.

Shan, T.C., & Hua, W.W. (2006). Solution Architecture of N-Tier Applications. In Proceedings of 3rd IEEE International Conference on Services Computing (pp. 349-356). California: IEEE Computer Society."

The Open Group (2008). *The Open Group Architecture Framework*. Retrieved May 18, 2008 from http://www.opengroup.org/architecture/togaf8/index8.htm

Zachman, J.A. (1987). A framework for information systems architecture. *IBM Systems Journal, 26*(3), 276-295.

Chapter XVI
Object–Oriented Software Design Patterns Applied to IT Management Theory

Eric Tachibana
National University of Singapore, Singapore

David Ross Florey
Merrill Lynch Global Business Technology, Singapore

ABSTRACT

Since the mid to late 1990's, object-oriented software design patterns have proven to be a powerful tool in support of software design and product management. However, the usefulness of the methodology need not be restricted to the technical domain alone. In fact, the design pattern methodology represents a powerful tool that can also be used in support of it management at a business level. In this paper, we discuss the design pattern methodology, provide an example of how the methodology could be implemented to solve a business problem, the multivariate vector map (mvm), and then apply the mvm pattern to the problem of choosing an it outsourcing strategy as a means to demonstrate its effectiveness to it managers and to it outsourcing vendors

INTRODUCTION

Since they were first introduced in the mid to late 1990's, Design Patterns for object-oriented software development have become a powerful force in software engineering. However, the efficacy of Design Patterns need not be limited to the technical realm.

In this chapter, we present a broad paradigm through which business managers can apply the object-oriented Design Pattern methodology to help solve strategic management problems and to better predict the market outcomes of their choices.

We will begin the discussion by briefly recounting the history of Design Patterns in software engineering. Next, we will discuss and define Design Patterns themselves and explain how the Design Pattern paradigm is used effectively in object-oriented software development.

Having defined our base of reference, we will then explore the ways in which the Design Pattern paradigm can be applied to the process of strategic management decision-making by examining how several popular management decision-making tools can be refactored as Design Patterns.

Finally, we will propose our own Design Pattern, the Multivariate Vector Map (MVM), and demonstrate its effectiveness by applying it to the problem of strategic IT Outsourcing. In support of the case study, we have gathered data from a large multinational IT Services company based in Singapore that was able to provide the information and statistics required for the generation and implementation of the MVM Design Pattern.

WHAT ARE DESIGN PATTERNS?

Over the last decade, Design Patterns have emerged at the forefront of object-oriented software engineering and have inspired dozens of books, conferences, online communities, and well-designed software solutions.

Although the conceptual origins of Design Patterns were being postulated in the early 1990s by several sources, it was the groundbreaking book, *"Design Patterns: Elements of Reusable Object Oriented Software"* by Gamma, Helm, Johnson and Vlissides, affectionately known as the Gang of Four (GoF), which truly launched the Design Pattern paradigm into the popular consciousness. [FOWLER, 5]

The core thesis argued by the GoF explains that rather than solving every software engineering design problem from first principles, good designers reuse abstracted designs developed (and copied) throughout their careers. When

software architects discover designs that work, they continue using those designs over and over again. In the words of the GoF,

"These patterns solve design problems and make object-oriented designs more flexible, elegant, and ultimately reusable ....A designer who is familiar with such patterns can apply them immediately to design problems without having to rediscover them. ...Once you know the pattern, a lot of design decisions follow automatically." [GoF, 1]

Of course, the recognition of 'good' designs within software architecture was no epiphany. Any of the almost two dozen design patterns cataloged in the GoF's revolutionary book were all designs that any senior, seasoned architect of the era would have intuitively recognized. The GoF's truly novel contribution to the field was their definition of a paradigm with which to understand the process of recognizing, documenting, communicating and implementing Design Patterns. As they explain it,

"The purpose of [our] book is to record experience in designing object-oriented software as design patterns. Each design pattern systematically names, explains, and evaluates an important and recurring design. Our goal is to capture design experience in a form that people can use effectively." [GoF, 1]

The benefits of using design patterns for object-oriented software engineering have proven to be numerous and significant.

For one, while the object-oriented paradigm addressed reusability at the algorithm and object level, Design Patterns make it easier to reuse successful designs at the architectural level. This result is faster development turnaround and more reliable code.

In addition, Design Patterns make more starkly visible the assumptions and consequences of design choices. This elevates the process of coding from fire-fighting to architecture, allowing developers to think more strategically about their designs. As noted by Shalloway and Trott, "developers are freed from the tyranny of dealing with details too early." [S&T, 84]

Further, representing proven techniques as formal Design Patterns rather than describing them loosely merely through intuition or 'experience', means improved communication, documentation, and maintenance as a result of shared terminology. This, in turn, makes systems more accessible to developers of new systems or to new developers. Using Design Patterns means that passing "knowledge" between people is streamlined and made more accurate. For example, a developer on a team need only declare that he intends to implement a "Factory Pattern" and a huge amount of information about his design intentions and their consequences will immediately and effectively be communicated to all other team members.

Finally, Design Patterns codify best-practices and help to ensure that there is maximum reuse of industry experience and accumulated knowledge by junior, intermediate, and senior professionals alike. Design Patterns are living, breathing artifacts of experience in that rather than being codified and frozen in place, they are starting points for extended dialog, open to continuous improvement and refinement from a variety of sources over time. In this way, they function as a basis for collaboration, analogous to written language in allowing knowledge to be imprinted and shared over space and time so that instead of constantly reinventing the wheel, we can benefit from the experience of others, past and to come.

In *Design Patterns*, the GoF originally proposed 13 elements to define any Design Pattern. More recent authors have simplified the GoF Framework down to 8. Consider Table 1.1 that was adapted from Shalloway and Trott, [S&T, 83]

Table 1.1. The core structure of a design pattern

ELEMENT	DESCRIPTION
Name	Many authors have remarked on the importance of pattern naming. Typically a pattern's name must convey the essence of the pattern effectively. Good names, as has been shown historically, become core components of the vocabulary and folklore of the field.
Intent	A pattern's intent defines its purpose. Typically, the intent is captured as a short statement that explains what the pattern does and the rationale and intent behind it.
Problem	Every design pattern must solve a certain type of problem faced by an engineer. In the literature of Design Patterns, problems are typically described as scenarios that depict situations in which the patterns are applicable and how to recognize those situations.
Solution	The Solution defines the pattern itself and how the pattern can be used to solve the problem just stated
Participants & collaborators	Explains the variables or entities that effect the implementation of the pattern
Consequences	This section includes an analysis of the forces at work in the pattern and documents the trade-offs that might be required when one chooses to use the pattern. Note that consequences can be good, bad, or neutral
Implementation	Usually sample code that provides an example as well as supporting text explaining pitfalls, hints, or techniques that might be useful.
Generic structure	A diagram that depicts the essential components of the pattern

All object-oriented software design patterns are defined rigorously using this format and, as noted in Section 4, we also use this format to define management design patterns.

APPLICATION OF DESIGN PATTERNS IN MANAGEMENT

Of course, despite the recent attention paid to the discipline of Design Patterns in software engineering, the theories upon which Design Patterns rely are not new. Nor are they specific to software.

The roots of the pattern movement come from a wide array of sources, stemming at least all the way back to Plato's musings on the nature of form and reality in the allegory of the Cave found in *"The Republic"*. However, most modern-day pundits would point to the works of Christopher Alexander as the watershed for Design Patterns in software engineering.

Christopher Alexander was a professor of architecture at the University of California at Berkeley during the early 1990s. As part of his own studies, Alexander published a series of 'pattern language' books that defined his paradigm for recognizing, defining and cataloguing patterns in architecture. These works today are considered the prototypes for pattern books for the software engineering world, and much of the subsequent paradigmatic work, including the rows in Table 1.1, are drawn from his initial efforts. As noted by many authors, Alexander's phrase, "a quality without a name" is often quoted as an attribute that all good software patterns should have. [Fowler, 6]

At the heart of Alexander's works was a search for the meaning of quality. As explained by Shalloway and Trott, Alexander was challenged by the question,

"Is beauty truly in the eye of the beholder, or would people agree that some things are beautiful and some things are not. What makes us know when an

architectural design is good? Is there an objective basis for such a judgment - a basis for describing our common consensus?" [S&T, 76]

Ultimately, Alexander's answer to the question was yes, there was an objective basis, beyond taste or personal aesthetics, within architectural systems that could measure beauty through a quantifiable objective basis. This method would ultimately lead him to patterns.

Of course, Alexander's exploration of patterns was couched inside a study of architecture. He began by making observations of all manner of living spaces that people have erected, from individual buildings to towns and streets to more exotic creations. Over time, he tells us, repeatable patterns emerged from the data and commonalities became clear in all forms of constructs.

As was explained by Shalloway and Trott,

"Architectural structures differ from each other, even if they are of the same type. Yet even though they differ, they can still be of high quality. Alexander understood this. He knew that structures couldn't be separated from the problem they are trying to solve. Therefore, in his quest to identify and describe the consistency of quality in design Alexander realized that he had to look at different structures that were designed to solve the same problem. Alexander found that by narrowing his focus in this way, he could discover similarities between designs that were high quality. He called these similarities patterns." [S&T, 77]

Alexander defined patterns as,

"solutions to a problem in a context. Each pattern describes a problem which occurs over and over again in our environment and then describes the core of the solution to that problem, in such a way that you can use this solution a million times over, without ever doing it the same way twice." {ALEXANDER, X]

As with architects, anthropologists have pondered the same issues over the last 40 years. One branch of cultural anthropology,

"suggests that within a culture, individuals will agree to a large extent on what is considered to be a good design, what is beautiful. Culture makes judgments on good design that transcend individual beliefs. A major branch of cultural anthropology looks for such patterns to describe the behaviors and values of a culture." [S&T, 76]

Examples include the structuralist movement pioneered by Claude Levi Strauss, in which meaning naturally forms into pairs of binary opposites whose very contrast defines both elements in sharp relief while binding them as a dyad. Levi Strauss applied these structuralist patterns broadly, throughout different cultures of the world and different elements within cultures, providing a new way of seeing culture not as amorphous and atomistic, but as an interaction of patterns and forms. [WIKI-STRAUSS]

Also in the cultural realm, Richard Dawkins invented, or discovered if you like, the concept of memes. Memes are the cultural equivalent of genes, which of course are the ultimate biological pattern, defining our very physical makeup. Dawkins asserted that cultural patterns are no less real and relevant, and that their formation and replication formed a basis both for communication and investigation. [WIKI-DAAWKINS]

Finally, patterns have been instrumental in Organizational Behavior with usage stemming at least as far back as Carl Jung whose work inspired a slew of Personality Sorter patterns including the well-renowned Meyers-Briggs Personality Types and the Keirsey Temperament Sorter [LEPLANTE, 15]

Given the groundings of design pattern theory in the liberal arts, it makes sense that the framework should be applicable to management science. In fact, today's management theory landscape appears very similar to the world of software engineering in the early 1990's.

Management models abound, but the discipline lacks a paradigm through which to organize patterns themselves into a meta-level analysis of the models. If the management science discipline can gain as much from an investigation at this meta-level as the object-oriented software discipline did, then further investigation is very much warranted.

To help the reader understand this, Table 1.2 provides a summary of some of the more common patterns used in management science discourse, but which have been refactored as Design Patterns.

It is important to restate as we conclude our discussion of Design Patterns in management science that as was the case in the object-oriented software design space, management models themselves are not at all new.

The key benefit of an investigation of Design Patterns is not necessarily any one individual implementation of a pattern (such as the BCG matrix as an implementation of the Quadrant Pattern). Instead, the benefit is to allow an investigation of the models at an abstract level to understand how, when, and where they can be applied to management strategic decision making.

A SAMPLE MANAGEMENT DESIGN PATTERN: THE MULTIVARIATE VECTOR MAP

Having spent the first half of this discussion focusing on the Design Pattern paradigm, we now provide an example of the process of identifying, describing, and using a new Design Pattern. As was said above, the reader should focus first on the process and utility rather than the details of the Design Pattern.

As is often said, patterns are not created, they are discovered. One way in which management theory patterns can differ from software patterns

Table 1.2. Management design patterns

ASPECT	PATTERN		
Name	S-Curve	Quadrant	Perceptual Map
Intent	Describes repeatable, phased changes to variables over time (life span)	Helps managers make strategic decisions based on two-variable analysis	Positions entities relative to each other based upon 2-4 variables and represents relative changes in positioning over time
Problem	Many entities within the business environment are subject to changes over time. Managers need a pattern to help them represent these time-based metamorphoses	Managers need a simple tool to help them make strategic decisions. Often, for the sake of speed and simplicity, decision criteria may be reduced to two dimensions	Managers need a way to compare multiple entities over time along 2-4 qualitative axes of differentiation in order to track more complex market movements
Solution	Uses an s-curve to represent the life cycle where points along the curve from left to right represent changes over time	Uses a 2x2 grid to generate 4 strategic choices. Then plots a position against the two axes to solve for the recommended strategy	Plots entities against two axes and size and/or color and tracks movements in positioning over time using arrows
Participants & collaborators	Time/effort x variable that is evolving (such as performance)	2 variables of the managers choice as well as 4 strategic choices	2-4 variables of comparison as well as 2 or more entities to be positioned
Consequences	• Naturalistic and emergent but predictive and quantitative view of management that provides flexible, but sometimes, high level lens into strategy	• Simplicity is both a strength and a weakness	• Strong visualization tool • Does not deal well with the unexpected • Works more effectively when comparing qualitative variables
Implementation (Examples)	Product &, industry life cycle curves, Emergence of disruptive technologies, Gartner Hype Cycle	BCG Matrix, Ansoff's Product / Market Grid, Ofman's Core Quadrants, Porter's Competitive Strategies Grid, Gartner Magic Quadrant	Competitive positioning Maps, Market Segmentation Maps
Generic Structure			

is in their generation. While, as with software patterns, management theory patterns can take existing abstractions and attempt to apply them to other contexts, the examples in Section 3 being germane, the generation of new patterns is a somewhat different matter as we are not looking necessarily at formal design decisions as with software, but more often at unstructured or semi-structured data as pertains to successful and unsuccessful strategic decisions.

Primarily, to be useful, patterns must align with actual data. There are two methods of performing this step, inductive and deductive. An inductive pattern is more or less a hypothesis put forward based on management theory and experience. Given the input variables, this pattern must then be tested against historical successes and failures to prove, disprove, and/or refine the pattern. Then, it must be applied across domains to verify its validity as a meta-tool.

For example, a manager might have a strategic theory that at a certain threshold, high margin product sales merit additional investment in sales staff. Let's say his hypothesis, based on intuition, is that for margins of 30% or higher, growing sales staff by 50% will lead to overall revenue and profit benefits even after reflecting the additional overhead costs associated with hiring. In order to test this hypothesis, the manager can formulate the theory as a pattern, say a Quadrant with the staff increase on the y axis and the margin on the x axis. He postulates that the sweet spot for growth will be in the top right, when margin is above 30% and growth is 50% or below.

The next step in this example would be to test the hypothesis against real-world data. In this example, we can suppose that the manager has access to data from multiple sales divisions over time and can plot the data points on the grid, with successful cases mapped as a dot and unsuccessful cases, those in which profit did not increase within one year, mapped as an x. The results of this exercise might prove or disprove the hypothesis, but will be valuable in either case. Once iterated a sufficient number of times for the data to cluster in a meaningful way, the pattern would be considered tested and would be useful for ongoing strategic decision making.

A deductive method, on the other hand, would first rely on observing patterns in raw data, e.g. by use of pattern recognition algorithms and/or

rigorous quantitative analysis. This method will find parallels between data clusters and successes and failures. These clusters can then be abstracted, formed into a pattern, and tested and refined as above.

An example of the deductive method could be simple or complex, but because the algorithms and statistics that would be used for the deductive approach are beyond the scope of this discussion, for our purposes we will not delve into the details of the methodology. Rather, we will hold the pattern-recognition analysis as a black box.

Thus, let's assume that a manager has a large amount of unstructured data on the situation described above, including profit margins and sales staff growth but does not have any intuition about the meaning of that data. We can assume for the sake of argument, that our "black box", a pattern recognition algorithm or a diligent quantitative analysis, could identify data clusters using various statistics. In this case, the manager iterates several rounds of deductive analysis before a pattern is recognized – when profit margins are high enough growth in sales staff leads to successful returns. Again, the final result of the process is the pattern itself, which can then be used for strategic decision making.

It is important to note that the method for generating the pattern, whether inductive or deductive, is more or less unimportant as the pattern, once discovered, enters into the feedback loop of retesting and refinement. Once the pattern holds up to the rigors of this process and can be predictive of success or failure based on relevant inputs, it can be generalized as a tool and applied to various contexts with customization. The efficacy of the approach is made clearer in the examples above that employ the magic quadrant pattern, which has been used successful time and time again and in numerous varied situations. Again, as in software patterns, management theory patterns are simply abstractions of solutions that have worked in one context and can be reused in other contexts.

As discussed above, patterns are not a novel approach to management theory, which uses many approaches to abstract rules and representations to transform data to information and again, to actionable knowledge driving a solution set. As such, by applying the techniques of software patterns to management theory, managers will benefit from the ways that Design Patterns frame problems in useful ways and allow for repurposing some of the tools and methods that have been developed in the software community to a paradigm of management theory.

The sample pattern that we have developed for this investigation is the Multivariate Vector Map (MVM). This sample pattern is purely used in this context to demonstrate the possible utility of such patterns to management theory and should be considered work-in-progress.

As with all patterns, it should be approached as a template, more or less useful in different situations, and freely challenged or modified to suit a specific management problem being addressed. See Exhibit A.

Generally, there will be two major steps in the creation of any MVM

1. Define the map topology
2. Define the vectors

The definition of vectors on the other hand, is a two-stage process. From basic math we know that vectors have two components,

1. A numeric value
2. A direction

The creation of the map topology follows iterations of inductions and deduction. Successful and unsuccessful results should tend to cluster in meaningful ways. One can either form areas on the map as solutions and then test with results,

Exhibit A.

ELEMENT	DESCRIPTION
Name	Multivariate Vector Map
Intent	The aim is to take a basic combination of input values, factor them together as vectors and apply their solution to a grid with a predetermined topology of strategic choices to help managers make the right choices given their unique business contexts
Problem	In management, there is often a wide array of quantitative data and qualitative comparisons, that defy the visualization and contextualization required to justify specific strategic choices or solutions to an existing problem. While the Quadrant pattern is fairly well-recognized, it lacks the finesse to handle truly multivariate situations and also limits the solution domain to four solutions.
Solution	This pattern seeks to frame inputs as values to add as vectors to arrive at a map point defining a strategic solution.
Participants & collaborators	The two key steps in applying this pattern are choosing relevant inputs and converting those inputs into relatively-scaled vector, then building the topography of the solution map.
Consequences	If properly applied, the multivariate vector map reduces complex analysis to a simple, easy to explain, graphical solution. However, if not properly developed and tested, the results may mislead.
Implementation	Refer to Case Study in Section 5, IT Services Solution
Generic structure	Refer to Figure 1.1.

or take data and map successes and failures to ascertain which solutions cluster together as successes in particular points on the map. Once a few iterations are performed, the topology should be refined enough to be used as a pattern for new data points to be entered and evaluate the applicable solution based on the MVM.

In the case of our analysis, the MVM was actually derived deductively from data forming the case study below, which should also help illustrate its use. It is important to note however that in this context, it is more appropriate to simplify the pattern and its use due to space constraints, as well as to more clearly show the concept without getting lost in an inordinate amount of detail.

Finally, it is important to mention that while we decided to limit the map topology to 4 solutions for the purposes of this discussion, the MVM pattern is not limited in any way to the number of solutions, nor to the use of a Quadrant-based solution map. The MVM would be just as useful, for example, using clouds, overlapping circles, or any other form of topology. With deductive analysis, quite unique and unexpected patterns will tend to arise from clusters of data.

For the numerical values, the critical factor is to scale the input values more or less evenly across all vectors. Thus, for example, if you have a dollar value for one vector and a time value for another vector, if the dollar values vary between $1 and $1000 and the time from 10 to 100 days, you'll want to make the dollar vector scale by units of $100 and the time by units of 10 days. This gives more or less comparable values so that the results don't skew too wildly on the map.

The second issue to address with vectors is their direction. Ideally, the inputs will vary in a predictable way versus each other, whether inversely, complementarily, or additively. For example, in situations where economies of scale preside, cost and volume should vary inversely, meaning that the vectors will be diametrically opposed. These relationships among vectors' directions will allow them to usefully interact in combining to indicate a position on the map. Typically, as will be demonstrated in Section 5, the direction of vectors will be governed by the map topology.

DESIGN PATTERNS BY EXAMPLE: USING MVMS TO ANALYZE DECISIONS ABOUT IT OUTSOURCING

Given the importance as well as the real and perceived complexity of strategic IT services outsourcing in S.E. Asia (both from a supplier and a buyer perspective), and because both authors had access to industry data, it was natural to focus our research on this domain. The following case study addresses a basic problem in the industry – **what form of IT Service solution is appropriate to any given particular environment?**

In today's hyper-competitive and globalized market, all businesses that use IT services in performing core functions, from banks to farms, face the problem of how best to source and supply IT services to meet business goals in a way that is tailored to their business goals, capabilities, and resources. [BRAGG, 1]

The same issue applies in reverse to IT service providers – which organizations (or market segments) are the best potential customers for specific solutions based on their IT environment? How should any one IT Service provider segment the total market? [BRAGG, 14]

By deriving and applying the MVM Design Pattern to this problem, customers and providers can have greater confidence in a best-fit solution based upon a bounded rigorous methodology.

As was mentioned in Section 4, application of the MVM begins first with an analysis of the solution topology. In the case of the IT Services market, we are quite fortunate because the map topology is fairly well defined by the industry itself. The typical decision space for IT service provision generates 4 generic solutions:

- **In-house** –An organization supports its business using its own IT environment, its own people, and its own management
- **Out Tasking** – an organization supports its business needs by employing external contract staff, possibly in addition to in-house staff, to manage and run its own IT environment.
- **Managed Services** – an organization employs an IT Service provider to staff and provide a degree of management in fulfilling IT services. That is, the organization's business is supported by its own IT environment, however, the environment is managed by the provider, using the provider's people
- **Outsourcing** – an organization employs an IT Service provider to completely accept responsibility for all, or an area, of its IT infrastructure, including management by contracted service levels. This solution in essence makes the service provider the organization's IT department, governed by business goals and overall IT strategy codified as service levels. In many cases, the organization transfers people and capital equipment to the provider.

The correct selection and application of these solutions has been the subject of much debate as IT infrastructures grow in cost, complexity, and importance and as outsourcing gains popularity as a viable option. However, in many instances, there is great uncertainty about the appropriate solution, and when an inappropriate solution is selected, many problems arise for both organizations hoping to outsource and their outsourcing service providers. As a result of the lack of a strategic decision-making tool, there has been a well-reported backlash against outsourcing and we believe some of the lack of confidence is avoidable by applying more rigorous methods to the selection process itself. [WIKI-OUT] In particular, using the MVM design pattern can result in stronger, more relevant decisions.

Whatever the case, the MVM topology is based on a set of four solutions. It is important to note here that to some degree, the map positions are arbitrary since the weightings and direction of the vectors will be based on the solutions. But as noted above, from industry best practice and from experience we can say that Managed Services and Outsourcing are more similar and should be proximate to each other. If we place them both at the top left and top right of the grid respectively, then we need to look at the other two solutions in relation to them to propose their relative position.

Since both In-House and Outsourcing solutions are managed by a team in which IT managers and staff are from a single organization, they would appropriately by nearer each other. The remaining section next to Outsourcing is bottom right, so we place In-House there. This leaves Outtasking to the bottom left. This is a simplified topography – you might well have more solutions grouped in less symmetrical ways, but for our purposes, this topography should show the MVM in action.

Figure 1.1 depicts the MVM solution grid for the IT outsourcing market.

Having defined the map topology based upon industry practice, MVM analysis next calls for a definition of the vectors of differentiation. In our study, the vectors of differentiation selected to generate our data set were chosen because 1) management felt that they represented a statistically significant subset of possible data points, 2) our target company only captured certain data points and 3) the point of the study was to demonstrate the methodology of applying the Design Pattern paradigm to management strategy rather than to generate a complete and tested pattern, and, as a result, a key goal was to simplify the set for clarity and convenience.

It is worth mentioning that we believe that in refining the MVM for this specific domain question, it would be useful to abstract the study across more companies and additional vectors of differentiation however this was beyond the scope of this study

With that said, the data points are all very relevant to the process and the actual Design Pattern did support management intuition and experience.

Thus, with no further ado, the vectors that we used for the case study are as follows:

- **Criticality** was defined as a measure of how critical the IT services provided are to business functions.
- **Specificity** is a measure of the degree of proprietariness of the infrastructure/applications.
- **Complexity** is a measure of the heterogeneity of the technical environment.
- **Scale** is a measure of staff/infrastructure size.

In regard to these four vectors, it is important to pause here to reference back to Section 4. As was mentioned there, all vectors have 1) a value and 2) a direction. Thus, the next step in the implementation of the MVM pattern is to define the vector values. But recall that because vectors must be measured in the same scale, we must also harmonize the scales across all four vectors. That is, if we say that the set of companies examined has a range of scale (staff and/or systems) from 100 to 1000, a complexity from 2 to 13, a specificity from 0 to 8, and finally criticality from USD50K/week to USD900K/week; then we align the unit values to approximate a range of 1-10, we can arrive at the values given above.

Scaling was done as follows:

- **Criticality** was defined as a measure of how critical the IT services provided are to business functions. The vector unit values are based on the financial impact in hundreds of thousands of USD per week to service interruption to 1.
- **Specificity** was defined as a measure of how bespoke the environment is, measured by the percentage of highly modified platforms and critical applications. Vector unit values were taken on a 10% to 1 basis.
- **Complexity** was defined as a measure of the number of platforms employed, by OS and critical application. Vector unit values were taken on a one to one basis.

Figure 1.1. MVM grid for the IT outsourcing market

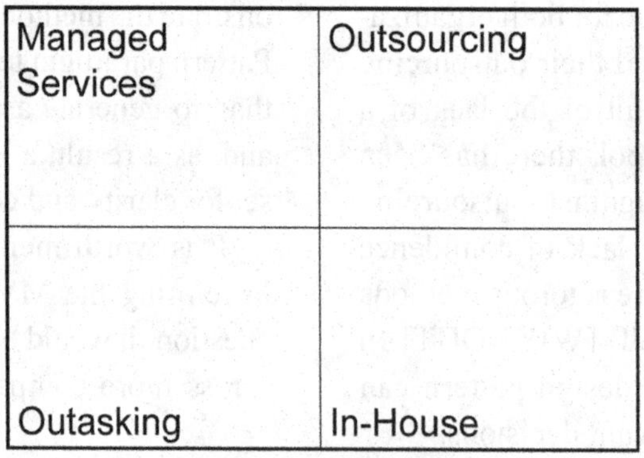

Managed Services	Outsourcing
Outasking	In-House

- **Scale** was measured in terms of the number of staff and the number of critical systems (servers, desktops, and software applications) available in the infrastructure. Unit values were taken in groups of 100 (100 staff or 100 critical systems equal 1 vector unit).

Thus, for example, consider one of the following study companies:

Company X is a pharmaceutical company with manufacturing facilities in Singapore.

Other than the ERP systems supporting the production lines, the majority of the IT infrastructure is fairly non-critical, including mostly admin, logistics, and finance support systems. However, because of the costs associated with manufacturing bottlenecks, a profitability analysis yields a cost of US$400,000 per week of downtime

The scale of the operations is also fairly small including about 50 IT staff supporting about 150 systems.

In addition, while the company does employ a fairly standardized Standard Operating Environment (SOE), for historical reasons there are 4 separate operating environments including Windows XP, AS400, UNIX, and LINUX.

Finally, the infrastructure is highly specific. With the exception of the ERP environment, most of the environment is standard office suites, applications .

Following our rules defined above, the company was given the following scores:

Criticality – 4
Scale – 2
Complexity – 4
Specificity – 5

As was mentioned in Section 4, the next step in the MVM design pattern is to assign directionality to each vector.

To some degree, the directionality was determined inductively based first upon management

experience and then tested against the data set in order to refine it and validate it. The following section records the decision criteria that went in to defining vector directions.

- **Criticality** reflects the business impact and means that cost is less decisive (because downtime is so expensive). As a result, the specialist expertise and flexibility of an external provider can be helpful to avoid outages. On the other hand, a highly developed in-house staff is also a viable option. Ultimately, the fact that the vector is being pulled two ways yields a sloped direction. Although simplistic, for the purposes of our analysis, we chose to define the slope at a 45 degree angle upward to the right which reflected that outsourcing is strongly preferred over Out-tasking, but Managed Services and In-House solutions both receive partial inclinations.

- **Specificity** This vector points in the exact opposite direction from Scale. In fact any vector which dis-incentivizes an outsourcing solution would point downward. In the group of vectors identified Specificity would be in this category as a highly proprietary environment, developed by in-house staff, would be exceedingly difficult for an external service provider to manage and would usually only be an Outsourcing candidate if the scale was large enough to be overwhelming for a customer organization to manage on its own.

- **Complexity** - Heterogeneous environments are more difficult to manage and tend to work better if the team is monolithic, which is the case in both outsourced and in-house solutions where management and staff are all from the same organization so better coordination of efforts can be achieved. Therefore, the direction for this vector is horizontal to the right.

- **Scale** is slightly more straight-forward. Large-scale environments tend to be good candidates for outsourcing as they require a large number of staff and would represent a concomitantly large management distraction, especially for a non-IT company. Therefore, in the study we assigned to the scale vector an upwards direction, or 90 degrees from a horizontal axis, and used this as a reference direction for vectors that tend to lead to an outsourcing solution.

Figure 1.2 represents the directionality visually

With the 1) map topology, 2) vector scaled values and 3) vector directionality, we are ready to apply the MVM Design Pattern to actual decisions.

While the study included only 10 customers of our single IT Outsourcing vendor, for the purposes of demonstration we provide the analysis of 4, as they represent a fairly diverse and interesting set of solutions that test the efficacy of the pattern well. It is worth noting that details have been altered to protect the anonymity of the companies involved.

Company 1

Criticality – 2
Specificity – 10
Complexity – 10
Scale – 2

Figure 1.3 provides a graphical representation of the solution grid for Company 1.

Company 1 is a high-end technology research facility. Like the Pharmaceutical example in Section 4, while the systems are important to the ongoing profitability of the business, downtime is not particularly expensive. Specifically, Criticality was measured at 2.

On the other hand, Specificity and Complexity reached their maximum values. The infrastructure heterogeneity is driven by the need to develop products on a variety of platforms, but this also means the staff are highly technically skilled. Because this is a development environment, by definition all the applications are completely proprietary and developed in-house.

Finally, the scale of operations is fairly low as R&D tends to require smaller infrastructures. This was supported by the actual data.

Ultimately, one can see from the MVM that for this company, in-house staffing should be the preferred solution and this company would not be a good candidate for the sales representative of an IT Services vendor.

This makes sense intuitively as it is a small environment, highly modified, with a highly complex but less mission critical set of systems as outages have minimal impact as long as data is backed up since none of the applications are live. A small team can manage this environment, but they must be specialized.

Figure 1.2. Vector directionality

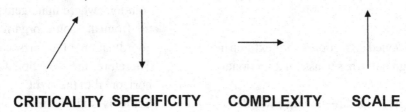

CRITICALITY SPECIFICITY   COMPLEXITY   SCALE

Figure 1.3. MVM for Company 1

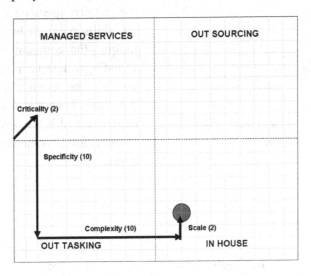

Company 2

Criticality – 10
Specificity – 10
Complexity – 10
Scale – 10

Figure 1.4 provides a graphical representation of the map solution for Company 2.

This situation is quite different from Company 1. This company is a large bank with numerous servers on various platforms running highly proprietary applications. Needless to say, the infrastructure is as mission critical as exists, with millions of dollars of transactions running through the systems. While the backup and disaster recovery regimes mitigate the frequency and impact of downtime, any outage has a high monetary impact. This company can benefit from the economies of scale a service provider can provide in outsourcing, with the benefits including backfill, remote support, and increased general background knowledge, as well as a pool of skilled resources.

Company 3

Criticality – 1
Specificity – 1
Complexity – 1
Scale – 10

Figure 1.5 provides a graphical representation of the map solution for Company 3.

Company 3 runs a call center, with replicated workstations and quite a few racks of identical network equipment. This environment is very large, but it is very generic given the scale, and is virtualized using blade servers and standard operating environments.

In this case, a Managed Service solution can provide an external team to oversee the infrastructure to mitigate the impact of a high number of headcount being taken on by the customer, but since the infrastructure is simple and relatively non-critical, the organization can manage the external team relatively easily.

Company 4

Criticality – 1
Specificity – 5
Complexity – 1
Scale – 1

Figure 1.6 provides a graphical representation of the map solution for Company 4.

Company 4 is a small game-design workshop, with a fairly specialized infrastructure. Because the skills required to manage the systems are unique, the company relies on finding correspondingly unique resources. If the company employs the resource directly, the management will likely have little knowledge of the platform expertise and if the resource must be replaced, the recruiting overhead can be high in finding the appropriate staff.

Figure 1.4. MVM for Company 2

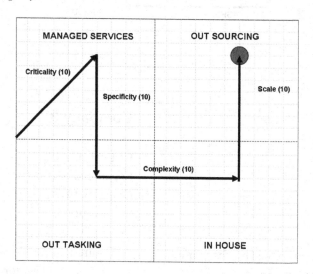

Figure 1.5 MVM for Company 3

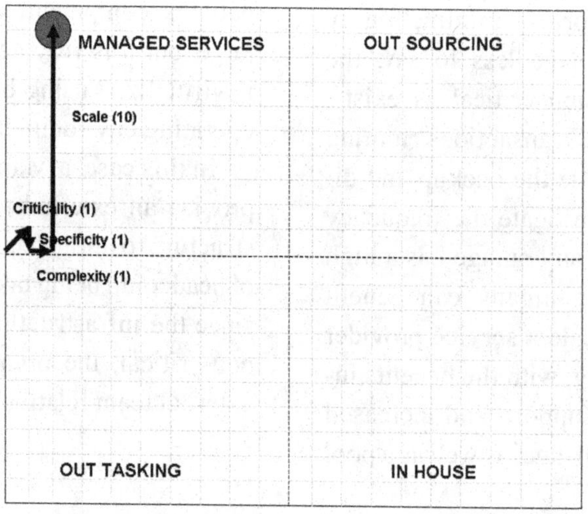

Using a service provider does not interfere with the management process since in this case it is relatively hands off, and the task of finding and/or replacing the specialized skills is handed off to an outside company that is more experienced in recruiting for such roles., this scale might not even require full-time employees, so contracting staff from a third party is much more cost effective.

CONCLUSION

It is finally worth mentioning that these are relatively extreme cases, and also simplified to illustrate the utility of the pattern, but conceptually the strategic decisions driven by the use of the MVM should be well-supported by relevant market data. Use of the model should increase the confidence level both of the organization and the supplier that their IT service partnership is an appropriate, sustainable, and supportable one.

These decisions are often made by management based on intuition and market trends. Intuition is as good or bad as the experience and knowledge of the manager making the decision, so this tool can aid managers, good and not so good, by allowing them to approach the problem at the correct level of abstraction and relevance. A CIO should not be looking at an asset list and employee roster, with numerous other detailed data points, but needs to focus on the real strategic bird's eye view of the situation when making such a critical decision.

Market trends can be useful, but only if interpreted properly, which is usually more beneficial in hindsight. Hype and bust curves are obviously misleading, and strategic market trends as a guide implicitly rely on the market performing a useful amount of analysis, that if it takes place at all is seldom transparent to outside organizations. Market data is far more useful when analyzed in context, using proven methods and tools. In the case of outsourcing, market trends have varied wildly, with success of implementations varying almost as much. In this environment, CIO surveys and the like become less reliable.

Figure 1.6. MVM for Company 4

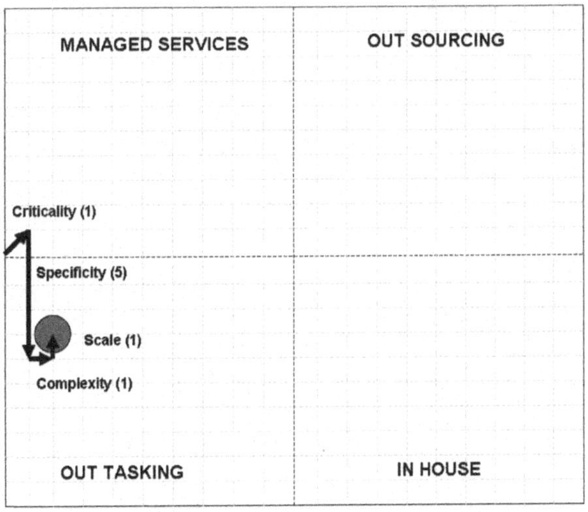

ADDITIONAL POSSIBLE CASE STUDY

Another area of great debate and consternation is the pricing of products and services. The MVM pattern could potentially be applied successfully to this problem as well.

For example, one could use the inputs of market size, market share, innovation, and value and create a map topology divided into market segments such as market leader on the high end, to mainstream, budget, or disruptor. Of course, this would take as much analysis and testing to derive as any other pattern, but we put it forward here to show other potential areas the pattern could address.

Ultimately, individual MVMs can be more or less useful, but the power lies in the application of the Design Pattern Paradigm to management theory in order to allow a more formalized method for developing and communicating strategic analysis in the management field.

REFERENCES

Alexander, C., & Ishikawa, S. (1977). *A Pattern Language*. New York: Oxford University Press.

Bragg, S. M. (2006). *Outsourcing*. Hoboken, NJ: John Wiley and Sons.

Fowler, M. (1997). *Analysis Patterns: Reusable Object Models*. Indianapolis, IN: Addison-Wesley.

Gamma, E., Helm, R., Johnson, R., & Vlissides, J. (2000). Design Patterns: *Elements of Reusable Object-Oriented Software (Paperback)*. Boston, MA: Addison-Wesley.

http://en.wikipedia.org/wiki/Claude_Levi-Strauss

http://en.wikipedia.org/wiki/Outsourcing

http://en.wikipedia.org/wiki/The_Selfish_Gene

Laplante, P. A., & Neill, C. J. (2006). *Antipatterns: Identification, Refactoring, and Management*. Boca Raton, FL: Auerbach Publications.

Shalloway, A., & Trott, J. R. (2005). *Design Patterns Explained: A New Perspective on Object-Oriented Design*. Boston, MA: Addison-Wesley.

Section V
Further Readings

Chapter XVII
The Interplay of Strategic Management and Information Technology

Zaiyong Tang
Louisiana Tech University, USA

Bruce Walters
Louisiana Tech University, USA

ABSTRACT

The authors trace historical developments in the fields of information technology (IT) and strategic management. IT's evolution from the mainframe era to the Internet era has been accompanied by a shift in the strategic emphasis of IT. In the early days, IT's contribution to the organization was largely information provision, monitoring and control. Current research at the intersection of IT and strategic management increasingly highlights the impact of IT in terms of informing strategic decisions and enabling information flow vis-à-vis all manner of organizational processes. We believe these fields are ripe for research focusing on their complementary impact on organizational performance.

INTRODUCTION

We live in an age in which the value of information and knowledge has far surpassed that of physical goods. Information resources have become a key differentiator of successful businesses. Information technology (IT) and information systems (IS) are now integrated in almost every aspect of business, from planning to analysis and design, operations management and strategic decision making. Even for those businesses not in information industries, information plays a vital role in supporting their business functions, from routine operations to strategizing. John

Naisbitt (1982) theorized that information would be the driving force for organizations. Companies that manage information well are more likely to maintain a competitive advantage against their peers. Because information has become a major force in driving business activities, Evans and Wurster (2000) proclaimed that every business is in the information business.

IT and IS have experienced dramatic changes in the last few decades. Their major role in business has shifted from tools to support "back-office" operations to an integrated part of business strategies and the maintenance of core competencies. Strategic management, as the process of business strategy formulation and strategy implementation, is concerned with establishing goals and directions, and developing and carrying out plans to achieve those goals. As organizations evolve, so do their strategies and strategic management practices. In recent years, IT has become increasingly important in strategic management. IT and IT-enabled systems are now indispensable in supporting business strategies. In this chapter, we examine the evolution of information technology and strategic management, and their interplay in the last 50 years. We start with a review of major theories and development in both strategic management and IT, and then explore how IT has become an enabler for strategic management. We also discuss research issues in IT-enabled strategic management, and suggest future directions in this cross-disciplinary research field.

STRATEGIC MANAGEMENT

Strategic management is concerned with managerial decisions and actions that determine the long-term prosperity of the organization. An organization must have a clear strategy and its strategy must be carefully developed and implemented to match its resources and environment in the pursuit of its organizational goals. Two meanings behind the often-used term "strategy," as Lowell Steele

(1989) pointed out, are the ideational content of strategy and the process of formulating strategy. The former refers to the array of options that one uses to compete and survive, and the latter refers to the planning that leads to the construction of the strategic plan. Thus, IT-enabled strategic management must address the role IT plays in strategy content options and priorities, strategy formulation processes and strategy implementation processes. Strategic management focuses on identifying the direction of an organization, and designing and instituting major changes needed to gear the organization towards moving in the established direction.

Early research in strategic management started in the 1950s, with leading researchers such as Peter Drucker, Alfred Chandler and Philip Selznick. Drucker (1954) pioneered the theory of management by objectives (MBO). He is also one of the first to recognize the dramatic changes IT brought to management. He predicted in the 1960s the rise of knowledge workers in the information age (Drucker, 1968). Alfred Chandler (1962) recognized the importance of a corporate-level strategy that gives a business its structure and direction; as he put it, "structure follows strategy." Philip Selznick (1957) established the ground work of matching a company's internal attributes with external factors.

In the 1970s, theories of strategic management primarily focused on growth, market share and portfolio analysis. A long-term study aimed at understanding the Profit Impact of Marketing Strategies (PIMS) was carried out from the 1960s to the 1970s. The study concluded that a company's rate of profit is positively correlated with its market share. This is a result of economies of scale (Buzzell & Gale, 1987). As companies pursued larger market share, a number of growth strategies—such as horizontal integration, vertical integration, diversification, franchises, mergers and acquisitions, and joint ventures—were developed. As will be discussed later, those strategies are even more widely used today, with the facilitation of information and networking technologies.

Another shifting of strategic focus occurring in the 1970s was the move from sales orientation towards customer orientation. Researchers such as Theodore Levitt (1983) argued that businesses should start with the customer proposition. The right approach is to find out how to create value for customers and then make the products and services that meet the needs of the customers, rather than trying to sell to customers once the products are created.

In the 1980s, strategic management theories were largely geared towards gaining competitive advantages. Michael Porter (1980, 1987) proposed a number of very influential strategic analysis models, such as the five-forces model of competition, the value chain and generic competitive strategies. Porter suggested that businesses need to choose either a strategy of cost leadership (with lowest cost), product differentiation or market focus. Research has demonstrated that both market share leaders and niche market players may obtain high financial returns while most companies without a coherent strategy did not (e.g., Levinson, 1984). Adopting one of Porter's generic strategies helps a company to avoid the so-called "stuck-in-the-middle" problem. Many of Porter's ideas have been implemented in modern corporate strategic management frameworks. Strategic IS applications, such as supply chain management, are based on efficient value chain management and forming strategic alliances to maintain competitive advantages.

Lester (1989) suggested that companies sustain their strategic positions in the market by following seven best practices: continuously improving products and services, breaking down barriers between functional areas, flattening organizational hierarchies, strengthening relationships with customers and suppliers, effectively using technology, having a global orientation and enhancing human resource quality. Various information technologies have been used to support those best practices.

Hamel and Prahalad (1990) popularized the idea of core competencies. They argued that companies should devote their resources to a few things that they can do better than the competition, and relegate non-core business operations to business partners. This laid the foundation for outsourcing, which has gained in popularity since the late 1990s. The wide spread of information and network technologies has reduced the time and geographic barriers of outsourcing business functions to other companies.

Reengineering, also known as business process redesign, calls for fundamental changes in the way business is carried out. Traditional companies are organized around functional business areas, which often leads to limited communication and cooperation, as well as redundancy due to functional overlap. Hammer and Champy's book, *Reengineering the Corporation,* makes a convincing case for restructuring business resources around whole business processes rather than functional tasks (Hammer & Champy, 1993). IT and IS have become both an impetus and a facilitator for reengineering projects.

In the 1990s, researchers increasingly recognized the importance of customer relationship management (e.g., Gronroos, 1994; Sewell & Brown, 1990). Computer and network technologies have played a key role in making customer relationship management efficient and effective. Along the line of improving value to the customers, mass customization provides competitive advantages (Pine & Gilmore, 1997). Reaching and custom-serving individual customers are only feasible with the proliferation of information and communication technologies.

Peter Senge (1990), in his book, *The Fifth Discipline,* popularized the concept of the learning organization. The rationale in creating a learning organization is that the business environment has become more dynamic and complex. Companies must have the ability to learn continuously and adapt to the changing environment. People in a learning organization need to continuously expand their capacity to become more productive or to maintain their level of competency.

The Greek philosopher Heraclitus said nothing is constant but change. Indeed, Toffler (1970) has recognized that not only is Heraclitus still right, but the rate of change is accelerating. Hamel (2000) believes that all strategies decay over time; thus, organizations need to reexamine their strategies and strategic management practices. Moncrieff (1999) argues that strategic management is a dynamic process. Strategy is partially deliberate and partially unplanned. Recently, many researchers have recognized that organizations are complex adaptive systems in which multiple agents set their own goals, share information, collaborate and interact with one another (Axelrod & Cohen, 1999; Dudik, 2000; Landsbergen, 2005). Two foreseeable trends are: 1) more IT-enabled interactions among human agents in the complex adaptive systems, and 2) agent activities moving from purely human interaction to interactions involving artificial intelligent agents.

THE EVOLUTION OF IT

IT can be defined as technology applied to the creation, management and use of information. Any technology that deals with information gathering, processing, storing and dissemination is considered IT. Earlier examples of IT include pigeon carriers and sending messages by fire and smoke. By definition, IT does not have to be computer-based. However, practically speaking, today's IT is largely built on computer hardware and software applications. Thus, in the following, while we review IT development in the past, we focus on computing-related technologies.

An early and relatively sophisticated computing device was the abacus, invented around 500 B.C. in Egypt. Blaise Pascal invented the first mechanical calculating machine for adding and subtracting in 1642. A milestone in computing

machine development was Charles Babbage's difference machine that could perform trigonometric and logarithmic operations. The first electronic computer, ENIAC (electronic numerical integrator and calculator), was developed in 1946. Commercially available computers began in the early 1950s, with IBM as the leading vendor.

One of the milestones in the computer industry was the arrival of the IBM System/360 in 1964. The System/360 was a family of computers running the same operating systems and using the same peripherals. Thus, companies could start with a less capable model and expand the capacity with more powerful models without the need to replace system software and peripheral components. Easy adoption through inter-changeability of hardware and software prompted significant growth of computer system usage in business in the 1960s and 1970s (with later models, such as the System/370). IBM first started unbundling software from hardware by selling software separate from its computer in 1969. That set the stage for the launch of an independent software industry. The fast growth of packaged software applications, in turn, prompted the growth of computer hardware.

The next major event in the computer industry was the birth of personal computers (PCs) in the mid-1970s. Intel introduced the first semiconductor microchip (the Intel 4004) in 1971. However, PCs were not widespread until the early 1980s, when IBM launched its standardized PC (known as the IBM PC). The IBM PC became "Machine of the Year," taking the place of traditional "Man of the Year" on the cover of *Time Magazine* in 1983. Other computer vendors jumped on the IBM PC bandwagon by producing IBM-compatible PCs. During the decade of the 1980s, the number of PCs grew more than 100 fold to more than 100 million (Gantz, 2004).

The continued growth of the PC industry is driven by the well-known Moore's Law, which stipulates that the number of transistors per silicon chip doubles roughly every 18 months; hence, the corresponding performance of the central processing unit—the brain of microcomputers. Gordon Moore, co-founder of Intel Corp., made that stipulation in 1965. Amazingly, Moore's Law has described the state of affairs for the last four decades. The power of exponential growth resulted in dramatic cost and performance improvement of computer hardware. Once scarce and expensive, computer systems are now abundant and inexpensive because of the availability of desktop computer, laptop computers, and even handheld computing devices. Low-cost computing changed organizational computing architecture from centralized computing to distributed computing systems in the 1980s.

In the history of IT, the 1990s is perhaps best known as the decade of Internet booming. The Internet started as the U.S. Department of Defense's ARPAnet, with the aim of creating a distributed computer network that can withstand a nuclear attack. In the 1970s and 1980s, the Internet was used mainly by academics and scientists, and was not accessible largely to the general public because its use, although open, required substantial learning of arcane application protocols. Two major events led to the explosive growth of the Internet. The first was the development of the World Wide Web (WWW or the Web) by Tim Berners-Lee, a researcher at the CERN Institute in Switzerland in 1990, and the second is the arrival of (largely free) graphic Web browsers. The Web made it possible to link information resources all over the world on the Internet. Users could retrieve information without knowing the whereabouts of the information by simply following the hyperlinks (or links). However, initial access to the WWW was text-based; hence, its richness in content and usability were limited. The WWW took off after 1993 when the first graphic Web browser, Mosaic, was released by the National Center for Supercomputing Applications (NCSA) at the University of Illinois at Urbana Champaign. The ensuing Internet growth was unprecedented in the history of technology development. Internet users grew from a few thousand to more than 300 million during the 1990s. As of June 2005, there were more than 938 million Internet users worldwide (www.internetworldstats.com/stats.htm).

The Internet provides a low-cost way of connecting virtually everyone in modern society to an open and shared common network. The wide accessibility of the Internet has created numerous opportunities for businesses and brought fundamental changes to the way businesses operate. The value of a network increases with the square of the number of users connected to the network. This is known as Metcalfe's law, attributed to Robert Metcalfe, one of the inventors of the widely used Ethernet standard and founder of 3Com Corporation (Applegate, Austin, & McFarlan, 2003). The Internet has changed the landscape of competition by lowering the barriers for small- and medium-size companies to reach markets that were traditionally accessible only to large corporations.

Since the late 1990s, mobile computing based on wireless network technologies has gained much momentum. Intelligent appliances, such as cellular phones, personal digital assistants and other handheld computing devices, are becoming a significant part of the IS infrastructure. IDC predicts that the number of mobile devices connected to the Internet will surpass that of Internet-connected computers by the end of 2006. The total number of networked devices may approach 6 billion by 2012 (Gantz, 2004). Ubiquitous computing that allows "anytime, anyplace" access to information resources will bring dramatic changes to the business environment.

The Internet has already created fundamental changes in the business world. The WWW brought the first revolution in our networked society. Many believe that the next major development of the Web may be network intelligence through Web services. The non-profit Internet governing organization W3C defines Web services as the programmatic interfaces for application to application communication on the Web. Web services create a promising infrastructure to support loosely coupled, distributed and heterogeneous applications on the Internet (Nagarajan, Lam, & Su, 2004). Applications based on Web services can be described, published, located and invoked over the Internet to create new products and services based on open Internet protocols such as HTTP, XML and Simple Object Access Protocol (SOAP). The significance of Web services is that system-to-system communications can be automated; hence, building business alliances and virtual organizations becomes much easier than with current Internet technology.

IT AS AN ENABLER FOR STRATEGIC MANAGEMENT

Although strategic management and IS developed in parallel over the last 50 years, the two fields have also had substantial impact on each other. The interaction and co-evolution of the two fields have experienced significant increase in recent years. In this section, we will examine such interaction and co-evolution through the motivations and development of computer-based IS used in businesses.

The short history of computer IT development can be divided into three eras: the mainframe era from the 1950s to the 1970s, the microcomputer era from the 1980s to the early 1990s, and the Internet era from the 1990s to the present. The mainframe era is characterized by centralized computing, where all computing needs were serviced by powerful computers at the computer center. The proliferation of microcomputers led to decentralized computing. Computing resources become readily accessible to more users. This is a period that witnessed improved user performance and decision-making quality. When computer networks became pervasive in the Internet era, decentralized computing evolved to distributed computing, where computing resources are located in multiple sites, as in decentralized

systems, but all of the computing resources are connected through computer networks. People in the Internet era are far more empowered than in previous eras, because they have access to not only technology tools as before, but also to shared knowledge from others. Table 1 summarizes the IS and their motivations during those three IT evolution eras. Although IS are separately listed in the three eras, we must point out that the lists are not mutually exclusive. In particular, in the Internet era, businesses are still heavily dependent on systems conceptualized and developed in earlier eras, such as TPS, MIS and DSS.

Clearly, the role of business IS has evolved and expanded over the last 5 decades. Early systems in the 1950s and 1960s were used primarily for dealing with business transactions with associated data collection, processing and storage. Management information systems (MIS) were developed in the 1960s to provide information for managerial support. Typical MIS are report based, with little or no decision-making support capabilities. Decision support systems (DSS) first appeared in the 1970s. They offer various analytical tools, models and flexible user interface for decision support at solving difficult problems, such as planning, forecasting and scheduling. Executive support systems (ESS) are specialized DSS designed to support top-level management in strategic decision making (O'Brien, 2005).

The 1990s saw an increased emphasis on Strategic Information Systems as a result of the changing competitive environment. Competitive advantage became a hot strategic management topic. IT and IS were developed to support business strategic initiatives. The commercialization of the Internet in the mid 1990s created an explosive growth of the Internet and Internet-based business applications. Using the Internet standards, corporations are converting their old incompatible internal networks to Intranets. Also based on Internet standards, Extranets are built to link companies with their customers, suppliers and other business partners (Chen, 2005).

Table 1. IT evolution and strategic management relevance

	Mainframe Era 1950s to 1970s	Microcomputer Era 1980s to early 1990s	Internet Era 1990s to present
Dominant technology	Mainframes, stand-alone applications, centralized databases	Microcomputers, workstations, stand-alone and client-server applications	Networked microcomputers, client-server applications, Internet technology, Web browser, hypertext, and hypermedia
Information systems	Transaction processing systems (TPS), management information systems (MIS), Limited decision support system (DSS)	Comprehensive decision support system (DSS), executive support systems (ESS), enterprise resource planning (ERP) business intelligence (BI), human resource management (HRM), expert systems (ES)	Supply chain management (SCM), customer relationship management (CRM), knowledge management (KM), strategic information systems (SIS), multi-agent systems (MAS), mobile information systems
IS motivation	Efficiency	Effectiveness	Business value
Strategic management relevance	Provide information for monitoring and control of operations	Provide information and decision support for problem solving	Support strategic initiatives to transform organizations and markets

Adopted from Applegate, Austin, and McFarlan (2003)

What kind of information systems would be considered strategic information systems? Although strategic support systems are almost exclusively used for top executives dealing with strategic problems, a strategic information system can be any type of IS that plays a key role in supporting business strategies. McFarlan's strategic grid defines four categories of IT impact: Support, Factory, Turnaround and Strategic (Applegate, Austin & McFarlan, 2003). When the IT has significant impact on business core strategy, core operations or both, the corresponding IS are considered strategic information systems. Thus, various information systems may be dealt with in strategic management.

Many researchers have written on the strategic importance of information and knowledge in the networked economy. Nasbitt (1982) observed that the world was transforming from an industrial to an information society, and IT would dominate the economic growth of developed nations. Quinn (1992) argued how knowledge- and service-based systems are revolutionizing the economy. Shapiro and Varian (1999) discussed information-based products and services, and how to use information to maximize economic gain.

IT and IS have made it possible to access vast amounts of information easily and quickly. Systems such as enterprise resource planning (ERP) give managers the ability to monitor the operation of the entire organization in real time. Executive information portals have allowed senior managers to take a much more comprehensive view of strategic management than ever before. Tools such as the balanced scorecard (Kaplan & Norton, 1992) give a holistic view of the business performance by integrating factors in multiple business functions.

In the last few years, business process management (BPM) software has been designed with the intent of closing gaps in existing ERP deployments. As companies are increasingly faced with problems associated with incompatible functional systems from different vendors, enterprise application integration (EAI) has become an important research. BPM systems have been deployed to lower the cost and complexity of application and data integration. Another recent development is Web services enabled by standards-based protocols (such as XML, SOAP, UDDI and WSDL). The wide acceptance of Internet protocols also led to the emergence of service-oriented architectures (SOA). SOA focus on building robust and flexible systems that provide services as they are requested in a dynamic business process environment. Instead of being programmed in advance, services are generated, brokered and delivered on the fly. Figure 1 presents a timeline that lists major developments in strategic management and IT/IS. Although the two fields have progressed in their separate paths, there are many instances where their paths crossed. As shown in Table 1 and the discussion following it, the motivation of IS has shifted from efficiency to effectiveness, and in the Internet era, to value creation. On one hand, IT is playing a more active and important role in strategic management. On the other hand, strategic management concerns have influenced the development of IS. In many cases, the theories and principles of strategic management led the way of IS development. IT and IS, in turn, have made it more feasible for those theories and principles to be practiced in businesses.

IT ALIGNMENT WITH BUSINESS STRATEGIES

IT in business has evolved and become increasingly integrated with business organizations. Strategic management now encompasses corporate strategy, functional business strategy, information strategy, and IT strategy, as shown in Figure 2. For most businesses, their strategies form a multi-level hierarchy. At the very top is corporate strategy, which sets the direction for corporate-level decision making. Below corporate strategy, there are functional strategies, business

unit strategies and operational strategies. Building a comprehensive strategic IT plan that aligns with the business strategy is essential to ensuring the success of the organization.

Numerous researchers have indicated that IT alignment with business strategy is vital to achieve expected results. Sabherwal and Chan (2001) studied the benefit of alignment between business and IS strategies, and concluded that the alignment can improve business performance. They also developed a framework that can be used to analyze the level of alignment between business and IS strategy. Symons (2005) claimed that IT alignment has been one of the top three issues confronting IT and business executives for more than 20 years. Symons reported that a recent poll of CIOs and business executives revealed that the alignment of IT and business goals is their no. 1 or 2 priority. Measuring the degree of IT alignment has been difficult for many businesses. Borrowing the idea from the Capacity Maturity Model (CMM) of the Software Engineering Institute, Symons proposed a strategy alignment maturity model with five distinct levels:

- At the base level, called Nonexistent, there is IT alignment with business strategy. IT plays only a supportive role of operations.
- At the Ad hoc level, the need for IT alignment is recognized, but there is a lack of systematic approach. IT supports business goals on a case-by-case basis. There is no attempt to measure the success of IT alignment.
- At the Repeatable level, IT alignment is considered at the enterprise level. However, it is only implemented in some business units. Limited measures of IT alignment exist.
- At the Defined process level, IT alignment is systematically implemented throughout the enterprise, with appropriate policies and procedures to monitor and measure the benefits of the IT alignment.

Figure 1. Chronology of strategic management and IT development

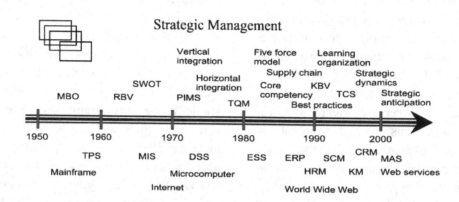

Obviously, IT alignment is one of the key issues in strategic management. However, IT alignment is more than simply formulating IT strategy to fit the business strategy. Business strategy is future oriented and subject to external forces and environmental uncertainty. IT alignment should build adaptability into IT strategy. Furthermore, for some technology companies, IT may be the driver of corporate strategy (Clarke, 2001).

Strategic management is concerned with the long-term survival and prosperity of organizations. As the environment changes, organizations must also adapt to maintain their viability. Organizations evolve, and so do strategies. Thus, strategic management is also a learning process. There are four basic learning behaviors in strategy formulation; namely, natural selection, imitation, reinforcement and best reply (Young, 1998). In each of the four learning processes, IT and IS are becoming indispensable.

Natural selection stipulates that organizations that use high-payoff strategies have competitive advantages over those using low-payoff strategies. As a result, high-payoff strategies have a better chance to be continued by surviving organizations. Determining the payoff of strategies, thus, is very important in this kind of strategic learning behavior.

Imitation describes how organizations mimic the practices of successful peers in their industry. This is the cause of herding behavior in which the outcome is not clear, but organizations jump on the bandwagon, simply following what many of their peers are doing. A classic example is the dot.com boom during the late 1990s.

Reinforcement is concerned with how organizations monitor their own behaviors and favor the strategies that resulted in high payoffs in the past. In contrast to *natural selection, reinforcement* learning is based on one's own experience rather than others' experience.

Best reply is the behavior wherein organizations formulate their strategies based on what

- At the Optimized level, IT strategy is seamlessly aligned with business strategy at all managerial levels and in all business units. IT alignment processes have been extended to external best practices with other organizations. Measures of IT alignment and feedback mechanisms exist to ensure that IT alignment stays at this level.

Figure 2. Alignment of information technology with strategies

Adopted from Boddy, Boonstra, and Kennedy (2005).

they expect their competitors will do. Many of the popular competitive strategies, such as low-cost leadership and differentiation, fall into this category.

RESEARCH ISSUES IN IT-ENABLED STRATEGIC MANAGEMENT

There is no doubt that the application of IT and strategic information systems has aided businesses in gaining competitive advantages. However, the extent to which IT/IS helps businesses to succeed varies, as many other factors also contribute to the long-term performance. Kettinger and colleagues (1994) studied a large number of cases of strategic information systems and found that 40% of the companies had above-average performance in the short to intermediate term, while only 20% of the companies sustained long-term (10 years or more) competitive advantages. Thus, for many of those companies, their strategic investment in IT and IS did not achieve their long-term goals.

In 2003, *Harvard Business Review* published a controversial article titled "IT Doesn't Matter."

The author of the article, Nicolas Carr, contends that since IT cost has dropped precipitously in recent years, and now IT is widely accessible to businesses large and small, IT no longer provides a competitive advantage to businesses. Thus, companies should stop investing heavily in advanced IT products and services. Rather, they should spend the resources on reducing operational risks associate with IT (Carr, 2003). Although many scholars and industrial leaders, such as Warren McFalan, Richard Nolan, Paul Strassmann, John Brown, John Hagel and Vladimir Zwass (see Stewart, 2003), have debated Carr's view, and have shown evidence of the strategic importance of IT, it is generally agreed that IT alone is not enough to sustain strategic advantages. Although IT plays an important role, it is only one facet of the comprehensive framework of strategic management. As Clemons and Row (1991) argued, IT's value is not so much in its intrinsic properties, but in how it can be effectively deployed to support business strategies. Although numerous previous researchers have studied IT's importance and its strategic value (e.g., Clarke, 2001; Porter & Miller, 1985), there is a lack of strategic research on integrating IT into strategic management.

In recent years, IT-enabled business changes have become more frequent and more crucial. Prahalad and Krishnan (2002) have surveyed business executives in large companies and found that almost invariably, the executives indicated that the quality of their IT infrastructure fell short of their need and desire for strategic change. In such a case, (existing) IT became an impediment to innovations and other strategic initiatives. Many companies have started large IT projects, such as ERP, CRM and SCM projects, in their effort to revamp their business processes. However, as Prahalad and Krishnan (2002) pointed out, packaged enterprise systems are designed for stability in processes, not ability to evolve. One of the key issues in IT-enabled strategic management is creating an IT infrastructure that offers speed for change and flexibility needed for strategic management.

Understanding how businesses create and sustain competitive value from their investments in IT has been a challenge for strategic management researchers as well as IS researchers. A more comprehensive way of conceptualizing the interplay of IT and strategic management is needed. As more companies are transforming into e-businesses, obviously, information and communication technologies are becoming an integrated part of the organization. However, what is the role of IT in strategic management when computing and network become pervasive and IT becomes invisible? How will emerging IT, such as grid computing, Web services and SOA, change strategic dynamics of organizations? Those questions need to be addressed by both IS and strategic management researchers.

Clearly, the intersection of IT and strategy is ripe for research. Opportunities abound with regard to strategy making and strategy implementation enabled by IT. Research questions falling within the scope of interest could cover a wide range of issues, from various product/market approaches to strategic decision processes to diversification management to corporate governance, to name just a few. For instance, the pursuit of combination, or hybrid, business-level strategies may be more possible now with IT advances. Whereas Porter (1980, 1985) advised organizations generally to pursue one coherent strategy (e.g., the choice between low-cost and differentiation), the advent of flexible manufacturing and highly sophisticated customer database systems may provide more latitude at the business level. A worthy research question is to what extent, and in what contexts, combination forms of competitive advantage can indeed be pursued, and in what ways these strategies are enabled by IT. Likewise, strategic decision processes, such as environmental scanning, analysis and planning, have been aided immensely by the development of executive IS, Internet capabilities and real-time access to business intelligence. These developments enable richer and more abundant information to reach executives, but a key challenge is how to provide relevant information in the proper form and at the right time so the organization can capitalize on opportunities. To what degree might IT advances enable the optimum breadth and depth of information to enter the strategic decision process, given contingencies such as decision makers' characteristics and organizational strategy? These are examples of research questions that would merely begin to scratch the surface.

CONCLUSION

We have explored concepts and issues involving the use of IT as an enabler for strategic management. We discussed the parallel development of strategic management and IT, and their co-evolutions over the last 5 decades. In general, the theoretical research in strategic management has led the way in the co-evolution. IT and IT-enabled IS are developed to support strategic management needs. The fields are at a unique point in their development, enabling cross-disciplinary research of both practical and theoretical interest dealing with a vast array of organization process and performance issues. We hope the succeeding chapters are helpful in providing a start toward fruitful research agendas and in offering practical guidance to those who are responsible for implementation in organizations.

REFERENCES

Applegate, L.M., Austin, R.D., & McFarlan, F.W. (2003). *Corporate information strategy and management* (6th edition). New York: McGraw-Hill.

Axelrod, R., & Cohen, M. (1999). *Harnessing complexity: Organizational implications of a scientific frontier.* New York: Free Press.

Boddy, D., Boonstra, A., & Kennedy, G. (2005). *Managing information systems: An organisational perspective* (2nd edition). Harlow: Pearson.

Buzzell, R., & Gale, B. (1987). *The PIMS principles: Linking strategy to performance.* New York: Free Press.

Carr, N.G. (2003). IT doesn't matter. *Harvard Business Review, 81*(5), 41-49.

Chandler, A. (1962). *Strategy and structure: Chapters in the history of industrial enterprise.* New York: Doubleday.

Chen, S. (2005). *Strategic management of e-business* (2nd edition). West Sussex: John Wiley & Sons.

Clarke, S. (2001). *Information systems strategic management: An integrated Approach.* New York: Routledge.

Clemons, E.K., & Row, M.C. (1991). Sustaining IT advantage: The role of structural differences. *MIS Quarterly, 15*(3), 275-292.

Drucker, P. (1954). *The practice of management.* New York: Harper and Row.

Drucker, P. (1968). *The age of discontinuity.* New York: Harper and Row.

Dudik, E. (2000). *Strategic renaissance.* New York: Amacon.

Evans, P., & Wurster, T.S. (2000). *Blown to bits: How the new economics of information transforms strategy.* Boston: Harvard Business School Press.

Gantz, J. (2004). *40 years of IT: Looking back, looking ahead.* IDC special edition executive white paper. Framingham, MA: International Data Corp.

Gronroos, C. (1994). From marketing mix to relationship marketing: Towards a paradigm shift in marketing. *Management Decision, 32*(2), 4-32.

Hamel, G. (2000). *Leading the revolution.* New York: Plume (Penguin Books).

Hamel, G., & Prahalad, C.K. (1990). The core competence of the corporation. *Harvard Business Review, 68*(3), 79-91.

Hammer, M., & Champy, J. (1993). *Reengineering the corporation.* New York: Harper Business.

Kaplan, R.S., & Norton, D.P. (1992). The balanced scorecard: Measures that drive performance. *Harvard Business Review, 70*(1), 71-80.

Kettinger, W., Grover, V., Guha, S., & Segars, A.H. (1994). Strategic information systems revisited: A study in sustainability and performance. *MIS Quarterly, 18*, 31-55.

Landsbergen, D. (2005). IT-enabled sense-and-respond strategies in complex public organizations. *The Communications of the ACM, 48*, 58-65.

Lester, R. (1989). *Made in America.* Boston: MIT Commission on Industrial Productivity.

Levinson, J.C. (1984). *Guerrilla marketing: Secrets for making big profits from your small business.* New York: Houghton Muffin.

Levitt, T. (1983). *The marketing imagination.* New York: Free Press.

Moncrieff, J. (1999). Is strategy making a difference? *Long Range Planning Review, 32*(2), 273-276.

Nagarajan, K., Lam, H., & Su, S.Y.W. (2004). Integration of business event and rule management with the Web services model. *International Journal of Web Services Research, 1*(1), 41-57.

Naisbitt, J. (1982). *Megatrends.* New York: Warner Books.

O'Brien, J. (2005). *Introduction to information systems* (12th edition). Boston: McGraw-Hill/Irwin.

Pine, J., & Gilmore, J. (1997). The four faces of mass customization. *Harvard Business Review, 75*(1), 91-101.

Porter, M. (1980). *Competitive strategy.* New York: Free Press.

Porter, M. (1985). *Competitive advantage.* New York: The Free Press.

Porter, M. (1987). From competitive advantage to corporate strategy. *Harvard Business Review, 65*(3), 43-59.

Porter, M., & Miller, V. (1985). How information technology gives you competitive advantage. *Harvard Business Review, 63*(4), 149-160.

Prahalad, C.K., & Krishnan, M.S. (2002). The dynamic synchronization of strategy and information technology. *MIT Sloan Management Review, 43*(Summer), 24-33.

Quinn, J.B. (1992). *Intelligent enterprise.* New York: Free Press.

Sabherwal, R., & Chan, Y.E. (2001). Alignment between business and IS strategies: A study of prospectors, analyzers, and defenders. *Information Systems Research, 12*(1), 11-33.

Selznick, P. (1957). *Leadership in administration: A sociological interpretation.* Evanston: Row, Peterson.

Senge, P. (1990). *The fifth discipline.* New York: Doubleday.

Sewell, C., & Brown, P. (1990). *Customers for life.* New York: Doubleday Currency.

Shapiro, C., & Varian, H. (1999). *Information rules.* Boston: Harvard Business School Press.

Steele, L. (1989). *Managing technology.* New York: McGraw-Hill.

Stewart, T. (2003). Does IT matter? An HBR debate. *Harvard Business Review, 81*(6), 1-17.

Symons, C. (2005). IT and business alignment: Are we there yet? *Trends.* Cambridge, MA: Forrester Research.

Toffler, A. (1970). *Future shock.* New York: Bantom Books.

Young, H. (1998). *Individual strategy and social Structure: An evolutionary theory of institutions.* Princeton: Princeton University Press.

This work was previously published in IT-Enabled Strategic Management: Increasing Returns for the Organization, edited by B. Walters and Z. Tang, pp. 1-15, copyright 2006 by IGI Publishing (an imprint of IGI Global).

Chapter XVIII
Information Technology Portfolio Management:
Literature Review, Framework, and Research Issues

Ram Kumar
University of North Carolina – Charlotte, USA

Haya Ajjan
University of North Carolina – Charlotte, USA

Yuan Niu
University of North Carolina – Charlotte, USA

ABSTRACT

There is significant interest in managing IT resources as a portfolio of assets. The concept of IT portfolio management (ITPM) is relatively new, compared to portfolio management in the context of finance, new product development (NPD), and research and development (R&D). This article compares ITPM with other types of portfolio management, and develops an improved understanding of IT assets and their characteristics. It presents a process-oriented framework for identifying critical ITPM decision stages. The proposed framework can be used by managers as well as researchers.

INTRODUCTION

IT investments constitute a major portion of organizations' capital budgets in many organizations (Jeffery & Leliveld, 2004). However, some authors question the business value of IT (Carr, 2003), and the actual contribution of IT to organizational performance is the subject of debate (Kohli & Devaraj, 2003). IT managers are constantly un-

der pressure to justify their IT investments and demonstrate the business value of IT. For most companies, selecting a project that would fit the corporate strategy—and therefore maximize the business value—is a challenging process (Jeffery & Leliveld, 2004). In addition, the high failure rate of IT projects in many organizations is a cause for concern. A study by Standish Group showed that only 28% of IT projects succeed in 2004, compared to 34% a year earlier (Hayes, 2004).

Hence, there has been significant interest in effective management of information technology investments (Cimral & Lawler, 2002; Datz, 2003; Jeffery & Leliveld, 2004; Reyck, Grushka-Cockayne, Lockett, Calderini, Moura, & Sloper, 2005). Organizations recognize that they have portfolios of IT assets. Each component of the portfolio (e.g., applications, projects, and infrastructure) serves a different purpose and needs to be managed differently, while recognizing the interdependencies between these components. Several organizations have undertaken IT portfolio management (ITPM) projects (Datz, 2003; Jeffery & Leliveld, 2004; Weill & Vitale, 1999). An increasing number of vendors and consultants offering ITPM products, services, and books are beginning to appear (Fitzpatrick, 2005; Maizlish & Handler, 2005). However, organizations have different maturity levels when it comes to implementing ITPM (Jeffery & Leliveld, 2004). There are significant additional benefits that can be obtained from better understanding and implementation of ITPM (Weill & Aral, 2006).

From a research perspective, there are several studies that address portfolio management. These research studies span diverse fields, such as new product development (NPD) (Cooper, Edgett, & Kleinschmidt, 1997, 1999), research and development (R&D) (Dickinson, Thornton, & Graves, 2001), financial portfolio management (FPM) (Reilly & Brown, 2002), and IT (Jeffery & Leliveld, 2004). However, an analysis of similarities and differences between ITPM and other types of portfolio management is lacking in the literature. Such an analysis would help researchers, as well as managers, apply ideas from other types of portfolio management that can be used for ITPM.

From an MIS perspective, there are very few studies directly related to ITPM (Jeffery & Leliveld, 2004; Weill & Aral, 2006; Weill & Vitale, 1999). ITPM as a concept remains under-

developed. However, there are several streams of research that seem to be relevant to ITPM. These include business values of IT (Devaraj & Kohli, 2003), IT project management (Wallace & Keil, 2004; Wallace, Keil, & Rai, 2004), IT adoption and use (Jasperson, Carter, & Zmud, 2005; Venkatesh, Morris, Davis, & Davis, 2003), IT success (DeLone & McLean, 2003), strategic use of IT (Bhatt & Grover, 2005; Piccoli & Ives, 2005), strategic IS planning (Grover & Segars, 2005), business process change (Kettinger & Grover, 1995), and others. Hence, there is a need to better understand how these streams of research are related to ITPM, and further develop ITPM from a research perspective.

This article views an organization's IT portfolio as comprising a set of assets: IT infrastructure assets (the hardware and software that support IT applications such as servers, workstations, database software, and network infrastructure), application assets, project assets, and IT-related human resource assets. This view of the IT portfolio mirrors the way many organizations manage their IT assets, and is discussed in Section 3. Application, infrastructure, and project components of the IT portfolio are the focus of this article, since managing the human component of the IT portfolio is an important topic in its own right.

Jeffrey and Leliveld (2004, p. 41) define ITPM as "managing IT as a portfolio of assets, similar to a financial portfolio, and striving to improve the performance of a portfolio by balancing risk and return." This article views ITPM as *a continuous process to manage IT project, application, and infrastructure assets and their interdependencies, in order to maximize portfolio benefits, minimize risk and cost, and ensure alignment with organizational strategy over the long run.* This view of ITPM specifically recognizes different types of IT assets, the continuous process nature of ITPM, and identifies major dimensions (alignment, benefits, costs, risks, and interdependencies) that need to be considered in managing IT as a portfolio of assets. It is important to note that some researchers would consider alignment to be a type of benefit. However, identifying it as a separate characteristic of an IT portfolio helps to maintain focus on the important goal of aligning IT with organizational strategy.

This article focuses on the following questions:

i. What are the core concepts of (other types of) portfolio management?

ii. How do these core concepts apply to IT portfolio management?

iii. How do relevant, major, existing MIS research streams relate to ITPM?

iv. How do existing IT management practices relate to ITPM?

This article presents a cumulative body of relevant knowledge to aid future development of ITPM by addressing the above questions. It develops a conceptual framework for better understanding and managing ITPM by (a) reviewing and synthesizing related literature, (b) identifying core concepts of portfolio management that cut across financial, NPD, and R&D contexts (e.g., assets, alignment, costs, benefits, risks, interdependencies), and (c) developing these core concepts in an MIS context by integrating relevant ideas from MIS literature with ideas from other types of portfolio management. The proposed framework systematically identifies major steps and decisions in ITPM. It could be of use to researchers who are interested in further development of ITPM, as well as practitioners. Areas for future research are identified by using this framework to compare existing research in MIS with research in other types of portfolio management. The use of this framework in an organizational context is illustrated using an example.

The article is organized as follows: Section 2 provides a review of related literature from the fields of NPD, R&D, financial portfolio management, and MIS. Core concepts of portfolio management in the context of IT are discussed in Section 3. A framework for understanding ITPM decisions and processes is described in Section 4. An example to illustrate the use of the ITPM decisions and processes framework is provided in Section 5. Managerial Issues are discussed in Section 6. Conclusions are presented in Section 7.

LITERATURE REVIEW

Portfolio management is typically associated with financial assets. Besides finance, other fields such as NPD, R&D, and MIS have used portfolio management concepts. This section summarizes relevant research.

Financial Portfolio Management

Portfolio management in finance (Reilly & Brown, 2002) deals with managing a variety of asset classes (such as stocks, bonds, cash) in order to maximize return for some specified period of time, while attempting to minimize risk. Each asset class can contain a variety of subclasses. These include different types of stocks (small-cap, mid-cap, international, and so on) and different types of bonds (domestic, international, junk, short-term, long-term, inflation adjusted, and so on). These asset classes vary in terms of their risk-return characteristics, as well as liquidity. Risk-return characteristics of portfolios are different from those of individual stocks, and are influenced by the degree of correlation between assets in the portfolio.

Financial asset holders typically select a portfolio of assets in relation to their strategic goals (e.g., retirement) and risk tolerance. They periodically trade (buy and sell) assets in order to rebalance (ensure that their portfolio continues to be aligned with their strategic goals). Trading costs influence the frequency with which they trade. Relatively liquid assets can be traded at relatively lower trading costs. The value of each financial asset is typically determined by markets. Costs of these assets include actual asset costs, trading fees, and asset management fees (for managing or maintaining a portfolio). Effective management of a financial portfolio comprising different types of assets often results in higher expected returns with an acceptable level of risk over a defined time horizon.

Major research issues in financial portfolio management include portfolio selection, risk-return characteristics of different types of financial assets, portfolio management, the impact of trading costs, and a variety of other issues (Elton, Gruber, Brown, & Goetzmann, 2002).

NPD Portfolio Management

NPD portfolio components are projects which result in products that can be marketed. The literature suggests numerous reasons for the popularity of NPD portfolio management practices (Cooper & Edget, 2003). These include scarcity of organizational resources, project failure rate, and the misalignment between projects and strategic decisions. Many companies find portfolio management useful in providing them with systematic ways to decide which projects to undertake and to help them track the deployment of existing resources (Cooper & Edget, 2003; Cooper et al., 1999). Cooper, Edgett, and Kleinschmidt (2004a, 2004b, 2004c) examined best portfolio management practices in several organizations, and found that portfolio management approaches are related to higher organizational NPD performance. More specifically, research shows that high-performing companies (in terms of revenue percentage from new products or other metrics) have a higher proportion of innovative projects in their portfolio than low-performing companies. This emphasizes the importance of the mix of projects in a portfolio. The NPD literature contains several streams of research on portfolio management.

One stream extends financial portfolio management and microeconomic theory to incorporate the unique characteristics of new product investments. Leong and Lim (1991) developed a multiperiod portfolio evaluation framework based on financial portfolio concepts. Relevant financial concepts include the correlation between projects (divisions), interproject relations (synergies), changes in risk and returns over time, and the effect of buy/sell decisions on portfolio performance. Devinney and Stewart (1988) extended the microeconomic theory of the firm, while paying close attention to "interdependency between demand and supply in new product line investment." The model presented in their article takes into consideration the interaction between cost, revenue, and profitability of products.

Another stream of research presents different project selection methodologies a firm can use to maximize its return and achieve the right balance of projects. In a series of articles, Cooper et al. (1997, 1999) evaluate different project selection and value maximizing practices employed by a set of firms. Examples of these practices are: NPV, productivity index, and scoring models. Cooper et al. (1999) recommended the use of hybrid portfolio evaluation methods. Financial methods such as NPV, IRR, or productivity index, strategic methods, scoring models, and finally, bubble diagrams where projects can be viewed in terms of risk and reward can be used to evaluate projects (Cooper et al., 1999). Other combinations of methods can be used when evaluating and selecting new projects. For example, managers can use a mix of analytic hierarchy process (AHP) and simulations to help them decide on the best project, based on predefined criteria (Ayag, 2005). Loch and Kavadias (2002) developed a dynamic model of selecting new product lines using a marginal analysis approach. The dynamic model takes into consideration multiple factors, such as interaction of multiple product lines (substitution or complementary), resource synergies, uncertainties, potential size of the market segment, and management risk aversion.

R&D Portfolio Management

The use of portfolio management in R&D resource allocation began in the 1980s (Dickinson et al., 2001). Because high-technology firms cannot afford to develop one product at a time, they face the challenge of concurrently managing multiple R&D projects using shared resources (Verma & Sinha, 2002). The goal of R&D portfolio management is to optimize the resource allocation among projects in a way that balances risk, benefits, and align projects with corporate strategies (Dickinson et al., 2001). Components in a R&D portfolio are projects. Project selection and evaluation represent a major managerial effort in R&D portfolio management. Researchers have identified different types of interdependencies among R&D projects, such as resource interdependencies, outcome interdependencies, and benefit interdependencies (Chien, 2002; Verma & Sinha, 2002). Because of the existence of the various interdependencies, the combination of individually optimal projects does not necessarily constitute the optimal portfolio (Chien, 2002). Therefore, portfolio management techniques which take into consideration all possible projects at the same time are required.

There are a wide range of R&D portfolio management techniques with varying metrics and evaluation/selection methods. The metrics used to evaluate and select a project include quantitative (e.g., ROI) and qualitative (e.g., alignment with company strategy) measures. Different portfolio management techniques have been developed to evaluate different metrics. Mathematical and scoring/weighing models could be used when quantitative measures are available (Dickinson et al., 2001; Ringuest et al., 2000; Stummer et al., 2003). Matrix and charting could be used to explore qualitative measures (MacMillan & McGrath, 2002; Mikkola, 2001). Professional judgment is often considered another valuable

decision source in R&D portfolio management (Dickinson et al., 2001).

Portfolio Management in IT

The information systems literature contains few studies on portfolio management. Similar to research in other disciplines, researchers have examined methods and models to measure the risk and value of different portfolio components, such as project portfolio risk (McFarlan, 1981) and application health (Weill & Vitale, 1999). Others have presented models to select projects in an IT portfolio (Bardhan & Sougstad, 2004). Although several methods to measure the value and risk of IT portfolio components exist, many companies are missing the full benefits of ITPM. According to a survey of 1,000 CIOs—while 89% of them were aware of ITPM, and 65% believed that it yields significant business value—only 17% think they have realized ITPM's full value (Jeffery & Leliveld, 2004). Hence, companies could benefit from an improved understanding of ITPM. ITPM is not a new topic in information systems research; it goes back to the early 1970s, when researchers started studying information systems within the context of the entire organization (Lucas, 1973). Recently, there has been a renewed interest in the topic, given the challenges facing companies in managing their IT assets more effectively. This renewed interest is due, in part, to articles such as Carr (2003) that have questioned the business value of IT.

Jeffrey and Leliveld (2004) discussed best practices in ITPM based on a survey and interviews. They also suggest that an IT portfolio maturity model be used to characterize different levels of ITPM implementation in organizations. Weill and Broadbent (1998) classified IT assets into transactional assets, informational assets, strategic assets, and infrastructure assets. They illustrate that the relative proportion of these four types of assets in an organization is related to corporate strategy. For example, an organization whose business strategy is based on cost leadership would emphasize transactional assets, while an organization whose business strategy is based on agility would emphasize strategic assets. Weill and Aral (2006) emphasized that the effective implementation of ITPM in organizations is related to developing IT savvy, which is a set of five interrelated characteristics. Of these five characteristics, three (use of IT for internal and external communication, internet use, and digital transactions) are practices related to IT use, and two (companywide IT skills, and management involvement) are competencies.

UNDERSTANDING ITPM

Financial, NPD, R&D and IT Portfolios: Similarities and Differences

Financial, NPD, R&D, and IT portfolio management have similarities and differences. This section analyzes these similarities and differences using the following characteristics or dimensions of portfolios: portfolio components, strategic alignment, benefits, costs, risks, and interdependencies. An analysis of each dimension

includes a discussion of MIS research related to that dimension. This analysis forms the basis for the ITPM decision framework presented in the following section.

Portfolio Components or Assets

Asset types in the case of FPM include different types of stocks and bonds. Portfolio assets are typically projects in the case of NPD and R&D portfolios. However, there could be different types of projects, just as there are different types of stocks or bonds.

Asset classes in IT portfolios include projects, applications, and infrastructure.[1] Figure 1 illustrates the interrelationship between these three asset classes. Completed IT projects could result in applications (e.g., purchasing systems), or infrastructure components (e.g., messaging system). Infrastructure components, in turn, support applications.

Of these, IT projects have been extensively researched, particularly from project success and risk management perspectives (Schmidt, Lyytinen, Keil, & Cule, 2001; Wallace & Keil, 2004; Wallace et al., 2004) and continue to be an active area of research. MIS research on IT applications spans several streams. These include IT adop-

Figure 1. Relationship among projects, infrastructure, and applications

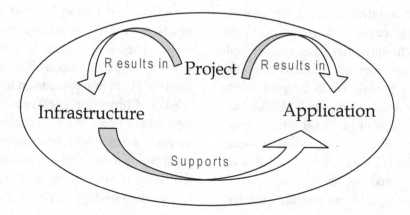

tion and use (Venkatesh et al., 2003), IT success (DeLone & McLean, 2003), and deriving business value from applications (Devraj & Kohli, 2003). Research on IT infrastructure is relatively new and includes streams, such as infrastructure value (Kumar, 2004), infrastructure flexibility (Byrd & Turner, 2000; Duncan, 1995), and infrastructure management (Weill & Broadbent, 1998; Weill & Vitale, 2002).

A benefit of viewing IT assets as projects, applications, and infrastructure is that it mirrors the way IT assets are managed in organizations. In the case of financial portfolios, groups of specialists manage different types of assets. For example, fixed income (bond) securities are managed by different groups of managers than equities or stocks. Similarly, in the case of IT portfolios, projects are typically managed by project and application development groups, applications are managed by support groups and infrastructure is managed by architects and network or infrastructure support

groups. While there is some job rotation between these groups, the organization structure in many IT organizations distinguishes between project or development groups, application support groups, and infrastructure support groups. Different (sometimes overlapping) skills are required for project management, application development, application support, and infrastructure support. Table 1 summarizes some key characteristics of IT assets. These characteristics are discussed in the following sections.

IT portfolios include architecture, project, and infrastructure subportfolios (Figure 2). Researchers studying project subportfolios have examined issues such as interdependent project evaluation (Bardhan & Sougstad, 2004) and use of different project management approaches depending on the type of project (Applegate, Austin, & McFarlan, 2006). Reyck et al. (2005) classified implementations of IT project portfolio management (PPM) into three stages and provide

Table 1. Key characteristics of projects, applications, and infrastructure assets

Characteristic	Projects	Applications	Infrastructure
Management responsibility	Project managers	Support groups	Architecture groups
Benefits	Determined as part of a business case.	Determined after implementation	Determined after implementation. Relatively difficult to determine
Costs (major)	Programming costs +purchased hardware/software costs + project management costs	Application license costs + support (labor) costs+ allocated infrastructure costs	License costs+ support (labor) costs
Risks (major)	Risks of the project not being completed on time, within budget, or not producing desired benefits	Risks of application downtime and risk of the application not being adopted or used as planned	Risks of infrastructure downtime
Alignment with Strategy	Projects are related to strategic goals (e.g. reduce cost)	Applications support strategic business processes	Strategic architecture decisions impact organizational performance

Figure 2. Information technology portfolio characteristics: components, alignment, benefit, cost, risk, and interdependency

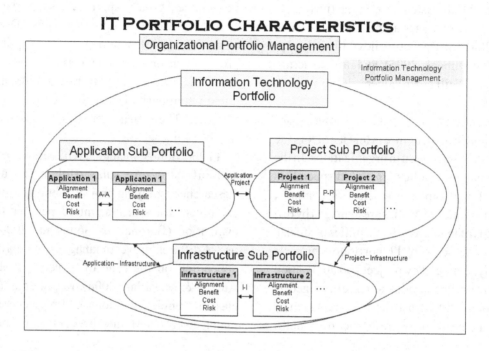

empirical evidence (based on European data) that adoption of PPM is highly correlated with improved project performance. Weill and Vitale (1999) proposed a framework for analyzing an organization's application subportfolio based on benefits and risk, and managing applications based on this analysis.

Characteristics of IT Portfolio Components

Strategic Alignment

All four types of portfolio management (FPM, NPD, R&D, ITPM) emphasize the need to align the portfolio with long-term goals or organizational strategies. However, there are some differences. NPD and R&D typically focus on a few products or processes. However, IT is sig-

nificantly more pervasive than NPD and R&D, because IT investments can impact a variety of processes or products. Some of the tools that have been proposed to align NPD and R&D projects with corporate strategy, such as scoring models, can also be used to align IT investments with corporate strategy. However, strategic planning for IT is likely to be more complex, and involves a variety of diverse stakeholders. MIS research (Grover & Segars, 2005; Newkirk & Lederer, 2006) which emphasizes the importance of a strategic information systems planning (SISP). This stream of research has identified important process elements of SISP (Newkirk & Lederer, 2006) and the results of successful SISP (Grover & Segars, 2005; Segars & Grover, 1998). SISP success measures include increased alignment, improved analysis and understanding of an organization's relationship with IT, improved cooperation, and important capabilities such as the ability to identify key problem areas and flexibility to adapt to unanticipated changes. Research on financial portfolios, NPD, R&D, and IT portfolios has recognized the need to have a mix of different types of assets in the portfolios. The mix of different types of assets would be related to an organization's strategic goals. As discussed earlier, Weill and Broadbent (1998) classify an organization's IT investments into transactional, informational, and strategic, and illustrate that the relative proportions of these types of assets is related to an organization's strategy. Weill and Aral (2006) provide empirical evidence of organizational benefits from planned portfolios that include strategic investments in IT.

Benefits

Organizations would typically like measurable financial benefits that could be quantified by means of financial calculations from all investments. Financial assets often have market-determined values. Hence, determining the value of a portfolio is relatively easy. However, the value of a portfolio could vary considerably over time. The value of NPD and R&D portfolios is typically based on projected project benefits. NPD project benefits are typically based on market research and projected sales. R&D project benefits could be more difficult to estimate, compared to NPD project benefits, depending on the type of R&D project, since R&D projects often require follow-up commercialization projects. Scoring models or financial measures are typically used to determine value, though several more sophisticated methods, often based on financial management, have been proposed, as have hybrid approaches.

There is an extensive body of literature on the business value of IT (Devaraj & Kohli, 2003). Several methods for evaluating the business value of IT projects have been proposed. These include traditional financial measures (Ross & Beath, 2002) and more sophisticated methods,

based on financial asset evaluation (Benaroch & Kauffman, 1999; Santos, 1991). However, it is well-recognized that it is often difficult to quantify the benefits of IT projects, particularly if they relate to infrastructure (Kumar, 2004). It has also been recognized that different types of evaluation methods may be appropriate, depending on the type of IT project (Ross & Beath, 2002). Hence, quantifying the benefits of a portfolio of IT projects can be difficult.

A growing body of literature exists on post hoc analysis of the business value of IT applications (Kohli & Devaraj, 2003). These studies typically use econometric analyses to determine the value of IT applications. The MIS literature recognizes that the business value of IT investments is influenced to a large extent by complementary investments in training and business processes (Weill & Aral, 2006), and by the extent to which an application is used in the organization (Devaraj & Kohli, 2003).

The business value of IT infrastructure investments can be particularly difficult to determine. Their value is determined in part by the value of applications they support, and in part by their ability to enhance organizational flexibility. Hence, relatively sophisticated techniques, such as those described in Kumar (2004), may be required.

In the case of financial portfolio management, it is possible to assign a value to a portfolio of assets. The total value of NPD and R&D portfolios can be estimated if projected financial metrics are available for projects. However, the total value (benefit) of an IT portfolio (comprised of projects, applications, and infrastructure) can be difficult to articulate, since different methods of determining the values of these portfolio components may be used at the portfolio component or subportfolio level, and determination of value is imprecise. Scoring models and approximate financial valuation using appropriate approximate techniques for projects, infrastructure, and applications is possible. Additional research on approaches to specifying portfolio value is required.

Costs

Costs of financial assets can be classified into acquisition costs, holding costs, and disposal costs. Acquisition costs include the purchase price and trading commissions. Holding costs typically include different types of asset management fees, which could vary depending on the type of asset (e.g., savings accounts, brokerage accounts). Disposal costs typically refer to commissions. In the case of NPD and R&D portfolios, organizations are concerned primarily with project costs. Completed projects result in products or services, which are then commercialized.

In the case of IT portfolios, IT projects are similar to NPD and R&D projects, in terms of project cost being the primary concern. The application and infrastructure assets that result from projects are similar to financial assets, in that one can think in terms of acquisition costs (could be the same as project costs), holding (or support) costs, and disposal costs for these assets.

Support (or holding, or management) costs for IT application and infrastructure assets have some important characteristics, which need to be emphasized. While support costs are typically a relatively small percentage of asset value in the case of financial assets, they can be a significant portion of total costs in the case of some application and infrastructure assets, and need to be carefully managed.

In the case of financial assets, organizations are not interested in tracking support costs for each individual asset. However, in the case of IT assets, organizations often incur significant infrastructure and support costs. Hence, they would like to assign these costs to different departments or user organizations. Chargeback or cost allocation systems are used for this purpose. Also, costs of one asset class (e.g., application or project) are related to those of another asset class (e.g., infrastructure), and hence, calculating total costs of an application or project might require some way of allocating or charging back cost of infrastructure assets to applications or projects. Chargeback of IT costs to users is a controversial topic, and user departments are not always satisfied with chargeback mechanisms and the behavior modifications that they induce (Drury, 2000). However, organizations continue to use chargeback systems (Quinlan, 2002), and with the growing trend towards IT being delivered as a service, it is likely that innovative methods of assigning shared costs of infrastructure to applications and users (Gerlach, Neuman, Moldauer,

Table 2. Interdependencies between IT portfolio components

	(Other) Approved and In-Progress Projects	(Other) Existing Applications	(Other) Existing Infrastructure components
New Project Proposals (depend on)	[1] For Shared resources Shared benefits	[2]For Shared resources Inputs (Application outputs)	[3]For Shared resources Inputs (Infrastructure outputs)
Existing Application (depends on)	[4] For Risk Reduction Reduced cost Benefit increase	[5] For Shared resources Inputs (application outputs)	[6]For Shared resources Inputs (infrastructure outputs)
Existing Infrastructure (depends on)	[7]For Risk Reduction Cost Reduction Benefit Increase	[8] For Shared resources	[9] For Shared Resources Inputs

Argo, & Frisby, 2002; Hoffman, 2005) merit additional research (Thornton, 2005).

Risk

Risk is often viewed as the possibility of deviation from an expected outcome (Wallace et al., 2004). Financial, NPD, R&D, and IT portfolios differ in terms of the magnitude and relative importance of different types of risks. Risks have been extensively studied in the financial domain, and are typically classified into market or systematic risks, and private or unsystematic risks. Market risk factors are typically correlated with the risks to the overall financial market, and include major economic factors such consumer confidence, oil prices, and interest rates. Market risk can be hedged by holding a diversified portfolio of securities. Private risk, on the other hand, is specific to individual projects, and is the result of factors that are not correlated with market risk. These include technical risks, project management risks, and organizational risks.

NPD portfolios typically have a significantly higher market risk compared to R&D portfolios, which have a significantly higher private risk (often technical risk). Risk factors of IT portfolios are likely to be primarily private risks. Also, the definition of risk and relevant risk factors could vary for project, application, and infrastructure subportfolios.

Risk, in the context of IT projects, can be defined as the possibility of an unfavorable outcome in terms of time, cost, or functionality of the final project deliverable (Wallace & Keil, 2004). There is an extensive body of literature on identifying risk factors for IT projects (Schmidt et al., 2001), and managing risk in IT projects (Schmidt, Lyytinen, K., Keil, & Cule, 2002; Wallace et al., 2004; Wallace et al., 2004; Westerman, 2005; Westerman & Walpole, 2005).

This article defines risk in the context of IT applications as *the likelihood of the application not delivering the expected business benefits.* Application risk factors include the risk of low adoption and use, and risk of application downtime. Risk of low rates of application adoption and use is often the result of behavioral factors and related to the MIS literature on IT adoption (Venkatesh et al., 2003) and IT success (DeLone

Table 3. A comparison of different types of portfolio management

Topic	Description	Page #
Asset classes	FPM: Different types of stocks, and bonds NPD and R&D: Projects ITPM: Projects, applications and infrastructure components	69
Management Model	FPM: Groups of specialists manage different types of assets (stocks, bonds etc.). NPD: Managed by multi-functional teams R&D: Managed by specialists ITPM: Specialized groups manage different types of assets (applications, projects, and infrastructure) with some overlap. Other business departments have different degrees of involvement depending on how IT governance is implemented.	69
Strategic Alignment	All four types of portfolio management (FPM, NPD, R&D, ITPM) emphasize the need to align the portfolio with long-term goals or organizational strategies	70
Process Change Impact	FPM, NPD and R&D typically focus on a few products or processes. ITPM investments relate to a variety of processes or products depending on project and application portfolios (sometimes involve the entire organization—enterprise wide system)	70

& McLean, 2003). Risk of application downtime could be related to security risks (Arora, Hall, Pinto, Ramsey, & Telang, 2004; Rainer, Snyder, Carr, & Houston, 1991; Sun, Srivastava, & Mock, 2006). It is important to note that there is a need for research that focuses on IT application risk from an integrated perspective that includes all types of IT assets.

Infrastructure risk can be defined in a manner similar to application risk as *the likelihood of the infrastructure not delivering the desired business benefits*. However, the business benefits of infrastructures are more difficult to measure when compared to those of applications. Infrastructure risks include natural disasters, terrorist attacks, power failure, software bugs, etc (Arora et al., 2004; Rainer et al., 1991; Sun et al., 2006). Thus,

Figure 3. A framework for understanding major steps and decisions in ITPM

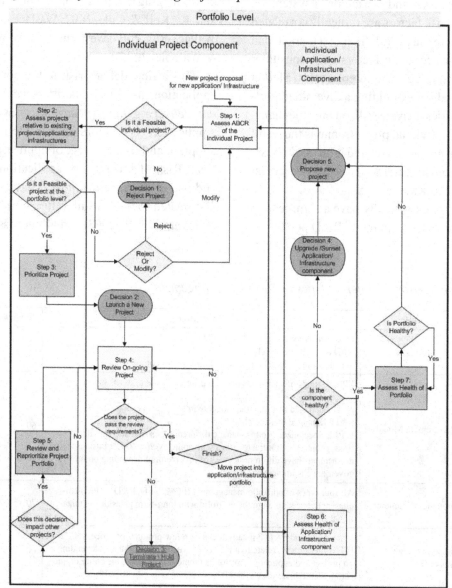

while risk has been studied in some contexts (e.g., project risk), IT risk management is an underdeveloped area, and there is a need for additional research that examines risk management in IT from an integrated perspective, and examines the relationships between project, application, and infrastructure risks. There is a growing recognition that IT risk management may be a valuable organizational capability (Westerman, 2005; Westerman & Walpole, 2005). Other disciplines such as operations management recognize the fact that risk management in their discipline is underdeveloped and encourage additional research in this area (Seshadri & Subrahmanyam, 2005).

Interdependencies

In general, interdependencies refer to situations where characteristics (alignment, benefits, costs, risks) of a portfolio asset depend on characteristics of another asset. Interdependencies have a major impact on the value of an IT portfolio over time. Interdependencies between assets have been extensively researched in finance. Project interdependencies have also been studied in NPD, R&D, and IT research. The relationship between projects may be positive (complement), negative (substitute), or zero (neutral) (Chien, 2002; Devinney & Stewart, 1988). Chien (2002) identified four types of interrelationships among projects: outcome or technical, cost or resource-utilization, impact or benefit, and serial (present-value) interrelationships. Outcome interrelationships occur when a project outcome depends on the other projects outcomes. Cost interrelationships exist in a portfolio when the total cost of the portfolio cannot be represented as the sum of the costs of the individual projects. Benefit interrelationships among the projects in a portfolio make the payoffs of the projects not additive. Serial interrelationships arise when time is considered as a factor in selecting the projects in a portfolio. Santhanam and Krypakis (1996) discussed three types of interdependencies involving IT projects: resource,

benefit, and technical. Resource dependencies involve shared resources such as hardware and software. Benefit interdependencies arise when projects are synergistic. Technical dependencies arise when completion of one project is dependant on completion of other projects, due to technical reasons.

The MIS literature differentiates between hard and soft dependencies (Bardhan & Sougstad, 2004). Hard dependencies exist when a capability developed for one project is required by one or more other projects. Soft dependencies are when a capability from one project supports or enhances capabilities of other projects. In general, however, the concept of interdependencies between different types of IT assets is underresearched in MIS, but extremely important if IT is to be managed as a portfolio of assets. Table 2 summarizes different types of interdependencies between IT assets. For example, Cell 1 in Table 2 indicates that new project proposals may depend on other approved and in-progress projects for shared resources (e.g., a common server or storage area network). It may also be possible that a new project proposal depends on some other project for shared benefits (an e-commerce project might depend on the completion of an infrastructure upgrade project for enhanced benefits). Cell 7 indicates a different type of dependency. An existing infrastructure component (e.g., server) might depend on a proposed security project for risk reduction. Similarly, the infrastructure might depend on an in-progress server consolidation project for cost reduction.

These interdependencies are also shown in Figure 2. Shared resources could include hardware, software, or personnel. A detailed analysis of different types of dependencies and their impact on ITPM decisions is an interesting research area. Other disciplines such as R&D management have recognized the need to understand dependencies in greater detail, and contain qualitative (Verma & Sinha, 2002), as well as quantitative studies (Dickinson et al., 2001) that result in improved

Table 4. Dependencies during different steps in the ITPM framework

	P	A	I
P	Step 2,5	Step 2,5	Step 2,5
A	Step 7	Step 7	Step 7
I	Step 7		Step 7

P: Project; A: Application; I: Infrastructure

understanding of different types of dependencies.

This section has summarized key issues in understanding ITPM. A comparison of major ITPM issues with other types of portfolio management is provided in Table 3. This table provides a comparative overview of different type of portfolio management and references to appropriate pages for additional detail.

ITPM DECISIONS AND PROCESSES

Implementing ITPM in organizations involves several interrelated business processes, such as processes for business case development, IS planning, and project management. Many organizations are likely to have some of these processes in place. Hence, it is possible to think of organizations being at different levels of maturity, as far as ITPM is concerned (Jeffery & Leliveld, 2004). This section presents a framework for understanding the relationships between different decisions that are part of ITPM. This framework was derived from the literature review by means of the following process:

a. First, different types of decisions relating to individual assets were identified from the MIS literature (e.g., project selection decisions).

b. Second, decisions relating to portfolios of IT assets (e.g., managing groups of projects) were identified from the NPD, R&D, finance, and MIS research.

c. Finally, relationships between different types of decisions (involving individual as well as portfolios) were iteratively developed through discussions between multiple researchers, and constant comparison with relationships discussed in the literature. For example, identifying new projects based on the health of a portfolio (relationship between Step 5 and Decision 7 in Figure 3) is discussed in Weill and Vitale (1999).

The following discussion also summarizes ideas from NPD, R&D, and MIS research that are relevant to each of the steps. The ITPM process consists of a series of interrelated steps. One or more steps could result in major ITPM decisions. The ITPM process consists of steps and decisions that pertain to *individual project components* of the portfolio (Step 1, Step 4, Decisions 1-3), steps and decisions that pertain to *individual application or infrastructure components* (Step 6, Decision 4), and steps and decisions that pertain to *the IT portfolio* (steps 2,3,5,7, and Decision 5). *While some of the steps in the framework are well-known, the combination of steps and decisions presented in Figure 2 represents a holistic process-oriented view of ITPM that is likely to be of value to researchers as well as managers.*

Step1:
Assess Alignment, Benefit, Cost, and Risk (ABCR) of Individual Projects

Ideas for IT projects[2] could be generated in multiple ways, depending on how IT governance is implemented (Weill, 2004). Sources of project ideas include the SISP process, business users, and IT personnel. A variety of approaches for evaluating individual projects have been proposed

Table 5. Summary of directions for future research

#	Directions for future ITPM Research	Page #
1	Methods of specifying the values of portfolio components	71-72
2	Improved methods of assigning shared costs of infrastructure to applications and users	72
3	Studies of risk management in IT from an integrated perspective and examines the relationships between project, application, and infrastructure risks	73
4	Qualitative and quantitative research on characterization and management of different types of interdependencies between different types of IT assets	74-75
5	Newer and better methods of evaluating the feasibility of individual IT projects	77
6	Additional research on methods to deescalate commitment to failing projects.	78
7	How to rebalance IT project portfolios in response to changes in individual projects.	78
8	Validation and extension of models of IT adoption and use	79
9	Comprehensive health assessment of IT assets	79
10	How ITPM fits within an overall IT Governance framework and roles and responsibilities of personnel involved in ITPM	80-81
11	The role of senior management in supporting ITPM	81
12	Issues of power and politics in ITPM decisions	81
13	Case studies of ITPM implementations	81

in the NPD, R&D, and MIS literature. These include traditional financial evaluation techniques, such as net present value, newer financial evaluation techniques, such as real options (Benaroch & Kauffman, 1999; Santos, 1991), the balanced scorecard (Martinsons, Davison, & Tse, 1999), as well as other techniques (Ross & Beath, 2002).

Traditional financial evaluation methods typically consider benefits and costs, but often underestimate the value of projects (Benaroch & Kauffman, 1999). Newer financial evaluation methods, such as real options, capture managerial flexibility in investment decisions (Benaroch & Kauffman, 1999), as well as uncertainty in cash flows (risk). However, parameter estimation is difficult. Scoring models or balanced scorecards can be used to capture strategic benefits (Martinsons et al., 1999). There is scope for additional research on newer and better methods of evaluating individual IT projects. It is important to note that feasibility in the context of the framework depends on the specific organization, and could

be a combination of economic, technical, operational, legal, and ethical factors.

Step 2:
Assess Project Fit Relative to Existing Applications/Infrastructures

Projects that are feasible in Step 1 need to be examined, relative to an organization's existing IT portfolio components (project, application, and infrastructure components). This type of analysis is best done by a committee made up of individuals from different business and IT units (ITPM Committee). In this step, organizations may reject or request modification of project proposals. Reasons for project modification or rejection could include similarity with existing IT portfolio components (redundancy), incompatibility with infrastructure standards, incompatibility with existing portfolio components, improved alignment with existing IT portfolio, and other actions that could enhance alignment, or benefit or reduce cost or risk of the IT portfolio. The committee may need to consider a variety of interdependencies between the proposed project and the existing IT portfolio (Table 2) and decide that the original project justification needs to be modified, since the individuals proposing the project were not aware of all the interdependencies. For example, the proposed project could have synergies with existing ITP components, thus reducing project cost and making the project more attractive. If, for example, a new portal project requires a Web infrastructure that is missing from the infrastructure subportfolio, then the project might be rejected or postponed until the infrastructure is acquired through a new project proposal. This step could be complicated and could benefit from additional research.

Step 3:
Prioritize Projects

Feasible projects can be prioritized using single criteria methods, based on a financial calculation, or using multiple criteria methods. Project prioritization has been extensively researched, and a variety of approaches have been proposed in the MIS, NPD, and R&D literature (Chien, 2002; Cooper et al., 1997; Dickinson, et al., 2001; Liberatore & Stylianou, 1995a; Liberatore & Stylianou, 1995b; Stummer & Heidenberger, 2003). These include scoring models, analytical hierarchy process, expert systems, mathematical programming, and hybrid methods that do not consider project interdependencies. More sophisticated methods consider interdependencies between projects. The R&D and NPD literature contains several approaches that consider interdependencies (Dickinson et al., 2001; Stummer & Heidenberger, 2003). Research on interdependent project selection and ranking in the MIS literature is limited. Santhanam and Krypakis (1996) propose a nonlinear programming model that considers resource, benefit, and technical interdependencies between projects. Bardhan

and Sougstad (2004) present a dynamic programming model that considers hard and soft project dependencies in prioritizing projects. There is considerable scope for additional research that examines the applicability of approaches proposed in the context of R&D or NPD to IT projects, and further development of other methods that consider project interdependencies. In addition to modeling-oriented research, qualitative research that illustrates different types of interdependencies and how to manage them (Verma & Sinha, 2002) will be useful.

Step 4:
Review On-Going (Individual) Projects

Projects which pass individual and portfolio-level examination will be accepted and moved to the implementation phase. Projects need to be actively managed to ensure results that are measured in terms of process and product outcomes (Wallace & Keil, 2004; Wallace et al., 2004a; Wallace et al., 2004b). IT projects are considered particularly difficult to manage, and there is an extensive body of literature on IT project management (Wallace & Keil, 2004; Wallace et al., 2004). Similar streams of research exist in the areas of R&D project management and NPD project management (Nobeoka & Cusumano, 1995; Santiago & Bifano, 2005). Termination of ongoing projects is often difficult, due to factors such as escalation of commitment (Keil, 1995; Keil & Mann, 1997; Keil, Truex, & Mixon, 1995). A study of methods to deescalate commitment to failing projects (Keil & Robey, 1999; Montealegre & Keil, 2000) is an interesting research area.

Step 5:
Review and Reprioritize Projects in the Portfolio

Business changes, technology changes, and a variety of project risks (Schmidt et al., 2002) result in projects being delayed, terminated, or refocused. Such changes impact other projects, as well as resource availability. IT managers are, therefore, faced with the need to rebalance their portfolio of projects dynamically (in relation to changes in some projects in the portfolio). While there is considerable research on individual IT projects, rebalancing IT portfolios in response to changes in individual projects is an underdeveloped research area. This step is similar to Step 3, in terms of evaluating interdependencies between projects. However, there are likely to be several resource reallocation decisions involved in addition to reprioritizing projects. These resource reallocation decisions should be based on a systematic analysis of the status of existing projects and possible new projects. However, such systematic analysis could be extremely complex. Also, since IT impacts almost every business process, unlike R&D and NPD, there are likely to be a larger number of IT projects, and a greater need for project reprioritization. Hence, IT portfolios are similar to financial portfolios with actively traded assets and a large number of buy and sell transactions due to—or in anticipation of—market changes. In actively traded financial portfolios, managers must frequently make decisions about reallocation of financial resources generated by sell transactions. In IT portfolios, managers must frequently make decisions about reallocation of resources as a result of cancelled, delayed, or refocused IT projects. However, the number and types of resources and their interdependencies involved in IT portfolio reprioritizations are likely to be greater than in the case of financial portfolios. Project reprioritization in MIS is an underresearched area that lends itself to modeling, as well as empirical studies.

Step 6:
Assess the Health of Application/ Infrastructure Components

Completed projects result in applications or infrastructure components or systems. An application or infrastructure component could be considered unhealthy, because it is not aligned with organizational goals, does not produce significant organizational benefits, is too expensive to maintain, too risky, or due to a combination of these factors. The MIS literature emphasizes the fact that systems resulting from completed projects may not be used as originally planned. There is extensive literature on IT adoption and use (Jasperson, Carte, Saunders, Butler, Croes, & Zheng, 2002; Jasperson et al., 2005; Venkatesh et al., 2003) and IT success (DeLone & McLean, 2003). System use problems can be provided by system users or technical support personnel through periodic surveys and/or analysis of technical support calls. It is important to have processes in place to systematically analyze the health of applications or infrastructure components. MIS literature in this area is limited. Weill and Vitale (1999) illustrate the use of risk return bubble diagrams to analyze the health of an application portfolio. Interesting research issues in this area include defining health of applications and infrastructure components, and designing processes and metrics to assess health. Validation and extension of existing models of adoption and use is relevant to this step.

Step 7:
Assess the Health of Portfolio and Balance

Assessing health of the IT portfolio considers different types of interdependencies in analyzing ABCR of the portfolio (unlike Step 2, which only considers dependencies involving a proposed project). Table 4 illustrates how different types of dependencies apply to different steps in the

ITPM framework. For example, project-project (PP), project-application (PA), and project-infrastructure (PI) dependencies are relevant during Steps 2 and 5.

This step is closely related to SISP (Grover & Segars, 2005). Approaches such as critical success factors or value chain analysis can be used as part of the assessment. However, SISP methodologies often focus on alignment and benefits, and do not integrate cost and risk. There is an increasing emphasis on the risk of an organization's IT portfolio as a result of increased organizational dependence on IT, and increased likelihood of security attacks. Issues such as threat assessment, disaster recovery planning, and regulatory compliance are part of this step. Organizational performance and increasing emphasis on the business value of IT (Carr, 2003) could drive projects to reduce the cost of the IT portfolio.

Managers may be interested in knowing what the total support costs of the portfolio are, which applications are the most expensive to support, which are the most risky applications are, or what the risk-return characteristics of applications are, or what the major risks of the portfolio are, and how they can be mitigated as part of ITP balancing. Additional research which guides balancing decisions is required.

The results of portfolio health assessment could be portfolio balancing decisions to upgrade or sunset applications or other types of projects. It is important to realize that unlike IT portfolios, where assets can be disposed of relatively easily, there is significant cost associated with implementing IT portfolio balancing decisions. Besides hardware and software costs, such balancing decisions could include costs of personnel reassignment and training. There is considerable scope for additional research on integrated approaches to assessing the health of an IT portfolio and balancing the portfolio based on health assessment. Such approaches should consider alignment, benefits, costs, and interdependencies.

ILLUSTRATIVE EXAMPLE

This section provides a brief example to illustrate how managers might use the ITPM Decision Framework in Figure 3. DigiBank is a major financial institution. The CEO and CIO of the organization have seen some articles about ITPM, and believe they could benefit from better managing their IT assets through ITPM. DigiBank has some processes in place for managing IT assets. However, the CEO and CIO believe there is considerable scope for more systematic management of IT assets. They are unsure about what constitutes ITPM, how it is different from what they are doing now, and what is involved in implementing ITPM.

Figure 3 presents a process which the CIO or (other managers) can use to systematically question existing IT management processes, identify strengths and weaknesses in existing processes and put in place additional processes needed to implement ITPM.

The process (Figure 3) starts with ensuring that each project that is proposed has a measure of alignment, costs, benefits, and risks (Step 1). The CIO realizes that Digibank has some processes for measuring project costs and benefits. Processes for measuring project risk exist, but need improvement. Processes for measuring project alignment need to be created. The discussion and references in Section 4 provide a starting point for improving project risk and alignment measurement.

On reviewing Steps 2 and 3 the CIO realizes the need to improve processes for comparing all proposed projects. They initiate a review of existing processes relating to these steps. The references relating to Steps 2 and 3 provide a starting point for fresh ideas. The CIO believes Digbank has good processes for project review (Step 4). However, decisions for project termination are not always consistent and could be improved, as is the case for reviewing and reprioritizing a portfolio of projects (Step 5). Digibank has a checklist and processes for Step 6. However, the CIO feels that decision making regarding upgrading or sunsetting a project could be improved. There are no processes in place for assessing the health of a portfolio of applications (Step 7) and references in Section 4, such as (Weill & Vitale, 1999) are a good starting point.

Having completed this exercise, the CIO of DigiBank feels that without Figure 3, systematic review of key steps and decisions needed to implement ITPM would have been considerably more difficult and would not have considered all the steps and decisions. Such a systematic review helps organizations assess their existing processes, relative to decisions and processes required for ITPM, and help them plan for ITPM implementations.

MANAGERIAL ISSUES

Practitioner articles regarding ITPM (Leliveld & Jeffery, 2003; Maizlish & Handler, 2005) mention that several organizations have implemented ITPM to varying degrees (maturity levels). Weill and Aral (2006) suggest that ITPM is a best practice. Surveys of chief information officers (Leliveld & Jeffery, 2003) regarding ITPM implementation reveal several managerial issues and challenges in implementing ITPM. Some interesting managerial issues for which related MIS literature in other implementation contexts exists are discussed below.

Management Support and IT Governance

ITPM projects are enterprise projects, because they involve multiple departments in addition to IT. Even within IT, there are likely to be different stakeholder groups, such as project managers, application support personnel, architects, and administration personnel with access to cost and contracting responsibilities involved in an ITPM project. Also, ITPM projects can be perceived

as IT projects and not business projects. While benefits to IT from a successful ITPM implementation may be expected, business units may be unclear as to why they should support an ITPM project. Successful ITPM projects are likely to require senior management or CXO (CEO, CFO, COO, and CIO) level support in order to resolve conflicts and ensure project success. Hence, the role of senior management and how they demonstrate support for ITPM is an interesting area of research. Prior research has recognized that power structures within an organization influence the type of senior management support required (Jasperson et al., 2002). How ITPM fits within an overall IT Governance framework, and roles and responsibilities of personnel involved in ITPM, is an interesting research area. This could build upon existing MIS literature on senior management support, and IT governance in other contexts (Brown & Grant, 2005; Peterson, 2004; Rau, 2004; Weill & Ross, 2005).

Relationship between IT and Business

Successful ITPM projects are likely to involve significant interaction between IT and business. These interactions are likely to occur during ITPM implementation as well as during ongoing management of the IT portfolio. Hence, recognizing differences between IT and business (Bassellier & Benbasat, 2004; Keil, Tiwana, & Bush, 2002; Peppard, 2001) and improving trust (Bushell, 2004; Gefen, 2004) are likely to be important in ensuring success of ITPM implementations. It is important to note that different stakeholders (e.g., business units, IT subunits) in an ITPM implementation may prefer outcomes (in terms of project selection or prioritization) that are best for them, while successful ITPM implementation is aimed at decisions that are best for the organization as a whole. This is likely to lead to conflicts between subunits. Hence, issues of power and politics are also likely to be important (Davenport,

Eccles, & Prusak, 1992; Hart & Saunders, 1997; Jasperson et al., 2002) for a variety of portfolio management decisions. Power and politics are also extremely important, because successful ITPM implementation requires sharing a variety of data across departmental boundaries. Examples of such data include cost data, contract clauses, application and infrastructure performance data, and project risk and success data.

Organizational Readiness and Change Management

Successful ITPM implementation in organizations could change several IT-related decision making processes in organizations. Examples of such processes include strategic planning, budgeting, project management processes, risk management processes, and application support processes. Hence, implementing ITPM can be viewed as business process change (Kettinger & Grover, 1995). Organizations differ significantly in their readiness to change (Guha, Groven, Kettinger, & Teng, 1997) and successful ITPM implementations are likely to involve active change management.

While a variety of research approaches are useful in studying managerial issues related to ITPM, case studies of ITPM implementations would be a particularly interesting and valuable area of future research. Such case studies would help to better understand "how" and "why" issues related to ITPM implementation (Yin, 1994).

CONCLUSION

The concept of managing IT as a portfolio of assets is gaining momentum, and is beginning to be considered a best practice (Jeffery & Leliveld, 2004). However, an analysis of what an IT portfolio is, how it is related to other types of portfolios, and how it should be managed is underdeveloped in MIS research. This article represents an attempt to present a cumulative body of relevant knowledge to aid future development of ITPM.

This article makes several contributions. First, it compares ITPM with other types of portfolio management, and develops an improved understanding of IT assets and their characteristics. A review of relevant literature from multiple disciplines is used to develop an improved understanding of ITPM concepts, such as assets, alignment, costs, benefits, risks, and interdependencies. Second, it presents a systematic, process-oriented framework for understanding ITPM. The proposed framework identifies critical ITPM decision stages. This framework could be of use to practitioners of ITPM who are interested in effective ITPM implementations in organizations, as well as researchers who are interested in further theoretical development of ITPM. An illustrative example of the use of this framework is provided. Third, the article integrates ideas from other types of portfolio management, as well as different streams of MIS research into ITPM decisions and management of ITPM implementations. This integration of research streams helps to identify a cumulative body of ITPM-related knowledge that exists and facilitates further development of ITPM. Several ideas for future ITPM research (summarized in Table 5) are identified.

REFERENCES

Applegate, L., Austin, R. D., & McFarlan, W. (2006). *Corporate information strategy and management: Portfolio approach to managing IT projects*. Boston: Mc Graw Hill.

Arora, A., Hall, D., Pinto, C. A., Ramsey, D., & Telang, R. A. (2004). Measuring the risk-based value of IT security solutions. *IEEE IT Professional, 6*(6), 35–42.

Ayag, Z. (2005). An integrated approach to evaluating conceptual design alternatives in a new product development environment. *Inter-*

national Journal of Production Research, 43(4), 687–713.

Bardhan, I., & Sougstad, R. (2004). Prioritizing a portfolio of information technology investment projects. *Journal of Management Information Systems, 21*(2), 33-60.

Bassellier, G., & Benbasat, I. (2004). Business competence of IT professionals: Conceptual development and influence on IT-business partnerships. *MIS Quarterly, 28*(4), 673–694.

Benaroch, M., & Kauffman, R. J. (1999). A case for using real options pricing analysis to evaluate information technology project investment. *Information Systems Research, 10*(1), 70–86.

Bhatt, G. D., & Grover, V. (2005). Types of information technology capabilities and their role in competitive advantage: An empirical study. *Journal of Management Information Systems, 22*(2), 253–278.

Brown, A. E., & Grant, G. G. (2005). Framing the frameworks: A review of IT governance research. *Communications of AIS, 15*(38), 696–712.

Bushell, S. (2004). At last a way to build trust. *CIO Magazine*. Retrieved January 27, 2008, from http://www.cio.com.au/index.php?id=677506899&fp=16&fpid=0

Byrd, T. A., & Turner, D. E. (2000). Measuring the flexibility of information technology infrastructure: Exploratory analysis of a construct. *Journal of Management Information Systems, 17*(1), 167–208.

Carr, N. (2003). IT doesn't matter. *Harvard Business Review,* 5-12.

Chien, C.-F. (2002). Portfolio-evaluation framework for selecting R&D projects. *R&D Management, 32*(4), 359-368.

Cimral, J., & Lawler, M. (2002). *White article: Getting started with portfolio management.* Prosight.

Cooper, R. G., & Edgett, S. (2003). Overcoming the crunch in resources for new product development. *Research Technology Management, 46*(3), 48–59.

Cooper, R. G., Edgett, S. J., & Kleinschmidt, E. J. (1997). Portfolio management in new product development: Lessons from the leaders-I. *Research Technology Management, 40*(6), 43–53.

Cooper, R. G., Edgett, S. J., & Kleinschmidt, E. J. (1999). New product portfolio management: Practices and performance. *The Journal of Product Innovation Management, 16*(4), 333–352.

Cooper, R. G., Edgett, S. J., & Kleinschmidt, E. J. (2004a). Benchmarking best NPD practices -I. *Research Technology Management, 47*(1), 31–43.

Cooper, R. G., Edgett, S. J., & Kleinschmidt, E. J. (2004b). Benchmarking best NPD practices-II. *Research Technology Management, 47*(3), 50–59.

Cooper, R. G., Edgett, S. J., & Kleinschmidt, E. J. (2004c). Benchmarking best NPD practices - III. *Research Technology Management, 47*(6), 43–55.

Datz, T. (2003). Portfolio management: How to do it right. *CIO Magazine*. Retrieved January 27, 2008, from, http://www.cio.com/archive/050103/portfolio.html

Davenport, T. H., Eccles, R. G., & Prusak, L. (1992). Information politics. *Sloan Management Review, 34*(1), 53–65.

DeLone, W. D., & McLean, E. R. (2003). The DeLone and McLean model of information systems success: A ten-year update. *Journal of Management Information Systems, 19*(4), 9–30

Devaraj, S., & Kohli, R. (2003). Performance impacts of information technology: Is actual usage the missing link? *Management Science, 49*(3), 273–289.

Devinney, T. M., & Stewart, D. W. (1988). Rethinking the product portfolio: A generalized investment. *Management Science, 34*(9), 1080–1096.

Dickinson, M., Thornton, A., & Graves, S. (2001). Technology portfolio management: Optimizing interdependent projects over multiple time periods. *IEEE Transactions on Engineering Management, 48*(4), 518–527.

Drury, D. H. (2000). Assessment of chargeback systems in IT management. *INFOR, 38*(3), 293–313.

Duncan, N. B. (1995). Capturing flexibility of information technology infrastructure: A study of resource characteristics and their measure. *Journal of Management Information Systems, 12*(2), 37–57.

Elton, E. J., Gruber, M. J., Brown, S. J., & Goetzmann, W. N. (2002). *Modern portfolio theory and investement analysis*. Wiley.

Fitzpatrick, E. W. (2005). *Planning and implementing IT portfolio management: Maximizing the return on information technology investments*. IT Economics Corporation.

Gefen, D. (2004). What makes an ERP implementation relationship worthwhile: Linking trust mechanisms and ERP usefulness. *Journal of Management Information Systems, 21*(1), 263–288.

Gerlach, J., Neuman, B., Moldauer, E., Argo, M., & Frisby, D. (2002). Determining the cost of IT services. *Communications of the ACM, 45*(9), 61–67.

Grover, V., & Segars, A. (2005). An empirical evaluation of stages of strategic information systems planning: patterns of process design and effectiveness. *Information and Management, 42*(5), 761–779.

Guha, S., Groven, V., Kettinger, W. J., & Teng, J. T. C. (1997). Business process change and organizational performance: Exploring an anteced-ent mode. *Journal of Management Information Systems, 14*(1), 119–154.

Hart, P., & Saunders, C. (1997). Power and trust: Critical factors in adoption and use of electronic data exchange. *Organization Science, 8*(1), 23–42.

Hayes, F. (2004). Chaos is back. *ComputerWorld*. Retrieved January 27, 2008, from, http://www.computerworld.com/managementtopics/management/project/story/0,10801,97283,00.html

Hoffman, T. (2005). Running IT operations like a business not so easy. *ComputerWorld*. Retrieved January 27, 2008, from http://www.computerworld.com/managementtopics/management/it-spending/story/0,10801,100135,00.html

Jasperson, J., Carte, T. A., Saunders, C. S., Butler, B. S., Croes, H. J. P., & Zheng, W. (2002). Power and information technology research: A metatriangulation review. *MIS Quarterly, 26*(4), 397–459.

Jasperson, J., Carter, P. E., & Zmud, R. W. (2005). A comprehensive conceptualization of the post-adoptive behaviors associated with IT-enabled work systems. *MIS Quarterly, 29*(3), 525–557.

Jeffery, M., & Leliveld, I. (2004). Best practices in IT portfolio management. *MIT Sloan Management Review, 45*(3), 41–49.

Keil, M. (1995). Pulling the plug: Software project management and the problem of project escalation. *MIS Quarterly, 19*(4), 421–447.

Keil, M., & Mann, J. (1997). The nature and extent of IT project escalation: Results from a survey of IS audit and control professionals (Part 1). *IS Audit and Control Journal, 1*(1), 40–48.

Keil, M., & Robey, D. (1999). Turning around troubled software projects: An exploratory study of the deescalation of commitment to failing courses of action. *Journal of Management Information Systems, 15*(4), 63–87.

Keil, M., Tiwana, A., & Bush, A. (2002). Reconciling user and project manager perceptions of IT project risk: A Delphi study. *Information Systems Journal, 12*(2), 103–119.

Keil, M., Truex, D. P., & Mixon, R. (1995). The effects of sunk cost and project completion on information technology project escalation. *IEEE Transactions on Engineering Management, 4*(42), 372–381.

Kettinger, W., & Grover, V. (1995). Towards a theory of business process change management. *Journal of Management Information Systems 12*(1), 9–30.

Kohli, R., & Devaraj, S. (2003). Measuring information technology payoff: A meta-analysis of structural variables in firm-level empirical research. *Information Systems Research, 14*(2), 127–145.

Kumar, R. (2004). A framework for assessing the business value of information technology infrastructures. *Journal of Management Information Systems, 21*(2), 11–32.

Leliveld, I., & Jeffery, M. (2003). *White article: IT portfolio management challenges and best practices.* Kellogg/DiamondCluster.

Leong, S. M., & Lim, K. G. (1991). Extending financial portfolio theory for product management. *Decision Sciences, 22*(1), 181–194.

Liberatore, M. J., & Stylianou, A. C. (1995). Expert support systems for new product development decision making: A modeling framework and applications. *Management Science, 41*(8), 1296–1316.

Liberatore, M. J., & Stylianou, A. C. (1995). Toward a framework for developing knowledge-based decision support systems for customer satisfaction assessment, an application in new product development. *Expert Systems with Applications, 8*(1), 213–228.

Loch, C. H., & Kavadias, S. (2002). Dynamic portfolio selection of NPD programs using marginal. *Management Science, 48*(10), 1227–1241

Lucas, H. C. J. (1973). A descriptive model of information systems in the context of the organization. *DATA BASE, 5*(2-3-4), 27–39.

MacMillan, I. C., & McGrath, R. G. (2002). Crafting R&D project portfolios. *Research Technology Management, 45*(5), 48–59.

Maizlish, B., & Handler, R. (2005). *IT portfolio management: Unlocking the business value of technology.* Wiley.

Martinsons, M., Davison, R., & Tse, D. (1999). The balanced scorecard: A foundation for the strategic management of information systems. *Decision Support Systems, 25*(11), 71–88.

McFarlan, W. (1981). Portfolio approach to information systems. *Harvard Business Review, 59*(5), 142–150.

Mikkola, J. H. (2001). Portfolio management of R&D Projects: Implications for innovation management. *Technovation, 21*(7), 423–435.

Montealegre, R., & Keil, M. (2000). De-escalating information technology projects: Lessons from the denver international airport. *MIS Quarterly, 24*(3), 417–447.

Newkirk, H. E., & Lederer, A. L. (2006). The effectiveness of strategic information systems planning under environmental uncertainty. *Information and Management, 43*(4), 481–501

Nobeoka, K., & Cusumano, M. A. (1995). Multiproject strategy, design transfer, and project performance: a survey of automobile development projects in the U.S. and Japan. *IEEE Transactions on Engineering Management, 42*(4), 397–409.

Peppard, J. (2001). Bridging the gap between the IS organization and the rest of the business: Plotting a route. *Information System Journal, 11*(3), 249–270.

Peterson, R. (2004). Crafting information technology governance. *Information Systems Management, 21*(4), 7–22.

Piccoli, G., & Ives, B. (2005). IT-dependent strategic initiatives and sustained competitive advantage: A review and synthesis of the literature. *MIS Quarterly, 29*(4).

Quinlan, T. (2002). The Value of an IT Chargeback System. *Journal of Bank Cost and Management Accounting, 5*(3), 16–30.

Rainer, R. K., Snyder, Charles A., & Carr, Houston H. (1991). Risk analysis for information technology. *Journal of Management Information Systems, 8*(1), 129–148.

Rau, K. G. (2004). Effective governance of IT: Design objectives, roles, and relationships. *Information Systems Management, 21*(4), 35–42.

Reilly, F. K., & Brown, K. C. (2002). *Investment analysis and portfolio management.* South-Western College Pub.

Reyck, B. D., Grushka-Cockayne, Y., Lockett, M., Calderini, S. R., Moura, M., & Sloper, A. (2005). The impact of project portfolio management on information technology projects. *International Journal of Project Management, 23*(7), 524–537.

Ringuest, J., Graves, S., & Case, R. (2000). Conditional stochastic dominance in R&D portfolio selection. *IEEE Transaction on Engineering Management, 47*(4), 478–484.

Ross, J., & Beath, C. (2002). Beyond the business case: New approaches to IT investment. *Sloan Management Review, 43*(2), 51–59.

Santhanam, R., & Kyparisis, J. (1996). A decision model for interdependent information system project selection. *European Journal of Operational Research, 89*(2), 380–399.

Santiago, L., & Bifano, T. (2005). Management of R&D projects under uncertainty: A multidi-mensional approach to managerial flexibility. *IEEE Transactions on Engineering Management, 52*(2), 269–280.

Santos, B. L. D. (1991). Justifying investments in new information technologies. *Journal of Management Information Systems, 7*(4), 71–90.

Schmidt, R., Lyytinen, K., Keil, M., & Cule, P. (2001). Identifying software project risks: An international Delphi study. *Journal of Management Information Systems, 17*(4), 5–36.

Schmidt, R., Lyytinen, K., Keil, M., & Cule, P. (2002). Perceptions of IT project risk: A Delphi study. *Information Systems Journal, 12*(2), 103–119.

Segars, A., & Grover, V. (1998). Strategic information systems planning success: An investigation of the contruct and its measurement. *MIS Quarterly, 22*(2), 139–163.

Seshadri, S., & Subrahmanyam, M. (2005). Introduction to the special issue on risk management in operations. *Production and Operations Management, 14*(1), 1–4.

Stummer, C., & Heidenberger, K. (2003). Interactive R&D portfolio analysis with project interdependencies and time profiles of multiple objectives. *IEEE Transactions on Engineering Management, 50*(2), 175–183.

Sun, L., Srivastava, R. P., & Mock, T. J. (2006). An information systems security risk assessment model under the Dempster--Shafer theory of belief functions. *Journal of Management Information Systems, 22*(4), 109–142

Thornton, M. (2005). Exfoliating dated IT assumptions. *Computerworld.* Retrieved January 27, 2008, from, http://www.computerworld.com/managementtopics/management/story/0,10801,105607,00.html

Venkatesh, V., Morris, M. G., Davis, F. D., & Davis, G. B. (2003). User acceptance of information technology: Toward a unified view. *MIS Quarterly, 27*(3), 425–478.

Verma, D., & Sinha, K. (2002). Toward a theory of project interdependencies in high tech R&D environments. *Journal of Operations Management, 20*(5), 451–468.

Wallace, L., & Keil, M. (2004). Software project risks and their impact on outcomes. *Communications of the ACM, 47*(4), 68–73.

Wallace, L., Keil, M., & Rai, A. (2004a). How software project risk affects project outcomes: An investigation of the dimensions of risk and an exploratory model. *Decision Sciences, 35*(2), 289–321.

Wallace, L., Keil, M., & Rai, A. (2004b). Understanding software project risk: A cluster analysis. *Information & Management, 42*(1), 115–125.

Weill, P. (2004). Don't just lead, govern: How top-performing firms govern IT. *MIS Quarterly Executive, 3*(1), 1-17.

Weill, P., & Aral, S. (2006). Generating premium returns on your IT investments. *Sloan Management Review, 47*(2), 39–48.

Weill, P., & Broadbent, M. (1998). *Leveraging the infrastructure*. Boston, Massachusetts: Harvard Business School Press.

Weill, P., & Ross, J. (2005). A matrixed approach to designing IT governance. *MIT Sloan Management Review, 46*(2), 26–34.

Weill, P., & Vitale, M. (1999). Assessing the health of an information systems applications portfolio: An example from process manufacturing. *MIS Quarterly, 13*(4), 601-624.

Weill, P., & Vitale, M. (2002). What IT infrastructure capabilities are needed to implement e-business models? *MIS Quarterly Executive, 1*(1), 17–34.

Westerman, G. (2005). What makes and IT risk management process effective. *MIT Sloan School of Management Center for Information Systems Research, 5*(3B), 1–3.

Westerman, G., & Walpole, R. (2005). Working article: PFPC: Building an IT risk management competency. *CISR,* 1–13.

Yin, R. (1994). *Case study research: Design and methods*. Beverly Hills, CA: Sage Publishing.

ENDNOTES

[1] Our discussion of asset classes and sub-portfolios (projects, applications, infrastructure components) is different from that of Broadbent and Weill (1998) who classify IT investments as infrastructure, transactional, informational, or strategic. Our approach is analogous to classifying financial portfolios as consisting of stock, bond and cash assets or sub-portfolios. Broadbent and Weill's approach is similar to classifying financial portfolios as conservative, balanced, and aggressive. Both approaches to classifying portfolios are used.

[2] A project proposal can be a request to build a new application/infrastructure component or an upgrade request for a current infrastructure/application component.

[3] This research was funded in-part by a grant from the Belk College of Business UNC-Charlotte.

This work was previously published in Information Resources Management Journal, Vol 21, Issue 3, edited by M. Khosrow-Pour, pp. 64-87, copyright 2008 by IGI Publishing (an imprint of IGI Global).

Chapter XIX
IT Portfolio Management:
Implementing and Maintaining IT Strategic Alignment

Brian H. Cameron
The Pennsylvania State University, USA

ABSTRACT

Information Technology Portfolio Management (ITPM) is a topic of intense interest in the strategic management of IT. In ITPM, IT synchronization with corporate business strategy is operationalized by the application of the principles of financial portfolio management to IT investments. This perspective is crucial to the continual alignment of business strategy and IT investments. Portfolio management is the discipline of managing projects together as a portfolio that meets stated corporate goals and objectives (Combe & Githens, 1999). It facilitates the optimization of resource allocation and development investment across multiple projects. This chapter investigates current techniques and issues for managing IT project portfolios and aligning those portfolios with the strategy of the business. The models and concepts presented are regarded as a starting point for dialogue and further research among IT project researchers and practitioners.

INTRODUCTION

Projects are used by companies to convert corporate strategy into new services, processes and products needed for the success and viability of the organization (Benko & McFarlan, 2003). Selecting the right projects through which to implement corporate strategy is a critically important process. Yet, selecting projects that support corporate strategy is often cited as an area of extreme weakness in many organizations. This misalignment of strategic planning and tactical operations is particularly acute in many IT organizations today (Bonham, 2005).

According to Rosser (2001), the IT portfolio approach suggests that alignment occurs in three ways. By definition, this approach forces engagement between the business and IT. It raises that engagement from a typically myopic review of individual projects to a more complete review that looks across all projects in the context of a comprehensive business strategy. Finally, the IT portfolio approach greatly reduces the emotional aspects of the project prioritization discussion and replaces it with criteria grounded in the business strategy.

ITPM is becoming an indispensable communication tool that helps business executives understand the visible impact IT operations have on business performance (Archibald, 2003). An IT portfolio is a set of managed technology assets, process investments, human capital assets and project investments allocated to business strategies according to an optimal mix based on assumptions about future performance (Benko & McFarlan, 2003). One of the goals of ITPM is to maximize value and risk tradeoffs in optimizing the organization's return on investment (ROI).

Under ITPM, all of an organization's IT projects are placed in a single repository, where the risk and reward of each project is reviewed and quantified. Using these metrics, senior management can then prioritize each project.

Portfolio management is not a new concept for business and IT organizations (Jeffery & Leliveld, 2004). However, in many organizations, portfolio management is typically used as a metaphor for prioritizing projects (Cooper, Edgett, & Kleinschmidt, 1998). Project portfolio management offers much more to the organization than simple project prioritization. Many of the financial analysis tools that financial portfolio managers utilize can be directly applied to the management of IT investments in infrastructure, applications, hardware, people, information, processes and projects. These analytic tools provide a view of investment alternatives based on cost vs. return and link IT investment decisions to business goals and objectives.

ITPM is important because most organizations have more project ideas than they have physical or financial resources to carry them out (Archer & Ghasemzadeh, 1999). In a similar vein, Cooper, Edgett and Kleinschmidt (2000, p. 19) write: "Pipeline gridlock plagues many IT portfolios. There are simply too many projects and not enough resources to do them well." Anell and Jensen (1998) observed that in-house projects have a tendency to make themselves permanent and that even failed projects show a surprising capacity for survival in many organizations. Existing models of ITPM are designed to help address this project overpopulation problem. However, some authors argue that this is only one side of a two-sided coin, of which the other side involves the active cultivation and nurturing of potential projects before they enter the traditional project portfolio management framework. A similar paradigm shift has taken place in the literature on risk management, in which the traditional view was that all risks are detrimental to projects. Now, the balance of opinion has shifted to acknowledge risk as a source of positive opportunities as well as negative effects (Charette, 2002).

Projects and potential projects typically pass through many stages of screening and prioritization before they are approved. For example, project portfolio management theory determines well-defined project checkpoints (or gates) where projects can be formally or informally challenged against established criteria. These checkpoints are used to determine if a project should be continued, accelerated, put on hold or canceled in the light of changing circumstances. Recent ITPM literature reveals that in many businesses this process is frequently less systematic and less rigorously enforced than portrayed in the models. As a consequence, many organizations are placing an increased emphasis on methodologies and processes that serve to better align projects with business strategy (Artto, Martinsuo, & Aalto, 2001). This disconnection between the corporate strategic direction and the portfolio of projects that will bring that strategy to fruition remains a deep source of concern to many chief executives today (Combe, 1998; Junttila, Ekholm, & Matilainen, 2001; Sharpe & Keelin, 1998).

To contribute to this dialogue and work towards achieving full economic benefit from ITPM, this chapter presents models, issues and best practices as well as published portfolio theories and case studies. ITPM is a relatively young discipline and the material presented is intended to serve as a starting point to promote dialogue, participation and further research. The chapter begins with an exploration of the current research on ITPM and motivations for the increased interest in ITPM today. The focus then moves to a discussion of the importance of aligning IT and business strategies and the importance of evaluating IT investments to ensure that those investments are aligned with one or more business strategies. From here, the chapter explores best practices and issues surrounding construction of the IT portfolio plan and associated IT portfolio. Next, an examination of IT portfolio, project and asset management issues and strategies is presented. The next section of the chapter delves into IT portfolio assessment and explores portfolio management techniques that help ensure that the IT portfolio is continually aligned with the strategy of the business. A discussion of the issues and strategies surrounding the effective communication and governance of the IT portfolio as well as a brief discussion of future trends in ITPM round out the chapter.

BACKGROUND

The product of the strategic planning process in most organizations is the strategic plan. However, the strategic process remains unrealized without proper implementation. Project management was defined by Turner (1996) as the art and science of converting vision into reality. This definition highlights the strength of the relationship between strategy creation, project management and strategy implementation. It is the confluence of these disciplines that has evolved into the modern science of project portfolio management. A literature review on project portfolio management

by Poskela, Korpi-Filppula, Mattila and Salkari (2001) presents a hierarchical relationship between strategy, project portfolio and individual projects. Referring to authors such as Archer and Ghasemzadeh (1999), Anell and Jensen (1998) and Turner (1999), they describe the role and purpose of project portfolio management as (1) a tool to implement the organization strategy; (2) a process for the projectification of business strategy; (3) a means to balance overall risk; and (4) a tool for optimizing resource allocation across projects.

Although relatively young as a discipline, ITPM has greatly matured in the last few years (Martinsuo, 2001). The number of organizations exploring ITPM as a way of adding value to their bottom line continues to grow each year, with projects increasingly viewed as "building blocks" in the design and execution of strategy (Project Management Institute, 2000). Sommer (1998) argues that any organization that funds, manages and allocates resources to more than one project has by definition a project portfolio (whether the organization is aware of it or actively manages it). Martinsuo (2001, p. 43) supports this view, stating, "Many project firms have succeeded probably without ever knowing that they manage a portfolio."

ITPM has been utilized by leading companies to make their enterprises more agile and competitive. Rather than locking in an annual budget, companies can create one list of necessary operating expenditures. They can then devote the rest of their money to an IT venture fund, the money from which can be shifted rapidly as opportunities arise and change. Portfolio management changes IT strategy from the old reactive paradigm to a sense-and-respond model of operation. As a result, ITPM theory, techniques and best practices are emerging areas of interest to IT researchers and industry leaders today (Combe & Githens, 1999).

Companies that become industry leaders share a common trait—they understand and exploit their specific source of value to customers. The strategy of these companies emphasizes excellence and prioritizes IT investments according to one of three value disciplines: product leadership, customer intimacy or operational excellence. Treacy and Wiersema (1995) argue that no company can be all things to all people. The company must identify a unique value that it alone can deliver to a chosen market by being dominant within one of these value disciplines.

Treacy and Wiersema (1995) crafted a simple but effective framework to guide strategic planning and help manage the IT investment portfolio of companies. Leadership in each of these disciplines delivers different types of value to customers, thereby requiring different types of IT investment unique to that value discipline. For example, product leadership may require research/development and engineering investment priorities, customer intimacy may require investment in CRM systems and techniques, and operational excellence may require that investments ensure superior price/performance quality at various price points.

Yet, defining and investing in a dominant value discipline does not mean that companies can neglect other disciplines. Once a priority is established, companies must ensure that they also remain competitive in other areas. Market leadership can also be derived from companies that efficiently integrate interdependent processes across these value disciplines. Even when not recognized as a leader in one of these specific disciplines, a company can create a source of customer value through effective systems integration. Efficient processes balanced across product differentiation, customer intimacy and operational excellence also build value by satisfying unique customer requirements, such as custom development, build-to-order opportunities or just-in-time manufacturing markets. Emphasis on external efficiency becomes of utmost priority with the growing trend to outsource many business processes and operations.

In an era of information-driven business op-portunities and increased demand for business flexibility, IT alignment with the business has a new meaning and new level of importance: the ability to support and at times drive sudden direction changes to capitalize on changing market opportunities. According to Rosser and Potter (2001), the alignment of IT and business strategy is the No. 1 concern of chief executive officers (CEOs) today. CEOs of fast-growth companies frequently indicate that IT is crucial for their success. The implication is that companies are working at a competitive disadvantage when their IT organizations are not aligned with business strategy.

To align with business strategy, the IT organization must be able to sense and respond, essentially becoming a fast collaborator with the CEO and business unit leaders. Critical to achieving this alignment is focusing on the impact of exemplary relationship management (Datz, 2003). This customer-centric focus causes IT organizations to move from supporting the business to becoming a business within a business, where the IT organization effectively competes and cooperates with outsourcers. In this model, outsourcing is a strategic decision, made in conjunction with the IT organization during the strategic planning process. There should be a direct relationship between business strategy and management of the IT portfolio of projects in place to implement that strategy. However, the seamless correlation between strategy and the project portfolio to ensure that the projects that will have the biggest impact on the desired strategic change are being undertaken in an orderly manner and with appropriate priority remains an inexact science in most organizations today (Archer & Ghasemzadeh, 1999; Dietrich, Poskela, & Artto, 2003; Dye & Pennypacker, 1999; Kaplan & Norton, 2001).

A review of the strategy and alignment literature reveals that most strategists have focused their efforts on various forms of strategic planning, strategic analysis and strategy formulation elements. The area of strategy implementation, which deals with operationalizing strategic plans, has been largely neglected (Roberts & Gardiner, 1998). The process for operationalizing strategic plans is still largely unexplored territory. It is difficult to envision how successful strategic plans can be devised in the absence of knowledge about how they are to be implemented. A comparison of the definitions of strategic planning and project management provides an indication that the two disciplines are compatible and, often, inseparable. A typical definition of strategic planning is, "a set of decision rules which guide the organization's resource allocation process, taking into account both the short and long term, with emphasis on allocating resources in uncertain conditions to achieve future objectives. The organization which uses a form of strategic planning does not simply react to events in the present, but considers what should be done in order to achieve future objectives" (Scott, 1997. p. 11).

Hartman (2000) approaches strategy from the project manager's perspective, suggesting that the best project and portfolio managers know how their projects support the corporate strategy and that they use this knowledge to help them obtain needed support and resources to succeed. The condition of knowing about the organization's strategy is imbued through a process of legitimate peripheral participation within the organization's historical and cultural mechanism for creating strategy (Lave & Wenger, 1991). There is little doubt that ITPM can be an effective tool for the implementation of strategic plans (Roberts & Gardiner, 1998), but the variability of current practice makes it clear that better and more explicit methodologies are needed to ensure that IT projects and investments are well aligned with the strategy and direction of the business.

ALIGNING IT INVESTMENTS WITH CORPORATE STRATEGY

The heart of the IT strategic planning process is arriving at a series of objectives or initiatives that provide guidance for selecting, maintaining and discontinuing IT projects (Luftman, 1996). IT project management strives to ensure that projects deliver results on time and budget. IT project management alone does not ensure that an organization is spending its resources in the right areas and doing the right projects. ITPM strives to ensure that the organization is doing the right projects and has enough of the right resources properly allocated to projects.

Selecting the right projects is only one element of organizational success. As Figure 1 suggests, strategic planning, ITPM, and IT project manage-

Figure 1. The strategic alignment cycle

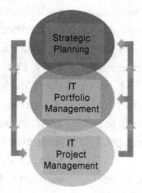

ment must be synchronized, with strong, bi-lateral communications. Through the strategic planning process, the organization and individual business units determine their direction and identify key goals and objectives (Weill & Broadbent, 1997). This process provides the foundation for the selection of projects and assignment of resources (portfolio management). After the portfolio of projects is selected, the organization needs to apply its knowledge, skills, tools and techniques to create the products or services through the practice of sound project management. The strategic alignment of corporate strategy and IT investments is not possible without this interconnected approach to strategic planning, portfolio management and project management (Heldey, 1997).

Companies strive to balance the opposing objectives of fiscal restraint and investment risk. This is not a new challenge, as companies have always struggled with this issue. This challenge has been exacerbated in recent years by various management and economic shortfalls that have constrained the availability of capital, limited investments and tightened budgets in many organizations more than usual. To effectively manage these competing objectives, companies must adopt strategic planning practices that identify and exploit strengths while fostering greater alignment with the business objectives of the organization's internal and external stakeholders (Santhanam & Kyparisis, 1995). Many organizations fail to build on their success and stray from targeted strategic objectives or fail to foster and build consensus among their stakeholder groups.

The resulting implications serve to create undesirable effects on customer satisfaction, financial performance and market share. Therefore, all stakeholder groups should start from common ground and create strategic plans based on general agreement as to what the relative strengths of an organization are and how to consistently manage an investment strategy to further enhance and exploit growth. This does not mean homogeniz-ing the business objectives of the stakeholder groups to eliminate competition among these groups. Competition fuels innovation, but it also often creates redundancy that increases overall costs. This redundancy often fails to trigger the potential economies of scale of earlier IT investments; hence, the opposing objectives.

Therefore, it is critical to structure strategic planning processes such that the source of corporate value is specified. This is accomplished by identifying, prioritizing and exploiting strategic investments according to customer intimacy, product differentiation or operational excellence that create a leading position within an industry (Jiang & Klein, 1999). No single organization can command a leadership position across all three of these areas. It is also imperative that management select and control investments using project portfolio management practices. This must take place to enhance and exploit an organization's source of value. Portfolio management provides the practices and principles needed to evaluate the relevant risks and rewards of various investment alternatives as they relate to stated strategic objectives, thereby facilitating conflict resolution across stakeholder groups (Solomon, 2002).

These principles and practices act as building blocks for strategic planning processes and are used to guide relevant IT investment decisions. This approach helps build consensus throughout an organization (among both its internal and external stakeholders) by clarifying and ranking investments relative to one another by distinguishing their value to operate, expand or transform the business. When these principles are practiced consistently, their use aligns business objectives and priorities across disparate groups, minimizes redundant efforts and reduces competition among limited investment resources.

CREATING A TECHNOLOGY EVALUATION FRAMEWORK

With the rapid rate of technological change, a strategic process for evaluating new technologies is needed in all organizations today. Modern organizations need the ability to transform, grow and move in new directions. They also need the mental ability to embrace transformation. Every investment and project has to be viewed in terms of the level of maturity of the organization. IT organizations must align IT actions (e.g., outsourcing, process improvements, re-engineering, technology migration, etc.) with business mandates (e.g., reduce costs, reduce waste, increase efficiency, become more customer focused, etc.) and turn strategies into results (Luftman, 1996). IT organizations should be on the forefront of determining and tracking long-term measures that provide a balanced view of the company. This transformation will require a focus on planning, organizational structures and performance. IT leadership must balance market and technology vision with market and technology reality and core organizational competencies.

To effectively identify, evaluate and integrate new technologies, the organization must first decide how much to invest in research and development (R&D). The issue of how much to spend in R&D has become elusive as organizations focus on cost cutting, workforce issues and maintaining current assets (Weill & Broadbent, 1998). The organization needs to utilize IT to innovate in order to produce value for its customers. Although technology itself is a driver for innovation and growth, successful transitions are driven by successful communication. Innovation and costs must be managed through the transition. Once the IT organization is transformed into a business within a business, its people start to feed innovation and provide options for moving the organization forward (Rosser & Potter, 2001).

Organizations that have successful frameworks in place for identifying, evaluating and implementing new technologies maintain a value creation culture where everyone in the organization knows who the customer is and what the value focus of the organization is to the customer (Weiser, 1994). These organizations also recognize that good decision-making requires alternatives—they do not simply take the first option that comes along and run with it; they want their employees to think out of the box. Change is viewed as positive and productive, and uncertainty is embraced (Spradlin & Kutoloski, 1999). Successful technology evaluation frameworks require an outside-in strategic perspective that examines factors outside of the organization and how they affect the business.

This perspective requires systems thinking that views the organization holistically, encourages open-information flows to all levels of the organization, and fosters the empowerment of management at all levels. Strategic decision-making that utilizes disciplined portfolio management processes and principles is at the core of successful strategic framework implementations (Kerzner, 2001). The principles that enable the organization to be innovative are not necessarily things that the organization does; they are ways of approaching and thinking about business investments and projects.

BUILDING THE IT PORTFOLIO PLAN

Projects undertaken by the organization should be a reflection of the organization's business strategy and able to be directly linked to the components of the business strategy that they support (Cooper, Edgett, & Kleinschmidt, 1997a). IT is often highly complex and difficult for non-specialists to understand. It is crucial for business executives to understand enough about IT to make significant and far-reaching strategic decisions. ITPM forges a critical link between the strategic planning process and the project management process, enabling management to reach consensus on the best use of resources by focusing on projects strategically aligned with the goals of the business.

An IT portfolio is more than a set of projects. It is comprised of a set of managed technology assets, process investments, human capital assets and project investments allocated to business strategies according to an optimal mix based on assumptions about future performance (Solomon, 2002). One of the goals of ITPM is to maximize value and risk tradeoffs in optimizing the organization's ROI. ITPM is an optimal way to categorize, capture and communicate IT value in business language. Value is achieved from the right balance of risk-and-reward decisions. Through this process, potential risks are identified and the likelihood of occurrence and severity of consequences are determined (Visitacion, 2003).

Identifying scenarios and evaluating risks leads to high-value IT portfolios. ITPM is the continuous process of selecting and managing the optimum set of project-oriented initiatives to deliver maximum value to the organization. Historically, ITPM has consisted of an intensive point-in-time review, with the goals of determining the current state of affairs and of making recommendations for changes in the project portfolio. These endeavors are highly labor intensive, and the results are extremely time-sensitive. While valuable in terms of the information it offers, this process typically produces static reports with relatively short shelf lives (Gliedman, 2002). A better process for ITPM is a continuous process of selecting and managing the optimum set of project-oriented investments that deliver maximum business value. Continuous ITPM begins with the development of a plan outlining how broad and deep the portfolio should be (objectives), what measurable expectations exist, and the risk and reward boundaries. Precursors to these activities include determining the IT organization's readiness to develop and benefit from ITPM, determining the IT organization's capabilities to successfully implement ITPM (including several capability assessments) and the

development of an overall organizational charter for ITPM (Miller, 1997).

Over time, the project portfolio may deviate from the stated organizational objectives, resulting in disproportionate levels of spending among projects that may not fully align with current strategic objectives. As a result, the actual strategic investment may vary significantly from the intended strategy. Strategic alignment analysis will uncover opportunities to improve the overall portfolio strategic alignment through modifications to the project portfolio. The portfolio plan is developed to define the portfolio investment strategy and structure. This plan includes categories into which investments will be split, the target investment mix across those categories and goals (risk/reward tradeoffs) for the portfolio (Buss, 1999). Triggers that will cause the portfolio to be re-evaluated and potentially rebalanced are also determined.

Underlying ITPM is the fundamental belief that IT property (e.g., hardware, software, data) and expenditures should not necessarily be considered costs or expenses—instead, they should be viewed as assets and investments that have unique value to yield measurable returns over time and managed as such (Broadbent & Weill, 1997). In addition, ITPM is both an analytical technique used to evaluate investments and a managerial tool used to prioritize and allocate IT resources. An IT portfolio must be prioritized for its ability to (1) consider assets and investments for their efficiencies to support day-to-day operations, (2) consider assets and investments that support the expansion of the business by improving asset use or migrating to more effective/efficient processes, and (3) consider assets and investments that seek new business opportunities.

Once the investments are listed, the organization can finalize the initial scope and depth of the portfolio management implementation. For some organizations, simply categorizing IT investments and using the portfolio as a communication tool is enough, whereas other organizations elect to apply the detailed statistical and management process disciplines of portfolio management to their business and IT investments (Rosser, 2001). Scale often drives the scope of ITPM implementations: Smaller IT groups can follow a simple portfolio management implementation; larger IT groups will benefit from the rigor and discipline of a detailed process. In either case, using a formal implementation process will accelerate business recognition of IT value and provide the most effective basis for ensuring the appropriate IT organizational structure.

According to Bonham (2005), the most basic use of ITPM is for communication of the elements of the IT portfolio in a business framework. Organizations starting ITPM often position the process as a communications tool. This perspective will focus the organization on the initial scope and business dialogue needed to create a single repository of categorized IT investments. This inventory will include IT assets and projects categorized for business-appropriate dialogue. Project prioritization, business case justification, basic IT governance and relationship management processes start to take shape as a result of the communication fostered by ITPM.

As portfolio management matures within the organization, individual ITPM within the IT group emerges. This level of ITPM allows for the active management of a portfolio—proactively balancing risk and reward. The initial target is usually a thematic (e.g., enterprise resource planning/ERP, CRM) sub-portfolio of IT assets and projects. Larger-scale IT groups will find it beneficial to appoint an overall portfolio manager to ensure coordination across portfolios. These groups typically combine relationship management (including change and problem management), services and products creation and delivery, and planning and measurement responsibilities.

After the organization develops a comfort level and competencies utilizing ITPM with a sub-portfolio of IT assets and projects, it typically advances ITPM across the entire IT organization (Bonham, 2005). This level of ITPM seeks to integrate all of the IT organization's assets, projects, resources and processes into one IT organization-wide investment portfolio. The process integration knowledge gained by assessing the deployment of ITPM at an individual sub-portfolio level is used to prepare the portfolio management plan covering the entire IT organization. IT organizational processes must be mature and integrated for this level of ITPM to be successful.

Once ITPM is engrained within the IT organization, portfolio management across the entire enterprise is typically the next evolutionary stage in portfolio management maturity. At this level of ITPM, the processes of the IT organization are no longer separate from business processes (Luftman, 1996). IT planning is fully integrated into business planning. Business planning cycles are dynamic, in contrast to the usual static yearly cycles. At this level of ITPM, the focus is on creating highly collaborative, high-performing, enterprise-wide operations that optimize the organization's portfolio of assets, projects, processes and resources. Business and IT organizational structures are merged into one organizational structure that has integrated portfolio management into its planning and management processes (Rosser & Potter, 2001).

CREATING THE IT PORTFOLIO

The first step in implementing portfolio management is to appropriately categorize the organization's IT investments. A portfolio is a categorized set of assets and investments. The items in a portfolio are typically classified by the level of risk vs. expected benefits, the current fair value of the investment and the expected investment life cycle. The IT portfolio will consist of activities/processes, projects and assets (e.g., liquid vs. illiquid, expense vs. capital, hard vs. soft, goodwill). The asset and project portfolios should be closely linked (e.g., a major improvement to an asset is a project) (Cooper, Edgett, & Kleinschmidt, 1997b).

Many organizations employ a three-category model for asset and project categorization: operate the business, expand the business and transform the business (Heldey, 1997). Organizations should adapt these categories to their particular context—taking into account their risk tolerance and process maturity. Gray areas between each category will exist and need to be managed within the linked value management, portfolio management, project prioritization and business case justification processes. Operate-the-business investments are needed to keep the business functioning. Spending in this category provides mission and business-critical services. Common spending entities in this category include electricity, lighting, heating/air conditioning, telephone dial tone, network services, IT vendor support and disaster recovery. Typical external influences that modify spending decisions in this category include business climate changes and corporate events or activities (e.g., mergers, acquisitions, divestitures) (Bonham, 2005).

Expand-the-business investments are needed to grow the organization's scope of products and services. Investments in this category might include software upgrades, adding incremental capacity or developing skills within the staff through additional training and other efforts. Spending in this category affords new levels of process efficiency and effectiveness that the business perceives it will need in the future and which the current assets cannot deliver. Assets in this category influence business performance through process agility (effectiveness), or through the ability to respond to new service requests in significantly less time than predecessors were able to respond. Transform-the-business investments involve project-based spending that creates new IT services that broaden an enterprise's ability to enter new markets. Emphasis in this category is on the speed required to gain control of a new market via first-mover advantage (Luehrman,

1998). Sample investments include new business ventures, mergers and acquisitions, new products, major new business initiatives and business process outsourcing.

Categorizing IT investments implies first listing the investments and grouping them by business unit and by overall shared services/products. Implementing portfolio management in such an environment can be considered business unit by business unit, with the shared-services IT portfolio considered one business unit. Given the typical scale and scope of CRM and ERP projects, significant value to the business is returned by applying portfolio management to the IT investments at the business unit level. As the organization-s portfolio management experience matures, grouping business unit portfolios together and managing them holistically is the natural evolution of applying the discipline of ITPM (Miller, 1997).

During the categorization process, information that the organization needs to make portfolio categorization decisions is compiled. This information takes many forms and comes from a variety of sources. Often, there exists a list of currently active projects and another "wish list" of requested or proposed projects awaiting further review. Some of these projects will have detailed work plans and many of the larger projects will have extensive scope and business case documentation that can be leveraged. Also, interviews and discussions with stakeholders will uncover information on otherwise "unknown projects" to complete the portfolio categorization process (Grochow, 1996).

Rather than focusing on detailed task assignments and project schedules, the data collected should be high-level. The data collection focus should be on capturing information that will be used in the categorization process. The information gathered is both quantitative and qualitative and generally contains information about projects, schedule and cost estimates, budgets, strategic initiatives, dependencies, expected benefits, risks, relative priority, value and ranking (Meredith

& Samuel, 1995). Information about available roles, resources, costs, skills and other important organizational information is also captured during the categorization process. Investment value is achieved from the right balance of risk and reward. Identifying potential risks, determining their likelihood of occurrence and determining the severity of consequences are essential parts of the portfolio creation process (Smith, 1996).

The appropriate mix of investment categories must be a dynamic business decision driven by market requirements, competition, internal requirements, business strategies and so forth. The belief that a proper mix exists is a dangerous assumption or strategy. The operate-expand-transform mix is neither a destination nor a primary performance indicator. Setting a good portfolio mix and managing toward it creates momentum and a performance culture that manages velocity metrics rather than a static portfolio mix. IT organizations that view management of the IT portfolio in this fashion are most apt to maximize their value to the business (Bonham, 2005).

According to Rosser (2001), typical IT portfolio mix ranges are 50%-80% operate the business, 10%-35% expand the business, and 0%-25% transform the business. When a high-performing organization makes a significant capital investment, its mix will typically shift significantly to the operate-the-business category. However, just because it is now spending more in this category, it does not cease being a high-performing organization. The operate/expand/transform mix is not an indicator of performance capability. The mix is only an indicator of current financial flexibility. For example, current spending on transformation is not what indicates transformation capabilities. That emphasis may be a last-minute, frantic attempt to avoid a catastrophe.

Technology's breadth, depth and upgrade cycles are making it difficult for IT organizations to cover the entire, ever-expanding IT list of organizational needs (Shoval & Giladi, 1996). The ITPM approach allows management to identify which

elements of the core IT competencies—planning, marketing, integrating, maintaining and human capital management—should be housed internally and which should be selectively outsourced. This process also assists in deciding which elements of which competencies are non-discretionary and which are discretionary. Building competencies should follow the strategic plan, which also implies a short-, medium-, and long-term planning horizon that must be considered (Visitacion, 2003). During this process, planners must evaluate their existing portfolio of assets to determine whether they can be further exploited for strategic advantage or whether additional investments are needed. This is where the delicate balance between fiscal control and strategic investment creates the greatest source of internal debate.

The assets of a typical IT portfolio consist of applications (e.g., ERP & CRM), data and information (e.g., customers, products, financials), services assets (e.g., consulting, engineering, security), infrastructure (e.g., servers, storage, networks), operations (e.g., data centers, help desks) and human capital. Assets are typically segmented into core, non-discretionary, discretionary, strategic and venture categories (Visitacion, 2003). Core assets are necessary expenses to enable operation of the IT organization (e.g., power, facilities, maintenance). Non-discretionary assets are typically forced expenditures caused by regulatory compliance, expansion or the need to replace outmoded or worn-out assets. Spending activity in this category centers on expanding existing capacity to meet growth requirements rather than to introduce new services.

Discretionary assets are required expenses to upgrade or replace existing assets (e.g., platforms, application versions). Spending in this category affords new levels of process efficiency and effectiveness that the business perceives it will need in the future and which current assets cannot deliver. Strategic assets are typically designed to support a growth or transformation business strategy (e.g., CRM, product life-cycle management, supplier relationship management) (Luftman, 1996). This category includes project-based spending that creates new IT services to deepen an enterprise's existing market penetration (e.g., expand market share). Venture assets are typically used to incubate future business opportunities or experiment with the transformation of business models or product/service lines (Gliedman, 2002). This category includes project-based spending that creates new IT services to broaden an enterprise's reach to enter new, untapped markets.

MANAGING THE IT PORTFOLIO

After the portfolio categories are established, each investment is placed in the appropriate category based on the risk-and reward decisions made in the IT portfolio plan. A strong portfolio measurement process is valuable for assessing actual IT portfolio performance against targets set in the planning phase and outlining discrepancies. Monitoring triggers should be established that signal potential portfolio problems. Following a formal portfolio management process will allow the organization to optimize the return on the overall IT investment portfolio and maximize its use in creating business innovation.

The key disciplines of planning and strategy, future-state planning and project management all overlap at the central core of the IT portfolio (Ghasemzadeh, Archer, & Iyogun, 1999). The planning and strategy discipline enables innovation and manages the business related to the particular asset portfolio, while future-state planning designs the evolution of the portfolio. The portfolio management process consists of two interrelated cycles: asset portfolio management and project portfolio management, both driven by business and IT strategies. These, in turn, frame the enterprise prioritization process for the identification, creation, acquisition or deployment of the assets (Bonham, 2005).

The asset cycle continually seeks to optimize the value that the assets are able to generate by identifying improvement, optimization, creation/acquisition and innovation opportunities. Optimal timing for asset disposal/retirement is understood and planned for upfront at asset creation or acquisition. Any projects necessary for asset creation/acquisition/improvement are identified and passed to the project portfolio management cycle. Asset usage is monitored to ensure optimal return, and value generated is assessed regularly to drive the appropriate use/retirement/enhancement strategy (McFarlan, 1981). The typical asset portfolio will include applications (ERP, CRM, e-mail, etc.), data and information, services, hardware, processes and human capital.

The project cycle actualizes the prioritized business transformation opportunities identified in business/IT planning and asset improvement identification. New projects are added either as recently identified and prioritized opportunities or as previously developed scenarios whose triggering event has occurred. Project adjustments (accelerate, slow down, retire) may also occur based on regular reviews of the projected value that the project will generate (Visitacion, 2003). Organizations should re-evaluate the business cases for both ongoing and non-triggered projects and take appropriate action to optimize the portfolio's value. This re-evaluation should occur on a regular basis, preferably quarterly. As projects enter the portfolio, their implementation is overseen and managed. Delivered projects' value is measured and assessed against initial expectations. Modified/created assets are transferred to the asset portfolio and managed as previously described.

According to Spradlin and Kutoloski (1999), portfolios should be managed with a life-cycle mindset, including stages such as portfolio goal setting, portfolio performance measurement and closing the cycle by adjusting and rebalancing the portfolio appropriately (adding, accelerating, decelerating and exiting portfolio components). The asset and project portfolios and their management processes should be embedded into the business and IT ecosystems. Building robust portfolio management capabilities is a staged process, tied to business and IT process maturity.

Performance improvement options (e.g., shifting resources from one project to another, developing new skills, providing user training) are developed by the governance body that oversees the portfolio management process (Miller, 1997). The project portfolio is continually reviewed with respect to strategic direction and external factors. This process involves defining and monitoring status metrics to keep projects on track and ensuring that executives and stakeholders are engaged. Adjustments to the project portfolio are made as strategic and operational plans change. Continuous monitoring of the project portfolio leads to frequent fine-tuning and occasional major shifts in the portfolio.

Project costs are summarized across multiple investment categories and compared with industry benchmarks to create baselines, set targets and balance the project portfolio. Most importantly, project value is captured and summarized to evaluate and maximize the value of the entire project portfolio (Rosser, 2001). An inventory of all projects is conducted to properly assess resource demands and ensure that the organization has enough resources to make the project portfolio achievable. The projects are mapped to the business strategies for a better view of the portfolio's strategic alignment.

Maximizing value, finding balance and aligning with corporate strategy while ensuring achievability in the project portfolio is challenging. Focusing on any one of these four goals in the absence of the others will lead to very different results. For example, fully maximizing the value of the project portfolio may lead to a poorly balanced portfolio that is neither aligned with the organization nor feasible. Therefore, optimization should be approached as an interactive review process to optimize the project portfolio in the

face of multiple (and possibly conflicting) goals (Luehrman, 1998).

This process begins with a review of the findings uncovered during the portfolio analysis. Strategic alignment issues may have been identified, or over-allocated (or mis-allocated) resources may indicate that the project portfolio is not realistic or feasible. Clear objectives should be defined that target desired organizational outcomes before any changes are made to the project portfolio. A cost and resource impact analysis will assist in uncovering portfolio adjustments needed before an achievable project portfolio is achieved. The process continues by reviewing portfolio strategic alignment and balance. Trade-offs are considered through multiple iterations of this process and final portfolio adjustments are made to arrive at the optimal project portfolio (Bonham, 2005).

The result of an iterative review process is an optimized project portfolio based on specific goals and constraints. Testing the impact of multiple what-if conditions on the project portfolio is an important element in the ongoing optimization process. The main benefit of what-if analysis is the potential to discover creative solutions by modeling the project portfolio under a variety of different conditions (Spradlin & Kutoloski, 1999). For example, this what-if analysis allows management to test the schedule and cost impacts of slowing a project, accelerating a project or canceling a project.

The main goal of scenario planning is to model a range of possible external impacts on the project. This form of modeling is in many ways a structured what-if analysis for selecting from multiple options. In scenario planning, each scenario is defined as a collection of what-if conditions and their outcomes. For portfolio optimization, scenario planning allows planners to choose from several equally valid project portfolios by determining which of the portfolios is best equipped to handle the range of possible external factors.

The ITPM process is designed to create the optimal IT project portfolio within the environmental, political and technological constraints of the organization. In most cases, this means that the final portfolio will be sub-optimal in some respects, but it will be the best project portfolio that the organization can implement at that particular point in time. Optimizing the project portfolio requires a collaborative approach to reviewing and adjusting the portfolio. Reaching consensus in this process can be challenging due to the number of variables involved. Real-time what-if analysis in a group setting is usually not very efficient. However, the scenario planning process can help focus the discussion on the merits of the alternatives (Ross & Beath, 2002). This process requires that the decision makers define the scenarios and associated constraints. Next, the project portfolio analysts construct multiple alternative portfolios off-line, ensuring that each alternative is achievable given the current constraints. After the merits of each alternative portfolio are discussed, a consensus decision or direction for refining the alternatives is typically achieved.

MANAGING PROJECTS AND ASSETS WITHIN THE IT PORTFOLIO

Project management is a proven technique to manage key attributes about a project, including scope, time, cost, quality, communication, risk, human capital, procurement and integration (The Standish Group, 2003). These attributes are tracked throughout the design, engineering, development and deployment phases of a project. Activity timelines, resource schedules and funding commitments are common mechanisms to track in this process (e.g., budget vs. actual expense). This enables managers to respond to the unplanned impact that these constraints have on project goals. The orientation of project management is typically inwardly focused and not sensitive to external influence.

Portfolio management is a structured technique to categorize, evaluate, prioritize, purchase and manage an organization's projects and assets (e.g., hardware, software, human capital, processes) (Pastore, 2003). It is based on current and future economic drivers, as well as on the acceptable value/risk balance desired by the business. Portfolio management enables a responsiveness to market dynamism not provided by project management. This includes dynamic modeling and the updating of prioritization for project and service enhancements, as well as the updating of funding decisions driven by constraints imposed by the business.

Project portfolio management is a macro-level control mechanism to ensure that enterprise strategies are operationalized (Bonham, 2005). Strategic change occurs through change projects. However, for the macro-level portfolio to be effective, the micro level (i.e., successful project executions) must be refined. Micro-level change control occurs through project management. Effective project management enables better control over the allocation of scarce resources, manages change more effectively, improves the image of IT by delivering on expectations, improves customer satisfaction through effective change control and expectation management, and attempts to contend with emerging challenges. Project management provides consistent processes, appropriate metrics and needed control. Project management is the most critical enabler of a successful project portfolio (Solomon, 2002). In the absence of project management, the project portfolio is merely a collection of unbridled initiatives supporting common objectives.

Enterprise project management capabilities provide for the proper rollup of project information into the IT project portfolio. When projects are completed, consistent project management methods should enable the state change from IT projects to IT assets, promoting better IT asset portfolio management. Project costs, projected benefits and expected asset life cycle can be consistently transferred into the asset portfolio via consistent project management methods, enabling more effective asset portfolio management. Project tracking information incorporated in this manner often translates into hard-dollar productivity gains (Grochow, 1996).

ASSESSING IT PORTFOLIO EXECUTION

Most organizations utilize financial models to determine the value of their projects. Many of these models use financial metrics that consider the value of money invested over time and the cost of the company's capital, such as net present value (NPV) and the internal rate of return (IRR), to evaluate the cost of implementing projects, along with a stream of future projected revenues or other benefits (Visitacion, 2003). The projected financial benefits may take a variety of forms, such as expected revenue growth and/or operating cost reductions. Though financial modeling is an important component of determining project value, it is not the only aspect of value that should be considered. Non-financial benefits (improved customer satisfaction, reduced defects, increased market share, etc.) can be quantified and evaluated using non-financial metrics. Scoring models are an effective metric that use non-financial ratings to produce a form of value measurement that can account for a variety of financial and non-financial benefits (Buss, 1999). As companies become more sophisticated in their processes to measure value, they often evolve mixed value measurement processes and tools that combine traditional financial metrics with non-financial scoring metrics to prioritize projects.

According to Combe and Githens (1999), there are two major challenges in determining the value of a project. The first is to define a methodology that allows for comparison of the value of one project to another. Most projects have a number of intangible benefits that make comparing one proj-

ect to another difficult. In addition, large projects often have larger costs, so the net of the project benefits minus the project costs is important for accurate project comparison. The second major difficulty in determining project value is to account for the time value of costs and benefits. In general, project costs are incurred before project benefits are realized, and the value of the project benefits received today is worth more than it will be in the future.

Both of these issues are addressed in traditional financial models by converting costs and benefits into offsetting streams of discounted cash flows. NPV and IRR are the most commonly used financial models; however, a number of variants exist. NPV is widely considered the best absolute measure of value (Gardiner & Stewart, 2000). This financial model factors the opportunity cost of capital (or discount rate) into the equation for calculating economic value. IRR is not an absolute value, but rather a ratio (or rate). This ratio is useful for comparing dissimilar investments. IRR is also useful for making comparisons between different-sized projects, different periods and for making international value comparisons. The expected commercial value method is used to determine the commercial worth of each project to the business (Grochow, 1996). The expected commercial value calculation is based on a decision-tree methodology that considers the probabilities of both technical and commercial success, the strategic importance of the project, and the future stream of costs and benefits. Economic value-added is a value-based measurement technique that calculates after-tax cash flow generated by a project minus the cost of the capital required to generate the cash flow. Economic value-added is used to represent real profit vs. paper profit and report shareholder value, a major area of focus for many corporate strategies today (Buss, 1999).

In many cases, the benefits from each project do not start accumulating until the project has been completed, and then the benefits often extend months or maybe years beyond the end of the project. Therefore, to accurately measure a project's ROI, it is important to keep the project in the portfolio well past the completion date. After the actual costs and benefits for each project are captured, the same financial models used to estimate value (e.g., NPV, IRR) can be used to calculate a project ROI over a given period of time. The capturing of actual costs and benefits at a project level allows for the calculation of the ROI for the entire project portfolio (Gliedman, 2002). This provides an objective measure of the value that the project portfolio is producing and also helps executives understand how to align the projects in the portfolio.

Financial models typically utilize only a few key criteria for calculating value. Scoring models, on the other hand, may use many more criteria in assessing a project's value. Scoring models have the added benefit of using subjective measures to calculate project value. These models can be more complex to implement, since they often rely on decision makers to provide much of the data in the form of ratings assigned through a review process. With scoring models, projects are typically rated on a number of questions or criteria that constitute superior projects. These ratings are weighted and totaled to produce a single score. This score is used as a proxy for the value of the project to the organization. This value proxy incorporates strategic alignment and balance considerations beyond pure financial measures (Jiang & Klein, 1999). The Productivity Index is a financial scoring model that utilizes expected commercial value, technical risk and remaining R&D expenditures to derive a financial value index that can be used for ranking projects in the portfolio. The Dynamic Rank Ordered List is another scoring model that utilizes a ranking technique that combines financial and subjective ratings and ranks projects accordingly (Gliedman, 2002).

The need to accurately define the portfolio's value has led to the creation of activity models for project and asset costing. A shift from industrial

activity with 80% fixed and 20% variable costs to information management with 20% fixed and 80% variable costs has created IT management uncertainties (e.g., competitor innovation, staffing shortages and changing customer demands) (Rosser, 2001). Innovation, management capability, employee and customer relationships, quality and brand value explain a significant proportion of a company's value, and IT managers must learn to model these intangibles to effectively contribute to business value. Activity Based Costing (ABC) is the instrument that many leading organizations are using to fully allocate, value and communicate IT services, products and costs.

ABC is an alternative to traditional accounting methods and allows an organization to identify activity centers and assign costs to products and services based on the number of events or transactions involved in the process of providing a product or service. One of the goals of ABC is to determine the actual cost associated with each product and service produced by the organization without regard to the organizational structure. With costing based on activities, the cost of performing each activity in a project can be ascertained and evaluated. The premise behind ABC is that controlled change cannot be initiated in a company that does not measure its processes and activities (Rosser, 2001). Strong leadership cannot compensate for poorly understood processes. Organizational agility and learning require investing in processes, products and services that offer sustainable advantages, and ABC captures the information needed by management to make effective decisions. By supplementing accounting measures with non-financial data about strategic performance and activity details of strategic plans, companies can communicate objectives and provide incentives for managers to address long-term strategy.

ASSESSING NEW TECHNOLOGIES

Organizations view technology in two ways: continuous and discontinuous. Continuous technologies are built on what already exists in the organization. Discontinuous technologies come from R&D activities and offer radically new approaches to problems. Trend linkage is a critical piece for forecasting new technologies and their impact on an organization. The balance between people and technology is an important consideration in this process. There is a delicate balance between what organizations and individuals do and the way in which new technologies are introduced and used. Forecasting requires making decisions within a framework of uncertainty, and uncertainty implies risk. Navigating new technologies from a risk to an opportunity requires a good understanding of the primary value that the technology creates for the organization. The alignment of the organization's IT strategy with its business strategy is crucial for managing the risks and realizing the value associated with new technologies.

Managing the IT portfolio entails examining how much risk an organization can afford and applying the appropriate IT financial investment strategy. Many organizations today are using a real-options approach to the financial analysis of new technologies. A real-options approach depends on the business impact of the initiatives themselves and the forecasted impact of the initiatives. It accounts for future opportunities and the uncertainty involved with new technologies, which traditional project measures like NPV do not (Luehrman, 1998).

Traditional financial planning tools and techniques (DCF, NPV, ROI, IRR, etc.) are incomplete and do not give a sufficient view of risk and reward in today's volatile, fast-moving world (Copeland, 2001). Many organizations are evolving the current, mostly financial process to a risk/reward-balanced scorecard approach. This approach is enhanced with options and portfolio management best practices borrowed from the financial industry used for valuing and managing the organization's IT investments.

Real options analysis (ROA) treats strategies as chains of related business options that should be separated and quantified. According to Luehrman (1998), the process consists of four steps:

1. **Uncovering real options:** Real options are usually buried inside complex webs of interdependent investments. To expose option opportunities, scenario analysis is frequently used to identify variables that could significantly alter outcomes. Cash-flow patterns are also examined for investment peaks that may signal opportunities to change paths.

2. **Gathering the data necessary to value real options:** Accurate quantification of real options requires data on several variables:

   - The cost/benefit ratio of the option
   - The exercise price
   - The value of the underlying asset
   - Time to expiration
   - The risk-free rate of return
   - The uncertainty (e.g., standard deviation) of projected returns.

3. **Calculating the value of the option:** This step employs tools common to financial option analysis to quantify a real option's dollar value.

4. **Using the analysis to create beneficial strategies:** Add the value of real options to the value of the same project as calculated by traditional analyses. Develop dynamic strategies that convince the organization to change behaviors.

ROA enables the chief information officer (CIO), often working in conjunction with the chief financial officer (CFO), to provide improved business strategy advice to the business units. It combines static financial calculations with a time-phased view of the value of implementing the projects in portfolio at different times in the future. A major challenge in this process is to provide a realistic assessment of the risk associated with each option. The benefits of ROA are agility, a sense-and-respond ability to adapt the business value of the project portfolio to changing conditions as they happen, the ability to consider deferring the decision to continue and the ability to quantify the value of deferring as an input to the decision-making process.

ROA also enables a more accurate assessment of the value of long, large multi-phased projects, such as ERP and CRM. Many organizations are beginning to use this more accurate assessment to assist their business units in increasing the accuracy and quality of their decisions, thus further illustrating the value of their IT organizations to the enterprise. The primary value of ROA is that it enables CIOs and their business unit colleagues to dissect and reassess a business and/or technology strategy. It enables them to break large, complex problems into smaller, simpler ones. It also helps them identify risk components and decide which ones to hold, hedge or transfer.

CASE STUDY: BRITISH AIRWAYS

In 1994, British Airways (BA) discovered that approximately one-third of its customers were dissatisfied with their flights. The company also discovered that less than 10% of these dissatisfied customers made contact with the company's customer relations department. Internal research established that a delay in responding to complaints led to a 30%-45% decline in possible intent to reuse BA. However, the effect of this decline in possible reuse intent on actual future behavior was not clear.

BA's CEO at the time, Colin Marshall, established a strategic focus of "putting the customer first"—which meant much more than just getting

to the destination on time. As a result, BA invested approximately U.S. $9 million in a system that enabled customers to register complaints faster. The company did not know the financial benefits of this system in advance and a cost-benefit analysis would not have produced meaningful results during the decision-making process. However, the intangible aspects of the project (particularly the fit with corporate strategy and improved customer information) meant even if the project generated no additional income, it provided a foundation for further projects to win back an estimated U.S. $800 million in potentially lost revenue that the dissatisfied customers represented. This case is an instance where the strategic considerations of a project were far more important than the short-term emphasis on revenues and costs.

COMMUNICATING THE IT PORTFOLIO

It is critically important that all stakeholders understand the IT portfolio plan and any changes made. This involves developing communication plans, delivering the messages to stakeholders and measuring communication success. Communication is a particularly critical part of the initial adoption of ITPM in an organization (Pastore, 2003). As the portfolio management process evolves into a continuous cycle of analysis and fine-tuning, the portfolio changes become less significant and the adjustment process becomes more efficient through standard practice. When implementing large changes to the project portfolio, there is risk of pushing the organization into a long adjustment period of very low productivity as plans are adjusted. Clearly communicating the changes required to move to the newly optimized project portfolio, as well as the logic behind the decisions, is critical to minimizing any down time associated with the change in strategic direction.

According to Visitacion (2003), effective communication serves two objectives. First, it clearly outlines the changes and unambiguously defines the new direction. The new project portfolio represents a top-down plan that sets direction and constraints to guide the bottom-up planning activities. The new direction and constraints, along with any assumptions, must be clearly conveyed to make the detail planning as efficient as possible. Second, communication provides the rationale for project teams to make changes in support of the "bigger picture." Ensuring project teams understand their role and their contribution to the value, balance and alignment of the project portfolio is important for building buy-in and support. Buy-in is not a black-and-white issue, but rather a matter of degrees. The more buy-in and support obtained, the more efficiently the changes will be implemented and sustained.

IT PORTFOLIO GOVERNANCE

Bigelow (2003) argues that portfolio management is critical to project justification and governance. The role and importance of governance in organizations has increased steadily over the last 10 years, reflecting a rise in complexity and uncertainty in the internal and external environments that confront organizations (Williams, 2003). The principles and theories of governance concerning accountability, responsibility, direction and control are expressed by the Asian Development Bank (1998) as four fundamental pillars of governance:

- **Accountability:** The capacity to call officials to account for their actions.
- **Transparency:** Entails low-cost access to relevant and material information.
- **Predictability:** Results primarily from laws and regulations that are clear, known in advance, and uniformly and effectively enforced.

- **Participation:** Needed to obtain reliable information and to serve as a reality check and watchdog for stakeholders.

IT governance is about assigning decision rights and creating an accountability framework that encourages desirable behaviors in the use of information and technology. ITPM is a powerful tool for IT governance that requires close connections among principles, processes, people and performance (Datz, 2003). As IT services are increasingly embedded in business operations, the IT focus shifts from cost efficiency to operational effectiveness and business process enhancement. To develop a strategic role within the business, the IT organization needs to pass through several phases, from being an order taker to becoming an integrated business partner with the rest of the company's activities (Prahalad & Krishnan, 2002). To make this evolution, the IT organization must educate the business about the services it provides (in terms of costs, quality, time to market, value, and risks involved), while constantly managing and maintaining a balanced portfolio of assets and projects that support the business.

It is critical to stress that IT governance is enterprise-wide governance, meaning that it requires both the IT organization and the rest of the business to be active participants. Gaining business unit participation in IT governance is a critical success factor for establishing a project priority scheme (Bonham, 2005). Effective IT risk management entails both top-down and bottom-up risk-management practices. Top-down management addresses risk in a granular, synchronous fashion, supporting executive-level decisions around portfolio initiation, investment strategies, progress review and value strategies. The focus is on understanding risks before plans are defined or operationalized. Conversely, bottom-up management concentrates on performing detailed, continuous assessment of risk and deals with day-to-day operational risks. Together, they provide a 360-degree, multidimensional view of risks that considers an organization as a whole.

The heart of IT portfolio governance is the strong connection between principles, processes, people and performance. Processes and principles, the heart of organizational culture and governance, are fundamental to ITPM (Kirsch, 1997). IT portfolio governance must establish enterprise-wide governing principles to articulate governance guidelines within which expected behaviors occur within the enterprise. In many organizations, the IT portfolio manager role is initially fulfilled by the CIO and functional vice presidents or directors. A governing body should be created that includes senior IT and business unit leaders, which develops the principles for governing appropriate for the organization.

The principles component of IT portfolio governance has two primary functions: principle development and principle compliance. A consistent set of principles must articulate the guidelines within which expected behaviors occur with the intent of directing the enterprise toward an acceptable level of commonality (Miller, 1997). Examples of IT portfolio principles include the decision that IT investments are classified as either assets or projects, that investments will be divided into categories meaningful to the business and relevant to the IT organization (operate-expand-transform) and that the investment mix is to be defined by an IT portfolio steering committee, with balancing and tuning recommendations made by the IT organization.

A set of consistent, enterprise-wide processes must be defined to execute the governing principles. These processes can broadly be grouped into operational processes, administration processes, financial processes, logistics processes and strategic processes. Effective IT portfolio governance requires governing bodies to ensure that relevant principles and processes are developed, adhered to and evolved over time. These groups include the executive steering committee, IT steering committee, IT architecture team, enterprise program management office and various

centers of excellence. The most overlooked and ill-managed aspects of IT portfolio governance are the controlling of performance (controls and checks) of the various IT governance processes and the monitoring of compliance with established principles (Meredith & Samuel, 1995).

Executive steering committees are special committees usually appointed by the CEO or board of directors of an organization to carry out specified tasks and submit findings and recommendations. IT steering committees are usually tasked with identifying projects and establishing IT plans and priorities. These committees are typically comprised of business unit and IT representatives. The IT architecture team makes technology policy, design and implementation recommendations and typically reports to the IT steering committee. Typical areas of responsibility include database, hardware, information, security, software and data center operations. The enterprise program management office oversees enterprise-level projects that are typically interrelated or interdependent to eliminate duplicate work and allow for staffing and decisions across the projects.

Centers of excellence (COEs) replace the traditional relationship between IT and business, where business advocates request IT services, define needs to IT representatives, and then test and implement new or revised systems. In a COE model, some traditional IT functions shift into the COE, including business process design, integration management, and enterprise application business functional configuration and programming. The essential function of the COE is to drive continual business benefit through optimization of business processes, optimization of end-user competency, and the continued coherence and integration of functionality and data through all processes.

The COE is typically run by the enterprise program management office, which typically reports to the CIO and IT steering committee. Although the IT COE may reside within the IT organization, it is made up of elements from across the organization. COEs are typically organized by workgroups bound by common themes, policies, requirements, procedures, process owners and core IT functions. COE workers share goals, standards, performance measures, tasks and management. COEs help to ensure tight business and IT alignment.

Effective IT portfolio governance mitigates conflict between long- and short-term goals. An enterprise can neither be focused just on the tactical, day-to-day decisions to promote immediate revenue and profit, nor can it focus only on the strategic, future-oriented vision of the enterprise to promote long-term growth and persistence. To transform while performing, conflicts between these opposing forces must be mitigated. Good governance practices also create a climate of trust and increase agility and freedom of action. Individual trust, decision-making and empowerment must be fostered within the governance structure for effective portfolio governance.

IT portfolio governance should not become so formal and rigid that no decisions are ever reached. Effective IT portfolio governance must include people from all parts and varying levels of the organization, participating in both policy development and policy compliance. Participation breeds communication, which breeds comprehension, which breeds buy-in, which breeds compliance. Governance provides a structured forum for discussing and communicating the strategies, goals, priorities and principles of an organization, as well as the expected impact on the enterprise (Visitacion, 2003).

The most distinguishing and important characteristic of well-functioning IT portfolio governance is the existence of a true culture of portfolio management within the organization (Bonham, 2005). Culture, rather than business strategy or technologies, is the catalyst behind process and commitment. The heart of organizational culture is a common set of values that the entire organization believes in and adheres to. A healthy culture strives to create an organization wherein individuals are empowered and that promotes information facilitators and contributors, not controllers. In this environment, risk-taking is encouraged and failure is viewed as a learning opportunity. Culture is the key factor in successfully moving the value perceptions of the IT organization from cost center to value center.

Governance is evolutionary. Over time, more or less formal means of governance will be required to meet expected results. Ongoing measurement of governance policies and their impact on the enterprise is required to determine how governance must evolve. Effective IT portfolio governance is a key factor in achieving business value from IT investments and providing transparent pathways for different levels of involvement, decision making, and allocation and acceptance of responsibilities. It is critical to carefully think through the governance principles and processes implemented in an organization to ensure that they facilitate achievement of the business value sought from the organization's IT investments. The implemented principles and processes must be consistent with the business model, leadership culture and corporate governance policy and direction (Luftman, 1996). The IT portfolio governance policy must include all of the relevant governing principles, processes, management structures and performance metrics that enable business and IT executives to integrate business and technology planning and implement and monitor key business and technology initiatives.

FUTURE TRENDS

According to The Standish Group (2003), less than 5% of Global 2000 corporations currently utilize portfolio management practices that manage business and IT investments as one portfolio. Today, many organizations are recognizing the value of embracing the portfolio management approach, which starts at the basic level of using portfolios as a communication vehicle (50% of the Global 2000) and evolves to utilizing portfolio management within the IT group on a sub-portfolio of IT assets (35% of the Global 2000). Organizations in the next, more advanced level of ITPM evolution holistically manage the entire set of IT investments as one portfolio across the entire IT organization (10% of the Global 2000) (Rosser & Potter, 2001). As more IT and business unit executives realize the strategic importance of ITPM, the above percentages are projected to increase significantly within the next 5 years. Even so, most organizations have a long way to go before they are able to truly create a highly collaborative, high-performing, enterprise-wide operation that optimizes the organization's portfolio of assets and projects.

There are many challenges to effective ITPM. Organizations that view IT as an expense rather than as an investment, will unlikely be able to reach more advanced levels of ITPM. In addition, according to Rosser and Potter (2001), 89% of companies today are flying blind, with virtually no portfolio metrics in place except for finance; 84% of companies either do not conduct business cases for any of their IT projects or perform them only on select, key projects; and 84% of companies are unable to adjust and realign their budgets with business needs more than once or twice a year.

Companies need to create a true culture of portfolio management within the organization before ITPM can be successful (Kerzner, 2001). Culture, rather than technology or business strategies, is the catalyst behind commitment and process. The aforementioned statistics suggest that commitment and process need to be greatly enhanced in many organizations before ITPM can have any lasting effect on the organization and its strategic objectives.

CONCLUSION

Strategic planning needs to be a continuous, collaborative process. Strategic planning is no longer a 5- or 10-year vision-setting exercise. It is a way of looking at conditions and initiatives that are just 1 to 3 years out. The process of strategic planning needs to occur continuously in organizations. The corporate strategic plan should serve as a commitment platform for IT initiatives (Heldey, 1997). Strategic planning needs to become a core competency of the organization for its long-term success. A strong CIO with vision is required to assist in building the strategic planning competency of the organization. Building stovepipes (one person does one thing, another person does another thing and they never talk), treating planning as an ad hoc process, making planning a one-time event and failing to measure initiatives will cause the organization fail in the strategic planning process. ITPM is a disciplined process that helps to ensure that the strategic planning process is successfully conducted, implemented and maintained.

ITPM is one of the most effective methods to reduce IT costs, yet maintain strategic value (Pastore, 2003). ITPM provides a process for selecting the highest-value initiatives and optimizing against budget, human resource, risk and other constraints. The benefits of the ITPM discipline are numerous. ITPM allows for unambiguous choices based on business impacts and measurable benefits. The ITPM process quantifies IT value by linking IT initiatives to the organization's business strategy, provides management accountability for realizing forecast benefits and provides a process to track and report on benefits realization.

ITPM requires that all IT-related costs be identified and classified using an effective IT asset inventory that facilitates accurate cost and value measurement. Adoption of a structured governance process and agreement across the enterprise on formal IT investment criteria are key to decision-making in a responsive approval process that is adaptable to changing business needs. The IT investment decision-making process must be defined and must consider short- and long-term impacts, cross-divisional impacts, business justification, benefit realization, strategic contribution, risk, compliance with regulatory mandates and conformity with technology architecture and direction.

ITPM is rapidly becoming an essential tool that enables business leaders to understand the visible impact IT operations have on business performance (Datz, 2003). IT synchronization with corporate business strategy is cited as the No. 1 concern of IT executives worldwide today. ITPM is increasingly recognized for its potential to support the continual alignment of business strategy and IT investment. As a result, leading corporations are placing a greater emphasis on ITPM as they attempt to make their enterprises more agile and competitive in today's global, hyper-competitive business environment.

CASE STUDY: HARRAH'S ENTERTAINMENT INC.

Many organizations struggle to measure the real value of IT projects and assets in their portfolios. The IT and business leaders at Harrah's in Las Vegas have developed a system of IT portfolio management that provides for robust financial projections as well as monitoring, measuring and tracking capabilities. Harrah's utilizes this system to accurately estimate the costs and benefits of IT projects and to track the business value that they create.

Harrah's rigorous approach to IT portfolio management, with its built-in metrics, excellent execution and strong follow-up, has led to impressive performance. Project throughput has nearly tripled from 112 projects in 2001 to 324 in 2003. In 2003, the aggregate of projects in excess of $100,000 (88% of total IT expenditures) came in

at 9% under budget. Seventy-seven percent of all projects came in on time, on budget and on target, while 83% hit two of those criteria. In comparison, The Standish Group reports that only 16.2% of IT projects, conducted in companies of comparable size to Harrah's, meet their time, budget and targeted performance objectives.

"It's a combination of structure and flexibility," says CIO Tim Stanley. "We have crisp operating procedures and structures, but we maintain the flexibility to constantly align with business, be responsive as things change, and really be able to go after the big hitters." Stanley says the success of Harrah's IT portfolio management process is largely about strategic alignment. "Alignment is, frankly, pretty hard," he says. And while aligning each business unit with IT is challenging, "pulling it all together into an overall corporate strategy is the secret to our success," Stanley says.

REFERENCES

Anell, B., & Jensen, T. (1998). Managing project portfolios. *Proceedings of the International Research Network on Organizing by Projects (IRNOP).* Calgary: The University of Calgary.

Archer, N., & Ghasemzadeh, F. (1999). An integrated framework for project portfolio selection. In L.D. Dye & J.S. Pennypacker (Eds.), *Project portfolio management* (4th edition, pp. 207-216). West Chester: Center for Business Practices.

Archibald, R.D. (2003). *Managing high-technology programs and projects.* New York: John Wiley & Sons.

Artto, K., Martinsuo, M., & Aalto, T. (2001). Project portfolio management—Suggestions for future research. In K.A. Artto, M. Martinsuo, & T. Aalto (Eds.), *Project portfolio management.* Helsinki: Project Management Association (PMA).

Asian Development Bank. (1998). *Annual re-*

port.

Benko, C., & McFarlan, F.W. (2003). *Connecting the dots: Aligning projects with objectives in unpredictable times*. Boston: Harvard Business School Press.

Bigelow, D. (2003). Trend watch: Want to ensure quality? Think project portfolio management. *PMNetwork, 17*(1), 16.

Bonham, S.S. (2005). *IT project portfolio management*. Norwood: Artech House.

Broadbent, M., & Weill, P. (1997). Management by maxim: How business and IT managers can create IT infrastructures. *Sloan Management Review, 38*, 77-91.

Buss, M. (1999). How to rank computer projects. In L.D. Dye & J.S. Pennypacker (Eds.), *Project portfolio management* (4th edition, pp. 183-192). West Chester: Center for Business Practices.

Cash, J.I. (May 1995). British air gets on course. *Informationweek*, 140.

Charette, R. (2002). *The state of risk management 2002: Hype or reality?* The Data & Analysis Center for Software (DACS) and Cutter Consortium.

Combe, M.W. (1998). Project prioritization in a large functional organization. In L.D. Dye & J. S. Pennypacker (Eds.), *Project portfolio management* (4th edition, pp. 310-318). West Chester: Center for Business Practices.

Combe, M.W., & Githens, G.D. (1999). Managing popcorn priorities: How portfolios and programs align projects with strategies. *Project Management Institute seminars and symposium proceedings*, 67-78.

Conrad, J. (August, 1997). It pays to think big. *Computerworld*, 40-42.

Cooper, R.G., Edgett, S.J., & Kleinschmidt, E.J. (1997a). Portfolio management for new product development: Lessons from the Leaders-I. *Research Technology Management, 40*(5), 16-28.

Cooper, R.G., Edgett, S.J., & Kleinschmidt, E.J. (1997b). Portfolio management for new product development: Lessons from the Leaders-II. *Research Technology Management, 40*(6), 21-23.

Cooper, R.G., Edgett, S.J., & Kleinschmidt, E.J. (1998). *Portfolio management for new products*. Boston: Addison-Wesley.

Cooper, R.G., Edgett, S.J., & Kleinschmidt, E.J. (2000). New problems, new solutions: Making portfolio management more effective. *Research Technology Management, 43*(2), 18-33.

Copeland, T. (2001). The real-options approach to capital allocation. *Strategic Finance, 20*(3), 36-47.

Datz, T. (May 2003). Portfolio management: How to do it right. *CIO Magazine*, 21-30.

Dietrich, P., Poskela, J., & Artto, K.A. (2003). Organizing for managing multiple projects—a strategic perspective. *Proceedings of the 17th Nordic Conference on Business Studies*, Reykjavik, Iceland.

Dye, L.D., & Pennypacker, J.S. (Eds.) (1999). *Project portfolio management: Selecting and prioritizing projects for competitive advantage*. West Chester: Center for Business Practices.

Gardiner, P.D., & Stewart, K. (2000). Revisiting the golden triangle of cost, time and quality: The role NPV in project control, success and failure. *International Journal of Project Management, 18*(4), 251-256.

Ghasemzadeh, F., Archer, N., & Iyogun, P. (1999). A zero-one model for project portfolio selection and scheduling. *The Journal of Operational Research Society, 50*(7), 745-755.

Gliedman, C. (2002, January). *Managing IT risk with portfolio management thinking*. Cambridge: Giga Information Group.

Grochow, J.M. (1996, August). Chaos theory and project estimates. *PC Week*, 5-7.

Heldey, B. (1997). Strategy for the business portfolio. *Long Range Planning, 10*(1), 9-15.

Jeffery, M. & Leliveld, I. (2004). Best practices in IT portfolio management. *MIT Sloan Management Review, 45*(3), 40-49.

Jiang, J., & Klein, G. (1999). Information systems project selection criteria variations within strategic classes. In L.D. Dye & J.S. Pennypacker (Eds.), *Project portfolio management* (4th edition, pp. 193-206). West Chester: Center for Business Practices.

Junttila, M., Ekholm, J., & Matilainen, R. (2001). Sonera's motives to corporate level project portfolio management development. In K.A. Artto, M. Martinsuo, & T. Aalto (Eds.), *Project portfolio management*. Helsinki: Project Management Association (PMA).

Kaplan, R.S., & Norton, D.P. (2001). *The strategy-focused organization*. Boston: Harvard Business School Press.

Kerzner, H. (2001). *Strategic planning for project management using a project management maturity model*. New York: John Wiley & Sons.

Kirsch, L.J. (1997). Portfolios of control modes and IS project management. *Information Systems Research, 8*(3), 215-239.

Lave, J., & Wenger, E. (1991). *Situated learning: Legitimate peripheral participation*. Cambridge: Cambridge University Press.

Luehrman, T.A. (1998, September-October). Strategy as a portfolio of real options. *Harvard Business Review*, 91-93.

Luftman, J.N. (1996). *Competing in the Information Age: Strategic alignment in practice*. New York: Oxford University Press.

Martinsuo, M. (2001). Project portfolio management: Contingencies, implementation and strategic renewal. In K.A. Artto, M. Martinsuo, & T. Aalto (Eds.), *Project portfolio management*. Helsinki: Project Management Association.

McFarlan, F.W. (1981). Portfolio approach to information systems. *Harvard Business Review, 59,* 142-150.

Melymuka, K. (2004, May). Harrah's: Betting on IT value. *Computerworld*, 18-22.

Meredith, J.R., & Samuel, J.M. (1995). *Project management: A managerial approach*. New York: John Wiley & Sons.

Miller, B. (1997). Linking corporate strategy to the selection of IT projects. *Project Management Institute 28th annual seminars & symposium proceedings,* 56-65.

Pastore, J.A. (May, 2003). The case for portfolio management. *CIO Magazine,* 12.

Poskela, J., Korpi-Filppula, M., Mattila, V., & Salkari, I. (2001). Project portfolio management practices of a global telecommunications operator. In K.A. Artto, M. Martinsuo, & T. Aalto (Eds.), *Project portfolio management*. Helsinki: Project Management Association.

Prahalad, C.K., & Krishnan, M.S. (2002). The dynamic synchronization of strategy and technology. *MIT Sloan Management Review, 43*(4), 24-33.

Project Management Institute. (2000). *Guide to the project management body of knowledge (PMBOK)*. Project Management Institute.

Roberts, A., & Gardiner, P.D. (1998). Project management and strategy implementation. *Proceedings of the 3rd International Research Network on Organizing by Projects,* 317-323. Alberta: University of Calgary.

Ross, J.W., & Beath, C.M. (2002). Beyond the business case: New approaches to IT investment. *MIT Sloan Management Review, 43,* 51-59.

Rosser, B. (October, 2001). *The Gartner Portfolio Management Tool for IT investment*. Stamford: Gartner Research.

Rosser, B., & Potter, K. (2001). *IT portfolio management and survey results*. Stamford: Gartner Research.

Santhanam, R., & Kyparisis, J. (1995). A multiple criteria decision model for information system project selection. *Computer Operations Research, 22*(8), 807-818.

Scott, A. (1997). *Strategic planning*. Edinburgh: Pitman Publishing/Edinburgh Business School.

Sharpe, P., & Keelin, T. (1998). How SmithKline Beecham makes better resource-allocation decisions. In L.D. Dye & J.S. Pennypacker (Eds.), *Project portfolio management* (4th edition, pp. 88-94). West Chester: Center for Business Practices.

Shoval, P., & Giladi, R. (1996). Determination of an implementation order for IS projects. *Information Management, 31*(2), 67-74.

Smith, H. (1996, December). Hitting the project mark. *InfoWorld, 32*.

Solomon, M. (2002, March). Project portfolio management. *Computerworld*, 14-16.

Sommer, R.J. (1998). Portfolio management for projects: A new paradigm. In L.D. Dye & J.S. Pennypacker (Eds.), *Project portfolio management* (4th edition, pp. 311-320). West Chester: Center for Business Practices.

Spradlin, C.T., & Kutoloski, D.M. (1999, March-April). Action-oriented portfolio management. *Research Technology Management, 27*.

The Standish Group. (2003). *Chaos chronicles, version 3.0*. West Yarmouth: The Standish Group.

Treacy, M., & Wiersema, F. (1995). *The discipline of market leaders: Choose your customers, narrow your focus, dominate your market*. New York: Perseus Book Group.

Turner, J.R. (1996). Editorial: International Project Management Association global qualification, certification and accreditation. *International Journal of Project Management, 14*(1), 1-6.

Turner, J.R. (1999). *The handbook of project-based management* (2nd edition). London: McGraw-Hill.

Visitacion, M. (April, 2003). *Process and tools: The nuts and bolts of project portfolio management*. Cambridge: Giga Information Group.

Weill, P., & Broadbent, M. (1997). Management by maxim: How business and IT managers can create IT infrastructures. *Sloan Management Review, 38*(3), 77-92.

Weill, P., & Broadbent, M. (1998). *Leveraging the new infrastructure: How market leaders capitalize on information technology*. Boston: Harvard Business School Press.

Weiser C.R. (1994). Best practice in customer relations. *Consumer Policy Review*, 130-137.

Williams, T. (2003). *Corporate governance: A guide for fund managers and corporations*. Provenance Investment & Financial Services Association Limited. Westpac Banking Corporation.

Chapter XX
IT Portfolio Management:
A Pragmatic Approach to Implement IT Governance

Muralidharan Ramakrishnan
Process Symphony, Australia

ABSTRACT

This chapter is intended primarily for managers who are preparing to implement portfolio management concepts in an organization and students of IT Project Management courses at the Masters level, who wish to understand the difference between Project and Portfolio Management. As IT Governance is gaining importance, the IT department should not be surprised if they are given a mandate from the senior management to implement a Governance framework. Portfolio Management principles are the foundations of building an effective governance. While there is literature available discussing portfolio management at the conceptual level, there is not enough available which translates these concepts into tactical implementation. This could be because implementation differs between organizations and there is no one size fits all solution. However, practitioners can benefit from discussing implementation approaches that can be tailored to suit individual needs. This chapter shows one of the many ways to implement a portfolio management framework.

INTRODUCTION

The chapter is divided into four sections.

The chapter commences with a hypothetical case study designed to illustrate that perceptions and personal preferences dominate IT Investment decisions. The case study highlights the need for structured decision making. This section also introduces IT Governance and portfolio management concepts.

The next section introduces a portfolio management life cycle consisting of three phases: *evaluation, monitoring,* and *benefits realization.* The section analyses the processes and techniques in each phase. This section provides guidance in the application of portfolio management concepts.

The third section consists of a real life case study; an application of one phase in the portfolio management life cycle, viz, *evaluation*, in a cross-government environment. The study analyses the "investment evaluation framework" proposed by the office of chief information officer (OCIO) in the Government of South Australia. The purpose is to show the application of a portfolio management framework in an organization and the associated challenges.

The final section summarizes the chapter and analyses the future trends in IT Portfolio Management.

IT PORTFOLIO MANAGEMENT CONCEPTS

Opening Case

Robert Malcolm felt the need to make an important decision for IT Governance meeting the following day. Three different departments were fighting for already stretched funds to initiate new projects into their departments. The operations manager, Julie, wanted to replace an ageing infrastructure; Raj, the marketing manager, was arguing a case for a new CRM system; and Darren wanted to enhance a functionality of the pay-roll system.

Robert knew he could not fund all the three projects. He could empathize with Julie, as he had been performing her role previously, before he was promoted to CIO. But he also knew that Raj would put a very convincing case, which could impress the CEO. Robert did not know much about the payroll system, so it is out-of-question for now, he thought. Well, not really, as the CFO might throw his weight behind Darren.

Robert wished he had a clear evaluation process to decide between these competing projects. He knew that if one of the on-going projects were stopped, that would free up some additional money. But, in his organization, once a project was approved, there was no way it could be terminated mid way.

It was not that Robert was facing issues only with the new projects. He was having some issues from previous projects also. The organization had developed a Website that would increase the online revenue from one of their products. But by monitoring the Web statistics he realized that it did not attract enough visitors. He was aware that the organization had changed its strategy and gave higher priority to another product. However, Robert still incurred expenditure to maintain the Website. Terminating the Website had been on his *to do* list for the past six months, but he did not have time to execute the decision.

Robert knew what to do as a short term *fix*. He would play the political game and give his support to the CEO's favourite project. At the same time, he decided to explore the available process methodologies that would help him to solve the *real* problem.

Need for IT Governance

For many enterprises managing Information Technology (IT) has always been a challenge. It is critical to a business that the IT investments are managed effectively. Research shows that top-performing enterprises generate returns on their IT investments up to 40% greater than their competitors (Weill, 2004). IT Governance ensures that IT investments are prioritized and monitored throughout their life cycle.

Another driver for IT Governance in the wake of corporate scandals like Enron and Worldcom is the renewed interest in Corporate Governance. As IT cuts across all the organizational functions, Corporate Governance cannot be complete without IT Governance. The scandals also pushed regulators in the US to introduce the Sarbane-Oxely act requiring new levels of accountability and traceability (Maizlish & Handler, 2005)

The IT Governance Institute (ITGI) (IT Governance Institute, n.d.) is one of the organizations that promote Governance standards. The institute has developed *Control Objectives for Information and related Technology* (COBIT®) and Val IT™ framework. Val IT (Val IT, 2006, p. 10), states that *"there is an increasing demand from board and executive management for generally accepted guidelines for decision making and benefits realisation related to IT-enabled business investments"*. The need for transparency in IT investments is reflected in the following industry reports (Val IT, 2006, p. 10):

- *A 2002 Gartner publication claimed that 20 percent all expenditure on IT is wasted, representing on a global basis, annual value destruction of US $600 billion.*
- *A 2004 IBM survey of Fortune 1000 CIOs reported that, on average, 40 percent of all IT spending brought no return to their organisations.*
- *A 2004 Standish report found that only 29 percent of all IT projects succeeded while the remainder were either challenged or failed.*

In summary, we need IT Governance because:

- It is a critical component of Corporate Governance.
- Well managed IT investments create more business value.
- A lack of perceived transparency in IT investments by the senior management.

Defining IT Governance

COBIT® defines IT Governance as follows:

IT Governance is the responsibility of executives and the board of directors and consists of the leadership, organisational structures and processes that ensure that the enterprise's IT sustains and

extends the organisation's strategies and objectives. (COBIT 4.1, 2007, p. 5)

Peter Weill (Weill, 2004, p. 8) defines IT Governance as "specifying the decision rights and accountability framework to encourage desirable behaviour in the use of IT."

Combining these definitions we can say that IT Governance is about structured decision making on IT Investments by the right people. Val IT expands the IT Investment decisions as "Four Ares" (Val IT, 2006, p. 9) as follows:

- *Are* we doing the right things?
- *Are* we doing them the right way?
- *Are* we getting them done well?
- *Are* we getting the benefits?

Figure 1 shows the "Four Ares" model proposed by Val IT™ (Val IT, 2006, p. 9).

How Do the Methodologies Fit?

The industry frameworks and best practices are mapped against the *Four Ares* in Table 1.

As we can see, many frameworks focus on the *delivery* aspect of IT, but very little on strategic alignment, architecture and value aspect of IT. It is because, as an evolving field, IT has been plagued with delivery issues. The industry methodologies and best practices tried to enforce a discipline in developing and implementing IT solutions. Now, the business stakeholders are asking the other *Four Ares* questions. We need a framework that addresses the entire life cycle of an IT investment. Portfolio Management is a concept that deals from choosing the right IT investment, monitoring the implementation and capturing the business benefits.

IT Portfolio Management: Concept

The concept of IT portfolio management is derived from the *financial portfolio investment model*.

As shares are evaluated before investing, the IT portfolio management model proposes the evaluation of any IT investment before it is initiated. The high growth, risky shares (riskier IT projects), need to be balanced against low risk, low return (low risk maintenance IT projects). IT Portfolio management aims to provide a holistic view of IT Investment across the enterprise so that the management can take informed decisions.

In shares investment, share prices are monitored through out an investment. Decisions to hold, buy or sell are taken depending upon a share's performance. IT portfolio management is similar. IT Investments need to be monitored throughout their life cycle. Decisions to continue, modify or stop an investment need to be taken throughout its life cycle.

Portfolio Management: Definition

The Project Management Body of Knowledge defines project, program, and portfolio management as follows (PMBOK®, 2000):

Project management is the application of knowledge, skills, tools and techniques to project activities to meet project requirements.

A program is a group of related projects managed in a coordinated way to obtain benefits and control not available from managing them individually.

Portfolio is a collection of projects or programs and other work that are grouped together to facilitated effective management of that work to meet strategic business objectives. The projects or programs in the portfolio may not necessarily be interdependent or directly related.

Val IT states: "The goal of portfolio management is to ensure that an organisation's overall portfolio of IT-enabled investments is aligned with and contributing optimal value to the organisations strategic objectives..." (2006, p. 14).

Portfolio management is strategic in nature. It is concerned more about doing the *right projects* than *executing the projects correctly.* In fact, Portfolio Management can terminate a project, which is being executed efficiently, if the project's benefits are no longer aligned with the strategic objectives of the organization.

Illustration of Portfolio Management

Portfolio Management enables senior management to better track the business benefits of a project, not only when the project was initiated but throughout its life cycle. For example, consider a company that specializes in building high-speed passenger catamarans. They have decided to build a new catamaran, in order to introduce a new service across a river.

The portfolio board has approved the construction of the catamaran, and project is progressing on time and, within budget. The project manager has announced that they have across a new technology which will make the catamaran operations cost effective. From the project management point of view, it will be a successful project.

During the portfolio management review, the senior management noted that the Government has sanctioned construction of a bridge across the river. If this bridge were constructed, it would reduce the catamaran traffic drastically. So the senior management decided no longer to invest in construction of the catamaran.

How many times has a *successful* IT project been terminated in your organization because the organization's strategic direction has changed?

PORTFOLIO MANAGEMENT LIFE CYCLE

This section deals with implementing a portfolio management framework in an organization. The portfolio management life cycle has three phases

1. Evaluation of IT Investments.
2. Monitoring the progress of IT investments.
3. Benefits realisation.

We will present a method to develop evaluation criteria for an IT Investment. It will be followed by a discussion on monitoring the progress of IT investments by establishing interface with project management structures. The benefits realisation process will be explained with an example.

Evaluation of IT Investments

It is very important for a business to have consistent evaluation while making decisions on IT investments. The evaluation criteria need to ensure that investment is aligned with strategic direction of the business and risks associated with the investments are clearly understood.

Developing an Evaluation Criteria

Developing evaluation criteria is the first step in IT Investment decision making. The evaluation should consider balancing the risks and rewards. There is no single way of developing the evaluation framework. We will explore one of the ways to develop a criterion.

In our approach, a business case will be *rewarded* if it is aligned with the strategic direction of the organization and it is financially sound. The reward score will be balanced against the risk score.

Overall Score = Reward Score / Risk Score

where

Reward Score = Strategic Direction Alignment * Financial Worth

such that

Overall Score = Strategic Direction * Financial Worth / Risk Score.

This evaluation scores can be used to create a portfolio view of all the IT Projects in an organization. The portfolio view will give an idea about the risk profile of the organization and potential improvement opportunities. Figure 3 illustrates a portfolio view based on risk and reward.

We will examine the individual scoring of each of the components that determine the overall score.

Strategic Alignment

Strategic alignment deals with an assessment of the degree of alignment that a proposal demonstrates against a business's strategic direction. An organization can have many business objectives that are aligned with the vision of the organization. When a new IT investment is proposed, it is important that stakeholders understand how the investment will impact on business objectives. Figure 2 illustrates the traceability between the IT Initiatives and the strategic vision of an organization.

It should be noted that one initiative could be aligned to more than one business objective. Also, it may be difficult for some objectives to demonstrate the alignment to strategic objectives. In Figure 2, IT Initiative-1 is aligned with business objectives 1 and 2. IT Initiatives 2 and 3 are aligned with business objective 3. IT Initiative 4 is not aligned with any of the business objectives. Similarly, business objective-4 does not have any IT initiatives that are supporting it.

It does not mean that an IT Initiative cannot be undertaken by the organization if it is not aligned with any of the business objectives. In a dynamic business environment, a decision can be taken to implement an initiative based on many other factors. However, portfolio management processes ensure that senior management is making informed decisions.

Figure 1 Val IT™ "Four Ares" Framework. Source: Val IT © 2006 IT Governance Institute. All rights reserved. Used with permission.

The **strategic** question. Is the investment:
• In line with our vision
• Consistent with our businesss principles
• Contributing to our strategic objectives
• Providing optimal value, at affordable cost, at an acceptable level of risk

The **architecture** question. Is the investment:
• In line with our architecture
• Consistent with our architectural principles
• Contributing to the population of our architecture
• In line with other initiatives

The **value** question. Do we have:
• A clear and shared understanding of the expected benefits
• Clear accountability for realising the benefits
• Relevant metrics
• An effective benefits realisation process

The **delivery** question. Do we have:
• Effective and disciplined management, delivery and change management processes
• Competent and available technical and business resouces to deliver:
  – The required capabilities
  – The organisational changes required to leverage the capabilities

Table 1. Industry frameworks alignment with Four Ares

Four Ares	Methodologies
Are we doing the right things?	Val IT
Are we doing them the right way?	The Open Group Architecture Framework (TOGAF), COBIT
Are we getting them done well?	COBIT, ITIL, CMMI, ISO/IEC 20000, Six Sigma, PRINCE2, PMBOK
Are we getting the benefits?	Val IT

Figure 2. Portfolio view based on risk and reward

High

Reward

Low Risk – High Reward Preferred category	High Risk- High Reward Risks need to be managed
Low Risk- Low Reward Maintenance projects	High Risk – Low Reward Avoid projects in this category

Low   Risk   High

Table 2 shows a generic scoring guideline that scores a business case from 1 to 4 by evaluating the alignment against a business objective.

Financial Worth

The next step in determining a *reward* score is to evaluate an initiative from financial point of view. The Net Present Value (NPV) of an investment is a simple criterion for deciding whether or not to undertake an investment (Ross, 2002). NPV answers the question of how much cash an investor would need to have today as a substitute for making an investment. If the net present value is negative, taking on an investment today is not financially justified.

The NPV can be translated to a scoring range of 1 to 4. An example is shown in Table 3. Each organization needs to tailor how financial benefits translate to individual scores.

While the NPV concept is widely used in the financial world, in IT investment decisions it is rarely used. One of the main reasons is that practitioners find it difficult to quantity benefits in financial terms because most IT Initiatives are viewed as a technical challenge without analysing the problems from business/financial perspective.

Risks Assessment

One of the "Four Ares" is "Are we doing them the right way?" (Val IT, 2006, p. 9). This is an architecture question that ensures the proposed business investment is:

- In line with the organization's enterprise architecture.
- Consistent with the organization's architectural principle.
- Contributing to the population of the architecture.
- In line with other initiatives.

If a solution is not aligned with the architecture, then it is a risk to the business. For example, the business cost of maintenance can become high or the solution can become a security risk.

The IT Architecture is the organising logic for data, applications, and infrastructure, captured in a set of policies, relationships and technical choices to achieve desired business and technical standardisation and integration (Weill & Ross, 2004, p. 30).

Enterprise Architecture is the description of the current and/or future structure and behavior of an organization's processes, information systems,

Figure 3. Strategic alignment

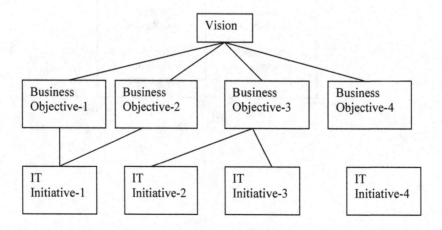

Table 2. Scoring guideline

High

Score	Interpretation
1	Business case addresses some components of a business objective
2	Business case address all the components of a business objective
3	Business initiative is applicable to a subsection of organization
4	Business initiative is applicable across the entire organization

Table 3. Financial worth scoring example

Score	NPV Value
1	Negative
2	< $5000
3	$5001 <$10000
4	$10,001 <$50,000

personnel and organizational subunits, aligned with the organization's core goals and strategic direction. (Enterprise Architecture-Wikipedia, n.d.). As the technology changes are faster than ever, if the standards are not set, technology integration and business process alignment will become a critical issue often affecting the operational costs.

If an organization does not have enterprise architecture defined, at least technical standards need to be documented and followed. For example, an organization can state that it will follow Microsoft platform for sales and support and UNIX platforms for technical development area. If a new business case is proposing to introduce a UNIX platform for a sales team, then the scoring for architecture risk will be high. The risk score will flag that the maintenance costs of a nonstandard technology will be high. This will enable the organization's governance to take an informed decision about the investment.

An example of architectural risk evaluation scoring is shown in Table 4.

Investment Evaluation: Summary

Investment prioritisation is one of the difficult processes to implement in portfolio management. It might require a cultural change in the organization if it is not used to formal decision making already. If the process is properly implemented, it will take away the political games and lobbying.

An investment evaluation assumes there is a Governance framework and decision making body responsible for IT investment decision making. The decision making body should be represented by the senior management and should have sufficient financial authority to take decision. The business should have commitment to make the formal decision making process happen.

ITIL® (Best Practice for Service Delivery, 2001, p. 59) states:

"Why does the IT organisation budget have be so large?"

"How much will it cost to implement and run this new system?"

..

*These are examples of the questions asked inside and outside an IT organisation, often in emotive situations, such as project over-runs or during periods of loss of critical services. The answer is often: "We are doing the best we can with the money that we have"; but....**is that true?***

Is that true? This is an introspective question to the IT community. To answer it IT practitioners

Figure 4. Hierarchical project structure Source: Adapted from Managing Successful projects with Prince2 (1998, p. 18)

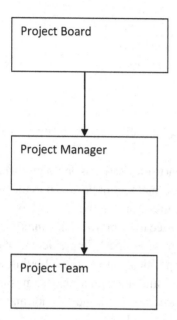

need to show the business that IT investments are aligned with the business direction and generate positive returns.

Monitoring the Progress of IT Investments

Once the IT Investment decisions are made, the implementations need to be managed as projects.

The progress monitoring can be built into the project management methodology. One of the widely used project methodology, Projects in Control Environments (PRINCE2), proposes that the projects need to be governed by a Project Board (Prince2.org.uk, 2007). The project board will review the business cases at regular intervals to ensure that the projects are still relevant to the strategic needs of the organization. *Figure 3* shows the project board structure hierarchy.

If an organization has already implemented a project board structure, similar to Prince2, it will be easier to implement an IT Investment monitoring process. However, it should be noted that Project Board cannot fulfil all the Portfolio Management monitoring requirements. There need to be a body at a higher level that oversees all the projects across the portfolio. Figure 4 shows a typical Portfolio Management board structure.

The role of the Portfolio Management board is to supervise the performance of the project board and advise the project, if there are any changes in the strategic direction of the organization. The Portfolio Management board need representation from the senior management of the organization. It should have the authority to terminate a project, if needed.

The Portfolio Management board should not duplicate the Project Board function. Prince2 (1998, pp. 22-23) defines the project board functions as follows:

- Provide overall direction and management of the project
- Accountable for the success of the project
- Approves all major plans and authorizes any deviations
- Authorizes the next stage of the project
- Ensures required resources are committed

The Portfolio board sits one step above the project board. The Portfolio board functions are:

- Receive progress reports from all the project boards
- Receive self assessment health-check reports from all the projects, through the boards
- Advise the project boards, if any changes in the strategic direction of the organization
- Advise the project boards, if any new projects are initiated in the organization
- Advise the project boards, if any changes in the budget allocation
- Advise the project boards, if any projects are terminated in the organization
- Advise any technology changes

Figure 5. Portfolio board structure

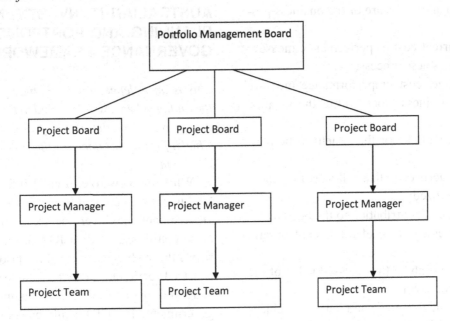

Investment Monitoring: Summary

The investment monitoring process is built on the foundations of project management. The investment monitoring process oversees the project execution of an IT investment. The investment monitoring ensures that the approved IT project is aligned with business objectives throughout the implementation.

Ideally, the investment monitoring authority should be able to terminate an IT investment when it is no longer aligned with the business objectives. In order to deliver this mandate, it is important that the organization body responsible for investment monitoring has sufficient authority to terminate or change the scope of an investment.

Benefits Realization

Once the IT Initiative is delivered, it is important to monitor the benefits and compare with what

had been promised in the initial business case. If this process, is omitted then business cases fall into the trap of over promising and under delivering. The organization will also gain knowledge on the reasons for not achieving the estimated benefits.

Like other portfolio management processes, there is no single way to implement the benefits monitoring. We will analyse a practical implementation of an Australian Government agency.

The New South Wales Government's Chief Information Office (http://www.gcio.nsw.gov. au/library/guidelines/769) proposes a Benefits realisation register (Appendix A) to track the benefits. The register contains the following:

- A description of the benefit to be achieved;
- The person responsible for realizing the benefit;

- A description of the current situation or performance measure of the business process;
- The current cost or performance measure of the business process;
- The target cost or performance measure of the business process after the planned change;
- The target date for the benefit to be realized;
- The trigger or event that will cause the benefit to be realized;
- The type of contribution to the business;
- The assessed value of the benefit or saving;
- Comments about the assessed value of the benefit or saving;
- State which strategic and corporate objectives and Results and Services Plan (RSP) outcomes are supported by the benefit;
- State how the benefit contributes to achieving strategic and corporate objectives and RSP outcomes;
- The value of the benefit realized and the date this is achieved.

Benefits Realization: Summary

Benefits realization ensures that the IT Investment delivers the benefit as stated in the business case. Some of the challenges in implementing the benefits monitoring process are:

- Lack of ownership of benefits realisation, as the IT project would have been completed before the realisation commences
- Difficulty in identifying the benefits
- Difficulty in isolating the benefits of a single project
- Political reasons that prevent one from admitting that the project did not achieve what was promised

CASE STUDY: SOUTH AUSTRALIAN IT INVESTMENT, PLANNING AND PORTFOLIO GOVERNANCE FRAMEWORKS

This is an independent case study prepared by the author. The views expressed in the case study do not represent the views of the Office of the Chief Information Officer or the South Australian Government.

When the new role of chief information officer (CIO) was created in the South Australian Government, the Government knew that it would be an uphill task for the CIO to bring the necessary culture change. Some of his priorities were to set a direction for IT investment prioritization and to improve and coordinate IT planning across government. The CIO would be responsible for streamlining the IT Investment decision-making process across the South Australian Government. This would be a challenging task, due to a number of factors, including a generally negative perception on IT's ability to deliver the required outcomes, the wide variety of existing agency and whole of Government processes, competing priorities for funding, diversity in IT investment needs, the Government's focus on transparency of decision making and audit comments.

The South Australian Government spends approximately $500 million on IT, or around 7 percent of the State's total budget per annum. Despite the significance of this expenditure across Government, IT planning is not as mature as planning for others functional areas, such as finance and HR. (ICT[1] Planning Framework, 2006, p. 4). So, it was not really a surprise when the South Australian Government's Auditor General Report in 2003, (Auditor Report, 2003) was quite critical on IT investment decision making and project execution. However, the Government of South Australia took this report seriously and decided to address these issues in a systematic way.

Creation of Office of CIO

The office of CIO (OCIO) was created to coordinate the whole of Government ICT planning and investment. The CIO reports directly to the minister for infrastructure.

The OCIO stipulates that the planning, execution and reporting of the ICT Projects are a business responsibility. The OCIO facilitates the coordination of ICT investment across agencies by publishing a suite of frameworks that set the minimum requirements to be complied with by all the South Australian Government agencies.

The OCIO Website (OCIO, n.d.) states the following key responsibilities:

ICT planning and investment

- Whole of Government strategic planning and prioritisation of ICT investment for business needs
- Guidance of strategic procurement process across Government
- Promotion of best practice ICT planning across agencies
- Use of ICT innovation to transform service delivery

Program Coordination

- Oversight of programs in alignment with across Government ICT strategy
- Oversight of the development and management of common ICT applications across Government, where appropriate
- Promotion of integrated service delivery and business integration initiatives across Government

Advice

- Provision of advice to the Minister for Infrastructure, Cabinet, Chief Executives and Senior Management on the value of ICT to business, the management of ICT investments and the effective use of ICT as a business tool
- Participation in a number of senior cross-government and cross-jurisdictional committees

ICT Portfolio Governance Life Cycle

The South Australian Government's ICT Governance framework (ICT Planning Framework, 2006) covers the entire life cycle of the ICT Investments. It has five distinct phases listed below:

- Strategic business and ICT planning
- Investment prioritisation and budgeting
- Projects and program portfolio management
- ICT operation and maintenance
- ICT asset renewal, replacement or retirement

Among these life cycle processes, we will examine "Investment Prioritisation and Budgeting" as an example of implementing the portfolio management framework discussed in chapter 3.

Investment Prioritisation and Budgeting

This is the first process area to be deployed by the OCIO as it was considered as a high priority need. The investment prioritisation is a key aspect of IT Governance on how the investment decisions are made. To effectively prioritize investments and ensure a balanced portfolio, each investment proposal needs to address a consistent set of criteria.

The OCIO's investment evaluation (ICT Investment Prioritisation Framework, 2005) includes assessing and considering the comparative weight of three dimensions in addition to cost:

- **Strategic alignment:** the degree of alignment that the business proposal demonstrates against an agency's strategies
- **Value:** the degree of business improvement that will be achieved
- **Risk Evaluation:** evaluation of business risks, delivery risks and benefits realisation risks

The introduction of business criteria for ICT investment evaluation provided a way for decision makers, who are largely not ICT experts, to understand the value proposition, contribution and scope of ICT proposals. Each of the dimensions has it's own practical challenges.

Strategic Alignment

All new South Australian Government ICT Initiatives should be aligned with the State strategic directions as set out in the SA Strategic Plan (SA Strategic Plan, n.d.) and with whole of Government policies and standards

For example, agencies need to demonstrate that their ICT initiatives are contributing to the specific targets for each of the six strategic objectives, outlined in South Australia's strategic plan:

- Growing prosperity
- Improving well being
- Attaining sustainability
- Fostering creativity
- Building communities
- Expanding opportunity

While value and risk are rated numerically, based on a preset evaluation scale, alignment with strategic direction is difficult to quantify. How does one determine the degree of strategic alignment for an IT infrastructure upgrade?

Initiatives are thus profiled into different categories, ranging from strategic to infrastructure. Each of these profiles will have different properties and strategic initiatives are expected to show a

higher degree of strategic alignment than infrastructure or hardware replacement initiatives.

For example, an "ICT Infrastructure upgrade" business case that can not show a high degree of alignment with any of the strategic initiatives, will not be rejected, provided it meets all other criteria. In the end, the purpose of evaluation is not to "score" high ratings in all the three dimensions but to balance the risk and benefits of different investment types to create a balanced portfolio.

Value Assessment

The criteria for evaluating the business value of the proposal are (ICT Investment Prioritisation Framework, p. 9):

- Business improvement value
- Systems improvement value
- Organizational improvement value
- Other business benefits
- Financial value

Each of the criteria has detailed scoring guidelines so that there is consistency in the evaluation. For major business cases, the agencies need to complete Net Present Value (NPV) to demonstrate the financial worth of the ICT Initiative.

Risk Evaluation

The risks are assessed against the following criteria (ICT Investment Prioritisation Framework, p. 9):

- Business risk
- Benefits realisation risk
- Architectural alignment risk
- Project Management risk

Benefits realisation is one of the challenging areas to track as intended benefits need to be stated clearly before investment and measured after implementation of an initiative. Many businesses find it hard to quantify or express the business benefits of an IT initiative and to have measurement systems in place, to track the benefits once the project is completed.

Case Study: Summary

OCIO has made progress in the development and deployment of its IT portfolio governance frameworks. Experience from implementation and agency feedback will now be used to update the frameworks and progress towards future stages of maturity.

Some of the "lessons learnt" are:

- Do not force "alignment" to the evaluation criteria
- Make it clear that getting "high score' is not the purpose of evaluation
- Educate the business leaders in evaluation process; Show that the evaluation criteria, will guide decision making thought process
- Provide feedback to agencies, especially if the business case is rejected, clearly identifying the improvement opportunities

OCIO plays only a facilitator role in the deployment of the process. For example, the OCIO cannot create a "full portfolio" view across Government, as not all the investments go through the cabinet submission. In future, the agencies need to create their own ICT portfolio views and feed that information to the OCIO so that the "big picture" across south Australian government can be developed.

The main benefit of the Investment Evaluation framework is the transparency it provides across Government IT investments. Before implementation of the framework, there would have no visibility on the spending of the allocated IT budget by the agencies. The Investment Evaluation provides this visibility, which is a key step in achieving good Governance.

SUMMARY AND FUTURE TRENDS

We started the chapter with a hypothetical case study. If Robert had read the chapter he would have realized that, his organization lacked evaluation, monitoring and benefits realisation processes.

According to Garter (2007, p. 1), the project and portfolio management (PPM) has grown rapidly and morphed since mid-2006. It also states *"even as large enterprises seek expanded IT planning and control with PPM as a key enabler, PPM value has become apparent to organisations of all sizes... "*. It also warns that before choosing software for implementation, the organization should spend effort in changing roles, developing skills and implementing processes. The reports predict that integration of project portfolio, IT service and application life cycle management (ALM) into a coherent IT planning and Control (ITPC) offering is under way.

The industry methodologies also respond to the needs of the market. As pointed out in the introduction the IT Governance Institute has developed COBIT and Val IT methodologies that supports end-to-end IT investment lifecycle. Information Technology Infrastructure Library (ITIL) version 3 covers the entire life cycle of IT services, including service strategy, design, transition, operation and continual service improvement. According to the Office of Government Commerce (OGC) (OGC, n.d.), ITIL version 3, emphasizes Business and IT integration and Value Network Integration, which are essentially portfolio management concepts.

In summary we can conclude that the tools are maturing in portfolio management market space. Industry methodologies, processes are being developed that support portfolio management. However the real challenge is, people, especially senior decision makers, accepting the structured way of evaluating, monitoring, and realizing the benefits of an IT investment. If this acceptance does not happen, the portfolio management will be just another bureaucratic overhead.

REFERENCES

Auditor Report (2003). Retrieved May 15, 2008, from http://www.audit.sa.gov.au/02-03/itrep/summary.html

COBIT 4.1 (2007). *COBIT 4.1 excerpt: Executive summary and framework.* IT Governance Institute

Enterprise Architecture – Wikipedia (n.d.). Retrieved May 15, 2008, from http://en.wikipedia.org/wiki/Enterprise_Architecture

Gartner (2007). *Magic quadrant for IT project and portfolio management 2007, Gartner RAS core research note G00149082*, Matt Light, Daniel B, Stang

ICT Investment Prioritisation Framework (2005). *ICT investment prioritisation framework-Version 1.0.* Government of South Australia

ICT Planning Framework (2006). *SA government ICT planning framework.* Government of South Australia

IT Governance Institute (n.d.). Retrieved May 15, 2008 from http://www.itgi.org

ITIL® (2001). *Best practice for service delivery.* United Kingdom: Office of Government Commerce.

Luftman, J., Bullen, C., Liao, D., Nash, E., & Nuewmann, C. (2004). *Managing the information technology resource: Leadership in the information age.* Upper Saddle River, NJ: Pearson Education Inc.

NSW Government Chief Information Office Benefits Register (n.d.). Retrieved May 15, 2008 from http://www.gcio.nsw.gov.au/documents/Sample%20Benefits_register.pdf

Office of Government Commerce (n.d.). Retrieved May 15, 2008, from http://www.best-management-practice.com/Online-Bookshop/IT-Service-Management-ITIL/ITIL-Version-3/

OGC PRINCE2 (n.d.). Retrieved May 15, 2008 from http://www.ogc.gov.uk/methods_prince_2.asp

PRINCE2 (1998). *Managing successful projects with PRINCE2.* London: The Stationery Office.

SA Strategic Plan (n.d.). Retrieved May 15, 2008, from http://www.stateplan.sa.gov.au/

South Australia Office of CIO (n.d.). Retrieved May 15, 2008, from http://www.cio.sa.gov.au/

Val IT (2006). *Enterprise value: Governance of IT investments.* IT Governance Institute

Weill, P. & Ross, J. W. (2004). *IT governance: How top performers manage IT decision rights for superior results.* Boston: Harvard Business School Press.

ENDNOTE

[1] **ICT:** information and communication technology; In this case study the abbreviations IT and ICT will be used interchangeably

APPENDIX: IT BENEFITS REGISTER

Description of the Benefit to be Achieved	Person Responsible for Realising the Benefit	Description of Current Situation/ Performance of the Business Process	Current Cost / Performance Measure of the Business Process	Target Cost / Performance Measure after the Planned Change	Target Date for the Benefit to be Realised	Triggers or events that will cause the Benefit to be Realised	Type of Contribution to the Business	Assessed Value of the Benefit or Saving	Comment about the Assessed Value	Strategic and Corporate Objectives and RSP outcomes Supported by this Benefit	Contribution of this Benefit to Achieving the Strategic and Corporate Objectives and RSP outcomes	Value of the Benefit Realised and Date Achieved
Example from a project to implement an intranet and internal E-mail system												
Reduce the amount of paper used to distribute information to staff.	Chief Information Officer	All information to staff is distributed in hard copy.	2,000 reams of paper per year are used to distribute information to staff at a total cost of $11,000.	All information to staff is distributed on the intranet and via e-mail.	June 2002	Intranet and e-mail systems deployed. All staff are trained in and have access to the intranet and e-mail systems. All information to staff is published on the intranet and distributed via e-mail.	Cost Reduction	$11,000 pa		Reduce administrative costs by 10% per year.	Value of benefit contributes a reduction in administrative costs.	
Example from a project to implement an HR Employee Self Service (ESS) system												
Reduce the cost of processing sick leave forms.	Director, Corporate Services	Sick leave forms are generated and processed manually.	24,410 forms processed per year at a total cost of $317,800 ($13.00 per form).	ESS introduced to reduce processing costs to $0.73 per form.	January 2003	ESS System deployed. All staff are trained in and have access to the ESS system.	Cost Reduction Increased productivity	$300,000 pa	Remaining administrative cost relates to staff time to update their own leave records.	Reduce administrative costs by 10% per year.	Value of benefit contributes a 0.3% p.a. reduction in administrative costs.	
Example from a project to develop an internet Website												
Satisfy an increasing demand for information without increasing costs	Chief Information Officer	Requests for information taken by phone are sent by mail. Requests are also made in person over the counter. Demand is increasing by 10% per year.	100 items of information are requested per day (26,000 per year) and cost $5 per item to satisfy or $130,000 per year.	2,600 items of information accessed via the website in first year.	June 2000	Website established and documents published. Availability of website is advertised via 'phone-hold' message, and branch signage.	Cost avoidance increased productivity	$13,000 pa	Increased demand for information satisfied without increasing resources.	Reduce administrative costs by 10% per year.	Value of benefit avoids increases in administrative costs to satisfy increasing demand for information.	7,800 items of information accessed via the website in the first year with $39,000 value of costs avoided. Benefit achieved June 2000.

Chapter XXI
Planning and Control and the Use of Information Technology in Mental Healthcare Organizations

I.J. Baars
Maastricht University, The Netherlands

G.G. Van Merode
Board of Maastricht University Medical Center & Maastricht University, The Netherlands

INTRODUCTION

Demand for mental healthcare increases. Simultaneously, the need for more patient oriented processes increases and the market develops towards more competition among providers and organizations. As a result of these developments, mental healthcare organizations are becoming more aware of efficiency and effectiveness. Often, they choose to transform to more process oriented organizations, which require changes in planning and control systems and information technology (IT). However, little is known about the required planning and control systems and IT for mental healthcare.

We argue that IT for planning and control of mental healthcare organization needs to be adaptive and support short term planning. IT has to be adaptive to be able to support first and second order control which is needed for planning and control of mental healthcare processes. Short term planning or reactivity is needed to deal with stochasticity and variability as present in mental healthcare. These subjects are further described in the background.

This article reports the results of two studies on the use of standard care processes and IT for planning and control of mental healthcare processes. The results give insight in the needed functionalities of IT and planning and control of mental healthcare processes. The first study

Table 1. Control models

Control model condition	Unambiguous objectives	Measurable output	Known effects	Repetitive activities
Routine control	+	+	+	+
Expert control	+	+	+	-
Trial and error control	+	+	-	+
Intuitive control	+	+	-	-
Judgmental control	+	-	+/-	+/-
Political control	-	+/-	+/-	+/-

+ = *condition is present*

is a case study in a center for multidisciplinary (mental) youth care. This center implemented care programs and an automated planning tool. We studied the success of this implementation and particularly the fit between the care programs and the planning tool. In the second study we studied the characteristics of ambulant mental healthcare processes and the actual and preferable use of planning and control models and IT.

BACKGROUND

Mental healthcare is often multidisciplinary and includes several professionals, disciplines, and departments within one or more organizations which all need to be planned and controlled. Consequently, the object of control is mainly professionals and patients, but also resources like rooms. We define planning as the determination

Figure 1. First and second order control

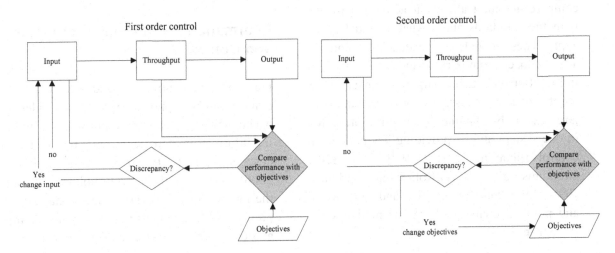

of what should be done and control as the process that assures that the planned results are obtained (Van Merode, Groothuis, & Hasman, 2004).

According to Hofstede (1981), the way non-profit organizations, such as mental healthcare organizations, can be planned and controlled depends on the type of processes. The type of process can be determined by answering the following questions: is the output measurable? Are the objectives unambiguous? Are the effects of management interventions known? And, can the activities be repeated? The type of processes determines the control model and instruments (e.g., protocols, case management and budgeting) that can be applied.

Hofstede (1981) defines six different control models, as shown in Table 1. The more standardized, well-defined, and structured the processes are, the more routine control can be used.

A mental healthcare organization consists of various processes. These processes are possibly different and thus need different control models. To select a control model that best suits a situation, processes have to be analyzed. Especially the distinction between routine and less routine processes is important here.

Routine processes can use standards and can be controlled by routine control or, when the activities cannot be repeated, by expert control. For routine control, and marginally for expert control and trial-and-error control, models that compare automatically what actually happens with the standards about what should happen apply. These models use feedback for control. The feedback from relevant indicators provides information that can be compared with targets. A number of care processes can be coordinated to a large extend by planning and control integrated in one system and by providing feedback from control to planning (Hofstede, 1981; Van Merode, Groothuis et al., 2004; Van Roth & Van Dierdonck, 1995). Moreover, for intuitive and judgmental and political control only vague models exist (Hofstede, 1981).

An example of control by feedback in mental healthcare is a protocol for the process of the treatment of depression. This protocol describes that the target of the indicator "number of sessions" is 15. If a patient receives 17 instead of the targeted 15 sessions, this is evaluated. Several actions can be undertaken to meet the target of 15. One such an action is adapting the input of the process so that the 15 sessions are not exceeded. This is first order control (Figure 1).

A problem with first order control can be that the aim becomes to keep the activity on target at any cost. To overcome this problem, a second order feedback loop that can periodically adjust the targets of the first order feedback loop is necessary (Figure 1). A second order feedback loop provides information (e.g., by new insights or outcome of evaluations) that enables decisions on the appropriateness of the target. By means of a second order feedback loop, the interventions of the first order loop can be overruled. With that, the targets of the process can be adapted so that the outcome better fits the targets. In our example of 15 sessions where the output did not meet the target of 15 sessions, the target of the standard can be changed to, for example, 17 sessions. An advantage of second order feedback is that it can cover more complex organizational control situations. Furthermore, variability and stochasticity can be accounted for with a second order feedback loop.

Information Technology for Planning and Control

Planning and control by feedback on performances can be supported by IT. IT provides the backbone for collecting, compiling, and utilizing information on patients, activities, methods, costs, and results (Porter & Olmsted Teisberg, 2006). Because of the multidisciplinary care and the involvement of several professionals, disciplines, and departments that need to be planned and controlled, a central automated system for planning and control might be needed. In industry Enterprise Resources Planning systems are often used for this purpose. Enterprise Resource Planning (ERP) systems attempt to integrate all corporate information in one central database, and information can be retrieved from many different organizational positions and in principle they allow any organizational object to be made visible (Dechow & Mouritsen, 2005).

Likewise, for healthcare, ERP systems can integrate many functions such as patient scheduling, human resource management, workload forecasting, and management of workflow (Jenkins & Christenson, 2001). However, when implementing ERP systems in an organization, several implementation and structural problems can occur, for example, ERP may not fit the structure of the organization.

Implementation and structural problems may occur in healthcare because ERP systems require fixed, deterministic processes and ignore alternative processes (Van Merode, Groothuis et al., 2004). But in healthcare, stochasticity (e.g., patients not showing up) and variability (e.g., demands for care differ between several individual patients) exist. Because of the existence of stochasticity and variability, a more reactive decision making technology or short term planning systems as, for example, Advanced Resource Planning (ARP), better suit the less deterministic processes (Vandaele & De Boeck, 2003; Van Merode, Groothuis et al., 2004). Another possibility for planning and control in mental healthcare is to physically separate deterministic processes suitable for ERP from nondeterministic processes requiring a more reactive decision making, or short term planning, technology.

PLANNING AND CONTROL AND THE USE OF IT IN MENTAL HEALTHCARE ORGANIZATIONS

To study the possibilities of planning and control and the use in mental healthcare organizations, we performed two case studies. Here we present the results of these two case studies.

Case 1: Planning Tool and Care Programs

In the multidisciplinary youth (mental) healthcare center, processes were standardized by care programs. The aim of the care programs was to plan processes more efficient and effective, and also to improve the patient-oriented way of working. A care program is defined as a framework with which organizations, professionals, and patients should comply and it is used to get a patient-oriented organization of a well described target group. It integrates the activities between different disciplines, professionals, and departments and indicates the way the care should be given, by which professional, in which setting, and with what frequency (Berg, Schellekens et al., 2005).

Care programs consist of several standardized modules. The planning of a care program, that is, which modules will be performed, is done based on the demand of the patient. Further, for planning and control of the activities of a module, each module contains a Bill of Resources (BOR), which is described in the protocol of the module.

A BOR is derived from a Bill of Materials that is used by ERP systems. However, mental healthcare includes more than materials such as professionals and patients. Therefore, the use of a BOR is more appropriate for healthcare organizations (Van Roth & Van Dierdonck, 1995). In the center, a BOR defined the location, type of activity, professional, and patient.

Because of the multidisciplinary care, the coordination of the care programs was complex. Automated support might reduce this complexity. Therefore, IT, that is, the planning tool, was used for planning and control of activities of patients and professionals. The planning tool was a software application, intended to support working with care programs. The features of the care programs, such as the involvement of several professionals and departments and the standardization of modules, require certain functionalities of the planning tool. The planning tool contained the following functionalities: a BOR to plan activities, an event handler to react to ad hoc changes by revising timetables and re-arranging activities, an electronic organizer, and a control function for process control by first order feedback and second order feedback.

To test the functionalities in relation to the care programs, the planning tool was tested in a pilot. The evaluation of the pilot was done with a document analysis, interviews with all those involved, and analysis of e-mails to and from the planning tool helpdesk.

The results of the evaluation show that the fit between the standardized care programs and the planning tool was insufficient. The main cause was the noncompliance of the professionals with the standard modules because they feared inflexibility in performing their activities due to the standardization and first order control. However, the professionals did have some flexibility in planning. They could use the event handler to react to ad hoc situations and they had the possibility to deviate from the standards to react to variability which is second order control. But the results show that the flexibility possibilities were not known and not used by the professionals.

As the results illustrate, the characteristics of care processes and the functionalities of IT must fit to function. In this case, the IT demands a certain amount of standardization while in daily practice the professionals require flexibility in performing their activities. Therefore standardization

and flexibility have to be balanced. Because the professionals did not comply with the standard modules of the care programs, and did not know of, or use, the possible flexibility, we do not know for sure that the care programs and the IT did not fit. It seems also due to implementation problems of the IT and care programs that professionals did not comply and did not have knowledge about the possibilities of second order control.

Professionals do need some planning freedom to be able to react to the present variability and stochasticity. A planning and control system, including the IT, need to support this in an efficient way. In the second case study, we studied the actual use and the possibilities of a planning and control model which is based on performance measurement and second order feedback.

Case 2: Optimizing Planning and Control in Ambulant Mental Healthcare Centers

Due to increasing competition in mental healthcare, planning and control based on performances is needed. Therefore routine control is necessary and processes have to fulfill the characteristics as described by Hofstede (1981). But as shown in the evaluation of the planning tool, also flexibility in planning is needed.

The case study of four ambulant mental healthcare centers presents information about characteristics of their processes and the planning and control models as used. These results are used for recommendations that can guide mental healthcare organizations in their planning and control and the use of IT. These are presented in the conclusion.

In this case study, we first described the present processes by using process mapping techniques. Next, we assessed these processes on the uncertainty of demand, supply, and the service process itself, complexity of coordination, and staff inflexibility. These three factors determine the efficiency and adaptation possibilities of a process (Van Merode, Molema, & Goldschmidt, 2004). These factors incorporate the conditions of Hofstede's (1981) model.

The results of this study showed that most of the processes were not planned and controlled in a consistence way. Three of the four ambulant mental healthcare centers hardly used performance indicators to monitor the processes. The uncertainty and complexity were high and instruments, like protocols or IT, to decrease the unnecessary uncertainty and complexity were hardly used. One center did use care programs. However, the opportunities for planning and control of these care programs were not used to their full extent. Besides, a planning and control system based on feedback did not exist. This center had the most extended IT software. Nevertheless, this software was not used to monitor the results of the processes with performance indicators. Therefore, planning and control based on feedback was not performed. IT use for planning and control was very minimal in all four centers.

FUTURE TRENDS

In mental healthcare organizations, we mainly see two developments. The first is that many mental healthcare organizations continue in their old ways in organizing their care, that is, that no standards or IT are used. However, a second development is that, because of growing attention for more efficiency in mental healthcare, more and more mental healthcare organizations standardize their processes by, for example, the introduction of care programs.

Standardization can be very fruitful in decreasing unnecessary uncertainty in care processes. However, mental healthcare organizations often do not change their organization structure simultaneously with the introduction of care programs. Additionally, IT with planning and control functionalities is underused. The use of IT for integrated planning and control will prob-

ably increase. But, what we observe in somatic healthcare is that (standard) ERP packages are implemented while they do not suit the situation. These ERP systems are often implemented without a change in organization structure. By the lack of the fit between the organization, processes, and ERP systems, this can result in many problems. New, adaptive, software is there but is not successful.

As we claimed in the introduction, first and second order control should be supported by IT. Therefore IT has to be adaptive and support short term planning or reactive decision making. However, mental healthcare organizations are not yet interested in this kind of technology. In the future, mental healthcare organizations consider IT more to profit from care programming and, as a result, work more efficient and effective.

CONCLUSION

Mental healthcare organizations are on their way to more efficiency in their processes; yet IT is still underused for planning and control.

As shown in the first case study, processes and IT must fit. In this center, the organization thought that planning and control was possible with routine control supported with information technology. The care programs met the conditions for first order control and second order control. However, in the pilot it did not work out as intended.

In the second study, we observe that almost no use is made of possibilities of standardization and feedback for control purposes. Moreover, IT is hardly used for planning and control purposes. As a result, the ambulant mental healthcare centers miss the possibility to direct the outcome of processes to a certain target, and efficiency is not optimal. As a result, the centers miss the opportunities to be competing on the (regulated) market.

The results emphasize the need to carefully consider process characteristics before introducing a planning and control system. Careful consideration is needed to avoid type I and type II errors. Type I errors occur when opportunities for routine planning and control (with standardization and IT) are not used by management. However, some processes are not deterministic and cannot be controlled with routine models. When they are controlled with routine models anyway, type II errors occur. To avoid either type I or type II errors, a fit between standardization and flexibility has to been found. Hofstede (1981) states that type I errors often occur in not-for-profit organizations because the concern for cost and effectiveness is often missing. However, mental healthcare is subject of social and political developments resulting in the need to be more aware of efficiency and effectiveness. Therefore we assume that type II errors may occur in future more often.

The results also show the necessity of balancing between process standardization and the flexibility of the working practice. Routine models can be applied for processes in mental healthcare in certain circumstances. Nevertheless, routine models need to use second order control because not all activities can be planned in advance due to variability and stochasticity. This balance between standardization and flexibility has to be considered carefully before fully implementing care programs and a central planning and control system integrated in IT. To be able to balance between flexibility and efficiency by means of care programs, the organization structure also has to be changed and IT has to be adaptive.

We recommend the following to develop more efficient processes in mental healthcare organizations. First, performance indicators should be developed to be able to compete in the (regulated) market. Simultaneously, time horizons should be distinguished in which planning and control on several different levels (e.g., establishing different care programs by board 3 years, planning of professional 6 weeks) can be defined. Next, processes need to be distinguished on uncertainty and complexity of the process. The difference in

characteristics of a process (more or less routine) decides on the possibility of standardizing processes. After that, the processes that satisfy the possibilities for routine control need to be standardized and a BOR should be described. For the actual control on performances, a system based on first order control and second order control must be developed and adaptive IT that supports short term planning or is reactive is needed to support the planning and control.

The use of these recommendations helps in finding a balance between standardization, use of IT, and flexibility. In addition, IT interacts with the social system and the working practice and, therefore, it is necessary to tailor both. However, it is a process of trial and error and therefore requires adaptive IT.

REFERENCES

Berg, M., Schellekens, W., et al. (2005). Bridging the quality chasm: Integrating professional and organizational approaches to quality. *International Journal Quality of Healthcare, 17*(1), 75-82.

Dechow, N., & Mouritsen, J. (2005). Enterprise resource planning systems, management control and the quest for integration. *Accounting, Organizations and Society, 30,* 691-733.

Hofstede, G. (1981). Management control of not-for profit activities. *Accounting, Organizations and Society: An International Journal Devoted to the Behavioural Organizational & Social Aspects of Accounting, 6,* 193-211.

Jenkins, E.K., & Christenson, E. (2001). ERP (enterprise resource planning) systems can streamline healthcare business functions. Healthcare Financial Management, 55(5), 48-52.

Porter, M.E., & Olmsted Teisberg, E. (2006). Redefining healthcare. *Creating value-based competition on results.* Boston, MA: Harvard

Business School Press.

Vandaele, N., & De Boeck, L. (2003). Advanced resource planning. *Robotics and Computer Integrated Manufacturing, 19,* 211-218.

Van Merode, G.G., Groothuis, S., & Hasman, A. (2004). Enterprise resource planning for hospitals. *International Journal of Medical Informatics, 73*(6), 493-501.

Van Merode, F., Molema, H., & Goldschmidt, H. (2004). GUM and six sigma approaches positioned as deterministic tools in quality target engineering. *Accreditation and Quality Assurance, 10,* 32-36.

Van Roth, A., & Van Dierdonck, R. (1995). Hospital resource planning: Concepts, feasibility and framework. *Production and operations management, 4*(1), 2-29.

KEY TERMS

Adaptive Information Technology: Information Technology that can be adapted to changing circumstances in finding a balance between processes and IT.

Care Program: A care program is a framework where organizations, professionals, and patients should comply with and is used for patient-centered organization of a well described target group. It integrates the activities between different disciplines, professionals, and departments (Berg, Schellekens et al., 2005).

Control: The process that assures that the planned results are obtained.

Enterprise Resource Planning System: Enterprise Resource Planning systems attempt to integrate all corporate information in one central database, and information can be retrieved from many different organizational positions and in principle they allow any organizational object to be made visible (Dechow & Mouritsen, 2005).

Feedback: Information about the output is fed back to the input.

Planning: Determination of what should be done.

Reactive Decision Making: Decision making based on reacting to unexpected situations due to variability and stochasticity.

Short Term Planning: Planning on short terms with data about monthly, daily, and hourly demand and meaning full statistical distributions to be able to deal with stochasticity and variability.

Chapter XXII
Examining the Approach Used for Information Technology Investment Decisions by Practitioners Responsible for IT Planning in Namibia

Karna Naidoo
University of KwaZulu-Natal, South Africa

ABSTRACT

Despite the technological progress made by organisations in Namibia, the impact of IT has not been studied. The existing definition of IT is not comprehensive enough to include all relevant IT expenditures. No return calculations are made, though managers are showing growing concern at the increasing IT costs. The purpose of this article is to determine what organisations in Namibia use as basis for investing in IT. In interviews with six organisations in Namibia, it was determined how they define and manage their investment in IT. Some conclusions can be drawn, the first being that organisations need to look at their definition of IT to include all aspects of IT like communication systems, maintenance, etc. the second implication is that somebody must be appointed to take responsibility for managing the IT investment.

INTRODUCTION

Throughout history, progress in technological behaviour had profound social significance—regardless of whether it was based on mere intuition, trail-or-error, or scientific approach. Machiavelli as *cited* by Bass (1990) made the following comment about systems in general: "There is nothing more difficult to plan, more doubtful of success, nor more dangerous to manage than the creation of a new system. For the initiator has the enmity of all who would profit by the preservation of the old system and merely lukewarm defenders in those who would gain by the new one."

We now realise that information systems (IS) are the centre of a new business reality in the 1990s.

The impact of the IT revolution is a phenomenon that is affecting every aspect of Third World societies. This revolution increasingly affects anything from the way organisations conduct business to the organisation of schools. The impact can even be stronger than the impact of gaining independence by drastically changing the course of economic development in a county. The major problem is that the use of IT is not fully understood nor studied in the Third World countries in order to yield meaningful insights.

PREVIOUS ATTEMPTS TO QUANTIFY IT EXPENDITURE

Although there has been some growth in the usage of IT over the last couple of years, no analysis of the impact of IT on sales, costs, and profits of organisations has been made in Third World countries. It is, however, important that organisations inform themselves of the impact of IT usage on operating results and profitability. Strategies can then be developed in order to gain a competitive advantage.

Weill and Olson (1989) use case studies of organisations to determine how IT is defined, how IT investments are measured, tracked, and what other factors control IT investment decisions. Some important issues emerged from their study, namely that managers must adopt a broad definition of IT and that IT expenditures can be measured and tracked against a convenient base (revenues, total expenses, or management control costs). Weill et al. believe that attention must be paid to certain factors concerning any important IT investment, namely: managers' commitment to IT, previous organisational experience with IT, user satisfaction with systems, and the turbulence of the political environment of the organisation. A literature study based on a graphical cost/benefit approach to computer systems selection was presented by Shoval and Lugasi (1988). They note that stages, like analysing the needs of the system

and defining its requirements and attributes, need attention.

Ahituv and Neumann (1990) state that any attempt to assess the value of information should be closely linked to the decision supported by the information. They noted that the selection of criteria to use in comparative analysis is the easier part in cost/benefit analysis. The complicated part is to identify all the elements which form part of cost and benefits, and determining how to measure (or estimate) all those elements.

Kwong and Mohammed (1985) suggest the use of a computerised index (CI) that can quantitatively evaluate the impact of computerisation on profitability and, in the process, develop an indicator to the extent and sophistication of computerisation. The organisations used show that an increasing degree of computerisation is generally associated with an increasing profitability margin as indicated by the CI—even in the short term.

In his study involving experienced users, Davis (1989) suggests the use of determinants, the most important one being that if potential users believe that a given application is useful, they may simultaneously believe that the system is difficult to use and that the performance benefits of usage are outweighed by the efforts of using the application.

In conclusion, it can be said that IT investment uses resources of organisations. There are no consensus of the definition of IT and the measurement of its tangible and intangible benefits. This makes IT investment difficult to manage.

CASE STUDY RESULTS

Six mini case studies were conducted to help understand how organisations define and manage their IT investments in Namibia. The six organisations compose of five large profit-making organisations, while the sixth organisation is a part of the educational system in Namibia. A lengthy, semi- structured interview was conducted with the senior representatives in information systems of each organisation. Every attempt was made to keep the identity of the organisation and sensitive information confidential.

Primary questions covered the following:

- What does the organisation regard as part of their IT?
- How do they manage and track IT investments?
- From where does the impetus for buying IT equipment start?
- What factors influence IT investment decisions?

Organisation 1—Education

Organisation 1 is in the field of tertiary education in Namibia. The interviewee is the director of the computer bureau. According to him IT is defined to include only hardware and software. During the past two years, the budget for purchasing IT equipment was drastically cut. All purchases of IT equipment were done from savings in department's budget. IT is tracked in a combined centralised and decentralised way, but no attempt is being made to include relatively small expenditures. IT equipment is not captured on the tracking of the investment if a department buys IT equipment from own savings. No ROI is calculated although departments are assessed on an output vs. input basis (output could be preparation for lectures while input could be space, equipment, number of persons in the department etc.).

The impetus to buy IT equipment originates from departments who identify a need, get top management's permission, and proceed to buy the equipment. Political considerations do play a significant part in decisions to invest in IT. The management of the IT investment is done on a partly centralised and partly decentralised basis. There is no link between the buying of IT equipment and the strategy and the strategy of the organisation.

Organisation 2—Transport

Organisation 2 is a large organisation in the transport sector. The interviewee is the chief clerk who controls IT. The interviewee noted that the process of investing resources in IT is the responsibility of individual divisions. IT is defined as all hardware and software. The productive capacity of the IT is planned in order to allow maximum advantage of their investment. The interviewee believes that investment in IT could be maximized but stated that no real attempt is being made to do so. No return calculations are made on the investment and there are decentralised tracking of the investment. He noted that political issues do play part in decisions to invest in IT. The impetus to invest in IT comes from a central point. If the need for II is recognised, he has to be notified. There is no link between investment in IT and the strategy for the organisation.

Organisation 3—Banking

Organisation 3 is a geographically dispersed commercial bank. The interviewee is a member of the management of the bank. The bank includes hardware and software in its general view of IT. No productive capacity planning for IT is being done in the bank. The bank keeps track on all levels of IT equipment in a combined centralised and decentralised basis. This is done as no simple measure is considered enduring enough in terms of accuracy. The bank's decision to invest in IT is done at corporate level the following inputs from base. Every department manages its own IT.

The interviewee stated that political considerations play a big part in the decision to invest in IT. According to him, there definitely is a link between the buying of IT equipment and the strategy of the organisation.

Organisation 4—Insurance

Organisation 4 is a local firm who handles all sorts of insurance for a large clientele basis. The interviewee is the manager of the financial department. Their definition of IT includes hardware and software. No productive capacity or any tracking of their IT equipment was done. They do not conduct return calculations on their IT investment because they consider it too complicated. All IT equipment in their possession is managed from a central position.

Political considerations do play a part in their decision to invest in IT and tat is why top management takes all decisions regarding IT investments. There is a link between the strategy the organisation employs and decisions to invest in IT or not.

Organisation 5—Consumer Products

Organisation 5 is a large manufacturing organisation in the consumer products industry. The interviewee is the manager of the information department. According to the interviewee, the definition includes all PC-hardware and software as well as all consumables. Productive capacity is planned in advanced as management wants to see IT equipment put to use. All IT equipment is managed in a centralised way. No return calculations are done on the investment in IT. The decision to invest in IT comes from management. He also said that political considerations play no part in decisions to invest in IT. There is a link the decision to buy IT equipment and the strategy for the organisation.

Organisation 6—Insurance

Organisation 6 is a large multi-national insurance organisation with three major businesses, namely individual insurance, group insurance, and investment. The interviewee is the computer consultant to the organisation. The definition of IT does not include consumables but encompasses all hardware and software. Decentralisation of the organisation is the reason why managers of the organisation decided to decentralise the management of IT. No return calculation is made on IT investments. Political considerations play a part in the decision to buy IT equipment. The impetus to buy IT usually comes from managers and the lower-hierarchy based on what their opposition is doing and how they define their strategy.

ANALYSIS OF KEY FACTORS

The Definition and Tracking of IT

The majority of organisations viewed hardware and software as the only part of its investment in IT. There seems to be a trend to keep the definition of IT as narrow as possible.

IT Investment Management

Organisations track IT expenses with varying degrees of success. Tracking is done mainly on the basis of comparing it with budgeted amounts for the specific year and taking care not to exceed the budgeted amount. Another problem could be that It investments by departments are not captured on the overall picture of the organisation. No return calculations on investments are done as people tend to think it is too difficult. The total hardware appeared as assets in the asset register though some organisations did not keep track of software expenses at all.

Political and Other Influences

Political considerations are important factors in most organisations and have significant impact on the acquisition of IT equipment. These considerations sometimes overshadow the technical and economic considerations and are becoming more important. In most cases the impetus for investment was taken by managers. This was not necessarily connected to a decision to incorporate more IT into the organisation. In all (but two) organisations there was no link between IT and the strategy for the organisation.

IMPLICATIONS OF THE FINDINGS

The implications from the findings are: (1) Define and track IT as IT expenditures increase the need for a definition for IT becomes an important issue. This must be broadened to include all cost aspects of IT; and (2) the calculation of the return on investments in IT can be complex as no real cash flow is available.

RECOMMENDATIONS

Organisations in a Third World country like Namibia must realise that they have to manage their IT investment by:

1. **Defining and tracking IT investments:** Redefine the definition of IT so that it includes all expenditures, such as hardware, software, people, consumables, training, and maintenance. There must be accurate recording of this expenditure over time against a convenient base such as revenues or staff employed, etc.
2. **Looking at IT investment and return:** To justify IT investment poses a problem for many organisations. Return on investment (ROI) calculations sometimes does not apply to certain IT investments because it is difficult to determine a definite income stream. Managers must, however, recognise that ROI calculations are not always relevant for all IT investments. They must remember that some IT investments could be essential to the organisation's survival. Lastly, managers must keep in mind that the total IT investment needs to be calculated if they want to see the effect of the IT investment on the organisation.
3. **Concentrating on organisational issues:** Issues that must be liked into are: Top management commitment to IT; previous experience with IT; user satisfaction with systems; and the political environment of the organisation.

CONCLUSION

It was found that IT definitions are not comprehensive enough. The problem could be that organisations do not sit down and constructively plan their investment in IT. I had the feeling that organisations in Namibia have no idea of the total amount of resources invested in IT. Another factor is that this investment is not managed satisfactorily and that nobody wanted to take responsibility for managing IT investment. My final conclusion is that workshops must be organised and people educated in the concepts of managing IT investment.

REFERENCES

Ahituv, N., & Neumann, S. (1990). *Principles of information systems for management* (3rd ed.). Dubuque: WC Brown Publishers.

Bass, B. M. (1990). *Handbook of leadership* (3rd ed.). New York: The Free Press.

Davis, F. J. (1989, September). Perceived usefulness, perceived ease of use, and user acceptance of IT. *MIS Quarterly.*

Kwong, H. C., & Mohammed, M. Z. (1985). Profit impact of computerisation. *Hong Kong Computer Journal.*

Shoval, P., & Lugasi, Y. (1988). Computer systems selection. *Information and Management, 15.*

Weill, P., & Olson, M. H. (1989, March). Managing investment in IT: Mini case examples and implications. *MIS Quarterly*.

Compilation of References

Adeoti-Adekeye, W. B. (1997). The importance of management information systems. *Library Review, 46*(5).

Agarwal, R., & Tanniru, M. (1992). Assessing the organizational impacts of Information technology. *ITJM, Special Issue on the Strategic Management of Information and Telecommunication Technology* (pp. 626-643).

Ahituv, N., & Neumann, S. (1990). *Principles of information systems for management* (3rd ed.). Dubuque: WC Brown Publishers.

Aitken, I. (2003). *Value-driven IT management*. Computer Weekly: Professional Series. Oxford, Butterworth-Heinemann.

Akella, J., Kanakamedala, K., & Roberts, R. P. (2006). 2006 Survey on CIO agenda in 2007. McKinsey & Company, Silicon Valley.

Alexander, C., & Ishikawa, S. (1977). *A Pattern Language*. New York: Oxford University Press.

Alexandrou, M. (2002). *Supply chain management (SCM) definition*. Retrieved on 18 February 2007, www.marioalexandrou.com/glossary/scm.asp

Allen, A. B., Juillet, L., Paquet, G., & Roy, J. (2001). E-Governance and Government Online in Canada: Partnerships, People and Prospects. *Government Information Quarterly, 18*, 93-104.

Allert J., & Kleiner, B. H. (1997). Developments in Computer-based information systems, *Logistics Information Management, 10*(5).

Al-Mashari, M., & Zairi, M. (2000). Supply-chain re-engineering using enterprise-resource planning (ERP) systems: An analysis of a SAP R/3 implementation case. *International Journal of Physical Distribution & Logistics Management, 30*(¾), 296-313.

American Productivity & Quality Center (APQC, 2007). *Open Standards Benchmarking Collaborative Database for Information Technology*, APQC, Houston, TX, retrieved 18 March 2007 www.apqc.org..

Amidon, D. M. (1997). *Innovation Strategy for the Knowledge Economy: The Ken Awakening*. Boston, MA: Butterworth-Heinemann.

Anand, V., Manz, C., & Glick, H. (1998). An organizational memory approach to information management. *Academy of Management Review, 23*(4).

Anderson, J. C., & Gerbing, G. W. (1988). Structural Equation Modeling in Practice: A Review and Recommended Two-step Approach. *Psychological Bulletin, 103*, 411-423.

Anderson, M. C., Banker, R. D., & Ravindran, S. (2003). The new productivity paradox. *Communications of the ACM, 46*(3).

Andriessen, D. (2001). *Weightless wealth*. Paper for the 4th world congress on the management of intellectual capital. Mc Master University, January 17 – 19, Hamilton, Ontario.

Anell, B., & Jensen, T. (1998). Managing project portfolios. *Proceedings of the International Research Network on Organizing by Projects (IRNOP)*. Calgary: The University of Calgary.

Ansoff I. (1987). *Corporate Strategy*. London, UK: Penguin Books.

Ansoff I. (2007). *Strategic Management*. Classic edition. London, UK: Palgrave Macmillan.

Anthony, R. N. (1965). *Planning and Control Systems: A Framework for Analysis*. Graduate School of Business, Harvard University.

Applegate, L. M., McFarlan, F. W., & McKenney, J. L. (1996). *Corporate Information Systems and Management: Text and Cases*. Boston, MA: Richard D. Irwin..

Applegate, L., Austin, R. D., & McFarlan, W. (2006). *Corporate information strategy and management: Portfolio approach to managing IT projects.* Boston: Mc Graw Hill.

Applegate, L.M., Austin, R.D., & McFarlan, F.W. (2003). *Corporate information strategy and management* (6th edition). New York: McGraw-Hill.

April, J., Glover, F., & Kelly, J. (2003). Optfolio-A Simulation Optimization System for Project Portfolio Planning. In S. Chick, T. Sanchez, D. Ferrin & D. Morrice (Ed.), *Proceedings of the 2003 Winter Simulation Conference* (pp. 301-309).

April, J., Glover, F., Kelly, J., & Laguna, M., (2003). Practical Introduction to Simulation Optimization. In S. Chick, T. Sanchez, D. Ferrin and D. Morrice, (Ed.), *Proceedings of the 2003 Winter Simulation Conference* (pp. 71-78).

Archer, N. P., & Ghasemzadeh, F. (1996). *Project Portfolio Selection Techniques: A Review and a Suggested Integrated Approach* (Innovation Research Working Group Working Paper No. 46). Hamilton, Ontario: McMaster University.

Archer, N. P., & Ghasemzadeh, F. (1999). An Integrated Framework for Project Portfolio Selection. *International Journal of Project Management, 17*(4), 207-216.

Archer, N. P., & Ghasemzadeh, F. (1999). An Integrated Framework for Project Portfolio Selection. *International Journal of Project Management, 17*(4), 207-216.

Archibald, R.D. (2003). *Managing high-technology programs and projects.* New York: John Wiley & Sons.

Argris, C. (1991). Management information systems: The challenge to rationality and emotionality. *Management Science, 291.*

Armstrong, J. S., & Overton, T. S. (1977). Estimating Nonresponse Bias in Mail Surveys. *J. Marketing Res., 14,* 396-402.

Arora, A., Hall, D., Pinto, C. A., Ramsey, D., & Telang, R. A. (2004). Measuring the risk-based value of IT security solutions. *IEEE IT Professional, 6*(6), 35–42.

Artto, K., Martinsuo, M., & Aalto, T. (2001). Project portfolio management—Suggestions for future research. In K.A. Artto, M. Martinsuo, & T. Aalto (Eds.), *Project portfolio management.* Helsinki: Project Management Association (PMA).

Asian Development Bank. (1998). *Annual report.*

Atrill, P., & McLaney, E. (2004). *Accounting and Finance for Non-Specialists* (4th ed.). England: Prentice Hall.

Aubert, A. B., Dussault, S., Patry, M., & Rivard, S. (1999). Managing the risk of IT Outsourcing. In *CD-ROM Proceedings of the 32nd Hawaii International Conference on System Sciences.* Los Alamitos: IEEE Computer Society.

Aubert, A. B., Patry, M., & Rivard, S. (1998). Assessing the Risk of IT Outsourcing. In *Proceedings of the 31st Hawaii International Conference on Systems Sciences* (pp. 685-692). Washington: IEEE Computer Society.

Auditor Report (2003). Retrieved May 15, 2008, from http://www.audit.sa.gov.au/02-03/itrep/summary.html

Auer, T., & Reponen, T. (1997). Information systems strategy formulation embedded into a continuous organizational learning process. *Information Resources Management Journal, 10*(2), 32-43.

Avison, D., Jones, J., Powell, P., & Wilson, D. (2004). Using and validating the strategic alignment model. *Journal of Strategic Information Systems, 13,* 223-246.

Axelrod R. (1976). *Structure of Decision: The Cognitive Maps of Political Elites.* Princeton, NJ: Princeton University Press.

Axelrod, R., & Cohen, M. (1999). *Harnessing complexity: Organizational implications of a scientific frontier.* New York: Free Press.

Ayag, Z. (2005). An integrated approach to evaluating conceptual design alternatives in a new product development environment. *International Journal of Production Research, 43*(4), 687–713.

Bacharach, S. B., & Aiken, M. (1977). Communication in Administrative Bureaucracies. *Acad. Management J., 20*(3), 365-377.

Badawy, M. K. (1998). Technology management education: alternative models. *California Management Review, 40*(4).

Bakos, Y., & Treacy, M. (1986). Information technology and corporate strategy: A research perspective. *MIS Quarterly, 10*(2), 107-119.

Ballantyne, P. (2000). Managing Relationships: A Key Information Management Capacity. *Information and Capacity Building, 7,* October 2000, ECDPM

Banini, G. A., & Bearman, R. A. (1998). *Application of fuzzy cognitive maps to factors affecting slurry rheology. International Journal of Mineral Processing, 52,* 233 – 244.

Barabba, V. P., & Zaltman, G. (1991). *Hearing the Voice of the Market: Competitive Advantage through creative use of Market Information.* Harvard Business School Press.

Bardhan, I., & Sougstad, R. (2004). Prioritizing a portfolio of information technology investment projects. *Journal of Management Information Systems, 21*(2), 33-60.

Barney, L. D., & Danielson, M. (2004). Ranking Mutually Exclusive Projects: The Role of Duration. *The Engineering Economist, 49*, 43-61.

Barsdale, H., & Darden, B. (1971). Marketers' attitudes toward the marketing concept, *Journal of Marketing, 35*, 29-36.

Bass, B. M. (1990). *Handbook of leadership* (3rd ed.). New York: The Free Press.

Bassellier, G., & Benbasat, I. (2004). Business competence of IT professionals: Conceptual development and influence on IT-business partnerships. *MIS Quarterly, 28*(4), 673–694.

Basu, V., Hartono, E., Lederer, A. L., & Sethi, V. (2002). The impact of organizational commitment, senior management involvement, and team involvement on information systems strategic planning. *Information and Management, 39*(6), 513-524.

Beardsley S. C., Johnson, B. C., & Manyika, J. M. (2006). Competitive advantage from better interactions. *The McKinsey Quarterly, 2.*

Beaumont, J. R., & Walters D. (1991). Information management in service industries: Towards a strategic framework. *Journal of Information Systems, 1.*

Benaroch, M., & Kauffman, R. J. (1999). A case for using real options pricing analysis to evaluate information technology project investment. *Information Systems Research, 10*(1), 70–86.

Benaroch, M., (2002). Managing Information technology Investment Risk: A Real Options Perspective. *Journal of Management Information Systems, 19*(2), 43-84.

Benjamin, R. I., & Levinson, E. (1993). A Framework for managing IT enabled Change. *Sloan Management Review*, (pp. 23-33).

Benjamin, R. I., de Long, D. W., & Morton, M. S. S. (1990). Electronic Data Interchange: How much Competitive Advantage? *Long Range Planning, 23*(1), 34-40.

Benjamin, R. I., Rockart, J. F., Morton, M. S. S., & Wyman, J. (1984). Information Technology: A Strategic Opportunity. *Sloan Management Review*, (pp. 3-10).

Benko, C., & McFarlan, F.W. (2003). *Connecting the dots: Aligning projects with objectives in unpredictable times.* Boston: Harvard Business School Press.

Bennett, M. (2002). *Outsourcing overlooks staff.* Retrieved November 18, 2005, from http://www.computing.co.uk/itweek/news/2084685/outsourcing-overlooks-staff

Benson, R. J., Bugnitz, T., & Walton, B., (2004). *From business strategy to IT action: right decisions for a better bottom line.* Hoboken, N.J., Wiley.

Bentler, P. M. (1995). *EQS Structural Equations Program Manual.* Multivariate Software, Inc. Encino, CA.

Berg, E. (1993). *Rethinking technical cooperation: reforms for capacity building in Africa.* Washington, DC: UNDP/DAL

Berg, M., Schellekens, W., et al. (2005). Bridging the quality chasm: Integrating professional and organizational approaches to quality. International Journal Quality of Healthcare, 17(1), 75-82.

Berger, P. L., & Luckmann, T. (1966). *The Social Construction of Reality.* Garden City, NY: Anchor Books.

Bezdek, J. (1993). Editorial, Fuzzy models - what they are, and why. *IEEE Transactions on Fuzzy Systems, 1.*

Bhatnagar, S. (2004). E-Government: Lessons from Implementation in Developing Countries. *Regional Development Dialogue, 24*, UNCRD, Autumn Issue 164-174.

Bhatt, G. D., & Grover, V. (2005). Types of information technology capabilities and their role in competitive advantage: An empirical study. *Journal of Management Information Systems, 22*(2), 253–278.

Bigelow, D. (2003). Trend watch: Want to ensure quality? Think project portfolio management. *PMNetwork, 17*(1), 16.

Bjornsson, H. & Lundegard, R. (1990). Corporate Competitiveness and Information Technology. *European Management Journal,* 10(3), 460-475.

Blackler, F. (1995). Knowledge, knowledge work and organizations: An overview and interpretation. *Organization studies, 16*(6).

Blechar, J. M., & Sinur, J. (2006). Magic Quadrant for Business Process Analysis Tools.

Bleistein, S., J., Cox, K., Verner, J., & Phalp, K.T. (2006). B-SCP: A requirements analysis framework for validating strategic alignment of organisational IT based on strategy, context, and process. *Information and Software Technology, 48*, 846-868.

Blili, S., & Raymond, L. (1993). Information technology: threats and opportunities for small and medium-sized enterprises. *International Journal of Information Management, 13*(6), 439-448.

Block T. R., & Frame J. D. (2001). Today's Project Office: Gauging Attitudes. *PM Network, 15*(8), 50-53.

Blomstrom, M. (1986). Foreign Investment and Productive Efficiency: The Case of Mexico. *Journal of Industrial Economics, 35*(1), 97-110.

Blum, C., & Roli, A., (2003). Metaheuristics in combinatorial optimization: Overview and conceptual comparison. *ACM Computing Surveys, 35*(3), 268–308.

Boddy, D., Boonstra, A., & Kennedy, G. (2005). *Managing information systems: An organisational perspective* (2nd edition). Harlow: Pearson.

Bolles D. (2002). *Building Project Management Centers of Excellence*. New York, NY: AMACOM.

Bonham, S. S. (2005). *IT Project Portfolio Management*. Norwood, MA: Artech House.

Boudreau, M., Gefen, D., & Straubm D. W. (2001). Validation in Information Systems Research: A State-of-the-Art Assessment. *MIS Quart., 25*(1), 1-24.

Boyatzis, R. (1982). *The Competent Manager*. New York: Wiley.

Boykin, R. F. (2001). Enterprise resource-planning software: a solution to the return material authorization problem. *Computers in Industry, 45*, 99-109.

Boynton, A. C., Jacobs, G. C., & Zmud, R. W. (1992). Whose Responsibility is IT management? *Sloan Management Review*, (pp. 32-38).

Bragg, S. M. (2006). *Outsourcing*. Hoboken, NJ: John Wiley and Sons.

Brancheau, J. C., Janz, B. D., & Wetherbe, J. C. (1996). Key issues in information systems management: 1994-95 SIM Delphi results. *MIS Quarterly, 20*(2), 225-242.

Braunerhjelm, P., & Carlsson, B. (2003). Introduction: Regional Growth, Clusters and Institutions. *Industry and Innovation, 10*(1), 1-3.

Bridges, N. D. (1999). Project Portfolio Management: Ideas and Practices. In Dye, D. L., & Pennypacker S. J. (Eds.), *Project Portfolio Management* (pp. 45-54). West Chester, PA: Center for business Practices.

Broadbent, M., & Weill, P. (1997). Management by maxim: How business and IT managers can create IT infrastructures. *Sloan Management Review, 38*, 77-91.

Brown, A. E., & Grant, G. G. (2005). Framing the frameworks: A review of IT governance research. *Communications of AIS, 15*(38), 696–712.

Brown, I. T. (2004). Testing and extending theory in strategic information systems planning through literature analysis. *Information Resource Management Journal, 17*(4), 20-48.

Browne, M., & Cudeck, R. (1993). Alternative Ways of Assessing Model Fit. K. A. Bollen & J. S. Long (Eds.), *Testing Structural Equation Models*. London, UK: Sage Publications.

Brynjolfsson, E., & Hitt, L. (1998). Beyond the productivity paradox. *Communications of the ACM, 41*(8), 49-55.

Bureau of Labor Statistics (2004). *Global Insights, International Labor Organization*. United Nations, World Bank.

Burn, J. (1997). Information systems strategies and the management of organizational change. *Journal of Information Technology, 8*, 205-216.

Burn, J. M. (1991). Stages of growth in strategic information systems planning (SISP). *Proceedings of the 24th Annual Hawaii International Conference on System Sciences*, Kanai, HI, Januatu.

Bushell, S. (2004). At last a way to build trust. *CIO Magazine*. Retrieved January 27, 2008, from http://www.cio.com.au/index.php?id=677506899&fp=16&fpid=0

Buss, M. (1999). How to rank computer projects. In L.D. Dye & J.S. Pennypacker (Eds.), *Project portfolio management* (4th edition, pp. 183-192). West Chester: Center for Business Practices.

Buzzell, R., & Gale, B. (1987). *The PIMS principles: Linking strategy to performance*. New York: Free Press.

Byrd, T. A., & Turner, D. E. (2000). Measuring the flexibility of information technology infrastructure: Exploratory analysis of a construct. *Journal of Management Information Systems, 17*(1), 167–208.

Byrd, T. A., Lewis, B. R., & Bryan, R. W. (2006). The leveraging influence of strategic alignment on IT investment: An empirical examination. *Information & Management*, (43), 308-321.

Cadle, J., & Yeates, D. (2004). *Project Management for Information Systems* (4E ed.). Prentice Hall.

Campbell, D. T., & Fiske, D. W. (1959). Convergent and Discriminant Validation by the Multitraitmultimethod Matrix. *Psychological Bulletin, 56*(1), 81-105.

Cantwell, J.(1989). *Technological Innovation and Multinational Corporations*. Oxford: Basil Blackwell.

Cardy, R. L., & Selvarajan, T. T. (2006). Competencies: Alternative frameworks for competitive advantage. *Business horizons, 49*. Elsevier.

Carlson, J. R., & Zmud, R. W. (1999). Channel Expansion Theory and the Experiential Nature of Media Richness Perceptions. *Acad. Management J., 42*(2), 153-170.

Carlsson, B., & Mudambi, R. (2003). Globalization, Entrepreneurship, and Public Policy: A System View. *Industry and Innovation, 10*(1), 103-116.

Carmines, E. G., & McIver, J. P. (1981). Analyzing Model with Unobserved Variables. In G. W. Bohrnstedt and E. F. Borgatta (Eds.), *Social Measurement: Current Issues*. Beverly Hills, CA: Sage Publications.

Carr, N.G. (2003). IT doesn't matter. *Harvard Business Review, 81*(5), 41-49.

Cash, J.I. (May 1995). British air gets on course. *Informationweek*, 140.

Caves, R. E. (1974). Multinational Firms, Competition and Productivity in HostCountry Markets. *Economics, 41*, 176-93.

Cecchini, S., & Raina, M. (2004). Electronic Government and the Rural Poor: The Case of Gyandoot. *Information Technologies and International Development, 2*(2), 65–75.

Cecil, J., & Goldstein, M. (1990). Sustaining competitive advantage from IT. *McKinsey Quarterly, 4*, 74-89.

Chaffey, D. (2004). *E-Business and E-Commerce* (2 E ed.). Prentice Hall.

Champy, J. (1996). *Reengineering Management: The Mandate for New Leadership*. New York/NY: HarperCollins.

Champy, J., & Hammer, M. (2001). *Reengineering the Corporation: A Manifesto for Business Revolution*. New York/NY: Harper Collins.

Chan, Y. E., Huff, S. L., & Barclay, D. W. (1997). Business Strategic Orientation, Information Systems Strategic Orientation, and Strategic Alignment. *Inform. Systems Res., 8*, 125-150.

Chandler, A. (1962). *Strategy and structure: Chapters in the history of industrial enterprise*. New York: Doubleday.

Chandler, A. D. (1962). *Strategy and Structure*. Cambridge, MA: MIT Press.

Charette, R. (2002). *The state of risk management 2002: Hype or reality?* The Data & Analysis Center for Software (DACS) and Cutter Consortium.

Chatzkel, J. (2002). Conversation with Alex Bennet, former deputy CIO for enterprise integration at the U.S. Dept. of Navy. *Journal of Knowledge Management, 6*(5)

Chen M., & Nunmaker J. (1989). *Integration of organisation and information systems modelling: An object-oriented approach*. In Proceedings of the 22nd Hawaii International Conference on Systems Science, Jan.

Chen, I. J. (2001). Planning for ERP systems: analysis and future trend. *Business Process Management Journal, 7*(5), 374-86.

Chen, S. (2005). *Strategic management of e-business* (2nd edition). West Sussex: John Wiley & Sons.

Cherry Tree & Co. (2002). Business Intelligence – the missing link. Retrieved 18 March 2007, www. cherrytreeco.com

Chien, C.-F. (2002). Portfolio-evaluation framework for selecting R&D projects. *R&D Management, 32*(4), 359-368.

Choe, J. (2003). The effect of environmental uncertainty and strategic applications of IS on a firm's performance. *Information & Management, 40*, 257-268.

Chou, H., & Jou, S. (1999). MIS key issues in Taiwan's enterprises. *International Journal of Information Management, 19*, 369-387.

Churchman, C. W. (1971). *The Design of Inquiring Systems: Basic Concepts of Systems and Organizations*. New York: Basic Books.

Ciborra, C. (2005). Interpreting e-government and Development Efficiency, transparency or governance at a distance? *Information Technology and People, 18*(3). 65-75.

Ciborra, C., (1997). De Profundis? Deconstructing the concept of strategic alignment. *IRIS conference* (http://iris.informatik.gu.se/conference/iris20/60.htm).

Cicmil, S. J. K. (1997). Critical factors of effective project management. *The TQM Magazine, 9*(6), 390-6.

Cimral, J., & Lawler, M. (2002). *White article: Getting started with portfolio management.* Prosight.

Clarke, S. (2001). *Information systems strategic management: An integrated Approach.* New York: Routledge.

Cleland, I. D. (1999). The Strategic Context of Projects. In Dye, D. L., & Pennypacker S. J. (Eds.), *Project Portfolio Management* (pp. 3-22). West Chester, PA: Center for Business Practices.

Clemons E. K., & Row M. C. (1991). Sustaining IT advantage: The role of structural differences, *MIS Quarterly*, September.

Clemons, E. (1991). Evaluation of strategic investments in information technology. *Communications of the ACM, 34*(1), 22-36.

Clemons, E.K., & Row, M.C. (1991). Sustaining IT advantage: The role of structural differences. *MIS Quarterly, 15*(3), 275-292.

COBIT 4.1 (2007). *COBIT 4.1 excerpt: Executive summary and framework.* IT Governance Institute

Cohen, J. M. (1993b). *Building sustainable public sector managerial, professional and technical capacity: A framework for analysis and intervention.* Development Discussion Paper 473. Cambridge. MA: Harvard Institute for International Development.

Cohen, L., & Young, A. (2005). *Multisourcing: Moving Beyond Outsourcing to Achieve Growth And Agility.* Boston: Harvard Business School Press.

Combe, M.W. (1998). Project prioritization in a large functional organization. In L.D. Dye & J.S. Pennypacker (Eds.), *Project portfolio management* (4th edition, pp. 310-318). West Chester: Center for Business Practices.

Combe, M.W., & Githens, G.D. (1999). Managing popcorn priorities: How portfolios and programs align projects with strategies. *Project Management Institute seminars and symposium proceedings,* 67-78.

Compeau, D. R., & Higgins, C. A. (1995). Computer Self-Efficacy: Development of a Measure and Initial Test. *MIS Quart.,* 189-211.

ComputerWeekly (2006, May 9). ComputerWeekly CIO Index, *ComputerWeekly,* 14-15.

Conlon, G. (2006). How do you create customer devotion? *1 to 1 weekly,* Issue December 11, 2006, retrieved 20 March 2007www. 1to1media.com/doc ID=29937,

Conrad, J. (August, 1997). It pays to think big. *Computerworld,* 40-42.

Conroy, J. (2007). *7 Challenges of Implementing a Content Management System.* Retrieved 12 30, 2007, from http://www.cmswire.com/cms/enterprise-cms/7-challenges-of-implementing-a-content-management-system-001848.php

Cooper, R. (2001). *Winning at New Products: Accelerating the Process from Idea to Launch.* New York, NY: Harper Collins Publishers.

Cooper, R. G., & Edgett, S. (2003). Overcoming the crunch in resources for new product development. *Research Technology Management, 46*(3), 48–59.

Cooper, R. G., Edgett, S. J., & Kleinschmidt, E. J. (1997). Portfolio Management in New Product Development: Lessons from the Leaders, Phase I. *Research Technology Management, 40*(5), 16-28.

Cooper, R. G., Edgett, S. J., & Kleinschmidt, E. J. (1998). Best Practices for Managing R&D Portfolios, *Research Technology Management, 41*(4), 20-33.

Cooper, R. G., Edgett, S. J., & Kleinschmidt, E. J. (1999). New product portfolio management: Practices and performance. *The Journal of Product Innovation Management, 16*(4), 333–352.

Cooper, R. G., Edgett, S. J., & Kleinschmidt, E. J. (2004). Benchmarking best NPD practices -I. *Research Technology Management, 47*(1), 31–43.

Cooper, R., & Kaplan, R. S. (1988). Measure costs right: make the right decisions. *Harvard Business Review, 66*(5), 96- 103.

Cooper, R.G., Edgett, S.J., & Kleinschmidt, E.J. (1997). Portfolio management for new product development: Lessons from the Leaders-I. *Research Technology Management, 40*(5), 16-28.

Cooper, R.G., Edgett, S.J., & Kleinschmidt, E.J. (1997). Portfolio management for new product development: Lessons from the Leaders-II. *Research Technology Management, 40*(6), 21-23.

Cooper, R.G., Edgett, S.J., & Kleinschmidt, E.J. (1998). *Portfolio management for new products.* Boston: Addison-Wesley.

Cooper, R.G., Edgett, S.J., & Kleinschmidt, E.J. (2000). New problems, new solutions: Making portfolio management more effective. *Research Technology Management, 43*(2), 18-33.

Copeland, T. (2001). The real-options approach to capital allocation. *Strategic Finance, 20*(3), 36-47.

Corporate Portfolio Management Association. (2007). *CPMA Member Survey Results & Research.* Retrieved November 1, 2007, from http://www.corporateportfoliomanagement.org.

Cox, A. W. (1996). Relational competence and strategic procurement management: towards an entrepreneurial and contractual theory of the firm. *European Journal of Purchasing and Supply Chain Management, 2*(1), 57-70.

Craiger, J. P., & Coovert, M. D. (1994). Modeling dynamic social and psychological processes with fuzzy cognitive maps. *Proceedings of the IEEE International Conference on Fuzzy Systems,* 1873 – 1877.

Craiger, J. P., Goodman, D. F., Weiss, R. J., & Butler, A. B. (1996). Modeling organizational behavior with fuzzy cognitive maps. *International Journal of Computational Intelligence and Organizations, 1,* 120 – 123.

Cresswell, A. M., Burke, G. B., & Pardo, T. A. (2006) *Advancing return on investment analysis for government IT: A public value framework.* Albany, NY: University at Albany, SUNY, Center for Technology in Government. Retrieved September 17, 2006 from http://www.ctg.albany.edu/

Cullen, D. (2003). *Inland Revenue sacks EDS.* Retrieved January 17, 2004, from http://www.theregister.co.uk/content/archive/34454.html

Cullen, S., & Willcocks, L. P. (2004). *Intelligent IT Outsourcing: Eight Building Blocks to Success.* Great Britain: Butterworth-Heinemann.

Cunningham, N. (2001). a model for the role of information systems in strategic change within healthcare organizations. *Organizational Development Journal, 19,* spring, 93-105.

Cuthbert S., & Tran V. N. (2005). *Vietnam E-Government Roadmap Study.* ADB Technical Assistance 4080 Program for Vietnam Office of the Government (OOG), Decision 112 State Administration Computerisation Committee (SAMCom).

Daft, R. L., & Lengel, R. H. (1984). Information Richness: A New Approach to Managerial Information Processing and Organization Design. In B. Staw and L. Cummings (Eds.), *Research in Organization Behavior.* Greenwich, CT: JAI Press.

Dahl, R. A. (1958). A Critique of the Ruling Elite Model. *American Political Science Review, 52*(2), 463-469.

Dai, Q., Kauffman, R. J., & March, S. T. (2004). Valuing IT middleware infrastructure with real options. Working paper, *Carlson School of Management, University of Minnesota,* Minneapolis.

Datz, T. (2003). Portfolio management: How to do it right. *CIO Magazine.* Retrieved January 27, 2008, from, http://www.cio.com/archive/050103/portfolio.html

Davenport, T. H. (1994). Saving IT's Soul: Human-Centered Information Management. *Harvard Business Review,* March-April 1994, pp. 119-131.

Davenport, T. H., & Prusak, L. (1998). *Working Knowledge, How Organizations Manage What They Know.* Boston, MA: Harvard Business School Press.

Davenport, T. H., & Short, J. E. (1990). The new industrial Engineering: Information Technology and Business Process Redesign. *Sloan Management Review,* Summer 1990, pp 11-26.

Davenport, T. H., Eccles, R. G., & Prusak, L. (1992). Information politics. *Sloan Management Review, 34*(1), 53–65.

Davila, T., Epstein, M.J., Shelton, R. (2006). *Making Innovation Work - How to Manage IT, Measure IT and Profit from IT.* Upper Saddle River, NJ: Wharton School Publishing.

Davis, F. J. (1989, September). Perceived usefulness, perceived ease of use, and user acceptance of IT. *MIS Quarterly.*

Davis, L. (1987). *Genetic Algorithms and Simulated Annealing.* London: Pitman.

De Jager, A., & Clarke, D. (2001). Building Local and Sustainable Capacities for ICT Development. *Approaches to ICT Development, 10,* July 2001, ECDPM.

De Looff, L. A. (1995). Information Systems Outsourcing decision-making: A framework, organisational theories and case studies. *Journal of Information Technology, 10,* 281-297.

Dechow, N., & Mouritsen, J. (2005). Enterprise resource planning systems, management control and the quest for integration. Accounting, Organizations and Society, 30, 691-733.

Dedrick, J., Gurbaxani, V., & Kraemer, K. (2003). Information technology and economic performance: A critical review of the empirical evidence. *ACM Computing Surveys, 35*(1), 1- 28.

DeLisi, P. S (1990). Lessons from the Steel Axe: Culture. Technology and Organisation Change. *Sloan Management Review, 32*, (1), 83-93.

Deloitte (2005). *Calling a Change in the Outsourcing Market: The Realities for the World's Largest Organizations.* Retrieved January 08, 2006, from http://www.deloitte.com/dtt/cda/doc/content/us_outsourcing_callingachange.pdf

DeLone, W. D., & McLean, E. R. (2003). The DeLone and McLean model of information systems success: A ten-year update. *Journal of Management Information Systems, 19*(4), 9–30

Dennis, A. R., & Wixom, B. H. (2001-2002). Investigating the Moderators of the Group SupportSystems Use with Meta-Analysis. *J. Management Information Systems, 18*(3), 235-257.

Deshpandé, R., & Farley, J. U. (1998). Measuring market orientation: generalization and synthesis. *Journal of Market-Focused Management, 2*(3), 213-232.

Deshpandé, R., Farley, J. U., & Webster, F. E. (1993). Corporate culture, customer

Devan, J., Klusas, M., & Ruefli, T. (2007). *The Elusive Goal of Corporate Outperformance. The McKinsey Quarterly*, Retrieved October 25, 2007 from http://www.mckinseyquarterly.com/The_elusive_goal_of_corporate_outperformance_1994.

Devaraj, S., & Kohli, R. (2003). Performance impacts of information technology: Is actual usage the missing link? *Management Science, 49*(3), 273–289.

Devinney, T. M., & Stewart, D. W. (1988). Rethinking the product portfolio: A generalized investment. *Management Science, 34*(9), 1080–1096.

Dibbern, J., Goles, T., Hirschheim, R. A., & Jayatilaka, B. (2004). Information Systems Outsourcing: A Survey and Analysis of the Literature. *The DATA BASE for Advances in Information Systems, 35*(4), 6-102.

Dickerson, & Kosko, B. (1994). Fuzzy virtual worlds. *AI Experts*, 25-31.

Dickinson, M., Thornton, A., & Graves, S. (2001). Technology portfolio management: Optimizing interdependent projects over multiple time periods. *IEEE Transactions on Engineering Management, 48*(4), 518–527.

Dietrich, P., Poskela, J., & Artto, K.A. (2003). Organizing for managing multiple projects—a strategic perspective. *Proceedings of the 17th Nordic Conference on Business Studies*, Reykjavik, Iceland.

Dinsmore, P. C. (1993). *The AMA Handbook of Project Management.* New York, NY: AMACOM.

Dirks, P. (1994). MIS investments for operations management: relevant costs and revenues. *International Journal of Production Economics*, 35

DoD C4ISR Architecture Working Group. *C4ISR Architecture Framework*, Version 2.

Doerner, K., Gutjahr, W. J., Hartl, R. F., Strauss, C., & Stummer, C., (2002). *Pareto Ant Colony Optimization: A metaheuristic approach to multiobjective portfolio selection.* Kluwer Academic Publishers, Printed in the Netherlands.

Dougherty, V. (1999). Knowledge is about people, not databases. *Industrial and Commercial Training, 31*(7).

Drucker, P. (1954). *The Practice of Management.* New York: Harper Collins Publishers, Inc.

Drucker, P. (1968). *The age of discontinuity.* New York: Harper and Row.

Drucker, P. F. (1980). Managing the Information Explosion. *The Wall Street Journal, 10,* 25-30.

Drucker, P. F. (1995). The information that executives truly need. *Harvard Business Review*, January-February 1995, pp. 54-63

Drury, D. H. (2000). Assessment of chargeback systems in IT management. *INFOR, 38*(3), 293–313.

Dudik, E. (2000). *Strategic renaissance.* New York: Amacon.

Duff, W. M., & Assad, M. C. (1980). *Information Management: An Executive Approach.* London: Oxford University Press (p. 243).

Dufner, D., Holley, L., & Reed, B. (2005). Models for U.S. state government strategic information systems planning. *Proceeding of the 38th Hawaii International Conference on Systems Sciences*, 1-9.

Duncan, N. B. (1995). Capturing flexibility of information technology infrastructure: A study of resource characteristics and their measure. *Journal of Management Information Systems, 12*(2), 37–57.

Dye, L. D., Pennypacker, J. S. (1999). An Introduction to Project Portfolio Management. In Dye, L. D., & Pennypacker J. S. (Eds.), *Project Portfolio Management* (pp. xi-xvi). West Chester, PA: Center for Business Practices.

Dye, L.D., & Pennypacker, J.S. (Eds.) (1999). *Project portfolio management: Selecting and prioritizing projects for competitive advantage.* West Chester: Center for Business Practices.

Earl, M. J. (1989). *Management Strategies for Information Technology.* Prentice Hall.

Earl, M. J. (1996). The Chief Information Officer: Past, Present, and Future. In M. J. Earl (Ed.), *Information Management: The Organizational Dimension.* New York: NY: Oxford University Press, Inc.

Earl, M. J. (1993). Experiences in strategic information systems planning. *MIS Quarterly*/March.

Earl, M. J. (1996). The Risks of Outsourcing IT. *Sloan Management Review, 37*(3), 26-32.

Earl, M., & Vivian, P. D. (1993). *The Role of the Chief Information Officer: A Study of Survival.* London: London Business School.

Ebrahim, Z., & Irani, Z. (2005). E-Government adoption: architecture and barriers. *Business Process Management Journal, 11*(5), 589-611.

Eden, C., Ackerman, F., & Cropper, S. (1992). *The analysis of cause maps. Journal of Management Studies, 29*(3), 309 – 324.

El-Mhied, M. T., & Abu-Tieh, E. M. (2005). *Knowledge Management: Nurturing Culture, Innovation And Technology.* North Carolina, USA: World Scientific Publishing Co. Pte. Ltd.

El-Shinnawy, M., & Markus, M. L. (1998). Acceptance of Communication Media in Organizations: Richness or Features? *IEEE Transactions On Professional Communication 41*(4), 242-253.

Elton, E. J., Gruber, M. J., & Padberg, W., (1976). Simple Criteria for Optimal Portfolio Selection. *The Journal of Finance, 31*(5), 1341-1357.

Elton, E. J., Gruber, M. J., Brown, S. J., & Goetzmann, W. N. (2002). *Modern portfolio theory and investement analysis.* Wiley.

Englund, R. L., Graham R. J., & Dinsmore, P. C. (2003). *Creating the Project Office: A Manager's Guide to Leading Organizational Change.* The Jossey-Bass Business & Management Series. New York, NY: Wiley.

Enterprise Architecture – Wikipedia (n.d.). Retrieved May 15, 2008, from http://en.wikipedia.org/wiki/Enterprise_Architecture

European Commission, (1995). *Green Paper on Innovation.* COM (95) 688 final. European Commission.

European Commission, (2004). Innovation Management Studies: Published Studies: Innovation Management. *Innovation Management and the Knowledge-Driven Economy.* Retrieved February 3, 2006, from http:/cordis.europa.eu/int/innovation-policy/studies/im_study6.htm.

European Commission, Enterprise DG (2004). *The Enterprise Directorate General - Activities and goals, results and future directions.* European Commission.

Evans, P., & Wurster, T.S. (2000). *Blown to bits: How the new economics of information transforms strategy.* Boston: Harvard Business School Press.

Eyal, J. (2004). *Armies Inc.* Retrieved June 08, 2004, from http://straitstimes.asia1.com.sg/world/story/0,4386,255062,00.html

Fahey, L., & Randall. R. M. (1998). *Learning from the future.* London: John Wiley.

Farbey B., Land F., & Targett, D. (1993). *How to Assess your IT Investment: A Study of Methods and Practice.* Oxford: Butterworth-Heineman.

Federal Office of Management and Budget. *Federal Architecture Framework.* http://www.feapmo.gov/fea.asp.

Feeny, D. F., Edwards, B. R., & Simpson, K. M. (1992). Understanding the CEO/CIO Relationship. *MIS Quart.,* 435-448.

Felton, A. (1959). Making the marketing concept work. *Harvard Business Review,* (pp. 55-65).

Fernandez, S., & Rainey, H. (2006). Managing successful organizational change in the public sector. *Public Administration Review, 66*(2), 168-176.

Filenet P8. (2006, November). *The Synergy between BPM and SOA.* White Paper.

Fisher, R. (1930). *The Genetical Theory of Natural Selection.* Oxford: Clarendon Press.

Fitzpatrick, E. (2005). *Planning and implementing IT portfolio management.* Gaithersburg, MD: IT Economics Corporation.

Fountain, J. F. (2001). *Building the Virtual State: Information Technology and Institutional Change.* Washington, DC: Brookings Institution Press.

Fowler, A., & Jeffs, B. (1998). Examining Information Systems Outsourcing: A Case Study from the United

Kingdom. *Journal of Information Technology, 13,* 111-126.

Fowler, A., & Pryke, J. (2003). Knowledge management in public service provision: The child support agency. *International Journal of Service Industry Management, 14*(3).

Fowler, M. (1997). *Analysis Patterns: Reusable Object Models.* Indianapolis, IN: Addison-Wesley.

Framel, J. E. (1990). Managing Information costs and Technologies as Assets. *Journal of Systems Management, 41*(2), 12-19.

Frenzel, C. W., & Frenzel, J. C. (2004). *Management of Information Technology* (4th ed.). Cambridge: Course Technology.

Gable, G. (1998). Large package software: a neglected technology? *Journal of Global Information Management, 6*(3), 3-4.

Gale, B. T. (1994). *Managing Customer Value: Creating Quality and Service that Customer Can See.* New York: The Free Press, Simon & Schuster.

Galliers R. D. (1993). Towards a flexible information architecture: integrating business strategies, information systems strategies and business process redesign. *Journal of Information Systems, 3.*

Galliers, R. D. (1991). Information systems strategic planning myths reality and guidelines for successful implementation systems planning. *European Journal of Information Systems, 1*(1), 55-64.

Gamma, E., Helm, R., Johnson, R., & Vlissides, J. (2000). Design Patterns: *Elements of Reusable Object-Oriented Software (Paperback).* Boston, MA: Addison-Wesley.

Ganeshan, R., & Harrison, T. P. (1995). *An introduction to supply chain management.* Retrieved 22 May 2006, http://lcm.csa.iisc.ernet.in/scm/supply_chain_intro.html

Gantz, J. (2004). *40 years of IT: Looking back, looking ahead.* IDC special edition executive white paper. Framingham, MA: International Data Corp.

Gardiner, P.D., & Stewart, K. (2000). Revisiting the golden triangle of cost, time and quality: The role NPV in project control, success and failure. *International Journal of Project Management, 18*(4), 251-256.

Gareis, R. (2003). *Competencies in the Project-oriented organization,* IPMA World Congress, Moscow, Russia.

Gareis, R., Huemann, M. (2000). Project Management Competences in the Project-oriented Organisation. In Turner J. R., & Simister S. J. (Eds.), *The Gower Handbook of Project Management.* Aldershot, UK: Gower.

Garey, M., & Johnson, D., (1979). *Computers and Intractability: A Guide to the Theory of NP-Completeness.* San Francisco: H.W. Freeman & Company.

Gartner (2007). *Magic quadrant for IT project and portfolio management 2007, Gartner RAS core research note G00149082,* Matt Light, Daniel B, Stang

Gbaje, E. S. (2007). Implementing a National Virtual Library for Higher Institutions in Nigeria. *LIBRES Library and Information Science Research Electronic Journal, 17*(12), 1-15.

Gefen, D. (2004). What makes an ERP implementation relationship worthwhile: Linking trust mechanisms and ERP usefulness. *Journal of Management Information Systems, 21*(1), 263–288.

Gefen, D., Straub, D. W., & Boudreau. M. (2000). Structural Equation Modeling and Regression: Guidelines for Research Practice. *Comm. AIS, 4*(7), 1-78.

General Accounting Office (1997). *High Risk Series. Information Management and Technology,* GAO/HR-97-9, February 1997

General Services Administration (2003). *Performance-Based Management: Eight Steps to Develop and Use Information Technology Performance Measures Effectively.* Retrieved May 06, 2005, from http://www.gsa.gov/gsa/cm_attachments/GSA_DOCUMENT/eight_steps_R2GX2-u_0Z5RDZ-i34K-pR.doc

George, M. et al. (2005). *Fast Innovation - Achieving Superior Differentiation, Speed to Market and Increased Profitability.* New York, NY: McGraw-Hill.

Georgopoulos, V. C., Malandraki, G. A., & Stylios, C. D. (2002). A fuzzy cognitive map approach to differential diagnosis of specific language impairment. *Artificial Intelligence in Medicine, 679,* 1-18.

Gerlach, J., Neuman, B., Moldauer, E., Argo, M., & Frisby, D. (2002). Determining the cost of IT services. *Communications of the ACM, 45*(9), 61–67.

Ghasemzadeh, F., Archer, N. (1999). Project Portfolio Selection Techniques: A Review and a Suggested Integrated Approach, In Dye, D. L., & Pennypacker S. J. (Eds.), *Project Portfolio Management* (pp. 207-238). West Chester, PA: Center for business Practices.

Ghasemzadeh, F., Archer, N., & Iyogun, P. (1999). A zero-one model for project portfolio selection and scheduling. *The Journal of Operational Research Society, 50*(7), 745-755.

Ghoshal, S., & Kim, S. K. (1986). Building effective Intelligence Systems for Competitive Advantage, *Sloan Management Review*, Fall 1986, pp. 49-58.

Gibson, C. F., & Nolan, R. L., (1974). Managing the Four Stages of EDP Growth. *Harvard Business Review, 52*(1), 76-88.

Gil-Garcia, J. R. (2005). Exploring the success factors of state website functionality: An empirical investigation. *Proceedings of the 2005 national conference on digital government research* Atlanta, Georgia: Digital Government Research Center.

Gliedman, C. (2002, January). *Managing IT risk with portfolio management thinking.* Cambridge: Giga Information Group.

Gliedman, C., & Brown, A. (2004). *Defining IT Portfolio Management: Holistic IT investment Planning.* Cambridge, MA: Forrester Research Inc.,

Glover, F., & Laguna, M., (1997). *Tabu Search*, Kluwer Academic Publishers, Boston.

Glover, F., Laguna, M., & Marti, R. (2003). Scatter Search. *Advances in Evolutionary Computing: Theory and Applications.* New York Springer-Verlag, (pp. 519-537).

Goh, A. (2004). Enhancing Organizational Performance through Knowledge Innovation: A Proposed Strategic Management Framework. *Journal of Knowledge Management Practice*, October 2004.

Goldberg, D. E. (1989). *Genetic algorithms in search, optimization and machine learning.* New York: Addison-Wesley.

Goldman, C. (1999). Align Drive–Expert Advice. *CIO Magazine*, January, 5.

Goodstein, J., Boeker, W., & Stephan, J. (1996). Professional Interests and Strategic Flexibility: A Political Perspective on Organizational Contracting. *Strategic Management Journal, 17*(7), 577-586.

Gordon, S., & Tarafdar, M. (2007). How do a company's information technology competences influence its ability to innovate?, *Journal of Enterprise Information Management, 20*(3), 271-290.

Gotoh, K., Murakami J., Yamaguchi, T., & Yamanaka, Y. (1989). Application of fuzzy cognitive maps to supporting for plant control. *Proceedings of the SICE Joint Symposium of 15th Systems Symposium and 10th Knowledge Engineering Symposium*, (pp. 99-104).

Gottschalk, P. (2001). Key issues in IS management in Norway: an empirical study based on Q-methodology. *Information Resources Management Journal, 14*(2), 37-45.

Grant, R. (1991). The Resource-Based Theory of Competitive Advantage: Implications for Strategy Formulation. *California Management Review, 33*(3), 114-135.

Grant, R. (2007). *Contemporary Strategy Analysis.* VI edition. Oxford, UK: Blackwell Publishing.

Grochow, J.M. (1996, August). Chaos theory and project estimates. *PC Week*, 5-7.

Gronroos, C. (1994). From marketing mix to relationship marketing: Towards a paradigm shift in marketing. *Management Decision, 32*(2), 4-32.

Groot, R., Smits, M., & Kuipers, H. (2005). A Method to Redesign the IS Portfolios in Large Organizations. *The 38th Hawaii International Conference on System Sciences.*

Groumpos, P. P., & Stylios, C. D. (2000). Modeling supervisory control systems using fuzzy cognitive maps. *Chaos, Solitons & Fractals, 11*, 329-336.

Grover, V., & Segars, A. (2005). An empirical evaluation of stages of strategic information systems planning: patterns of process design and effectiveness. *Information and Management, 42*(5), 761–779.

Guha, S., Groven, V., Kettinger, W. J., & Teng, J. T. C. (1997). Business process change and organizational performance: Exploring an antecedent mode. *Journal of Management Information Systems, 14*(1), 119–154.

Hackathorn R. C., & Karimi J. (1998). A framework for comparing information engineering methods. *MIS Quarterly*/June.

Hadfield, W. (2006). *Sainsbury's transfers IT back in-house.* Retrieved May 09, 2006, from http://www.computerweekly.com/Articles/2006/05/09/215869/Sainsbury%e2%80%99s+transfers+IT+back+in-house.htm

Haeckel, S. H. (1987). *Presentation to the Information Planning Steering Group.* Cambridge, MA: Marketing Science Institute.

Hamel, G. (2000). *Leading the revolution.* New York: Plume (Penguin Books).

Hamel, G., & Prahalad, C. K. (1989). Strategic Intent. *Harvard Business Review, 67*(3), 63-78.

Hamel, G., & Prahalad, C.K. (1990). The core competence of the corporation. *Harvard Business Review, 68*(3), 79-91.

Hammer, M., & Champy, J. (1993). *Reengineering the corporation.* New York: Harper Business.

Hannes, K. (2000). Linking intangible resources and competition. *European Management Journal, 18*(1).

Harder, P. (2002). *A Conversation with Dr. Harry Markowitz,* Retrieved by Gantthead.com.

Hariharan, A., & Cellular, B. (2005). Crtical Success Factors for Knowledge Mnangemnt: Fifteen Common Challanges and how to overcome them. *KM review, 8*(2), 16-20.

Harris, K., & Casonato, R. (2002). *Where is the Value on Investments in IT?* (No. SPA-17-2345): Gartner, Inc.

Hart, P., & Saunders, C. (1997). Power and trust: Critical factors in adoption and use of electronic data exchange. *Organization Science, 8*(1), 23–42.

Hassard, J., & Sharifi, S. (1989). Corporate Culture and Strategic Change. *Journal of General Management, 15*(2), 4-19.

Hatcher, L. (1994). *A Step-by-Step Approach to Using the SAS System for Factor Analysis and Structural Equation Modeling.* Cary, NC: SAS Institute.

Hayes, F. (2004). Chaos is back. *ComputerWorld.* Retrieved January 27, 2008, from, http://www.computerworld.com/managementtopics/management/project/story/0,10801,97283,00.html

Hayward, R. G. (1987). Developing an information systems strategy. *Long Range Planning, 20*(2).

HBR (2003). Does IT Matter?: An HBR Debate. *Harvard Business Review,* June 2003.

Healy, T.J., & Linder, J.C. (2004). *Outsourcing in Government: The Path to Transformation.* Retrieved June 23, 2004, from http://www.accenture.com/xdoc/en/ideas/institute/pdf/outsourcing_in_gov.pdf

Hebert, B. (2002). Tracking Progress. *New Zealand Management, 49*(1), 24-27.

Heeks, R. (2001a). *Understanding e-Governance for Development.* Working Paper Series Paper No. 11 IDPM U. of Manchester.

Heeks, R. (2001b). *Building e-Governance for Development: A Framework for Nation and Donor Action.* Working Paper Series Paper No. 12 IDPM U of Manchester.

Heeks, R. (2003). *Most e-Government-for-developing Projects Fail: How Can Risks Be Reduced?* iGovernment Working Paper Series, Paper no. 14.

Heeks, R. (Ed.) (1999). Reinventing Government in the Information Age: International Practice in IT-Enabled Public Sector Reform. Routledge: London.

Hefferman, R., & LaValle, S. (2006). Advocacy in the customer focused enterprise: The next generation of CRM done right. *Executive Handbook,* NY: IBM Global service, IBM Corporation.

Heldey, B. (1997). Strategy for the business portfolio. *Long Range Planning, 10*(1), 9-15.

Henderson, J. C., & Venkatraman, N. (1993). Strategic alignment: Leveraging information technology for transforming organisations. *IBM Systems Journal, 32*(1).

Hendriks, P. H. J., & Vriens, D. J. (1999). Knowledge-based systems and knowledge management: friends or foes? *Information and Management, 35*(2).

Heo, J., & Han, I. (2003). Performance measures of information systems in evolving computing environment: An empirical investigation. *Information & Management, 40.*

Hewitt, E. (2003). A National Strategy for Developing Countries. *COMNET-IT Forum Newsletter of Comm Network of IT for Development.*

Hiderbrand, M. E., & Grinde, M. S. (1994). *Building sustainable capacity: challenges for the Public Sector*: Cambridge, MA: Harvard Institute for International Development/UNDP.

Higa, K., Sheng, O. R. L., Shin, B., & Figueredo ,A. J. (2000). Understanding Relationships Among Teleworkers' E-Mail Usage, E-Mail Richness Perceptions, and E-Mail Productivity Perceptions Under a Software Engineering Environment. *IEEE Transactions On Engineering Management, 47*(2) 163-173.

Hildreth, P., Wright, P., & Kimble, C. (1999). Knowledge Management: are we missing something? In *Information Systems – The Next Generation,* L. Brooks & C. Kimble (Eds.), pp. 347-356.

Hilton, E. (1992). How neural networks learn from experience. *Scientific American 267,* 144 – 151.

Hise, R. T. (1965). Have manufacturing firms adopted the marketing concept? *Journal of Marketing, 29,* 9-12.

Hitt, L., & Brynjolfsson, E. (1996). Productivity, business profitability, and consumer surplus: Three different measures of information technology value. *MIS Quarterly, 20*(2), 121-140.

Hitt, M. A., Ireland, R. D., & Hoskisson, R. E. (2005). *Strategic Management: Competitiveness and Globalization* (6th Edition), Versailles, KY: South-Western.

Ho, A.T-K. (2002). Reinventing local governments and the e-government initiative", Public Administration Review, 62(4), 434-44.

Ho, L., & Atkins, A. (2006). IT Outsourcing: Impacts and Challenges. In B. Walters and Z. Tang (Eds.). *IT-Enabled Strategic Management - Increasing Returns for the Organization* (pp. 244-274.). United States of America: Idea Group Inc.

Ho, L., Atkins, A., & Eardley A. (2005). Emergent Trends of Outsourcing and Strategic Framework Techniques. In G. Kotsis, D. Taniar, S. Bressan, I.K. Ibrahim, & S, Mokhtar. (Eds.), *Proceedings of the 7th International Conference on Information Integration and Web-based Application & Services* (pp. 433-444). Austrian Computer Society.

Ho, L., Atkins, A., Prince, I., & Sharp, B. (2006). Alignment of a Strategic Outsourcing Framework to Practitioner Case Studies. In Z. Irani, O. D. Sarikas, J. Llopis, R. Gonzalez, & J. Gasco (Eds.), *CD-ROM Proceedings of the European and Mediterranean Conference on Information Systems*. EMCIS Press.

Hoffer, J., George J., & Valacich J. (2005). *Modern System Analysis and Design 5th Ed.* NewYork, USA: prentice hall.

Hoffman, T. (2005). Running IT operations like a business not so easy. *ComputerWorld*. Retrieved January 27, 2008, from http://www.computerworld.com/managementtopics/management/itspending/story/0,10801,100135,00.html

Hofstede, G. (1981). Management control of not-for profit activities. Accounting, Organizations and Society: An International Journal Devoted to the Behavioural Organizational & Social Aspects of Accounting, 6, 193-211.

Holland, J. H. (1975). *Adaptation in natural and artificial systems: an introductory analysis with applications to biology, control and artificial intelligence*. University of Michigan Press.

Hong, T., & Han, I. (2002). Knowledge-based data mining of news information on the Internet using cognitive maps and neural networks. *Expert Systems with Applications, 23*, 1-8.

Hoos, H. H., & Stützle, T. (2004). *Stochastic Local Search: Foundations and Applications*. Elsevier/Morgan Kaufmann, San Francisco, CA.

Houtzagers, G. (1999). Empowerment, using skills and competence management. *Participation and Empowerment: An International Journal, 7*(2).

Hsaio, R., & Ormerod, R. (1998). A new perspective on the dynamic of IT-Enabled strategic change. *Information Systems Journal, 8*(1), 21-52.

http://en.wikipedia.org/wiki/Claude_Levi-Strauss

http://en.wikipedia.org/wiki/Outsourcing

http://en.wikipedia.org/wiki/The_Selfish_Gene

Hubbard, D. (2007). *How to measure anything: finding the value of intangibles in business*. John Wiley & Sons.

Huber, G. H. (1991). Organizational learning, the contributing process and the literature, *Organization Science, 2*(1).

Huizenga, E. (2005). *Innovation Management in the ICT Sector*. New York, NY: John Wiley & Sons.

Hunter, M. G., Long, W. (2002). Information Systems and Small Business: Lessons from the Entrepreneurial Process. In M. Khosrow-Pour (Ed.), Issues and Trends of IT Management in Contemporary Organisations. Idea Group Press

ICT Investment Prioritisation Framework (2005). *ICT investment prioritisation framework-Version 1.0*. Government of South Australia

ICT Planning Framework (2006). *SA government ICT planning framework*. Government of South Australia

IEEE Standard 1003.0-1995. (1995). *IEEE Guide to the POSIX Open System Environment*. http://standards.ieee.org/reading/ieee/std_public/description/posix/1003.0-1995_desc.html

Improving Mission Performance Through Strategic Information Management and Technology: Learning from Leading Organizations. (1994). (pp. 1 - 50): United States Government Accountability Office, Washington, D.C.

Infocomm Development Authority of Singapore website: http://www.ida.gov.sg.

Information Technology Investment Management: A Framework for Assessing and Improving Process Maturity. (2004). (pp. 1 - 138): United States Government

Accountability Office, Washington, D.C. *The standard for portfolio management* (2006). Newtown Square, PA: PMI Publications.

Institute for Enterprise Architecture Developments. (2004). *Extended Enterprise Architecture Framework.*.

Institute For Enterprise Architecture, Trends in Enterprise Architecture 2005 (2005, December). *How are organizations progressing? Report of the Third Measurement Developments, Edition 1.0.*

Irani, Z., Sharif, A., Love, P. E. D., & Kahraman, C. (2002). Applying concepts of fuzzy cognitive mapping to model: The IT/IS investment evaluation process. *International Journal of Production Economics, 75,* 199-211.

IT Governance Institute (n.d.). Retrieved May 15, 2008 from http://www.itgi.org

ITIL® (2001). *Best practice for service delivery.* United Kingdom: Office of Government Commerce.

Ives, B., & Learmonth, G. P. (1984). The information system as a competitive weapon. *Communications of the ACM, 27*(12), December.

Ives, B., Olson, M. H., & Baroudi, J. J. (1988). The measurement of user information satisfaction. *Communications of the ACM, 26*(10)

Jaeger, P. T., & Thompson, K. M. (2003). E-Government around the world: Lessons, challenges, and future directions. *Government Information Quarterly, 20,* 389-394.

Jagannathan, R., & Ma, T. (2003). Risk Reduction in Large Portfolios: Why Imposing the Wrong Constraints Helps. *The Journal of Finance, 58*(4), 1651-1638.

Jang, S. Y. (1989). Influence of Organizational Factors on Information Systems Strategic Planning. *Unpublished Dissertation.* University of Pittsburgh.

Jarvenpaa, S. L., & Ives, B. (1991). Executive Involvement and Participation in the Management of Information Technology. *MIS Quart.,* 205-227.

Jarvenpaa, S. L., & Ives, B., (1994). The global network organization of the future: Information management opportunities and challenges. *Journal of Management Information Systems, 10*(4), 25-57.

Jasperson, J., Carte, T. A., Saunders, C. S., Butler, B. S., Croes, H. J. P., & Zheng, W. (2002). Power and information technology research: A metatriangulation review. *MIS Quarterly, 26*(4), 397-459.

Jasperson, J., Carter, P. E., & Zmud, R. W. (2005). A comprehensive conceptualization of the post-adoptive behaviors associated with IT-enabled work systems. *MIS Quarterly, 29*(3), 525-557.

Jeffery, M. & Leliveld, I. (2004). Best practices in IT portfolio management. *MIT Sloan Management Review, 45*(3), 40-49.

Jeffery, M., & Leliveld, I., (2003). Best Practices in IT Portfolio Management. *Sloan Management Review, 45.*

Jenkins, E.K., & Christenson, E. (2001). ERP (enterprise resource planning) systems can streamline healthcare business functions. Healthcare Financial Management, 55(5), 48-52.

Jiang, J., & Klein, G. (1999). Information systems project selection criteria variations within strategic classes. In L.D. Dye & J.S. Pennypacker (Eds.), *Project portfolio management* (4th edition, pp. 193-206). West Chester: Center for Business Practices.

Jones, M. C., Taylor, G. S., & Spencer, B A. (1995). The CEO/CIO Relationship Revisited: An Empirical Assessment of Satisfaction with IS. *Inform. & Management, 29,* 123-130.

Joreskog, K. G. D., & Sorbom, D. (1989). *LISREL 7: A Guide to the Program and Applications.* 2nd Ed., SPSS, Inc, Chicago, IL.

Jovanović, P., Mihić, M., & Petrović, D. (2007). Social Implications of Managing Project Stakeholders. In Feng Li (Ed.), *Social Implications and Challenges of e-Business* (pp. 130-144). Hershey, PA: Information Science Reference.

Junttila, M., Ekholm, J., & Matilainen, R. (2001). Sonera's motives to corporate level project portfolio management development. In K.A. Artto, M. Martinsuo, & T. Aalto (Eds.), *Project portfolio management.* Helsinki: Project Management Association (PMA).

Kahai, S. S., & Cooper R. B. (2003). Exploring the Core Concepts of Media Richness Theory: The Impact of Cue Multiplicity and Feedback Immediacy on Decision Quality. *J. Management Information Systems, 20*(1), 263-299.

Kahn, H. (1985). *Thinking about the Unthinkable in the 1980s.* New York: Simon & Schuster.

Kahn, H., & Wierner, J. (1968). *The year 2000: a framework for speculation on the next 33 years.* New York: Macmillan.

Kane, H., Ragsdell, G., & Oppenheim, C. (2006). Knowledge Management Methodologies. The Electronic Journal of Knowledge Management, *4*(2).

Kang, S., & Choi, L. J. (2003). Using fuzzy cognitive map for the relationship management in airline service. *Expert Systems with Applications, 26*, 545-555.

Kanungo, S. (2005). Using Process Theory to analyze direct and indirect value-drivers of information system. *Proceedings of the 38th Hawaii International Conference on System Sciences.*

Kaplan, J. D. (2001). White Paper: Strategically Managing Your IT Portfolio. *PRTM's Insight*, April 1.

Kaplan, J. D. (2005). *Strategic IT portfolio management: Governing enterprise transformation.* Pittiglio Rabin Todd & McGrath (PRTM), Inc.

Kaplan, R. S., & Norton, D. P. (1992). The Balanced Scorecard - Measures that Drive Performance. *Harvard Business Review*, (Jan-Feb), 71-79.

Kaplan, R. S., & Norton, D. P. (1996). *Translating Strategy into Action: The Balanced Scorecard.* HBS Press.

Kaplan, R. S., & Norton, D. P. (1997). *Balanced scorecard.* 17. ed. Rio de Janeiro: Campus.

Kaplan, R. S., & Norton, D. P. (2001). *The Strategy Focused Organization.* HBS Press.

Kaplan, R. S., & Norton, D. P. (2004). *Strategy Maps: Converting Intangible Assets into Tangible Outcomes.* HBS Press.

Kaplan, R.S., & Norton, D.P. (2001). *The strategy-focused organization.* Boston: Harvard Business School Press.

Karahanna, E., & Limayem, M. (2000). E-Mail and V-Mail Usage: Generalizing Across Technologies. *J. Organizational Computing and Electronic Commerce, 10*(1), 49-66.

Kardaras, D., & Karakostas, B. (1999). The use of fuzzy cognitive maps to stimulate the information systems strategic planning process. *Information and Software Technology. 41*(4), 197-210.

Kardaras, D., & Karakostas, B. (1999). A Modeling Approach for Information Systems Evaluation Based on Fuzzy Cognitive Map. *Proceedings of the 5th International Conference of the Decision Sciences Institute. Integrating Technology and Human Decisions: Global Bridges into the 21st Century.* Athens, Greece.

Kearns, G. S., & Lederer, A. L. (2000). The effect of strategic alignment on the use of IS-based resources for competitive advantage. *Journal of Strategic Information Systems, 9*, 265-293.

Keen, P. G. W. (1991). *Shaping the Future: Business Design Through Information Technology*, Boston, MA: Harvard Business School Press.

Keil, M. (1995). Pulling the plug: Software project management and the problem of project escalation. *MIS Quarterly, 19*(4), 421–447.

Keil, M., & Mann, J. (1997). The nature and extent of IT project escalation: Results from a survey of IS audit and control professionals (Part 1). *IS Audit and Control Journal, 1*(1), 40–48.

Keil, M., & Robey, D. (1999). Turning around troubled software projects: An exploratory study of the deescalation of commitment to failing courses of action. *Journal of Management Information Systems, 15*(4), 63–87.

Keil, M., Tiwana, A., & Bush, A. (2002). Reconciling user and project manager perceptions of IT project risk: A Delphi study. *Information Systems Journal, 12*(2), 103–119.

Keil, M., Truex, D. P., & Mixon, R. (1995). The effects of sunk cost and project completion on information technology project escalation. *IEEE Transactions on Engineering Management, 4*(42), 372–381.

Keith, R. J. (1960). The marketing revolution. *Journal of Marketing,* January, 35-38.

Kelton, W. D., & Law, A., (1991). *Simulation Modeling & Analysis.* New York: McGraw Hill, Inc.

Kempner, T. (1976). *Handbook of Management.* Penguin, Harmondsworth (p. 216)

Kenny, D. A. (1987). *Statistics for the Social and Behavioral Sciences.* Boston, MA: Little, Brown, and Company.

Kersten, B., & Verhoef, C., (2003). IT Portfolio Management: A Banker's Perspective on IT. *Cutter IT Journal, 16*(4), 34-40.

Kerzner, H. (2001). *Strategic planning for project management using a project management maturity model.* New York: John Wiley & Sons.

Kerzner, H. (2003). *Project Management.* Eight edition. New York, NY: John Wiley & Sons.

Kettinger, W., & Grover, V. (1995). Towards a theory of business process change management. *Journal of Management Information Systems 12*(1), 9–30.

Kettinger, W., Grover, V., Guha, S., & Segars, A.H. (1994). Strategic information systems revisited: A study in sustainability and performance. *MIS Quarterly, 18,* 31-55.

Kettunen, J., & Kantola, I. (2005). Management information system based on the balanced scorecard. *Campus-wide Information System, 22*(5).

Killen, C., Hunt, R., & Kleinschmidt. E. (2008). Project portfolio management for product innovation. *International Journal of Quality & Reliability Management, 25*(1), 24-38.

King J. L., & Kraemer K. L. (1984). Evolution and organisational information systems: An assessment of Nolan's stage model. *Communications of the ACM, 27*(5).

King, R. C., & Xia, W. (1997). Media Appropriateness: Effects of Experience on Communication Media Choice. *Dec. Sci., 28*(4), 877-910.

King, W. R. (1995). The payoff from IS strategic planning. *Information Systems Management, 2*(3), 66-68.

King, W. R. (2002). IT capabilities, business processes and impact on the bottom line. *Information Systems Management, 19*(2).

Kirchmer, M., & Scheer, A.W. (2004). Business Process Automation — Combining Best and Next Practices. In A. W. Scheer, F. Abolhassan, W. Jost, & M. Kirchmer, (Ed.), *Business Process Automation—ARIS in Practice,* Berlin, New York and others.

Kirsch, L.J. (1997). Portfolios of control modes and IS project management. *Information Systems Research, 8*(3), 215-239.

Kishore, E., Rao, H. R., Nam, R., Rajagopalan, S., & Chaudhury, A. (2003). A Relationship Perspective on IT Outsourcing. *Communications of the ACM, 46*(12) 87-92.

Kleinknecht, A., & Mohnen, P., ed. (2002). *Innovation and Firm Performance - Econometric Explorations of Survey Data.* Hampshire, UK: Palgrave.

Kline, S. J., & Rosenberg, N. (1986). An Overview of Innovation. In Landau, R., & Rosenberg, N., (Eds.), *The Positive Sum Strategy* (pp. 275-305). Washington, DC: National Academy Press.

Kloppenborg, T., & Opfer, W. (2002). The current state of project management research: Trends, interpretations and predictions. *Project Management Journal, 33*(2), 5-18.

Kock, N. (2001). Compensatory Adaptation to a Lean Medium: An Action Research Investigation of Electronic Communication in Process Improvement Groups. *IEEE Transactions On Professional Communication, 44*(4) 267-285.

Kohli, A. K., & Jaworski, B. J. (1990). Market orientation: The construct, research propositions and managerial implications. *Journal of Marketing, 54*(April), 1-18.

Kohli, R., & Devaraj, S. (2003). Measuring information technology payoff: A meta-analysis of structural variables in firm-level empirical research. *Information Systems Research, 14*(2), 127–145.

Kokko, A. (1992). *Foreign Direct Investment, Host Country Characteristics, and Spillovers.* Ph.D. dissertation, Stockholm School of Economics.

Konno, H., & Yamazaki, H., (1991). Mean-Absolute Deviation Portfolio Optimization Model and its Applications to Tokyo Stock Market. *Management Science, 37*(5), 519-531.

Koski, T. H. A. (1988). Competitive Advantage and the IT Industry. *European Management Journal, 6*(2), 340-357.

Kosko, B. (1986). *Fuzzy Cognitive Maps. International Journal of Man-Machine Studies, 24,* 65-75.

Kosko, B. (1990). *Fuzzy Thinking: the New Science of Fuzzy Logic.* Flamingo Press.

Kotler, P. (1977). From sales obsession to marketing effectiveness. *Harvard Business Review,* November-December.

Kotler, P. (1999). *Kotler on marketing.* Simon & Schuster.

Kotler, P. (2003). Marketing management: an Asian perspective, Prentice Hall, 1999.

Kovacevic, A., & Majluf, N. (1993). Six stages of IT Strategic Management. *Sloan Management Review,* Summer 1993, 77-87.

Kruchten, K. (2003). *The Rational Unified Process: An Introduction.* 3rd Edition, Massachusetts: Addison Wesley.

Kueng, P., Meier, A., & Wettstein, T. (2000). *Computer-based performance measurement in SMEs: Is there an option. Institute of Informatics,* Paper 00-11 (Internal Working Paper), University of Fribourg, Fribourg.

Kumar, R. (2004). A framework for assessing the business value of information technology infrastructures. *Journal of Management Information Systems, 21*(2), 11–32.

Kwahk, K.-Y., & Kim, Y.-G. (1998). A Cognitive Model Based Approach for Organizational Conflict Resolution. *International Journal of Information Management, 18*(6), 443-456.

Kwak, Y. H., & Ibbs, C.W., (2000). Assessing Organization's Project Management Maturity. *Project Management Journal, 5*, 32-43.

Kwong, H. C., & Mohammed, M. Z. (1985). Profit impact of computerisation. *Hong Kong Computer Journal.*

Lacity, M. C., & Willcocks, L. P. (1995). Interpreting Information Technology Sourcing Decisions from a Transaction Cost Perspective: Findings and Critique. *Accounting, Management and Information Technologies, 5*(3/4), 203-244.

Lalakota, R., & Robinson, M. (1999). *E-business: Roadmap for Success.* Reading, MA: Addison-Wesley.

Landsbergen, D. (2005). IT-enabled sense-and-respond strategies in complex public organizations. *The Communications of the ACM, 48*, 58-65.

Laplante, P. A., & Neill, C. J. (2006). *Antipatterns: Identification, Refactoring, and Management.* Boca Raton, FL: Auerbach Publications.

Lau, C. W., & Pun. K. F. (2000). Assimilation of a strategic information system to gain competitiveness, *Logistics Information Management, 13*(5).

LaValle, S., & Scheld, B. (2004). *CRM Done Right: Executive Handbook for realizing the value of CRM.* NY: IBM Global service, IBM Corporation.

Lave, J., & Wenger, E. (1991). *Situated learning: Legitimate peripheral participation.* Cambridge: Cambridge University Press.

Learned, E.P., Christensen, C.R., Andrews, K.R., & Guth, W.D. (1965). *Business Policy: Text and Cases.* Homewood: Irwin.

Lederer A. L., & Sethi V. (1991). Critical dimensions of strategic information systems planning, *Decision Sciences, 22.*

Lederer A. L., & Sethi V. (1998). The implementation of strategic information systems planning methodologies. *MIS Quarterly*/September.

Lederer, L. A., & Gardiner, V. (1992). The process of strategic information planning. *Journal of Strategic Information Systems,* 1(2).

Lederer, L. A., & Salmena, H. (1996). Toward a theory of strategic information system planning. *Journal of Strategic Information Systems, 5.*

Lee, A. S. (1994). Electronic Mail as a Medium for Rich Communication: An Empirical Investigation Using Hermeneutic Interpretation. *MIS Quart.,* 143-150.

Lee, G. G., & Pai, R. J. (2003). Effects of organizational context and inter-group behaviour on the success of strategic information systems planning: an empirical study. *Behaviour and Information Technology, 22*(4), July-August, 263-280.

Lee, G., & Bai, R. (2003). Organizational mechanisms for successful IS/IT strategic planning in the digital era. *Management Decision* 41/1, (2003).

Lee, S. M., & Hong, S. (2002). An enterprise-wide knowledge management system Infrastructure. *Industrial Management and Data Systems,* 102/1.

Lee, S., & Han, I. (2000). Fuzzy cognitive map for the design of EDI controls. *Information & Management, 37,* 37-50.

Leek, C. (1997). Information systems frameworks and strategy, *Industrial Management and Data Systems,* 97/3.

Lee-Kelley, L., & James, T. (2003). E-Government and Social Exclusion: An Empirical Study. *Journal of Electronic Commerce in Organisations, 1*(4), 1-16.

Leifer, R. (1988). Matching computer-based information systems with organizational structures, *MIS Quarterly, 12*(1).

Leliveld, I., & Jeffery, M. (2003). *White article: IT portfolio management challenges and best practices.* Kellogg/DiamondCluster.

Lengel, R. H. (1983). Managerial Information Processing and Communication-Media Source Selection Behavior. *Unpublished Dissertation.* Texas A&M University.

Leong, S. M., & Lim, K. G. (1991). Extending financial portfolio theory for product management. *Decision Sciences, 22*(1), 181–194.

Lertwongsatien, C., & Wongpinunwatana, N. (2003). E-commerce adoption in Thailand: an empirical study of Small and Medium Enterprises (SMEs). *Journal of Global Information Technology Management, 6*(30), 67-83.

Leslie, K., Loch, M., & Schaninger, W. (2006). Managing Your Organization by the Evidence. The McKinsey Quarterly, Retrieved August 14, 2007 from http://www.mckinseyquarterly.com/Managing_your_organization_by_the_evidence_1829.

Lester, R. (1989). *Made in America.* Boston: MIT Commission on Industrial Productivity.

Levine, H.A. (1999). Project Portfolio Management: A Song without Words? *PM Network, 13*(7), 25-27.

Levinson, J.C. (1984). *Guerrilla marketing: Secrets for making big profits from your small business.* New York: Houghton Muffin.

Levitt, T. (1969). Marketing Myopia. *Harvard Business Review,* July-August, 45-56.

Levitt, T. (1983). *The marketing imagination.* New York: Free Press.

Li, E.Y., & Chen, H. G. (2001). output-driven information systems planning: a case study. *Information and Management, 38*(3), 195-199.

Liberatore, M. J., & Stylianou, A. C. (1995). Expert support systems for new product development decision making: A modeling framework and applications. *Management Science, 41*(8), 1296–1316.

Liberatore, M. J., & Stylianou, A. C. (1995). Toward a framework for developing knowledge-based decision support systems for customer satisfaction assessment, an application in new product development. *Expert Systems with Applications, 8*(1), 213–228.

Lin, M., Zhu, R., & Hachigian, N. (2001). *Beijing's Business E-Park.* World Bank.

Lind, M. R., & Zmud R. W. (1991). The Influence of a Convergence in Understanding Between Technology Providers and Users on Technology Innovativeness. *Organization Sci., 2*(2), 195-217.

Linenberg, Y., Stadlker, Z., & Arbuthnot, S., (2003). Optimising Organisational Performance by Managing Project Benefits. *PMI Global Congress 2003*, Europe.

Loch, C. H., & Kavadias, S. (2002). Dynamic portfolio selection of NPD programs using marginal. *Management Science, 48*(10), 1227–1241

Loo, R. (1996). Training in Project Management a powerful tool for improving individual and team performance. *Team Performance Management: An International Journal, 2*(3), 6-14.

Lounser, D. K. (1991). *Capacity development – A conceptual overview.* Paper presented at a workshop on Capacity Development at the Institute of Governance, Ottawa, Canada.

Lucas, H. C. J. (1973). A descriptive model of information systems in the context of the organization. *DATA BASE, 5*(2-3-4), 27–39.

Luehrman, T.A. (1998, September-October). Strategy as a portfolio of real options. *Harvard Business Review,* 91-93.

Luftman, J. N., Lewis, P. R., & Oldach, S. H. (1993). Transforming the enterprise: The alignment of business and information technology strategies. *IBM Systems Journal, 32*(1), 198-221.

Luftman, J. N., Papp, R., & Brier, T. (1996). *Business and IT in harmony: Enablers and Inhibitors to alignment.* (http://hsb.baylor.edu/ramsowner/ais.ac.96/papers/papp. htm Oct 2000).

Luftman, J., Bullen, C., Liao, D., Nash, E., & Nuewmann, C. (2004). *Managing the information technology resource: Leadership in the information age.* Upper Saddle River, NJ: Pearson Education Inc.

Luftman, J.N. (1996). *Competing in the Information Age: Strategic alignment in practice.* New York: Oxford University Press.

MacKenzie, L. (2003). The Challenges of Implementing Enterprise GIS at the City of Fort Worth. *ESRI International Users Conference* . ESRI.

MacMillan, I. C., & McGrath, R. G. (2002). Crafting R&D project portfolios. *Research Technology Management, 45*(5), 48–59.

Mahesh, K., & Suresh, J. K. (2004). What is the K in KM Technology? *The Electronic Journal of Knowledge Management, 2*(2).

Mahmood, M. A, & Soon S. K. (1991). A comprehensive model for measuring the potential impact of information technology on organisational strategic variables. *Decision Sciences, 22*.

Maizlish, B., & Handler, R. (2005). *IT portfolio management: Unlocking the business value of technology.* Wiley.

Malhotra, Y. (1996). Organizational learning and learning organizations: An overview. available at: http:/brint. com/papers/orglrng.htm

Malmgren, K. (2003). *Epilepsy Care Across Europe and Key Concerns.* Retrieved June 22, 2004, from http://www. bbriefings.com/pdf/14/lth031_p_MALMGREN.PDF

Mancey, A. (2000). Building a National Information and Communication Network. *Information and Capacity Building, 7*, October 2000, ECDPM.

Mansell, R., & Wehn, U. (1998). Knowledge Societies: Information Technology for

March, J. G. (1962). The Business Firm as a Political Coalition. *Journal of Politics, 24,* 662-678.

Markowitz, H. (1952). Portfolio selection. *The Journal of Finance, 7,* 77-91.

Markowitz, H. (1959). *Portfolio Selection, Efficient Diversification of Investment.* (2nd edition in 1991), Basil Blackwell, New York.

Markowitz, H. M. (1991), *Portfolio Selection.* London, UK: Basil Blackwell.

Markus, M. L. (1994). Electronic Mail as the Medium of Managerial Choice. *Organization Sci. 5*(4), 502-527.

Martin, J. (1989). *Strategic Information Planning Methodologies.* 2nd edition, Englewood Cliffs, NJ

Martinsons, M., Davison, R., & Tse, D. (1999). The balanced scorecard: A foundation for the strategic management of information systems. *Decision Support Systems, 25*(11), 71–88.

Martinsuo, M. (2001). Project portfolio management: Contingencies, implementation and strategic renewal. In K.A. Artto, M. Martinsuo, & T. Aalto (Eds.), *Project portfolio management.* Helsinki: Project Management Association.

Massy, W.F. (1999). *The ABCs of Course-Level Costing.* Retrieved May 08, 2005, from http://www.nwmissouri. edu/sloan/CostBook/CourseLevelCosting.html

Maurer, D., & Büch, P. (2007, March). From Business Process Design to Enterprise Architecture, ARIS Expert Paper.

McClure, D. L. (2001). *Electronic Government: Challenges Must Be Addressed with Effective Leadership and Management.* GAO-01-959T, Testimony before the Senate Committee on Governmental Affairs, on behalf of the U.S. General Accounting Office.

McDermott, R. (1999). Knowing is a Human Act: How Information Technology Inspired but cannot deliver Knowledge Management. *California Management Review,* Summer 1999.

McFarlan F.W., & McKenney J.L (1983) *Corporate Information Systems Management: The issues facing senior executives.* Illinois: Richard D. Irwin Inc.

McFarlan, F. W. (1981). Portfolio approach to information systems. *Harvard Business Review* (September-October), 142-150.

McFarlan, F. W. (1984). Information Technology changes the way you compete, *Harvard Business Review,* May-June 1984 pp. 210-226.

McFarlan, F.W. (1981). Portfolio Approach to Information Systems. *Harvard Business Review, 59*(5), 142-150.

McGrath, G. R., & Macmillan, I. C. (2000). Assessing Technology Projects Using Real Options Reasoning. *Research Technology Management, 43*(4), 35–49.

McIvor, R. (2000). A practical framework for understanding the Outsourcing process. *Supply Chain Management: An International Journal, 5*(1), 22-36.

McLellan, K. L., Marcolin, B. L., & Beamish, P. W. (1995). Financial and Strategic Motivations Behind IS Outsourcing. *Journal of Information Technology, 10*(4), 299-321.

McLeod, J. M., & Chaffee, S. H. (1973). Interpersonal Approaches to Communication Research. *American Behavioral Scientist,* 469-499.

McNamara, C. (1972). The present status of the marketing concept. *Journal of Marketing, 36, 50-57.*

Medaglia, A. L., Graves, S. B., & Ringuest, J. L. (2007). A multiobjective evolutionary approach for linearly constrained project selection under uncertainty. *European Journal of Operational Research, 179*(3), 869-894.

Melarkode, A., From-Poulsen, M., & Warnakulasuriya, S. (2004). Delivering Agility through IT, *Business Strategy Review,* Autumn 2004.

Melymuka, K. (2004, May). Harrah's: Betting on IT value. *Computerworld,* 18-22.

Mentz, J. C. N. (1997). *Personal and Institutional Factors in Capacity Building and Institutional Development,* ECDPM Working Paper No. 14, Maastricht: ECDPM.

Mentzas, G. (1997). Implementing an IS strategy - a team approach. *Long Range Planning, 30*(1), 84-95.

Meredith, J.R., & Samuel, J.M. (1995). *Project management: A managerial approach.* New York: John Wiley & Sons.

Meredith, R. J., & Mantel, J. S., Jr. (1999). Project Selection. In Dye, D. L., & Pennypacker S. J. (Eds.), *Project Portfolio Management* (pp. 135-168). West Chester, PA: Center for Business Practices

Meta Group (2002). *Centralizing Management of Project Portfolios.* Meta Group, January 29.

Mihić, M., & Petrović, D. (2004). Project-oriented managers – results of the new approach to managers' education. In proceedings of International Scientific Days, *European Integration: Challenge for Slovakia* (pp. 720-725). Nitra, Slovakia: Slovak Agricultural University.

Mikkola, H. (2001). Portfolio management of R&D projects: implications for innovation management. *Technovation, 21*(4), 23-35.

Miller, B. (1997). Linking corporate strategy to the selection of IT projects. *Project Management Institute 28th annual seminars & symposium proceedings,* 56-65.

Miller, M. D., & Gibson, M. L. (1995). The CIO as an Integrative Strategist. *Information Strategy: The Executive's Journal,* 35-40.

Millett, D. (1996). Critical Success Factors in Expert System Development: Case Study. *Sigcpiu sigmis '96,* (pp. 214-222). Denver Colorado USA: ACM.

Mills, C. (2004). *Outsourcing - The latest research from the public and private sectors.* Retrieved January 07, 2005, from http://www.conferencepage.com/outsourcing4/downloads/CliffMills.pdf

Miranda, E. (2003). *Running the Successful Hi-Tech Project Office.* Boston, MA: Artech House.

Moncrieff, J. (1999). Is strategy making a difference? *Long Range Planning Review, 32*(2), 273-276.

Montealegre, R., & Keil, M. (2000). De-escalating information technology projects: Lessons from the denver international airport. *MIS Quarterly, 24*(3), 417–447.

Moon, M. J. (2002). The evolution of e-government among municipalities: rhetoric or reality. *Public Administration Review, 62*(4), 424-33.

Morgan, P. (1993). *Capacity development: An Overview* Paper presented at a workshop on Capacity Development at the Institute of Governance, Ottawa, Canada.

Morris, P. (1997). *The Management of Projects.* London, UK: Thomas Telford.

Moskowitz, K., & Kern, H. (2003). *Managing IT as an Investment.* Prentice Hall.

Mukherji, A. (2002). The evolution of information systems: their impact on organizations and structures. *Management Decision,* 40/5.

Muller, N. J. (1999). Managing Service Level Agreements. *International Journal of Network Management, 9*(3), 155-166.

Muller-Merbach, H. (2006). Three kinds of knowledge, reflecting Kant's three kinds of action, *Knowledge Management Research and Practice, 4.*

Muralidhar, K., Santhanam, R., & Schniederjans, M., (1988). An optimization model for information system project selection. *Journal of Management Science and Policy Analysis, 6*(1), 53–62.

Nagarajan, K., Lam, H., & Su, S.Y.W. (2004). Integration of business event and rule management with the Web services model. *International Journal of Web Services Research, 1*(1), 41-57.

Naisbitt, J. (1982). *Megatrends.* New York: Warner Books.

Nam, K., Rajagopalan, S., Rao, H. R., & Chaudhury, A. (1996). A Two-Level Investigation of Information Systems Outsourcing. *Communications of the ACM, 39*(7), 36-44.

Namasivayam, S. (2004). Profiting from Business Process Outsourcing. *IT Professional, 6*(1), 12-18.

Narayanan, V. K. (2001). *Managing Technology and Innovation for Competitive Advantage.* Upper Saddle River, New Jersey: Prentice-Hall.

Narver, J. C., & Slater, S. F. (1990). The effect of a market orientation on business profitability. *Journal of Marketing, 54*(October), 20-35.

Nath, R. (1989). Aligning MIS with the Business Goals. *Inform. & Management, 16,* 71-79.

National Research Council (1987). *Management of Technology: The hidden competitive advantage,* Report of the Task Force on Management of Technology. Washington: National Academy Press..

Ndou, V. D. (2004). E-Government for Developing Countries: Opportunities and Challenges. *Electronic Journal of Information Systems in Developing Countries, 18*(1), 1-24.

Neo, B. S. (1988). Factors Facilitating the Use of Information Technology for Competitive Advantage: An Exploratory Study. *Inform. & Management, 15,* 191-201.

Neumann, S. (1994). *Strategic Information Systems: Competition Through Information Technologies.* New York, NY: Macmillian College Publishing.

Newkirk, H. E., & Lederer, A. L. (2006). The effectiveness of strategic information systems planning under environmental uncertainty. *Information and Management, 43*(4), 481–501

Newkirk, H., Lederer, A. L., & Srinivasan, C. (2003). *Strategic information systems planning: too little or too much?, 12,* 201-228.

Nobeoka, K., & Cusumano, M. A. (1995). Multiproject strategy, design transfer, and project performance: a survey of automobile development projects in the U.S. and Japan. *IEEE Transactions on Engineering Management, 42*(4), 397–409.

Nonaka, I. (1991). The Knowledge-Creating Company, *Harvard Business Review*, November – December 1991.

Nonaka, I., & Takeuchi, H. (1995). *The Knowledge-Creating Company: How Japanese Companies Create the Dynamics of Innovation*. New York: Oxford University Press.

Norton, D., & Kaplan, R. (2003). *The Strategy-Focused Organization*. Boston, MA: Harvard Business School Press.

NSW Government Chief Information Office Benefits Register (n.d.). Retrieved May 15, 2008 from http://www.gcio.nsw.gov.au/documents/Sample%20Benefits_register.pdf

O'Brien, J. (2005). *Introduction to information systems* (12th edition). Boston: McGraw-Hill/Irwin.

O'Connor, A. D. (1993). Successful strategic information systems planning. *Journal of Information Systems, 3*.

O'Shaughnessy, B. (2002). *Challenges of Implementing GIS in a gas utility*. Retrieved 12 30, 2007, from GIS for Oil & Gas Conference : http://www.gisdevelopment.net/proceedings/gita/oil_gas2002/papers/boshauhnessy.asp

Oates, J. (2004). *Inverclyde IT staff fight outsource threat*. Retrieved June 03, 3004, from http://www.theregister.co.uk/2004/06/15/inverclyde_strike/

Object Management Group. *Model Driven Architecture*. http://www.omg.org/mda.

OECD (2001). Engaging Citizens in Policy-Making: Information, Consultation and Policy Participation. *Puma Policy Brief No. 10.*

OECD, Directorate for Science, Technology and Industry, Industry Committee (1991). *OECD Proposed Guidelines for Collecting and Interpreting Technological Innovation Data*. Paris, France: OECD.

OECD, Eurostat (2005). *Oslo Manual - Guidelines for Collecting and Interpreting Innovation Data*, Joint Publication, 3rd Edition. OECD/European Communities.

Oesterle, H. (1991). Generating Business Ideas Based on Information Technology. In Clarke R. & Cameron J. (Ed.), *Managing Information Technology's Organisational Impact II*. Elsevier/North-Holland, Amsterdam.

Office of Government Commerce (n.d.). Retrieved May 15, 2008, from http://www.best-management-practice.com/Online-Bookshop/IT-Service-Management-ITIL/ITIL-Version-3/

OGC PRINCE2 (n.d.). Retrieved May 15, 2008 from http://www.ogc.gov.uk/methods_prince_2.asp

Overby, S. (2006). *Outsourcing: Big Deals, Big Savings, Big Problems*. Retrieved February 08, 2006, from http://www.cio.com/archive/020106/outsourcing.html

Palvia, P. C. (1995). A Dialectic View of Information Systems Outsourcing: Pros and Cons. *Information & Management, 29*, 265-275.

Papp, R. (2001). *Strategic information technology: Opportunities for competitive advantage*. IDEA publishing Group.

Parker, M. M., Benson, R. J., & Trainor, H. E. (1988). *Information Economics: Linking business performance to Information Technology*. New Jersey: Prentice Hall.

Parsons, G. L. (1983). Information Technology : A new competitive weapon, *Sloan Management Review*, Fall 1983, pp. 3-14.

Pastore, J. A. (May, 2003). The case for portfolio management. *CIO Magazine, 12.*

Pearlson, K. E. (2001). *Managing and using Information Systems: A Strategic Approach*. New York: John Wiley & Sons Inc.

Pearlson, K. E., & Saunders, C. S. (2004). *Managing and using Information Systems: A Strategic Approach* (2nd ed.). United States of America: John Wiley & Sons.

Peppard, J. (2001). Bridging the gap between the IS organization and the rest of the business: Plotting a route. *Information System Journal, 11*(3), 249–270.

Peppers & Rogers (2006). *Customer-Focused Self-Service: Building the Balanced Business Case*. white paper 2006, Peppers and Rogers, www.1to1.com.

Perry, L. T., Stott, R. C., & Smallwood, W. W. (1993). *Real Time Strategy: Improvising Team Based Planning for a Fast-Changing World*. New York: John Wiley & Sons Inc.

Peterson, R. (2004). Crafting information technology governance. *Information Systems Management, 21*(4), 7–22.

Petridis, V., & Syrris, V., (2007). Machine Learning Techniques for Environmental Data Estimation. In V. G. Kaburlasos, & G. X. Ritter (Ed.), *Computational Intelligence Based on Lattice Theory* (pp. 195-214).

Peyret, H. (2007, April 25). *The Forrester Wave™: Enterprise Architecture Tools, Q2 2007.*

Piccoli, G., & Ives, B. (2005). IT-dependent strategic initiatives and sustained competitive advantage: A review and synthesis of the literature. *MIS Quarterly, 29*(4).

Pimchangthong, D., Plaisent, M., & Bernard, P. (2003). Key issues in information systems management: A comparative study of academics and practitioners in Thailand. *Journal of Global Information Technology Management, 6*(4), 27-44.

Pine, J., & Gilmore, J. (1997). The four faces of mass customization. *Harvard Business Review, 75*(1), 91-101.

Plattner, B. (2004). Crtical Success Factors in Engineering Education: Some Observation and Examples. *Information Knowledge Systems Management*, (4), 179-190.

Porter M. (1996). What Is Strategy? *Harvard Business Review, 74*(60), 61-78.

Porter M. E. (1980). *Competitive Strategy.* Free Press.

Porter M. E., & Millar V. E. (1985). How information gives you competitive advantage. *Harvard Business Review*, July-August.

Porter, M. (1980). *Competitive strategy.* New York: Free Press.

Porter, M. (1987). From competitive advantage to corporate strategy. *Harvard Business Review, 65*(3), 43-59.

Porter, M. (1990). *The Competitive Advantage of Nations.* Free Press.

Porter, M. (1998). Location, Clusters, and the 'New' Micro-Economics of Competition. *Business Economics, 33*(1), 7-13.

Porter, M. E. (1996). What is strategy? *Harvard Business Review*, Nov-Dec., 61-78.

Porter, M., & Miller, V. (1985). How information technology gives you competitive advantage. *Harvard Business Review, 63*(4), 149-160.

Porter, M.E., & Olmsted Teisberg, E. (2006). Redefining healthcare. Creating value-based competition on results. Boston, MA: Harvard Business School Press.

Porter, M.F. (1979). How Competitive Forces Shape Strategy. *Harvard Business Review, 57*(2), 137-145.

Porter, M.F. (1980). *Competitive Strategy.* New York: The Free Press.

Poskela, J., Korpi-Filppula, M., Mattila, V., & Salkari, I. (2001). Project portfolio management practices of a global telecommunications operator. In K.A. Artto, M. Martinsuo, & T. Aalto (Eds.), *Project portfolio management.* Helsinki: Project Management Association.

Prahalad, C. K., & Hamel, G. (1990). The Core Competence of the Corporation. *Harvard Business Review, 68*(3), 79-91.

Prahalad, C.K., & Krishnan, M.S. (2002). The dynamic synchronization of strategy and technology. *MIT Sloan Management Review, 43*(4), 24-33.

Prahalad, C.K., & Krishnan, M.S. (2002). The dynamic synchronization of strategy and information technology. *MIT Sloan Management Review, 43*(Summer), 24-33.

Pramongkit, P., & Teay, S. (2002). Strategic IT Framework for Modern enterprise by using Information Technology Capabilities. *Proceedings of 2002 IEEE International Engineering Management Conference (IEMC – 2002),* Cambridge UK

Pramongkit, P., & Teay, S. (2002). Strategic IT Framework for Modern enterprise by using Information Technology Capabilities. *Proceedings of 2002 IEEE International Engineering Management Conference (IEMC – 2002).* Cambridge UK

Pramongkit, P., Teay, S., & Boonmark, S. (2000). Analysis of Technological Learning for Thai Manufacturing Industry *Technovation: The International Journal of Technological Innovation and Entrepreneurship, 20*(4), 189 – 196.

Prekumar, G., & King, W.R. (1994). The evaluation of strategic information system planning. *Information and Management, 26*, 327-340.

Preston, D., Karahanna, E., & Rowe, F. (2006). Development of Shared Understanding between the Chief Information Officer and Top Management Team in U.S. and French Organizations: A Cross-Cultural Comparison. *IEEE Transactions on Engineering Management. 53*(2), 191-206.

PRINCE2 (1998). *Managing successful projects with PRINCE2.* London: The Stationery Office.

Project Management Institute. (2000). *Guide to the project management body of knowledge (PMBOK).* Project Management Institute.

Purdue University, *The Purdue Enterprise Reference Architecture*, http://pera.net

Putman, J. R. (2001). *Architecting with RM-ODP*. New Jersey: Prentice Hall PTR.

Quinlan, T. (2002). The Value of an IT Chargeback System. *Journal of Bank Cost and Management Accounting, 5*(3), 16–30.

Quinn, J. B., & Hilmer, F. G. (1994). Strategic Outsourcing. *Sloan Management Review, 35*(4), 43-55.

Quinn, J.B. (1992). *Intelligent enterprise*. New York: Free Press.

Rachev, S. T., Ortobelli, S., & Schwartz, E. (2004). The Problem of Optimal Asset Allocation with Stable Distributed Returns. In Krinik, A., & Swift, R. J. (Ed.), *Stochastic Processes and Functional Analysis. Dekker Series of Lecture Notes in Pure and Applied Mathematics* (pp. 295–361).

Raghunathan, B., Raghunathan, T. S., & Qiang, T. (1999). Dimensionality of the Strategic Grid Framework: The Construct and its Measurement. *Information Systems Research 10*(4) 343-355.

Raghunathan, T. S., Gupta, Y. P., & Sundararaghavan P. S. (1989). Assessing the Impact of IS Executives' Critical Success Factors on the Performance of IS Organizations. *Information & Management, 17*, 157-168.

Rai, A., Patnayakuni, R., & Patnayakuni, N. (1997). Technology investment and business performance. *Communications of the ACM, 40*(7), 89-97.

Rainer, R. K., Snyder, Charles A., & Carr, Houston H. (1991). Risk analysis for information technology. *Journal of Management Information Systems, 8*(1), 129–148.

Ranganathan, C., & Kannabiran, G. (2004). Effective Management of Information Systems function: an exploratory study of Indian organizations. *International Journal of Information Management, 24*(3).

Rau, K. G. (2004). Effective governance of IT: Design objectives, roles, and relationships. *Information Systems Management, 21*(4), 35–42.

Ravi, R., Bingham, B. J., Rowan, L., Danilenko, A., & McStravick, P. (2005). *Worldwide and U.S. Business Process Outsourcing (BPO). 2005-2009 Forecast: Market Opportunities by Horizontal Business Functions*. 33815, IDC.

Raymond, L. (2003). Globalization, the knowledge economy, and competitiveness: A business intelligence framework for the development SMEs. *Journal of American Academy of Business, 3*(1/2), 260-269.

Reich, B. H., & Benbasat, I. (1996). Measuring the Linkage Between Business and Information Technology Objectives. *MIS Quart., 20*(1), 55-81.

Reilly, F. K., & Brown, K. C. (2002). *Investment analysis and portfolio management*. South-Western College Pub.

Remenyi, D. S. J. (1991). *Strategic Information Systems Planning*. NCC Blackwell.

Reyck, B. D., Grushka-Cockayne, Y., Lockett, M., Calderini, S. R., Moura, M., & Sloper, A. (2005). The impact of project portfolio management on information technology projects. *International Journal of Project Management, 23*(7), 524–537.

Rice, R. E., D'Ambra, J., & More, E. (1998). Cross-Cultural Comparison of Organizational Media Evaluation and Choice. *J. Communication, 48*(3) 3-26.

Richardson, T. (2004). *Bradford IT staff vote to strike*. Retrieved June 02, 2004, from http://www.theregister.co.uk/2004/01/21/bradford_it_staff_vote/

Ringuest, J., Graves, S., & Case, R. (2000). Conditional stochastic dominance in R&D portfolio selection. *IEEE Transaction on Engineering Management, 47*(4), 478–484.

Roberts, A., & Gardiner, P.D. (1998). Project management and strategy implementation. *Proceedings of the 3rd International Research Network on Organizing by Projects, 317-323*. Alberta: University of Calgary.

Robson, W. (1997). *Strategic Management & Information Systems* (2nd ed.). London: Pitman Publishing.

Rockart, J. F., & Morton, M. S. S. (1984). Implications of Changes in Information Technology for Corporate Strategy. *Interfaces,* Jan 1988 pp. 84-95.

Rockart, J. F., & Short, J. E. (1989). IT in the 1990s: Managing Organizational Interdependence. *Sloan Management Review,* Winter 1989, pp. 128-136.

Rogers, E. M., & Kincaid D. L. (1981). *Communication Networks*. New York: The Free Press.

Rogerson, S., & Fidler, C. (1994). Strategic Information Planning System: its adoption and use. *Information Management and Computer Security, 2*(1).

Rosemann, M. (1999). ERP software characteristics and consequences. *Proceedings of the 7th European Conference on Information Systems*, Copenhagen.

Ross, J., & Beath, C. (2002). Beyond the business case: New approaches to IT investment. *Sloan Management Review, 43*(2), 51–59.

Ross, T. (2004). *Fuzzy Logic with Engineering Applications*. John Wiley, 2nd edition.

Rosser, B., & Potter, K. (2001). *IT portfolio management and survey results*. Stamford: Gartner Research.

Russell, A. (2003). *Managing High-Technology Programs and Project*. New York, NY: John Wiley & Sons.

SA Strategic Plan (n.d.). Retrieved May 15, 2008, from http://www.stateplan.sa.gov.au/

Sabherwal, R., & Chan, Y.E. (2001). Alignment between business and IS strategies: A study of prospectors, analyzers, and defenders. *Information Systems Research, 12*(1), 11-33.

Sabherwal, R., & Kirs, P. (1994). The Alignment Between Organizational Critical Success Factors and Information Technology Capability in Academic Institutions. *Decision Sci., 25*(2) 01-330.

Sabherwal, R., Jeyaraj, A., & Chowa, C. (2006). Information system success: Individual and organizational determinants. *Management Science, 52*(12), 1849-1860.

Salton, G. (1975). *Dynamic Information and Library Processing*. London: Prentice-Hall International, (p. 523).

Sankar, Y. (1991). Implementing Information technology: A Managerial Audit for Planning change, *Journal of Systems Management, 42*(11), 32-37.

Santhanam, R., & Kyparisis, G. J., (1995). A multiple criteria decision model for information system project selection. *Computers and Operations Research, 22*(8), 807–818.

Santhanam, R., & Kyparisis, J. (1996). A decision model for interdependent information system project selection. *European Journal of Operational Research, 89*(2), 380–399.

Santiago, L., & Bifano, T. (2005). Management of R&D projects under uncertainty: A multidimensional approach to managerial flexibility. *IEEE Transactions on Engineering Management, 52*(2), 269–280.

Santos, B. L. D. (1991). Justifying investments in new information technologies. *Journal of Management Information Systems, 7*(4), 71–90.

Sanwal, A. (2007). *Optimizing Corporate Portfolio Management: Aligning Investment Proposals with Organizational Strategy.* New York/NY: John Wiley & Sons, Inc.

Scheer, A. W. (1998). *ARIS — Business Process Frameworks*, 2nd edition, Berlin, New York and others.

Scheer, A. W. (2004). 20 years of business process management: From ideas to innovation. Process World.

Scheer, A. W. (2004, July). ARIS Value Engineering Concept, White Paper.

Schein, E. H. (1992). The Role of the CEO in the management of change: The case of information technology. In T. A. Kochan & M. Useem, (Eds), *Transforming Organizations*. Oxford: Oxford University Press.

Schmidt, R., Lyytinen, K., Keil, M., & Cule, P. (2001). Identifying software project risks: An international Delphi study. *Journal of Management Information Systems, 17*(4), 5–36.

Schmidt, R., Lyytinen, K., Keil, M., & Cule, P. (2002). Perceptions of IT project risk: A Delphi study. *Information Systems Journal, 12*(2), 103–119.

Schmitz, J., & Fulk, J. (1991). Organizational Colleagues, Media Richness, and Electronic Mail. *Communication Res., 18*(4), 487-523.

Schneider, M., Shnaider, E., Kandel, A., & Chew, G. (1998). Automatic construction of FCMs. *Fuzzy Sets and Systems, 93*, 161-172.

Schniederjans, M., & Santhanam, R., (1993). A multi-objective constrained resource information system project selection method. *European Journal of Operational Research, 70*(2), 244–253.

Schware, R., & Deane, A. (2003). *Deploying E-Government programs: The strategic importance of 'I' before 'E'", info, 5*(4), 10-19.

Schwartz, P. (1991). *The art of the long view*. New York: Doubleday.

Scott, A. (1997). *Strategic planning*. Edinburgh: Pitman Publishing/Edinburgh Business School.

Segars, A. H., & Grover, V. (1999). Profiles of strategic information systems planning. *Information Systems Research, 10*(3), 199-232.

Segars, A., & Grover, V. (1998). Strategic information systems planning success: An investigation of the contruct and its measurement. *MIS Quarterly, 22*(2), 139–163.

Seltzer, L. (1999). The Virtual Office. *PC Magazine*. October 19.

Selznick, P. (1957). *Leadership in administration: A sociological interpretation*. Evanston: Row, Peterson.

Senge, P. (1990). *The fifth discipline*. New York: Doubleday.

Seshadri, S., & Subrahmanyam, M. (2005). Introduction to the special issue on risk management in operations. *Production and Operations Management, 14*(1), 1–4.

Sewell, C., & Brown, P. (1990). *Customers for life*. New York: Doubleday Currency.

Shalloway, A., & Trott, J. R. (2005). *Design Patterns Explained: A New Perspective on Object-Oriented Design*. Boston, MA: Addison-Wesley.

Shan, T., & Hua, W. (2006, September). *Solution Architecture of N-Tier Applications*. 3rd IEEE Conference on Services Computing (SCC 2006).

Shapiro, C., & Varian, H. (1999). *Information rules*. Boston: Harvard Business School Press.

Sharif, N. (1995). *The Evolution of Technology Management Studies: Techno-economics to Techno-metrics*. Professorial lecture at Asian Institute of Technology, 23. March 1995

Sharp B., Atkins A., Ho L., Kothari H., & Paul D. (2005). Intelligent Agent Concepts for Outsourcing Decision-Making in Customer Service Operations. In P. Iasias, & M. B. Nunes (Eds.), *Proceedings of the IADIS International Conference WWW/Internet* (Vol I., pp. 215-221). IADIS Press.

Sharpe, P., & Keelin, T. (1998). How SmithKline Beecham makes better resource-allocation decisions. In L.D. Dye & J.S. Pennypacker (Eds.), *Project portfolio management* (4th edition, pp. 88-94). West Chester: Center for Business Practices.

Short, J., Williams, E., & Christie, B. (1976). *The Social Psychology of Telecommunications*. London: Wiley.

Shoval, P., & Giladi, R. (1996). Determination of an implementation order for IS projects. *Information Management, 31*(2), 67-74.

Shoval, P., & Lugasi, Y. (1988). Computer systems selection. *Information and Management, 15*.

Shupe, C., & Behling, R. (2006). Developing and Implementing a Strategy for Technology Deployment. *The Information Management Journal*, July and August.

Singlemann, P. (1972). Exchange as Symbolic Interaction: Convergences Between Two Theoretical Perspectives. *American Sociological Rev., 37*, 414-424.

Smaczny, T. (2001). IS an alignment between business and IT the appropriate paradigm to manage IT in today's organization? *Management Decision, 39*(10), 797-802.

Smith C. (2003). Corporate Social Responsibility: Whether or How? *California Management Review, 45*(4), 52-76.

Smith, H. (1996, December). Hitting the project mark. *InfoWorld, 32*.

Solomon, M. (2002, March). Project portfolio management. *Computerworld*, 14-16.

Sommer, R. (1999). Portfolio Management for Projects: A New Paradigm. In Dye, D. L., & Pennypacker S. J. (Eds.), *Project Portfolio Management* (pp. 55-60). West Chester, PA: Center for business Practices.

Sommer, R.J. (1998). Portfolio management for projects: A new paradigm. In L.D. Dye & J.S. Pennypacker (Eds.), *Project portfolio management* (4th edition, pp. 311-320). West Chester: Center for Business Practices.

Sorteberg, I., & Kure, O. (2005). The use of service level agreements in tactical military coalition force networks. *IEEE Communications Magazine, 43*(11), 107-114.

South Australia Office of CIO (n.d.). Retrieved May 15, 2008, from http://www.cio.sa.gov.au/

Sowa, J. F., & Zachman, J. A. (1992). Extending and formalizing the framework for information systems architecture. *IBM Systems Journal*, 31(3).

Spradlin, C.T., & Kutoloski, D.M. (1999, March-April). Action-oriented portfolio management. *Research Technology Management, 27*.

Steele, L. (1989). *Managing technology*. New York: McGraw-Hill.

Stewart, T. (2003). Does IT matter? An HBR debate. *Harvard Business Review, 81*(6), 1-17.

Stošić, B. (2004). Application of PATTERN Method in Innovation Projects Management. In I. Travnik (Ed.), *3rd Central and South East Europe Project Management Network Conference, Project Management Paving the Way to European Union*, (E:\papers\p22.pdf). Bratislava, Slovakia: SENET.

Strassmann, P. A. (1990). The Business Value of Computers-An Executive's Guide. *The Information Economics Press*. Connecticut, USA: New Canaan.

Straub, D. W. (1989). Validating Instruments in MIS Research. *MIS Quart., 13*(2), 147-169.

Straub, D., & Karahanna, E. (1998). Knowledge Worker Communications and Recipient Availability: Toward a Task Closure Explanation of Media Choice. *Organization Sci., 9*(2) 160-175.

Stummer, C., & Heidenberger, K. (2003). Interactive R&D portfolio analysis with project interdependencies and time profiles of multiple objectives. *IEEE Transactions on Engineering Management, 50*(2), 175–183.

Stylios, C. C., & Groumpos, P. P. (1999). Fuzzy Cognitive Maps: a model for intelligent supervisory control systems. *Computers in Industry, (39)*, 229 – 238.

Sun, L., Srivastava, R. P., & Mock, T. J. (2006). An information systems security risk assessment model under the Dempster--Shafer theory of belief functions. *Journal of Management Information Systems, 22*(4), 109–142

Sustainable Development. Oxford University Press.

Sweetin v Coral Racing (2005). *Industrial Relations Law Reports (UK) Vol. 252.*

Symons, C. (2005). IT and business alignment: Are we there yet? *Trends.* Cambridge, MA: Forrester Research.

Symons, C. (2005). *IT Strategy Maps: A Tool for Strategic Alignment.* Cambridge, MA: Forrester Research Inc.

Synnott, W. R. (1987). The Information Weapon. Wiley.

Syrris, V., & Petridis, V. (2008). Classification through Hierarchical Clustering and Dimensionality Reduction. *IEEE World Congress on Computational Intelligence,* Hong Kong.

Taber, R. (1991). Knowledge processing with fuzzy cognitive maps. *Expert Systems with Applications, 2*(1), 83 – 87.

Taber, R. (1994). *Fuzzy cognitive maps model social systems. AI Expert, 9*, 18-23.

Tallon, P., & Kraemer, K. (2003). *Investigating the relationship between strategic alignment and business value.* Hershy, PA: IDEA Publications (pp. 1-22).

Tan, A. (2007). Business Process Reengineering in Asia: A Practical Approach. Second Edition, Prentice Hall.

Tan, F., & Gallupe, R.B. (2006). Aligning Business and Information Systems Thinking: A Cognitive Approach. *IEEE Transactions on Engineering Management, 23*(2), 223-237.

Tanaka, K. (1997). *An Introduction to Fuzzy Logic for Practical Applications.* Springer Verlag.

Tapscott, D. (1996). The Digital Economy. New York: McGraw Hill.

Tapscott, D., & Caston, A. (1993). *Paradigm Shift : The New Promise of Information Technology.* McGraw-Hill Inc.

Tate, P. (1999, Dec 98-Jan 99). The Big Spenders. *Information Strategy,* 30-37.

Tavakolian, H. (1989). Linking the information technology structure with organizational strategy: a survey. *MIS Quarterly, 13*(3).

Teay, S. (2005). Quality Assurance and Strategic Implementation in educational institutions: A Holistic Alliance? *JIRSEA (Journal of Institutional Research South East Asia, 3*(1) 24-40.

Teay, S. (2007). Integrated Curriculum QMIPS – Curriculum Quality Management, Information and Planning Systems. *ASAIHL Journal, 10*(1).

Teay, S. (2007). *Strategic Capital Capacity and Capability Management of IS/IT.* under review for publication in Handbook in Strategic Information Technology and Portfolio Management, Institute of Systems Science, National University of Singapore

TechRepublic & Smith, T. (2000). *IT Project Management Research Findings.* Louiville, KY: TechRepublic.

Teo, T. S. H., & Ang, J. S. K. (2000). How useful are strategic plans for information systems. *Behavior and Information Technology, 19*(4), 275-282.

Teo, T. S. H., & King, W. R. (1997). Integration between business planning and information systems planning: an evolutionary-contingency perspective. *Journal of Management Information Systems, 14*(1), 185-224

Teo, T., & Ang, J. (1999). Critical Success Factors in the alignment of IS plans with business plans. *International Journal of Information Management, 19*, 173-185.

The Open Group. *The Open Group Architecture Framework,* http://www.opengroup.org/architecture/togaf8/index8.htm.

The Standish Group. (2003). *Chaos chronicles, version 3.0.* West Yarmouth: The Standish Group.

Thomas, R. J. (1993). *New Product Development: Managing and Forecasting for Strategic Success.* New York, NY: Wiley.

Thompson Jr., A. A., & Strickland III, A. J. (2005). *Crafting and Executing Strategies – The Quest for Competitive Advantage: Concepts and Cases.* 14th Edition, 2005, McGraw-Hill Irwin.

Thornton, M. (2005). Exfoliating dated IT assumptions. *Computerworld.* Retrieved January 27, 2008, from, http://www.computerworld.com/managementtopics/management/story/0,10801,105607,00.html

Thorton, G. C., & Byham, W. C. (1982). *Assessment centers and managerial performance.* New York: Academic Press.

Tidd, J., Bessant, J., & Pavitt, K. (2001). *Managing Innovation.* Chichester, UK: John Wiley & Sons.

Toffler, A. (1970). *Future shock.* New York: Bantom Books.

Trainor, E. (2003). From the president's desk. *SIM Top Ten List* (http://www.simnet.org).

Traynor, I. (2003). *The Privatisation of War.* Retrieved June 08, 2004, from http://www.guardian.co.uk/international/story/0,3604,1103566,00.html

Treacy, M., & Wiersema, F. (1995). *The discipline of market leaders: Choose your customers, narrow your focus, dominate your market.* New York: Perseus Book Group.

Trevino, L. K. (1987). Message Equivocality, Media Selection, and Manager Performance: Implications for Information Systems. *MIS Quart., 1*(1), 355-366.

Trott, P. (2005). *Innovation Management and New Product Development.* London, UK: Prentice Hall.

Turner, D., & Crawford, M. (1994). Managing current and future competitive performers: The role of competency. In G. Hamel and A. Heene (Eds.), *Competency-based competition: Strategic Management series* (pp. 241–254). Chichester, England: Wiley.

Turner, J.R. (1996). Editorial: International Project Management Association global qualification, certification and accreditation. *International Journal of Project Management, 14*(1), 1-6.

Turner, J.R. (1999). *The handbook of project-based management* (2"d edition). London: McGraw-Hill.

UNCED (1992). *Capacity Building – Agenda 21's definition* (Chapter 37, UNCED, 1992)

UNDP (1991). Symposium on "A Strategy for Water Sector Capacity Building" Deft, The Netherlands in 1991.

Val IT (2006). *Enterprise value: Governance of IT investments.* IT Governance Institute

Van de Ven, A. H., & Walker, G. (1984). The Dynamics of Interorganizational Coordination. *Admin. Sci. Quart., 29,* 598-621.

Van Der Heijden, K. (2005). *Scenarios: the art of strategic conversation.* 2.ed. London: John Wiley.

Van Merode, F., Molema, H., & Goldschmidt, H. (2004). GUM and six sigma approaches positioned as deterministic tools in quality target engineering. Accreditation and Quality Assurance, 10, 32-36.

Van Merode, G.G., Groothuis, S., & Hasman, A. (2004). Enterprise resource planning for hospitals. International Journal of Medical Informatics, 73(6), 493-501.

Van Roth, A., & Van Dierdonck, R. (1995). Hospital resource planning: Concepts, feasibility and framework. Production and operations management, 4(1), 2-29.

Vandaele, N., & De Boeck, L. (2003). Advanced resource planning. Robotics and Computer Integrated Manufacturing, 19, 211-218.

Venkatesh, V., Morris, M. G., Davis, F. D., & Davis, G. B. (2003). User acceptance of information technology: Toward a unified view. *MIS Quarterly, 27*(3), 425–478.

Verhoef, C. (2002). Quantitative IT portfolio management, *Science of Computer Programming, 45*(1), 1–96.

Verhoef, C. (2005). Quantitative aspects of outsourcing deals. *Science of Computer Programming, 56*(3), 275 - 313.

Verma, D., & Sinha, K. (2002). Toward a theory of project interdependencies in high tech R&D environments. *Journal of Operations Management, 20*(5), 451–468.

Visitacion, M. (April, 2003). *Process and tools: The nuts and bolts of project portfolio management.* Cambridge: Giga Information Group.

Viswanathan, N. (2006). *The Technology Strategies for Integrated Business Planning Benchmark Report.* Boston, MA: Aberdeen Group, www.Aberdeen.com.

Von Krogh, G., Roos, J., & Slocum, K. (1996). An Essay on corporate epistemology. In G. von Krogh and J. Roos (Eds), *Managing Knowledge: Perspectives on Cooperation and Competition.* London: Sage Publication.

Wallace, L., & Keil, M. (2004). Software project risks and their impact on outcomes. *Communications of the ACM, 47*(4), 68–73.

Wallace, L., Keil, M., & Rai, A. (2004a). How software project risk affects project outcomes: An investigation of the dimensions of risk and an exploratory model. *Decision Sciences, 35*(2), 289–321.

Wallace, L., Keil, M., & Rai, A. (2004b). Understanding software project risk: A cluster analysis. *Information & Management, 42*(1), 115–125.

Walter, J., Gutjahr, S. K., & Reiter, P. (2007). A VNS Algorithm for Noisy Problems and Its Application to Project Portfolio Analysis. In J. Hromkovic et al. (Ed.), *Lecture Notes in Computer Science, Stochastic Algorithms: Foundations and Applications 4665* (pp. 93-104), Springer-Verlag Berlin/Heidelberg.

Ward, J., & Peppard, J. (2002). *Strategic Planning for Information Systems* (3rd ed.), New York: John Wiley & Sons Inc.

Ward, J., Griffiths, P., & Whitmore, P. (1990). *Strategic Planning for Information Systems.* Wiley.

Warriner, C. K. (1970). *The Emergence of Society.* Dorsey, Homewood: IL.

Watson, E. E., & Schneider, H. (1999). Using ERP systems in education. *Communications of the Association for Information Systems,* 1, 2-44.

Watson, R. T. (1990). Influences on the IS Manager's Perceptions of Key Issues: Information Scanning and the Relationship with the CEO. *MIS Quart.,* 217-231.

Watson, R. T., Kelly, G. G., Galliers, R. D., & Brancheau, J. C. (1997). Key issues in information systems management: an international perspective. *Journal of Management Information Systems,* 13(4), 91-115.

Webster, G. (1999). Project definition – The missing link. *Industrial and Commercial Training,* 31(6), 240-244.

Webster, J., & Trevino, T. K. (1995). Rational and Social Theories as Complementary Explanations of Communication Media Choices: Two Policy Capturing Studies. *Acad. Management J.,* 1544-1572.

Weick, K. (1979). *The Social Psychology of Organizing.* Reading, MA: Addison Wesley.

Weill, P. & Ross, J. W. (2004). *IT governance: How top performers manage IT decision rights for superior results.* Boston: Harvard Business School Press.

Weill, P. (1990). Strategic investment in information technology: An empirical study. *Information Age,* 12(3), 141-147.

Weill, P. (2004). Don't just lead, govern: How top-performing firms govern IT. *MIS Quarterly Executive,* 3(1), 1-17.

Weill, P., & Aral, S. (2006). Generating premium returns on your IT investments. *Sloan Management Review,* 47(2), 39–48.

Weill, P., & Broadbent, M. (1997). Management by maxim: How business and IT managers can create

IT infrastructures. *Sloan Management Review,* 38(3), 77-92.

Weill, P., & Broadbent, M. (1998). *Leveraging the infrastructure.* Boston, Massachusetts: Harvard Business School Press.

Weill, P., & Olson, M. H. (1989, March). Managing investment in IT: Mini case examples and implications. *MIS Quarterly.*

Weill, P., & Ross, J. (2005). A matrixed approach to designing IT governance. *MIT Sloan Management Review,* 46(2), 26–34.

Weill, P., & Vitale, M. (1999). Assessing the health of an information systems applications portfolio: An example from process manufacturing. *MIS Quarterly,* 13(4), 601-624.

Weill, P., & Vitale, M. (2002). What IT infrastructure capabilities are needed to implement e-business models? *MIS Quarterly Executive,* 1(1), 17–34.

Weill, P., Subramani, M., & Broadbent, M. (2002). Building IT Infrastructure for Strategic Agility. *MIT Sloan Management Review,* Fall 2002.

Weinstein, L. (2004). Inside Risks: Outsourced and out of control. *Communications of the ACM,* 47(2), 120.

Weiser C.R. (1994). Best practice in customer relations. *Consumer Policy Review,* 130-137.

Wesh, J., & White, J. (1981). A small business is not a little big business. *Harvard Business Review,* 59(4), 213-223.

Westerman, G. (2005). What makes and IT risk management process effective. *MIT Sloan School of Management Center for Information Systems Research,* 5(3B), 1–3.

Westerman, G., & Walpole, R. (2005). Working article: PFPC: Building an IT risk management competency. *CISR,* 1–13.

Wheelen, T. L., & Hunger, J. D. (2004). *Strategic Management and Business Policy.* 9th Edition, 2004, Pearson Prentice Hall

Whitley, R. (2002). Developing innovative competences: The role of institutional frameworks, *Industrial and Corporate Change,* 11(3), 497-528.

Wilkinson, L. (1995). How to build scenarios. *Wired,* (September), 4-10.

Willcocks, L. P., Feeny, D., & Islei, G. (1997). *Managing IT as a Strategic Resource.* Berkshire: McGraw Hill Book Company.

Willcocks, L. P., Fitzgerald, G., & Lacity, M. C. (1996). To Outsource IT Or Not? Recent Research on Economics and Evaluation Practice. *European Journal of Information Systems, 5*(3), 143-160.

Williams, L. T. (1997). Planning and Managing the information system – A manager's guide. *Industrial Management and Data Systems,* 97/5.

Williams, T. (2003). *Corporate governance: A guide for fund managers and corporations.* Provenance Investment & Financial Services Association Limited. Westpac Banking Corporation.

Winston, W. (2000). *Financial Models Using Simulation and Optimization: A Step-By-Step Guide With Excel and Palisade's Decision tools Software.* Palisade.

Wiseman, C. (1985). *Strategy and Computers,* Dow Jones Irwin.

Woodfuffe, C. (1992). What is meant by competency? In R. Boam & P. Sparrow (Eds.), *Designing and achieving competency.* New York: McGraw-Hill.

World Bank (2003) World Development Indicators, http://www.worldbank.org/data/wdi2003/

Wysocki, R. (2004). *Project Management Process Improvement.* Boston, MA: Artech House.

Xirogiannis, G., Stefanou, J., & Glykas, M. (2004). A fuzzy cognitive map approach to support urban design. *Expert Systems with Applications, 26,* 257-268.

Yang, C., & Huang, J. (2000). A decision model for IS Outsourcing, *International Journal of Information Management, 20,* 225-239.

Yen, D. C., Chou, D. C., & Chang, J. (2002). A synergic analysis for Web-based enterprise resources-planning systems. *Computer Standards & Interfaces, 24*(4), 337-46.

Yeoman, B. (2003). *Soldiers of Good Fortune.* Retrieved June 08, 2004, from http://www.motherjones.com/news/feature/2003/05/ma_365_01.html

Yetton, P. (1997). False prophesies, successful practice, and future directions in IT management. In C. Sauer, P.

Yetton, et al., (Eds), *Steps to the Future.* San Francisco: Jossey-Bass.

Yin, R. (1994). *Case study research: Design and methods.* Beverly Hills, CA: Sage Publishing.

Yong, J. (2005). *E-Government in Asia.* Second Edition, Times edition.

Yoon, K. P., & Naadimuthu, G. (1994). A make-or-buy decision analysis involving imprecise data. *International Journal of Operations and Production Management, 14*(2), 62-69.

Young, H. (1998). *Individual strategy and social Structure: An evolutionary theory of institutions.* Princeton: Princeton University Press.

Zachman, J. A. (1987). A framework for information systems architecture. *IBM Systems Journal,* 26(3).

Zachman, J. A. (1997 March). Enterprise architecture: The issue of the century. *Database Programming and Design,* pp. 2-5.

Zachman, J. *Zachman Framework.* http://www.zifa.com.

Zhang, W. R. Chen, S. S., Wang, W., & King, R. S. (1992). A cognitive-map-based approach to the coordination of distributed cooperative agent. *IEEE Transactions on Systems, Man, & Cybernetics, 22,* 103-114.

Zhang, W. R., Chen, S. S., & Bezdek, J. C. (1989). *Pool2: a generic system for cognitive map development and decision analysis, 19*(1), 31-39.

Zhu, K., & Weyant, J. P. (2003). Strategic decisions of new technology adoption under asymmetric information: A game-theoretic model. *Decision Sciences, 34*(4), 643–675.

Zmud, R. W., Lind, M. R., & Forrest, W. Y. (1990). An Attribute Space for Organizational Communication Channels. *Inform. Systems Res., 1*(4) 440-457.

Zorkoczy, P. (1981). *Information Technology: An Introduction.* London: Pitman (p.157).

Zuboff, S. (1988). *In the Age of Smart Machines: The future of Work and Power.* New York, NY: Basic books.

About the Contributors

Albert Wee Kwan Tan was an assistant professor in the college of graduate studies at the University of Wollongong, Dubai. His research interests are in reverse logistics, process modelling and reengineering and information technology to coordinate supply chain. He holds an MBS from the National University of Ireland and a PhD in supply chain management from the Nanyang Technological University. His research works have been published in the *International Journal Physical Distribution and Logistics Management, the International Journal Logistics Systems and Management, the International Journal Logistics Management and the Asia Pacific Journal of Marketing and Logistics.* He is also serving as a member of the editorial board for several journals in the field of Information Systems and Decision Science. He is now managing a post graduate program in The Logistics Institute, National University of Singapore.

Petros Theodorou holds a PhD and a PostDoct in finance and strategy of information systems and an HBSc in economics. Theodorou is currently an adjunct professor of corporate finance in Athens University of Economics and Business in the Department of Economics and a senior researcher in the Department of Strategy and Planning, Public Power Corporation (DEH/PPC S.A). His previous working experience was in computer logic, Astron/PEP, etc. and on the board of directors in various firms. His teaching experience was at the Technological Educational Institution of Thessaloniki, Technological Educations Institution of Piraeus and had the position of Assistant Professor at the Technological Educational Institution of Kavala in the Department of Management. Furthermore, worked as a researcher at the Aristotle University in the Department of Economics and at the University of Macedonia in the Department of Applied Informatics. Theodorou is a member of NYA, Economic Chamber of Greece, Management of Technology Organization, Who's is Who Marquis etc.. He has published as author and co-author in various sources such as IGI Global, Elsevier Science, The University Publishers of Crete, *International Journal of Management Science, Journal of Cases on Information Technology* and in many conference proceedings.

* * *

Asim Abdel Rahman El Sheikh was awarded his master's degree in operational research from London School of Economics & Political Science, University of London. Later he was awarded his PhD in simulation and modeling. Currently he is dean of the Faculty of Information Systems & Technology, The Arab Academy for Banking & Financial Sciences, Jordan. Author of two books and more than 35 papers, his research interest areas software piracy, software outsourcing, simulation modeling, and SW engineering.

Evon M. O. Abu-Taieh is a PhD holder in simulation. A U.S. graduate for both her Master of Science and bachelor's degrees with a total experience of 19 years. Author of many renowned research papers in the Airline and IT, PM, KM, GIS, AI, Simulation, Security and Ciphering. Editor/author of book: *Utilizing Information Technology Systems Across Disciplines: Advancements in the Application of Computer Science* (IGI Global, USA). Editor/author: *Handbook of Research on Discrete Event Simulation Environments: Technologies and Applications* (IGI Global, USA). Guest Editor, *Journal of Information Technology Research (JITR),* editorial board member: *International Journal of E-Services and Mobile Applications (IJESMA)* and *International Journal of Information Technology Project Management (IJITPM)* and *International Journal of Information Systems and Social Change (IJISSC).* Editor/author of book: *Simulation and Modeling: Current Technologies and Applications* (IGI Global, USA). Developed some systems like: Ministry of transport databank, auditing system for airline reservation systems and Maritime Databank among others in her capacity as head of IT department in the ministry of transport for 10 years. Furthermore worked in the Arab Academy in her capacity as Assistant Professor, Dean's Assistant and London School of Economics (LSE) Director. Appointed many times as track chair, reviewer in many international conferences: IRMA, CISTA, and WMSCI. Enjoys both the academic arena as well as the hands on job.

Tony Atkins is principal lecturer in Applied Computing in the Faculty of Computing, Engineering and Technology at Staffordshire University. He has an MSc in computing science and an MSc in process engineering and a PhD in bioengineering. He is a chartered engineer in both computing, and mineral and petroleum engineering and has taught and supervised PhD programmes in both disciplines in the UK, and at the University of Wollongong Australia and Virginia Polytechnic Institute and State University in the United States. He is also a Churchill Fellowship in Bioengineering and Environmental Engineering and has several patents in bioengineering and waste recycling with embedded real time systems covering the UK, EU, Australia and US. His main interests include IT outsourcing and service management and Knowledge Management Systems (KMS). Other interests include mobile & RFID business technology in waste recycling in the construction industry, supply chain management (SCM) and mobile technological application to the ageing population. He has published over 100 refereed publications consisting of journals, chapters in books, and conferences with his research students.

Jeihan M. Auda Abu-Tayeh is a head of the International Agencies & Commissions Division at the Jordanian Ministry of Planning and International Cooperation. In her capacity, she has the opportunity to maintain sound cooperation relations with the World Bank Group, as well as the UN Agencies, in order to extend to Jordan financial and technical support for developmental projects through setting appropriate programs and plans, building and improving relations with those organizations. This is achieved through loans and aids programs, by means of designing *project proposals*, conducting *Problem & Needs Assessment* for the concerned Governmental and Non-Governmental Jordanian entities, followed by active participation in extensive evaluation processes, conducted by either the UN Country Team, or the World Bank Group Country Team. She acquired her bachelor's in Pharmaceutical Science and Management from *Al-Ahlyya Amman University.* Furthermore, in 2002, she got her M.B.A. with emphasis on *"International Marketing & Negotiations Technique",* with outstanding G. P. A. of 3.87 out of 4 *(with honors)* from *Saint Martin's College,* State of Washington; USA.

Léo Faller Becker has a bachelor's degree in information systems by Catholic University of Pelotas, obtained in 2007, and works as system analyst in His interests include IT management and IT applied to organizational management.

David Florey's career in technology management ranges from marketing and product development to senior management in hardware, software, and IT services, in both start ups and Fortune 500 companies. He has also worked as a contributor or editor for several technology and general interest publications, and as a university lecturer. Having spent the last 17 years in the U.S., Taiwan, and Hong Kong, David currently works in Singapore managing in-house software development for a U.S. MNC in the financial services sector.

Luke Ho is an executive in the Ministry of Home Affairs (Singapore), where he advises on fiscal allocation and formulates budgetary policies for the nation's 13 Prison institutions. He holds a PhD, Master by Research (Distinction) and Bachelor of Science (1st Class Honours) in computing science from Staffordshire University (UK), where he is a research affiliate. His main research interests are in strategic frameworks, outsourcing as well as Risk Management and Horizon Scanning (RAHS).

Winnie Hua is a principal consultant/architect in CTS Inc. She holds an advanced degree in computer science with about 20 year project and consulting experience on a wide range of leading-edge technologies. As a solution/lead architect, she has led lifecycle design and development of large-scale e-commerce systems on diverse platforms using a variety of cutting-edge technologies and unified/agile methodologies. She has initiated/participated in applied research on various emerging web technologies, and has published several books and numerous technical papers. Affiliated with many professional associations, she frequently speaks in conferences/seminars and co-founded the Developers' Forum and Charlotte Architecture & Technology Symposium (CATS).

Anthony Ioannidis is an assistant professor of management at the Department of Business Administration, Athens University of Economics and Business, Greece. He has previously taught at the University of Patras, Greece, University of La Verne California, Athens Campus, and Baruch College, The City University of New York. He holds a BS from the University of Athens, Greece, and an MBA, an MPhil, and a PhD from Baruch College, The City University of New York. He also possesses working experience as management consultant with leading consultancy firms in the United States and Greece, in the areas telecommunications, media and technology. His current research interests include strategy formation, organizational design, entrepreneurship, and Public-Private Partnerships, with emphasis in the Technology, Media, and Telecommunications (TMT) sector.

Alice M. Johnson is an assistant professor in the School of Business and Economics at North Carolina Agricultural and Technical State University. She holds a BA in business administration from Winston-Salem State University, an MS in personnel and industrial relations from Winthrop University, an a PhD in decision sciences and information systems from the Gatton College of Business and Economics at the University of Kentucky. She has over 10 years of industry experience. Her major research area is information systems strategy. Her research has appeared in the *Journal of Management Information Systems*, *Information Systems Management*, and various conference proceedings.

Bill Karakostas is a senior lecturer at the School of Informatics at the City University, London. Dr. Karakostas holds a BSc (Hons) in computer engineering from the University of Patras, Greece, an MPhil and a PhD from the Department of Computation at the University of Manchester Institute of Science and Technology (UMIST), England. He has been leading research projects in IS/IT for over 15 years and he has published extensively in the areas of software engineering and IS modelling and e-commerce technologies. He is scientific advisor in IT to English and Greek companies.

Dimitris K. Kardaras is an assistant professor in information management in the Department of Business Administration, at the Athens University of Economics and Business (AUEB), Athens, Greece. He holds a BSc (Hons) in informatics and a BSc (Hons) in management both from the Athens University of Economics and Business, an MSc in information systems engineering and a PhD in information systems from the Department of Computation at the University of Manchester Institute of Science and Technology (UMIST), England. Dr. Kardaras has participated to many research projects in IS/IT since 1990 and he has been teaching in IS courses for over 12 years. He has published journal and conference papers in the areas of IS planning, fuzzy cognitive maps, IS modelling and e-commerce. He is advisor to Greek companies on information management.

Albert L. Lederer earned his MS and PhD from the Ohio State University, and his BA from the University of Cincinnati. He has over ten years of full-time industry experience. Before becoming a Professor at the University of Kentucky, he served on the faculties of the University of Pittsburgh and Oakland University, and taught at Ohio State. The focus of his research for two decades continues to be strategic information systems planning. His work has appeared in the *Information Resources Management Journal, Journal of End User Computing, MIS Quarterly, Information Systems Research, Communications of the ACM*, and elsewhere.

Stanley Loh is a professor in the Catholic University of Pelotas and in the Lutheran University of Brazil. He also works in InText Mining Ltda, a brazilian company that develops technology for text analysis. He has a PhD degree in Computer Science, obtained in 2001 at the Federal University of Rio Grande do Sul. He has done researches in recommender systems, data-text-web mining and technology applied to knowledge management.

Marko Mihić is an assistant professor at the Faculty of Organizational Sciences, University of Belgrade. He is member of board of Serbian Project Management Association. He received his PhD from University of Belgrade. His current research interests include project management, e-project management, corporate strategy and change management. He has published over 50 papers on various management topics and took part on several research projects for Ministry of Science, Republic of Serbia. Besides academic work, Marko works as a consultant for Government of Serbia and numerous companies.

Subhradeep Mohanty is a director at American Express and manages the three year financial outlook for the company. During his five years at the firm, he has performed a variety of roles with responsibilities including strategic planning & analysis, reengineering and econometrics. He has a rich international experience, having worked in USA, India, Hong Kong, Singapore and Australia. Subhradeep also has a background in credit risk management and was responsible for developing innovative, risk-weighted products for one of the leading banks in India. He holds an MBA from Indian Institute of Management,

Ahmedabad and a Bachelor's degree in Engineering from Indian Institute of Technology, Chennai - two of the most prestigious academic institutions in Asia.

TRAN Van Nam is an associate professor at the National Economics University (NEU), Vietnam and currently head, Department of Business Law, Faculty of Law, NEU. He graduated from Hanoi Law University, holds an MBA from Boise States University; a Master of Law (LL.M) from the University of Turin and got his PhD in management from the Hanoi NEU. He was a Fulbright visiting lecturer at the University of Washington School of Law for the 2002-2003 school year. Dr. Tran is also an arbitrator at the Vietnam International Arbitration Center (VIAC). His research interests are international trade law; intellectual property and legal aspects of e-transactions.

Dejan Petrović is an associate professor of management at the Faculty of Organizational Sciences, University of Belgrade (Serbia) and visiting professor at several universities in the country and abroad. His research interests include project management, strategic management, project appraisal and change management. He is a general secretary of Serbian Project Management Association, member of Council of Delegates of International Project Management Association and member of editorial board of international journal *Management*. He has been a consultant for wide variety of public and private organizations and he has published books and articles in refereed journals.

Ramiro Saldaña is a teacher in the Catholic University of Pelotas, Brazil, at the courses of Information Systems and Tourism. He has an MSc in production engeneering obtained in 1999 by the Federal University of Santa Catarina. His interests include information systems, organizational management and planning and technological applications to tourism.

Anand Sanwal is currently a managing director with Brilliont (www.brilliont.com). He is the former vice president, Investment Optimization and Strategic Business Analysis, at American Express where he was responsible for building, managing and leading the company's corporate portfolio management effort managing several billion dollars of per annum discretionary investment and project spending. It is widely recognized as the most ambitious corporate portfolio management undertaking within a large- or mid-size corporation. In this role, he also oversaw the CFO's strategic planning group and the company's first-ever $50MM Chairman's Innovation Fund. American Express was recently recognized as the most innovative financial services company by Fortune Magazine for these efforts. He is the author of the book *Optimizing Corporate Portfolio Management: Aligning Investment Proposals with Organizational Strategy* (Wiley, April 2007) which features a foreword by former American Express CFO, Gary Crittenden. He is a recognized thought leader on corporate portfolio management and innovation speaking frequently to research organizations including *CFO Magazine*, the Beyond Budgeting Round Table, CFO Executive Board, Corporate Portfolio Management Association, and Gartner amongst others. He has worked with leading pharma, high-tech, healthcare, financial services, manufacturing and public sector institutions to assist them in developing and strengthening their corporate portfolio management and innovation processes and strategies and his work has been featured in *Business Finance Magazine*, *BPM Magazine*, *The Journal of Accounting & Finance*, The Deal Previous to his current role at Brilliont and his prior role at American Express, he worked in venture capital. He also worked oversees in London for an internet company and prior to that was based in Mumbai, India and Shanghai, China as a strategy/operations consultant for a mid-size chemical firm. He graduated from the Wharton School of Business with a degree in Finance and Accounting and also has a degree in Chemical Engineering from the University of Pennsylvania. Thoughts and additional discussion on corporate portfolio management, innovation, reengineering and corporate stupidity are found at his Investile Dysfunction blog at http://brilliont.com/blogs/id/.

Tony Shan is a renowned expert working in the computing field for over 20 years with extensive experience on architecture engineering, technology strategies, portfolio rationalization, and system designs in a number of multi-million dollar IT projects in a broad range of industries. He has initiated advanced research on emerging computing technologies, resulting in an invention patent and several patent-pending initiatives as well as many unified methodologies and platform models for adaptive enterprise system development. He has played a principal strategist role in leading establishing IT strategies and architecture blueprints, coupled with pragmatic technology roadmaps and enterprise architecture standards/policies, for IT governance and portfolio/asset management in Fortune 100 international organizations. He serves as a mentor/advisor on leading-edge technologies, architecture, and engineering in various technical committees, and teaches a wide variety of courses as an adjunct professor and professional trainer. In addition to dozens of top-notch technical publications, he has authored more than 10 books on Internet technologies. He is a member of numerous professional associations and honorary society, a frequent keynote speaker and Chair/Advisor/Panel/Program Committee member in prominent conferences/workshops, an editor/editorial advisory board member of IT research journals & books, as well as a founder of several user groups and forums.

Teay Shawyun is an associate professor in strategic management with a previous assistant professorship in management of technology. He has a PhD in management of technology from the Asian Institute of Technology, Thailand. Presently, he is the deputy director of the Office of QMIPS (Quality Management, Information and Planning Systems). He has more than 25 years academic experience teaching MIS, IT and strategic management at the undergraduate and graduate programs in Assumption University and other public universities, and also has been a resource person for various training programs to doctors, academics, business professionals, government officials and NGO personnel on topics ranging from strategic management, performance management, quality assurance, leadership, and teambuilding. His 10 years business experience in marketing and EDP positions covers the spectrum of transportation, hotel, and telecommunication industries. His research interest is in Management of Technology, Strategic Management and Performance Management approaching them from the strategic and organizational aspects and from an interdisciplinary, integrative and holistic approach.

Cuthbert Shepherdson is an international e-government consultant and trainer. He has been based in Vietnam for the last 3 years providing e-Government consulting for projects funded by Asian Development Bank (ADB) and World Bank. Cuthbert hold a Master of Technology Management from the Griffith University, Australia. He is also an Associate Trainer in Singapore for the Singapore Civil College focusing on E-Government. Cuthbert's research interest include e-Government for developing countries, e-Governance, business processes redesign, change management for IT deployment and knowledge management. Cuthbert is a Director in KDI Asia Pte Ltd, a management consultancy company in Singapore in charge of the e-Government practice.

Nikolaos Skarpetis is a PhD candidate at the Department of Shipping, Trade and Transport, University of the Aegean and General Manager of *Spirit S.A. e-Business & Communications Engineering.* Nikolaos holds a BSc and an MSc in mechanical engineering from the National Technical University (NTUA) in Greece. His current research interests include business process reengineering, business performance measurement, enterprise architecture, and organizational design, with emphasis in the Technology, Media, and Telecommunications (TMT) sector.

Syrris Vassilis has studied mathematics at the Aristotle University of Thessaloniki (BA), business management at the Hellenic Management Association (Postgraduate studies) and artificial intelligence: knowledge-based systems at the University of Edinburgh (MSc). Currently completing PhD in the Aatomation and Robotics Lab, Faculty of Electrical and Computers Engineering, Aristotle University of Thessaloniki. I am also working as assistant tutor in the Aristotle University of Thessaloniki, as laboratorial instructor in the Technological Educational Institute of Thessaloniki and as a high-school teacher with a private college in Thessaloniki. I have also participated and run European Community programmes related to education, informatics and professional occupation. Research interests are: machine learning, robotics, automation, evolutionary algorithms, fuzzy logic, e-learning, intelligent tutoring systems, symbolic representation, data manipulation and statistical analysis.

Eric Tachibana has been an entrepreneur focusing on the financial services space for the last 12 years - creating, building, and eventually exiting, successful small companies in Silicon Valley, Singapore, Malaysia, Thailand, and the UK. Today Tachibana continues his entrepreneurial endeavors as a regional angel investor, strategic adviser, and mentor for early-stage entrepreneurial ventures, serving as founding non-executive director for seven companies regionally. An author of 8 books on technology development and innovation management, and a professor at the National University of Singapore business school, Tachibana continues to focus on cutting edge theory and implementation.

David Van Over is the chair of The College of Graduate Studies at The University of Wollongong – Dubai and is a professor of Information Technology. He has held similar positions at several other universities, including The University of Georgia, The University of Idaho, The University of Houston, and Sam Houston State University. He was the Director of IT, International Operations at Milchem, Inc. He has been a consultant with Deloitte and Touche and IBM where he specialized in strategic IT in the government sector. He has published over forty research articles in the areas of individual and group decision support, strategic use of IT, and IS/IT pedagogy.

Index